The Word

Grammar

Punctuation and Mechanics

THE HARPER HANDBOOK
OF COLLEGE COMPOSITION

Third Edition

THE
HARPER
HANDBOOK

OF COLLEGE COMPOSITION

GEORGE S. WYKOFF, Professor of
English, Purdue University, and
HARRY SHAW, Formerly Director,
Workshops in Composition, New York
University

Harper & Brothers
Publishers, New York

CONTENTS

Contents

Contents

Contents

TABLES

FOREWORD

A course in freshman English—depending upon a freshman's precollege training—means many things to many people, as it should. For some teachers its important aim is training students to read critically and carefully. For others the course provides opportunity to teach literature, a sort of survey leading to advanced or specialized literary work. With still others first-year English constitutes an approach to aesthetics, a method of fostering "good taste." And some instructors use the discipline of the course to emphasize speaking or listening or principles of clear thinking.

We are content to agree with any of these approaches. Yet many years of classroom experience have convinced us, since primary emphasis must be placed somewhere, of one unassailable charge against the first-year English course: in attempting much, it sometimes accomplishes too little.

We believe that the needs of most beginning college students, perhaps all, are best served by genuinely solid work, under supervision, in thinking, writing, and rewriting. *The Harper Handbook of College Composition* has these major aims: *to help students to think and write correctly, clearly, effectively, and appropriately, and to assist teachers in achieving these aims for their students.* Such objectives, we hold, are important and significant. Learning to think clearly and learning to write correctly, clearly, effectively, appropriately, are worth-while intellectual processes valuable not only in composition classes but in all other outreachings of the mind. Furthermore, writing that is routine, correct, and clear is not enough; any correct, clear, competent writing can be also effective, interesting, and even artistic.

In most of this textbook, whenever the information has been available, we have relied upon various dictionaries which through their prefatory articles and their consulting editors have the backing and approval of the foremost linguistic authorities in the United States. To

ix

reputable dictionaries English teachers constantly refer their students. We have tried, perhaps sometimes in vain, to avoid the minor embarrassments that occur or might occur when what the teacher or handbook says disagrees with what the student's reputable dictionary says.

In the two preceding editions and the present edition we have tried to follow the advice given by Alexander Pope:

> Be not the first by whom the new are tried,
> Nor yet the last to lay the old aside.
> —*Essay on Criticism*, II, 135, 136

Our attempts to follow this advice lead us to make the same comment that W. Cabell Greet made about following a middle course for pronunciation in *The American College Dictionary:* "This middle course may grieve young radicals and old conservatives, but it is hoped that it will please the judicious" (page xx).

Our attitude toward language and usage is that stated in the conventional definition of good English: written and spoken English used correctly, clearly, effectively, appropriately in carrying on the business, professional, and social affairs of our country. In applying this definition to various parts of this handbook, we have been influenced by the prefaces of dictionaries to which we refer students: for example, we apply more widely the attitude toward pronunciation expressed in *Webster's New Collegiate Dictionary* (page ix), i.e., that correctness is a flexible term, that a word or expression is correct and standard when it is in actual use by a sufficient number of cultivated people or when it "prevails among the educated and cultured people to whom the language is vernacular."

We also agree with the comments made by one of our consultants, Professor George E. Grauel of John Carroll University—bearing in mind that appropriateness is also an important characterizing word:

1. Good usage *is not* merely numerical preponderance among all users of the language any more than correctness of surgical technique is a matter of decision by a Gallup poll.

2. Good usage *is* a matter of preponderant usage among the informed users of the language.

3. The *occasional* use of a form or construction by an "elite" speaker or writer does not in itself establish the practice as equally good or desirable with the forms or constructions *heavily favored* by good writers and speakers. Even careful users of the language are guilty of errors or indulge in

occasional eccentricities; for teaching purposes, the conventionally preponderant practices of good writers and speakers are best.

The Harper Handbook of College Composition is filled with specific recommendations and definite suggestions. If some consider them to be rules and regulations, such may be the needs of students seeking positive answers. Agreeing that much about language and grammar is descriptive, we believe that the application of this information is prescriptive, that much that is prescriptive is necessary in giving directions to students about writing. Our belief, further, is that improvement in thinking and writing involves replacing bad habits with good, that learning composition—or any intellectual or social activity—is necessarily negative in part.

Experience suggests no ideal plan of organization or order of assignments in freshman English. Any teacher will naturally follow the order of assignments which he has found most satisfactory and will vary this order from year to year according to the needs of his or her students. Since many students are weak in more than one division of writing, we recommend prompt assignment of the two prefatory chapters in this book dealing with communication and early themes. The six major divisions of the text ("The Theme," "The Paragraph," "The Sentence," "The Word," "Grammar," and "Punctuation and Mechanics") may be taken up in any order. The authors have each started at various times with every one of the six divisions save punctuation.

As a textbook for teaching, *The Harper Handbook of College Composition* has three purposes: to serve as a text for profitable use in the classroom; to serve as a text for independent use and consultation on the student's desk; and to serve as a text useful to the teacher in marking themes and to the student in making corrections. The second purpose explains partly the predominating use of the imperative mode (for variety, at the risk of being considered inconsistent, we have occasionally been impersonal or used the passive voice). The last purpose explains some of the detail in certain sections, on the comma, for example, Section 88; our own experience has been that a student learns more from a specific reference than he does from searching for an answer in several pages of print. We have therefore tried to be thorough in treating all varieties of student errors; we naturally do not expect any student to memorize detail of this kind or any teacher to assign it for memorization. Instead, we believe that such thoroughness allows the teacher to pinpoint a specific mistake rather than to mark beside an error some vague symbol which explains the trouble only in part.

In conclusion, we have done everything we (and our colleagues and consultants) could do to make the book as easy to use, as sensibly comprehensive, as flexible, and as attractive as possible. If our efforts are successful, we owe much to those who have shared their experiences: to former teachers, and to students from whom we have learned much. Many of these students have permitted us to use, anonymously, both their good and their bad writing; some have been unconscious victims. Most of the illustrations and exercises in this handbook are based upon or have been adapted from a careful perusal of some 12,000 freshman themes, thanks to colleagues who have lent us many of their already carefully marked and graded papers. Experience has shown us that exercises from such themes, and not synthetic ones, are usually best for student use. A teacher can find, in any set of freshman themes, numerous and effective exercise materials, impressive to students because vices and virtues of the writing are their own.

Particularly do we extend our hearty thanks to the gifted and experienced teachers—many present or former users—whose suggestions and advice have immeasurably improved this book. Names of 42 of these were recorded in the Foreword of the first and second editions. For this new edition we have received suggestions from other eminently successful teachers who have used the book in their classrooms. We can give only this record, inadequate as it is, of our indebtedness to the following: Richard Braddock, State University of Iowa; B. Bernard Cohen, University of Wichita; George E. Grauel, John Carroll University; Jewell McCracken, East Tennessee State College; H. J. Sachs, Louisiana Polytechnic Institute; John Timmerman, Calvin College and Seminary; and Eric M. Zale, Eastern Michigan University. For invaluable suggestions on the revision of "Using the Library" (Section 18), we express our deep indebtedness to Anne L. Corbitt, Reference Librarian, New York University.

We are also appreciative of the frank comments and constructive suggestions of some 80 staff members of the Department of English at Purdue University.

Finally, we can never adequately express our appreciation to two most efficient helpers, Brenta H. Wykoff and Jocelyn T. Shaw.

GEORGE S. WYKOFF

HARRY SHAW

PART I.

GETTING UNDER WAY

1. YOU
AND THE PROCESS
OF COMMUNICATION

The affairs of the world—its business and its pleasure—are carried on through communication: the exchange and interchange of thoughts and ideas between two people or more. It is even possible for one person to commune or communicate with himself.

The means of communication are various. Messages are conveyed through pictures, including painting, graphic representation, photographs, sketches, cartoons; through sculpture; through architecture; through music; through dancing. The most common medium is language: the written or printed page and the spoken word. Communication can be limited to two persons, or it can be extended to hundreds or thousands or millions. With large numbers of people, communication takes the form of "mass media": books, magazines, newspapers; radio and television; motion pictures, in which obviously, as in TV, words and pictures combine.

Applied to language, communication consists of two major divisions: (1) writing and reading, (2) speaking and listening.

Achieving communication is like the use of the telephone and radio because a sender and a recipient are involved. The writer writes for, or sends to, a reader; the reader reads or receives what the writer sends. The speaker speaks for a listener; the listener receives what the speaker transmits. Between sender and receiver is the material transmitted. When the recipient understands what the sender has wanted to convey, communication is successfully completed. The more clearly and effectively the reader or listener understands the subject, the more successful the communication.

3

The process is illustrated by the following diagram:

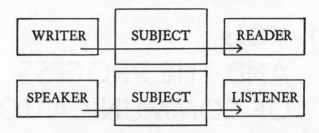

Through all parts of effective communication runs the thread of straight thinking—a clear, orderly plan and arrangement of ideas, and attention to methods of correct reasoning—so that conclusions are based on sufficient evidence and are not seemingly correct but actually unsound. Writers and speakers are responsible for logical thinking in their parts of the communication process; readers and listeners must avoid being misled by illogical thinking in what they read or hear. (See also Section 12c.)

If you kept account for a week of your communication activities, what would the results be? How much time do you spend reading? Writing? Speaking? Listening? The percentages might show that the time spent in writing activities is rather small, that somewhat more time is spent in reading, and that most time is spent in speaking and listening. Such statistics would not prove any area of communication unimportant, for each demands certain skills of the user if he is to make the process of communication successful.

When you write, read, speak, or listen, therefore, you are engaged in one of the four parts of communication. So closely are these parts related that the skills you develop in any one contribute to your mastery of the others. Although this handbook is designed to assist you in writing, your mastery of written language can be more easily and quickly attained if you give adequate attention to speaking, reading, and listening.

WRITING

Your written papers express ideas. You record these ideas for your own use, as in note taking or diary entries, or, more commonly, you write to convey ideas to a reader or readers: your instructor, classmates, or some other designated person or persons.

For effective communication of ideas, a *controlling purpose* and *ample content* are needed, but even with these a paper may fail unless it passes a final test of its worth: Does it correctly, clearly, effectively, and appropriately convey ideas from writer to reader? Correctness, clearness, effectiveness, and appropriateness are essential to a well-written paper. If one of these is lacking completely, or to an unusual degree, the paper is weak. Remember, also, that readers get no help from a writer's voice, gestures, or facial expression. Words must accordingly conform to accepted spelling, carry the maximum meaning to keep the reader's attention, be arranged to present the writer's ideas accurately, and be punctuated to provide the clearness normally achieved by the intonation of a speaker's voice.

A well-written paper, therefore, must be *correct* in its (1) grammar, (2) punctuation, (3) mechanics, and (4) spelling, and it must be *correct, clear, effective,* and *appropriate* in its (5) diction, (6) sentence construction, and (7) paragraph structure. A passing-grade paper is reasonably correct, and any careful user of a composition handbook and a good dictionary can achieve correctness, which is or should be assumed in formal and informal writing designed for readers both inside and outside college or university boundaries. An *excellent* paper, assuming *correctness,* has as chief merits *clearness, effectiveness,* and *appropriateness;* writing a paper possessing these qualities is a real achievement.

The writer, not the reader, must make communication successful. "Easy writing makes hard reading, but hard writing makes easy reading." A much-loved and highly successful teacher of writing used to add: "You may think you have done enough if you write so that you can be understood. Well, you haven't. You must write so that *you can't be misunderstood.*"

SPEAKING

Correctness, clearness, effectiveness, and appropriateness apply to both written and spoken communication, the aspects of communication which are the "sending" part. For speaking, the same emphasis is needed on controlling purpose and ample content, and on grammar, diction, sentence construction, and paragraph structure—a structure usually made clear in speaking by means of key words like "in the next place," "for example," "as a result," and "finally." The speaker need not worry about punctuation marks or misspellings; unlike the writer, however, he must be concerned about pronunciation, for it is as unforgivable for him to mispronounce words as it is for the writer to misspell.

The speaker has one other responsibility. A writer can expect—perhaps unreasonably—his reader to reread materials which he does not immediately understand or from which his attention has wandered. A spoken communication is given once, and unless it is received by the listener as the speaker desired, communication fails. Except in conversation, the speaker has no opportunity to repeat. He must, therefore, be immediately clear and effective.

Successful speaking, like successful writing, comes through constant practice, but for the technical details of speaking (such as use of voice, gestures, audience approach, type of speech) formal instruction is necessary through the aid of both teacher and textbook.

Can speaking help you in writing? Certainly. Since you speak on many more occasions than you write, your habits of correct, clear, effective, and appropriate speaking assist materially in correct, clear, effective, and appropriate writing. On the negative side, watch your speaking, your conversation especially, in order to avoid serious errors in grammar and word use. Such errors easily become habits and are frequently carried over into writing.

READING

As reader you are at the other end of the communication process, "receiving" through printed or written words what some other writer communicates. Your part in the process cannot be passive, unless you read merely to be entertained or to skim through for an idea here and there. If you are reading for information and instruction, you are an *active* reader and have at least one of three major purposes: (I) to understand the content of the reading material; (II) to evaluate it, agreeing or disagreeing, or possibly agreeing only in part; (III) to use the reading material for improving your own writing and speaking.

So important has effective reading become that books are available on the subject, and colleges and universities are adding courses and counselors to help students improve. The aid thus given is called *developmental reading;* it is designed for the comparatively slow or average or even superior reader, in order to help him increase his reading speed and comprehension of what he reads. If such help is not available, you can improve your reading effectiveness through specific directions, such as the following:

I. *In reading for information about ideas and content, use the following suggestions:*

1. Read and understand the title. Look also for any subtitle, prefatory note by the author, material about the author, any introductory summary, any footnotes giving additional information.

2. Determine the kind of reader (degree of education, occupation, age level, sex) for whom the author is writing. Determine also how well the author has adapted his material to this reader and what the occasion or circumstances were for his writing.

3. Look for a sentence or a paragraph in which the author gives his central purpose. Whether it is expressed or implied, formulate it in your own words. Look also for a sentence or paragraph in which the author summarizes his content, the *theme* sentence or the *theme* paragraph.

4. Look for mechanical aids that the author uses to help you: subheads; numbering of sections (I, II, III, etc.); blank spaces between sections; italicized words or sentences; paragraph divisions.

5. Read the article, chapter, or section rapidly. Next, try to recall what you have read. Next, reread the material paragraph by paragraph. Near the beginning, as suggested in Suggestion 3 above, look for a sentence or a paragraph in which the author summarizes his content or in which he gives the *theme* or central thought and the point of view he uses in developing it. Underline the topic sentence or topic phrase or topic word of each paragraph. Notice how these topics are developed within each paragraph (see pp. 220–231). Use pen or pencil to indicate which paragraphs belong together. Look for transitional devices (see pp. 84–87) indicating how successive paragraphs are linked or change the direction of the discussion. Note the length of the paragraphs and account for any which are extremely short or extremely long. Also, in your reading or rereading, circle key words in each paragraph.

6. As you read, underline words whose meaning you do not know and whose meaning you cannot guess from the context. Look them up

in a good dictionary, choose the definition which fits the context, and write it in the margin.

7. Make a formal outline (see pp. 48–58) of the material, using for main heads and subheads the underlining and grouping which you have done according to Suggestion 5.

II. *In evaluating what you have read—deciding to what extent you accept it, believe it, let it influence your thinking or guide your actions—answer the following questions:*

1. Is the author an authority? An expert witness? Is he close enough to the situation he is writing about to know it thoroughly? Has he had sufficient experience?

2. Is the author biased? Or is he sufficiently detached from the situation to give an objective view?

If you are reading expository or argumentative nonfiction, ask yourself, in addition:

3. Does the author present data to support generalizations?

4. Does the author reason logically, avoiding common fallacies? (See Section 12c.)

In fiction, the means an author uses are characters, setting, plot, philosophy, and, often, manners and customs. If you are reading fiction, ask yourself:

1. Has the author succeeded in creating an illusion of reality?

2. Has the author helped me to understand myself and my fellow human beings better than before?

III. *In reading to help yourself write and speak correctly, clearly, effectively, and appropriately, use the following suggestions:*

1. Occasionally underline a word or a group of words and identify it grammatically by definition and use. Assist your review of grammar by choosing various grammatical terms and looking for examples of these in your reading.

2. Look at the punctuation marks in three or four paragraphs. Do they follow conventional principles of punctuation? If any marks are used in a striking or unconventional manner, give a reason for their use, the purpose they serve.

3. Look on each page for three or four examples of words spelled according to rules and for words which are exceptions to rules.

4. Underline a certain number of words which you know and which are effectively used. Underline a certain number of words which you

do not have in your active vocabulary but which you will hereupon add with the aid of your dictionary.

5. Study a number of the sentences. Examine them for their use of phrases and clauses, of subordination and coordination. Determine which sentences are simple, complex, compound, compound-complex (see pp. 508–516). Which are loose or periodic (see pp. 517–518)? Which use inverted word order? What is the proportion of long and short sentences? Examine the ways in which sentences begin and end. Use all this material for a brief analysis of the author's style and compare it to that of your own written work.

6. Restudy the author's paragraphs according to Suggestion 5, p. 7. Apply to your own paragraphs whatever methods of effective paragraphing the author has used.

7. Study the author's use of title, *theme* statement, controlling purpose, point of view, and plan of organization. If these are clear and effective, adapt them to your own writing.

LISTENING

Listening, perhaps the most common form of communication, is difficult to utilize effectively. Most people have only an inaccurate idea of what they have heard, partly because of lapses in attention and partly because memory is faulty. Listeners normally have one opportunity to hear what is spoken. Therefore, aside from conversation and informal talks for entertainment, some note taking is advisable when you listen to classroom lectures, formal speeches, radio addresses, panel discussions, and the like. Good notes are not mere verbatim reports of what is said; in fact, a knowledge of shorthand does not insure good note taking, for you must think and understand as well as record.

To profit from listening, your notes should follow specific suggestions or contain answers to specific questions.

Listening to classroom lectures.

Lecture notes have various uses, as possible sources for themes, material for basic research, or review material for examinations, for example. In listening to and taking notes on lectures, you have to think and write rapidly. Thus, taking lecture notes is more difficult than making notes on reading.

The majority of students take lecture notes in bound or loose-leaf notebooks; some prefer using cards or card-size slips of paper (3 x 5, 4 x 6, or larger). Whatever the mechanical method, keep together all the notes taken in a single course. Record the date and the subject of each lecture. Utilize the following aids:

1. "Stop, look, and listen" before you write. Do not record the introductory words dealing with a subject unless they are really important; wait until the point can be summarized.

2. Do not try to take down everything the lecturer says. The best lecture notes contain a *summary* of what was said.

3. Abbreviate in order to save time. Make up a list of abbreviations, such as c̄ for "with"; ∴ for "therefore"; = for "equal"; & for "and"; tr. for "translation," etc.

4. Read over your notes on a lecture as soon as possible after they are taken. If they are difficult to read, or if your abbreviations may later lose meaning, write them out clearly, at once.

Listening to speeches.

1. What was the occasion for the speech? What were the circumstances under which it was given?

2. Was the address given before a miscellaneous group or a specialized one (college assembly, classroom lecture group, specific society, etc.)? Was it appropriate or inappropriate for its audience?

3. What was the subject of the speech? Did the speaker give early a phrase or sentence stating his central theme?

4. What was the purpose of the speech: to entertain, inform, convince, persuade, or incite to action? Did the speaker use chiefly logical and intellectual materials or did he make an emotional appeal?

5. What materials did the speaker use in support of his central theme? How did he organize them? How did he indicate his plan of organization? (Watch for such clues as "In the second place," "A third reason is," "As an example," "By way of contrast," etc., and for other linking or transitional devices.)

6. How did the speech begin (challenging statement, personal experience, anecdote, quotation, historical incident, etc.)?

7. What devices were used to hold attention throughout the speech (specific examples, personal experiences, definitions, allusions, questions, humor, familiar or unusual materials, repetition, stories or anecdotes or incidents, etc.)?

The Process of Communication

8. How did the speech end (concise summary, repetition of central theme, quotation, appeal for belief or action, etc.)?

9. What striking or unusual words were used? Did the general tone seem impartial or were words used to "slant" the subject in a given direction? List these striking, unusual, or "slanting" words.

Listening to radio, television, and movie programs.

Two popular forms of "receiving" are radio and television. Programs in these media are primarily for entertainment. Some combine information and entertainment, but you will probably take notes only on a formal radio or TV address. If your listening is to be active and critical, you must answer three basic questions: (1) What *kind* of program is it (news broadcast, news commentary, radio drama, dramatized biography, address, etc.)? (2) What is *the general purpose* (information, inspiration, argument, etc.)? (3) At what *general* or *specific* class of listeners is it aimed? If this information can be obtained before the time of listening, the listening process is facilitated and strengthened.

Most useful in learning to write, speak, read, and listen effectively are news broadcasts and commentator programs. Such programs provide lessons in selection of materials, differentiating conjecture and opinion from facts, and evaluating the speaker's impartiality or bias.

Note also these devices: the use of short sentences, the placing of transitional devices at the beginning of sentences, the use of simple and vigorous words, repetition to make ideas effective, and, in general, the use of a conversational tone.

In listening to radio or TV drama, try to discover (either before or early in the broadcast) what kind of drama is being presented: light, serious, farcical, satirical, biographical, etc. Determine the central theme of the play and state it in a sentence or two. What contributions are made by the announcer or commentator and by the different characters? In addition to their appearance, how do what they say and the way they say it help to characterize them, make them definite, vivid, convincing? What sound effects are used and what specific purposes do they serve? Note also how music influences the mood or tone of the play, indicates passage of time or change of scene, and sometimes even replaces words.

Movie programs, like TV programs, are varied, but their major

11

contribution is dramatic presentation. What similarities and differences exist between radio drama and movies or television? In these latter two, note how sound and sight, hearing and seeing, complement each other: as an experiment close your eyes for part of the program and hold your ears shut for a part. How much did you miss? Again, answer for yourself questions about the type of drama, subject matter, central theme, development of character. Also, since you are seeing as well as hearing, determine how well the speeches are adapted to each speaker. For good critical and active listening to movie and television programs, some advance preparation is easy through reviews and comments in newspapers and magazines. (For discussion of written criticism in general, see p. 133.)

As outlined above, informal listening and careful formal listening contribute to clearness and effectiveness of writing, for they give you experience in organizing and evaluating ideas.

2. YOUR FIRST THEMES

Regularly through your freshman year and in later college assignments you will be required to write papers of varying length. The chief purpose of this writing is to establish and confirm habits of correctness, clearness, effectiveness, and appropriateness in written work, so that in future years your writing will measure up to standards expected of one with your degree of education.

FRESHMAN ENGLISH

Your college writing will begin in the first week or two of your freshman year with formal training in a freshman English class. The aim of this course is to give you practice in correct, clear, effective, appropriate expression of your own ideas, emotions, reactions, thoughts. It is not a course designed for training professional writers. Hundreds of thousands of students preceding you have benefited from such a course, have improved in their writing. Why not you? The course makes no demands beyond the ability of the ordinary student. Your instructor will grade your written work by giving you constructive criticism and by marking all your major errors and many of your minor ones. As you profit by this criticism and as you eliminate these errors, your writing will conform to acceptable standards of "good English"—written and spoken English used correctly, clearly, effectively, appropriately in carrying on business, professional, and social affairs in our country.

ATTAINING STANDARDS OF GOOD ENGLISH

"Good English" is a broad term, and what is "good English" at one time and place may not be "good English" at another time and place. A discussion of language and the occasions for its variations in use is given on pages 356–360 and pages 454–456.

Here it is sufficient to say that good English is correct, clear, effective, appropriate English in speaking and writing. Applied to writing, what do these characterizing words mean?

Correct writing is free of errors in grammar, spelling, punctuation, diction, mechanics—serious or ludicrous or even minor errors that distract your reader from your subject.

Clear writing permits no possibility of confusion: it is understandable with no difficulty by the reader for whom it is written.

Effective writing makes a favorable impression on the reader because it catches and holds his attention, so that he remembers it with pleasure and profit.

Appropriate writing is adapted to the reader—his age, education, interests, understanding; it is suitable for the occasion and the purpose of its creation.

To attain these standards of good English, you need *constant* practice in writing. You will get limited practice by writing papers in your freshman English course. You cannot, however, make much progress by letting your first draft be your final draft or by giving either your first or your last draft a hasty rereading before calling it finished. Nor can you establish satisfactory habits by writing carefully only one or two papers a week for freshman English. Careful planning, composing, rereading, and checking—these steps you should apply to everything you write, even to the letters you send to relatives and friends. The best teacher and the best textbooks can only assist; they can never do the work for you.

WHAT IS A GOOD THEME?

A good theme, as indicated in the preceding section, is correct, clear, effective, and appropriate—qualifying adjectives which describe or relate to content, organization, diction, grammar, punctuation, and spelling.

Depending upon the observance or violation of the foregoing principle, a theme can be labeled "superior" (graded A or B), "average" (graded C), or "unacceptable" (graded D, E, or F).

Worth serious study is the chart on page 16. It explains in some detail the characteristics of superior, average, and unacceptable papers.

X SEVEN PRACTICAL SUGGESTIONS FOR WRITING THEMES

How can you improve in theme writing? The following suggestions apply to both early and succeeding papers.

1. Follow the work-sheet method of preparing a paper or a theme—a method designed to help you write easily, effectively, even quickly and painlessly. (See pp. 23, 24.)

2. *Analyze* the theme subject carefully. What are its possibilities? List as many divisions of the subject as you can. Determine your *central purpose*. Good *purposeless* writing does not exist. (See pp. 37–44.)

3. *Gather ample content* for the fulfillment of your central purpose. Draw upon your own experience and the experience of others as revealed in newspapers, magazines, books, and conversation. Make use of your own observation, curiosity, imagination, and reflection. (See pp. 45–47.)

4. *Arrange* the material you have collected. Reject all that is irrelevant to your purpose and classify what remains. Good themes have been written without the aid of a formal outline, but no good theme has ever been written which did not have a definite plan of some sort. (See pp. 48–59.)

5. Write your first draft, slowly and thoughtfully if that is the best way for you; or rapidly, if you want to get your thoughts on paper and then spend time on their improvement. Revise your first draft; better still, entirely rewrite it. Remember that good writing usually is good only through *rewriting*. Keep asking yourself: Have I tested my paper for its *organization* and the *relevance* of all material to my subject? Will my reader see exactly what I have in mind? Will he be

TABLE I. GRADING STANDARDS IN FRESHMAN COMPOSITION[1]

	CONTENT	ORGANIZATION: Rhetorical and Logical Development	DICTION	ORGANIZATION: Sentence Structure	GRAMMAR, PUNCTUATION, SPELLING
Superior (A-B)	A significant central idea clearly defined, supported with concrete, substantial, and consistently relevant detail	Theme planned so that it progresses by clearly ordered and necessary stages, and developed with originality and consistent attention to proportion and emphasis; paragraphs coherent, unified, and effectively developed; transitions between paragraphs explicit and effective	Distinctive: fresh, precise, economical, and idiomatic	Sentences skillfully constructed (unified, coherent, forceful, effectively varied)	Clarity and effectiveness of expression promoted by consistent use of standard grammar, punctuation, and spelling
Average (C)	Central idea apparent but trivial, or trite, or too general; supported with concrete detail, but detail that is occasionally repetitious, irrelevant, or sketchy	Plan and method of theme apparent but not consistently fulfilled; developed with only occasional disproportion or inappropriate emphasis; paragraphs unified, coherent, usually effective in their development; transitions between paragraphs clear but abrupt, mechanical, or monotonous	Appropriate: clear and idiomatic	Sentences correctly constructed but lacking distinction	Clarity and effectiveness of expression weakened by occasional deviations from standard grammar, punctuation, and spelling
Unacceptable (D-F)	Central idea lacking, or confused, or unsupported with concrete and relevant detail	Plan and purpose of theme not apparent; undeveloped or developed with irrelevance, redundancy, or inconsistency; paragraphs incoherent, not unified, or undeveloped; transitions between paragraphs unclear or ineffective	Inappropriate: vague, unidiomatic, or substandard	Sentences not unified, incoherent, fused, incomplete, monotonous, or childish	Communication obscured by frequent deviations from standard grammar, punctuation, and spelling

[1] From *Joint Statement on Freshman English in College and High School Preparation* (p. 4), by the Departments of English of Ball State Teachers College, Indiana State Teachers College, Indiana University, and Purdue University. Used by permission.

interested in my presentation? Have I made my writing clear, effective, and appropriate?

6. After completing Step 5, *reread* your theme for errors in mechanics, grammar, punctuation, spelling, and diction. If you find that you are making several kinds of errors, reread several times for similar errors of a specific kind: once for misspellings, once for punctuation errors, once for errors in grammar, and so on. If your paper has been written outside class, make a final, clean, error-free draft to turn in.

7. *Proofread* your final draft, pencil or pen in hand, pointing to every word and punctuation mark. Reading aloud, when possible, helps, for it slows down your proofreading speed, and your voice helps you to find errors that your eyes overlook.

How long should you spend in the preparation of a paper? No one can say. Subjects vary in difficulty. Students differ in their abilities: some write easily and rapidly; others write slowly and laboriously. However, every student should spend *at least two hours* on each 400- or 500-word assignment. If you make serious errors in your writing, work at them first. If you have few such errors, work at them and concentrate also on improving your sentences and word choice. Usually the only answer to the question "How can I make my themes better?" is the uninspired but true "Take more time."

AIDS IN ATTAINING STANDARDS OF GOOD ENGLISH

To help you attain standards of good English, your instructor will give during your freshman English course some review or memory-refreshing assignments in grammar, punctuation, spelling, diction, and sentence construction. Unfortunately, these assignments cannot be given simultaneously, nor can they always be given in the order in which you may need them. Your early writing may show errors in spelling, diction, punctuation, or grammar, while your assignments are dealing with the whole theme, choice of subject, planning, or paragraphing. You may feel aggrieved that your themes are being graded down for errors that you have not yet studied in your review assignments or classwork. When this happens, *your* task is to follow conscientiously the directions for revision given in Section 15f. Also,

1. Utilize fully any comment your instructor makes on your themes.

Note carefully the errors he marks and reference numbers indicating sections of this handbook. Through his aid you will find where your weaknesses lie, and you can make necessary revisions and avoid the same errors in later themes.

2. Keep a record of your most common errors in writing (see chart on third page from back cover) and consult it each time you have any writing to do.

3. Master the directions concerning the elimination of the error or errors that you are making. A worthy ideal is to try never to make the same mistake twice, or even the same kind of mistake.

4. Make a "correction sheet" for every paper that is returned to you. Since this is an important part of revision, it is discussed in detail on pages 119–122.

SERIOUS ERRORS TO BE AVOIDED

For rapid improvement in writing, concentrate on avoiding the serious errors mentioned below. If any of these appear in your writing, consult immediately the pages listed.

1. IMPROPER CHOICE AND LIMITING OF SUBJECT

Have you chosen a subject and narrowed it so that, in the number of words at your disposal, you have given your reader a clear and complete account of what he expects? (See pp. 28–33.)

2. FAULTY PLANNING

Have you followed an orderly plan in the writing of your paper? Have you made a brief written or mental outline, divided your subject into related parts, and written a paragraph on each? (See pp. 48–59.)

3. IMPROPER PARAGRAPHING

Is each of your paragraphs an adequate treatment of one division of the subject? Does any paragraph include material that belongs elsewhere in the paper? Or omit material necessary to clear development? Or include illogically material needed in some other paragraph? Is any paragraph too long or detailed? Too short and concise? (See pp. 212–249.) Seven guides for self-checking your paragraphs are given on pages 210–211.

4. SENTENCE FRAGMENTS

Have you written any unjustifiable sentence fragments and thus misled your reader into expecting a complete statement instead of an incomplete one? (See pp. 264–271.)

5. FUSED SENTENCES

Have you combined two sentences with no punctuation between, and thereby confused your reader by not indicating to him where one complete thought ends and another begins? (See pp. 281–282.)

6. "COMMA SPLICES"

Have you avoided making any unjustifiable comma splices? A "comma splice" confuses the reader because a comma is used incorrectly to separate two sentences, or, in grammatical terms, a comma is used between two independent clauses not joined by one of the simple conjunctions, *and, but, or, nor, neither, yet.* (See pp. 275–279.)

7. MISUSE OF SEMICOLON

Have you misused the semicolon by using it to set off a dependent clause or a phrase? Ordinarily, the semicolon serves the same purpose as the period: to indicate the end of one complete thought and the beginning of another; it is this "break" in thought that your reader expects when he sees a semicolon. One guide is this: no period, no semicolon. Setting off dependent clauses or phrases with semicolons leads to the same confusion caused by the *sentence fragment.* (See pp. 662–667.)

8. OTHER SERIOUS ERRORS IN PUNCTUATION

Have you used the apostrophe correctly in forming the possessive case? (See Section 94)

Have you made other serious and confusing errors in punctuation? When in doubt about the correct mark to use, see "Glossary of Applied Punctuation" (Section 100).

9. SERIOUS ERRORS IN GRAMMAR

Have you avoided serious errors in grammar which distract your reader's attention from what you are saying to the way you are saying it?

a. *Have you made subjects and predicates agree in number?* This is a subtle principle more easily violated than observed, partly because of the position of the subject, or the way nouns form their plurals, or the way two or more members of a compound subject are connected. (See pp. 534–540.)

b. *Have you used adjectives and adverbs correctly and not used an adjective when you should have used an adverb, or vice versa?* (See pp. 595–599.)

c. *Have you used the correct form of the verb?* Serious errors in verb use, in addition to misusing singular-plural forms, are mistaking the past tense for the past participle, or vice versa, and confusing similar verbs like *lay—lie, sit—set, raise—rise.* (See Sections **71g, 79.**)

d. *Have you used the correct case forms of pronouns when these are the objects of verbs or prepositions or the subjects of elliptical statements?* (Section **75d, h, i.**)

10. SERIOUS ERRORS IN SENTENCE CONSTRUCTION

After checking for correctness, have you reread each sentence for possible changes for greater clearness, effectiveness, appropriateness? For assistance, see "Glossary of Sentence Errors" (Section **50**). Have you avoided mixed and illogical constructions? (See Section **35c, d, e, f, g.**) Have you carelessly omitted words? (Section **35a, b.**)

11. SERIOUS ERRORS IN WORD CHOICE (DICTION)

Have you used words or groups of words incorrectly? In revising, can you choose clearer, more effective, more appropriate words than those already used? (See pp. 402–476.)

12. MISSPELLING

Have you checked the spelling of all words about which you are in doubt? Have you carefully proofread for any misspellings due to carelessness?

REMINDER: Only after a theme has been carefully planned, written, rewritten, and proofread for all kinds of errors will it approach correctness in its grammar, punctuation, mechanics, spelling, diction (including idiom), and sentence and paragraph structure. Study *systematically* and *conscientiously* the handbook sections dealing with your particular weaknesses so as to forestall making errors.

PART II.

THE HARPER HANDBOOK

THE
THEME

"English" is difficult for some students and easy for others, but everyone can learn to write and speak competently if he is earnest in his efforts and will devote time and energy to mastering his *own* language. After all, except for the non-English born, English is our native tongue, and we should take pride in using it correctly,[1] clearly, effectively, appropriately.

Anyone expecting to be able to write and speak competently through all the years of his life needs on his desk two, and possibly three or four, source books: a good handbook of composition or communication, a reliable dictionary, and, if one expects to do much speaking or letter writing, good guides to public speaking and to business and social correspondence.

Through study of principles of writing in the theme, paragraphs, sentences, words, business and social letters you approach language competency: "Good English—written and spoken English used effectively in carrying on the business, professional, and social affairs of our country."

To learn to write correctly, clearly, effectively, and appropriately you may require a semester of theme writing, or longer, depending upon your background training and the time and energy you may or may not have given to the problem in the past. You, like everyone, can improve your writing if you conscientiously try. You can eliminate certain errors and become aware of others to guard against by doing

[1] *Correct, correctly, correctness* are used throughout this book not in an absolute sense but in the meaning permitted by every standard dictionary: "in accordance with an acknowledged or accepted standard; according to recognized usage."

carefully the exercises at the end of the various sections which follow. Such exercises are no substitute for writing, since *the only way to learn to write is to write.*

Other sections of this book deal with the paragraph, the sentence, and the word. This section deals with the theme, or composition, and with specific approaches to writing such longer units. A common definition of a theme, or paper, or article, is that it is a series of related paragraphs (sometimes one paragraph) dealing with one subject or one part of a subject.

To write competently, even *painlessly,* many students have found effective the following process, pursued step by step:

Prepare a number of work sheets, 5½ by 8½ inches in size (half-size standard stationery), a desirable size since each work sheet will contain all necessary step-by-step information.

Work Sheet 1. On this sheet put preliminary miscellaneous information: number of the theme; date due; number of words required; reader or readers aimed at; general title; specific title, or titles, if given (otherwise, several specific titles suggested by the general title); general tone of paper (see Section **4f**); *theme* sentence, the sentence summarizing the content of the theme you plan to write.

Work Sheet 2. Here put your preliminary analysis for possible content (see Section **4d**). List 15 to 25 items you might include, each of which might serve as topic or subject for a paragraph.

Work Sheet 3. From the 15 to 25 items on Work Sheet 2 make a tentative outline (see Section **6**). Your outline can be changed later, if necessary, as you develop it in writing.

Work Sheet 4. On this work sheet write topic sentences, one for each paragraph that you plan for your theme. The number will depend upon the major divisions of your outline. Preferably, make each topic sentence a simple sentence (see Section **23**).

Work Sheet 5, and *6, 7, 8, 9,* etc., depending upon the number of paragraphs, using one work sheet for each paragraph. On each work sheet copy a topic sentence from Work Sheet 4. Expand this into an adequate paragraph (see Section **24**).

When you have expanded the last topic sentence into its paragraph, you have written your theme. Do your revising and correcting on these work sheets. Add necessary transitions between paragraphs. When you are satisfied with your revisions and corrections, copy your material on regular theme paper. Make a final rereading of your theme before you turn it in. Your instructor may ask for a final draft of your outline to turn in with your theme. He may also wish to see all your work sheets.

But before you turn your theme over to a reader, ask these questions about your writing:

→ 1. Does my theme have a *central purpose?*
→ 2. Have I carefully *analyzed* the subject?
→ 3. Does my theme have *ample* content?
→ 4. Is the content *arranged* logically and effectively?
→ 5. Is my theme *unified?*
→ 6. Is my theme *clear* to my reader?
→ 7. Have I used adequate *transition* between sentences and between paragraphs?
→ 8. Does my theme have *interest?* Is my content presented effectively so that it makes a *definite appeal* to the reader?
→ 9. Have I *adapted* my material to my reader and made it *appropriate?* Have I kept my reader constantly in mind?
→10. Is my theme *correct* in all mechanical and grammatical details?

If you can truthfully answer "yes" to these ten questions, your task is completed. Otherwise, you need the guidance and constructive criticism that both your instructor and your textbook give. None of these requirements is beyond the ability of any serious student who will work intelligently, industriously, and faithfully. The following sections are designed to help you give "yes" answers to the foregoing questions.

MANUSCRIPT FORM

1. Neatness and legibility are important in papers which you submit. Many a good composition has received a poorer grade or made a poorer impression than its actual content deserved because it was so improperly prepared and so sloppily written that the reader lost patience in trying to decipher it. Conversely, many a mediocre theme has received a comparatively high grade because of its neatness and legibility. Here, then, are some suggestions for the preparation of your final draft.

1a. Conform to specific standards in preparing manuscript.

If in your English composition or other classes you are given particularized directions for the preparation of manuscript, follow those directions. Otherwise, use the following as a guide.

1. *Paper.* Use standard-sized stationery, 8½-by-11 inches in size. Ruled paper is convenient for longhand, but most standard paper is unruled. Use paper of good quality, preferably white bond, to take ink without blurring. Write on one side only.

2. *Title.* Write the title on the first line, or about two inches from the top of the page. Center the title. Capitalize the first word and all other important words in the title (see Section 97a). Do not use a period after the title, but use a question mark or exclamation point if necessary for interrogative or exclamatory titles.

3. *Beginning.* Begin the theme about one inch below the title. If the paper is ruled, write on each line; if unruled, leave about one-half inch between lines.

4. *Margins.* Leave a margin of at least one inch on the left side of each page. Standard theme paper may have a margin of one inch ruled off; leave a similar blank space on paper not having this vertical line. Leave a margin of about a half-inch at the right. Make the margins even and fairly uniform down the page. At the bottom, leave a margin of at least one inch.

5. *Indentations.* Indent the first line of every paragraph about one inch. Use indentations of equal length for all paragraphs in the same paper. Make no exception if you have occasion to use *numbered* paragraphs. On the second page and following pages, indent the first line *only* if it is the beginning of a paragraph.

Indicate a paragraph division not shown by indentation by placing the sign ⁋ or ℙ before the word beginning the paragraph. Cancel a paragraph division by writing "No ⁋" or "No ℙ" in the margin. But, in general, avoid the use of these paragraph symbols. Preferably, recopy the entire page, correcting the indentation.

6. *Insertions.* Use a caret ($_\wedge$) when inserting an omitted expression (see Section 92f).

7. *Cancellations.* Draw a straight line through material you wish to cancel. Do not use parentheses or brackets to cancel words. These marks have their own particular uses (see Section 92) and should never be used to indicate deletion.

8. *Order.* Number your pages with Arabic numerals in the upper right-hand corner of each page. Arrange the pages in proper order: 1, 2, 3, etc. No reader likes to open a manuscript and find page 2 or page 3 before him.

9. *Endorsement.* With pages in proper order, page 1 on top, fold the theme lengthwise through the middle. On the right-hand side of the back of the last page write your name, course, instructor's name, date, and number of the paper. Write these items in the order desired by your department or your instructor.

NOTE: For other "basic mechanics" in the preparation of manuscript, see "The Hyphen" (Section 93), "Capitals" (Section 97), "Abbreviations" (Section 98), "Italics" (Section 96), and "Numbers" (Section 99).

1b. Make your handwriting legible.

Illegible writing taxes the patience of a reader and causes him to give so much attention to the words themselves that his thought is turned away from the important ideas which should engage his interest. Make your handwriting easily readable by

1. *Not crowding your writing.* Do not run words together; do not run consecutive lines too closely together; do not crowd writing at the bottom of a page.

2. *Not leaving gaps in words.* The consecutive letters in a word should be joined.

3. *Forming your letters carefully and correctly.* Dot every small-letter *i* and *j*. Cross every *t*. Make small letters *m* and *n* and *u* distinct, and small letters *a* and *o*. Do not carelessly write small letters as capitals, or capitals as small letters (see Section 97g).

4. *Writing with a good pen, using black or blue-black ink, and writing legibly.* Avoid the reader's possible comment on your theme: "This *looks* interesting, but I can't *read* it!"

1c. If possible, type your themes and other written work.

Not only is typescript more legible than handwriting, but errors are also more easily detected in typescript than in handwriting. Observe the following conventions in typing:

1. Do not use onionskin paper for your reader's copy; use onionskin only for the carbon copy you keep.

2. Indent paragraph beginnings either 5 or 10 spaces.

3. Leave margins at both the left and right: an inch or an inch and a half at the left, about an inch at the right.

4. Leave a blank space of an inch at the bottom of each page.

5. Double-space all lines (single-space only in business letters, which have double-spacing only between paragraphs. See p. 728).

6. To form a dash, use two hyphens (--). To form an exclamation point, use period (.) or apostrophe (') and then backspace and use, respectively, apostrophe (') or period (.). (Late models of typewriters have these punctuation marks.)

7. After terminating marks of punctuation (period, question mark, exclamation point), use the space bar twice or thrice; after internal punctuation marks, including the period after abbreviations and initials, use it once. Before and after the dash (—) use no spaces.

8. For numbers, use the small letter l for Arabic one, the capital I for Roman one, and, if your typewriter has no zero, the capital O for zero.

The endorsement on a typewritten manuscript is usually placed in the upper left-hand corner of the first page. If the paper is folded, it should also be endorsed like a handwritten theme (see "Endorsement," 1a).

1d. Avoid numerous and unsightly erasures and corrections.

1. *Recopying.* Everyone is likely to make errors even in preparing a final draft. If such errors are numerous, it is far better to recopy an entire page than to leave it filled with blots, blurs, and canceled and inserted words. If only one or two corrections must be made on a page, follow the directions given above (1a) under "Indentations," "Insertions," and "Cancellations."

2. *Proofreading.* Every manuscript should be reread carefully for errors of all kinds, especially for careless errors. ("Oh, I knew better than that" is slim excuse for the writer.) Though typescript makes detection of errors easier, typed papers often contain more errors than papers written in longhand because of the insidious way in which letters seem to change places and because of careless proofreading. For a guide to proofreading, see Section 15.

3. *Final Draft.* Always reread the final draft of a manuscript before passing it on to a reader.

THEME TOPICS

2. Every writer has had the experience of writing something with great care, something which pleased him and seemed to be correct and clear, only to find that others derived neither pleasure nor profit from reading it. Although everything has interest for somebody, some objects are inherently more interesting than others and can be presented more effectively.

Students manage to turn in both conventional and outstandingly interesting themes when definite topics are assigned by their instructors, but they are often puzzled when required to write on topics of their own choosing. Five simple tests enable you to choose subjects that you can handle effectively (Section 2a, b, c, d, e).

2a. Choose a topic of interest to yourself.

To write effectively you must be interested in your material. Vagueness, aimlessness, dullness, and sketchiness are evidence of uninterested writing; force and vigor are present when you are wrapped up in your subject and let yourself go. You can write more vigorously and interestingly about people and activities that you have been associated with, either pleasantly or unpleasantly, than you can about people and activities that you have known about only through the experience of others.

For example, you may not have been interested in labor unions, but if members of your family or intimate friends have been favorably or adversely affected by labor unions, you are likely to discover that unions are an interesting topic.

Do not neglect, either, the possibilities of subjects suggested by your reading or by your conversations with others.

You necessarily will write several themes on topics in which you are not greatly interested, an experience not uncommon for any speaker or writer. Usually, however, even when theme topics are assigned by your instructor, you can choose a limited part of the subject that comes closest to your interests.

2b. Choose a topic of interest to your readers.

Except on rare occasions, like keeping a diary or taking notes, all writing is done primarily for a reader or a group of readers, with the purpose of giving information or entertainment, or both. Far more important than yourself as writer are your readers, who may be your classmates, friends, relatives, readers of campus publications, or instructor. Your theme may be specifically required as a class exercise, but you can indicate for what type of reader you intend it. Your instructor then becomes a "reader over your shoulder," who visualizes himself as one of your designated readers and judges whether your writing is appropriate.

A writer, like a salesman, has to sell his ideas to his readers. He will profitably spend considerable time in analyzing the likes and dislikes of his readers, their backgrounds, their general range of information on the chosen subject. He will plan ways to interest them in his material or to present in new or different ways material in which they are already interested.

In general, the following subjects and limitations of these subjects have a genuine appeal for most people:

1. *Timely topics:* recent events, new ideas, or late facts, or the development of some old idea through contact with recent developments.

2. *People:* unique, prominent, well-known, or unforgettable; also, personal reminiscences, reactions, and reflections.

3. *Life, property, and welfare:* important matters which involve the life and property of others and which have a relation to the reader's own welfare—ideas, perhaps, concerning "life, liberty, and the pursuit of happiness."

4. *Places:* historical, unusual, scenic, even uncommon features of common places and familiar features of familiar places.

5. *Travel:* both places themselves and actual experiences and people encountered in getting from place to place—on foot, by auto, by train, by boat, by plane.

6. *Conflict:* contests between people, between man and nature, between man and space, and conflicts within the individual.

7. *Amusements, hobbies, recreation:* radio, television, movies, recordings; growth of, development of, interest in, pleasure in, and profit from hobbies; spectator and participation sports, games, directions for playing games, exciting or dramatic episodes in sports.

8. *Occupations:* what they are, how they came into being, what they involve, what they mean in terms of money and happiness.

9. *Religion:* reasons for one's beliefs, a personal creed, attitudes toward the soul and immortality, a code of ethics.

10. *Nature:* in all its animate and inanimate appearances—animals, plants, flowers, trees, metals, atoms, geology, astronomy, etc.

11. *The universe:* God-made and man-made planets and satellites, radiation, interspace exploration, men and animals in space.

12. *Manufacturing:* factory visits, machines, mechanisms, processes, directions, recipes.

NOTE: You may be aided in choosing topics by keeping in mind four general purposes of writing: to tell a story (narrative); to give a picture in words (description); to explain (exposition); or to convince (argumentation). See Section 16.

2c.　Choose a topic about which you know something.

Just as you cannot expect to handle a tool, instrument, or machine efficiently and expertly without some previous experience or some first-hand acquaintance, so you cannot expect to write effectively without some experience and firsthand acquaintance with the topic of the com-position. Most current magazine articles and nonfiction books, and fiction too, are based on many months or years of direct observation, study, and personal familiarity with the materials treated. Every writer goes to his own experience—to those things he knows or has thought about or seen or heard. You, likewise, can do so profitably and effectively.

2d.　Choose a topic which you can treat adequately.

You should have in mind, in choosing a topic, approximately the length of the paper you plan to write. A short paper requires a limited subject; a longer paper naturally permits a broader subject, a more extended treatment, a wider point of view, the inclusion of more details.

The word *theme* implies a single, well-defined *phase* of a subject. You cannot write an effective 500-word theme on a subject which requires 5,000 words. If you choose a broad subject and fail to limit it, you are likely to write sketchily and superficially. "College Fraternities," "Professional Football," "Chicago," and "Aviation" are examples of such topics. A small composition on a large subject is necessarily a fragmentary, disconnected, ineffective treatment.

General topics or broad subjects must therefore be narrowed. "The Duties of a Fraternity Pledge," "How Professional Football Players Are Recruited," and "When in Chicago, See the Planetarium" are ex-amples of such limitation. "Aviation" is a hopelessly broad subject; limited to "Aviation in America," it is still too large, even for a book; "The Career of Wilbur Wright" might be developed in a very long paper; "Wilbur Wright's First Flight" would be more suitable for ordinary-length theme treatment.

2e. Choose a topic which is concrete and specific.

Even though you have a topic which can be adequately treated in the number of words allotted, many topics are uninteresting because they are general, vague, or abstract. If any of these words describe your selection, restudy it to make it concrete and specific.

Consider these successive narrowings of a broad general subject, in the light of a student's interest, observation, and experience. The asterisk (*) indicates the broader subject which is narrowed in the next group of topics.

Very general:	College Activities.
General:	Fraternities and Sororities.
	Physical Activities.
	Intellectual Activities.
	Social Activities.
	Studies in College.
	*Student Organizations.
Less general:	Our Intramural Sports.
	College Dramatics.
	Week Ends on the Campus.
	Departmental Clubs (Science, Chemistry, French, Debating, etc.).
	Interest Clubs (Camera, Model Railroads, Painting, Ceramics, etc.).
	*Musical Organizations.
Fairly specific:	Our Student Chorus.
	Our All-Campus Musical Show.
	Student Dance Bands.
	Impromptu Music
	Broadcasting Music to the Dormitories.
	*Our Glee Club.
Limited:	How I Joined the Glee Club.
	Why I Joined the Glee Club.
	How to Become a Member of the Glee Club.
	What Our Glee Club Does.
	How Our Glee Club Helps Our College.
	Join Our Glee Club and See Our State!
	Let's Sing!

2f. Be prepared to write on assigned topics.

Many composition subjects in your classes will be assigned. They may need some adaptation or limitation; they may need none. Writing on assigned subjects is excellent experience and practical training for post-college work, since much routine writing (and speaking) is done on assignment. Answers to letters, research reports in business and industry, papers read before specific groups, newspaper reporting, feature articles, and many nonfiction articles in general and trade magazines are examples of assigned materials.

EXERCISES

NOTE: In addition to the theme subjects just below, some 150 theme topics are suggested in the exercises at the end of Section **16**, p. 135.

A. For each of the 12 classes of subjects on pp. 30–31, make a list of 5 to 10 limited topics, each suitable for a 350-word to 500-word theme.

B. Using the following as general subjects, for each write three to five limited topics which you think will interest specific readers whom you designate: Animals, Athletics, Atoms, Bravery, Business, Campus Activities, Childhood, Contests, Education, Food, Friends, Health, Heroes, Illness, Medicine, Memories, Music, Nature, Night, One Week, Personal Experience, Recreation, Relatives, Soil Conservation, Sorrow, Success, Superstition, Tall Stories, Vacations, Weather.

C. Using the following as general subjects, for each write three to five limited topics which you think will interest specific readers whom you designate: Airplanes, Ancestors, Automobiles, Birthdays, Cities, Cooking, Country, Crises, Dormitories, Dramatics, Embarrassments, Etiquette or Good Manners, Failure, Favorites, Fishing and Hunting, Future, History, Jobs, Jokes, Military Service, Money, Patriotism, Photography, Radio and TV, Reading, Sportsmanship, Taking Stock, Teachers, Thoughtfulness, Water.

D. Using the following official or unofficial American holidays as general subjects, for each write three to five limited topics which you think will interest specific readers whom you designate: New Year's Eve, New Year's Day, Lincoln's Birthday, Washington's Birthday, St. Patrick's Day, Good Friday, Easter, April Fool's Day, May Day, Memorial Day, Fourth of July, August Vacation Days, Labor Day, Columbus Day, Homecoming, Halloween, Armistice Day (Armed Services Day), Thanksgiving, Christmas Eve, Christmas Day.

E. Prepare a list of 10 limited theme topics designed to be developed by telling a story (narrative); 10 to be developed by giving a picture in words (description); 10 to be developed by explaining (exposition); 10 to be developed by convincing (argument).

F. List 10 incidents in your life which, expanded, would be interesting to your readers, your instructor, and the members of your class.

G. List five subjects about which you think you know details not known to your classmates.

H. Apply the five tests (Section **2a, b, c, d, e**) for topics to the following suggestions for themes and suggest what readers you have in mind:

1. An interview with a well-known campus personality.
2. An account of a visit to a law court during a trial.
3. The history, including a description, of a building on your campus.
4. A description and character sketch of a well-known employee of your college.
5. A description of a college cafeteria during the luncheon hour.
6. Description of college "types": the athlete, the bluffer, the TV fan, the hi-fi enthusiast, the "odd" character.
7. A commentary upon a popular radio or TV program.
8. A criticism of a motion picture currently being shown.
9. An account of the conversation among a group of friends after a college dance.
10. A commentary upon the "easiest" and the "most difficult" courses and professors in the college.
11. Favorite magazines and newspapers.
12. Personalities of high school and college teachers.
13. Likes and dislikes (radio announcers, tabloid newspapers, practical jokes, eight-o'clock classes, dormitory life, etc.).
14. An account of how you budget your time for a day, a week, a month of college life.
15. What you want to be, and to be doing, 10 years from now.
16. Politics on the campus.
17. The greatest personal disaster you can imagine.
18. A list of five books, with reasons for their choice, which you would choose for a summer's reading.
19. Desirable qualities you want your friends or roommate or future wife or future husband to have.
20. The ideal preparation for college.

THE TITLE

3. A well-chosen title helps you stick to your subject throughout a theme, reminding you that all material included should bear upon the subject. It is also an effective means of gaining the reader's attention. Most of us are led to read a certain book, magazine article, or story because of its attractive title. Give your theme a good title and you have taken an important step in making the whole composition effective.

3a. Avoid confusion of title and subject.

The term *subject* is broader and more inclusive than the word *title*. If your instructor asks for a composition on "Reading Habits," he has assigned a *subject,* not a *title,* and you should sharpen this subject to a more specific title. Conversely, if the actual title is assigned, you must discover precisely what subject it covers. Do not assume that the title of a specific paper is the same as a general subject which has been assigned. The best titles indicate not a general subject but the actual *theme* of the composition.

3b. Use clear and effective phrasing in the title.

Your title, of course, cannot mention everything a theme contains, but it should indicate, or give at least a hint of, the contents. Do not announce a title and then develop ideas which have no relation to it. Above all, do not use a title, no matter how catchy, which is deliberately misleading.

1. *Avoid long titles.* As a title, "Browsing Among Magazines" is certainly more effective than "How to While Away an Afternoon Among the Magazines in the Periodical Room of the Belvedere Library." Lovers of William Wordsworth's poetry refer to a well-loved poem as "Tintern Abbey" rather than by the title the poet gave it: "Lines Composed a Few Miles Above Tintern Abbey, on Revisiting the Banks of the Wye During a Tour, July 13, 1798."

2. *Rephrase vague and commonplace titles.* Titles like "College Football Is Overemphasized," "A Camping Trip," "Contemporary Etiquette," and "The Importance of Using Short Words" can be rephrased for greater concreteness and uniqueness: "Dollar Marks on the Gridiron," "Alone in a Civilized Wilderness," "Best Foot Forward," and "Little Words, but Mighty."

At the other extreme, however, titles which puzzle or mislead are questionable. To be clear, a title should be short, informative, definite. In addition, to be effective, it must be fresh and provocative. A survey of many titles shows three frequently used kinds:

Informative titles, which tell exactly and concretely the content:
The Method of Scientific Investigation.
How to Stay in College.
What Should Colleges Teach Women?
The American Student as I See Him.
Why an Airplane Flies.

Suggestive titles, which become clear as the reader uses a little imagination:
The Great Sports Myth. (A criticism of American sports)
That Burrowing Bean. (An article about peanuts)
Snapshot of America. (A brief survey of American culture)
Ten-Gallon Hero. (An article on the American cowboy)

Intriguing titles, which neither tell nor suggest but which later become clear:
Is It Anyone We Know? (An article criticizing advertisements designed to appeal to women)
Farewell, My Lovely! (An article expressing regret at the passing of a once nationally popular automobile model)
A Game of Wild Indians. (An investigation of an outbreak of typhoid fever)
No Tears, No Good. (A reminiscence of judging a motion picture by the tears the spectators shed)
Look Out, Here I Come! (A study of the reasons for our increasing number of automobile fatalities; another article on the subject was titled —*And Sudden Death!*)

3c. Place and punctuate the title correctly on the page.

Center the title on the page, on the first line of ruled paper or two inches from the top of unruled paper. Leave a space between the title and the first line of the theme. (See Section 1a.)

Capitalize important words (see Section 97a), but do not italicize the title or enclose it in quotation marks unless it is itself a quotation or unless you quote it in the theme (see Section 951).

Do not place a period after the title; use a question mark or exclamation point if the title is a question or an exclamation.

3d. Avoid vague, indirect reference to the title in the first sentence of the theme.

The title is independent of the composition. The first sentence, therefore, should be complete in its meaning, self-explanatory, without need for reference to the title. Avoid vague reference of words like *this, that, such* in your opening lines. (See Section 8a, also.)

Ineffective, less clear beginnings:
1. This is one of the best books I own, and I find it invaluable.
2. It was in the winter of 1960 when it happened. I was driving . . .
3. From early childhood I have been interested in this subject.
4. I was not exactly a tourist when I visited these countries.
5. Many times I have asked myself this same question.

Improved beginnings:
1. My dictionary is one of the best books I own, . . .
2. My most serious accident occurred in the winter of 1960.
3. From early childhood I have been interested in music.
4. I was not exactly a tourist when I visited England, Scotland, and Ireland.
5. Many times I have asked myself whether a college education is worth the price.

EXERCISES

A. Buy, or consult in your library, current copies of three or four magazines like *The Saturday Evening Post, Esquire, The American Scholar, The Atlantic Monthly, Harper's Magazine.* Look at the titles of the articles; then skim through the content of these articles and decide whether the titles are commonplace, intriguing, novel (or too novel), appropriate. Copy those titles that you think skillfully chosen and put in parentheses the general subject of the articles.

B. Follow the procedure listed in Exercise A but apply it to the short stories in the same magazines.

C. Apply the directions in the last two sentences of Exercise A to 10 articles in your book of readings.

D. If your book of readings has short stories, apply the directions of Exercise B to 10 of these stories.

ANALYSIS OF SUBJECT

4. The first step in writing a theme, after you have chosen or been assigned a subject and have limited it, is a careful analysis of the subject. You should understand what the subject involves by asking and satisfactorily answering certain questions. Your answers can well· be your *controlling purpose* in planning and writing. You need an objective other than completion of a required assignment, since good purposeless writing does not exist.

Consider carefully answers for these important questions:

→1. How long is my paper to be?

→2. For what reader or readers am I to write? (The teacher is a "reader over your shoulder," an adviser, a kind of editor.)

→3. What is my specific purpose in writing this paper, the purpose which controls and centralizes my writing? Can I express the content of my planned paper in a single summarizing sentence, a thesis sentence, a theme-topic sentence?

→4. What do I already know about the subject? Where can I find additional material, and what kind of material do I need?

→5. What type of writing will best suit my subject: narrative, descriptive, expository, argumentative? (See Section 16.)

If you use the work-sheet method, put such information on Work Sheet 1. (See p. 24.)

4a. Begin your analysis on the basis of the number of words you are to write.

Themes vary in length. Some are 250 or 300 words, others are 500 words or 1,000 words, and long research papers may extend to 5,000 or 8,000 words. Choice of subject, narrowing of a fairly broad subject, choice of details, and plan of organization to be followed—all these are directly affected by the number of words you are to write.

4b. Make your analysis according to your prospective reader.

Nearly every piece of writing is a project for communicating to someone a series of thoughts and emotions. That "someone" may be a specially chosen individual, like the recipient of a business or friendly letter, or he may be one of a group. However, a group should not be too large, too broad. Such labels as "the average reader," "anyone interested," "city people," "college students," "high school graduates," "average driver," "a job hunter," "a stranger," "a person who intends to take a vacation" include people of such varied interests and backgrounds that a composition aimed at them can at best be general. Narrow "the reader" or "the group" for whom you are writing. Make sure, too, that your choice of reader is appropriate. It is inappropriate to choose a reader whom you talk to a dozen times a day, such as your roommate, or, if you live at home, a member of your family.

Writing aimed at an appropriate person or group is likely to be clear, concise, and effective. Your English teacher tries to judge how appropriately and effectively you have written for the reader or readers you have designated. For example, a theme on "My Background in English" may be written for your present English teacher to indicate the strong and weak points of your training. It may be written for your high school principal, suggesting changes in the course for students going to college. It may be written to your former high school English teachers and may give critical evaluation of their courses in the light of your present course.

4c. Determine the central purpose of the theme.

Before you begin to write, state in a single sentence (which may or may not be included in the theme later) your central purpose, your controlling idea. To play upon words, what is the *theme* of your theme? Write a *thesis* statement, a *topic sentence* for the paper, a sentence, either general or specific, that summarizes your entire material. Until you have done this, you have not fully or clearly defined your purpose. (For examples of thesis statements. see pp. 49–51.)

On the general subject, "A Camping Trip," you might clarify your purpose and procedure by jotting down for your own guidance:

Limited subject:	"Advice to a Young Camp Leader."
Possible title:	"Let's Take the Boys Camping."
Reader:	A camp leader who is starting his first summer of service.
Length:	1,000 words.
Thesis sentence (general):	Boys between 12 and 15 enjoy most those group activities—especially out of doors—which call for vigorous physical and mental exertion.
Or	
Thesis sentence (specific):	Kinds of recreational activities that appeal to boys between 12 and 15 years of age are (1) athletic and competitive (softball, tennis, swimming, horseshoes); (2) athletic and social (rowing, canoeing, hiking, woodcraft); (3) handicrafts; (4) mental (reading appropriate books, group discussions).

This material, also, might go on Work Sheet 1. The specific thesis sentence aids in making an outline; see pp. 58–59 for the outline developed from the specific thesis sentence above.

4d. In determining your central purpose, list 15 to 25 details that you might possibly use.

Make an inventory of what you know of the subject or make specific plans to find out more. (See Section 5.)

Put your inventory into words. Make a list of, say, 15 to 25 items that *might* be included and that *might* serve as the topic for a paragraph each. The items at first listing may come in no special order, for you will later prepare from them a revised list.

For example, in a theme on "When in Chicago, Visit the Planetarium," your list might include:

1. What a planetarium is.
2. History of the Planetarium.
3. Location.
4. Cost.
5. Description of building (exterior).
6. Description of building (interior).
7. Special exhibits.
8. Special lectures.
9. Maintenance of Planetarium.
10. Personnel.
11. Comparison of Chicago's Planetarium and New York's.
12. Value of planetariums.
13. Mechanics of the projecting machine.
14. Famous astronomers who have lectured there.
15. Best days to go ("free" days or "fee" days).
16. Necessity of making two or three visits.
17. My outstanding experiences there.
18. My personal recommendations to the visitor.

Or, on a simpler subject, like "Meet My High School," "The High School I Attended," or "Important Facts Concerning My High School," your list might include, as they come to mind:

1. Size.	8. Kinds of teachers.
2. Building.	9. Courses of study.
3. Location.	10. College prep courses.
4. History and name.	11. Commercial courses.
5. Number of students.	12. Vocational courses.
6. Kinds of students.	13. Athletic program.
7. Number of teachers.	14. Basketball championships.

15. Publications.
16. Social activities.
17. Class trips.

18. Dramatic presentations.
19. Musical activities.
20. English courses.

Naturally you would not include all such details in your theme nor in this first-draft order. But such a listing gives you an overview and suggests details to include or exclude. Your central purpose, after a study of the Planetarium list, might be limited to giving directions for reaching the Planetarium and to calling attention to special exhibits and lectures. From the list about your high school, your central purpose might be an evaluation of extracurricular activities, or a discussion of how well your high school studies and activities prepared you for college.

Using the work-sheet plan, you would put this material on Work Sheet 2.

4e. Choose a consistent method of development.

Even when you have sharply limited your subject to fit the number of allotted words, when you have chosen a specific reader or readers, and when you have made a list of possible items to include, you must do still more in your analysis. You must choose some method of development and treatment which will most clearly and effectively accomplish your purpose.

You may wish to narrate (anecdote, history, biography, etc.); to describe (details of persons or places); to explain (give directions, define, classify, tell how a mechanism works or a process develops, etc.); or to argue (give reasons for and against, give advantages and disadvantages, show the need for or value of, etc.). Or one type of development may be aided by another: in an expository paper, the use of specific narrative incidents, descriptive details, or comparisons and contrasts. (See Section 16.)

4f. Maintain a consistent tone or style.

Find a word or two (an adjective or noun, or two adjectives) which describe your purpose and planned treatment. Keep the characterizing term constantly in mind as you write; let your own choice of words be guided accordingly. When you have finished writing, check your written material for consistency with the specific descriptive word or phrase. Among such, the following are examples: *serious, dignified, solemn, formal, elevated, critical, humorous, flippant, facetious, light, light-hearted, cheerful, genial, gentle, conversational, chatty, familiar, breezy, racy, witty, breathless, whimsical, tranquil, peaceful, sad, mournful, eerie, persuasive, contentious, pungent, ironical, satirical, savage, vitriolic, cantankerous.* In the following three examples, notice the differences in tone:

Former President Woodrow Wilson used a *serious* and *dignified* tone in defining *liberty:*

> What is liberty?
> I have long had an image in my mind of what constitutes liberty. Suppose that I were building a great piece of powerful machinery, and suppose that I should so awkwardly and unskillfully assemble the parts of it that every time one part tried to move it would be interfered with by the others, and the whole thing would buckle up and be checked. Liberty for the several parts would consist in the best possible assembling and adjustment of them all, would it not? If you want the great piston of the engine to run with absolute freedom, give it absolutely perfect alignment and adjustment with the other parts of the engine, so that it is free, not because it is let alone or isolated, but because it has been associated most skillfully and carefully with the other parts of the great structure.
> What is liberty? You say of the locomotive that it runs free. What do you mean? You mean that its parts are so assembled and adjusted that friction is reduced to a minimum, and that it has perfect adjustment. We say of a boat skimming the water with light foot, "How free she runs," when we mean, how perfectly she is adjusted to the force of the wind, how perfectly she obeys the great breath out of the heavens that fills her sails. Throw her head up into the wind and see how she will halt and stagger, how every sheet will shiver and her whole frame be shaken, how instantly she is "in irons," in the expressive phrase of the sea. She is free only when you have let her fall off again and have recovered once more her nice adjustment to the forces she must obey and cannot defy.
> Human freedom consists in perfect adjustments of human interests and human activities and human energies.[2]

A *solemn* and *reflective* tone was used in *The Spectator,* No. 26, after Joseph Addison visited the tombs of the great and near-great in Westminster Abbey, London:

> When I am in a serious humour, I very often walk by myself in Westminster Abbey, where the gloominess of the place, and the use to which it is applied, with the solemnity of the building, and the condition of the

[2] From "The Liberation of a People's Vital Energies," *The New Freedom.* Copyright, 1913, Doubleday, Page & Company.

people who lie in it, are apt to fill the mind with a kind of melancholy, or rather thoughtfulness, that is not disagreeable. I yesterday passed a whole afternoon in the churchyard, the cloisters, and the church, amusing myself with the tombstones and inscriptions that I met with in those several regions of the dead. Most of them recorded nothing else of the buried person, but that he was born upon one day and died upon another: the whole history of his life being comprehended in those two circumstances that are common to all mankind. I could not but look upon these registers of existence, whether of brass or marble, as a kind of satire upon the departed persons, who had left no other memorial of them, but that they were born and that they died. They put me in mind of several persons mentioned in the battles of heroic poems who have sounding names given them, for no other reason but that they may be killed, and are celebrated for nothing but being knocked on the head. The life of these men is finely described in Holy Writ by *the path of an arrow,* which is immediately closed up and lost. . . .

I know that entertainments of this nature are apt to raise dark and dismal thoughts in timorous minds, and gloomy imaginations; but for my own part, though I am always serious, I do not know what it is to be melancholy, and can therefore take a view of nature in her deep and solemn scenes with the same pleasure as in her most gay and delightful ones. By this means I can improve myself with those objects, which others consider with terror. When I look upon the tombs of the great, every emotion of envy dies in me; when I read the epitaphs of the beautiful, every inordinate desire goes out; when I meet with the grief of parents upon a tombstone, my heart melts with compassion; when I see the tomb of the parents themselves, I consider the vanity of grieving for those whom we must quickly follow. When I see kings lying by those who deposed them, when I consider rival wits placed side by side, or the holy men that divided the world with their contests and disputes, I reflect with sorrow and astonishment on the little competitions, factions, and debates of mankind. When I read the several dates of the tombs, of some that died yesterday, and some six hundred years ago, I consider that great day when we shall all of us be contemporaries, and make our appearance together.

By contrast, in a tone of *vitriolic satire,* abundantly illustrated throughout his masterpiece, *Gulliver's Travels,* Jonathan Swift[3] writes about the human race. His hero, Gulliver, is a captive among people 60 feet tall and has just boasted about his country's government, religion, elections, courts of justice, army, and history; to this boasting, the Brobdingnagian king replies:

[3] For comment on Jonathan Swift as a writer, see p. 434.

. . . you have made a most admirable panegyric upon your country; you have clearly proved that ignorance, idleness, and vice are the proper ingredients for qualifying a legislator; that laws are best explained, interpreted, and applied by those whose interest and abilities lie in perverting, confounding, and eluding them. I observe among you some lines of an institution, which in its original might have been tolerable, but these half erased, and the rest wholly blurred and blotted by corruptions. It doth not appear from all you have said, how any one virtue is required towards the procurement of any one station among you; much less that men are ennobled on account of their virtue, that priests are advanced for their piety or learning, soldiers for their conduct or valour, judges for their integrity, senators for the love of their country, or counsellors for their wisdom. As for yourself (continued the King), who have spent the greatest part of your life in traveling, I am well disposed to hope you may hitherto have escaped many vices of your country. But by what I have gathered from your own relation, and the answers I have with much pains wringed and extorted from you, I cannot but conclude the bulk of your natives to be the most pernicious race of little odious vermin that nature ever suffered to crawl upon the surface of the earth.

Part II, Ch. vi, *Gulliver's Travels* (1726)

EXERCISES

A. Comment on the following as the readers for whom papers in the past have been written, according to students in freshman English classes. Which seem appropriate or inappropriate, which too general, and which properly specific? (1) Anyone who has an older sister. (2) Anyone who has a young brother. (3) Anyone with patience. (4) People who have not lived on a farm. (5) Any unmarried person. (6) Basketball lovers. (7) Anyone interested in traveling to Mexico. (8) A boy or girl, 14 to 17 years old. (9) A pen pal in England. (10) Anyone not from New York City.

B. Make a list of five theme subjects suitable for treatment in 250 to 500 words; five for treatment in 1,000 to 1,500 words; and five for treatment in 4,000 to 6,000 words.

C. Choose one subject from each of the three length groups in Exercise B and write a sentence or two for each, stating your central purpose (see Section **4c** and Section **6f**).

D. For one subject chosen in Exercise C, list 15 or 20 details that you might consider using in developing the theme.

E. For each of the subjects chosen in Exercise C, indicate your probable method of development (see Section **4e**).

F. Choose five of the *tones* listed in Section **4f**, and for each list three theme subjects which might be developed illustrating the particular tone chosen.

G. Restrict the following broad subjects to some phase which can be treated within the limits of an assigned theme-length paper:

1. Communism in America—Past and Present.
2. The Cosmetics Industry (or some other industry).
3. Clothes.
4. My College Career.
5. Games of Chance.
6. Campus Politics.
7. Athletics.
8. Academic Activities.
9. Misunderstandings Between Americans and Europeans.
10. Week-End Recreations.
11. National and State Parks.
12. TV Advertising.
13. Atomic Energy.
14. Atomic Weapons.
15. Space Research.

H. Using one of the limited subjects you have prepared for Exercise G, discuss various methods of development to suit different purposes and different kinds of readers.

I. Make a list of 10 subjects which are likely to be uninteresting to your fellow students. Mention methods of analysis and treatment which might make these subjects interesting.

CONTENT

5. A successful theme depends upon effort to collect material *before* you begin to write. In gathering this material, keep in mind the necessity of giving specific details to bolster the theme idea. One of the most lamentable weaknesses in the content of student themes is the tendency to make general statements with little use of concrete material or evidence to support the central idea or position. (See Section **24b, d.**)

5a.   Gather content from your own thought and experience.

Many students believe that their own ideas and experiences are not significant or interesting. Actually, as you are interested in what others say to you, others are interested in what you say to them. Significant and interesting materials are available from your own *experience, observation, curiosity, imagination,* and *reflection.* Indeed, every writer necessarily puts something of himself into everything he writes, his own ideas, reactions, and observations. An excellent source of content, therefore, is one's self.

5b. Gather content from the thought and experience of others.

Although you necessarily gather content from yourself, you should not neglect the material you may derive from others.

The easiest and perhaps most pleasant way of getting material for themes from other people is *discussion.* This may take the form of an *interview,* in which the ideas of the interviewed person constitute almost the whole of the theme. Or it may be merely a *conversation* with a member of your family, an acquaintance, or an instructor, in which there is an interchange of ideas, a give-and-take resulting in clarified and expanded thought. Classroom discussions are often an excellent source of material for compositions.

Another important way of getting content is *reading.* Magazines, newspapers, and books are almost inexhaustible sources of material which may be utilized. Half-formed ideas of your own may be intensified and expanded by reading. Entirely new phases of thought may be suggested, which, when put through the hopper of your mind, can legitimately be used as your own. A fruitful source of material, a combination of conversation and reading, is discussing with your classmates and instructor the ideas, and their significance, in book-of-readings assignments.

For special information a *letter of inquiry* to a company or to a recognized authority may provide valuable content, a method especially useful for a longer research paper. Likewise, you may obtain material for themes from *radio* and *television programs, motion pictures,* and *plays.* Although these are usually listened to or seen, not read, they do constitute the experiences and thoughts of other people and are fertile sources of content. Using these various sources, especially discussion and reading, you can write why you agree or disagree, or what your own opinions and beliefs are.

But in drawing upon the experiences and reflections of others, be careful to make them your own by assimilating the ideas and expressing them in your own words, unless you quote directly. When you make use of an idea new to you, either in your own or in quoted words, acknowledge your indebtedness. Sometimes a phrase is sufficient: "As Woodrow Wilson points out in his definition of 'liberty' in *The New Freedom, . . .*" or "These novelists, Joseph Warren Beach says in *American Fiction, 1920–1940,* were profoundly affected by the social conditions. . . ." Sometimes—in a research paper, for example—fuller acknowledgment is necessary; for the proper method and forms of documentation in research papers, see Section **20f.** You must avoid the charge of plagiarism—that is, taking the ideas and words of another and passing them off as your own.

EXERCISES

A. For each of the following groups make a list of five limited subjects which can be developed using your own thought, experience, and observation:

1. Past and Present Physical Activities.
2. Past and Present Social Activities.
3. My Environment (home, community, college).
4. Recreation and Avocation.
5. Education.
6. Vocational Experiences (full-time; part-time)
7. Financial Responsibilities.
8. Religion.
9. Politics.
10. Philosophy of Life.

B. Mention some experience or an incident that could be used in developing a theme based on one of the following topics:

1. Intercollegiate Football Should (Should Not) Be Abolished.
2. Activities and Studies Do Not Mix.
3. Buying Textbooks.
4. Earning and Saving Money.
5. The Value of a Time Budget.
6. Kindness to Animals.
7. A "Never Again" Experience.
8. The Earth from Above.
9. Drive-Ins.
10. Safe Automobile Driving.

OUTLINES AND OUTLINING

6. After analyzing your subject and gathering ample content, you must consider the problem of arranging your material. Order is important: a confusing arrangement will puzzle your reader.

The most frequently used method to insure clear ordering of parts in a theme is an outline: a sort of blueprint, a framework for the builder-writer of the theme; in one sense it is a recipe which contains the names of ingredients and the order in which they should be used. Outlines need not be elaborate or overly detailed: for very short papers, only the main heads or the main heads with the first division of sub-heads; for longer papers, from a half-page to a page or a page and a half. Outlines are only a guide to the writer, to be consulted as he writes, to be varied when other important ideas are suggested in the actual writing. In fact, as you write, you may find certain changes in plan effective and necessary.

Why have outlines? Many instructors require them for submitted themes because they know that a theme must be clearly ordered and proportioned to be effective, and because an outline aids the advisory reader as well as the writer in grasping organization. Certainly, no one can write an orderly composition without using *some kind* of outline, mental or written, actual or implied.

An outline existing only in the student's mind is of no help for a teacher who would like to make constructive suggestions about ordering and subdivision of ideas. Even a brief outline might well be written, and written *before* you write the theme. Only apparently logical is any student's statement that he cannot make an outline until he finishes his theme and knows what he has said. Would you like to live in, buy, and be proud of a house which the contractor built first and then made plans for after he knew what the house contained?

Three types of outlines are *topic outline, sentence outline,* and *paragraph outline;* each serves its own special purpose.

Preliminary to these three types of outlines is the "scratch" (or impromptu) outline, which is useful when time is short or the writer under pressure, as in planning a short class theme or preparing good answers for an essay type of examination. Five minutes can be profitably spent in making such an outline: listing a number of points, major and minor, directly or indirectly related, and then quickly, with lines or numbers or both, indicating the relative and logical order of these points. With more time, the writer can develop the "scratch" outline into a topic or sentence outline.

6a. Use a topic outline to make clear to yourself the arrangement of your ideas.

The topic outline consists of words, phrases, or dependent clauses, not sentences. It has meaning to the writer for immediate use; perhaps six weeks later he will not know what the topics mean. Such an outline may be very simple:

MY MOST MEMORABLE DAY

I. The evening before
II. The day itself
III. The morning after

WHY "GO ON" WITH LATIN?[4]

I. The popular reason why people go on with any subject (136 words)
II. The practical reason why people go on with any subject (75 words)
III. The attractive reason why people go on with any subject (148 words)
IV. The effective reason why people go on with any subject (134 words)
V. Application of "the effective reason" to Latin (199 words)
  A. An enlightened perspective (97 words)
  B. An accompanying sense of intellectual mastery (102 words)

NOTE: The figures in parentheses indicate how proportion and proper length (see Section 7b) can be achieved. In addition, in the article written from this outline, an introductory paragraph had 44 words and a concluding paragraph had 59 words.

The topic outline may be more elaborate, more detailed:

CAMPUS VERSUS CLASSROOM[5]

Thesis sentence: "Campus Versus Classroom" contrasts the scholarship activities of the classroom and the extracurricular activities

[4] For a 995-word article from this outline, see Warren E. Black, "Why 'Go On' with Latin?" in *School and Society,* LXIX (May 7, 1949), 334–335.

[5] For a 2,800-word article from this outline, see Burges Johnson, *Campus Versus Classroom,* 1946. The outline is based on the selection "Campus Versus Classroom," in *Readings for Opinion,* 2nd ed., pp. 282–293, edited by Earl Davis and William C. Hummel (Englewood Cliffs, N.J., 1960). A paragraph outline of this selection appears in Section 6c.

of the campus; it shows how little actual time there is for academic training, how extracurricular activities conflict with activities of the classroom, and how there may eventually be a solution in their merger.

I. The problem of the classroom (scholarship)
  A. Vacation
    1. Its length
    2. Its lack of relation to post-college life
    3. Its supposed justification
    4. Why it persists
  B. The college "year" (32 weeks) and the time that is lost
    1. Enrolling and examinations (over 5 weeks)
    2. "Hell Week"
    3. Athletic program
    4. A "prom"
    5. "Senior Week" or "Junior Week"
    6. The cut system
    7. Saturday holidays
II. The problem of the campus (its activities)
  A. Its war with scholarship
  B. What its activities are
  C. Woodrow Wilson on the life and work of a college
  D. The confusion of the two (campus and classroom) in the minds of administrators
III. Possible solutions to the problems
  A. The original old-world setup
    1. Not wanted
    2. Probably not workable
  B. A complete merger of campus and classroom

6b.   **Use a sentence outline to make clear to yourself and to a reader the arrangement of ideas.**

The *sentence outline* consists of grammatically complete sentences. Such an outline should be clear, now and later, to the writer; it should be equally clear to any reader who would make constructive suggestions. For this latter reason many teachers insist upon sentence outlines. The outline may be simple:

My Most Memorable Day

I. I spent the previous evening putting my soap-box racer into perfect condition.

II. I won all my preliminary heats, won the semifinals, and came in first in the finals.

III. I was greeted with a parade in my home town and given all kinds of civic honors.

The outline may also be more elaborate, more detailed:

UNIVERSITY DAYS[6]

Thesis sentence: I never could pass botany, but I passed all the other courses that I took at the university: economics, physical education, and military drill.

I. I never could pass botany.
   A. I was unable to see through a microscope.
   B. I repeated the course.
      1. The professor vowed that he would make me see.
      2. I did see, but it was only the reflection of my own eye.

II. I did not like economics but I managed to pass it.
   A. I had my own troubles with the course.
   B. They were nothing to the troubles of a football tackle, Bolenciecwcz.

III. I had more anguish in gymnasium work than I had in botany and economics.
   A. I could not see to do the exercises or play the games.
   B. I could not pass the swimming requirement.
   C. I disliked the physical examination.

IV. I did not have the trouble with journalism that a certain agricultural student had.

V. I had trouble passing the military drill requirement.
   A. We drilled with outmoded rifles and studied Civil War tactics.
   B. I spent four years on military drill.
   C. I had one moment of military glory in the presence of General Littlefield.
   D. I had an interesting interview with General Littlefield the next day.

NOTE 1:   Use declarative sentences in the sentence outline for clearness. Interrogative sentences are usually uninformative; exclamatory sentences are somewhat unusual and inappropriate; imperative sentences, only when appropriate, are clear.

NOTE 2:   Unless carefully phrased, even declarative sentences may not be clear; such sentences should outline content, not procedure.

[6] For this well-known and widely reprinted essay, see James Thurber, *My Life and Hard Times* (New York, 1933).

AUTO ACCIDENTS

Not clear:
    I. The major causes of accidents will be discussed.
    II. Methods of preventing accidents will be presented.
    III. Suggestions for making the methods effective will be given.

Clear:
    I. Auto accidents are caused by both mechanical and human failures.
    II. Accidents can be reduced by careful check of cars and greater responsibility by drivers.
    III. City officials, police, school authorities, and clergymen can lead in a campaign to make effective the suggestions for fewer accidents.

6c. Use a paragraph outline primarily as a first step in outlining the work of others.

The paragraph outline consists of groups of sentences—perhaps, but not necessarily, topic sentences (see Section 23), indicating the contents of whole paragraphs.

Such an outline is valuable to the writer only when the theme is to consist of two, three, four, or five paragraphs. His outline consists of his topic sentences or summarizing sentences, usually designated by Arabic numbers.

The paragraph outline is especially useful as a first step in outlining someone else's work, such as a magazine article or book chapter. Topic sentences are chosen, or summary sentences are written, to present the thought of successive paragraphs in a selection being studied. From these sentences a topic outline or sentence outline can be built which reveals major and minor divisions.

Here, as an example, is a paragraph outline of James Thurber's "University Days"; from this outline the sentence outline on page 51 was prepared:

1. I could not pass botany because I could not see through a microscope.
2. I tried again a year later.
3. The professor was sure that he could teach me to use the microscope.
4. We tried every adjustment known to man, but we did not succeed.
5. I did not like economics but I managed to pass the course, with less trouble than Bolenciecwcz, the tackle on the football team.

6, 7, 8, 9, 10, 11, 12, 13 (dialogue). With encouragement from the pro-
    fessor, Bolenciecwcz answered one question correctly.
14. Gymnasium work was worse for me, for I could not see without glasses
    and I disliked swimming and the physical examination; I finally passed
    anyway.
15. Haskins, a student from a farm, was not a success in journalism.
16. Ohio State required two years of military drill, with outmoded equip-
    ment and Civil War tactics.
17. I failed military drill at the end of each year and was still taking it as
    a senior.
18. By executing one command correctly, I became a corporal.
19. General Littlefield summoned me to his office the next day, but the
    interview did not lead anywhere.

Here, as another example, is a paragraph outline of Burges Johnson's
"Campus Versus Classroom"; from this outline the topic outline on
pages 49–50 was prepared.

1. The serious-minded boy who goes away to college dreams that he is
   about to dedicate four years of his life to higher education.
2. Tradition says that 20 of the annual 52 weeks shall be given over to
   "vacation," perhaps on the theory that a student needs to regain the
   physical strength he has lost in long hours of hard study.
3. Today this long break in the college year is continued partly from habit
   and partly because it has become a vested right of the teacher, whose
   underpayment in salary is counterbalanced by overpayment in leisure.
4. I should like now to examine the 32 weeks in terms of classroom and
   study hours, in the prewar era.
5. One-sixth of the time of the classroom has been taken from it for the
   business of organization and tests.
6. Then come other fixed demands made by the campus and enforced by
   tradition.
7. A "prom" with attendant house parties is more than an evening dance
   after the day's work is over.
8. In many colleges "Senior Week" or "Junior Week" is a fixture, with
   festivities supplanting study for five or six consecutive days.
9. In order to regularize student attendance, or from some other reason
   now known to God alone, each individual student is allowed a fixed
   number of unexplained and pre-excused "cuts" to provide for emer-
   gencies. . . . All of these drains upon class time have reduced the 32
   weeks to 22.

10. I add to this list the Saturday holidays which are a matter of routine at a majority of our universities and colleges.
11. It seems that activities which began spontaneously as outlets for youthful energy in a day when the campus and the surrounding community offered too little variety have now jelled into conventional forms.
12. These activities have not only been thieves of time, but they have been at war with scholarship, many of them secretly and some of them openly and brazenly.
13. The list is long, and if some champion denies the war, the answer is: then why is the activity not a part of the curriculum and an adjunct of the classroom?
14. All of them (the list) are potential enemies of the classroom, and all are actual enemies in one college or another.
15. "*Life* at college," wrote Woodrow Wilson, "is one thing, the *work* of the college another, entirely separate and distinct."
16. A fundamental absurdity of our undergraduate administration is this: it will not admit frankly that classroom instruction is no longer its sole excuse or even its chief excuse for being.
17. The fact is that in ruling over two separate jurisdictions an administrator confuses them in his own mind or thoughtlessly allows them to clash with each other.
18. Many worth-while experiments in college organization have been tried, but no American college has dared to try going all the way back to the original old-world setup; this would mean devoting itself solely to the business of scholarship.
19. Probably such an experiment in American undergraduate college administration has not been tried because no one wants it; it would not work, the chief reason being the immaturity of American college boys and girls.
20. President Hopkins once remarked that the most effective college would be a combination of orphanage and penal institution.
21. The representatives of the former republic of Czechoslovakia, after visiting many American colleges, assembled at Vassar College to compare notes and draw up a message of advice to Czechoslovak students who might follow them.
22. The Czech women observed that the life of the campus did much to develop self-reliance and initiative in American women students.
23. My only reason for suggesting that an undergraduate college might try the experiment of complete indifference to campus life is to bring out in sharper relief the obvious alternative—that some college might try bringing about a complete merger of campus and classroom.

6d. Make your outlines correct in form.

Since the purpose of an outline is to show the structure (the plan, the arrangement) of a piece of writing, mechanical correctness, so-called, is important only as it serves this purpose. Actually, outline form is neither correct nor incorrect; writers in the past have followed certain conventions, and these conventions are described in this and the next section.

The outline, whether topic, sentence, or paragraph, is based on division of material into parts. Analysis of your subject shows major divisions and the order in which you can .best discuss them. You make these divisions the foundations of your outline and examine them to determine what subtopics you need to include to make the discussion complete.

The examples of outlines in Section **6a, b,** and **c** show the conventional use of symbols, indentation, and punctuation.

In making the *topic outline,* follow these directions:

1. Indicate the major divisions by using Roman numerals, I, II, III, IV, etc. Begin flush at the left margin.

2. Indicate the first series of subdivisions under each main division by using capital letters, A, B, C, D, etc., indented equally.

3. Indicate the next series of subdivisions (if needed) by Arabic numbers, 1, 2, 3, 4, etc., also equally indented; and if still further subdivisions are needed, use small letters, a, b, c, d, etc., equally indented. But do not divide too minutely; avoid excessive detail; keep the number of main headings and major subdivisions to a minimum, consistent with clearness, order, and meaning.

4. Use a period after each symbol. Periods at the ends of topics are optional, but be consistent in their use or omission.

In making the *sentence outline,* follow the directions given just above for the topic outline. The only difference is the use of some terminating mark of punctuation—period, question mark, exclamation point—at the end of all divisions and subdivisions.

In making the *paragraph outline,* use Arabic numbers. Roman numerals would serve, but for some 30 to 50 paragraphs the numbering is complicated (see Section **99e**). A period follows the symbol; a period or a question mark comes at the end of the sentence. The beginning of each sentence may be indented, or it may begin flush at the left margin, with run-over lines indented.

6e. Make your outlines consistent in their divisions and their wording.

A few words and phrases jotted down at random are not an outline. A usable outline requires thought. You must give it a consistent structure if the theme you write from it is to be well arranged and clear. Therefore, you must critically examine your first draft of the outline and carefully revise it. Remove repetitions and overlappings; add specific details where necessary; remove illogical relationships; rearrange parts for more effective organization.

To attain these aims in outlining, follow these suggestions:

1. Be sure that the first or any main heading *does not repeat the title.*

Wrong: Advice to a High School Student

     I. Advice to a high school student
    II. Types of courses to take in high school

How to Be a Good Friend

     I. Friend—a definition
    II. Types of friends
       A. Fair-weather friends
       B. True friends
    III. How to be a good friend
       A. Be loyal
       B. Be sincere
       C. Be helpful
    IV. Rewards in being a good friend

2. Use *parallel phrasing* (see Section 44) to make your outline divisions clear and effective: use words or the same kind of phrases or clauses or sentences for all main divisions and subdivisions. Do not use a word for one topic and a phrase or dependent clause for another, and do not mix the two kinds of outlines, topic and sentence.

Who I Am

Wrong:	Improved:	Improved:
I. About my name	I. My name	I. What my name is
II. About my home	II. My home town	II. Where I come from
III. Occupation	III. My occupation	III. What I am doing

56

3. Do not put in a subhead any matter that should be in a larger division, and do not put in a main heading any matter that should be in a subdivision.

MEET MY ROOMMATE

Wrong:	Wrong:
I. Physical appearance	I. Physical appearance
A. His name	II. Height, weight, age, complexion
B. His outstanding character trait	
C. His worst fault	

4. Remember that outlining is division, that subdivision means *division into at least two parts.* If a single minor topic must be mentioned, express it in, or as part of, its major heading, or add another coordinate minor topic.

Wrong:
WHY ACCIDENTS HAPPEN

    I. Major reason for accidents
      A. Drivers at fault
   II. Minor reason for accidents
      A. Roads and highways at fault
  III. Proposed solution
      A. Better driver training

Do not artificially seek a subdivision B or a subdivision 2 to correspond to a possible A or 1. Carry a single subdivision in your mind or make it part of the larger division. Some teachers accept and advise a single subdivision when it is to serve as one example or one illustration, since an outline can be a plan of additions as well as of divisions; however, such an example or illustration can usually be incorporated as part of a larger division.

Advisable:

    I. Major reason for accidents: drivers at fault
   II. Minor reason for accidents: roads and highways at fault
  III. Proposed solution: better driver training

Advisable:
KINDS OF RESTAURANTS

  I. Those specializing in American food
 II. Those specializing in foreign foods

(*Cont'd*)   A. Italian (Antonelli's in Pittsburgh for spaghetti)
                   B. Chinese (Fu Yung in St. Louis for chop suey)
                   C. Swedish (Swenson's in Detroit for smörgåsbord)

5. *Avoid meaningless headings* such as *Introduction, Body, Conclusion.* If you know what these parts are to contain, put your ideas into words and use them as headings. Avoid even such headings as *Reasons, Causes, Results, Effects,* unless you accompany them with explanatory material or subheads.

6. If your theme is to contain short introductory and concluding paragraphs, you need not indicate such paragraphs by outline topics. For example, the article written from the outline "Why 'Go On' with Latin?" on page 49 has a brief introductory paragraph of 44 words and a brief concluding paragraph of 59 words.

6f.   Use a <u>thesis sentence</u> in the preparation or development of your outline.

Many writers like to use a *thesis sentence,* one sentence providing the gist of the whole paper or a kind of topic sentence (see Section 23) not for one paragraph but for all. The thesis sentence may summarize a writer's thinking before he begins making his outline, or it may serve to tie together his various thoughts after the outline has been written. Your teacher may ask you to prepare a thesis sentence and to place it between title and outline. Examples of thesis sentences are given preceding the outlines for "Campus Versus Classroom" and "University Days," on pages 49–50 and page 51.

You may, of course, write your thesis sentence from a tentative or final outline. If you thoughtfully prepare your thesis sentence first, it may make easy your preparation of an outline. Study the closeness of the thesis sentence and the outline of "Campus Versus Classroom," pages 49–50, and of "University Days," page 51. Note also in these and in the example below that the main-heading topics or sentences add up to the thesis sentence.

The specific thesis sentence for "Let's Take the Boys Camping," page 39, develops into the following outline:

    I. Participation in competitive athletics
       A. Soft ball (team effort)
       B. Swimming (two or many competitors)
       C. Tennis and horseshoes (two or four contestants)

II. Sharing of noncompetitive athletic activities
   A. Rowing and canoeing
   B. Hiking and woodcraft
III. Instruction in handicrafts (woodcarving, carpentry, ceramics, cooking)
IV. Guidance in mental activities
   A. Reading appropriate books
   B. Participating in group discussions

EXERCISES

  A. Rewrite the following outlines, eliminating all errors:

(1)   ARE COLLEGE BOYS STUDENTS?

I. Definition of word *student.*
   a. Reference to several dictionaries.
II. Many boys come to college to engage in athletics.
   A. Some come to enjoy the social life.
   B. Others to keep from working.
III. A minority come to get a real education.
   1. Preparation for various professions.
      a. Medicine, dentistry.
         1. Law, teaching.
IV. Summary and Conclusion.

(2)   THREE 4-H ACTIVITIES

I Junior leadership
  a) age
  b) experience
  C) girls' and boys' projects
II Clothing
  a) Age

B) experience
C) Time
D) Cost
III Freezing
  a) where purchased
  B) Cost

(3)   AN INTRODUCTION TO THE FIELD OF
        TEACHING HOME ECONOMICS

I. Introduction to the Field of Teaching Home Economics.
  A. Cooking

B. How to sew
C. Drawing and ceramics

(4)   MEET MY ROOMMATES

I. Roommates   d. Physical and Mental character-
  a. Their names and where their   istics
    home towns are   e. What I like about them
  b. Their hobbies   f. What I dislike about them
  c. What we have in common

(5)   SOME POPULAR SUPERSTITIONS

I. Introduction   II. Body   III. Conclusion

(6)   THREE AIRPLANE RIDES

I. First was slow and gentle   II. Long   III. Wild

(7)   CHRISTMAS AT HOME

  I. Christmas at Home   II. Opening my presents
    A. A delightful occasion   III. Christmas Day

(8)   MY FIRST GUN

A. Out Hunting   C. Getting shot
B. Showing my Cousin   D. Lesson Learned

(9)   TWELVE DEGREES BELOW ZERO

  I Really cold
    A. 12 degrees below
    B. froze my ears going to school
    C. have to walk through cold part of campus
  II Had to get up
    A. wanted to go back to bed
    B. brother wore 4 pairs pants and 3 shirts
  III Going to drive to school
    A. Battery cracked
    B. wheels frozen
    C. Every class clear across campus
    D. Had a cold for 3 weeks

(10)   The High School I Attended

I. Bldgs	1. Kind of teachers
a. size	2. No. of teachers
b. location	IV. Course of Study
II. Students	1. College prep
No. of	2. General course
Kind of Students	3. Vocational study
III. Teachers	

B. Make correct topic outlines for the three themes indicated by the topics you chose in Exercise C on page 44.

C. Make a correct sentence outline for five themes that you could write on the topics chosen in Exercise B on page 44.

D. Make a paragraph outline of one of the essays in your book of readings.

E. Change the paragraph outline (Exercise D) into a sentence outline.

F. Change the sentence outline (Exercise E) into a topic outline.

G. After you have prepared the topic outline (Exercise F), write after each of your main divisions and subdivisions the number of words used by the author. Study this word-numbered outline with the essay or article from the point of view of proper or inadequate proportion.

PROPORTION

7. The principle of proportion is simply that of giving any part of a theme the space and attention which are appropriate to your reader and to your subject.

7a. Develop divisions of a theme in proportion to their importance.

Proportion concerns the amount of space, or details of treatment, for the various parts of a composition. It requires that the development given each division of a theme—each paragraph or each group of paragraphs—be in accord with the relative importance of the division. Note the word *relative;* importance is not absolute. In determining which parts of a theme should be developed at length and which less fully, you must be guided by the *purpose* of the theme and the *readers* for whom it is written. Ordinarily, do not give disproportionate space to less closely related or minor sections of your theme or to material which your reader already knows. Ordinarily, also, give greater space to sections which may be difficult to understand otherwise or which are to be emphasized.

If, for example, your purpose in writing on "TV Advertising" is to show that such advertising is overdone, your theme will be badly proportioned if you devote more than half the space to a discussion of the origin and growth of general advertising and only a small part of the composition to the central theme. Similarly, if you are writing a theme on "Campus Customs" for your classmates, you can appropriately give less space to many important details well known to them than if you are writing on the same subject for a group of high school students. Even for your classmates, if you argue for the abandonment of certain customs and the retaining of others, the ones you wish to change will get more space than the ones with which you have no quarrel.

7b. Use an outline to give your theme proportion.

A good outline enables you to achieve proper order and assists you in achieving proportion and appropriate length—an adequate number of words for each major division and subdivision for purposes of clearness and effectiveness.

Careful planning helps you to write a well-balanced paper, neither too long nor too short. If you do not follow some guide to proportion, you may write a narrative of five pages, of which four deal with relatively unimportant details and only one with the really important part of the story. Or in an expository theme, you may write 400 words of introductory material and then realize that you have only 100 left, into which you may attempt to compress important ideas which needed most of the 400-word space.

As a practical suggestion for proportion, place in parenthesis marks after each part of your outline the number of words you plan to write on that division or subdivision. The sum of the subdivision words should equal the major division; the sum of the major divisions should equal the total number of words required. This allocation is, of course, only tentative; you may find expansion or contraction necessary. (For an example of such allocation, see the outline of "Why 'Go On' with Latin?" on p. 49.)

EXERCISES

A. Count the number of words in each paragraph of three of your recent themes. Put the numbers after the appropriate divisions in the outlines for these themes. Comment in a paragraph or two on your use of proportion, giving consideration to both subject and reader.

B. Among other errors the following theme lacks proportion. Why?

WHAT I EXPECT TO GET FROM COLLEGE BESIDES FACTS

I. Important to study, but many other things just as important.
II. Points one can learn at a big university.
III. College is a basis for later life.

When I knew that I was coming to Purdue, I was very thrilled with the idea of coming to a big university. I realize that it is extremely important to study hard in college and to learn everything I possibly can, but I also believe that I am at Purdue for a great many other reasons.

In high school, I had a certain group of friends that I "palled around with" all the time. All my friends lived in the same city and had been brought up just as I had. Also, our beliefs and ideas were pretty much the same. When a person goes to a big school like Purdue, they meet all kinds of people from places all over the world. To me, this is a marvelous experience because you must learn to get along with people whose beliefs and ideas are much different from others.

If people would really take to heart what another person says or believes, although maybe they don't agree, I know they would learn something that would be of great value to them in later life.

Before I came to Purdue, I had never been away from home. Now, I feel more or less on my own, knowing that I have to make all my own decisions and work out all my problems without the wonderful help of my mother or dad.

I believe that every person at Purdue should be in an extracurricular activity. People can certainly receive valuable information by working with others, and activities are a splendid way of expressing one's ideas.

College not only gives one a chosen profession, but a basis for later life. I expect to learn a great deal more than I already know and what I learn, I will remember for a lifetime.

BEGINNING THE THEME

8. After gathering, outlining, and proportioning content, you must *begin* the composition. The body of a theme is naturally important, but so are beginnings and endings because they are first and last impressions. These should be direct, clear, effective, and appropriate, not abrupt or wordy. If such material is not carefully composed, the theme lacks proportion.

8a. Avoid a beginning referring indirectly and vaguely to the title.

Remember the advice given under Section **3d**: the opening sentences of a theme should be self-explanatory. The reader should not have to refer to the title for the meaning of "This subject . . . ," "On this trip . . . ," "Such an accident . . . ," "These evils. . . ." Here are four improved understandable opening sentences of the foregoing:

Collecting matchbooks as a hobby is fascinating.

On our trip to Mexico we met interesting people and saw memorable scenes.

A head-on collision of two automobiles traveling at high speed is the worst kind of motor accident.

The evils of TV advertising are numerous.

8b. Avoid unnecessary formal introductions.

Write an introduction if and when your theme requires one. Usually, only long papers require a formal beginning giving extended definition of terms, history of the subject, or a long statement of its significance. Do not make a series of general statements or give needless explanations and details.

8c. Avoid wordy beginnings.

Many writers ramble for some time before they warm to their subject. They seem to be building a platform from which to "take off." By the time the reader reaches the "take-off point," he has lost interest in the subject.

Look at the second or third paragraph of your theme. If your theme really begins there, you can throw away everything before it.

Occasionally, a student labors through much introductory material and finally turns up something worth talking about near the end. He stops at that point; he should make this his starting point.

8d. Avoid beginnings that are too abrupt.

Contrasting with the wordy beginning is the beginning which is too abrupt. Do not bewilder your reader by beginning so abruptly that he is unable to understand what follows. If preliminary details are needed, give them.

Direct, clear, effective, and appropriate beginnings serve one major purpose: orientation. At the end of your first paragraph, ask yourself: "Does my reader have his bearings in the discussion? Does he know where he is and in what direction he is moving?" If your answer is "No," throw away what you have written and try again.

For clear and effective beginnings the happy medium between *too much* and *too little* is assurance that your reader will continue reading with interest and pleasure.

8e. Begin themes directly and clearly.

Here are four direct and clear beginnings, avoiding false starts and loose generalities:

1. *Repetition of the title in the opening sentence.*

The evils of TV advertising project like pinnacles above the lesser evils of other forms of advertising.

2. *Rephrasing or paraphrasing the title in the opening sentence.*

Of all forms of advertising, that broadcast by TV is the most brazen and least effective.

3. *A setting or framework within which the subject will develop.*

Everyone is familiar with TV broadcasting, but not everyone realizes that many TV programs not only give information and entertainment but also enrich those who prepare, present, and pay for them.

4. *A summary or outline paragraph enumerating the main divisions to be discussed.*

TV advertising is guilty of four deadly sins: the sin of exaggeration, the sin of false taste, the sin of usurpation, and the sin of greed.

These four beginnings, respectively, are further illustrated in the following opening sentences:

1. The method of scientific investigation is nothing but the expression of the necessary mode of working of the human mind. . . .
—Thomas Henry Huxley, "The Method of Scientific Investigation"

2. The White Star liner *Titanic,* largest ship the world had ever known, sailed from Southampton on her maiden voyage to New York on April 10, 1912. . . .
—Hanson W. Baldwin, "R.M.S. *Titanic*"

3. At this moment of time, when humanity stands upon the threshold of space and has already launched its first vehicles beyond the atmosphere, there is a centuries-old question which presses more and more urgently for an answer. In almost any astronomy book you will find a chapter devoted to the subject: "Is there life on other worlds?"—the answer given depending upon the optimism of the author and the period in which he is writing (for there are fashions in astronomy as in everything else).

—Arthur C. Clarke, "Where's Everybody?"

4. Having finished one semester at Atwood University, I believe that the three most important things I have learned are the following: how to study properly, how to work together with other people, and how to assume responsibilities.

—Student theme, "A Review of My First Semester in College"

The direct beginning—a kind of topic sentence for the whole composition—immediately informs the reader by giving the central thought or *theme* of the theme.

8f. Begin themes effectively by use of the appropriate kind of sentence.

A good beginning gains the reader's attention and so interests him that he wishes to continue reading. Direct and clear beginnings, like those suggested in Section 8e, are usually effective. The kind of sentence or sentences used—declarative, imperative, interrogative, and exclamatory—expressing meaning and purpose, can add clearness and effectiveness.

1. *Declarative sentence.*

In this age few tragedies are written. . . .

—Arthur Miller, "Tragedy and the Common Man"

2. *Imperative sentence.*

Come with me for an autumn tour of the sights and sounds of Great Smoky National Park.

—Student theme, "The Great Smokies in Autumn"

3. *Exclamatory sentence.*

Wagons west!

—Norman Wilkinson, "The Conestoga Wagon"

4. *Interrogative sentence, i.e., a direct question alone or as part of a context statement.*

Does the spread of American prosperity threaten quality? Are we achieving a mass of second-rate education, second-rate culture, second-rate thinking, and squeezing out the first-rate?
—FREDERICK LEWIS ALLEN, "The Spirit of the Times"

5. *Sentence containing a condition.*

If you were suddenly chosen from a group and asked to make an informal luncheon talk, or address a business meeting, or even speak to millions of people over radio and TV, how would your voice sound to your listeners?
—STEPHEN S. PRICE, "Put Your Best Voice Forward"

8g.   Begin themes effectively by use of an appropriate personal pronoun.

Impersonal beginnings and those using the third-person pronoun, singular or plural, are effective; equally effective is the use of the first and second person pronoun.

1. *First person (I, we).*

The day I was graduated from college I believed—modestly, and yet with a nice warm glow of conviction—that I was an educated young woman. I had salted away an impressive supply of miscellaneous information. My mind, after constant limbering up with fancy mental gymnastics, was as supple as a ballerina. I was all set to deal with Life.
—MARION WALKER ALCARO, "Colleges Don't Make Sense"

We do not think enough about thinking, and much of our confusion is the result of current illusions in regard to it. Let us forget for the moment any impressions we may have derived from the philosophers, and see what seems to happen in ourselves. . . .
—JAMES HARVEY ROBINSON, "On Various Kinds of Thinking"

2. *Second person (you).*

It finally happened. After months, maybe years of watching the other fellow squirm on a platform, you've been called upon to make a speech. . . .
—ANONYMOUS, "Our Speaker Is . . ."

NOTE 1: From the examples given, you notice that the beginnings illustrated in Sections **8f** and **8g** may be and often are combined, as in the following, one "direct question—we" beginning and one "direct question—you" beginning:

Of what use is a college training? We who have had it seldom hear the question raised—we might be a little nonplused to answer it offhand. . . .
—WILLIAM JAMES, "The Social Value of the College-Bred"

Have you ever wondered what you would say if you were suddenly called upon to defend the human race?
—NORMAN COUSINS, "Don't Resign from the Human Race"

NOTE 2: Use the *you* beginning carefully and appropriately, not as an impertinent or buttonholing device to involve your reader by mechanical means. Make sure that the *you* is a genuine and appropriate address to your reader, that the *you* and the problem stated really concern him.

Ineffective and inappropriate for most readers:
Have you ever built a bird house?
Have you ever climbed a mountain peak in the Himalaya Mountains?
Did you know that the air we breathe is often called ozone?

Appropriate:
Your local, state, and national taxes are high and may go higher? What are you going to do about them? (Group of tax-paying citizens)
Are you observing the necessary precautions for safety in your school laboratory? (Laboratory students)
Your eyes are your most precious possession. Learn about them and their proper care. (College students)

8h. Begin themes effectively by varying the content of the beginnings.

An effective beginning must use one of the kinds of sentences illustrated in Section 8f, and it may use one of the pronoun approaches illustrated in Section 8g. Sometimes, as already seen, two kinds or more may be combined.

Effective beginnings also use different kinds of content—*alone* or *in combination*. These are illustrated in the opening sentence or sentences of many magazine articles, chapters of books, and the excerpts or selections chosen for books of readings. Some of the most frequently used content-beginnings are the following; compare them with the titles given after the authors' names:

1. *A significant or startling statement.* Such a statement should not be used for attention and interest alone; it should have some connection with what is to follow.

The greatest single obstacle to human happiness is not disease, or war, death, or even hunger. It isn't jealousy. It *is* superstition.
                                        —PHILIP WYLIE, "Witchcraft Is Hurting You"

Podunk, as a place name, is older in American history than New York, Philadelphia, and Baltimore, and only six years junior to Boston, yet the lexicographers still pass it over with titters, and try to give the impression that the place itself is a mere hypothetical entity, like the square root of minus zero. . . .
                                        —H. L. MENCKEN, "The Podunk Mystery"

2. *Timely news events or seasonal occurrences.*

This is the time of year [fall] when students all over the country are discovering that the courses they are taking are not what the college catalogues said they were. . . .
                                        —REED WHITTEMORE, "College Catalogues"

3. *Reference to a historical event.*

More than three centuries ago a handful of pioneers crossed the ocean to Jamestown and Plymouth in search of freedoms they were unable to find in their own countries, the freedoms we still cherish today: freedom from want, freedom from fear, freedom of speech, freedom of religion. . . .
                                        —SEYMOUR ST. JOHN, "The Fifth Freedom"

4. *An illustrative incident or anecdote, personal or impersonal.*

A bright-eyed woman, whose sparkle was rather more of eagerness than of intelligence, approached me at a party one afternoon and said, "Why do you hate women, Mr. Thurber?" I quickly adjusted my fixed grin and denied that I hated women; I said I did not hate women at all. But the question remained with me, and I discovered when I went to bed that night that I had been subconsciously listing a number of reasons why I do hate women. It might be interesting—at least it will help to pass the time—to set down these reasons, just as they came up out of my subconscious.
                                        —JAMES THURBER, "The Case Against Women"

During the second week in August, 1946, an elderly man, a middle-aged woman, and a boy of ten dragged themselves, singly and painfully, into the Presbyterian Hospital, in the Washington Heights section of Manhattan, where their trouble was unhesitatingly identified as typhoid fever. This diagnosis was soon confirmed by laboratory analysis, and on Thursday morning, August 15th, a report of the outbreak was dutifully telephoned to the Department of Health. . . .

—Berton Roueche, "A Game of Wild Indians"

5. *A combination of narrative and descriptive details.*

Late last autumn, when the first snow flurries dusted across the northern half of the United States, an estimated three million pairs of knees began to twitch. This mass flexing was the first symptom of a seasonal phenomenon that has progressed in twenty years from the status of a foreign foolishness to that of a national mania. Although still in early stages of development, this phenomenon has reversed migratory instincts, cut scars in the faces of ancient mountains, created an economic revolution in rural areas, upped the income of the medical profession, and released several million inmates of modern society into flights of ecstatic freedom.

—Eric Swenson, "Let Fly Downhill"

6. *An observed experience.*

Everyone has heard people quarreling. Sometimes it sounds funny and sometimes it sounds merely unpleasant; but however it sounds, I believe we can learn something very important from listening to the kind of things they say.

—C. S. Lewis, "Right and Wrong as a Clue to the
Meaning of the Universe"

7. *References to people—contemporary or historical, prominent or unknown.*

When I was in St. Augustine, Florida, in the winter of 1932, Helen Keller appeared at the Cathedral Lyceum, and I went to see and hear her there, drawn by curiosity, such as one feels for any world-famous person.

—Van Wyck Brooks, "Helen Keller"

In a dim hut in the Wild Arctic Circle region of Sweden, an area of impenetrable forests and howling storms, a doctor knelt by a stricken patient to wrestle with death.

—Ralph Wallace, "Doctor at the End of the World"

8. *Directly or indirectly quoted material of some kind or the report of a conversation.*

There is a characteristic saying of Dr. Johnson: "Patriotism is the last refuge of a scoundrel." The saying is cynical, many will even call it brutal; yet it has in it something of plain, robust sense and truth. We do often see men passing themselves off as patriots, who are in truth scoundrels; we meet with talk and proceedings laying claim to patriotism, which are these gentlemen's last refuge. We may all of us agree in praying to be delivered from patriots and patriotism of this sort. . . .

—MATTHEW ARNOLD, "Numbers; or The Majority and the Remnant"

"Nobody warned me about a thing before I went to a near-slum district in Brooklyn," the young schoolteacher said. "I was full of ideals, and after six months I was certain I just couldn't stand another day of it. I made myself stick—I told myself that my ideals wouldn't be worth much if I didn't fight for them, and I stayed on for four years before I gave up. . . ."

—*Time* Magazine, "Boys and Girls Together"

NOTE: Much overused is the beginning using a quotation from a dictionary. Avoid such beginnings as "According to the dictionary . . . ," "*Webster's New Collegiate Dictionary* says that . . . ," etc.

9. *Creation of suspense.*

My career as a mining engineer has this much in common with many success stories—it was founded on an accident. Otherwise, there is no comparison, because mine is not a success story.

—EMILY HAHN, "B.Sc."

In Moulmein, in Lower Burma, I was hated by large numbers of people— the only time in my life that I have been important enough for this to happen to me.

—GEORGE ORWELL, "Shooting an Elephant"

10. *Posing a problem.*

I wish to argue an unpopular cause: the cause of the old, free elective system in the academic world, or the untrammeled right of the undergraduate to make his own mistakes. . . .

—HOWARD MUMFORD JONES, "Undergraduates on Apron Strings"

From my boyish days I had always felt a great perplexity on one point in *Macbeth*. It was this:—The knocking at the gate which succeeds to the murder of Duncan produced to my feelings an effect for which I never could account.

—THOMAS DE QUINCEY, "On the Knocking at the Gate in *Macbeth*"

These illustrations show, obviously, that content-beginnings often overlap. For example, the following combines quotation and a reference to history and to a famous leader:

> Once, in the course of his magnificent wartime broadcasts [1940–1945], Winston Churchill introduced certain lines from "Say Not the Struggle Naught Availeth," by the English poet, Arthur Hugh Clough. The reader may remember them. They ended: "But westward, look, the land is bright."
> —CLIFTON FADIMAN, "The Art of Quotation"

EXERCISES

(See end of Section 9)

ENDING THE THEME

9. Like the beginning, the ending is an important position. Because it contains the last words that the reader sees, it should be emphatic and effective. Unfortunately, an effective ending is more difficult to write than an effective beginning, and many themes and articles which begin strongly end weakly or on a minor note.

9a. Avoid unnecessary formal or rambling conclusions.

The most important thing to remember in ending themes is this: When you have said all you intended to say, stop. A short composition usually requires no formal conclusion; a summarizing or rounding-off sentence suffices. A rambling and wordy ending destroys the effect of what has been said. Except in argumentative writing, little excuse exists for concluding statements like "thus we see" and "in conclusion, let me state."

Try to find a concise effective ending (see Section 9c), but if you cannot, stop anyway instead of trailing off or padding. Apply the story of the guest, at the end of a long evening, lingering at the door mumbling: "There was something else I wanted to say," to which the hostess replied, "Perhaps it was 'Good-by.'"

9b. Avoid abrupt, incomplete, or confusing endings.

Like an effective beginning, an effective ending is a happy medium between the formal or rambling conclusion and the too abrupt or incomplete one. Your theme should leave an impression of completeness, of having rounded out a discussion and reached a goal. Avoid a weak, minor-note ending.

A confusing ending introduces a totally new subject or unrelated material in the concluding sentences or paragraph. The reader naturally does not see how such material adds anything to the preceding discussion.

To avoid an abrupt, incomplete, or confusing ending, bring your reader back to some phase of the main thought or leave him with a thought that is a real and related contribution to the subject.

9c.   End themes effectively.

Like effective beginnings, effective endings use the appropriate kind of sentence, the appropriate personal pronoun, and the appropriate kind of content. These various specific methods—*alone* or *in combination*—are illustrated in the following closing sentences; compare them with the titles of the articles:

1. *Use of the appropriate kind of sentence.*

. . . Remember, then, that the more you study and learn in high school, the less trouble you will have when you come to college. [Imperative sentence]

—Student theme, "Advice to a High School Freshman"

The "mass mind" is a delusion. How many dictators have been amazed when their rule, which seemed so strong, has collapsed in a few hours, without a friend? [Interrogative sentence]

—Joyce Cary, "The Mass Mind: A Piece of Modern Nonsense"

2. *Use of the appropriate personal pronoun.*

The public as a whole—that is, the public barring the Intellectual Snobs—shows its sensible preference for having its artists in sufficient possession of their faculties to put us all, and immediately, in possession of their meaning. The artist who does not know his own intentions is a pretender. If he does know them and cannot express them, he is merely incompetent.

I hope I have made myself plain.

—Ivor Brown, "The Case for Greater Clarity in Writing"

And, reader and writer, we can wish each other well. Don't we after all want the same thing? A story of beauty and passion and truth?

—Eudora Welty, "The Reading and Writing of Short Stories"

The gift of a liberal education—which will still be a gift, no matter how much you or your parents pay for it—is the gift of a careful, continuous further training in being generous-minded and generous-hearted. "Liberal" means generous and "liberal" means free. Your powers and the development of your powers through the help of parents, teachers, arts, books are given you essentially, through all these channels, by the grace of God. By training your talents intensively and giving of them generously, you return a little thanks for a tremendous gift.

—JEREMY INGALLS, "Catching Up with the Human Race"

We ought when we put down a book to feel a deeper sense of completion of self, not of escape from it. We ought to understand that self better and feel in closer accord with it and more content with it. If we do, then the book is literature, and literature has made its contribution to life.

—PEARL BUCK, "Literature and Life"

3. *Reference to or restatement of title or central idea.*

. . . Only the free can be educated, but only the truly educated will find the spiritual spark of genius and morality necessary to remain free.

—SIDNEY J. FRENCH, "Only the Educated Shall Remain Free"

4. *A summarizing or clinching of the theme of the article.*

. . . He is that rare statesman—perhaps the only great one of his time— who has kept his feet in the mud of today but his eyes on the stars of tomorrow.

—HANSON W. BALWIN, "Churchill Was Right"

5. *An outline sentence or paragraph enumerating the main divisions that have been discussed.*

Friendliness and enthusiasm are twin horses for your chariot in reaching your listeners' minds and hearts. Look and act as if you're pleased to face this group. To add it all up: 1) have something important to say; 2) prepare carefully; 3) deliver your talk convincingly, sincerely.

—ANONYMOUS, "Our Speaker Is . . ."

6. *A direct or indirect quotation.*

John Dewey, a worshiper in the temple of science, said "the future of our civilization depends on the widening spread and deepening hold of the scientific habit of mind." But perhaps there is more truth in an old wisecrack of Oliver Wendell Holmes: "Science is a good piece of furniture for a man to have in an upper chamber provided he has common sense on the ground floor."

—ANTHONY STANDEN, "They Say It's Wonderful"

7. *A generalized statement or logical conclusion growing out of the material presented.*

One is forced to the conclusion that the American woman—according to the advertisements—has a wonderful life until she's twenty-five. After that she'd better be dead.

—AGNES ROGERS ALLEN, "Is It Anyone We Know?"

With these freedoms, my generation will have a good chance of solving problems raised by the destructive and rebellious among us. I have no doubt that from among the juvenile lawbreakers of today will come new law-makers, judges, theologians, philosophers, while from among those who at this moment appear the dullest, the most docile, and the quietest will come new revolutionaries, philosophers, artists, and prophets, who can inspire future generations. In other words, my generation is not in such bad shape as some might think.

—TOM SLINKARD, "A Teen-Ager Talks Back"

8. *A statement of significance, some new or practical application, or a linking of the subject with some matter of current interest.*

One thing is certain: men are no longer taking grass for granted, and we have only begun to discover what may be done with the commonest and potentially the most valuable of all our plants.

—MILO PERKINS, "Grass Made to Your Order"

You can't escape reading fifteen minutes a day, and that means you will read half a book a week, two books a month, twenty a year, and 1,000 or more in a reading lifetime. It's an easy way to become well read.

—LOUIS SHORES, "How to Find Time to Read"

No one knows. Nor can any one safely predict. We are at about the same stage in atomic energy today as those in the field of electricity attempting to predict its future uses only ten years after Franklin experimented with his kite.

—GORDON DEAN, "Atomic Energy for Peace"

9. *Offering a warning.*

Most important of all, the contest for technical pre-eminence must not lead us into the trap of encouraging that type of technician who has been called the "skilled barbarian"—the specialist tightly fitted into his own slot and serenely indifferent to the "unscientific" turmoil in which the rest of us live. Such a luxury we can ill afford.

—George S. Odiorne, "The Trouble with Engineers"

. . . There is hope that law, rather than private force, may come to govern the relations of nations within the present century. If this hope is not realized, we face utter disaster; if it is realized, the world will be far better than at any previous period in the history of man.

—Bertrand Russell, "The Future of Man"

10. *Suggesting a course of action or giving advice.*

Educators now find that what was once the recreation of students in school has been transformed into a responsibility of the educational system to supply the public with entertainment. It is essential that educators carry through a fundamental revision of concepts of athletic management appropriate to this transformation.

—Harold W. Stoke, "College Athletics: Education
or Show Businesss"

We can make America safe for tree farms only by making every citizen take personal responsibility for keeping fires out of the woods.

—William B. Greeley, "Man-Made Fires"

9d. Compare the beginnings and endings of your papers for clearness, effectiveness, and appropriateness.

Well-organized and well-written content should be an extensive link between a clear, effective, appropriate beginning and a clear, effective, appropriate ending. The beginning should lead smoothly into the body of the content, which should lead smoothly into the ending.

The following examples are excellent for their harmony of beginning, middle, and ending:

Anecdote beginning and statement-of-significance ending.

Not long ago a 96-year-old woman was brought into a New York hospital with a broken hip. Fifteen years ago she would immediately have been put in a cast and immobilized in bed. And—since old people tolerate immobility poorly—the odds were that she would have been dead in two weeks.

Instead, she was taken to the operating room. There the hip was pinned together with a long nail driven down through the center of the bone. She was out of bed the next day and out of the hospital twelve days later, her hip usable and well on the mend.

. . . . .

The great increase in operating-room and surgical-care personnel is chiefly a reflection of the growth of conservative practices in surgery; there are simply too many ways in which the patient must be safeguarded for the surgeon and a nurse or two to do the job. Burdensome as in some ways they are, the new means of protecting the patient have brought surgery to new heights of daring in saving life and health.

—LEONARD ENGEL, "The Healing Knife"

Direct-quotation beginning and direct-quotation/giving-advice ending.

"Do not let your studies interfere with your college education." This motto is the student's semi-humorous way of expressing his semi-conviction that studies do not count—that the thing to go in for is "College Life."

. . . . .

The undergraduate who is eager to excel in his life-work and who is brave enough to face the facts will take down that sign: "Do not let your studies interfere with your college education," and replace it with this one: "Do not let your college life interfere with your life's ambition." The boy without ambition will take for his motto, "Let well enough alone," oblivious to the fact that boys who are content to "let well enough alone" never do "well enough."

—WILLIAM T. FOSTER, "Should Students Study?"

Significant-statement beginning and significant-statement ending.

The strength of a nation, to a large degree, rests in its ability to meet successfully the never-ending succession of problems that arise. This is true in agriculture just as in other phases of our national life. The problems of today are the successes of tomorrow. They are, when rightly viewed, stepping stones along the road to progress rather than stumbling blocks to compound our complexities.

. . . . .

As agriculture continues to make great forward strides, it will not be because of mere legislation. It will be because the people on the farms—together with our scientists—all push forward the march of progress in an atmosphere of freedom that has made our agricultural plant one of the modern wonders of the world.

—EZRA TAFT BENSON, "A Workable Farm Policy"

EXERCISES

A. Choose five articles from your book of readings and study their beginnings: (1) What methods do they use to begin directly and clearly (Section **8e**)? (2) What methods or combination of methods do they use to gain effectiveness (Section **8f, g, h**)? (3) Have you found other methods in addition to those listed in Sections **8e, f, g, h**?

B. Apply the directions given in Exercise A to all articles in one issue of a magazine such as *The Atlantic Monthly, Harper's Magazine, The Saturday Evening Post, Holiday, The National Geographic Magazine.*

C. From articles in magazines or in your book of readings, find two examples each of beginnings using (1) declarative sentence, (2) imperative sentence, (3) interrogative sentence, (4) exclamatory sentence.

D. Examine the endings of the articles that you chose in Exercise A. (1) What methods of effective ending are used (Section **9c**)? (2) Are there other methods in addition to those listed in Section **9c**?

E. What methods of effective ending are used in the articles that you consulted for Exercise B? Are other methods used in addition to those listed in Section **9c**?

F. From articles in magazines or in your book of readings find five examples of beginnings and five examples of endings using personal pronouns. Label the kinds of pronouns.

G. From articles in magazines or in your book of readings find three examples each in which *both* beginnings and endings are effective.

H. Which of the following beginnings are clear and effective and which are not? Give your reasons.

1. Many people want to know the answer to the question of how to live happily.
2. Have you ever thought of what life on the earth was like ten million years ago?
3. The title of this theme suggests a number of important matters.
4. I think this is one of the most important questions a high school graduate can ask himself. (Theme title: "Am I Ready for College?")
5. It happened last Fourth of July. Several friends and I were planning a day at the lake.
6. Millions and millions of cells make up the human body, and each cell must function properly. When a great number of similar cells group together, tissue is formed. Organs are formed from similar tissues, and finally, after further complex advancements, a complete human body is formed. I made my debut in Houston, Texas, on May 9, 1944. That

event was quite an important thing for me. . . . (Theme title: "About Myself")

7. We went to Wright-Paterson Air Force Base, Dayton, Ohio, in a school bus. Eight boys from my own Explorer Scout Unit joined 17 boys from various other units at Shelbyville, Indiana, which is near my home. At about 8 that evening, we started a busy ride for a 3-day experience that I will always remember. (Theme title: "My First Visit to an Air Force Base")

8. Three important steps toward effective studying are selecting a definite place to study, planning ahead, and concentrating.

9. A rocket to the moon was a dream of yesterday, it is a possibility of today, and it will be a reality of tomorrow.

10. I have known my roommate for only three weeks, but I wish I had never met him at all.

I. Which of the following endings are clear and effective and which are not? Give your reasons.

1. Experiments in teaching tricks to animals are most enjoyable for me. Why don't you try them? You might enjoy them, too.

2. The decision I have made is the biggest decision I shall ever have to make. Do you think it was a wise decision?

3. I like my roommate and find him most interesting. I even think, if I try hard, I can live with him for the rest of the year.

4. Then the band began to play the recessional, and the line of graduates began to move. I smiled, and we walked forward to meet tomorrow. (Theme title: "Graduation Day")

5. In the two adjoining towns, which are only five or six miles away from my home, several churches can be found.

6. These facilities and many more like them make Oakmont a wonderful town in which to live.

7. We have also raised a few turkeys in the past few years.

8. The pharmacist also has high standards to go by. He is always polite to customers, and he must be accurate in his work with prescriptions.

9. After this brief introduction, I hope that you know a little more about the Philadelphia of the past and of the present.

10. From recent rocket experiments, we see that a dream of yesterday is a possibility of today and will be a reality of tomorrow.

UNITY (ONENESS)

10. Unity means *oneness, singleness of purpose,* or, as the *New World Dictionary* defines it, "an arrangement of parts or material that will produce a single, harmonious design or effect in an artistic or literary production." Unity applies to the theme, to the paragraph (Section 25), and to the sentence (Section 34).

A *theme* (a short paper, a composition in words) contains and treats a *theme* (subject of a discussion, meditation, composition). Keep in mind constantly "the *theme* within the *theme*" so that you will be sure of treating a *single* phase of one subject. A composition should clearly and fully develop this one phase, should stick to the oneness of its central idea, should be guided by its controlling purpose. If it does, it has unity.

10a. Discuss in your theme only one phase of a subject.

A writer is not likely to violate unity so grossly as to discuss completely unrelated subjects, such as a game of professional football in a composition whose theme is the horrors of nuclear warfare. The danger is that he may thoughtlessly slip from one phase of his subject into another phase which is remotely related but which has no bearing upon the central theme. Nothing is more confusing or irritating to a reader than the insertion of irrelevant detail whose connection with the main theme is not clear.

The principle of unity in a longer piece of writing is violated in three ways:

1. An irrelevant introduction or a useless conclusion is tacked on to meet a word quota (see Sections **8b, 9a**).

2. Material which has nothing to do with the subject is included merely for its own sake or for padding. When a student has a scarcity of ideas and a great need for words, he may fill a paragraph or two with material that deals with a phase of the subject other than the one being treated. As an illustration, many student-written book reviews give too much space to facts about the author and too little space to the book. A student writing on the subject "The Ingenuity of Robinson Crusoe on the Desert Island" began his theme: "Before giving a discussion of Robinson Crusoe's ingenuity on the deserted island, I think it well to

give the main facts of Daniel Defoe's life." Over half the paper was devoted to Defoe's biography.

3. Material is included which bears on the general subject but which has little bearing on the particular topic discussed. The writer, forgetting or ignoring his outline, may be misled by his train of ideas and may include a paragraph or paragraphs of material not necessary and not related. For example, the title of a theme is "My High School," and the particular phase of the subject is the *instruction* in the school. The purpose of the theme is to show that the school which the student attended furnished him with instruction enabling him to do his college work successfully. If in this composition the student includes paragraphs giving a discussion of the school building itself, attempting to point out that it is badly in need of repair, he has shifted the purpose, the central idea, of the theme.

Unity, then, as applied to the theme, means the use of paragraphs properly developing the subject. Violations of unity within the paragraph and within the sentence are discussed, respectively, in Sections 25 and 34.

10b.   Give your theme unity of purpose and tone.

In addition to treating a single phase of one subject, you should seek to achieve also a threefold general purpose:

1. If you wish to inform, amuse, interest, satirize, persuade, convince, or arouse to action, be consistent in this aim of your writing.

2. Decide on the basic form of writing that you will use (see Section 16). If you plan to write narration, do not overburden your writing with description. If you plan to explain, do not become involved in detailed arguments. If you plan to argue, do not introduce anecdotes which have little or no bearing on the evidence.

3. Make your theme consistent in its *tone* or *mood*. Do not unnecessarily mix tragedy and comedy, pathos and satire, humor and stateliness, reverence and irreverence, dignity and absurdity, or any two similar extremes. For examples: a serious paper on Abraham Lincoln's last day should not introduce the humorous anecdotes of which Lincoln was fond, nor should a fair-minded discussion of international relations on the campus include comical or satirical stories about any particular race or nation.

EXERCISES

A. Show how a theme may lack unity even if all its component sentences and paragraphs are themselves unified.

B. Discuss violations of unity in the following plan for a theme:

MY ROOMMATE'S FATHER

I. My roommate's father is an excellent dentist.

II. He studied hard while he was in college and dental school and took many scholastic honors.

III. His mother died during his last year at dental school.

IV. My roommate is not a good student; he is more interested in dancing and campus dramatics.

V. After he was graduated, my roommate's father studied abroad for several years.

VI. He now has a large and lucrative practice in Mobile.

VII. His health is poor, and he has engaged an assistant.

VIII. My roommate has many excellent characteristics.

C. Considering unity, discuss the place or use of the following paragraph—it was the third paragraph—in a theme on "City Life Is the Life for Me":

I have always enjoyed meeting people and having many friends. I believe that one may always benefit from one's acquaintances in one manner or another. Every acquaintance a person may make teaches that person something. The acquaintance may be a professor who will educate one from books, or a man whose pleasing personality may teach one to make life pleasant for other people, or maybe a self-centered egotist whose unpleasantness may teach one tolerance.

D. Why does the following theme lack unity?

THE INVENTOR OF THE AUTOMOBILE

I. The inventor of the automobile.

II. Menace to humanity.

III. Increasing popularity.

Credit is usually given to a group of men who were said to have invented the automobile. These fifteen or twenty inventors each contributed something toward the invention of the automobile. The period of years for the contributions of these inventors fell between the years of 1880 and 1903. These inventors gained significance by the invention of a horseless carriage or a motor-driven vehicle. However, the latest facts prove that a man named Siegfried Marcus should receive full credit for the invention. In 1861 the first automobile chugged down the street in a small town in Germany. This information has been presented quite recently, and has startled many automobile fans.

In the first years of automobiles, people were decidedly against them. Automobiles were declared a menace to humanity. Farmers were constantly suing drivers for scaring their chickens and horses. A few states tried to obtain laws against automobiles, but did not succeed.

As time went by, the public was gradually realizing that automobiles were becoming more useful. Roads and other conditions were now in favor of the automobile instead of against it.

COHERENCE AND TRANSITION

11. Coherence, meaning "holding together," is an essential quality of a good theme because without coherence no clear communication of thought passes from writer to reader. The thoughtful writer remembers that he is attempting to *transfer* ideas to a reader, to show him clearly that the whole theme has made orderly progress from beginning to end. In a coherent theme each paragraph must grow out of the preceding one, and each group of paragraphs dealing with one division of the theme must be clearly connected with other paragraph groups, just as within each paragraph each sentence is logically and coherently related to the sentences that precede and follow. A composition is coherent, therefore, when its parts have been so carefully woven together that the reader is never confused about the relationships of ideas.

11a.   Check your theme and your outline for orderly arrangement.

A series of steps unrelated or arranged in a puzzling order confuses your reader. Test each part of your outline; test the arrangement of paragraphs; test each sentence within each paragraph. Does each element lead logically and clearly to the element that follows? Make sure not only that you *have* order in the theme but that you *reveal* this order to the reader.

11b.   Do not leave any missing links in thought.

In writing a composition, remember that your reader cannot read your mind. The omission of ideas that are clear to you will leave him confused; you must include these ideas.

Sometimes connection between paragraphs, or between sentences in the same paragraph, is faulty because the writer fails to give all pertinent details of relation. For example, one paragraph may discuss the value of good roads, and the next may discuss good roads as a menace to life and property. The reader naturally asks "Why?" A link has been left out in the thought and must be filled in with, perhaps, a statement that good roads, because they are a temptation to speed and reckless driving, are a menace as well as an asset. Or a student, writing on "Rules for Safe Driving," may jump from a paragraph dealing with the running of red lights and stop signs to a paragraph discussing ice and snow. The relation of the two paragraphs should be made clear in some such manner as this: "In addition to observance of traffic lights and signs, certain precautions are necessary also because of road conditions."

Since good writing is characterized by skill in the revelation of thought relationships, transitional aids are indispensable to the writer who wishes clearly, smoothly, and effectively to *communicate* his thoughts, and the exact shadings of his thoughts, to his reader.

11c. Attain coherence by the use of transition.

Trans literally means *over, across, beyond, on* or *to the other side of. Transition,* in general, means passage or change from one position, part, place, state, stage, or type to another.

Applied to writing, transition means showing evidence of the links or bridges between related units. This evidence—a word, phrase, clause, sentence, or group of sentences—may link parts of sentences or two sentences; it may link paragraphs. When we say that a theme should be coherent, we mean in part that the paragraphs should be properly tied together. If the order of the sentences within the paragraph is clear and fully logical, then the secret of coherence lies in the uses of transitional devices between the paragraphs. The progress of thought must be actually *marked* so that the reader will immediately know when one point has been finished and another is taken up. Transition within or between sentences is discussed in Section 42; the following sections deal with transitions between paragraphs.

11d. Make the relationship between paragraphs clear by using transitional words, phrases, sentences, and short paragraphs.

Shifts in thought are always puzzling to a reader unless he is prepared in advance for them. Transitions are similar in function to signs on highways, such as "Curve, 100 yards" and "Slow Down; Double Lane Ends." By definition, a paragraph is a sentence or a series of sentences dealing with one part of a larger topic. When the discussion of this part has been finished, the careful, considerate writer informs his reader of that fact and prepares him for the next part of the discussion. Sometimes he finds it necessary to sum up what has been said. More often he uses the beginning of the new paragraph to point out the road to be followed: a continuation in the same direction, a pause to give examples, a reversing to show contrast, a paralleling to make a comparison. Such direction-pointing to the reader is a major aid to clearness and effectiveness.

Important as transitions are, they should be relatively brief and inconspicuous. Virtually a mechanical feature of style designed to make the machinery run smoothly and easily, they should not be labored or artificial, nor should they protrude so awkwardly that they distract the reader's attention from ideas. Since transition reveals relationships, transitional devices are inherent in the material, should grow out of the nature of the material, and need only be put into adequate words to show the already existing relationships.

Transitional devices to accomplish bridging between paragraphs are the following:

1. *Transitional words and phrases.* The following classification is not rigid but merely suggestive to show some of the kinds of relationships which transitional words and phrases serve:

In the same, or similar, or parallel direction: *and, again, moreover, furthermore, likewise, besides, similarly, again, another reason, in like manner, as I said, in addition.*

Comparison or example: *as an illustration, for instance, for example, let us compare, by way of comparison.*

Contrast: *but, yet, nor, neither, however, nevertheless, otherwise, whereas, on the other hand, on the contrary, in contrast, by contrast.*

Result or summary: *for, because, since, as, hence, accordingly, thus, therefore, consequently, in short, as a result, to summarize.*

Others: *in the first place, second, finally, meanwhile, while, then, in conclusion.*

Employed at the beginning of a paragraph, although not necessarily as the opening words, such connectives serve to link what is to follow with the thought in the preceding paragraph.

2. *Transitional sentences.* Such sentences come usually at the beginning, rarely at the end, of paragraphs, i.e., between integral parts of the theme. Examples:

> *The greatness of a college depends not only upon its buildings and equipment; it depends also upon its faculty and students.*

> *We have seen how words, phrases, and sentences can be used as transitional aids; let us now consider the transitional paragraph.* For clear and effective writing, . . .

3. *Transitional paragraphs.* Sometimes the shift in thought between two paragraphs, or two groups of paragraphs, is so marked that a word or phrase, or even a sentence, is not sufficient fully to indicate transition. In this situation a short transitional paragraph of one or two sentences may be used to look back to the preceding paragraph, to give a summary of what has been said, or to point forward to the paragraph which is to come and to suggest what is to follow. The second example under "Transitional sentences," just above, could have served as a transitional paragraph. The writer, considering effectiveness and appropriateness, must decide whether to paragraph such sentences separately or include them at the ending or, preferably, beginning of other paragraphs. In the following example, the italicized material is a transitional paragraph:

Four characteristics mark the good theme: correctness, clearness, effectiveness, and appropriateness. If a theme lacks any one of these elements, it is not a good theme; if it lacks more than one, or lacks any one to an unusual degree, it is a very poor theme.

These elements, then, are essential. It now remains for us to define each of these terms and apply them to such matters as diction, punctuation, and sentence structure.

A good theme must be correct in its diction. Correct diction implies . . .

11e.   **Make the relationship between paragraphs clear by repetition.**

Often transition may be shown by repetition of key words, especially key nouns, at the close of one paragraph and the beginning of the next— a method especially effective if the key word is also the subject of the composition. Pronouns are rarely effective for paragraph transitions. In fact, a fairly safe negative principle is this: Never begin a paragraph with a personal or demonstrative pronoun; the antecedent in the preceding paragraph is too far removed for the pronoun to be clear. Instead, an effective paragraph usually begins with a strong word or words, such as the topic of the paragraph and its relation to the topic of the theme. In the following examples, the repeated material is italicized.

. . . This concludes the author's explanation of *taxation*.
But *taxation* is not the only problem discussed by our *author*. Another problem is . . .

I have three reasons for believing in the *honor system*. In the first place, . . .
My second reason for believing in the *honor system* is . . .
Finally, I support the *honor system* because . . .

From these examples, you will note that a combination of methods of paragraph transition, Section **11d, e,** is not only possible but also coherent, clear, and effective.

EXERCISE

In your book of readings or in the nonfiction articles of a current magazine, look for examples of the kinds of transitional devices described in Section **11d.** Limit your search to transitional devices between paragraphs. Prepare for class a brief discussion of your findings.

CLEARNESS

12. Every writer can profitably apply the advice of Anthony Hope, British author of the novel *The Prisoner of Zenda:* "Unless one is a genius, it is best to aim at being intelligible."

Correctness, clearness, effectiveness, and appropriateness are essentials of all good writing, but clearness is perhaps the most important. An idea may be incorrectly and ineffectively expressed, but if it is understood by others, communication, the purpose of all writing, has been achieved.

On the other hand, a theme may be substantially correct in its writing and not be clear to the reader. It is theoretically impossible for writing to be effective without being clear; yet many a reader has read and reread material obviously correct and seemingly emphatic without being able to understand its central meaning.

Thus, because clearness is essential, nearly every section of this book deals with it. In addition, two specific suggestions (Section **12a, b)** and one general suggestion (Section 12c) for attaining clearness deserve particular attention.

12a. Restate in simple, direct language the meaning of any passage not clear.

A sentence or series of sentences may be clear to you but not to your reader. Put yourself in his place and read through his eyes. Perhaps your teacher as "reader over your shoulder" may imply, "This is almost or quite opaque," but he will probably say, "Now just tell me in your own words what you had in mind here." Such a secret thought and such a voiced comment concern the sentence or paragraph which is grammatically acceptable and seems to have a kind of meaning playing over its surface but which is still far from communicating anything definite. Use simple, direct language to make your meaning clear.

12b. Define all terms which are not completely clear.

A writer aiming at clearness never takes too much for granted; it is his responsibility to make sure that the reader understands.

Certain terms familiar to you may be foreign to your reader. Since thinking begins with terms (ideas, concepts, names), the reader cannot understand your thought unless he understands the terms used. Strange or unusual words may puzzle him; even in context he may be unable to guess their meaning. An attentive reader should, of course, look up words if he expects to grow in wisdom and word power, but the writer should not assume that all readers will take this trouble. Appropriateness of words for the occasion and to the reader is a fair test; you as writer should use words that you can reasonably expect the reader to understand.

If it is necessary to use technical words (terms peculiar to and generally understood only by members of a certain sect, class, or occupation), define them clearly. The following are not everyday words: *cassock, quinazoline, gravamen, counterpoint, idiopathy,* and *syncope.* If you use such words, define. Explain also common words used in a specialized way. But before defining, consider the reader or class of readers for whom you are writing; for example, if you are writing a paper for musicians, you need not explain words like *counterpoint.*

Even many common words that are seemingly clear can cause confusion. What do you mean precisely and what will your reader understand by *average person, typical college student, sincere, beauty, truth, justice, honor, patriotic, un-American?* (For clearness in word use, see Sections 61, 62, 63.)

12c. Test your statements for evidence of clear thinking.

Clear, orderly thinking must underlie effective writing and speaking. Its presence in the writing and speaking of others should similarly be evident as you read and listen.

In narrative (storytelling), description (word painting), and some forms of exposition (explanation), your material follows a clear, orderly plan—each part leading logically to the part that follows (see Section 6).

In other forms of exposition (such as fact finding and in accounts of experiments, in both of which a chain of reasoning is necessary to lead to a definite conclusion) and in argumentative writing or speaking (designed to convince or persuade of the truth or falsity of a proposal or statement), the process of clear thinking becomes more complicated than mere planning and arrangement.

Errors in thinking often occur in fact-finding and experiment-describing exposition and in argumentative writing and speaking, especially when writer or speaker is concerned with establishing his "case" and yields to the temptation to ignore, twist, or even falsify the evidence. Some are errors in logic; others simply violate, purposely or unconsciously, plain common sense. For clear and straight thinking, therefore, guard against the errors briefly discussed below when you write or speak.[7] Train yourself also to look for *observance* or *violation* of straight thinking in the writings and speeches of others: fruitful sources to use are political speeches, letters to newspapers and magazines, and advertisements.

Two common methods of clear thinking, used and violated every day, are *induction* and *deduction.*

[7] Those who do much writing and speaking of the kinds mentioned (exposition and argument) will find in the following books an excellent extended treatment of methods for attaining clear thinking:

Altick, Richard D. Ch. 3, "Patterns of Clear Thinking," *Preface to Critical Reading,* 4th ed. (New York, 1960).

Beardsley, Monroe C. *Thinking Straight: A Guide for Readers and Writers,* 2nd ed. (Englewood Cliffs, N.J., 1956).

Bilsky, Manuel. *Logic and Effective Argument* (New York, 1956).

Chase, Stuart. *Guides to Straight Thinking, with 13 Common Fallacies* (New York, 1956).

Sherwood, John C. *Discourse of Reason: A Brief Handbook of Semantics and Logic* (New York, 1960).

Induction seeks to establish a general truth, a comprehensive principle, an all-embracing conclusion. The inductive process begins by using observation of a number of specific facts; it classifies these facts, looks for similarities among them, and from a sufficient number of these facts or particulars draws a conclusion or "leads into" a principle. Once the principle is stated, other particulars or examples are sought to support or verify it. The movement is always *from the particular to the general.*

Deduction, on the other hand, seeks to establish a specific conclusion by showing that it conforms to or "leads down from" a general truth or principle. The movement, implied or expressed, is always *from the general to the particular.*

Consider some examples of these processes. Very early in the history of the human race men became convinced from their observation of many particular instances that no man lives forever, that sooner or later all men die. Through *inductive* thinking, then, mankind arrived at a general conclusion about itself, a conclusion that the Greek philosophers phrased: "All men are mortal." A generalization so well established that it no longer needs to be re-examined and tested to be widely believed is sometimes called a major premise, and is used as the starting point in a piece of *deductive* thinking. Thus in the light of the general truth that all men are mortal, we examine the particular truth that John Johnson is a man, and we come to the conclusion that John Johnson is mortal, that he will die sooner or later. This deductive process is as follows:

> Major premise: All men are mortal.
> Minor premise: John Johnson is a man.
> Conclusion: Therefore, John Johnson is mortal.

Through *inductive* reasoning the "laws" (here meaning "principles" or "descriptive, generalized statements") of any science, such as medicine, biology, chemistry, or physics, have been arrived at; and through *deductive* reasoning they are being applied every day in particular situations—the development of a vaccine, the manufacture of a complicated business machine, the preparation and launching of space rockets. Such reasoning can be virtually foolproof in pure and applied science; loopholes often occur in the social sciences (language, history, politics, economics, psychology), where human beings and human behavior are concerned. But even there, many reasonable conclusions can be reached.

For example, consider the "laws" or "rules" (i.e., principles) of language: pronunciation, grammar, word use, punctuation. Even with the perversity and variations among human beings, accounting for exceptions, enough examples exist to establish some generalizations. If you examine carefully words like *cat, catty, stem, stemmed, dim, dimmer, hot, hottest, cut, cutting, infer, inferred, admit, admitting, admittance,* etc., noting likenesses and differences before and after certain endings are added, you will reach the spelling conclusion or rule stated in Section 52e3.

So, too, with punctuation. Most students do not develop their own punctuation rules by *induction,* although they could if they wanted to spend the time and effort required. If you were to read several hundred pages of prose and make note of how commas are used, you would doubtless reach as one conclusion the principle that a comma is usually placed after an introductory adverbial clause, a *when* or *if* or *although* or *because* clause at the beginning of a sentence. This process is also *descriptive.* You could then apply the principle *deductively* to your writing, a process which is also *prescriptive.* Ordinarily, however, you will be content to accept the generalization from your instructor or from a handbook, doing your inductive thinking in fields where principles have not been so thoroughly investigated and established.

Trouble in clear thinking occurs with both induction and deduction.

1. The major error in induction is *hasty generalization:* observing only a few instances and then jumping to a dogmatic conclusion. What is the inductive evidence for labeling certain groups "absent-minded professors," "dumb athletes," "irresponsible women drivers," "teen-age gangsters"? Have enough specific examples been examined to justify such generalizations? What is the inductive evidence for "Every schoolboy knows . . ." or "All Americans realize . . ."?

Many proverbs and other general statements, as well as many popular superstitions, are often hasty-generalization errors, such as "Oh, well, you know how women are!" or "Isn't that just like a man?" or "Fools rush in where angels fear to tread" versus "Nothing venture, nothing have," or "Friday the 13th is always unlucky." A true proverb, warning also against all hasty generalizations, is this: "Let's remember that *one* swallow or *one* robin does not make a summer."

So, too, with *statistics* and *samplings.* When "statistics show . . . ," what statistics? Who gathered them? Under what conditions? If 100 students chosen at random (out of 12,000) are interviewed and a majority favor a certain policy, does this policy become the favored policy of the entire student body?

Also, if the generalization in the major premise of a syllogism is not true, any conclusion based upon it is unsound:

Invalid: All students who attend classes faithfully will receive high grades.
Henry attends classes faithfully.
Therefore, Henry will receive high grades.

2. The major error in deductive thinking is the *it-does-not-follow error* (*non sequitur*), which in precise language is limited to deduction and which should not be used loosely as a label for any error in clear thinking. *Non sequitur* is an inference or conclusion that does not follow from the materials or premises upon which it is apparently based. It usually occurs because one of the premises is not stated but implied, or assumed to be true. Thus, in "John Johnson is mortal because he is a man," the major premise, that all men are mortal, has been irrefutably established. But in the statement "Joe Brown is a poor student because he is an athlete," has the statement "All athletes are poor students" been proved true? A deductive conclusion, then, based on a false major premise is one example of the *non sequitur* error. Also, when the minor premise is only apparently related to the major premise, the *non sequitur* error occurs. For example, many great men have been wretched penmen, but is anyone justified in inferring from his own bad penmanship that he, too, is destined to greatness? Such errors often arise when in the expressed or implied syllogism the words *all, some,* and *only* are used or understood:

Valid: All members of X Club are snobbish.
Mary is a member of X Club.
Therefore, Mary is snobbish.
Invalid: All members of X Club are snobbish.
Sue is not a member of X Club.
Therefore, Sue is not snobbish.
Invalid: Some members of X Club are snobbish.
Mary is a member of X Club.
Therefore, Mary is snobbish.

Invalid: Only members of X Club are snobbish.
Sue is not a member of X Club.
Therefore, Sue is not snobbish.

Invalid: Only students who attend classes faithfuly receive high grades.
Henry received a high grade.
Therefore, he attended classes faithfully.

Other specific types of errors which may or may not relate to induction and deduction but which violate principles of clear thinking are the following:

3. A variation of the hasty-generalization error is the error of *post hoc, ergo propter hoc* (Latin for "after this, therefore on account of this"), a mistake in thinking which holds that a happening which precedes another must naturally be its cause, or that when one happening follows another, the latter is the direct result of the first.

Many popular superstitions began or continue in this way: "No wonder I had bad luck today; yesterday I walked under a ladder (or saw a black cat cross my path, or drew the number 13, or broke a mirror, etc.)." If you have a cold today, you must have got your feet wet yesterday. Day follows night, or night follows day—is one the cause of the other? The great ancient Roman Empire fell after the ascendancy of Christianity; would anyone argue that Christianity was the cause? Some hurricanes, floods, and tornadoes followed a series of American atomic-explosion tests? Were these tests the cause? Scientists competent in the field said no.

4. *Biased or suppressed evidence* should be guarded against in any attempt to think clearly. Evidence consists of facts which furnish ground for belief and which help to prove an assumption or proposition. The use of biased evidence results in unwarranted conclusions; it means that only evidence for one side of a problem is considered and that any evidence on the other side is suppressed or ignored. Suppression of evidence, in favor of another view or casting some doubt on our own presentation, is completely dishonest, as is any changing or falsifying of evidence, even slightly, to serve our own purpose.

Even *figures* or *statistics* can lie if evidence is biased or suppressed.[8] Much of the so-called truth about advertising, or national income, or the

[8] Darrell Huff's "How to Lie with Statistics," *Harper's Magazine,* August, 1950, gives an entertaining and revealing account of nine tricks by which statistical presentations can be made misleading.

value of sports, or similar materials designed to impress the public comes from biased sources, from paid propagandists and directly interested apologists. The testimony of enthusiastic fraternity members is insufficient in itself to support a contention that fraternities promote high scholarship; the evidence of girls who are not sorority members may be biased and insufficient to prove that sororities are socially undesirable.

Another excellent example of biased and suppressed evidence is the use of *a statement out of context,* ignoring any qualifying statements. An advertisement might describe a book as "at last, the great American novel," and ignore the complete statement: "This might have been, at last, the great American novel if the author had paid more careful attention to the development of his characters and the accurate portrayal of American life." Or an American statesman might be condemned for saying, "The United States will be a fifth-rate power in five years," unless we know that he also said in the same sentence, "if we do not keep in the forefront of scientific achievement and military preparedness."

5. *Not distinguishing fact from opinion* is an error appearing in much thinking. A *fact* is based on actuality and can be positively proved or verified. If it is a statistical fact—such as the population of a city, the number of students in a college or university, or the cost-of-living index for January in a specified year—it is the result of systematic enumeration and mathematical calculation. If it is a biographical or historical fact—the birth or death of George Washington, the outbreak of the Civil War, the stock market crash on October 29, 1929, the Normandy invasion in June, 1944, etc.—it is attested by a record of some sort: statements of witnesses or participants, a newspaper account, an entry in a private journal or letter, a government document, or, if we go back far enough in time, a tapestry, rock carving, or fossil. A generalization such as the one that all men are mortal is considered a fact only when the evidence in support of it is so overwhelming that its acceptance is virtually unanimous.

Opinion, on the other hand, is a personal inference or preference mingled in with a fact. That is, it is a belief, the value of which is determined by the validity of the facts which support it and the judgment of the person holding or expressing it. That Ernest Hemingway was "an American novelist" is a fact; that he was "the greatest novelist America has ever had" or that his *A Farewell to Arms* is "the greatest

American novel of the twentieth century" is only an opinion of those who hold it. Similarly, "a United States citizen," "the Rocky Mountains," "the Swiss Alps" can be proved facts, but the following statement is opinion: "A United States citizen who prefers the Swiss Alps to the Rocky Mountains is unpatriotic." A favorite trick of propagandists is to mingle opinions with facts and thus obscure the difference between them.

6. *Begging the question* consists in taking a conclusion for granted before it is proved or assuming in the premises what is to be proved in the conclusion. Common forms are *name calling, slanting,* and *shifting the meaning of a word.*

Name calling appeals to prejudice and emotion, not to intellect; its technical name is *argumentum ad populum,* using bad words to reject and condemn, good words to approve and accept. Our minds are so quick to accept epithets that we fail to look behind the propaganda. Frequently, name calling appears as sarcasm and invective. Examples: "wolf in sheep's clothing," "rabble rouser," "second-rate college," "profiteer," "bloated bondholder," "radical," "plutocrat."

Slanting, similarly, uses colored, unfairly suggestive words to create an emotional attitude for or against a proposal or movement or person; it is also *argumentum ad populum.* Examples: "saintly," "wise and experienced," "infallible," "progressive," "bigoted," "superstitious," "progress-obstructing," "lousy football player," "undemocratic fraternities and snobbish sororities," "unworkable and makeshift substitute," "dangerous proposal."

Shifting the meaning of a word consists in using the same ambiguous word several times with a shift in meaning that, it is hoped, will escape the reader or listener. College *unions* are one thing, labor *unions* are another. So, too, are *sport* and *sports. Literature* as *belles lettres* is not *literature* as the written record of the entire life and thought of a people, nor is *literature* in *journalistic literature* the same as *literature* in *A History of American Literature.* Should every citizen of the United States vote the *Republican* ticket because this is a great *republic,* or should he vote the *Democratic* ticket because this is a great *democracy*?

7. *Evading the issue* occurs most frequently in heated personal arguments but is common everywhere. It consists in ignoring the point under discussion and making a statement that has no bearing on the argument. If you tell your roommate that his study habits need improve-

ment, and he retorts that you do not handle your finances properly, he has ignored the question; he may be quite right but he has not won the argument. He has merely employed what logicians call *ad hominem* argument (argument against the person). Dealing with personalities rather than principles, *argumentum ad hominem,* seeks to discredit proposals by emphasizing alleged undesirable characteristics of men or groups who favor or are associated with those proposals. *Slanting* and *name calling* are also used for this purpose. Such argument is especially common in political campaigns where issues are not met squarely; a candidate or his supporters may attack the past record, character, and even family of his opponent without once confronting the issues themselves. Intelligent listeners or readers watch for such illogical thinking.

8. *Argument from testimonials and authority,* citing statements from historical people or well-known contemporaries, is not necessarily straight thinking. Hasty generalization, again, occurs in statements such as "Doctors say . . . ," "Science proves . . . ," and "Laboratory tests show. . . ." Or, specifically, George Washington or Abraham Lincoln may not be good authorities for solving economic, scientific, or even political problems of this atomic era. Is a well-known TV star's statement on automobiles better than the opinion of an unknown but experienced garage mechanic? Is an authority in one field an oracle of wisdom about any subject on which he speaks or writes or only on his specialty? Would an eminent surgeon, for example, be a good witness for or against an important intercollegiate athletic policy?

9. *Faulty analogy* occurs when we infer that because two objects or ideas are similar in one or more respects they must be similar in some further way. Analogy can be accurate and effective; otherwise, we could never make use of two rhetorical devices based upon it: simile and metaphor. When we use figurative-language analogy, however, we are not trying to prove something; we are trying to make something clear. When William Shakespeare wrote

> That time of year thou mayst in me behold
> When yellow leaves, or none, or few, do hang
> Upon those boughs which shake against the cold,
> Bare ruin'd choirs where late the sweet birds sang. . . .

he was not attempting to prove a point; he was seeking to give a vivid and moving picture of old age, and he succeeded memorably.

In an argument about social security, someone might say, "Look here. We don't do anything to help or protect or comfort trees when they lose their leaves and the autumn winds shake them. Why, then, should we provide assistance to old men and women?" If anyone were to argue thus, he would be so clearly committing false analogy as to make himself ridiculous. Sometimes even literal analogies are faulty because the stated points of similarity are not essential; they are either superficial or less important than the differences. Colleges are large and small, some with all men students, some with all women students, some coeducational. Will what has been effective in one kind of college necessarily be effective in another kind? Although a certain type of student government, say, the honor system, has worked well in a small college, it does not necessarily follow that it will work equally well in a state or city university of 20,000 or 30,000 students. Analogy, therefore, is more effective in other forms of discourse than in closely reasoned or argumentative writing. In all writing and speaking it is effective only as illustration; in most analogies differences outweigh similarities.

Errors in clear thinking (technically, fallacies in logic) not only are common but frequently overlap. You should try to find and analyze evidence; you should not permit emotional bias and prejudice to take the role of sound reason in your thinking, speaking, and writing; and you should not let unsound reason corroborate your prejudices. In short, you should attempt to acquire honest habits of thought and to express this honesty in speaking and writing.

12d. Revise or rewrite your material to show evidence of clear thinking.

Although you may have checked your statements according to the directions given in Section **12c**, your material may need further improvement. Your instructor may refer you to one of the following, to guide you in revising or rewriting parts of your paper:

1. The statement needs qualification; it is too sweeping or dogmatic. (This comment refers to assertions which are *not* necessarily false or hasty but simply cover too much ground too positively and need to be guarded with a limiting phrase such as "It is likely that," "As far as my observations go," "Some if not all," etc.)
2. The evidence supplied is pertinent but falls far short of proof.
3. Sometimes, paradoxically, you are too specific. More general or comprehensive reasons are needed to support certain kinds of conclusion.

4. Your argument is good so far as it goes, but it is quite unconvincing because you have failed to dispose of some obvious and overriding arguments that can be made on the other side.

5. The facts cited are not such as you can normally verify. You should supply informally in the current of your text some authority, occupational experience, or other reason why you should be believed. (This suggestion is different from documentation—see Section **20f, g;** it applies to the short, informal essay where footnotes would be out of order.)

6. You owe it to your reader not to waste time in naïve exploration of religious or philosophical questions that have been canvassed for thousands of years by experts without being brought to an issue. No logical conclusion on this point is possible because the assumptions with which you begin are untestable.

7. Your treatment here is obviously marked by particular bias and prior emotional commitment. This does not necessarily make your conclusions false but it does make them all suspect.

8. Your approach here is essentially moralistic and directive rather than analytical. No law exists against preaching, but distinguish preaching from investigation, analysis, and reasoning.[9]

EXERCISES

A. Explain, in a 350-word paper, what famed American inventor and former president of General Motors Research Corporation, Charles F. Kettering, meant when he said: "In America we can say what we think, and even if we can't think, we can say it anyhow."

B. Look through advertisements, letters to newspapers and magazines, and, if it is election time, some campaign speeches. Find 10 errors in clear thinking, label each, and tell why it is an error.

C. Tell why the examples of invalid reasoning in Section **12c2** are examples of the *non sequitur* error.

D. Without paying too much attention to the exact, logical names, explain any errors in clear thinking in the following sentences:

1. Every Saturday morning starts off with a bang because I have a math class at 9 o'clock.

2. The interior of the car indicated that it has been driven many miles.

3. Some athletes on our campus don't have the right attitude toward football; they put their studies ahead of their football practice.

4. There are probably many other things about people which I am sure I don't know about. Therefore, I will not attempt to discuss them.

[9] For these suggestions the authors acknowledge their indebtedness to Professor Macklin Thomas of the Chicago City Junior College.

5. Since I am from a small town, not many people get to go to college.
6. Some students on our campus are un-American; they converse in a language that I don't understand.
7. Our new neighbors must be rich; they own and drive the latest model of station wagon.
8. I was not reported "failing" at mid-term, and I am sure to pass this course at the end of the semester.
9. My college is primarily a liberal arts school; therefore, many students go out for extracurricular activities.
10. Coughex is like a doctor's prescription because it contains not one but many proven ingredients.
11. A U.S. senator, arguing against curtailment of debate in the Senate, said: "There is no more divine right to majority rule than there is divine right to monarchy."
12. In a conference on methods of helping elderly people, a physician said of a labor leader: "Some labor leaders obviously are more interested in saddling the people of this country with a system of socialized medicine than they are in helping those older people who really need help."
13. In national political campaigns, one party may send a "truth squad" to make speeches in cities where candidates of the other party have spoken. What definitions of *truth* are suggested by "truth squads"?
14. "As a humble follower in the steps of Abraham Lincoln, who founded our glorious party, every member of this community is politically and morally obligated to vote for me as the honorable mayor of this fair and beautiful city." (Adapted from a campaign speech; also, according to a national-magazine survey, this "fair and beautiful city" ranked seventh in the United States for crime and lawlessness.)
15. (True occurrence, names changed.) Henry Smith, 61 years old, a candidate for an important public office, was defeated by his rival, John Jones, aged 59. Throughout the campaign, Jones stressed in conversation and public speeches that Smith was a *sexagenarian*. Jones won easily. (In a 350-word paper, show why.)

E. What errors, logical or otherwise, are made in clear thinking in the following:

1. A student who is a scholar and nothing more will never get ahead in the world.
2. I should have taken a nap to compensate for the lack of sleep I received the previous night.
3. The students made pep signs to parade through the streets during the pep rally on Thursday night.

4. In our town we have an antique shop which displays this sign: "Antiques of the Past, Present, and Future."
5. "We have never been accused of being crooked in any sense for the entire 13 years of our salesmanship, and we know that you will change your opinion of us." (From an adjustment letter.)
6. The fatal accident occurred at the corner of Broadway and Ninth, just as the dead man attempted to cross.
7. My father was fatally injured in an airplane crash three years ago, but fortunately he recovered.
8. The only thing you have to know is how to count change. If you buy something for 27 cents and give the man a 50-cent piece, be sure to get 13 cents in change; the man could have made a mistake.
9. I grew up on a farm until I was six years old.
10. I had never worn a tuxedo with tails before joining the Glee Club.
11. Two years of military training are included in the freshman year.
12. Today's American society has changed considerably in the past century.
13. My roommate's actions made my temper flare to no end.
14. A good student is always working ahead and preparing himself in advance.
15. When Grandfather began farming, he was so poor that he had to plant every acre he owned, no matter how small it was.

F. With "clear thinking" as your guide, write a paragraph agreeing or disagreeing with the ideas in the following "single-paragraph" theme; its topic is expressed in the first sentence.

Living in a dormitory is preferable to living in a sorority house. I believe that if I lived in a sorority house, I would feel like a caged bird. For the first semester every year I would not be allowed to visit my friends in the dormitory because the sorority would be suspected of "dirty rush." Whenever the sorority arranged to have a trade party with a fraternity, I would be required to attend whether I wanted to or not, with a penalty of $5 hanging over my head if I didn't show up. I'd have to help to arrange parties and rush functions which would sometimes take so much time that I wouldn't be able to get anything else accomplished. It seems that these days almost every aspect of our lives is organized, and I am going to keep my social life my own to do with as I see fit.

G. With "clear thinking" as your guide, write a theme agreeing or disagreeing with the ideas expressed in the revised theme on pp. 259–261, "I Didn't Pledge a Fraternity."

H. As a discussion of "name calling," write a 350-word paper on the following: Emil Ludwig, in his biography *Napoleon*, shows how the Paris newspapers changed their name calling from the time the deposed Emperor Napoleon Buonaparte escaped from the island of Elba on March 1, 1815, until he arrived in Paris three weeks later.[10]

The monster has escaped from his place of exile.

The Corsican werewolf has landed at Cannes.

The tiger appeared at Gap, troops were sent against him, the wretched adventurer ended his career in the mountains.

The fiend has actually, thanks to treachery, been able to get as far as Grenoble.

The tyrant has reached Lyons, where horror paralyzed all attempts at resistance.

The usurper has dared to advance within a hundred and fifty miles of the capital.

Buonaparte moves northward with rapid strides, but he will never reach Paris.

Tomorrow Napoleon will be at our gates.

His Majesty is at Fontainebleau.

[The Emperor has reassumed his imperial duties in Paris.]

I. Read Robert Frost's well-known poem "Mending Wall" and write a 350-word paper on whether it means fences should or should not be built to insure friendly relations between neighbors. (This poem is reprinted in Exercise E, pp. 148–149.)

CONSISTENCY

13. To write clearly and effectively, a writer must be *consistent* in his approach to his material and in its development.

Consistency concerns *mood, style,* and *point of view,* this last a phrase here meaning (1) from what point, place, or position a view is obtained; (2) through whose eyes something is seen or through whose mind something is considered—one person's, another person's, or the eyes or minds of many persons.

13a. Be consistent in the personal point of view.

In discussing a subject, you may use one of four personal points of view. Your choice depends upon appropriateness to the reader or readers and appropriateness to the subject.

[10] Emil Ludwig, *Napoleon,* trans. Eden and Cedar Paul. Copyright, 1926, Boni & Liveright.

1. *The first person* (*I, my, mine, me, we, our, ours, us*), i.e., the person or persons writing or speaking. First person, singular or plural, is usually used in telling firsthand experiences, thoughts, decisions.

2. *The second person* (*you, your, yours*), the person or persons written or spoken to. Remember that the *you* should not be vague but should refer directly to your reader or readers (listener or listeners), in giving information, asking direct questions, making requests, giving invitations.

3. *The third person* (*he, his, him, she, her, hers, they, their, theirs, them*). Third person is used when you are writing (or speaking) about someone, male or female, or about some group.

4. *The impersonal,* from which point of view personal pronouns (1, 2, and 3, above) are replaced by indefinite pronouns (*one, everybody, anyone,* etc.—see Section **71d**), or nouns like *a person, a student,* or the passive voice (see Section **81**). The impersonal point of view is frequently used in descriptive, expository, and argumentative writing.

For the use of various points of view in writing narrative, see Section **16a**; for the use of personal pronouns in effective beginnings and endings, see Sections **8g** and **9c**.

NOTE: Do not carelessly shift the point of view in any discussion from *I* to *we* or *you* or *one,* or from any one of these to another. When a shift is necessary or effective, as it sometimes is, give your reader warning of what you are doing. (See Section **45e**.)

13b. Be consistent in a subjective or objective approach.

When you are *subjective,* you let your own feelings, emotions, prejudices control your attitude. You are personal: everything is seen through your eyes or through your mind as a thinking *subject.*

When you are *objective,* you refuse, or try to refuse, to let your own feelings, emotions, prejudices control your attitude. You are impersonal: everything is seen or considered outwardly, as it is related to the *object* of thought. An "objective test," for example, is a test on which the grader's own feelings or beliefs count for nothing; no matter who grades the test, the result is the same.

One kind of writing may demand a subjective approach and attitude. When it does, guard against letting any objective words or phrases creep in. Another kind of writing may demand an objective approach and attitude. When it does, guard against letting any subjective words or phrases creep in.

13c.   Be consistent in the use of a physical point of view.

A physical point of view concerns a point in *space* or a point in *time*. For certain kinds of writing you choose a point in *space* (inside or outside a building, an elevation, a point of the compass, etc.) or *time* (hour, season, weather, year) from which the subject is considered. The selection of a definite point of view is particularly important in descriptive and narrative writing. After you have chosen your position and time, do not needlessly shift them; and, when a shift is necessary, make such shift clear to your reader by using adequate transitional phrases.

If you are describing a building, for example, do not shift carelessly and without warning from the back to the front of it, or from the inside to the outside, or from one floor to another. The reader will be confused if he thinks that you are looking at the outside of the house and suddenly you begin to describe striking features of the interior.

A confusion in *time* is just as mystifying to the reader. Do not carelessly jump from one year to another or go suddenly from night to the afternoon of the next day. If the time is midwinter, do not without warning interject details about summer activities. (For consistency in the use of tense, see Section **45a**.)

Both space and time were ignored in the following; over a thousand miles disappeared between the two sentences:

> Not long after dawn the four survivors were picked up by a French naval ship some thousand miles off shore. To their surprise, they were immediately seized by the port authorities and clapped in jail to await trial.

13d.   Be consistent in the use of mental point of view.

For certain writing, especially expository and argumentative, you choose a mental point of view, a position or "point in the mind," as it were. You have heard about a doctor's point of view, a teacher's, a clergyman's, a lawyer's, a college student's, a high school student's, a child's. When you attribute views to such a person, make them consistent and appropriate. You would not expect a four-year-old child to say: "Honored and revered parent, will we all eventually live in an eleemosynary institution?"

13e

Furthermore, after you have chosen a mental point of view from which to consider a subject, keep this point of view constantly before you. If you are discussing intercollegiate athletic competition, you may properly present arguments for and against it, but you must make perfectly clear any shift from one side to the other. Similarly, if you are arguing that intramural sports are preferable to intercollegiate athletics, do not present arguments in favor of the latter unless you use them to further your central point. And do not subtly shift to a different phase of the subject, such as women's part in intramural sports, without indicating the shift. Never cause confusion in the mind of your reader about the mental point of view.

13e. Make your writing consistent in mood or mental impression.

Occasionally you will wish to establish a certain *mood* for your reader, to create a certain *impression* in his mind. To succeed, choose words and phrases which best express that mood.

A few of the many moods from which you can choose are *peacefulness, cheerfulness, lightheartedness, optimism, sarcasm, bitterness, anger, carelessness, sadness, hopelessness, pessimism, weirdness, gloom.* You can add many more. (See also Section 4f.)

Notice how the italicized words in the following build the mood or atmosphere or impression of gloom and fear and how inconsistent would be a statement about birds chattering gaily in the trees:

During the whole of a *dull, dark,* and *soundless* day in the *autumn* of the year, when the clouds hung *oppressively low* in the heavens, I had been passing *alone,* on horseback, through a *singularly dreary* tract of country, and at length found myself as the *shades of the evening* drew on, within view of the *melancholy* House of Usher. I know not how it was—but, with the first glimpse of the building, a sense of *insufferable gloom* pervaded my spirit. I say *insufferable;* for the feeling was *unrelieved* by any of that half-pleasurable, because poetic, sentiment with which the mind usually receives even the *sternest* natural images of the *desolate* or *terrible.* I looked upon the scene before me—upon the mere house, and the simple landscape features of the domain—upon the *bleak* walls—upon the *vacant* eye-like windows—upon a few *rank* sedges—and upon a few white trunks of *decayed* trees—with an utter *depression* of soul which I can compare to no earthly sensation more properly than to the after-dream of the reveller upon opium—the *bitter lapse* into everyday life—the *hideous dropping off of the veil.* There was an *iciness,* a *sinking,* a *sickening of the heart*—an *unredeemed dreari-*

ness of thought which no *goading* of the imagination could *torture* into aught of the sublime. What was it—I paused to think—what was it that so *unnerved* me in the contemplation of the House of Usher?

—EDGAR ALLAN POE, "The Fall of the House of Usher"

13f. Make your writing consistent in <u>physical impression</u>.

In addition to creating a mental impression, you will occasionally wish to create for your reader a *physical impression*. You appeal to one or more of the senses: sight, sound, smell, taste, touch. The impression you wish to create may be favorable, positive, pleasant, or it may be unfavorable, negative, unpleasant.

To create physical impression, use vivid, effective, sensation-appealing words (see Sections 63, 64): adjectives, nouns, verbs, adverbs. Notice in magazine advertising the words used to sell appetizing foods, fragrant perfumes, melodious music. Notice, also, in Section 14d, Charles Dickens' use of words to give the physical impression of *stagnant* and *extreme heat*.

In these few words—six to be exact—the physical impression of *taste* is made:

> Talk of joy: there may be things better than *beef stew* and *baked potatoes* and *home-made bread*—there may be——[11]
>
> —DAVID GRAYSON, "The Marsh Ditch," *Adventures in Contentment*

In the following, the dominant physical impression is one of *smell;* notice how the italicized words help make the appeal to that sense:

Of all hours of the day there is none like the early morning for *downright good odours*—the morning before eating. Fresh from sleep and unclogged with food a man's senses cut like knives. The whole world comes in upon him. A still morning is best, for the *mists* and the *moisture* seem to retain the *odours* which they have *distilled* through the night. Upon a *breezy* morning one is likely to get a *single predominant odour* as of *clover* when the wind blows across *a hay field* or of *apple blossoms* when the wind comes through the orchard, but upon a perfectly still morning, it is wonderful how the *odours* arrange themselves in upright strata, so that one walking passes through them as from room to room in a *marvellous temple of fragrance*. (I should have said, I think, if I had not been on my way to dig a ditch, that it was like turning the leaves of some *delicate* volume of lyrics!)

[11] From *Adventures in Contentment*. Copyright, 1925, by Doubleday, Doran & Company, Inc.

So it was this morning. As I walked along the margin of my field I was conscious at first, coming within the shadows of the wood, of the *cool, heavy aroma* which one associates with the night: as of *moist woods* and *earth mould.* The *penetrating scent* of the night remains long after the sights and sounds of it have disappeared. In *sunny spots* I had the *fragrance* of the *open cornfield,* the *aromatic breath* of the *brown earth,* giving curiously the sense of fecundity—a *warm, generous odour* of *daylight and sunshine.* Down the field, toward the corner, cutting in sharply, as though a door opened (or a page turned to another lyric), came the *cloying, sweet fragrance* of *wild crab-apple blossoms,* almost *tropical* in their *richness,* and below that, as I came to my work, the *thin acrid smell* of the *marsh,* the place of the *rushes* and *the flags* and *the frogs.*[12]

—DAVID GRAYSON, "The Marsh Ditch," *Adventures in Contentment*

13g. Make your writing consistent in style.

Think of *mood* and *impression* as the mental or physical atmosphere that a writer creates to surround his reader and wants the reader to receive. Think of *style,* which occasionally may include mood and impression, as mainly the manner in which a writer expresses himself. In that expression, variety of phrase, clause, and sentence patterns is not only consistent but desirable; consistency in style is also a matter of word choice. What kind of style are you aiming at? Formal? Dignified? Conversational? Simple? Archaic? Quaint? Whimsical? Flippant? Humorous? Breezy? Breathless? Concise? Whatever it is, be consistent in choosing and arranging words.

Notice how consistent is the concise, pithy style in this paragraph from Francis Bacon's essay "Of Studies":

Some books are to be tasted, others to be swallowed, and some few to be chewed and digested; that is, some books are to be read only in parts; others to be read, but not curiously; and some few to be read wholly, and with diligence and attention. Some books also may be read by deputy, and extracts made of them by others; but that would be only in the less important arguments, and the meaner sort of books; else distilled books are like common distilled waters, flashy things. Reading maketh a full man; conference a ready man; and writing an exact man. And therefore, if a man write little, he had need have a great memory; if he confer little, he had need have a present wit; and if he read little, he had need have much cunning, to seem to know that he doth not.

[12] *Ibid.*

Inconsistency in mood and style is illustrated by the following, suggested by H. L. Mencken's writing of "The Declaration of Independence in American" (see Exercise H, at end of this section):

Gentlemen: One hundred years ago my great-grandparents were peasants in eastern Europe. They were intelligent and hard-working. Inspired by their love for freedom and democracy, they emigrated to this great country of opportunity, and instilled their loves and ideals in their children. One of them, my grandfather, was so impressed that he was willing to die for America. In fact, he did, giving his life for his country in the Battle of Belleau Woods in France in 1918. I have never forgotten the examples Great-grandfather and Grandfather set for their descendants.

Now, times have changed. The idealism held by Great-grandfather and Grandfather seems to have been forgotten. When I think about it, I get hot under the collar. I want to blow my top. Too many lousy cowards are taking advantage of dear old Uncle Sam. I think he should kick the living daylights out of every such dirty bum. If the skunks don't like it here, let them scram back to where they came from.

EXERCISES

A. What is the *personal* point of view in several essays and short stories that you have read recently, either in your book of readings or elsewhere?

B. What is the *physical* point of view (in *space*) of some piece of description which you have read? Does this point of view shift? If so, explain.

C. What is the *physical* point of view (in *time*) of some narrative that you have read? Does this point of view shift?

D. What is the *mood* or *mental impression* created in one or more of several essays that you have studied recently? List some of the effective words and phrases used.

E. What is the *physical impression* created in one or more pieces of description which you have read? List some of the effective words and phrases used.

F. Write a paragraph in which you create *mood* or *mental impression* of one of the suggestions in Section **13e.**

G. Write a paragraph using words illustrating *a physical impression*, pleasant or unpleasant, suggested in Section **13f;** name the sense or senses you are appealing to.

H. "The Declaration of Independence" is an outstanding example of beautful and effective prose. In 1923 H. L. Mencken wrote a version in what he labeled "American." Below are given the closing paragraph of the original and Mencken's rewriting in American. Write a brief paper discussing (1) the difference in tone and style between the two versions and (2) consistency or inconsistency within each of the versions.

Original version:

We, therefore, the representatives of the United States of America, in general Congress assembled, appealing to the Supreme Judge of the world for the rectitude of our intentions, do, in the name and by the authority of the good people of these colonies, solemnly publish and declare that these united colonies are, and of right ought to be, free and independent states; that they are absolved from all allegiance to the British crown, and that all political connection between them and the State of Great Britain is, and ought to be, totally dissolved; and that, as free and independent states, they have full power to levy war, conclude peace, contract alliances, establish commerce, and to do all other acts and things which independent states may of right do. And for the support of this declaration, with a firm reliance on the protection of Divine Providence, we mutually pledge to each other our lives, our fortunes and our sacred honor.

Mencken's version in American:

Therefore be it resolved, That we, the representatives of the people of the United States of America, in Congress assembled, hereby declare as follows: That the United States, which was the United Colonies in former times, is now a free country, and ought to be; that we have throwed out the English King and don't want to have nothing to do with him no more, and are not taking no more English orders no more; and that, being as we are now a free country, we can do anything that free countries can do, especially declare war, make peace, sign treaties, go into business, etc. And we swear on the Bible on this proposition, one and all, and agree to stick to it no matter what happens, whether we win or we lose, and whether we get away with it or get the worst of it, no matter whether we lose all our property by it or even get hung for it.[13]

EFFECTIVENESS

14.   With the aid of textbooks and instructors, you can learn to write correctly and clearly, but correctness and clearness cannot assure effectiveness. Effective writing is not only clear and competent but also interesting, attractive, and artistic. In order to communicate ideas effectively, you must *interest* your readers by expressing ideas so as to gain and hold their attention.

[13] From *A Mencken Chrestomathy,* copyright, 1949, by Alfred A. Knopf, Inc.

The title of a well-known opera, *Aïda,* contains the letters of a memory device which can apply to writing: *A*—Attention; *I*—Interest; *D*—Desire; *A*—Action. That is, a theme should command the *attention* of the reader, then attract his *interest* so that he will *desire* to read it, perhaps agree or disagree with what is said, and then *do* what the theme suggests.

14a. Achieve effectiveness by conveying an actual sense of fact.

Many papers are not effective because of abstractness, indefiniteness. Good writing is definite, concrete: it contains specific details which arouse interest, it contains facts or conveys a sense of fact, and it tells what the facts are for.

A composition on taxation will hardly be effective so long as you abstractly discuss the theory of taxation. When you show that every one of us pays taxes in large or small amounts, even on small everyday items including food, and when you show also the concrete ways in which tax money is spent for local, state, and national services, your paper conveys an actual sense of fact and suggests what the facts are for.

Specific answers to the questions Who? What? Where? When? Why? How? are effective because they furnish realistic touches. To help you answer such questions and thus convey effectively an actual sense of fact:

→1. Enumerate specific details.

→2. Narrate specific and dramatic incidents and anecdotes.

→3. Use specific people as examples, whenever possible.

→4. Use comparison and contrast.

→5. Show definite relationships of causes and effects.

→6. Make occasional use of dialogue, or humor, or satire.

→7. When they are appropriate, make occasional use of a series of questions or exclamations, or a single question or a single exclamation.

→8. Be definite and concrete as much and as frequently as possible.

14b. Achieve effectiveness by variety of sentences and paragraphs.

Variety makes writing effective. Try using a variety of sentences: (1) those which vary in grammatical form, simple, compound, complex, compound-complex (Section 74a); (2) those which vary in meaning and purpose, declarative, interrogative, imperative, exclamatory (Section 74b); (3) those which vary in the use of suspense, loose and periodic (Section 74c); (4) those which vary in length, long, short (Section 49d); (5) those which vary their beginnings: some starting with the subject, others with one of numerous kinds of phrases, and others with dependent clauses (Section 48a).

So, too, with paragraphs: observing the principles of good paragraphing, vary the length of your paragraphs. Just as a reader tires of pages with no paragraph breaks at all, he loses interest in a group of paragraphs monotonously alike in length or in the kind of sentences they contain (Sections 28, 29).

14c.   Achieve effectiveness by the use of parallel structure.

Parallel structure means that two or more ideas, two or more parts of a sentence, are expressed in the same grammatical form: prepositional phrases, participial phrases, predicate phrases, dependent clauses, independent clauses, and the like. A simple example of parallelism is the oft-quoted line: "To err is human; to forgive divine," in which the subjects (two infinitives) and the two adjectives are balanced:

To err	is	human
To forgive	(is)	divine

(For more detailed discussion of parallelism within the sentence, see Section 44.)

Sometimes separate sentences and even paragraphs are made parallel. In the following, each sentence and the structure of each sentence in the first paragraph are parallel with each corresponding sentence and the structure of each sentence in the second paragraph.

Verse is patterned language. That is, verse is composition in which words are arranged according to a pattern, a form which is metrical, rhythmical. Verse may be mere doggerel, such as

"Here lies the body of Samuel Blank;
  He dropped a match in a gasoline tank."

These lines are verse because they consist of words arranged according to a pattern.

Poetry is patterned language, plus. That is, poetry is composition arranged in a pattern. But poetry is more than verse. It signifies high thought, imagination, or emotion.

> "Heard melodies are sweet, but those unheard
> Are sweeter; therefore, ye soft pipes, play on."

These lines are poetry because they are patterned language which contains genuine thought and imagination. All poetry is verse, but not all verse can be called poetry.

14d. Achieve effectiveness by the skillful repetition of words.

Skillful use of repetition can help to achieve effectiveness; faulty and useless repetition of words and ideas can prevent it (see Section 67). Reread the illustration of parallelism in Section 14c and note the effectiveness achieved by the repetition of words like *verse, patterned language, poetry.*

Notice how the repetition of the words *stare, stared, staring* adds to the physical impression of stagnant and extreme heat in the following:

Thirty years ago Marseilles lay burning in the sun, one day.

A blazing sun upon a fierce August day was no greater rarity . . . then than at any other time, before or since. Everything in Marseilles and about Marseilles, had *stared* at the fervid sky, and been *stared* at in return, until a *staring* habit had become universal there. Strangers were *stared* out of countenance by *staring* white houses, *staring* white walls, *staring* tracts of arid road, *staring* hills from which verdure was burnt away. The only things to be seen not fixedly *staring* and glaring were the vines drooping under their load of grapes. These did occasionally wink a little, as the hot air barely moved their faint leaves.

There was no wind to make a ripple on the foul water within the harbor, or on the beautiful sea without. The lines of demarcation between the two colors, black and blue, showed the point which the pure sea would not pass; but it lay as quiet as the abominable pool, with which it never mixed. Boats without awnings were too hot to touch; ships blistered at their moorings; the stones of the quays had not cooled, night or day, for months. Hindoos, Russians, Chinese, Spaniards, Portuguese, Englishmen, Frenchmen, Genoese, Neapolitans, Venetians, Greeks, Turks, descendants from all the builders of Babel, come to trade at Marseilles, sought the shade alike— taking refuge in any hiding-place from a sea too intensely blue to be looked at, and a sky of purple, set with one great flaming jewel of fire.

The universal *stare* made the eyes ache. Towards the distant line of Italian coast, indeed, it was a little relieved by light clouds of mist, slowly rising from the evaporation of the sea; but it softened nowhere else. Far away the *staring* roads, deep in dust, *stared* from the hillside, *stared* from the hollow, *stared* from the interminable plain. Far away the dusty vines

111

overhanging wayside cottages, and the monotonous wayside avenues of parched trees without shade, drooped beneath the *stare* of earth and sky. So did the horses with drowsy bells, in long files of carts, creeping slowly toward the interior; so did their recumbent drivers when they were awake, which rarely happened; so did the exhausted laborers in the fields. Everything that lived or grew, was oppressed by the glare, except the lizard passing swiftly over rough stone walls, and the cicala, chirping his dry, hot chirp, like a rattle. The very dust was scorched brown, and something quivered in the atmosphere as if the air itself were panting.[14]

14e. Achieve effectiveness through effective diction.

Aim at explaining, describing, or narrating from a *fresh* point of view; use vivid, concrete words which suggest feeling, which appeal to the reader's sense of shape, color, sound, touch, taste, and smell. Replace with more colorful, more expressive words the comparatively colorless verbs like *to be* (various forms), *to make, to have, to do, to cause, to seem.* Apply the suggestions for effective diction—using clear, emphatic, appropriate, concise, euphonious diction; avoiding trite diction, useless repetition, fine writing—discussed in Sections **63** through **68**.

14f. Achieve effectiveness by using the active voice instead of the passive voice.

Make your themes have life, move, or create an impression of movement, with the subjects of your sentences acting and not being passive or acted upon (see Section **81**). To say "The motor was started" or "The way was lost" is not so effective as "I started the motor" or "We lost our way." Use verbs in the active voice whenever you want to express or imply action, mental or physical, unless your purpose in a sentence is to represent the subject as being acted upon. Even in sentences emphasizing inanimate things, choose carefully the appropriate voice: "The fluid runs through the tube at a constant rate" is preferable to "The fluid is run through. . . ." When you have chosen the grammatical voice you want, be consistent: shifting from active to passive distracts your reader (see Section **45b**).

14g. Achieve clearness and effectiveness by applying a writing yardstick.

Several tests for clear and effective writing exist, but perhaps the best known, a scale for measuring reading difficulty, is that prepared by Dr.

[14] A description of Marseilles, France, in August, from Charles Dickens' novel *Little Dorrit.*

Rudolf Flesch in *The Art of Plain Talk*.[15] It can help any writer aiming at clearness and effectiveness. For main features of "The Writing Yardstick" as "a tool for more *effective* writing," study carefully page 114.

The directions, "How to Use the Writing Yardstick," may be summarized as follows:

1. Unless you want to test a complete letter or report, select several samples of about 100 words each, preferably not from the introduction or conclusion.

2. Count the words in the samples. Then count the sentences. Divide the number of words by the number of sentences. Count contractions and hyphenated words as one word. Numbers and letters separated by spaces should be regarded as single words. In counting sentences, tabulate each unit of thought as a sentence even though it is set off by colons or semicolons rather than periods.

3. Count the syllables in the samples. Divide the total by the number of words and multiply the result by 100. The result is the number of syllables for each 100 words. This, of course, is a rough measure. A more detailed test is described in *The Art of Plain Talk*.

4. Count the personal references. Divide the total by the number of words and multiply the result by 100. This gives the number of references per 100 words.

There are three types of personal references:

Personal pronouns, such as I, you, he, she, them, me, himself, ourselves, and yourselves.

Names of people. Count the entire name, including any title, as one reference.

Words referring to human beings or human relationships. Count only the following: aunt, baby, boy, brother, child, cousin, dad, daddy, dame, daughter, family, father, fellow, folks, friend, gentlemen, girl, guy, husband, kid, lad, lady, lass, madam, mamma, man, miss, mister, mother, nephew, niece, pal, poppa, parent, people (not peoples), sir, sister, son, sweetheart, uncle, wife, woman. Count as one personal reference combinations of these words such as baby boy and girl friend, and combinations using grand, great, step, and in-law.

[15] Published by Harper & Brothers, New York, N.Y., 1946.

GUIDEPOSTS TO MORE EFFECTIVE WRITING

1. Shorten your sentences to an average of 17 words.
2. Shorten your words so that they average about 150 syllables for each 100 words.
3. Use about six personal references per 100 words.

Reading Level	Very Easy	Easy	Fairly Easy	Standard	Fairly Difficult	Difficult	Very Difficult
Average sentence length in words	8	11	14	17	21	25	29
Syllables per 100 words	127	134	142	150	158	166	175
Personal references per 100 words	19	14	10	6	4	3	2
Typical magazines	Comics	Pulp	Sat. Eve. Post	The Reader's Digest	Literary	Scholarly	Scientific and professional

These factors are involved:

1. The *more words* in a sentence, the *more difficult* it is to read and understand that sentence.
2. The *more syllables* a word has, the *more difficult* it is to read and understand that word.
3. The *more personal references* in a passage, the *easier* it is to read and understand that passage.

The last line of the yardstick lists reading matter at each of several levels. The "standard" writing level is easily understood by most persons.

SOURCE: Adapted from Rudolf Flesch, *The Art of Plain Talk*, Harper & Brothers, New York, 1946. Used by permission of The Prudential Insurance Company of America.

EXERCISES

A. Choose an article from a current magazine. Prepare for discussion an analysis of the devices used for effectiveness in three of the paragraphs.

B. Analyze several articles in one issue of *Time* to determine its style.

C. The student theme below is an A theme, so labeled by a committee of teachers from Indiana's two state-supported colleges and two state-supported universities. Can you give reasons why the readers judged this an A theme? When you have done so, turn to the consensus of the readers, given in a note at the end of the theme. How does your estimate compare with theirs?

Saturday Invaders

There is quite an assortment of Saturday students found within a music school in a metropolitan area. Within the ivy-covered walls during the week, all is quiet as can be expected in a music school. Nearly all of the college students are students in every sense of the word. But, on Saturdays, pandemonium breaks loose with the invasion by "students" between the ages of five and eighteen.

There are very young children whose doting parents are aspiring for them to attain the heights of musical achievement. These children may be separated into two groups. There are those who are what their parents have hoped; there are also those who would rather be anywhere in the world but at a music school. To them, music is a thing to be unhappily endured. They are easily distinguished from one another at orchestra rehearsal. The first group listens with rapt attention to the conductor's instructions and explanations. With swinging feet that can't quite reach the floor, the others let their eyes wander over the faces of the people who are listening to the rehearsal. The heads of these erstwhile young musicians move as though on pivots, much to the consternation of the harassed conductor.

The high school students constitute the next large age group. There are, of course, a few near-geniuses, but very few. Most of them come stumbling through the corridor and up the stairs with only the score of last night's game fresh in their minds. Since they haven't had much time to practice during the week, and since even music teachers sometimes like to hear a play-by-play account of the latest basketball game, these team-happy musicians often manage to keep a rather one-sided conversation going for twenty-five minutes of their half-hour lesson periods. A full day of teaching of this type provides an unscheduled rest for these teachers.

Some of the high school music students play in the student orchestra also, sitting unashamedly beside and between some of the little geniuses. This is another basis for consternation on the conductor's part. How can he ever have an orchestra that looks balanced in size when a minute boy of nine years plays first chair cornet while a lanky high school senior plays second? As soon as a break in the rehearsal is declared, there is a unanimous stampede in the direction of the ice cream machine. This is the only time when it's impossible to distinguish the geniuses from the ordinary people.

Finally, Saturday draws to an end, and as the invaders begin to leave, the regular students begin to emerge, one by one, from their private practice rooms where they have spent most of the day, venturing out only for meals. Once again their chosen school assumes its intended form as an institution of learning.[16]

REVISION

15. "Good writing is good only because of good *rewriting*." Some students do not accept this statement; they maintain that when they really get started, they turn out first drafts which are superior to anything they have laboriously revised, or they recall having heard of successful writers who rarely rewrote. The truth is that most successful writers revise and rewrite, not once but many times.

Like professional writers, students differ in their abilities: some write easily and rapidly; others write slowly and painstakingly, revising as they go. Even a professional writer cannot plan, write, and proofread a paper all at one time. Perhaps the best plan to follow is this: First, gather material for your theme and then plan and arrange it. Next,

[16] Readers' comment: "The writer of this theme is able to profit by subtle and exacting suggestions for revision. His theme is well planned, and its plan is well executed. The first paragraph both defines the central idea and establishes the method of its development by contrast and classification. The second and third paragraphs then describe two different types of students and the problems each presents, characterizing each group with fresh, concrete, and carefully chosen detail. In the fourth paragraph the writer considers one of the problems presented by the simultaneous presence of the two types, and in the final paragraph he returns to the contrast between weekdays and Saturday students, effectively concluding his theme by exploiting at the same time the chronological pattern implicit in his topic. Each of his paragraphs is closely related to the central idea, and his transitions between paragraphs are smooth and effective. In addition to developing the idea by clearly marked stages, each of the paragraphs is itself carefully developed around a clearly apparent topic sentence. Although too many sentences begin with 'There,' the writer is, on the whole, skillful in giving variety and emphasis to his sentence-patterns. Similarly, his diction is often fresh and usually economical, but careful revision might have eliminated a few inaccuracies and ambiguities. In every other respect, this theme represents superior freshman writing."

Material in Exercise C from *Joint Statement on Freshman English in College and High School Preparation,* by the Departments of English of Ball State Teachers College, Indiana State Teachers College, Indiana University, and Purdue University. Used by permission.

write the theme with all the vigor and interest you can. If you are a
slow, methodical writer, you may wish to compose carefully each phrase,
clause, and sentence, checking for spelling, grammar, punctuation, and
word use as you go. Or if you want to get something down on paper,
as many writers do, and not break your train of thought, proceed as
rapidly as you can without paying special attention to grammatical,
stylistic, or mechanical details until your first draft is finished.

Simply follow the plan that best assures your writing a good theme.
After that, and preferably some time later, revise your theme carefully
before you make the final copy.

15a. Revise your theme for unity, coherence, emphasis.

Read your theme once to make sure that it is unified, coherent, and
effective as a whole. Delete any extraneous material; recheck to assure
that everything in the theme is relevant to the subject; rephrase all
vague or rambling thought; substitute specific details for broad generalities. Make clear transitions between paragraphs and between sentences within paragraphs (Sections 10, 11, 14, 25, 42).

15b. Revise your theme to secure better sentences.

Read again the preliminary draft to improve the sentences in phrasing and structure. Make certain that all sentences are unified and complete (Sections 31, 34); that all ideas are properly coordinated or subordinated (Sections 36, 37); that no unjustifiable "sentence fragments,"
unjustifiable "comma splices," or "fused sentences" remain (Sections
31, 32, 33); that the sentences are clearly and effectively phrased; that
the sentences are varied in structure (Section 48).

15c. Proofread your theme for accuracy and correctness.

In composing a first draft, you may frequently make careless slips
or you may neglect to check compositional matters about which you
are not sure. After you have written your first draft, reread it for accuracy of content and for correctness in writing.

1. Go through the theme once for the sole purpose of making sure
that all the words are *spelled correctly* (see Section 52).

2. Read the theme through again to insure *grammatical correctness.*

3. Read the theme through again to insure *correct punctuation.*

4. Read the theme again to insure *correct, clear, effective,* and *appropriate diction.*

15d. Revise after an interval of time.

Allow time to elapse between writing a paper and final revision. With sufficient time between the two steps, actual composition and rereadings, you notice errors not apparent when you just completed writing and see errors not seen before. You also approach your theme more objectively. Most of us can detect errors in another's work more easily than in our own. After a lapse of time, you see your writing almost as objectively as if it were the work of someone else.

Another helpful suggestion: Proofread aloud, if possible. Since your voice slows down your eyes, you see errors you have already missed, you catch harsh or awkward-sounding word combinations, and you detect involved sentences which need simplification and clarification.

15e. Proofread your final draft.

If you have carried out your revision thoroughly, flaws in the final draft are only those which result from slips of the pen or from errors in typing. Because such slips do occur, you need to proofread the final draft with care. Do this with pen or pencil in hand, pointing to every word and punctuation mark as you check its correctness. Read aloud this final draft also.

15f. Revise your graded and returned theme according to a specific plan.

As in many other activities, one does not improve merely by having his attention called to errors. He must correct those errors under supervision. So, too, with theme writing.

When your theme is graded and returned to you, follow a careful plan of revision as directed by your instructor. This plan may include the following:

1. Utilize fully any comment your instructor makes on your themes. Note carefully the errors he marks and reference numbers indicating sections of this handbook. Through his aid you will find where your weaknesses lie, and you can make the necessary revisions so as to avoid making the same errors in later themes.

2. Keep a record of the number and kind of your most common errors in writing. For your own guidance, use the Theme Record on the third page from the back cover. Consult it each time you have any writing to do. Your instructor may ask you to make a copy of the

Theme Record on a separate sheet, so that he can check it from time to time.

3. Master the directions concerning the elimination of the error or errors that you are making. A worthy ideal is to try never to make the same mistake twice, or even the same kind of mistake.

4. If errors occur in organization or in various types of sentence structure, you may be asked to rewrite and resubmit the theme. If errors are in spelling, grammar, punctuation, or diction, you may be asked to make corrections (a) on the theme itself, above or between lines, (b) on the back of the theme, or (c) on a separate sheet, labeled "Corrections for Theme No. —." Your instructor will indicate by some method, such as underlining the symbols, which errors are to be corrected, and he may further indicate by some mechanical device such as brackets [. . . .] or double parallel lines ||. . . .|| how much material is to be included on the correction sheet.

If you are asked to make out a correction sheet, follow the sample form given in Section **15g**. In the left margin put the symbol and handbook section number. In the left column copy the material from the theme exactly as it is; in the right column copy the same material but make sufficient change for the correction of the error. Do not, however, change the wording or phrasing so much that no apparent relation is evident between error and correction. Be sure to include enough in both columns so that both error and correction are immediately understandable, even weeks afterward, without further reference to the theme.

Correction sheets can be valuable guides in future writing. Save them and study them, both before you do additional writing and before you make final revision of succeeding themes. As the number of your correction sheets increases, you will have a personal guide to both the kinds of errors that you habitually make and the methods by which these errors can be corrected.

15g. Follow conventional practice in proofreading printed materials.

In anticipation of your future needs as a campus newspaper or magazine writer, or as a post-college author of articles or books, this section offers advice on preparing material for printing and on proofreading printed materials.

the/	Every man has in him possibility	*insert word*
?/?/	Every man they say has in him the possibility	*insert commas*
;/	Every man has in him the possibility but	*insert semicolon*
⊙/	Every man has in him the possibility	*insert period*
:/	They say Every man has in him the possibility	*insert colon*
?/	Has every man the possibility	*insert question mark*
∨/	Every mans possibilities lie within him	*insert apostrophe*
℣/℣/	Every man has in him the possibility	*insert quotation marks*
(/)/	Every man they say has in him the possibility	*insert parentheses*
H/	Some men sidestep the possibility	*insert hyphen*
m̄//	Every man that is, most has in him the	*insert em dashes*
₁/	Every man has in him the possibility	*insert superior number*
ℰ/	Every man has in him the possibility	*take out*
⌒/	Every man has in him the possi bility	*close up*
ℰ̂/	Every man has in him the possibillity	*take out and close up*
tr/	Every man in him has the possibility	*transpose*
stet/	Every man has in him the possibility	*stet, let it stand*
#/	Every man has in him thepossibility	*insert space*
⌒#/	Every man has in him the possibility	*close up and insert space*
∨∧∨/	Every man has in him the possibility	*even spacing*
☐/	Every man has in him the possibility	*indent one em*
¶/	purpose. Every man has in him the	*start new paragraph*
[/	[Every man has in him the possibility	*move to left*
]/	Every man has in him the possibility	*move to right*
℗/℗	Every man has in him the possibilities	*query to author*
cap/	every man has in him the possibility	*set in capitals*
sc/	Every man has in him the possibility	*set in small capitals*
lc/	Every Man has in him the possibility	*set in lower case*
rom/	Every *man* has in him the possibility	*set in roman*
ital/	Every man has in him the possibility	*set in italic*
bf/	Every man has in him the possibility	*set in boldface*
sp	Two out of 3 have in them the possibility	*spell out*
℥	Every man has in him the possibility	*invert*
wf/	Every man has in him the possibility	*wrong font*
℧/	Every man has in him the possibility	*push down space*
✕/	Every man has in him the possibility	*broken letter*
⎓/	Every man has in him the possibility	*straighten line*
‖/‖	Every man has in him the possibility	*align*

Proofreader's Symbols, Listed and Illustrated. (From Dorothy Thompson, *Author's Manual,* 2nd ed. Copyright, 1956, by Harper & Brothers.)

At recess Tom continued his flirtation with Amy with jubilant self satisfaction. And he kept drifting about to find Becky and lacerate her with the performance. At last he spied her but there was a sudden falling off of his mercury. She was sitting cosily on a little bench behind the schoolhouse looking at a picture-book with Alfred Tample—and so absorbed were they, and their heads so close over the book together, that they did not seem to be conscious of anything in the world besides. Jealousy ran red-hot through Tom's veins. He began to hate himself for throwing away the chance Becky had offered for a reconciliation. He called himself a fool, and all hard names he could think of. He wanted to cry with vexation. Amy chatted happily along, as they walked, for her heart was singing, but Tom's tongue had lost its function. He did not hear what Amy was saying, and whenever she paused expectantly he could only stammer an awkward assent, which was as often misplaced as otherwise. He kept drifting to the rear of the school house, again and again, to sear his eyeballs with the hateful spectacle there. He could not help it. And it maddened him to see as he thought he saw, that Becky Thatcher never once suspected that he was even in the land of the living. But she did see, nevertheless, and she knew she was winning her fight too, and was glad to see him suffer as she had suffered.

Amy's happy prattle became intolerable. Tom hinted at things he had to attend to; things that must be done, and time was fleeting. But in vain, the girl chirped on. Tom thought, "Oh, *hang* her, ain't I ever going to get rid of her!" At last he must be attending to those things—and she said artlessly that she would be "around" when school let out. And he hastened away, hating her for it.

"Any other boy!" Tom thought, grating his teeth. "Any boy in the whole town but that St Louis smarty that thinks he dresses so fine and is aristocracy! Oh, all right, I licked you the first day you ever saw this town, mister, and I'll lick you again! You just wait till I catch you out! I'll just take and—" And he went through the motions of thrashing an imaginary boy—pommeling the air, and kicking and gouging.

—MARK Twain, *Tom Sawyer*

Proofreader's Symbols, Applied. (From Dorothy Thompson, *Author's Manual,* 2nd ed. Copyright, 1956, by Harper & Brothers.)

121

1. Type your manuscript clearly, using a good ribbon. Double-space your material; double-space also quoted materials and footnotes. Use one side only of white paper, 8½ x 11 inches in size, and *never* use onionskin or other very thin paper, except for your carbon copy. Leave margins of an inch at top, right, and bottom, of an inch and a half at the left. Put your name and address in the upper left corner of the first page. Type the title in capitals about two inches from the top, and put under it your name as you want it printed. Number pages consecutively, top right or top center. Always keep a carbon copy.

CORRECTIONS FOR THEME NO. x

	Incorrect	*Correct*
sp 52e	admited	admitted
p 94a	a students first task	a student's first task
sp 52b	to many activities	too many activities
CS 32	Many a freshman becomes a reporter for the student newspaper, this activity aids him in his writing.	Many a freshman becomes a reporter for the student newspaper; this activity aids him in his writing.
SF 31	Another activity that everyone needs involves physical exertion. If he wants to keep in good physical condition.	Another activity that everyone needs involves physical exertion, if he wants to keep in good physical condition.
gr 76b	The major activity of many students are in the field of athletics.	The major activity of many students is in the field of athletics.
gr 75d	An individual activity appeals to my roommate and I.	An individual activity appeals to my roommate and me.
FS 33	Such in brief are our extracurricular activities every student should choose one of them and take an active part.	Such in brief are our extracurricular activities; every student should choose one of them and take an active part.

2. Typewrite material *exactly* as you want it. Your printer will follow your copy as you have it, misusing grammar, punctuation, spelling, and diction in accordance with your manuscript. For italicized words, underscore once; for small capitals, underscore twice; for large capitals,

type them as CAPITALS, or underscore three times; for boldface or blackface type, use one wavy line.

3. When you receive galley proofs (single-column sheets about 22 inches long), read them word by word, or even letter by letter, pointing to each with a pencil. If you make changes from your manuscript, you will receive an additional bill for those changes.

4. Mark all errors and indicate them also in the margin opposite. Use conventional proofreader's marks. See the illustrated list on page 120 and the symbols as applied on page 121. If these will not serve, write out your changes.

5. After you return the galley proofs, you may receive page proofs. Reread these carefully to be sure that all corrections on the galley proofs have been made, that no new errors occur, and that all errors previously missed are now marked. Any additional changes not in the galley proofs will also be made at your expense.

Finally, in all proofreading you, as author, bear full responsibility for seeing that all errors are marked and corrected.

EXERCISES

A. Make an honest analysis of the time spent on three of your themes written outside class. Estimate the amount of time spent on *preparation* for writing, the actual time spent in *writing,* and the time spent in *revising.*

B. Write a short paper discussing the meaning and application of the following statement: "Errors in writing hinder communication as much as stammering does in conversation."

C. Below are five short themes. The number under the title indicates when in the term they were written; "class" or "outside" means an impromptu theme in class or a theme written outside the classroom. Proofread each theme carefully, marking all the errors that you see and giving each theme a grade. Write for each theme a paragraph of comment that should aid the writers in future themes; comment also on whether outlines are correct and whether outlines would have helped the writers who did not make them.

(1) OUR LOCAL GRAIN MILL
(No. 2—Outside)

It was built beside a railroad and highway in the village of Thornhope, Illinois.

Most all farmers and stock raisers go there to buy feed and to get their grain ground. The mill handles most all kinds of feed and will mix your analysises of feed and grain anyway that you want.

It has storage bins for grain that farmers bring for sale. The mill manager then ships most of the grain, that he buys, by rail and some by truck. The rest of the grain he sells back to the farmers and stock raisers for feeding purposes.

They handle all kinds of merchandise such as fertilizer, coal, gas, seed, tile, fencing, and many other articles.

They will treat seed grain for the farmers.

The mill is not owned by one man, but by the farmers and stock raisers. Most all of them own some shares of it.

One of the best things I like about "Our Local Grain Mill" is that, it is a nice and friendly place. There you can meet and talk with your neighbors that in general have the same kind or similar kind of problems.

(2)   THREE SERIOUS ERRORS IN ENGLISH
(No. 5—Class)

There were three reasons why I didn't get through English 101 the first time. One of them being the sentence fragment. Time and time again I made this error. I did just about everything I could to prevent this error, but it seem to be a hopeless case. I could recognize the mistake when it was pointed out to me, but in proff reading I couldn't find them.

The sentence fragment gave me quite alot of trouble and kept my grades low; but another error, which put my grades down even lower, was spelling. In most cases it was'nt not knowing how to spell a paticular word, it was carelessness more then anything else. I would misspell "there" and "their" all of the time. I knew the differences between the two; I was just careless in writing them.

The last and biggest of my problems was the run-on-sentence. This I think was my biggest and worst mistake; if none of the other errors were on my themes you could be sure that the run-on-sentence was there to take care of the grade.

(3)   MEET ME
(No. 2—Outside)

Since my pre-high school life was rather uneventful, I shall enlighten you on my post grade school days.

I attended a small township high school in Frankton, Ohio, where I studied a pre-engineering curriculum fortified with as much mathematics as our high school offered. I majored in mathematics, science, English, and history and minored in Latin and agriculture (I was thinking of agricultural engineering).

During my first two years of high school I was perseverent toward my studies; however, during my junior and senior years my persistance ceased. I bought an automobile!

It seems that whenever a student acquires a car the student is converted to a "play-boy" and the studies are traded for dates. I was no different; I too became a "play-boy." This trait of mine has been highly debtrimental to me here at this university.

While still a high school freshman I decided that I would enter college following graduation. At the beginning of my second semester of my senior year I applied for admission. At this time I also applied to an out-of-state college in case my first choice refused to admit me.

This spring I was quite happy when I received my letter of acceptance. I was enrolled as a freshman engineering student.

College has been a big change for me. As I stated, I came from a small high school; therefore, the change into a large university left me almost bewildered. Other than the size of this school leaving me in a trance there are the studies which are also bewildering to me.

This seems to bring us to the present time. I'm now beginning my second semester of my freshman year.

My future plans are to study hard to raise my low index high enough to graduate in mechanical engineering. If I accomplish this feat I'd like to obtain a position at some motor-manufacturing company.

(4)   THE THINGS I DID NOT GET TO DO
                (No. 13—Class)

   I. See my old teachers.
  II. Looked for a job.
 III. Make some money.

Students coming back home for vacations always visited our high school when they came home. I had hopes of doing this when I got home for my first big college vacation. Not getting out of school here until December 22, 1960, didn't help me at all in seeing my old teachers and visiting my high school. Since the high school was closed for the vacation and many of the teacher's that I had in my last years of high school had gone away, I didn't have a chance to see my high school teachers.

Looking for a job that I will need when my first year of college is over was something very important that I didnt get to do over this vacation. The job that I have had the last few summers was on a construction project which has been completed. Dad said that he would see if some jobs would be available in the company that he is working for. If he can't get a job for me, then I will have to go home some weekend and see if I can get a job working for one of the big construction firms in one of the towns surrounding Lake Medley.

My hopes of making any money during the Christmas Vacation ended upon finding owt that our Vacation didn't begin until December 22. I had hopes of working in a men's clothing store, but by the time I got home, the Christmas buying was over.

(5)   MEET CHICAGO
                                      (No. 6—Outside)

I. Introduction to Chicago
II. Description of City
    A. Its layout
    B. Its parks
III. Sketch of City.
IV. Detriments
V. Conclusion

I'd like you to meet my home town, Chicago. To really introduce you to the city would take days and days, therefore it's nearly impossible to do anything now but give you a brief sketch of my favorite home.

Of course, you know the city has a "North Side", a "West Side", the "Loop", and last but not the least a "South Side" with Lake Michigan acting as a boundary line on the east of the city. Although Chicago has it's fill of parks we (the Southsiders) agree that our parks are the best. And who can dispute with us, for there is nothing as beautiful as the Loop at night seen from the vantage point of a lonely deserted beach.

Naturally the darkness of night hids some of the "Windy City's" dirt, but since the weather is so unpredictable the rain or snow will soon wash or cover this detriment. When people ask me how I can stand that filthy place, I can never find an answer. Maybe I'm crazy like the rest of the Chicagoans, or maybe I love the way the city reacts. I love the small town atmosphere of carolers at Christmas time; the bustling frantic shopping for last minute items in a bustling frantic department store as the whole town seems to be ready to burst with some of that lost Christmas spirit; the suppressed murmurings of children gazing in awe at some modern or ancient device in the Museum of Science and Industry; the sailors and their girls walking quietly in the park filled with blooming cherry trees; Buckingham fountain conceitedly showing it's splendid colors to a multitude of it's freinds; the people, young and old, lining up to drop their hard earned money into a box so that a child may someday walk without crutchs. All this I love and so much more that I'm afraid if I tell it you really might begin to think I'm quite conceited and that I'm hiding some of the facts, the true facts, about Chicago.

Yes, we have slums, horrible dirty places where ten humans exsist where two people could comfortably call home, but we are doing something about it and today you can see block after block of undefined rubble being cleared away and clear modern housing units going up in it's place.

Chicago has gansters and law breakers for which it is notorius, but I won't go into that as I can honestly say that I've never been afraid to walk home at night alone. If there are violators of law, I've never seen them. Now I'm not saying I haven't heard about them but . . . oh, lets drop this subject.

I can't write a conclusion for there isn't any. Chicago isn't concluded and never will be. We have just gotten started and if Texas doesn't watch out we may call her our suburb in another year or two.

THE BASIC FORMS OF WRITING

16. All writing can be classified as narration, description, exposition, or argument. *Narration* (or *narrative*) tells a story; *description* gives a picture in words or a sense impression; *exposition* explains; *argument* seeks to convince or persuade. No one form exists alone, pure and unmixed; for example, descriptive details may be used in narrative or in exposition; narration helps to clarify in exposition or argument; and argument may be used in exposition. Predominating tone, purpose, and style (Section **4c, f**) determine the classification.

Cutting across boundaries and classifiable by content are such varieties of writing as the précis (Section **17a-f**), the paraphrase (Section **17g-1**), the research paper (Section **20**), and letters (pp. 723–750).

Deceptively simple when so labeled, these basic forms of writing and their subdivisions vary in difficulty. The following discussion is brief; you can receive further help from examples in your book of readings, from class discussions and lectures, and from books, magazines, and articles on specific basic forms. For a guide to finding these in your library, see Section **18**.

16a. Use narration to tell a story, true or imagined.

Narration answers the questions What happened? How? When? Why? Where? With or by whom? It varies in length from extremely long to extremely short materials: novels, novelettes, dramas, biographies, autobiographies, histories, news stories, short stories, incidents, and anecdotes. Longer types of narrative are beyond the scope of freshman writing; some of the shorter ones, such as one-act plays, news writing, and short stories, require specialized study.

The plan or order in simple narrative is chronological: relating various events as they occurred in time. The narrative is told from a certain *point of view,* the phrase here meaning: Through whose eyes and thoughts do we get the story? Do we get it from a major character, from a minor character, or from an omniscient or all-knowing person such as the author, who knows all that his characters think, feel, and do, and who tells events and thoughts that could not possibly be known by *all* the other participants or characters? A story can be told in the first person (*I* or *we*), in the third person singular (*he* or *she*), or with multiple persons (*he, she,* and *they*). In writing narrative, the author must be consistent in point of view.

Shorter or shortened forms of narrative and narrative-exposition which you may choose or be assigned are the anecdote, incident, autobiography, interview, and profile.

1. The *anecdote* is a narrative bit told or written to illustrate a point. Its chief characteristic is that it presents individuals in an action which illustrates some definite idea, illuminates some aspects of personality or character. Dialogue, setting, characters are subordinate to the main point. The anecdote rarely stands alone but is a powerful method of making understandable a possibly difficult idea.

2. An *incident* is a short narrative told for its own sake. It deals with a single, simple situation. Its primary emphasis is upon the character of the narrator or some person involved in the action, or upon the action itself. The incident involves character, setting, action, and dialogue, but it is simple in structure, brief, and without undue emphasis upon dramatic conflict. Good examples are in the department "Life in These United States," in each month's *The Reader's Digest.* The following are examples:

One blue-and-gold afternoon in early fall, I was driving down a slope of the Alleghenies in western Virginia when I noted a police car following me.

Just before a turn in the highway the patrolman pulled ahead and motioned for me to follow him. Soon he indicated that we were to stop. I had no idea what I'd done wrong.

By the side of the road, looking down into a mountain hollow, lay a pool of still water, dappled by leaves. In the light and shadow I discerned several deer, partly reflected in the pool, motionless, the sun glinting on sleek coats and stately antlers.

Not a word was spoken for several minutes, then the trooper turned, touched his hat in salute and said, "Thank you, Sir! I *had* to show it to somebody."[17] (134 words; other examples run to 300 words)

We were distressed to learn that our friendly general store was changing hands. The courtesy and ability of Boyle, the man who owned it, had made him beloved by all. Tired of the cold winters, he was going to Florida and had sold out to Crosby, a man who had been in the merchant marine for 30 years.

A few months later I walked into the store and there was Boyle behind the counter. After a joyful reunion I wanted to know why he wasn't still in Florida.

"Didn't like it," he said. "Missed the people dropping in the store. I wrote Crosby and bought it back."

"Where's Crosby?" I asked.

Boyle chuckled. "He's just signed up in the merchant marine—for the longest voyage he could find."[18] (128 words; other examples run to 300 words)

3. In *autobiography* you give a rounded and understandable picture of yourself, just as in biography you give such a picture of another person. In analyzing your subject (*you*) and gathering material, give consideration to the following: a brief account of your heredity and environment—ancestry, birthplace, places of residence; a series of descriptions of people, places, and events, including education, which have genuinely influenced you; your social beliefs; your religious beliefs; your political beliefs; your moral beliefs; your interests, hobbies, likes, dislikes; your ambitions; your qualities of character; your future plans; your ideas of happiness. An autobiographical theme composed of these and similar important matters, arranged in what you consider a

[17] By T. H. Roane, in *The Reader's Digest,* September, 1960, p. 111. Used by permission.

[18] By Herman E. Wiener, in *The Reader's Digest,* November, 1960, p. 110. Used by permission.

clear and effective order, should be genuinely significant and revealing to both writer and reader.

4. The *interview* is a narrative account of some person's opinions, beliefs, and attitudes told through dialogue and direct quotation. The person need not be a "VIP"—"very important person"; almost anyone who has an interesting occupation or hobby is a good subject. Before the interview find out as much as you can about the person. Plan in advance questions to ask and topics which you would like discussed. According to circumstances, modify these as necessary during the interview. Be inconspicuous in the use of a notebook or in taking notes; try to rely upon your memory in the subject's presence. In writing the interview, avoid exclusive use of a "question and answer" style. Give something of the background of the person. Build your interview around some high point or central thesis of the conversation. Finally, be careful to insure the mechanical accuracy of your interview, such as the use of punctuation marks and the paragraphing of conversation.

5. The *profile* combines biographical material with character interpretation. The profile differs from biographical writing in that it contains more anecdotes, human-interest stories, and humorous or ironic comment. As its name indicates, it is not a full-length portrait; it merely seizes upon highlights and bears somewhat the relation to a full-length biography that a short story does to a novel. Anyone, regardless of who he is, is a potential subject for a profile.

Include in your profile more than merely "who's who" detail, which ordinarily constitutes a minor part of the whole. Be thorough in getting information, not only from the subject himself but from his friends and acquaintances, members of his family, his roommate, his enemies, his teachers or students. Do not make your profile didactic: you are not writing a sermon, a moral lecture, or a piece of propaganda. Build the major portion of the profile around some dominant characteristic of the subject. Account for his attitudes toward various topics. Use incidents, anecdotes, description of appearance and actions, direct quotations.

Follow some clear plan of organization. A good and typical profile may be written as follows: First, describe your subject's physical appearance and follow up with a few flashes of him in action—teaching a class, serving a customer, treating a patient, etc. After that, give a rapid story of his life, stressing details of heredity and environment which have an important bearing. Then come back to him as of the present, showing why he is important, interesting, amusing, bitter, frustrated, happy, or what not. Here develop his guiding philosophy of life, his primary motives, his aims and hopes, the worth of his actual achievements. Such an outline is merely a suggestion.

16b. Use description to give a picture or an impression.

Description tells how something looks, tastes, smells, sounds, feels, or acts. It deals with objects, people, places, scenes, animals, moods, or impressions. It may supplement narrative, exposition, or even argumentative writing. Its primary purpose is to indicate a mood, portray a sense impression, or give a picture in words.

1. Maintain a consistent point of view to make description clear and effective. As in narrative, choose through whose eyes and mind the subject is presented, and be consistent. Furthermore, are the materials described outside the person: concrete physical things that help the reader to *see,* or *hear,* or *smell,* or *taste,* or *touch?* Or are the materials within the mind; are you using a *mental* outlook, by which you create for the reader a specific mood or tone (Section 4f)?

2. Use "space order," ordinarily, in writing description. That is, choose some point in space or geography, from which point your description moves: from north to south or east to west; from left to right or right to left; from near to remote or remote to near; or, in personal description, from head to foot. Sometimes you develop description by beginning with prominent characteristics and moving to the less prominent.

3. For effective description, use words that appeal to one of the senses, pleasantly or unpleasantly, or that portray a mood: words of shape, size, color (*rectangular, bulbous, bluish*); sound words (*tinkling, harsh, melodious*); smell words (*pungent, acrid, rose-scented*); taste words (*sweet, sour, tangy, bitter*); touch words (*hard, hot, soft, cold, caressing, velvety*); mood words (*sad, brooding, mournful, melancholy*). Descriptive writing should have a single effect, provide a unified dominant impression.

4. A common form of descriptive writing is the *sketch,* a study of character or setting or mood. It contains little action or plot but places emphasis on descriptive details. Unlike the anecdote, it is not concerned with making a point or illustrating a thesis; unlike the incident, it

emphasizes characterization—person, setting, mood—to the virtual exclusion of action.

16c. Use exposition to explain or clarify or interpret.

Exposition includes the greatest part of what is written and read: textbooks; long and short magazine articles; newspaper editorials; and criticisms of books, motion pictures, radio and television programs, and musical compositions. Nearly all of these you may be called upon to write.

1. Follow a logical plan or order in writing exposition. Choose one of the following:

a. *Known to unknown.* Begin with what your reader knows and proceed to unknown material about which you give information.

b. *Simple to complex.* Begin with easily understood matters; proceed logically to the more difficult.

c. *Classification.* Divide your subject into its various parts according to a consistent, logical plan and discuss each part in order.

d. *Time.* Develop your subject according to the way its parts develop in time, as, for example, giving instructions on how to paint furniture or how to reach a certain place.

e. *Space.* Follow the order that the parts of your subject occupy in space; for example, discuss regional characteristics or particular attitudes or habits in various countries.

f. *Deductive.* Begin with a general statement or truth and show how it applies to specific or particular instances or examples.

g. *Inductive.* Discuss particular instances or examples from which you draw a general conclusion or make a generalized statement.

h. *Cause and effect.* Start with cause or causes and lead to results, or start with the effect or effects and explain by giving causes.

i. *Comparison or analogy and contrast.* Explain your subject, or some part of it, by using materials which show its similarity to some familiar object, or by using contrast, which emphasizes differences.

2. Choose the form of exposition which most appropriately and effectively develops your subject.

a. *Expanded definition.* Other than giving a simpler synonym to define a term, most definition assigns a term, especially a noun, to a general class (*genus*) and then shows how it differs (*differentia*) from other members of this class. In such definitions, use simple words;

exclude everything from the definition that does not belong in it; include everything that does belong; and avoid using any derivative of the term being defined. Expanded definition proceeds by giving further details or examples; by using comparison or contrast; by showing cause or effect; or by dividing the term into its component parts. A method of paragraph development, that by *definition,* is discussed in Section **24b.**

b. *Narrative exposition.* Explaining by telling a story and usually following a time order is commonly used in the explanation of a process. Subjects using the words *how, the method, the principle,* and the like, are developed by narrative exposition—for example, "How Petroleum Is Refined" and "Methods of Obtaining Penicillin from Mold."

c. *Giving directions.* An important subdivision of narrative exposition is giving directions. Subjects may be impersonal, "How to Ride a Bicycle," or personal, "How I Learned to Ride a Bicycle." In either, directions should be so clear that your reader will have no trouble in following them.

d. *Descriptive exposition.* Explaining by describing, and ordinarily using space order, is commonly used to make clear the working of mechanical objects like a spark plug, the telephone receiver, a fishing reel. Frequently, descriptive exposition and narrative exposition are used together; examples appear in any issue of a semitechnical or popular scientific magazine.

e. *Criticism.* Criticism is an estimation of worth or value, whether of a book, a magazine article, a movie, a radio or television program, or a musical composition. Ordinarily, as critic, you answer four questions: What was the author's purpose? What methods did he use in accomplishing his purpose: scope, characters, setting, kind of plot, dialogue, point of view, style, etc.? Was the purpose successfully accomplished? Was it worth accomplishing?

Always give some indication of content. Select a controlling idea and mold your review around it. Make some use of quotations or examples. Be specific; avoid vague terms. Do not hesitate to inject your ideas into the review. Make necessary qualifications, but avoid contradictions and afterthoughts which destroy the unity of purpose and tone of your review.

f. *Informal and formal essays.* The informal or personal essay is usually a friendly and conversational explanation of the writer's attitudes, opinions, or moods toward a specific subject, using some dominant tone such as whimsy, satire, irony, humor.

The formal essay or article, commonly labeled "magazine article," is a dignified and usually impersonal treatment of a serious subject; it may be descriptive or argumentative, but it is usually expository.

Examples of both informal and formal essay can be found in contemporary magazines: the former are fairly infrequent now; the latter, a preponderant or integral part of the contents of almost all modern magazines, are mainly specialized types of exposition. However, by following directions given for writing themes (choosing and limiting and analyzing subjects, Sections 2, 4; getting material, Section 5, and organizing, Section 6), and by adapting directions for writing the research paper (see Section 20), you should approach successful writing of the formal essay or article. Bear in mind only that it is now usually written in an appropriately popular style and, although based on fact, is not accompanied by the paraphernalia of documentation (footnotes and bibliography).

16d. Use argument to persuade or convince.

Formal argument, a complicated subject, uses four special steps: establishing the proposition, analyzing the proposition, formulating the argument, and preparing the brief (a form of outline).

Less formal argument—usually used in themes, magazine articles, and occasional newspaper editorials—is built around subjects containing the words "advantages," "disadvantages," "value," or "why": "The Advantages of Belonging to a Social Fraternity," "The Value of Intramural Athletics," "Why Mission College Should Abolish Final Examinations."

The order or plan in informal argument is classification: a listing of the reasons for or against, sometimes in the order of climax, i.e., progressing to the most important, sometimes in a more or less arbitrary order. Under each reason discuss the facts or materials, known as evidence, which support and establish that particular part of the argument. Guard against any weaknesses or errors that would destroy the effectiveness of the chain of reasoning or logical thinking (see Section 12c).

Make argumentative substance lead to an inevitable conclusion. But sometimes you may give both sides and leave the reader to make his own decision about the conclusion: "The Advantages and Disadvantages of Final Examinations."

EXERCISES

In writing on any of the following subjects, remember that you should have in mind, and indicate, a specific reader or limited group of readers (see Section **4b,** p. 38).

A. Examine three selections in your book of readings; determine how many of the four basic forms of writing (narration, description, exposition, argument) are contained in each selection.

B. From the vantage point of a window overlooking a busy street, observe details which are primarily expository, descriptive, argumentative, and narrative. For each type of writing, compile a list of 10 subjects based on your observation.

C. Write a 400-word narrative, preferably but not necessarily from personal experience, which exemplifies an old proverb. Do not explain the expository idea of the proverb; simply state at the end the proverb which the narrative exemplifies.

1. A stitch in time saves nine.
2. Better late than never.
3. He who hesitates is lost.
4. Little strokes fell great oaks.
5. Procrastination is the thief of time.
6. There's no fool like an old fool.
7. Fools rush in where angels fear to tread.
8. Pride goeth before a fall.
9. A rolling stone gathers no moss.
10. It's a long lane that has no turning.
11. He who laughs last laughs best.
12. Haste makes waste.
13. Make hay while the sun shines.
14. Two heads are better than one.
15. All's well that ends well.
16. A bird in the hand is worth two in the bush.
17. Half a loaf is better than no bread.
18. One good turn deserves another.
19. A friend in need is a friend indeed.
20. You can't have your cake and eat it too.

D. Write an anecdote to prove or disprove any one of the following statements:

1. Women are more emotional than men.
2. Men are better automobile drivers than women.
3. The most reckless drivers in the country are the group aged — to — years.
4. American traffic policemen are noted for their courtesy.
5. Young people are no ruder than their elders.
6. Chivalry among youth is nonexistent.
7. Few people have the courage of their convictions.
8. Most important people have inferiority complexes.
9. A loyal voter should always vote the straight party ticket.
10. One should never travel in a foreign country before he has seen all of the United States.
11. Informal education is more valuable than formal education.
12. A college should admit every high school graduate that applies.
13. Getting admitted to college is a difficult process.
14. Students should be allowed to choose all the courses they take.
15. The honor system on our campus is successful.
16. Our campus does not know the meaning of "campus politics."
17. Athletes receive special consideration from their instructors.
18. Participation in athletic activities develops good sportsmanship.
19. Students should be allowed to cut as many classes as they please.
20. Success in post-college life depends only upon the grades a student has made.

E. List five incidents in which you have recently been involved and which you think would be of general interest.

F. Read the department "Life in These United States," in several issues of *The Reader's Digest*. From your own experience write several similar incidents (limit, 300 words each).

G. Write a brief autobiographical theme (about 500 words) introducing yourself to your instructor.

H. If you do not write a fairly complete autobiography, you may be assigned (or wish to write) sections or divisions of your autobiography: Ancestry; Early Childhood; Environment; Early Education; College; Summer Activities; People, Places, and Events That Have Had Influence; Friends; Religion; Politics; Travel; Ambitions; Interests and Hobbies; Personal Characteristics; Ideals.

I. Choose someone on or near the campus who has a responsible position or who is known for some achievement or activity. Plan, carry out, and write an interview with this person. Suggestions: My College Adviser; A Receptionist or the Man (or Woman) at an Information Desk; An Interesting Teacher; A Coach; A Student Pastor; The Manager or Owner of a

Cafeteria or Restaurant; A Bookstore Owner or Manager; The Librarian; The President of — Class (or Organization); The Manager of — (a student activity); A Campus Band Leader; A Campus Policeman; A Janitor; A Night Watchman; A Bus or Taxicab Driver, etc.

J. Write a *profile* of one of the people mentioned in Exercise I or in Exercise N.

K. Copy from a guidebook a formal description of some place which you have visited. Then write a brief description in which you try to convey to the reader some idea of the *impression* the place made upon you. Make liberal use of your five senses.

L. Make each of the following specific; then write a brief, literal description of any two: A Drug Store or Department Store Lunch Counter; A Chemistry Laboratory; A Student Room; A Dentist's Office; A Bus Station; The College Cafeteria; A Professor's Office; A Chain Grocery Store; A Skyscraper; A Filling Station; Back Stage at a Theater; A Projection Booth; A Student's Notebook; An Airport; A Stadium; A Golf Course; A City Park; A Bridge; A Modernized Farm; A Mountain.

M. Assume that a friend of yours in a distant city has agreed to meet at the station someone he or she has never seen. Write for that friend an adequate description of a relative, your roommate, a classmate, or a close friend.

N. Make individual and write a character sketch of one of the following: A College Dean; A Typical Clubwoman; A Member of My Family; My Best Friend; The Cashier at a Motion Picture Theater; A Camp Counselor; A Fraternity Brother; A Coed; An Actress as She Appears in the Part of — (a specific character); Our Family Physician; A Good Teacher; My High School Principal; A Campus Leader; An Unforgettable Character; Campus Man (or Woman) of the Year.

O. Write an informal or expanded definition (300 to 500 words long) of one or more of the following: Dictatorship; A Roommate; An English Composition Class; A Theme; Hydroponics; A State Fair; Sorority Tea; Fraternity Rush; A Good Sport; The Ideal Wife (or Husband); Television; Student Government; 4-H Club; Campus Politics; Code of Honor; Rewriting; Radar; Cutthroat Competition; Scholars and Students; any limited term in sport (Lateral Pass; Offside; Strike; Let Ball; Three-Bagger; Technical Foul; Knockout; Hole in One; etc.).

P. Write a narrative exposition explaining one of the following processes:

1. How an Automatic Washing Machine Works (or any similar mechanism).
2. The Manufacture of Paper (or any similar process that you know about or have observed in a factory).
3. Producing an Amateur Play.

4. Dressing for a Formal Dance.
5. The Principle of Jet Propulsion.
6. Mimeographing.
7. Cooking with a Pressure Cooker.
8. Fluorescent Lighting.
9. The Method of Electing Class Officers.
10. Air Conditioning in the Home.

Q. Write a "giving directions" theme on one of the following:

1. How to Make a Tossed Salad (or some other appetizing food).
2. How to Lead a Boy Scout (Girl Scout) Troop.
3. How to Change an Automobile Tire.
4. How to Study Successfully.
5. How to Make an 8-O'clock Class.
6. How to Prepare for an Examination.
7. Rules for Driving in City Traffic.
8. A Guide to (or Through) a Building, Factory, Park, Campus, Historical Site, etc. (make definite).
9. Directions for Getting to (name some place).
10. How to Make a Strike in Bowling (or any other limited action in a sport).
11. How I Learned to Swim (or some other physical activity).
12. How I Budget My Time.
13. How I Earn My Spending Money.
14. How I Taught My Dog Tricks.
15. How I Developed My Hobby of —.

R. Write a theme for a named person on a subject beginning: "So You Want to Learn to. . . ."

S. Write a descriptive exposition on one of the following: Automatic Washer, Deep-Freeze Unit, Electric Fan, Camera, Opaque Projector, Movie Film, Ball Point Pen, Desk Calendar, Microscope, Lawn Mower, Can Opener, Storm Windows, Drawing Board, Model Airplane, Electric Shaver, etc.

T. Choose from each of the following groups one that you liked (or like) best and one that you liked (or like) least. Write a criticism of each: book (fiction), book (nonfiction), magazine, newspaper, movie, radio program, television program, musical composition, recording, dramatic production, short story.

U. Write a theme (argument) for a named person on one of the following subjects. Begin each title with the words "This Is a . . . ." Town You

Should Visit; Program (or Recording) You Should Hear; Meal You Would Enjoy; Girl (Boy) Whom You Should Know; Professor Whom You Should Have; Activity You Should Enter; Book You Should Read; Profession You Should Enter; Hobby You Should Have; TV Show (or Movie) You Should Not Miss.

V. Use, as topic sentences in three paragraphs illustrating argument, statements in Exercise D, above.

W. Complete each of the following as theme subjects to be developed as argument:

1. The Advantages of —.
2. The Disadvantages of —.
3. The Value of —.
4. Why I Am in Favor of —.
5. Why I Am Opposed to —.
6. Never —.
7. You Will Not Like (Enjoy) —.
8. Two Sides of the Question of —.
9. Three Reasons for (or Against) —.
10. Why—Should— (Example: Why Mission College Should Adopt the Honor System)

THE PRÉCIS AND THE PARAPHRASE

17. Many questions asked in conversation and on examinations require summarizing answers, an indispensable form of communication in modern college life. Each day we are called upon to give, in written or oral form, condensed versions of events, ideas, or impressions.

In fact, the method of summary is generally prevalent. A popular magazine, *The Reader's Digest,* is largely composed of summaries of more detailed articles in other periodicals, and the editorial technique involved (that of preserving so far as possible the exact wording of a full-length article but dropping out substantial portions of it) has been employed by other "digest" magazines. Certain periodicals publish digests of entire books. Radio and TV news commentators furnish what are essentially summaries of the latest news developments, and they say: "For further details, see your daily newspaper." Magazines such as *Time* and *Newsweek* contain short articles which are, in one sense, condensations of events. Business and industrial executives frequently ask employees to submit brief reports concerning developments in their departments or trends in business or research, or to write brief introductory summaries of longer reports. The illustrations need not be continued; every student could mention other examples of the use of summaries.

A summary, as a condensed version of a longer passage or a more extended account, has several names: *abstract, abridgment, condensation, digest, epitome, précis, résumé, synopsis,* and others. Distinctions between any two are of no great importance.

THE PRÉCIS

A précis (form both singular and plural, pronounced pray-see′) is a brief summary of the essential thought of a longer composition. It provides a miniature of the original selection, reproducing the same proportions on smaller scale, the same ideas, and the same mood and tone, so far as possible. The maker of a précis cannot interpret or comment; his sole function is to give a reduction of the author's exact and essential meaning. Nor can he omit important details.

Précis are effective in developing your capacities for *careful reading, constructive thinking,* and *exact writing.* The composition of a good précis is difficult and requires time and effort. In its making, follow these suggestions:

17a.   Select carefuly the material to be condensed.

Some selections can be reduced satisfactorily: novels, short stories, plays, speeches, magazine articles; but other materials are so short or so tightly knit that condensation is virtually impossible, such as Francis Bacon's essays, the style of which is especially compact and epigrammatic.

17b.   Read the selection carefully.

In order to group the central ideas, read carefully, analytically, and reflectively. In doing such reading, follow two steps:

1. Give the material a through and thorough reading once, to get a clear understanding of the whole.

2. Reread paragraph by paragraph, to get each paragraph topic and to note how it has been developed by various methods.

Look up the meanings of all words and phrases about which you are in doubt. Look for important or key expressions that must be used in your précis if it is to preserve the essential meaning and flavor of the original selection. Before starting to write, you must, to use Francis Bacon's phrase, "chew and digest" the selection, not merely "taste" it or "swallow" it whole in a single gulp. See how the material has been organized, what devices the writer has used, what kinds of illustrations support the main thought. You may want to question critically some of the writer's statements, but if your purpose is to write a précis, you must report faithfully and without comment what he has said.

17c.   Use your own words.

As you read, restate the main idea of each paragraph clearly and concisely. Quoting sentences, perhaps topic sentences, from each paragraph results in a sentence outline, not a précis. You must use your own words for the most part, although a little quotation is permissible; ordinarily, however, the phrasing of the original will not be suitable for your purposes. Once you have mastered the thought of the material, your problem is one of original composition: your own analysis and statement of the major thought.

17d.   Set limits to the number of words you use.

The length of a condensation cannot arbitrarily be determined, but for purposes of summary most prose can be reduced by two-thirds to three-fourths. A précis, therefore, should usually be about one-third to one-fourth as long as the original. Omit nothing of real importance but remember that the central aim of a précis is condensation.

17e.   Follow the plan of the original.

Follow the logical order of the original so that the condensation will be accurate. Thoughts and facts should not be rearranged; if they are, the essence of the original may be distorted. Give attention to proportion. Try to preserve the mood and tone of the original.

17f.   Write the précis in effective English.

The condensation should be a model of exact and emphatic diction and clear, effective sentence construction, because it must be intelligible to a reader who has not seen the original. Bring together with logic and with transitions your various summarizing statements. Transition from sentence to sentence must be smooth and unobtrusive, emphasizing the unity and coherence of the summarization. As you proceed, you may need to contract certain parts. Although the précis is not likely to be so well written as the original, it should read smoothly and possess compositional merit of its own.

NOTE: If you use a précis as part of a theme or research paper, document it in a footnote by giving details of your source (see Section 20f).

The following example of a précis was written by a student. Criticize it in the light of suggestions given above.

ORIGINAL

A third kind of thinking is stimulated when anyone questions our beliefs and opinions. We sometimes find ourselves changing our minds without any resistance or heavy emotion, but if we are told that we are wrong we resent the imputation and harden our hearts. We are incredibly heedless in the formation of our beliefs, but find ourselves filled with an illicit passion for them when anyone proposes to rob us of their companionship. It is obviously not the ideas themselves that are dear to us, but our self-esteem, which is threatened. We are by nature stubbornly pledged to defend our own from attack, whether it be our person, our family, our property, or our opinion. A United States Senator once remarked to a friend of mine that God Almighty could not make him change his mind on our Latin-America policy. We may surrender, but rarely confess ourselves vanquished. In the intellectual world at least, peace is without victory.

Few of us take the pains to study the origin of our cherished convictions; indeed, we have a natural repugnance to so doing. We like to continue to believe what we have been accustomed to accept as true, and the resentment aroused when doubt is cast upon any of our assumptions leads us to seek every manner of excuse for clinging to them. *The result is that most of our so-called reasoning consists in finding arguments for going on believing as we already do.*[19] [242 words]

—JAMES HARVEY ROBINSON, "On Various Kinds of Thinking"

PRÉCIS

A third kind of thinking occurs when we are told that our beliefs and opinions are wrong. We may have been heedless in their formation, but our self-esteem will not permit us to change. We may have to give, but we are not convinced. We do not study the origin of our beliefs; we believe as we have been accustomed to believe, and we seek arguments for continuing to believe as we already do. [75 words]

[19] From *The Mind in the Making*, by James Harvey Robinson. Copyright, 1921, by Harper & Brothers. Used by permission.

THE PARAPHRASE

The paraphrase is another type of report on reading required frequently in college work. Whereas a précis is a digest of the essential meaning of an original passage, a paraphrase is a full-length statement of that meaning: a free rendering of the sense of a passage, fully and proportionately, but in different words; or, as *Webster's New International Dictionary* says: "A restatement of a text, passage, or work, giving the meaning in another form, usually for clearer and fuller exposition." A paraphrase does not include translation from one language to another, the technical name for which is *metaphrase*.

The paraphrase is frequently used to make clear any material which is vague, obscure, or difficult, a process usually consisting of both simplification and modernization. You may have read a difficult poem or an abstruse discussion which you could not make sense of until you put it in your own words. After you did so, its meaning was clear, and you felt that you had actually translated the passage into your own thought. Much of the discussion in English and social science classrooms begins with paraphrasing ideas expressed in assignments from textbooks. In other words, as a student you have almost daily need for reshaping source material to suit your own discussional purposes.

Three common uses of paraphase, therefore, are the following: (1) paraphrasing technical, semitechnical, or otherwise difficult materials into understandable nontechnical English; (2) paraphrasing poems into clear prose; (3) paraphrasing poetry or prose of a bygone era into understandable present-day prose.

If the material to be paraphrased is poetry, remember: (1) A line of poetry is a *poetic* unit, not a *sense* unit; it need not be and very likely is not a sentence. As a first step, copy the poem as if it were prose; then reread it with special attention to the punctuation marks and the purposes they serve. (2) Poetry, for poetic reasons, often uses inverted, suspended, or transposed word order. Rearrange these words in normal, straightforward English word order: subject and modifiers, predicate and modifiers, object and modifiers.

In making a paraphrase, follow these additional suggestions:

17g. Study the original passage.

"Study" here means that you should read the original passage as often as necessary in order to approach understanding its full and exact meaning. It is impossible to paraphrase a passage until you are familiar with its purposes, organization, development, and essential content. Some phrases and sentences you will probably have to reread several times, carefully and reflectively, before their meaning becomes clear. If the passage contains obscure words and allusions, consult a dictionary or other reference book to determine their meanings.

17h. Use your own words.

Find understandable equivalents for words and phrases which are obscure, but do not strain for synonyms. Feel free to use words from the original material if their meaning is unmistakably clear, but do not hesitate to use your own words and phrases where simplification, clarity, or modernization requires them.

17i. Leave out nothing of importance.

A paraphrase is a restatement and, as such, should contain the thought of the original in its entirety. Omitting significant detail is a violation of the original and results in distortion.

17j. Add nothing which is not in the original.

A paraphrase is not designed to be a *full* interpretation, in which the paraphraser adds his own comments. Interpretation and explanation should be confined to making clear what the original author had in mind. Whether you like or dislike what the writer has said, whether you agree or disagree with him, whether you think his logic is sound or faulty—these considerations do not enter into the making of the paraphrase. Your making of a paraphrase does not mean that you, as a writer, cease to think; it means that your thinking produces a full-length statement of another's meaning.

17k. Retain the tone of the original.

As closely as clearness permits, follow the tone, mood, and atmosphere of the material being paraphrased. Changing the purpose, mood, treatment, or tone of the original may distort, parody, or give a wrong meaning. Obviously, as paraphraser, you can hardly hope to achieve the same mood and tone quality as the author of, say, a great poem, but try to preserve as much of these existing qualities as possible.

17l. Use effective English.

Any paraphrase of a good poem or prose passage is worth less than the original, but the better the paraphrase, the less the difference between it and the original. The making of a good paraphrase, just as of an effective précis, requires exact writing: correct, clear diction, effective sentence structure, and adequate transitions.

NOTE: If you use paraphrase as part of a theme or research paper, document it in a footnote by giving details of your source (see Section 20f).

The following is a paraphrase made by a student. Criticize it in terms of the suggestions given above.

ON FIRST LOOKING INTO CHAPMAN'S HOMER

Much have I travell'd in the realms of gold,
And many goodly states and kingdoms seen;
Round many western islands have I been
Which bards in fealty to Apollo hold.
Oft of one wide expanse had I been told
That deep-brow'd Homer ruled as his demesne:
Yet did I never breathe its pure serene
Till I heard Chapman speak out loud and bold:
Then felt I like some watcher of the skies
When a new planet swims into his ken;
Or like stout Cortez, when with eagle eyes
He stared at the Pacific—and all his men
Look'd at each other with a wild surmise—
Silent, upon a peak in Darien.

—JOHN KEATS

PARAPHRASE

I have read widely in the great classics of literature and have noted many examples of great poetry. I had often been told of the work of Homer and the poetry which he had created, but I never really understood or appreciated its great beauty and power until I read Chapman's translation. Then I felt as awed as some astronomer who unexpectedly discovers a new planet, or as surprised and speechless as Cortez (Balboa) and his followers when they saw the Pacific Ocean for the first time, from Panama.

EXERCISES

A. Write several précis of materials from your book of readings, selecting short articles, or two or three paragraphs from a longer selection. Include one narrative and one expository selection. Perhaps your instructor will prefer to make uniform assignments for all class members.

B. Select several articles in a recent or the current issue of *The Reader's Digest*. In your library obtain the magazines referred to. Write a comment on the shortened versions compared with the original versions.

C. Choose an article in a current magazine and condense it as *The Reader's Digest* would.

D. Write several précis of paragraphs or themes included in this book for other illustration purposes. See pp. 42–44; 111; 115–116; 220–231; 233–236.

E. If your book of readings includes poetry, write paraphrases of five of the shorter poems. Otherwise, write paraphrases of the following, according to the directions given in Section **17g-1.** Your instructor may also ask you to write a précis of each paraphrase.

(1)   From SONNETS
XXIX

When, in disgrace with Fortune and men's eyes,
I all alone beweep my outcast state,
And trouble deaf heaven with my bootless cries,
And look upon myself and curse my fate,
Wishing me like to one more rich in hope,
Featured like him, like him with friends possessed,
Desiring this man's art, and that man's scope,
With what I most enjoy contented least;
Yet in these thoughts myself almost despising,
Haply I think on thee; and then my state,
Like to the lark at break of day arising
From sullen earth, sings hymns at heaven's gate;
    For thy sweet love remembered such wealth brings
    That then I scorn to change my state with kings.
                            —WILLIAM SHAKESPEARE

(2)   HOW DO I LOVE THEE?

How do I love thee? Let me count the ways.
I love thee to the depth and breadth and height
My soul can reach, when feeling out of sight
For the ends of Being and ideal Grace.
I love thee to the level of every day's
Most quiet need, by sun and candlelight.
I love thee freely, as men strive for Right;

I love thee purely, as they turn from Praise.
I love thee with the passion put to use
In my old griefs, and with my childhood's faith.
I love thee with a love I seemed to lose
With my lost saints—I love thee with the breath,
Smiles, tears, of all my life!—and, if God choose,
I shall but love thee better after death.
                    —Elizabeth Barrett Browning

(3)   Sonnet I from DIVINA COMMEDIA

Oft have I seen at some cathedral door
A laborer, pausing in the dust and heat,
Lay down his burden, and with reverent feet
Enter, and cross himself, and on the floor
Kneel to repeat his paternoster o'er;
Far off the noises of the world retreat;
The loud vociferations of the street
Become an undistinguishable roar.
So, as I enter here from day to day,
And leave my burden at this minster gate,
Kneeling in prayer, and not ashamed to pray,
The tumult of the time disconsolate
To inarticulate murmurs dies away,
While the eternal ages watch and wait.
                    —Henry Wadsworth Longfellow

(4)   DOVER BEACH

The sea is calm to-night,
The tide is full, the moon lies fair
Upon the Straits;—on the French coast, the light
Gleams, and is gone; the cliffs of England stand,
Glimmering and vast, out in the tranquil bay.
Come to the window, sweet is the night air!
Only, from the long line of spray
Where the sea meets the moon-blanch'd sand,
Listen! you hear the grating roar
Of pebbles which the waves suck back, and fling,
At their return, up the high strand,
Begin, and cease, and then again begin,
With tremulous cadence slow, and bring
The eternal note of sadness in.

Sophocles long ago
Heard it on the Aegean, and it brought
Into his mind the turbid ebb and flow
Of human misery; we
Find also in the sound a thought,
Hearing it by this distant northern sea.

The sea of faith
Was once, too, at the full, and round earth's shore
Lay like the folds of a bright girdle furl'd;
But now I only hear
Its melancholy, long, withdrawing roar,
Retreating to the breath
Of the night-wind down the vast edges drear
And naked shingles of the world.

Ah, love, let us be true
To one another; for the world, which seems
To lie before us like a land of dreams,
So various, so beautiful, so new,
Hath really neither joy, nor love, nor light,
Nor certitude, nor peace, nor help for pain;
And we are here as on a darkling plain
Swept with confused alarms of struggle and flight,
Where ignorant armies clash by night.

—MATTHEW ARNOLD

(5)   MENDING WALL[20]

Something there is that doesn't love a wall,
That sends the frozen-ground-swell under it,
And spills the upper boulders in the sun;
And makes gaps even two can pass abreast.
The work of hunters is another thing:
I have come after them and made repair
Where they have left not one stone on a stone,
But they would have the rabbit out of hiding
To please the yelping dogs. The gaps I mean,
No one has seen them made or heard them made,
But at spring mending-time we find them there.

[20] "Mending Wall," from *Complete Poems of Robert Frost*. Copyright, 1930, 1949, by Henry Holt and Company, Inc. By permission of Holt, Rinehart and Winston, Inc.

I let my neighbour know beyond the hill;
And on a day we meet to walk the line
And set the wall between us once again.
We keep the wall between us as we go.
To each the boulders that have fallen to each.
And some are loaves and some so nearly balls
We have to use a spell to make them balance:
'Stay where you are until our backs are turned!'
We wear our fingers rough with handling them.
Oh, just another kind of out-door game,
One on a side. It comes to little more:
There where it is we do not need the wall:
He is all pine and I am apple orchard.
My apple trees will never get across
And eat the cones under his pines, I tell him.
He only says, 'Good fences make good neighbours.'
Spring is the mischief in me, and I wonder
If I could put a notion in his head:
'*Why* do they make good neighbours? Isn't it
Where there are cows? But here there are no cows.
Before I built a wall I'd ask to know
What I was walling in or walling out,
And to whom I was like to give offence.
Something there is that doesn't love a wall,
That wants it down.' I could say 'Elves' to him,
But it's not elves exactly, and I'd rather
He said it for himself. I see him there
Bringing a stone grasped firmly by the top
In each hand, like an old-stone savage armed.
He moves in darkness as it seems to me,
Not of woods only and the shade of trees.
He will not go behind his father's saying,
And he likes having thought of it so well
He says again, 'Good fences make good neighbours.'

—ROBERT FROST

USING THE LIBRARY

18. A library is virtually a laboratory where deposits of the written word and the graphic portrayal of thought preserved in manuscript, print, and picture are available to the reader, the investigator, and the creative worker. A knowledge of these resources and an understanding of their organization are prerequisites for your effective use and enjoyment of this library-laboratory.

As a first step, use a free hour for a trip to the library. Get its physical setup clearly in mind: number of rooms and their use (main reading room, study alcoves, and reserved-book room); labels on different offices of library personnel indicating the activities that make a library effective; different sections for reference books, new acquisitions, fiction, bound magazines, current magazines and newspapers, and the like. Stroll beside the reference shelves and note the kind and location of the books there.

Libraries differ in actual content and physical arrangement, but the basic principles which determine the organization of library resources have been sufficiently standardized to enable the student familiar with them to proceed with an investigation in any library.

Regulations established for its users by a particular library may appear in various forms. Before losing time by a trial-and-error method of learning to use your library, and especially before beginning research on any subject or for any paper or article, find out whether your library has a guide, handbook, or pamphlet which explains or interprets its organization.

Whether familiar or not with library organization, you should examine one or more of the following guides. The first, probably kept at the library reference desk, is comprehensive and invaluable.

Winchell, Constance M. *Guide to Reference Books,* 7th ed., 1951. *Supplement, 1950–1952, 1953–1955, 1956–1958.*

Barton, Mary M., comp. *Reference Books: A Brief Guide for Students and Other Users of the Library,* 4th ed. Baltimore, Md.: Enoch Pratt Free Library, 1959.

Cook, Margaret G. *The New Library Key.* New York: The H. W. Wilson Company, 1956.

Gohdes, Clarence. *Bibliographical Guide to the Study of the Literature of the U.S.A.* Durham, N.C.: Duke University Press, 1959.

Murphey, Robert W. *How and Where to Look It Up.* New York: McGraw-Hill Book Company, 1958.

Russell, Harold G., and others. *The Use of Books and Libraries,* 9th ed. Minneapolis: University of Minnesota Press, 1958.

Look up in these guidebooks some or many of the titles below, for the rich information given, such as full bibliographic details and helpful critical discussions of materials on various subjects.

In every library a student has at his disposal three important kinds of material: reference works, periodicals, and the general collection of books.

18a. Become familiar with the reference works in your library.

Unless you already know what books and magazine articles are suited to your research needs, you should start with condensed, authoritative articles in reference books. Any book may be used for reference purposes, but reference books "are usually comprehensive in scope, condensed in treatment, and arranged on some special plan to facilitate the ready and accurate finding of information."[21] Such works are usually located on shelves open to the student in the main reading room or in a nearby reference room.

The following lists contain titles of works which are likely to be most valuable to the undergraduate student. Several titles may deal with the same general or specific subjects, and your library is virtually certain to have one or more of these books. Remember, however, that the preparation of a reference book is expensive in time and money. It cannot be revised and reprinted very often. Sometimes, too, supplements are added, and sometimes revisions and new editions may be in progress but may take several years for completion. Always a good starting point, reference books may become dated, and you should supplement any dated material by consulting annual publications and current indexes. (See Section **18b.**)

I. Books of General Information

A. GENERAL ENCYCLOPEDIAS

Collier's Encyclopedia. 20 vols. (Kept up to date with an annual volume, *Collier's Year Book Covering National and International Events*.)
Columbia Encyclopedia, 2nd ed.
Columbia-Viking Desk Encyclopedia, 2nd ed.
Encyclopaedia Britannica. 24 vols. (Kept up to date with an annual

[21] Isadore G. Mudge, "Reference Work and Reference Books," in Constance M. Winchell, *Guide to Reference Books*, 7th ed. (Chicago, 1951), p. xvi. Mudge's brief introduction, pp. xv–xvii, gives valuable suggestions for consulting and studying reference books.

volume, *Britannica Book of the Year, a Record of the March of Events.*)

Encyclopedia Americana. 30 vols. (Kept up to date with an annual volume, *The Americana Annual, an Encyclopedia of Current Events.*)

Lincoln Library of Essential Information.

New International Encyclopaedia. 25 vols. (Kept up to date with an annual volume, *New International Year Book, a Compendium of the World's Progress.*)

Seligman, Edwin R. A., and Alvin Johnson, eds. *Encyclopaedia of the Social Sciences* (commonly known as E.S.S.). 15 vols. (Less comprehensive than the volumes listed above, it deals with many subjects directly and indirectly related to the social sciences. E.S.S. could just as well have been listed under the following section, "Books of and Guides to Special Subject Information.")

B. GENERAL DICTIONARIES

Funk and Wagnalls New Standard Dictionary of the English Language.

Murray, Sir James A. H., and others, eds. *A New English Dictionary on Historical Principles,* reissued as *The Oxford English Dictionary.* 13 vols. (Commonly referred to as the NED, N.E.D., OED, or O.E.D.)

Webster's New International Dictionary of the English Language.

C. YEARBOOKS, in addition to the annual yearbooks of the various encyclopedias (see A, above)

Annual Register: A Review of Public Events at Home and Abroad (British).

Europa Yearbook. 2 vols. (Vol. I, Europe; Vol. II, Africa, The Americas, Asia, Australasia.)

Information Please Almanac. (Miscellaneous information.)

International Yearbook and Statesmen's Who's Who.

Statesman's Year-book: Statistical and Historical Annual of the States of the World. (Over 90 annual volumes have been published.)

Statistical Abstract of the United States.

United Nations Yearbook.

World Almanac and Book of Facts. (Miscellaneous information.)

Some of these books have been published annually for many years; some are comparatively recent. Like most of the books listed in this entire section (18a), their general nature is evident from their title or from their subtitle. Outstanding events, changes, statistics, and progress in the fields of industry, government, literature, and education should be sought in these yearbooks for the period. The *Statesman's Year-book,* for example, gives data regarding the government, area, population, education, religion, and industries of every nation and state in the world, including the United States.

II. Books of and Guides to Special Subject Information

Twelve subject lists follow, containing titles of encyclopedias, dictionaries, and handbooks, as well as indexes to specialized magazines. The twelve groups of subjects are Biography, Business and Economics, Education, Drama and Theater, History, Language, Literature, Music and the Dance, Painting and Architecture, Philosophy and Psychology, Religion, and Science.

In the indexes to magazines, both in these lists and in Section **18b,** the words *cumulative* or *cumulation* mean "increasing by successive additions"; that is, lists of authors, titles, and subjects are arranged alphabetically and published in several issues of the index; then periodically—for example, quarterly, semiannually, annually, or over a two- or three-year period—all the lists are combined in one alphabet, and earlier separate issues are discarded.

The subject encyclopedias are especially useful for supplying a brief history of a special subject, together with a selected bibliography, i.e., a list of books, booklets, and articles about a certain subject or subjects, or about a person or persons. In general, therefore, you should prefer the special encyclopedias for subjects within their scope rather than the general encyclopedias. The "best" encyclopedia to use for a given topic often depends upon the phase of a subject being investigated.

In addition to the titles listed below, your library has many other handbooks, dictionaries, or encyclopedias. A random sampling reveals handbooks on the following: air conditioning, automotive engineering, aviation, civil engineering, electrical engineering, geography, heating and ventilating, history of science, industrial relations, marine Diesels, mechanical engineering, nuclear science and technology, plastics, portraits, radio electronics, radio engineering, rare metals, refrigeration engineering, sociology, songs, structural engineering, welding, and wool.

Among innumerable special bibliographies, i.e., lists of books and magazine articles, a random sampling shows bibliographies on these subjects: American mammals and birds, American natural history, ceramics, costume, detective short story, fairy tales, foreign affairs, handicrafts, labor, meteorites, North American folklore and folk song, papermaking, printing, stainless steel, swimming.

A. BIOGRAPHY

Amory, Cleveland, ed. *International Celebrity Register*.

Barnhart, C. L., ed. *New Century Cyclopedia of Names*. 3 vols.

Biography Index, 1946—. (A cumulative index to biographical material in books and magazines.)

Current Biography: Who's News and Why, 1940—. (Eleven monthly issues which are cumulated in one alphabet annually "of personalities prominent on the international scene, in the arts, sciences, industry, politics, education, and entertainment.")

Dargan, Marion. *Guide to American Biography, 1607–1933*. (Suggests original and secondary sources.)

Johnson, Allen, and Dumas Malone, eds. *Dictionary of American Biography*. 21 vols. (Commonly known as D.A.B. or DAB. It includes outstanding Americans who are no longer living.)

Kunitz, Stanley J., and Howard Haycraft, eds. *American Authors, 1600–1900*. (Includes 1,300 biographies and 400 portraits.)

Kunitz, Stanley J., and Howard Haycraft, eds. *British Authors Before 1800*. (Includes 650 biographies and 220 portraits.)

Kunitz, Stanley J., and Howard Haycraft, eds. *British Authors of the Nineteenth Century*. (Includes 1,000 biographies and 350 portraits.)

Kunitz, Stanley J., and Howard Haycraft, eds. *Twentieth Century Authors*, and *First Supplement*. (Includes over 1,850 biographies and 1,700 portraits.)

Preston, Wheeler. *American Biographies*. (Excludes living people.)

Stephen, Leslie, and Sidney Lee, eds. *Dictionary of National Biography*. 63 vols. originally; reissued in 22 vols. Several supplements. (Commonly known as D.N.B. or DNB. It includes outstanding Englishmen who are no longer living.)

Webster's Biographical Dictionary.

Who's Who (principally British). (Includes only living people.)

Who's Who in America. (Includes only living people. For those who have recently died, see earlier volumes or volumes entitled *Who Was Who in America*.)

Specialized books giving biographies of contemporary people in various fields and in foreign countries include *American Men of Science; Directory of American Scholars; Leaders in Education; Who's Who in*

American Art; Who's Who in Engineering; Who's Who in the Theatre; Who's Who of American Women; and "Who's Who" in the Middle West, Canada, France, Latin America, the United Nations.

Your library also has special bibliographies for biographical and critical materials about older authors. A random sampling shows special bibliographies of the following: George Ade, Cervantes, Geoffrey Chaucer, James Fenimore Cooper, Stephen Crane, Charles Dickens, Robert Frost, Thomas Hardy, Oliver Wendell Holmes, John Keats, Abraham Lincoln, Edgar Allan Poe, James Whitcomb Riley, Walter Scott, William Shakespeare, Booth Tarkington, Mark Twain, Walt Whitman.

B. BUSINESS AND ECONOMICS

Business Periodicals Index, 1958—. (A cumulative subject index to about 120 periodicals dealing with various business fields.)

Clark, Donald T., and Bert A. Gottfried. *Dictionary of Business and Finance.*

Munn, Glenn G. *Encyclopedia of Banking and Finance,* 5th ed., and *Supplement.*

C. EDUCATION

Alexander, Carter, and Arvid J. Burke. *How to Locate Educational Information and Data,* 3rd ed.

Education Index, 1929—. (A cumulative author and subject index to magazines, books, bulletins, and reports in the entire field of education.)

Educational Film Guide, 11th ed. (A classified subject list of 11,000 16mm. motion pictures, together with an alphabetical title and subject index. Semiannual supplements.)

Good, Carter V., ed. *Dictionary of Education.*

Monroe, Paul, ed. *Cyclopedia of Education.* 5 vols.

D. DRAMA AND THEATER

Baker, Blanch M., comp. *Theatre and Allied Arts.*

Dramatic Index, 1909–1949. (Until discontinued, an annual index to articles and illustrations, concerning the stage and players, in American and British periodicals.)

Firkins, Ina Ten Eyck. *Index to Plays,* 1800–1926, with *Supplement* to 1934. (The two volumes index 11,156 plays by 3,538 authors.)

Hartnoll, Phyllis, ed. *The Oxford Companion to the Theatre.*
Ottemiller, John H. *Index to Plays in Collections . . . 1900–1956,* 3rd ed.
(An index to 5,765 copies of 2,205 different plays by 1,148 different authors in 624 collections—from ancient times to the present.)
Shipley, J. T., *Guide to Great Plays.*
Sobel, Bernard. *The New Theatre Handbook and Digest of Plays.*
West, Dorothy H., and Dorothy M. Peake. *Play Index, 1949–1952.* (An index to 2,616 plays in 1,138 volumes.)

E. HISTORY

Adams, James Truslow, ed. *Dictionary of American History.* 6 vols.
Barzun, Jacques, and Henry F. Graff. *The Modern Researcher.*
Bury, J. B., and others, eds. *Cambridge Ancient History.* 12 vols.
Chambers, R. *The Book of Days.* 2 vols. (Old, but still interesting as "a miscellany of popular antiquities in connection with the calendar, including anecdotes, biography and history, curiosities of literature, and oddities of human life and character.")
Damon, Charles R., comp. *American Dictionary of Dates, 458–1920.* 3 vols.
Douglas, George W. *The American Book of Days.*
Dutcher, G. M., and others, eds. *Guide to Historical Literature.*
Guide to the Study of the United States of America.
Gwatkin, H. M., J. P. Whitney, and others, eds. *Cambridge Medieval History.* 8 vols.
Handlin, Oscar, and others. *Harvard Guide to American History.*
Harper's Encyclopaedia of United States History from 458 A.D. to 1912. 10 vols.
Keller, Helen Rex. *Dictionary of Dates.* 2 vols.
Morris, Richard B. *Encyclopedia of American History.*
Schlesinger, Arthur M., and D. R. Fox, eds. *A History of American Life.* 12 vols.
Ward, A. W., and others, eds. *Cambridge Modern History.* 13 vols. (*New Cambridge Modern History* in progress.)
Webster's Geographical Dictionary.
Writings on American History, 1906–1940, 1948—. (An annual index, arranged by author, title, and subject, to materials in books and periodicals dealing with United States history.)

F. LANGUAGE

Berrey, Lester V., and Melvin Van den Bark. *American Thesaurus of Slang: A Complete Reference Book of Colloquial Speech.*

Crabb's English Synonyms.

Craigie, Sir William A., and James R. Hulbert, eds. *A Dictionary of American English on Historical Principles.* 4 vols.

Evans, Bergen, and Cornelia Evans. *A Dictionary of Contemporary American Usage.*

Fowler, Henry W. *A Dictionary of Modern English Usage.*

Mathews, Mitford M., ed. *A Dictionary of Americanisms on Historical Principles.* 2 vols.

Nicholson, Margaret. *Dictionary of American-English Usage.*

Partridge, Eric. *A Dictionary of Slang and Unconventional English,* 4th ed.

Partridge, Eric. *Slang Today and Yesterday.*

Roget's *International Thesaurus of English Words and Phrases.* (Revised constantly and title may vary slightly.)

Webster's Dictionary of Synonyms.

G. LITERATURE

A.L.A. Index . . . to General Literature. (With *Supplement,* a guide down to 1910; a subject index, still useful for older books.)

Baker, Ernest A. *Guide to Historical Fiction.* (Lists about 5,000 novels dealing with the past, but its publication date, 1914, renders it useless for the last 50 years.)

Baker, Ernest A., and James Packman. *Guide to the Best Fiction, English and American, Including Translations from Foreign Languages.*

Barnhart, C. L., ed. *The New Century Handbook of English Literature.*

Bartlett, John. *Familiar Quotations.* (First published in 1855, the book has been constantly revised by succeeding editors.)

Bateson, F. W., ed. *Cambridge Bibliography of English Literature.* 4 vols. Vol. 5, *Supplement,* ed. by George Watson, also the editor of a condensed 1-vol. version, *The Concise Bibliography of English Literature, 600–1950.*

Blanck, Jacob, comp. *Bibliography of American Literature* (begun and continuing). 8 or 9 vols.

Book Review Digest, 1905—. (An index to reviews of some 4,000 general books appearing in some 75 American and British periodicals. It is published 11 times a year, but it is cumulative semiannually and annually.)

Burke, William J., and W. D. Howe, eds. *American Authors and Books, 1640–1940.*

Cary, M., and others, eds. *Oxford Classical Dictionary.*

Cook, Dorothy E., and Isabel S. Monro. *Short Story Index: An Index to*

60,000 Short Stories in 4,320 Collections, and Supplement. (Entries are listed by author, title, and subject.)

Cumulative Book Index: A World List of Books in the English Language, 1929—. (Author, title, and subject entries are in one alphabet. It is published monthly, except August, and cumulated frequently during the year, annually, and in four- or five-year cumulations. Information given includes publisher, price, and date of publication. For books in print before the Cumulative Book Index started, see United States Catalog, 1st, 2nd, 3rd, and 4th editions.)

Essay and General Literature Index, 1900—. (An index to essays and articles in volumes of collections of essays and miscellaneous works; supplements the A.L.A. Index, above; published semiannually.)

Funk and Wagnalls Standard Dictionary of Folklore, Mythology and Legend. 2 vols.

Granger, Edith. Index to Poetry. (The 4th edition, 1953, indexes 577 volumes of poetry anthologies.) Also Supplement.

Hart, James D. Oxford Companion to American Literature.

Harvey, Paul. Oxford Companion to Classical Literature.

Harvey, Paul. Oxford Companion to English Literature.

Hoffman, Hester R. Bessie Graham's Bookman's Manual, a Guide to Literature, 7th ed.

Hornstein, Lillian H., ed. The Reader's Companion to World Literature.

Leary, Lewis G. Articles on American Literature, 1900–1950.

Magill, Frank N., ed. Masterplots. First Series, 2 vols. Second Series, 2 vols. (Also published in a combined edition, 4 vols., as well as under the title Masterpieces of World Literature in Digest Form.)

Magnus, Laurie, ed. A Dictionary of European Literature Designed as a Companion to English Studies.

Mencken, H. L., ed. A New Dictionary of Quotations on Historical Principles from Ancient and Modern Sources.

Modern Humanities Research Association. Annual Bibliography of the English Language and Literature, 1920—.

Nield, Jonathan. A Guide to the Best Historical Novels and Tales, 5th ed. (Useful down to 1929.)

Nyren, Dorothy, ed. A Library of Literary Criticism: Modern American Literature.

Oxford Dictionary of Quotations.

Oxford History of English Literature (in progress).

Sanders, Chauncey. An Introduction to Research in English Literary History.

Shipley, Joseph T., ed. Dictionary of World Literature: Criticism—

Forms—Technique. (Also published under the title *Dictionary of World Literary Terms.*)

Smith, Horatio, ed. *Columbia Dictionary of Modern European Literature.* (Contains 1,167 articles by 239 specialists, dealing with later nineteenth- and twentieth-century authors; 31 literatures are represented.)

Sonnenschein, William S. *Best Books: A Reader's Guide to the Choice of the Best Available Books in Every Department of Science, Art, and Literature.* 6 parts. (Lists about 100,000 books. First appeared in 1887; final edition in 1910–1935.)

Spiller, Robert E., and others, eds. *Literary History of the United States.* 3 vols. *Bibliography Supplement,* ed. by Richard M. Ludwig.

Steinberg, S. H., ed. *Cassell's Encyclopaedia of Literature.* 2 vols.

Stevenson, Burton E. *The Home Book of Quotations, Classical and Modern.*

Stevenson, Burton E. *The Home Book of Shakespeare Quotations.*

Thrall, William F., and Addison Hibbard. *A Handbook to Literature.*

Trent, William P., and others, eds. *Cambridge History of American Literature.* 4 vols.

Ward, A. W., and A. R. Waller, eds. *Cambridge History of English Literature.* 15 vols.

Zesmer, David M. *Guide to English Literature.*

H. MUSIC AND THE DANCE

Apel, Willi. *Harvard Dictionary of Music.*

Baker, Theodore. *Baker's Biographical Dictionary of Musicians,* 5th ed.

Darrell, Robert D. *Schirmer's Guide to Books on Music and Musicians.*

Duckles, Vincent H., and H. S. Nicewonger. *A Guide to Reference Materials on Music.*

Feather, Leonard. *The Encyclopedia of Jazz.*

Grove's Dictionary of Music and Musicians, 5th ed. 9 vols.

Guide to Dance Periodicals, 1950—. (An index to dance magazines, each volume covering periods of from two to five years.)

Magriel, Paul D. *A Bibliography of Dancing.*

Music Index, 1949—. (A cumulative index to current music periodical literature.)

Oxford History of Music, 2nd ed. 7 vols. (*New Oxford History of Music* in process of publication.)

Scholes, Percy A. *Oxford Companion to Music.*

Thompson, Oscar, ed. *International Cyclopedia of Music and Musicians.*

I. PAINTING AND ARCHITECTURE

Art Index, 1929—. (A cumulative author and subject index to magazines and bulletins dealing with the fine arts, such as architecture, painting, ceramics, sculpture.)

Encyclopedia of World Art. 15 vols. (In progress.)

Fielding, Mantle. *Dictionary of American Painters, Sculptors, and Engravers.*

Fletcher, Banister F. *History of Architecture*, 16th ed.

Gardner, Helen. *Art Through the Ages*, 3rd ed.

Harper's Encyclopedia of Art: Architecture, Sculpture, Painting, Decorative Arts. 2 vols.

Lucas, Edna. *The Harvard List of Books on Art.*

Mallett, Daniel T. *Index of Artists: International-Biographical, Including Painters, Sculptors, Illustrators, Engravers and Etchers.*

Myers, Bernard S., ed. *Encyclopedia of Painting.*

Sturgis, Russell. *Dictionary of Architecture and Building: Biographical, Historical, and Descriptive.* 3 vols.

J. PHILOSOPHY AND PSYCHOLOGY

Baldwin, James M. *Dictionary of Philosophy and Psychology.* 3 vols.

English, Horace B., and Ava C. English. *A Comprehensive Dictionary of Psychological and Psychoanalytical Terms.*

Harriman, Philip L. *New Dictionary of Psychology.*

The Harvard List of Books in Psychology.

Runes, Dagobert D., ed. *Dictionary of Philosophy.*

Warren, Howard C. *Dictionary of Psychology.*

K. RELIGION

Barrow, John G. *A Bibliography of Bibliographies in Religion.*

Catholic Encyclopedia. 18 vols.

Catholic Periodical Index, 1930—. (A cumulative author and subject index to a selected list of Catholic periodicals.)

Ellison, John W., comp. *Nelson's Complete Concordance of the Revised Standard Version Bible.*

Gibbs, H. A. R., and J. H. Kramers. *Shorter Encyclopedia of Islam.*

Hastings, James, ed. *Dictionary of the Bible.* 5 vols.

Hastings, James, ed. *Encyclopedia of Religion and Ethics.* 13 vols.

Jewish Encyclopedia. 12 vols.

Miller, Madeleine S., and J. Lane Miller. *Harper's Bible Dictionary.*

New Schaff-Herzog Encyclopedia of Religious Knowledge. 12 vols.

Stevenson, Burton. *The Home Book of Bible Quotations.*
Strong, James. *The Exhaustive Concordance of the Bible.*
Universal Jewish Encyclopedia. 10 vols. (More up to date than the *Jewish Encyclopedia.*)

L. SCIENCE

Agricultural Index, 1916—. (A cumulative subject index to a selected but extensive list of agricultural magazines, books, and bulletins.)

Applied Science and Technology Index (formerly *Industrial Arts Index*), 1958—. (A cumulative subject index to about 200 periodicals dealing with applied science and technology subjects.)

Crane, E. J., and others, eds. *A Guide to the Literature of Chemistry,* 2nd ed.

Engineering Index, 1884—. (With changes over the years, this index has been since 1928 a selective subject-author index to periodicals in all engineering fields. It is published annually, but technical libraries receive weekly cards containing the information eventually published in the annual volumes.)

Hackh, Ingo W. D. *A Chemical Dictionary, Containing the Words Generally Used in Chemistry, and Many of the Terms Used in the Related Sciences* . . . , 3rd ed.

Hawkins, Reginald R. *Scientific, Medical, and Technical Books Published in the United States.*

Henderson, Isabella Ferguson, and W. D. Henderson. *Dictionary of Scientific Terms* (pronunciation, derivation, and definition of terms in biology, botany, zoology, anatomy, cytology, genetics, embryology, physiology), 6th ed.

Industrial Arts Index, 1913–1958. (A cumulative subject index, until discontinuation, to a selected but extensive list of business, finance, applied science, and technology periodicals, books, and pamphlets. See *Applied Science and Technology Index,* above.)

Jones, Franklin, ed. *Engineering Encyclopedia.* 2 vols. (Treats 4,500 important engineering subjects.)

Kirk, Raymond E., and others, eds. *Encyclopedia of Chemical Technology.* 15 vols.

McGraw-Hill Encyclopedia of Science and Technology. (An international reference work consisting of 15 vols. in progress.)

O'Rourke, Charles E. *General Engineering Handbook.*

Parke, Nathan G. *Guide to the Literature of Mathematics and Physics.*

Quarterly Cumulative Index Medicus, 1927—. (An author and subject index to medical magazines and books. For materials before 1927, see

Index Medicus, 1879–1899, 1903–1926, a classified index of medical literature.)

Space Encyclopedia: A Guide to Astronomy and Space Research.

Taylor, Norman. *Encyclopedia of Gardening, Horticulture and Landscape Design,* 2nd ed.

Technical Book Review Index, 1935—. (A guide to reviews of scientific and technical books in scientific, technical, and trade journals. It is published monthly except July and August, and is cumulative annually.)

Thorpe, Sir Jocelyn F. *Thorpe's Dictionary of Applied Chemistry,* 4th ed. 12 vols.

Van Nostrand's Scientific Encyclopedia.

18b.   Become familiar with indexes to periodicals.

If you are doing research on a subject of contemporary or revived interest or of recent occurrence, you need to consult magazine files and, perhaps, bound volumes of newspapers. Libraries usually display current issues of the best general magazines and some of special interest—some libraries even have special periodical rooms for such magazines—but older issues are bound in book form and can be obtained most easily after you have consulted index books which are a guide to the contents of the magazines.

In each of these indexes, look for directions to the reader, ordinarily given in the preface, so that you can interpret the entries and find your material without loss of time. The front of each index volume usually tells you which magazines are indexed and gives full instructions for use. For example, here are two entries from *Readers' Guide to Periodical Literature* and their meaning:

Author entry:

> **LINDBERGH, Charles Augustus, 1902-**
> Our best chance to survive. por Sat Eve Post
> 227:25 Jl 17 '54
> Thoughts of a combat pilot. pors Sat Eve
> Post 227:20-1+ O 2 '54

This entry means that during the time covered by this issue Charles A. Lindbergh (born 1902) published two articles. One, "Our Best Chance to Survive," with his portrait, was published in *The Saturday Evening Post* for July 17, 1954, in Volume Number 227, page 25. The second, entitled "Thoughts of a Combat Pilot," with portraits also, was published in *The Saturday Evening Post* for October 2, 1954, in Volume

Number 227, beginning on page 20, and continuing on page 21 and later pages. (For unbound magazines, the date of issue is your guide; when the magazines are bound into book form, the volume number is your guide, with the date of issue important only when each issue is paged separately.)

Subject entry:

> **COLLEGE students**
> Americans as students. P. Emmanuel. Atlan
> 194:59-62 Ag '54; Discussion. 194:77-9 O; 19
> N '54

This entry means that an article dealing with college students, entitled "Americans as Students," by P. Emmanuel, appeared in the *Atlantic Monthly* for August, 1954, pages 59 to 62; the volume number, when the magazine is bound, is Volume 194. Discussion of the article appeared in the October, 1954, issue, pages 77 to 79, and in the November, 1954, issue, page 19—both issues part of Volume 194.

In addition to the periodical indexes included in the lists of special subject information in Section **18a,** the most helpful of the other periodical indexes are those given below. To keep readers entirely up to date, with little loss of time for the reader, most of them are *cumulative* (see definition on p. 153).

1. *Annual Magazine Subject-Index,* 1907–1949. (A subject index, until discontinued, to a selected list—dealing mainly with history, travel, and art—of American and British periodicals and professional or cultural society publications.)
2. *Bibliographic Index, A Cumulative Bibliography of Bibliographies,* 1937—. (A subject index to separately published bibliographies and to bibliographies included each year in several hundred books and approximately 1,500 periodicals.)
3. *Bulletin of the Public Affairs Information Service,* 1915—. (A cumulative subject index to current books, pamphlets, periodicals, government documents, and other library material in the fields of economics and public affairs.)
4. *Facts on File,* 1940—. (A weekly world news digest with cumulative index, including world, national, and foreign affairs, Latin America, finance and economics, art and science, education and religion, sports, obituaries, and other miscellany.)
5. *Index to Legal Periodicals,* 1908—. (A cumulative subject and author index to articles in law journals.)

6. *International Index to Periodicals,* 1907—. (A cumulative author and subject index to articles in domestic and foreign periodicals dealing with literature, history, social science, religion, drama, and pure science. It is really a supplement to *Readers' Guide,* below.)

7. *The New York Times Index,* 1913—. (A cumulative guide to events of national importance by reference to day, page, and column of *The New York Times.* Material is entered by subjects, persons, and organizations. The only index to an American newspaper, it is an indirect guide to events in other newspapers.)

8. *Nineteenth Century Readers' Guide to Periodical Literature,* 1890–1899, with supplementary indexing, 1900–1922. 2 vols.

9. *Poole's Index to Periodical Literature.* 7 vols. (An index of articles, by subject only, in American and British periodicals from 1802 to 1906.)

10. *Readers' Guide to Periodical Literature,* 1900—. (A cumulative index, most useful to the general reader, to over 100 popular and semipopular magazines. Entries are according to author, subject, and fiction title.)

11. *Subject Index to Periodicals,* 1915—. (A cumulative index, arranged by subject, to articles in British magazines.)

18c.   Become familiar with the general collection of books in your library.

The most important part of a library is the main collection of books. To obtain them, you need to consult the card catalog, which is the index of the whole library. It consists of 3 x 5 inch cards filed alpha-

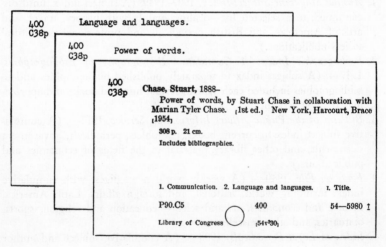

Sample Cards, Library Card Catalog.

```
PE2808
.M4
1936        Mencken, Henry Louis, 1880–
              ... The American language; an inquiry into the develop-
            ment of English in the United States, by H. L. Mencken.
            New York, A. A. Knopf, 1936.
              xi, 769, xxix. ₁1₁ p.  24½ cm.
              At head of title: 4th ed., cor., enl., and rewritten.
              "Proper names in America": p. 474–554.
              ———————— Supplement ɪ–ɪɪ ...  New York, A. A. Knopf,
            1945–48.
              2 v.  24½ cm.
              "First edition."
              Includes bibliographies.
                                    PE2808.M4  1936  Suppl.

              1. English language.     2. Americanisms.  3. Names — U. S.
            4. Names, Personal—        U. S.     ɪ. Title.
            PE2808.M4  1936              427.9                 36—27236
            Library of Congress         ₁54r48u⁹30₁
```

Specimen Library Card, Card Catalog.

betically in long trays or drawers in a series of filing cabinets; on the
front of each drawer is a label (for example, A—ABN) giving the
alphabetical limits of the cards there.

Book information is filed in the card catalog in three ways, by (1)
author, (2) title, and (3) subject. Each book in the library is therefore
represented in the card catalog by several cards, printed and supplied
by the Library of Congress and thus uniform in all libraries. These
cards are usually identical, except that certain lines may be typed across
the top, giving the title, joint author, or subject headings, i.e., entries
for the subject with which the book deals and which are obtained from
the Library of Congress card.

Illustrated are examples of one of the simpler cards in the card catalog. The typed numbers at the left are the call number of the book,
according to the Dewey Decimal Classification (see pp. 167–168). The
typed words show that one card is indexed by title, one by subject (this
book has also one other subject entry); one card is filed according to
author. The first line gives the author's last name, given name, and
date of birth. On the second, third, and fourth lines are the title, author's
name again, collaborating author, edition, place of publication, publisher, and year of copyright (no brackets around date would indicate
that the date is printed on the title page). Line 5 gives number of pages
and size (height) of the book in centimeters. Line 6 indicates that the

book has bibliographies. Line 7 tells that, in addition to the author card, the card catalog should have three additional cards, one under the subject "Communication," one under the subject "Language and languages," and one under title. In line 8, "P90.C5" is the call number of this book in libraries using the Library of Congress system; the middle number, "400," is the initial number for libraries using the Dewey Decimal Classification. The other figures have a specialized meaning intelligible only to librarians; for example, "54–5980" is the number of this card, when copies of it are ordered from the Library of Congress, which prepares and prints it. The round hole is for the insertion of a rod in the filing drawer so that if the drawer is accidentally dropped, some hundreds of cards are not hopelessly mixed up.

A library card with more complicated information (can you explain it?) is illustrated on page 165.[22] If you think that the information on any library card is important and you do not understand how to interpret it, ask a member of your library staff.

When you want a book, and you know the author or the title, you can easily get needed information from the author or title card. If you know neither author nor title, turn to the cards that list books dealing with the subject upon which you are working and make your choices from the collection there. If the author is not given, as may be true of many bulletins or pamphlets, or if there is no author, as is true of bound volumes of magazines, look for the title or the organization responsible for the publication.

In addition to revealing the resources of the library, the card catalog gives the call number by means of which each book is located on the shelves. This number appears in the upper left-hand corner (see illustrations) and corresponds exactly to the number placed on the cover and also inside the front cover of the book. Some libraries are so arranged that all or part of the books are placed on open shelves accessible to students. In other libraries the main collection is shelved in enclosed stacks. To obtain a book then, you fill out a "call slip" furnished by the library and present it at the Circulation or Loan Desk. On this

---

[22] Henry L. Mencken died in 1956, but the Library of Congress does not print new cards when an author dies. Any new edition of a deceased author's book requiring a new card or a card for a posthumously published book contains author's death year. Sometimes a particular library has a policy of typing in the death year on cards not having that information.

call slip write the call number of the book, author, title, and your own name and address; the library attendant will then obtain the book for you from the stacks.

If you have access to the book collection, you will discover that the books are arranged according to a definite system, the key to which is the first part of the call number. The two classification systems commonly used are the Dewey Decimal Classification and the Library of Congress Classification. Books classified by either system are arranged according to subjects treated.

In the Dewey Decimal Classification, the field of knowledge is arranged in 10 groups, including one group for reference books. Each major class as well as each subclass is represented by a three-digit number; further subdivisions are indicated by the use of numbers after a decimal point. The 10 main classes and some of the subclasses under the main classes are illustrated in the following:

000	General works	400	Linguistics	
	010 Bibliography	500	Pure science	
	020 Library science		510 Mathematics	
	030 General encyclopedias		520 Astronomy	
	040 General collected essays		530 Physics	
	050 General periodicals		540 Chemistry	
	060 General societies, museums		550 Geology	
	070 Journalism, newspapers		560 Paleontology	
	080 Polygraphy, general collections		570 Biology, anthropology	
	090 Rare books		580 Botany	
100	Philosophy		590 Zoology	
200	Religion	600	Applied science	
300	Social sciences		610 Medicine	
	310 Statistics		620 Engineering	
	320 Political science		630 Agriculture	
	330 Economics		640 Home economics	
	340 Law		650 Communication, business	
	350 Administration		660 Chemical technology	
	360 Associations and institutions		670 Manufactures	
	370 Education		680 Trades	
	380 Commerce, communication		690 Building	
	390 Manners and customs	700	Arts and recreation	
			710 Landscape gardening	
			720 Architecture	

730	Sculpture	870	Latin
740	Drawing, decoration, design	880	Greek
		890	Other literatures
750	Painting	900	History
760	Engraving	910	Geography, description, and travel
770	Photography		
780	Music	920	Biography
790	Amusements	930	Ancient history
800	Literature	940	Europe
810	American	950	Asia
820	English	960	Africa
830	German	970	North America
840	French	980	South America
850	Italian	990	Oceania and the polar regions
860	Spanish, Portuguese		

Examples of further subclassification:

Applied Science is numbered 600; Engineering, 620; Radio, 621. A book, *Microphone Technique for the Speaker,* by Verl Bratton, has as classification number 621.384193/B73m. The B73m is placed under the longer number; B is the first letter of the author's last name; m the first letter of the first word of the title.

American Literature is numbered 810–819; an edition of Henry Wadsworth Longfellow's *Evangeline* is numbered 811/L86e. British Literature bears the numbers 820–829; British Drama is 822; Elizabethan Drama is 822.3; an edition of Shakespeare's *Julius Caesar* is numbered 822.3/S5jA, in which the last letter, A, stands for *A*rden Edition.

The Library of Congress Classification uses letters of the alphabet followed by additional letters or by Arabic numerals. The main classes are these:

A	General works	K	Law
B	Philosophy, religion	L	Education
C	History, auxiliary sciences	M	Music
D	History and topography (except America)	N	Fine arts
		P	Language and literature
E and F	American history	Q	Science
G	Geography, anthropology	R	Medicine
H	Social sciences	S	Agriculture, plant and animal industry
J	Political science		

T Technology   V Naval science
U Military science   Z Bibliography and library science

The letters I, O, W, X, and Y have not yet been used and will allow for expansion by five additional classes. Each general class has sub-classes: PB—PH classifies modern European Languages; PN, PR, PS, and PZ classify, respectively, General Literary History, British Literature, American Literature, and Fiction and Juvenile Literature.

Under PS, for example, PS 303–324 is American poetry; PS 700 on, individual authors; PS 2250–2298, Henry Wadsworth Longfellow; PS 2263, Longfellow's *Evangeline.*

In filing cards in the card catalog, libraries in general observe the following rules:

All libraries file by entry, i.e., according to what appears first on the card, whether author, subject, or title. The articles *the, a, an* appearing as the first word of a title are ignored. Most libraries file letter-by-letter to the end of the word. This means that the title card, *The American Way,* is filed in front of the subject card AMERICANISMS, just as all cards beginning "New York" are filed in front of cards with "Newark" as the entry word. Libraries which file in strictly alphabetical order, of course, place *-isms* before *way* and *-ark* before *York*. Incidentally, encyclopedias, as well as library catalogs, differ in their entry system.

Books *about* an author—when his name is a subject entry, it is typed in black capitals or in red—are filed before or after all books *by* that author.

Cards for authors having the same last name as the entry word are filed according to the given name; always make a note of the first name, or at least the initials, of an author and of the exact title of the book you want.

Abbreviations and numerals are filed just as they would be if the words they represent were spelled out.

When the entry word is the same, all authors by that name-word precede all subjects, and all subjects precede all titles. For example, Washington, George (books by), WASHINGTON, GEORGE (books about), *Washington merry-go-round* (title) are entered in that order.

EXERCISES

A. After you have become familiar with your college or university library, choose two or three or four of the following sentences, or write similar ones.

Use each as the first sentence, the topic sentence, in a paragraph. Expand each sentence into a fair-sized paragraph, a half-page or three-fourths of a page long.

1. I have made my first visit to our library.
2. I have made a thorough tour of our library.
3. Several things impressed me about our library.
4. A library has many uses.
5. The ___ room in the library is an interesting place.
6. The library has a newspaper room.
7. The library has a periodical room.
8. The library has a study room.
9. The library has a main reading room.
10. The library has a reserved-book room.
11. The card catalog is very helpful.
12. Here are directions for borrowing books from the library.
13. Fiction books are kept in a special place.
14. *The New York Times* is both bound and kept on microfilm.
15. Our library has encyclopedias and other reference books.
16. Here are directions for finding material in bound magazines (or newspapers).
17. It is fun to browse through the bound magazines in the library.
18. You can even have dates in the library!
19. My high school (home town) has a satisfactory (unsatisfactory) library.
20. I have (hope to have) a private library.

B. Prepare, or answer, the following. Give, if not already indicated, the source of your information.

1. Make a floor plan of the main reading room of your college or university library, showing the location of the more general kinds of reference books such as encyclopedias, dictionaries, biographical books, magazine indexes.
2. Where in your library are kept bound magazines, current magazines, bound newspapers, current newspapers, novels, reserved books, the card catalog?
3. Go to your library and fill out call slips or cards for five nonfiction books you would like to read. Get one of the books and bring it and the other four call slips to class.
4. Make a list of five widely different alphabetical subject headings that are used in the following (choose three indexes that will help you in your chosen field): *Agricultural Index, Applied Science and Tech-*

nology *Index, Art Index, Bulletin of the Public Affairs Information Service, Business Periodicals Index, Drama Index, Education Index, Index to Legal Periodicals, Music Index, Quarterly Cumulative Index Medicus.*

5. Choose a word in the *New English Dictionary* (*Oxford English Dictionary*) with at least 20 lines of type, and prepare a brief account of its history.

6. Consult a dictionary of Americanisms and discuss a half-dozen words that have specialized meanings in America of the past or present.

7. Where would you find information about a prominent living person: musician, engineer, scientist, educator, scholar, American, British resident?

8. Who wrote the following and in what poems?
   a. "A little learning is a dangerous thing."
   b. "What is so rare as a day in June?"
   c. "In the spring a young man's fancy lightly turns to thoughts of love."
   d. "God's in His heaven—All's right with the world!"
   e. "Where ignorance is bliss, 'tis folly to be wise."
   f. "Bliss was it in that dawn to be alive,
      But to be young was very heaven!"

9. How many books were published last year on the subject of cookery, canals, landscape gardening, reading, oil, clothing?

10. Find the name, birthplace, birth date, and death date of a prominent nineteenth-century architect, a painter, a musician, a teacher, an inventor.

11. In your library what is the (a) most recent book by Ernest Hemingway, (b) most recent book about Ernest Hemingway, (c) most recent magazine article or story by Ernest Hemingway, (d) most recent magazine article about Ernest Hemingway, (e) most recent review of a book by Ernest Hemingway, (f) fullest and most interesting account of his death?

12. How many books does your library have about Alexander Graham Bell, Charles Dickens, John J. Pershing, Theodore Roosevelt, Woodrow Wilson?

13. Who are the authors of the following: *An American Tragedy, The Barretts of Wimpole Street, Leaves of Grass, The Rise of Silas Lapham, Vanity Fair?*

14. Who were the following? What did they do? When did they live? When did they die? (a) Thomas à Becket; (b) Thomas à Kempis; (c) Thomas Aquinas; (d) Thomas Browne; (e) Thomas Hughes; (f) Thomas Hardy; (g) Thomas Henry Huxley.

15. What system of classification is used in your college library? Get the call number of a book on each of the following: ceramics, education, poetry, travel, biography. What is the title of each book? When and where was it published? Who is the publisher?

C. Copy the following, leaving enough space where the dashes occur to fill in needed material. Then give the information asked for, after you have filled in the blanks or have had them filled in for you by your teacher.

1. Give the name, birth date, and death date of one of the persons whose biographies are given on page ___ of Volume ___ of the *Dictionary of American Biography*.

2. For the last word which is treated fully at the bottom of the first column (not carried over to the second column) on page ___ of Volume ___ of *A Dictionary of American English* give (1) its origin and (2) the sentence containing its earliest recorded use.

3. Give the volume and page number of the volume of the *Encyclopedia Americana* which discusses ___.

4. From the card catalog obtain the name of a book on ___ which was published in the 1950's.

5. According to the *Readers' Guide to Periodical Literature* for ___, did John Steinbeck in that year publish any stories in magazines? If so, list the titles of the stories, the magazines, and their dates.

6. Does your library have any copies of *Time* magazine for the year ___? Of *The New Yorker* for the year ___? Of *Newsweek* for the year ___?

7. Were any articles on ___ published during November, ___? If so, list one and the name and precise date of the magazine in which it appeared.

8. According to *The Engineering Index,* were any articles published in foreign magazines in ___ on ___? If so, list one, and the name, date of publication, and country in which it appeared.

9. Give page and volume number of an article in the *Encyclopedia of Religion and Ethics* on ___.

10. Give the name of the author, the title, and the publisher of the latest book about ___ listed in the card catalog.

D. Copy the following, leaving enough space where the dashes occur to fill in needed material. Find the information in your library, after you have filled in the blanks or have had them filled in for you by your teacher. Write after each of the 10 items the exact source of your information.

1. Give the birthplace, university attended, and date of death of ___.
2. ___ was the discoverer (or inventor) of ___.
3. ___ was first published the year ___, in the city of ___.

4. ___ University was founded in ___.
5. ___ was elected Vice-President of the United States in ___. He was a candidate of the ___ party.
6. The scenes of action in Shakespeare's play ___ are ___.
7. Two books about ___ are by, respectively, ___ and ___. For each, give the nationality of author and year and place of publication.
8. ___ is the manufacturing center in ___ of (the product) ___.
9. ___ of ___ University received his undergraduate college or university training at ___ and did his graduate study at ___. He holds the degrees of ___ from ___.
10. At one time or another ___ has been a part of, or has belonged to, three different countries: ___, ___, and ___.

E. For answers to the following questions, give the specific source of your information. Your instructor may follow the general plan of this exercise but may change the details.

1. How many books does your library have by Henry David Thoreau? How many books about him? How many books in which parts are devoted to him?
2. Where are the fiction books kept in your library? Where are the bound magazines kept?
3. Are the bound-magazine volumes listed in the regular card catalog or in a separate card-catalog file?
4. Who won (a) the National League baseball championship in 1954? (b) The American League baseball championship in 1959? (c) The winter and summer Olympic games in 1960? (d) The Rose Bowl football game on January 1, 1958; (d) The professional football championship in 1957?
5. When were the following born? Where? When did they die? What were they famous for? (a) Lew Wallace, (b) William Henry Harrison, (c) Captain Robert Gray, (d) Elizabeth Barrett Browning, (e) Susan B. Anthony.

TAKING NOTES

As a college student you will spend much time taking notes in your room, in the library, and in the classroom. Both now and later you will be faced with the problem of taking notes on books and articles for research or other subjects about which you may write, or for use in reviewing for examinations. You will need, too, to take usable notes on lectures and other speeches (see pp. 9–12). Much of your success depends upon your ability to takes notes which are really helpful.

19. Take careful notes from your reading.

Note taking should be a process of systematic thinking. Too frequently it is a hurried setting down of jumbled, carelessly selected ideas on scraps of paper, or miscellaneous jottings here and there in a notebook. If you wish to get maximum benefit from your reading, with intelligent labor-saving, you should organize both materials and methods of note taking, in order to preserve notes for possible use at any future time—for example, until a long paper is written or until an examination is over.

Materials. 1. Many instructors and students believe that the most efficient note taking is done on *cards* or *slips of paper* (3 x 5 or 4 x 6 inches, or larger), *one note to a card*. All notes taken are placed on similar cards, a heading is put on each card, and cards are filed for later reference. The advantage of this system is that all notes on the same subject, even when taken at widely separated intervals, can be kept together.

2. Some students prefer to take notes on full-size or half-size sheets of paper, or *loose-leaf notebook* paper. (Bound notebooks are usually unsatisfactory.) If you use such materials, keep notes on a particular book or article together and organize your notes on the various phases of the subject as you proceed.

Methods. More important than the materials are the methods employed. To save time and trouble later and to prevent a hodgepodge of quotations and undigested raw material, follow this technique, however tedious it may seem:

1. Before taking notes on a book, study its preface and table of contents. From these you learn the scope and purpose of the book. If you are going to read only one chapter from a book, or a magazine article, skim through it first, and then begin to read carefully and take notes. If the book has an index, save time by examining it for your particular subject or for related materials.

2. Record accurately and fully the details about the source of information: author, book, titles, article or chapter titles, magazine titles, dates, volume and page numbers, and the like.

3. Record accurately and fully the information itself. If you write a précis (p. 140) or a paraphrase (p. 143), check it on the spot with the original. If quoting directly, to use the material later for either direct quotation or summarizing, make a word-by-word check at once. Be careful to copy *exactly* all direct quotations, preserving original spelling and punctuation; mark clearly any such variations in your *first* notes, and do not forget to use quotation marks.

Your notes must be clear and full, or you will have to make trip after trip to the library to supply missing information. Get all the information *the first time*. Make your notes *clear,* so that you can read and understand them later; *full,* so that you can supply adequate information about sources in both footnotes and bibliography; *exact,* so that you can quote or paraphrase accurately; *organized,* so that you can make ready use of what you have assembled.

4. Condense your notes, which should be as full as needed but not so full that main ideas are obscured in a mass of detail. Make frequent use of topic sentences (see Section 23) and summaries (see pp. 139–142).

5. Rearrange and regroup your notes as your work proceeds. Keep your notes on a single subject together, not mixed with others even on the same general subject. This segregation is especially important whenever numerous books or articles are consulted.

If you are writing a research paper (see Section 20), you will of course be analyzing your subject and making, through your analysis and through the arrangement and grouping of your notes, a preliminary outline of your paper. In this way you will keep on the main track of the investigation and not be totally surprised at the end of your note taking by the manner in which your investigation has run away with you. You will also be more thoroughly prepared for the next major step in the preparation of your paper.

6. Be careful to distinguish fact and opinion in your reading and in the notes themselves. In weighing opinions, consider the facts upon which the opinions are based, the expert knowledge and possible bias of the author, and the date of publication of the material.

The specimen cards on page 176 illustrate use of the methods suggested. The upper right corner gives the general subject, the upper left the specific subject; then come a direct quotation, summary or paraphrase, and full bibliographical details. If a number of note cards

As Volunteer (Lincoln)

Black Hawk War

Two reasons for volunteering:
1. Job as clerk would soon be gone.
2. "And he was running for the legislature; a war record in any kind of war, would count in politics."
He enlisted; friends said they would elect him company captain.

P. 154
Carl Sandburg, Abraham Lincoln, the Prairie Years, Vol. I, N.Y.: Harcourt, Brace & Co., c. 1926.

As Captain (Lincoln)

Lincoln as captain drilled his men. One day he had two platoons advancing toward a gate.
Couldn't think of order to get them in column of two's. Commanded:
"This company is dismissed for two minutes when it will fall in again on the other side of the gate."

P. 155
Carl Sandburg, Abraham Lincoln, the Prairie Years, Vol. I, N.Y.: Harcourt, Brace & Co., c. 1926.

---

come from the same source, work out an abbreviated system whereby your bibliographical references will be explained by your preliminary or final bibliography cards.

Not all cards will be notes of material directly quoted. Some will be *précis*, summarizing in your own words the ideas of the source (see pp. 140–142). Some will be *paraphrases* giving a full-length statement of the source material (see pp. 143–145). All cards should be so complete that you need not return to the source to discover how much of the material is direct quotation, how much is paraphrase, or what the bibliographical facts are.

THE RESEARCH PAPER

20. The *research paper*—also called *investigative theme* or *term report* or *term paper*—is a long theme, usually from 1,500 to 6,000 words, assigned in most college courses requiring outside reading. More than a routine report, its purpose is to make a careful investigation of some subject and to present and interpret the source material in the light of the researcher's findings. It is, therefore, not merely a reading report based on several books or articles read more or less haphazardly, nor is it a jumbled series of quotations and paraphrases. In fact, you should learn how to put ideas of others into your own words and give proper credit, without overuse of short or extended direct quotations.

A good research paper is a carefully controlled study, which sets out with a definite purpose and accomplishes that purpose. Its preparation and writing depend upon four major steps: (1) choosing and analyzing the subject; (2) making a thorough investigation of the subject; (3) preparing an outline; and (4) writing and revising. As a preliminary to these four steps, review "The Theme," Sections 1 through 17, pages 25 to 145.

20a.   Choose and analyze your subject carefully.

1. Choose a subject in which you are already interested or in which you can become interested. Furthermore, do not select so abstruse or technical a subject that your readers cannot be interested.

2. Do not select too large or too small a subject. Some subjects can be treated adequately in 1,000 words; an attempt to develop such subjects in 5,000-word papers results in padding, repetition, dullness. On the other hand, do not choose a subject which cannot be handled in the assigned space.

3. Choose a topic upon which enough· has been written for you to obtain adequate information. Keep in mind the resources of the library in which you will do your investigating; for example, avoid a subject which will depend heavily upon back copies of magazines your library

does not have. Also, base your paper upon material from *several* sources: reference books, periodicals, books, perhaps newspapers, and personal interviews.

4. Select a central purpose, a controlling idea, and state it in a thesis topic or theme sentence. Any assembling of material presupposes the support of some proposition, some general statement or idea, and all the facts you gather should lead toward your conclusions, the important part of any research paper. You may have to change your attitude toward and treatment of your subject when you have assembled and digested your materials, for you should never start out with a rigid, preconceived idea that you want to establish in spite of all contrary facts and evidence. A research paper, like any theme, must develop one phase of a broad subject, fairly and convincingly, in order to achieve one central purpose.

5. Select, but modify if necessary, the basic type of writing for your research paper. Your report may be *descriptive exposition:* it may describe and explain the processes involved in the manufacture of some product. It may be *narrative:* a report of exactly what took place at a certain time or on a certain occasion in history. It may be *argumentative:* setting forth facts in favor of or opposed to some plan, movement, proposal, such as reasons for or against making 18 years the legal voting age in a particular state. Or it may be *analytical:* the component parts and significance of a somewhat abstract subject, or a limited comparison-contrast treating the likenesses and differences of two systems. But whatever type of writing you use, your research paper must accomplish a clear, unmistakable *purpose.*

Since choice of topic depends upon your interests and those of your prospective reader or readers, literally hundreds of topics are available, many suggested by these broad fields:

applied science	language
biography	literature
economics	manufacturing
education	politics
fine arts (music, painting, sculpture, ceramics, architecture, etc.)	psychology
	pure science
	religion
history	space exploration
land, sea, air	warfare

Other hundreds of subjects are possible from somewhat more limited but still general topics, as, for example:

An outstanding or memorable episode, or day, or month, or year in a well-known person's life (like "Lincoln the Soldier," pp. 193–201 below).
An account of the relatives of a famous person.
A man, or men, in public office: president, vice-president, senator, governor, etc.
The friendship of two well-known people, or some phase of that friendship.
A love affair of a famous couple.
The reception, influence, effect of some book, some invention, some process, or the reputation of such about 10, 25, 50, 100 years later.
The reputation of an author after 25, 50, or 100 years.
The major achievement(s) of a major (or minor) biologist, chemist, discoverer, explorer, soldier, inventor, manufacturer, speaker, traveler, writer, etc.
Famous scientific discoveries or inventions.
Interspace research and exploration: planets, satellites, rockets, animal-carrying rockets, man-carrying rockets, etc. (See "The Canals of Mars," below, pp. 201–208.)
The next 5 (10) years in space exploration, or the last 5 (10) years in space exploration.
Famous historical events, trials, sporting events, etc.
Famous or well-known battles or phases of battles (land, sea, air).
Famous or memorable shipwrecks, storms, fires, floods, cyclones, tornadoes.
Famous peacetime sea tragedies or famous wartime sea tragedies.
A famous structure, completed or proposed: harbor, canal, bridge, building, ship, tower, cathedral, pyramid, dam, tunnel, train, automobile, airplane, etc.
Famous places: summer resorts, winter resorts, health resorts, world capitals, cities, rivers, lakes, canyons, parks, etc.
Foods: nutritive value of foods, home freezing of fruits and vegetables, recent methods of food preservation, etc.
Language: British and American (Briticisms and Americanisms); Latin and Greek prefixes, suffixes, roots in English; slang; neologisms; localisms; dialect; logic and language; place names; long words vs. short words; spelling reform; making a dictionary, etc.

As suitable limitations of some of the foregoing, consider as examples:

The Presidential Campaign of 1960.
John F. Kennedy's First Day as President.

Lincoln's Son.
Robert Browning's Courtship of Elizabeth Barrett.
Noah Webster's First Dictionary.
Thomas A. Edison's Minor Inventions.
Abraham Lincoln and His Secretary of State, William H. Seward.
Early Results of the Discovery of Anesthesia.
Mark Twain's *Huckleberry Finn*—Its First Ten Years.
April 19, 1775 (or July 4, 1776, or April 6, 1917, or November 11, 1918, or December 7, 1941, etc.).
The First Kentucky Derby.
The Final Day of the Battle of Gettysburg.
The Sinking of the *Andrea Doria*.
The Straits of Mackinac Bridge.
Saratoga Springs a Century Ago.
A Tunnel Under the English Channel.
The Development of the First American Satellite.
Survival Under Atomic Attack.

20b. Make a thorough investigation of the subject.

The conscientious researcher ferrets out all information he can about a subject. A student, pressed for time, may not ascertain *all* the facts, but he should make as thorough search as possible for pertinent detail, by utilizing information from reference books, periodicals, the general collection of books in the library, and newspapers. It is an illusion that using an encyclopedia and writing a term paper are the same thing. A term paper has no real value unless it does more than merely dip into a subject.

In order to make a competent investigation of a subject:

1. Learn how to use efficiently the resources of your library: reference works, periodical indexes, the card catalog, and the general collection of books (see Section 18a, b, c). From these resources, notably the first three, prepare a preliminary bibliography on 3 x 5 inch cards, that is, a list of books and magazine or newspaper articles that are *likely* to contribute material, with one title to a card. You save time if you give complete information on this preliminary bibliography card, since it will serve as your information for your final bibliography. See page 181 for sample.

Note that the material is arranged in the order in which it would or does appear in a final bibliography (Section 20g), except that the publisher's name might not appear there. Note also that the card contains

Sandburg, Carl. <u>Abraham Lincoln:</u>
<u>the Prairie Years</u>.
2 vols. New York: Harcourt, Brace
& Company, 1926.

92
L63sa

Preliminary Bibliography Card.

the library call number—a timesaver if you have to return (and you usually will have to) to the book for further checking. Put this library call number on each preliminary bibliography card as soon as you begin your library search for specific materials.

2. Take careful notes from your reading (see Section 19). Give full details about sources after each note. If no confusion can result, use an abbreviated reference to the full information on your bibliography card.

20c.   Prepare an adequate outline for your paper.

When you have read and taken notes on available material, you can outline your research paper. It is helpful, however, if you have in mind early some general plan to follow, a plan you can adapt, change, and rearrange as you assemble material and become familiar with it. When you have worked long enough to reach definite conclusions and to see the framework of the whole structure, you can rearrange notes in final form, under appropriate headings, and from them prepare a topic or sentence outline. (See Section 6a, b.) The actual writing of the paper begins *only* after you have prepared and revised carefully such an outline.

In making an outline for your paper, bear in mind that the object of your investigation is to find out the facts, arrange and interpret them, and present conclusions based upon them. You are not necessarily a propagandist—rather, a discoverer of fact—but you must assimilate and absorb what seems to you the truth so that you can present it to a reader who will see what definite purpose you had in mind.

A tentative but general outline, adaptable for many but not all subjects, might include the following:

I. Purpose of investigation
II. Importance or significance of the subject
III. Background or history of the subject.
IV. Nature of the investigation (description of apparatus, procedure, results, chronological development, etc.)
V. Conclusions (generalized statements based on the investigation and rounding out of the paper)

20d. Write your research paper correctly, clearly, and forcefully.

After you have investigated the field thoroughly, organized your notes, and prepared an outline, you are ready to write. If you have taken careful notes and arranged them properly, your work is more than half done. To give the results of your study correct, clear, and effective expression, write the body of your paper as clearly and forcefully as you can; take great care with footnotes and bibliography; and revise your paper to insure correctness and accuracy.

A term report need not be dull and lifeless. If you have chosen an attractive subject and investigated it fully, you should have little difficulty in making your paper effective. An occasional bit of humor, vigorous diction, and neatly turned phrases add effectiveness to the thoroughness and accuracy which the paper must have. Careful investigation, forceful writing, and pleasant, easy reading need not be exclusive of one another.

20e. Revise your research paper carefully.

After you have written the report with all the vigor and interest which you can muster, and after you have correctly indicated the footnotes and bibliography (see Section 20f, g), you should put the report aside and forget about it for some time, several days if possible. After this "cooling" process, you will be able to come back to it with more impartiality than was possible just after you finished it. Your errors will be more apparent, and you can give the paper its final polishing. Also give it the rereadings suggested in Section 15, and add another for the sole purpose of making certain that footnotes are accurately and uniformly listed and that the bibliography is correctly and consistently arranged.

In addition to being correct, clear, effective, and appropriate, every investigative theme must be carefully documented. The following suggestions enable you to provide your paper with adequate and accurately listed footnotes and bibliography, *provided your notes on reading were carefully taken.*

20f.   Use footnotes to document your research paper adequately and properly.

The purpose of a footnote is to mention the authority for some fact stated or some material quoted, or to develop some point more or less incidentally referred to in the body of the paper.

Generally known facts do not require substantiation in footnotes, nor do well-known quotations, usually. With other materials you must avoid charges of plagiarism, and unless ideas and phrasing are completely your own, you should refer the reader to some source for your statement. To be entirely honest, you will acknowledge every source of indebtedness, even when no direct quotation is used.

Occasionally you may wish to develop, interpret, or refute some idea but do not wish an extended comment to interfere with the unity of your paper. Use a footnote, but, since footnotes for such purposes become distracting to the reader, do not use too many of them.

How many footnotes should appear in a research paper? Only as many as are necessary, in the light of the discussion above. One investigation may call for twice as many as another. Some pages may require a half-dozen or more footnotes, others may need none or only one or two. A good guiding principle is the following: Use footnotes to acknowledge credit where it is due and to supply discussion-explanations only when necessary for understanding.

1.   Adopt a standard form of footnote and be consistent in its use.

Methods of footnoting are numerous, but whatever system you employ should be consistent throughout your paper and immediately clear to any intelligent reader. The Modern Language Association of America *Style Sheet* favors the following forms—content, arrangement of details, punctuation—for books and periodicals.

For books: (1) *author's (or authors') name,* i.e., given name(s) followed by last name, followed by a comma; (2) *title of chapter or part of book cited,* enclosed in quotation marks, followed by a comma inside the final quotation marks (used when the article is part of a collection, anthology, etc.); (3) *title of the book,* in italics (i.e., underlined), followed by a comma—the title is taken from the title page of the book, not from the cover, and any subtitle is also underlined, with appropriate punctuation supplied, usually a colon; (4) *editor's or translator's name* (if any) in normal order, preceded by "ed." or "trans."—without parentheses—and followed by a comma; however, if the work of the editor or translator is considered of first importance, his name comes first in the footnote, followed by a comma, followed by "ed." or "trans." —without parentheses and without a comma following—then the title and a comma, and then "by" followed by the author's name; (5) *edition used,* whenever the edition is not the first, in Arabic numerals (e.g., 3rd ed.), followed by a comma; (6) *the series,* if book is part of a series, followed by a comma, followed by the number of this book in the series; (7) *the number of volumes* if more than one (e.g., 4 vols.), but this information is not needed if the reference is to be a specific passage instead of to the book as a whole; (8) *place(s) and date(s) of publication,* within parentheses, followed by a comma; if it is desirable, the publisher's name may be given, following the place of publication, preceded by a colon, and followed by a comma—many teachers and editors prefer omitting the publisher's name and others favor using it; (9) *volume number,* if one of two or more, in capital Roman numerals, preceded and followed by a comma; (10) *page number(s)* in Arabic numerals (unless the book or part of it referred to has small Roman numerals), preceded by a comma, followed by a period.

NOTE: Naturally, for many books used in preparing student-written research papers, certain of the foregoing items will not appear, especially (4), (6), and possibly (2).

For articles or stories in periodicals (first references): (1) *author's name,* given name(s) followed by last name, followed by a comma; (2) *title in full,* enclosed in quotation marks (not underlined), followed by a comma inside the final quotation marks; (3) *name of the periodical* (or its standard abbreviation, if any) in italics (i.e., underlined), followed by a comma; (4) *volume number* not using the abbreviation "Vol." but using capital Roman numerals, followed by a comma unless material in parentheses follows; however, for newspapers and for many weekly or monthly magazines which may or may not page each issue separately, the volume number may be omitted in favor of the complete date, enclosed in commas, followed by the use of "p." or "pp." and the page numbers in Arabic numerals; (5) *issue number* or *name,* if periodical is quarterly, like "Winter" or "Spring"; (6) *year,* preceded by month if needed (i.e., when each issue is paged separately), enclosed in parentheses, followed by a comma—between month and year use of a comma is optional; (7) *page number(s)* in Arabic numerals, not preceded by "p." or "pp." but followed by a period.

NOTE: The use of (5) above may be rare. Also, some teachers believe that if periodicals use Arabic numerals for their volume numbers, these should be used instead of Roman numerals, or when the Roman numerals become unwieldy, such as CCXXVII for 227.

The foregoing directions for footnotes are illustrated in the following examples:

BOOKS

A. Book by one author:
  [1] John R. Tunis, *This Writing Game* (New York, 1941), p. 26.
or
  [1] John R. Tunis, *This Writing Game* (New York: A. S. Barnes & Company, 1941), p. 26.

NOTE: If the author's full name has been given in the text, footnote reads:
  [1] *This Writing Game* (New York, 1941), p. 26.
and if both author's full name and title of book have been given in the text, the footnote reads:
  [1] New York, 1941, p. 26.

B. Books by two or more authors:
  [1] John Tasker Howard and Arthur Mendel, *Our American Composers* (New York, 1941), p. 82.

C. Book of two or more volumes:
  [1] Douglas S. Freeman, *George Washington* (New York, 1948), II, 142.

D. Book prepared by an editor:
  [1] Charles Mills Gayley, ed. *Representative English Comedies* (New York, 1916), I, xxiii.

[2] *Great French Romances,* ed. Richard Aldington (New York, 1946), p. 17.

E. A translation:
[1] Homer, *The Odyssey,* trans. George Herbert Palmer (Boston, 1891), p. 46.

ARTICLES (ESSAYS, STORIES)

A. From a magazine:
[1] Walter D. Edmonds, "Arrival of the Lily Dean," *The Saturday Evening Post,* CCX (May 7, 1938), 5.
or
[1] Walter D. Edmonds, "Arrival of the Lily Dean," *The Saturday Evening Post,* May 7, 1938, p. 5.
[2] Roger Angell, "A Walk in Washington," *Holiday,* XIX (May, 1956), 37.
or
[2] Roger Angell, "A Walk in Washington," *Holiday,* May 1956, p. 37.
[3] "What to Do about the Draft?" *Life,* XL (May 14, 1956), 69.
or
[3] "What to Do about the Draft?" in *Life,* May 14, 1956, p. 69.
(Note the alternate expression after the question mark, just above.)

B. From a collection:
[1] Katherine Mansfield, "Bliss," *A Study of the Short Story,* ed. Henry S. Canby and Alfred Dashiell (New York, 1935), p. 303.
[2] Burges Johnson, "Campus Versus Classroom," *Readings for Opinion,* ed. Earl Davis and William C. Hummel, 2nd ed. (Englewood Cliffs, N.J., 1960), pp. 282–293.

C. From a newspaper:
[1] "Summer's Children," *The New York Times,* June 19, 1954, p. 14.
[2] "The U.S. and Its Critics," *The New York Times,* April 15, 1956, Section 4, p. 8.

NOTE: The first reference above is to the daily edition, the second to the Sunday edition.

D. From an encyclopedia:
[1] "Edgar Allan Poe," *Encyclopaedia Britannica* (Chicago, 1958), XVIII, 103.

2. Use the following standard footnote abbreviations.

In footnotes in research papers, abbreviations are permissible and desirable. If the need for abbreviations occurs, employ these forms:

1. anon.   anonymous
2. ante   before
3. art. (plural, arts.)   article (articles)
4. bk. (plural, bks.)   book (books)
5. c.   copyright, copyrighted
6. cf.   compare. Never use "cf." in the meaning of "see."
7. ch. (plural, chs.)   chapter (chapters)
8. comp.   compiler, compiled
9. ed. (plural, eds.)   editor (editors)   edition (editions); ed. also means edited by
10. e.g.   for example
11. f. (plural, ff.)   following line (following lines), following page (following pages)
12. fig. (plural, figs.)   figure (figures)
13. *ibid*.   "the same." If a footnote refers to the same source as the one referred to in the footnote *immediately* preceding, the abbreviation *ibid*. (from the Latin *ibidem* meaning "in the same place") may be used. If the volume, page, title, and author are the same, use *ibid*. alone. If the volume and page differ, use, for example, *Ibid.,* III, 206. *Ibid*. usually comes at the beginning of a footnote and is capitalized for that reason only.
14. i.e.   that is
15. l. (plural, ll.)   line (lines)
16. *loc. cit.*   "the place cited." If the reference is to the *exact* passage covered by an earlier reference not immediately preceding, use *loc. cit.* from the Latin *loco citato* meaning "in the place cited"). Never follow *loc. cit.* with a page number.
17. MS (plural, MSS)   manuscript (manuscripts)
18. n. (plural, nn.)   note (notes)
19. N.B.   *nota bene*—"take notice, mark well"
20. *op. cit.*   "the work cited." After the first full reference to a given work, provided no other work by the same author is mentioned in the paper, succeeding references may be indicated by the author's surname, followed by *op. cit.* (from Latin *opere citato* meaning "in the work cited") and the volume and page. For comment on *op. cit.,* see Note 2 at the end of this list of abbreviations.
21. p. (plural, pp.)   page (pages)
22. par. (plural, pars.)   paragraph (paragraphs)

23. *passim.* To be employed when no specific page reference can be given; it means "everywhere," "throughout," "here and there."
24. pseud. pseudonym
25. pt. (plural, pts.) part (parts)
26. q.v. which see
27. sec. (plural, secs.) section (sections)
28. *sic.* thus, so. Used between brackets in someone's quoted material, to show that the material is followed exactly even if there is an error in spelling, grammar, punctuation, word use.
29. v. (plural, vv.) verse (verses)
30. vol. (plural, vols.) volume (volumes)

NOTE 1: The abbreviations *ibid., op. cit.,* and *loc. cit.,* and the words *passim* and *sic* are always italicized (underlined).

NOTE 2: Many teachers and editors believe that *op. cit.* is the most abused and overused of all abbreviations in research writing; they advocate, instead, the author's name alone with a short title for footnote references after the first. The following examples illustrate:

First entry:
    [1] Sir Arthur Quiller-Couch, *On the Art of Writing* (New York, 1930), p. 84.

Subsequent entry for the same book:
Allowed:
    [5] Quiller-Couch, *op. cit.,* p. 92.
Preferred:
    [5] Quiller-Couch, *Art of Writing,* p. 92.

First entry:
    [1] Clifton Fadiman, "Herman Melville," *The Atlantic Monthly,* CLXXII (October 1943), 88.

Subsequent entry for the same article:
Allowed:
    [4] Fadiman, *op. cit.,* p. 90.
Preferred:
    [4] Fadiman, "Melville," p. 90.

3. Place the footnote numeral and the footnote properly.

A footnote is referred to by an Arabic numeral placed above and to the right of the word to be commented upon. If reference is to a statement or a quotation, place the numeral at the end of the passage, and always after the punctuation.

Before the actual footnote at the bottom of the page repeat the number used in the text. Place it also above the line. Do not use asterisks or other symbols in place of Arabic numerals.

Number footnotes consecutively throughout the paper. Although a few writers number them anew for each page, most instructors and editors prefer the consecutive numbering plan, since it facilitates everyone's work—including the writer's—if the paper needs to be retyped after revision or to be prepared for printing.

Footnotes may be put at the bottom of pages, between lines drawn across the page in the manuscript proper, or all together at the end of the paper. Most instructors prefer the first or third method; the second method distracts from the continuity of reading. If footnotes are placed at the bottom of the page, do not crowd them. Unless otherwise instructed, you should apply the following:

1. Place footnotes at the bottom of each page.

2. Number them consecutively throughout the paper.

3. Separate the first footnote on a page by leaving three typed spaces, or their equivalent, between the text material and the footnote; do not draw a full or part line above the footnote.

4. If you type, use single spacing within each footnote and double spacing between footnotes.

20g. Use a bibliography to document your research paper adequately and properly.

A *bibliography* is a list of books or magazine or newspaper articles relating to a given subject and, in the research paper, placed at the end of the manuscript. It is usually a list, in one alphabet, or classified, containing the names of all the works actually quoted from or used generally in the paper and its preparation. Thus a bibliography may contain more references than the sum of all the footnote references. Every formally prepared research paper should contain a bibliography.

Arrange bibliographical items correctly and consistently, in regard to content, order of details in each item, and punctuation. Usage in the arrangement of bibliographies varies, but, subject to adaptation by your instructor, keep the following suggestions in mind as your guide; these recommendations are based on suggestions of the compiler of *The MLA Style Sheet* for the preparation of masters' and doctors' theses.

Arrange items alphabetically by last names of the authors. Each author's last name is followed by a comma, and then by his given name(s) or initial(s) as it appears in the source. If the author's name is not given or is not known, list the item alphabetically according to the first word (except *the, a,* or *an*) in the title. List titles by the same author alphabetically. When more than one work by the same author is cited, use a blank line about three-fourths of an inch long in place of the author's name after its first appearance. To make the author's name stand out (it may even be put in capital letters throughout), place it flush with the left margin, and indent all run-over lines.

Punctuation: A comma follows the author's last name and precedes his given name or initials. A period, not a comma, follows the complete name. If the person is the editor or compiler or translator, the abbreviation ed., comp., or trans. follows the name, and is separated from the name by a comma. The title of a book is followed by a period. The place and date of publication are *not* placed in parentheses, as they are in footnotes; note also that the publisher's name, which may be included in the footnote reference, is not included in the bibliography. The titles of articles and of the periodicals in which articles appear are treated as they are in footnotes (see p. 183), except that the inclusive pages (beginning and ending page) of the article should be shown. The use of italics in the bibliography for titles of books and of periodicals is the same as such use in footnotes.

If the items in a bibliography are numerous, you may classify them in groups: books, magazine articles, public documents, reports, and newspaper accounts. Such classification is given below, for purposes of illustration only. The preferred method is to have *all* bibliographical items in one alphabetical arrangement, as in the two research papers at the end of this section.

A sentence or phrase under each item is sometimes helpful and desirable. Such statements, indicating the scope or content of the book or article, comprise what is known as an *annotative* or *annotated bibliography.*

Place the bibliography at the end of the research paper, and begin it on a separate page, not on the last page of the text. Give it a title that fits it precisely, such as "List of Works Consulted," "List of Works Cited," "A Selected Bibliography," "A Brief Annotated Bibliography," or sometimes merely "Bibliography." It should include all your first references in footnotes. If the paper is typewritten, spacing is single or double, according to desire or instructions, but double spacing is preferable, and any run-over lines of a single item are indented. If the spacing is single, use double spacing between the items.

The following is an example of a short bibliography; as indicated, it is classified into "books" and "magazine articles" merely for illustration:

LIST OF WORKS CONSULTED

BOOKS

Allen, Hervey. *Israfel, the Life and Times of Edgar Allan Poe.* New York, 1934.

Boyd, Ernest. *Literary Blasphemies* (pp. 163–185). New York, 1927.

Campbell, Killis. *The Mind of Poe and Other Studies.* Cambridge, Mass., 1933.

"Edgar Allan Poe," *Encyclopaedia Britannica,* XVIII, 103–104. Chicago, 1958.

Ostrom, John Ward, ed. *The Letters of Edgar Allan Poe.* 2 vols. Cambridge, Mass., 1948.

Robertson, John W. *Edgar A. Poe: a Psychopathic Study.* New York, 1922.

———. *Bibliography of the Writings of Edgar A. Poe.* 2 vols. San Francisco, 1934.

Woodberry, George Edward. *Life of Edgar Allan Poe, Personal and Literary, with His Chief Correspondence with Men of Letters.* 2 vols. Boston, 1909.

MAGAZINE ARTICLES

Cooke, A. L. "Edgar Allan Poe—Critic," *Cornhill Magazine,* LXXII (November, 1934), 588–597.

Eaves, T. C. D. "Poe's Last Visit to Philadelphia," *American Literature,* XXVI (March, 1954), 44–51.

Huxley, Aldous Leonard. "Vulgarity in Literature," *Saturday Review of Literature,* VII (September 27, 1930), 158–159.

Macpherson, Harriet Dorothea. "Dumas and Poe Again," *Saturday Review of Literature,* VI (February 22, 1930), 760.

Wilson, James Southall. "Devil Was in It," *American Mercury,* XXIV (October, 1931), 215–220.

The foregoing suggestions should enable you to prepare and write an interesting and eminently satisfactory research paper. For those desiring more extended discussion, excellent and inexpensive booklets are available.[23]

Below are two student-written research papers. Their many merits, among which are their organization, content, and interest appeal, show that any student who will expend time, patience, and energy can produce research papers not only good in themselves but interesting to a wide variety of readers. One paper deals with one of the most prominent figures in American history; the other deals with an astronomical subject, now of increasing interest as space exploration develops; it is also of interest as an illustration of combining various opinions and theories. "Lincoln the Soldier" (approximately 1,900 words) and "The Canals of Mars" (approximately 1,850 words) were, respectively, Themes No. 12 and No. 9 in second-semester composition at the University of Illinois.[24] Both are reproduced in typewriter type.

As you study these examples bear in mind several facts: (1) Although they are here reproduced in typewriter type, these pages in typewritten manuscript form would have a page size of 8½-x-11 inches (standard size), with the lines double-spaced; each footnote would be single-spaced, with double spacing between footnotes. (2) Note how direct quotations are used within the body of the paper, not only in phrases and sentences but also in paragraphs. In manuscript form, quoted paragraphs would be single-spaced, preferably, or, if double spaced, would be indented an inch more on the left and an inch more

---

[23] Among such booklets are the following:

Hendrickson, John R. *Research Paper.* New York: Henry Holt & Company, 1957.

Hook, Lucyle, and Mary Virginia Gaver. *The Research Paper,* 2nd ed. Englewood Cliffs, N.J.: Prentice-Hall, Inc., 1952.

Miles, Leland, and Frank Baker. *A Brief Guide to Writing Term Papers,* rev. ed. Dubuque, Iowa: Wm. C. Brown Company, 1959.

Schmitz, Robert M. *Preparing the Research Paper,* 4th ed. New York: Rinehart & Company, Inc., 1957.

Sears, Donald. *Harbrace Guide to the Library and the Research Paper,* 2nd ed. New York: Harcourt, Brace and Company, 1960.

Turabian, Kate L. *A Manual for Writers of Term Papers, Theses, and Dissertations,* rev. ed. Chicago: The University of Chicago Press, 1955.

Williams, Cecil B., and Allan H. Stevenson. *A Research Manual,* rev. ed. New York: Harper & Brothers, 1951.

[24] "Lincoln the Soldier" and "The Canals of Mars" were published in *The Green Caldron: A Magazine of Freshman Writing,* University of Illinois, Urbana, Ill., the former in Vol. XVI (October, 1946), pp. 27–32, the latter in Vol. XXIX (October, 1959), pp. 18–22. The former is copyrighted by Charles W. Roberts. Both are used by the kind permission of the University of Illinois.

on the right. (3) Note the use of ellipsis periods within the quoted paragraphs, to indicate omissions (see Section **86g**). (4) Note in the footnotes that when two pages, even consecutive pages, are referred to, the documentation reads: "pp. 463–464." (5) The first paper has its footnotes at the bottom of each page, its bibliography at the end; the second paper has both footnotes and bibliography at the end. (6) In manuscript form, the papers would have the bibliography begin on a separate page at the end.

LINCOLN THE SOLDIER

Mortimer Hitt

Although Abraham Lincoln spent fifty-one days in the armed service of the United States, in the Black Hawk War, few writers have more than mentioned the fact, probably because of the general lack of authentic accounts and the meager wording of official reports and records of this phase of his career.

Lincoln was yet to be recognized by the world when hostilities broke out. To be sure, he already had made a name for himself in New Salem and Sangamon County. He was noted for his skill in athletics, particularly in wrestling, a sport in which he had held his own against all comers,[1] and he already was making plans for his political career.[2]

Carl Sandburg suggests that Lincoln enlisted for two reasons: first, he would soon lose his clerking job; and second, "he was running for the legislature; a war record, in any kind of war, would count in politics."[3] Whatever may have been his

---

[1] Leonard Swett, "Mr. Lincoln's Story of His Own Life," in Reminiscences of Abraham Lincoln by Distinguished Men of His Time, ed. Allen Thorndike Rice (New York, 1886), pp. 463–464.

[2] Carl Sandburg, Abraham Lincoln: The Prairie Years (New York, 1926), I, 154.

[3] Ibid.

motives, the fact remains that Lincoln, on the
twenty-first of April, 1832, enlisted in the
militia, which was at that time called into the
service of the national government.[4]

Lincoln was chosen captain by the men of his
company, in accord with the custom of those days.
An interesting account of his election is given by
Leonard Swett:

Together with the talk of organizing a company
in New Salem, began the talk of making Lincoln
captain of it. His characteristics as an athlete
had made something of a hero of him. . . . But when
the day of organization arrived, a man who had
been captain of a real company arrived in his
uniform, and assumed the organization of the
company. The mode of it was as follows: A line of
two was formed by the company, with the parties
who intended to be candidates for officers
standing in front. The candidate for captain
then made a speech to the men, telling them what
a gallant man he was, in what wars he had fought.
bled and died, and how he was ready again, for
the glory of his country, to lead them. Then
another candidate ; and when the speech-making was
ended, they commanded those who would vote for
this man, or that, to form a line behind their
favorite. . . .

When the real captain with his regimentals came
and assumed control, Lincoln's heart failed him.
He formed in the line with the boys, and after
the speech was made they began to form behind the
old captain, but the boys seized Lincoln, and
pushed him out of line, and began to form behind

[4] Abraham Lincoln, <u>Muster Roll of Captain Abraham
Lincoln's Company</u> (MS in State Historical Library,
Springfield, Illinois).

him . . . and when they counted back he had two
more than the other captain, and he became real
captain.[5]

His captaincy was the first electoral job he ever
held, and in his own words, it was "a success which
gave me more pleasure than any I have had since."[6]
That Lincoln was obviously untrained and inexperienced in the way of the military is evidenced
by an account of his drilling his company during
the first few days of his service. The men were
marching across a field, formed in what today most
probably would be termed a "company front," when
they came to a gate at the edge of the field. Lincoln, unable to recall the proper command for
getting the company into a column, shouted, "This
company is dismissed for two minutes, when it will
fall in again on the other side of the gate!"[7]
Lincoln's ignorance of drill regulations was not
the only thing that caused him trouble. He was
arrested and his sword was taken away from him for
a day because he broke a general order that forbade
the discharge of firearms within a radius of fifty
yards from the camp.[8] It may have been that he was
not familiar with the orders or that he was careless in judging his distance. Whatever the reason,
he showed clearly that he was not taking his responsibilities very seriously.
Lincoln's company was not amenable to discipline.
To his first order he received the reply, "Go to

[5] Swett, "Mr. Lincoln's Story," pp. 464-465.
[6] Abraham Lincoln From His Own Words and Contemporary Accounts, ed. Roy Edgar Appleman (Washington,
1942), p. 2.
[7] Sandburg, Abraham Lincoln, p. 155.
[8] William H. Herndon and Jesse W. Weik, Herndon's
Lincoln (Springfield, 1921), I, 95.

the devil, sir."[9] The attitudes of the men are
described very well by Theodore Pease:

> Allow the man whom they had recently honored by
> electing captain--a man whom they knew thoroughly
> as no better than themselves--allow such a one
> to take advantage of his position to direct an
> action undesirable to them? Incomprehensible! To
> the recently elected captain this point of view
> seemed entirely reasonable.[10]

Yet another example of the obvious lack of discipline is witnessed by the following incident. One
of the men broke into the officers' quarters one
night and stole a quantity of liquor which he
shared with his comrades. When the army began to
march the following morning, the men of Lincoln's
company dropped out right and left until only a few
remained in the ranks. It was late in the evening
before the entire company was together again. As a
result of the investigation that followed, Lincoln, though innocent of complicity in or knowledge of the affair, was arrested and forced to
undergo the humiliation of wearing a wooden sword
for two days.[11]

This theft may be partly excused on the grounds
that the men were not given adequate rations. Lincoln's company, between April 25 and May 17,
received the following:

Corn	118 bu., 18 pecks	Powder	1 keg
Meal	10 qts.	Lead	50 lbs.
Flour	1 bbl., 252 lbs.	Flints	265
Bread	66 lbs.	Candles	20

---

[9] Norman Hapgood, Abraham Lincoln, The Man of the
People (New York, 1900), p. 32.

[10] Theodore C. Pease, The Centennial History of
Illinois (Chicago, 1919), II, 161.

[11] Herndon, Herndon's Lincoln, pp. 95-96.

Salt	42 lbs.	Tape	144 yds.
Pork	1 bbl., 160 lbs.	Buckets	50
Whiskey	10½ gals.	Coffee Boilers	7
Sacks	48	Tin Pans	7
Blankets	3	Tin Cups	16[12]
Soap	[Amount unreadable]		

Some authors have mentioned that the men would make
expeditions to nearby farms, and return loaded
down with sundry items of food. This seems entirely
probable, for there were, including Lincoln and his
lieutenants, seventy men in the company. One can
readily see that the rations listed above would
hardly suffice for that number of active men for a
period of twenty-three days, let alone the additional ten days of their enlistment during which
time no rations were drawn.

The closest contact Lincoln had with the Indians
during the war was with an old Indian who had a
safe conduct from General Cass and who was captured
by some of the men. They were about to kill the
aged savage, but Lincoln intervened and saved his
life.[13] There are several accounts of this episode
by various reputable authors, but as none of them
is documented, it may be apocryphal.

On the twenty-seventh of May, Lincoln's company
was demobilized at Ottawa, Illinois, because of the
increasing dissatisfaction of the men.[14] Lincoln
and several of the other men from his company re-
enlisted for a period of twenty days in Captain

---

[12] William Thommas, Quarter Master's Book (MS
in State Historical Library, Springfield, Illinois), p. 14.

[13] Ida M. Tarbell, The Early Life of Abraham Lincoln (New York, 1896), p. 141.

[14] Isaac H. Elliott, Adjutant General's Report
(Springfield, 1902), IX, 100.

Elijah Iles' company of Independent Rangers,[15] a
company composed of generals, colonels, captains,
and other distinguished men of the disbanded army.
It was an unique organization--the men had no camp
duties and could draw rations as often as they
desired; their arms and equipment were of the best.
In the final analysis, Lincoln was much better off
as a private in this company than he had been as
captain of his old organization.[16] Captain Iles'
company saw no action whatever during the twenty
days of Lincoln's enlistment. In fact, though many
historians have written about the war, and more
still have written biographies of Lincoln, there is
no account of his individual actions during this
enlistment.

Lincoln's second period of enlistment ended on
the sixteenth of June, and although he re-enlisted
the same day, he was not actually mustered into
service again until the twentieth.[17] The officer who
mustered Lincoln into service the second and third
times was Major Robert Anderson, later to be com-
mander of Fort Sumter during the early part of the
Civil War. From his own account:

> I also mustered Abraham Lincoln twice into the
> service and once out. He was a member of two of
> the Independent companies which were not brigaded.
> The first time I mustered him into the service
> was at the mouth of the Fox River, May 29, 1832,
> in Captain Elijah Iles' company. . . . I mustered
> him out of the service at the "Rapids of the
> Illinois," June 16, 1832, and in four days after-
> wards, at the same place, I mustered him into
> service again in Captain Jacob M. Early's com-

[15] General Robert Anderson, Muster Rolls, etc.,
etc., Black Hawk War, 1832 (MS in State Historical
Library, Springfield, Illinois), p. 7.

[16] Tarbell, Early Life, p. 144.

[17] Anderson, Muster Rolls, p. 23.

pany. . . . Of course I had no recollection of
Mr. Lincoln, but when President he reminded me
of the fact.[18]

Surely if Lincoln had had any of the qualities of
a good soldier he would have been remembered by
some of the officers, such as General Anderson, and
most likely would have been promoted. Many of the
accounts build up Lincoln's accomplishments during
his military career into proportions far beyond
what seem to have been the actual facts as illustrated by surviving primary sources. The very fact
that he remained a private during his second and
third enlistments speaks for his military abilities.

BIBLIOGRAPHY

Anderson, General Robert. Letter dated May 10,
1870, to E. B. Washburn. (MS in State Historical
Library, Centennial Building, Springfield,
Illinois.)
---. Muster Rolls, etc., etc., Black Hawk War,
1832. (MS in State Historical Library, Centennial
Building, Springfield, Illinois.)
Appleman, Roy Edgar, ed. Abraham Lincoln From His
Own Words and Contemporary Accounts. Washington,
1942.
Arnold, Isaac N. Address: November 19, 1868.
Chicago, 1877.
---. The Life of Abraham Lincoln. Chicago, 1901.
Barber, Joseph. War Letters of a Disbanded Vol-
unteer. New York, 1864.
Barrett, Joseph H. Life of Abraham Lincoln. New
York, 1865.
Brooks, Noah. Abraham Lincoln: His Youth and Early
Manhood. New York, 1901.
---. Abraham Lincoln and the Downfall of American
Slavery. New York, 1908.

[18] General Robert Anderson, Letter dated May
10, 1870, to E. B. Washburn (MS in State Historical
Library, Springfield, Illinois), p. 4.

Browne, Francis F. The Every-Day Life of Abraham
   Lincoln. Chicago, 1913.
Collections of the State Historical Society of
   Wisconsin. Vol. XIV. Madison, 1898.
Dunne, Edward F. Illinois, The Heart of the Nation.
   Chicago and New York, 1933.
Elliott, Isaac H. Adjutant General's Report. Vol.
   IX. Springfield, 1902.
Ford, Governor Thomas. A History of Illinois. Vol.
   I. Chicago, 1945.
Hapgood, Norman. Abraham Lincoln, The Man of the
   People. New York, 1900.
Herndon, William H., and Jesse W. Weik. Herndon's
   Lincoln. Vol. I. Springfield, 1921.
Iles, Major Elijah. Sketches of Early Life and
   Times. Springfield, 1883.
Lincoln, Abraham. Muster Roll of Captain Abraham
   Lincoln's Company. (MS in State Historical
   Library, Centennial Building, Springfield,
   Illinois.)
Malone, Thomas J. "Soldiering with Captain Abraham
   Lincoln," American Legion Weekly, February 6,
   1925, pp. 5-6, 18-19.
Moses, John. Illinois, Historical and Statistical.
   Chicago, 1895.
Nicolay, John G., and John Hay. Abraham Lincoln, A
   History. Vol. I. New York, 1914.
Pease, Theodore C. The Centennial History of
   Illinois. Vol. II. Chicago, 1919.
Report and Collections of the State Historical
   Society of Wisconsin for the Years 1877, 1878,
   and 1879. Madison, 1879.
Report and Collections of the State Historical
   Society of Wisconsin for the Years 1883, 1884,
   and 1885. Madison, 1888.
Sandburg, Carl. Abraham Lincoln: The Prairie Years.
   Vol. I. New York, 1926.
Second Annual Report and Collections of the State

Historical Society of Wisconsin for the Year
1855. Madison, 1856.
Smith, George W. History of Illinois and Her
People. Vol. II. Chicago and New York, 1927.
Smith, Henry. "Indian Campaign of 1832," Military
and Naval Magazine of the United States, August,
1833, pp. 321-333.
Swett, Leonard. "Mr. Lincoln's Story of His Own
Life," in Reminiscences of Abraham Lincoln by
Distinguished Men of His Time, ed. Allen Thorn-
dike Rice. New York, 1886.
Tarbell, Ida M. The Early Life of Abraham Lincoln.
New York, 1896.
---. The Life of Abraham Lincoln. New York, 1900.
Thommas, William. Quarter Master's Book. (MS in
State Historical Library, Centennial Building,
Springfield, Illinois.)

THE CANALS OF MARS

By Robert Hoehn

For thousands of years, since it was first observed by Ptolemy in 272 B.C., the planet Mars has
been a source of great fascination and controversy.
Every prominent astronomer at some time during his
career has described and drawn conclusions concerning his findings about Mars. In 1840 A.D., Beer and
Maedler, a team of German astronomers, produced a
map of Mars showing four fine streaks. Fourteen
years later an Englishman named Dawes drew a sketch
of Mars showing eight or ten similar streaks. An
Italian astronomer, Father Angelo Secci, named
these streaks "canali" (meaning channels or
grooves) and today they are called canals because
of the corrupted English pronunciation of the
Italian word canali.[1]
Giovanni Virginis Sciaparelli, the director of
the observatory in Milan, is popularly admitted to

be the discoverer of the canals of Mars. This belief
is untrue, but Sciaparelli did add some important
facts to man's knowledge of the canals. First, his
map of Mars showed about forty complete canals.
These canals were from three hundred to several
thousand miles long, and eighteen to two hundred
miles wide. An interesting feature of the canals,
according to Sciaparelli, was the fact that every
one opened either into a "sea," or a "lake," another
canal, or into the intersection of a group of
canals.[2]

In 1879 Sciaparelli announced the "germination"
of the canal Nilus. This phenomenon was described
by Sciaparelli in this way:

> A given canal changes its appearance and is
> found transformed through all its length into
> two lines or uniform stripes more or less par-
> allel to one another, and which run straight
> and equal with the exact geometrical precision
> of the two rails of a railroad.[3]

Sciaparelli's findings turned out to be very con-
troversial. It is interesting to note that he took
no part in the arguments, but instead stated:

> We conclude, therefore, that the canals are
> such in fact and not only in name. The network
> formed by these was probably determined in its
> origin in the geological state of the planet,
> and has come to be slowly elaborated in the
> course of centuries. It is not necessary to
> suppose them the work of intelligent beings
> and, notwithstanding the almost geometric ap-
> pearance of all of their system, we are now
> inclined to believe them to be produced by the
> evolution of the planet, just as on earth we
> have the English Channel and the Channel of
> Mozambique.[4]

Sciaparelli's revelations caused astronomers to split into two groups. The first group denied the existence of the canals, saying that they were merely optical illusions. The second group accepted the idea of canals and put forth a whole series of theories explaining them.

Professor Percival Lowell, director of the observatory in Flagstaff, Arizona, was a member of the second group of "canal men." Lowell spent twelve years in study and observation of the canals. He found that there were about 437 canals running in straight lines along great circles of the planet. The fact that these canals were so precisely geometric and were joined together so perfectly led Lowell to believe that the canals were constructed by a race of intelligent beings. He contended that Mars is further along than the Earth in planetary evolution because it has no oceans or mountains and because almost three-fifths of the planet is a desert. The intelligent population of Mars, he believed, had foreseen the inevitable end of the planet and had established plans to meet it.

> With this motive of self-preservation . . . , and with a race equal to emergency we should expect to note certain general phenomena. Both polar caps would be pressed into service in order to utilize the whole available supply and also to accommodate most easily the inhabitants of each hemisphere. We should thus expect to find a system of conduits of some sort world-wide in its distribution and running at its northern and southern ends to termini in the caps. This is precisely what the telescope reveals.[5]

Professor Lowell's theories fascinated many laymen during the period in which they were published, but no professional astronomer would agree with him.

Another interesting theory about the canals was published by Professor Elihu Thompson. He believed that Mars was inhabited by a type of primitive animal. The changes of the Martian seasons cause the animals to migrate toward the poles, following the vegetation and the warm weather. Since there are no physical obstructions such as mountains or rivers on Mars, the yearly migrations followed the same path. Thompson believed that this repeated yearly fertilization on the paths of migration caused vegetation to grow, and left the rest of the planet a barren desert.[6]

Around 1907, the noted astronomer, William H. Pickering, who was a "believer" in the canals and a longtime observer of Mars, produced his "aerial deposition theory." Pickering agreed with Lowell and Thompson that water was very scarce on Mars. He stated that rain, sweeping across the planet, would cause vegetation to spring up along its course and thus produce uniform bands which would resemble canals. Many astronomers found fault with Pickering's theories because he didn't explain the "germination" or 'double-canal phenomenon. Pickering was one of the last "early" astronomers to present an explanation of the canals of Mars.[7]

The current theories concerning the canals of Mars are also very numerous. In 1950, Mr. Clyde Tombaugh, the discoverer of the planet Pluto, stated that he had observed the canals and put forth a theory to explain them. Mr. Tombaugh believes that the canals are due to faults in the Martian crust and that the seasonal changes are due to a hardy type of plant life which survives in these faults.[8] This theory is one of the so-called "physical explanations" of the canals, and it reminds us somewhat of the theory explained by the Swedish chemist Arrhenius around 1910.

Arrhenius said that the canals were caused by natural fissures and cracks which were made by earthquakes. These cracks on Mars are longer than those on earth because of the lower gravity and the thicker crust (for Mars is much older than Earth geologically). The seasonal changes in color are due to minerals in the fissures which change color with changes in temperature and humidity.[9]

In 1952 Gerard De Vaucouleurs, a noted French astronomer, proposed a theory which is accepted by some modern astronomers. He first explained that the mere existence of the dark areas of Mars shows that the surface cannot be dead. Vaucouleurs stated:

> A suggestion of continuous chemical surface action, for example by moist salt layers or similar [phenomena] modifying the color of the depositing dust, must be rejected because no such surface action would withstand the pouring in of the deposits for millions of centuries.
>
> Organic life probably in the form of vegetation defying the sand drifts and feeding on the dust appears to be the only explanation.[10]

Some of our modern astronomers still cling to the old theory that the canals of Mars are merely optical illusions. Dr. W. E. Finsen, who heads this group of non-believers, maintains that

> The strange canals of Mars may be only optical illusions. "The canals," first reported in 1877, have been described frequently by astronomers. But photographs have failed to show them clearly and I suggest, after new observations, that they are "figments" created by straining to see something.[11]

Modern methods of photography have turned most of the "non-believers" like Dr. Finsen into "believers." Dr. D. B. McLaughlin of the University of Michigan has discussed the importance of photography in observation of the canals:

> Photographs have been taken, upon which features of a generally linear character can be seen in the location of the canals as mapped by visual observers. The photographs and the "visible canals" on them prove that human perceptions are subject to the same fallibility and illusions, whether we view Mars directly through the telescope or look at a photograph.[12]

Dr. McLaughlin develops an entirely new theory of the formation of the canals. He thinks that the canals are made of volcanic ash placed in patterns by the trade and monsoon winds near the Martian equator and that the colors are produced by the chemicals which compose the volcanic ash.[13] McLaughlin's theory of the canals is a unique one, and very few of his contemporaries follow it.

On the other hand, the great majority of scientists and astronomers believe the assumptions of Dr. E. C. Slipher, an astronomer of the Lowell Observatory. Slipher easily crushes McLaughlin's theory, first of all by noting that the markings on the surface of Mars are absolutely immobile and that they grow larger or smaller during certain seasons. He also states that there is no evidence of volcanic action which would explain the faulting theories of certain scientists. Slipher represents many scientists when he says:

> To me, the best hypothesis still seems to be that the green areas represent vegetation able to grow through the yellow dust deposited upon it from time to time.
>
> In the light of our present knowledge, it appears that in Mars we are enabled to foresee what will overtake the earth in the fullness of time.[14]

There are many theories about the origin and development of the famous canals of Mars. Who can honestly say which of the hypotheses is true? Perhaps the mystery will be solved in the not too distant future by an increase in our theoretical and technical knowledge.

FOOTNOTES

[1] William H. Pickering, "Sciaparelli's Latest Views Regarding Mars," Annual Report of the Board of Regents of the Smithsonian Institution, 1894 (Washington, 1896), pp. 114-115.

[2] Ibid., pp. 122-123.

[3] Ibid., p. 125.

[4] Ibid., p. 124.

[5] Mars as the Abode of Life (New York, 1908), pp. 210-211.

[6] Willy Ley and Wernher Von Braun, The Conquest of Mars (New York, 1956), p. 64.

[7] Robert S. Richardson, Exploring Mars (New York, 1954), p. 151.

[8] Ibid., p. 152.

[9] Ley and Von Braun, pp. 74-75.

[10] Physics of the Planet Mars, trans. Patrick A. Moore (London, 1952), p. 137.

[11] "Mars Swings Close, Reveals More of Its Secrets," U.S. News and World Report, September 14, 1956, pp. 76-77.

[12] "New Interpretation of the Surface of Mars," Scientific Monthly, October, 1956, p. 177.

[13] Ibid., pp. 178-188.

[14] "New Light on the Changing Face of Mars," National Geographic Magazine, September, 1955, p. 436.

A SELECTED BIBLIOGRAPHY

Abbot, C. G. "The Habitability of Venus, Mars, and Other Worlds," Annual Report of the Board of

Regents of the Smithsonian Institution, 1920, pp. 165-171. Washington, 1922.

Levitt, I. M. A Space Traveler's Guide to Mars. New York, 1956.

Ley, Willy, and Wernher Von Braun. The Conquest of Mars. New York, 1956.

Lowell, Percival. Mars and Its Canals. New York, 1906.

---. Mars as the Abode of Life. New York, 1908.

McLaughlin, D. B. "The Geology of Mars," Sky and Telescope, XVI (February, 1957), 172.

---. "Interpretation of Martian Features," Sky and Telescope, XIII (September, 1954), 372.

---. "New Interpretation of the Surface of Mars," Scientific Monthly, LXXXIII (October, 1956), 176-188.

"Mars Swings Close, Reveals More of Its Secrets," U.S. News and World Report, XLI (September 14, 1956), 76-77.

"Martian Canals Seen," Science News Letter, LXVI (July 31, 1954), 77.

"Neighbor Is Nearer," Life, XLI (September 24, 1956), 36-39.

Pickering, William H. "Sciaparelli's Latest Views Regarding Mars," Annual Report of the Board of Regents of the Smithsonian Institution, 1894, pp. 113-139. Washington, 1896.

Richardson, Robert S. Exploring Mars. New York, 1954.

Slipher, E. C. "New Light on the Changing Face of Mars," National Geographic Magazine, CVIII (September, 1955), 426-436.

"The Universe: Close Up," Newsweek, XLVIII (August 20, 1956), 56.

Vaucouleurs, De, Gerard. Physics of the Planet Mars, trans. Patrick A. Moore. London, 1952.

---. The Planet Mars, trans. Patrick A. Moore. London, 1952.

THE
PARAGRAPH

Writing is a process of building. Letters of the alphabet are combined into words; words are linked to form phrases, clauses, and sentences; and sentences are combined to form paragraphs. Good themes or compositions are thus built with good paragraphs, which are fundamental to all good writing and which are predicated upon clear thinking.

Anyone can create good paragraphs who has ideas, will think clearly about them, will develop them, will relate them to one another, and will write and rewrite thoughtfully. You speak in words and sentences, but you usually think and write in larger units.

To achieve good paragraphs, therefore, you should understand the meaning, purposes, and characteristics of paragraphs and paragraphing.

DEFINITION AND CHARACTERISTICS

21a. Understand clearly the meaning and purpose of paragraphing.

A paragraph is usually a group of sentences developing either one single topic or a specific part of a larger topic. Sometimes, in serving an appropriate purpose, a paragraph may consist of only one sentence.

The purpose of a paragraph is to aid in communicating ideas by setting off the single topic which is developed or by providing clear distinctions between the separate parts of a longer composition. A complete theme or short paper may consist of one paragraph only (see Section 29d), or a theme or paper may have two or three or as many paragraphs as the writer decides are necessary to give his subject adequate treatment.

21b. Make your paragraphs correct, clear, effective, and appropriate.

A well-constructed paragraph has *correctness, clearness, effectiveness,* and *appropriateness*—characteristics dependent upon careful thinking.

Good paragraphing is essential for clearness. Properly separated groups of sentences enable the writer to plot his course and see the progress he is making. To the reader they make the structure and development of ideas easily apparent by serving as signposts or road markers to guide him along the paths of thought which the writer is developing. The reader, following the signs laid out to help him, obtains a grasp of the parts and of the whole which they constitute.

Good paragraphing is also essential for effectiveness, partly because readers easily tire unless a page of writing is broken into smaller units. The sign of the paragraph, *indentation,* helps, for the reader knows that he has completed a unified section of writing and can go on to another unit. Similarly, books, magazine articles, and even short stories are often divided into chapters or sections, or their parts are otherwise typographically set off from one another both to keep related ideas or parts of the action distinct and to furnish the reader a breathing space.

For convenience, preview, and ready reference, seven desirable paragraph characteristics are listed below; except for No. 7, each is discussed in later sections. These characteristics refer to the normal paragraph, that is, the paragraph as a group of related sentences. They do not apply to paragraphs *appropriate* for special purposes (see Section 29).

1. A good paragraph is *mechanically* correct. It is properly indented. It does not have part of a line left blank unless this blank line comes at the end of the paragraph. If dialogue is recorded, each paragraph correctly represents every change of speaker. (Correctness and appropriateness)

2. A good paragraph contains a *topic statement,* expressed or implied. (Clearness)

3. A good paragraph depends upon proper *analysis* of its topic; it contains a *body of thought,* not a mere fragment; it contains ample content. The well-developed paragraph is never sketchy or incomplete. (Clearness)

4. A good paragraph is *unified.* Oneness of purpose and content is essential; unrelated details are eliminated. Each paragraph contains the

words that belong with it, not with the preceding or following paragraph. (Clearness and effectiveness)

5. A good paragraph has its ideas arranged in proper *order*. Sentences in it are so worded and arranged that each sentence flows naturally out of the one that precedes it and leads naturally into the one that follows. (Clearness and effectiveness)

6. A good paragraph is well *proportioned* and has appropriate *length*. If the thought of the paragraph is important, the paragraph will be fairly long. If the paragraph discusses an idea, or a group of related ideas, of comparatively less importance, the paragraph will be shorter. Usually a series of short, choppy paragraphs, or a group of very long ones, should be avoided. (Effectiveness and appropriateness)

7. A good paragraph contains *transitional aids:* words, phrases, clauses, and sentences serving as links or bridges. The thoughts within paragraphs should make orderly, clear progress, and one paragraph should lead to another clearly, logically, and smoothly (see Sections 11 and 42). (Clearness and effectiveness)

MECHANICS

22.   The conventions of mechanical correctness in paragraphs are few and easily learned.

22a.   Indent the first line of every paragraph.

Indentation, although mechanical, is important. Indent the first line of every paragraph three-quarters of an inch or more; or, if you typewrite, about five or ten spaces. Exception: business letters using the block form usually do not have indented paragraph beginnings (see pp. 730–731).

The break of distinct paragraph indentation is a clear and effective aid to both writer and reader in recognizing the divisions of thought within the whole theme. Paragraph indentation also aids in reading; the break serves as a signal that a clear distinction between separate parts of the composition is about to be made.

Use indentations of equal length for all the paragraphs in the same theme. Make no exception for *numbered* paragraphs.

Avoid in general the use of the marks " ¶ " or " ℙ " and "no ¶ " or "no ℙ ," meaning, respectively, "a new .paragraph intended" and "not a new paragraph." Preferably, recopy the entire page, correcting the indentation.

Do not indent the first line of the second page or succeeding pages unless the indentation marks the beginning of a new paragraph.

22b. Do not leave part of a line blank within a paragraph.

Unless a new paragraph begins on the next line, do not leave part of a line blank within a paragraph. Blanks in lines which are not last lines of paragraphs mislead your reader, who expects such a break to finish the discussion of one phase of a subject. Furthermore, blanks in lines not only cause a jagged appearance but also make less efficient the mechanical process of reading—the eye, in sweeping over the line, has to make several extra movements in order to adjust itself and to transfer meaning to the brain. Margins at the left of the page should, of course, always be uniform for the same reasons and should not meander toward the right.

(For the conventional and appropriate use of very short paragraphs—conversation, short introductory and concluding paragraphs, transitional paragraphs, business letters, directions, summaries, conclusions, and recommendations—see Section 29.)

THE TOPIC SENTENCE OR STATEMENT

23. A topic sentence or statement gives the subject of the paragraph; it contains the heart of the idea which is to be, is being, or has been, developed. It contributes to unity, clearness, and effectiveness of the paragraph by expressing the central thought with which the group of sentences is concerned. It contains, however, only the main point or points of the paragraph, not every idea mentioned.

23a. Use a topic sentence or topic statement to aid in gaining paragraph unity.

The topic sentence, although so called, may not be a "sentence" at all. It is the statement containing the subject or topic, which may be expressed in various forms: (1) as one of the clauses in a compound sentence; (2) as the main clause of a complex sentence; (3) as a phrase within the sentence; (4) even as a single word; or (5) as a short, simple sentence—usually the most effective kind of topic sentence.

The reason for such flexibility is that a writer may use part of the sentence containing the topic to serve as transition or to indicate either the manner in which the topic is to be developed or the direction in which the discussion is to continue. Whatever its grammatical form, the topic sentence, or statement, always is or contains the subject of the paragraph.

Not every well-constructed paragraph contains an expressed topic sentence, but every good paragraph is so well knit that it at least *implies* one. The reader, reflecting, can sum up the central thought of the paragraph in his own "topic sentence." Perhaps a study, however, of a number of paragraphs would show that the clearest and most effective paragraphs are those in which the topic is expressed, and the least effective those in which it is implied. Consideration for the reader is certainly an argument in favor of an expressed topic.

A topic sentence or statement or word, therefore, is a guide to both writer and reader. For the writer, it is the guide by which he keeps on the subject and avoids introducing irrelevant material. It perhaps should be a simple sentence, at least in its first draft. Simple sentences are easier to phrase than other kinds, and a writer can write all the topic sentences or statements for a theme, or even a long paper, before he begins the more difficult task of developing them.

A well-planned topic outline, in which you have already decided the divisions to be expanded into paragraphs, will readily provide the key words for topic statements; a sentence outline will present topic sentences ready-made. The paragraph outline, usually made of others' writing, shows how other authors have composed their topic sentences. (See Section **6a, b, c.**)

As a check on the presence or absence of a paragraph topic and its effective phrasing, reread carefully each paragraph you write. Put in the margin the one or two words that are the subject of the paragraph. Or apply the methods of some textbooks which print in blackface type the paragraph topic at the beginning of the paragraph. If you follow any of these suggestions, be sure to eliminate from your final draft all such mechanical indications of the topic.

23b. Vary the kind of sentences containing the topic.

Although simple sentences are clear and effective as topic sentences, you can include topics in the phrases or clauses of compound, complex, and compound-complex sentences. Use mainly declarative sentences, but for variety, and when they are appropriate, use interrogative, exclamatory, or even imperative sentences. Any of these kinds of sentences can make a topic sentence which generalizes, or summarizes, or particularizes.

23c.   Vary the position of topic sentences within the paragraph.

Ordinarily, since the purpose of writing is clearness of communication, the first sentence of the paragraph, especially in expository and argumentative writing, should be or contain the topic. Your reader should be told immediately what he is to read about. Since a series of paragraphs beginning with topic sentences may become monotonous, you can experiment with placing a paragraph topic in the second, third, or fourth sentences and letting the earlier sentences lead up to it. Occasionally, your last sentence may be or contain the topic. Occasionally, too, you may repeat the thought of the topic sentence in other sentences in the paragraph.

Study the following examples. Note the unifying, clarifying effect of the topic sentences; note also their position and form. To emphasize their position, they are here italicized.

1. The topic sentence is the first sentence, a simple sentence, a declarative sentence; it tells what is to follow.

Two main courses of study are offered at Milldale High School. One is the academic course and the other is the commercial course. The high school freshman is required to choose the course he plans to follow during the next four years. The academic course consists of the subjects which are required for college entrance, such as written composition, English and American literature, mathematics, history, and some science. This course does not include typing, shorthand, or bookkeeping, although a student may elect one or more of these. The commercial course is designed for girls and boys preparing to become stenographers and secretaries. It does not include English literature or any of the sciences or higher mathematics courses. It is concerned mainly with the commercial courses, like shorthand, typing, bookkeeping, business English, and office etiquette.

—Student theme

2. The topic statement is the noun clause used as subject of the first sentence. It is repeated in the same words in the third sentence and in slightly different words in the sixth sentence.

What makes an airplane fly is not its engine nor its propeller. Nor is it, as many people think, some mysterious knack of the pilot, nor some ingenious gadget inside. *What makes an airplane fly* is simply its shape. This may sound absurd, but gliders do fly without engines and model airplanes do fly without pilots. As for the insides of an airplane, they are disappointing, for they are mostly hollow. No, *what keeps an airplane up* is its shape—the impact of the air upon its shape. Whittle that shape out of wood, or cast it out of iron, or fashion it, for that matter, out of chocolate and throw the thing into the air. It will behave like an airplane. It will *be* an airplane.[1]

3. The topic sentence is the fourth sentence; the sentences before and after it illustrate and expand the idea expressed.

Suppose, however, that we had called that same animal a "mongrel." The matter is more complicated. We have used a word which objectively means the same as "dog of mixed breed," but which also arouses in our hearers an emotional attitude of disapproval toward that particular dog. *A word, therefore, cannot only indicate an object, but can also suggest an emotional attitude toward it.* Such suggestion of an emotional attitude does go beyond exact and scientific discussion because our approvals and disapprovals are individual—they belong to ourselves and not to the objects we approve or disapprove of. An animal which to the mind of its master is a faithful and noble dog of mixed ancestry may be a "mongrel" to his neighbor whose chickens are chased by it.

—ROBERT THOULESS, "Emotional Meanings"[2]

4. In two brief paragraphs, by American soldiers in the United States Army, note the repetition of the topic, and, incidentally, the effective use of sentence fragments (Section **31a**) in the second example:[3]

Whenever I think of *what America means to me,* simple memories come to mind like pictures of Washington and Lincoln, a big dish of ice cream, or my warm bed at home. However, *America means* more. It *means* security—the opportunity of obtaining sufficient food, clothing, and shelter for loved ones and self. It *means* that I have no fear in the night. It *means* I'm able to attend the church of my choice. *America means* a choked-up feeling when I see Old Glory or hear the national anthem. *America* is my country.

—1st Lt. R. H. HENSTROM, USA

[1] Wolfgang Langewiesche, "Why an Airplane Flies," from *Life,* May 17, 1943. Copyright, Time, Inc.

[2] From *How to Think Straight,* by Robert H. Thouless. (New York: Simon and Schuster, Inc., c. 1939.)

[3] From *You and Your USA,* published by the Offices of Armed Forces Information and Education, Department of Defense, Washington 25, D.C. (1954).

As an American soldier now in Korea [1953–1954], *America means to me:* Superhighways on which to move swiftly. Freedom from want through factories, farms, and ever-increasing research into better things for better living. Freedom from fear, through the building of a strong defense against Communism. Freedom of speech, which enables each American citizen to strive for what he believes is right. I conclude, *America means to me,* and to millions of other Americans, *Faith* to live, *Hope* for the future, and *Charity* for others through the abundance of its riches.

—Pvt. Robert Dayhuff, USA

These illustrations indicate various positions for the topic sentence and a few of the ways in which it is expressed. Important to remember is this: One criterion of the good paragraph is that it must be so unified that its content is summarized in a topic sentence or clause, or can be when a topic is not expressed. Thus a writer can be certain that he has kept to the subject and that his reader can follow clearly the development of the paragraph thought.

EXERCISES

A. Underline the topic sentence or topic statement of each one of a number of paragraphs in (1) one of your textbooks; (2) an article in a current magazine; (3) an article in your book of readings. Discuss the position in the paragraph of these topic sentences and the kinds of sentences they are.

B. From your reading, select a seemingly well-constructed paragraph which has no topic sentence or topic statement. Give the implied topic.

C. By means of the author's topic sentences, make a paragraph outline of some essay in your book of readings. (See Section 6c.)

D. For each of five of the following theme subjects, write five or more simple sentences which could be used for topics of paragraphs developing the theme.

1. Why I Am Attending — College.
2. The Honor System on Our Campus.
3. The Best Way to Buy a Second-Hand Car.
4. The Most Remarkable Character in Our Town.
5. How to Improve in Writing.
6. Let's Ignore the Saturday Football Games.
7. Reading as a Substitute for Travel.
8. Why Golf Makes Walking Interesting.
9. See Your Dentist Twice a Year, but Your Doctor Only Once.
10. Are You Here to Study or to Have a Great Time?

E. Write 20 simple sentences to be used as topic sentences: five for narrative, five for description, five for exposition, and five for argument.

F. Using the following simple sentences as topic sentences, expand one or more into paragraphs of 150 to 300 words.

1. A good farmer can always make a comfortable living.
2. Basketball in our state is overemphasized.
3. It is women who make a home out of a house.
4. Careless driving is responsible for serious accidents.
5. Basketball is a better spectator sport than bowling (or some similar game).
6. Bowling (or some similar game) is a better sport for individuals than basketball (or some similar game).
7. Our college's greatest need is —.
8. May I recommend a good television (or radio) program?
9. Being the oldest (youngest, only) child in a family has its advantages (disadvantages).
10. A satisfactory roommate has few faults and many virtues.
11. High school English is different from college English.
12. The illness was diagnosed as —.
13. A traveler has many unusual experiences.
14. Life on a farm (in a city) has its exciting moments.
15. A budget is an efficient way to conserve time (or money).

G. Directions given in F.

1. The small farm is rapidly disappearing.
2. Every person past — years of age should carry life insurance.
3. I have three reasons for joining (not joining) a fraternity (sorority).
4. My hobby is —.
5. Intelligence is required in taking useful notes.
6. Being a Boy (Girl) Scout has meant much to me.
7. A good breakfast is the best way to start a day.
8. Appearances are sometimes deceiving.
9. Cutting classes can lead to serious trouble.
10. I did not take my high school studies seriously enough.
11. During the first week of college a freshman learns much.
12. Everyone should learn how to swim.
13. A slip of the tongue may be embarrassing.
14. Party telephone lines are frustrating.
15. A traveler is an adventurer at heart.

H. Directions in F.

1. May I introduce you to —?
2. The first day at college is a day to remember.
3. A woman would (would not) make a good President of the United States.
4. My dog has several fascinating tricks.
5. TV provides interesting entertainment.
6. Summer employment has several advantages.
7. Getting mail is one of the joys of campus life.
8. Honesty is a basic stone in the foundation of a good life.
9. I shall never forget my first airplane ride.
10. The voting age in the United States should be 18 years.
11. Driver education should be compulsory in high school.
12. Living at home has advantages (disadvantages) for the college student.
13. A farmer looks forward to the harvest season.
14. Regular study habits are necessary for success in college.
15. The modern kitchen is a miracle of mechanics.

CONTENT

24.   After you have determined the thought to be developed in the paragraph and put it in a topic sentence, expressed or implied, your problem is developing the thought. Topic sentences are only the beginning, the foundation, the summary of the thought to be presented. Neither hazy generalizations nor mere repetition of the central thought builds good paragraphs.

Clear and effective paragraphs are completely developed and contain an abundance of pertinent detail. Ineffective paragraphs are weak not because the central ideas are necessarily weak but because their content is thin, dull, and meaningless. In other words, fully developed paragraphs require genuine mental activity. An effective, clear theme is the sum total of a series of paragraphs rounded with ample content.

24a.   Gather content from your own thought and experience and from the thought and experience of others.

After phrasing the topic sentence, draw upon your own experience and the experience of others as revealed in newspapers, magazines, books, radio, TV, and conversation. Make use of your own experience, observation, curiosity, imagination, and reflection. Since a single paragraph may be either a complete short theme or one of a series of paragraphs making up a theme, the suggestions concerning content for the theme (Section 5) apply equally to the paragraph.

To this content apply also the analysis suggested for theme topics in Section 4. Your paragraph topic is simply a more limited subject: What are its component parts? What, from your various materials, will you jot down concerning it?

For example, for a long theme, "Important Facts Concerning My High School," designed to inform his freshman English instructor of his pre-college background, a student chose for one paragraph subject, "Courses of Study Offered." As a start and in no special order, his jottings consisted of the following:

1. Two main courses
2. Academic course
3. Commercial course
4. General course for a few weaker students
5. Time of choosing courses
6. Content of academic course (composition, literature, history, science, mathematics, etc.)
7. Content of commercial course (typing, shorthand, bookkeeping, business English, etc.)
8. Purpose of academic course
9. Purpose of commercial course

The following outline for the paragraph resulted from these jottings:

I. General information about courses
   A. Kinds
   B. Purpose
   C. Time of choosing
II. The academic course
   A. Subjects included
   B. Subjects not included
III. The commercial course
   A. Subjects included
   B. Subjects not included

For the paragraph as written from this outline, see page 214.

24b. Follow a consistent method, or methods, in developing the idea contained in the topic sentence.

By various methods you can expand a topic into an effective paragraph. Your method may vary with the four kinds of writing, narration, description, exposition, argument. Your topic sentence, if well chosen and phrased, will often indicate the most desirable method; sometimes it will suggest several methods, from which you choose the one that will most clearly, effectively, and appropriately accomplish your purpose. The choice of any one method does not exclude other methods of paragraph development; also, a short illustration—a sentence or two at the most—may always be inserted into the course of development by any method without destroying the unity of the paragraph or the directness of the thought.

Frequently used to develop a paragraph topic are the following: (1) particulars and details, (2) illustration or example, (3) comparison or contrast, (4) division, (5) causes or effects, (6) reasons and inferences, and (7) definition.

1. Development by *particulars and details* means expanding the idea contained in the topic by a series of specific details or concrete particulars, arranged in some logical order. Since any topic is broader or more general than its supporting material, every paragraph in a sense is developed by particulars and details. Apart from other methods, however, this method uses ideas related to or suggested by preceding ideas, and all taken together amplify, make vivid, make definite the topic. Notice how particulars and details support the topic, italicized, in the following paragraphs:

Miscellaneous *details:*

In an elevator, ascending with strangers to familiar heights, the breath congeals, the body stiffens, the spirit marks time. These brief vertical journeys that we make in a common lift, from street level to office level, past the missing thirteenth floor—they afford moments of suspended animation, unique and probably beneficial. Passengers in an elevator, whether wedged tight or scattered with room to spare, achieve in their perpendicular passage a trancelike state: each person adhering to the unwritten code, a man descending at five in the afternoon with his nose buried in a strange woman's back hair, reducing his breath to an absolute minimum necessary to sustain life, willing to suffocate rather than allow a suggestion of his physical presence to impinge; a man coming home at one A.M., ascending with only one other occupant of the car, carefully avoiding any slight recognition of joint occupancy. What is there about elevator travel that induces this painstaking catalepsy? A sudden solemnity, perhaps, which seizes people when they feel gravity being tampered with—they hope successfully. Sometimes it seems to us as though everyone in the car were in silent prayer.[4]

Narrative *details:*

The bare, indisputable facts in the life of Mary Todd Lincoln are few and simple. She was born of a good Kentucky family, in 1818, ten years after her husband. In 1839 she came to live with her sister, Mrs. Edwards, in Springfield. After a stormy courtship Lincoln married her in 1842. Her life then led her through Illinois law and politics to the White House, and the war, and the culminations of triumphant peace. All the triumph and hope were blasted by the assassination of her husband, and her remaining years, in spite of a brief sojourn to Europe, were darkened by sorrow and misfortune till a temperament, always impulsive and intense, was unbalanced to a point of oddity approaching and at times reaching actual derangement. She died in 1882.[5]

Descriptive *details:*

For *sounds in winter nights, and often in winter days,* I heard the forlorn but melodious notes of a hooting owl indefinitely far; such a sound as the frozen earth would yield if struck with a suitable plectrum, the very *lingua vernacula* of Walden Wood, and quite familiar to me at last, though I never saw the bird while it was making it. I seldom opened my door in a winter evening without hearing it; *Hoo hoo hoo, hoorer hoo,* sounded sonorously, and the first three syllables accented somewhat like *how der do;* or sometimes *hoo hoo* only. One night in the beginning of winter, before the pond froze over, about nine o'clock, I was startled by the loud honking of a goose, and, stepping to the door, heard the sound of their wings like a tempest in the woods as they flew low over my house. They passed over the pond toward Fair-Haven, seemingly deterred from settling by my light, their commodore honking all the while with a regular beat. Suddenly an unmistakable cat-owl from very near me, with the most harsh and tremendous voice I ever heard from any inhabitant of the woods, responded at regular intervals to the goose, as if determined to expose and disgrace this intruder from Hudson's Bay by exhibiting a greater compass and volume of voice in a native, and *boohoo* him out of Concord horizon. What do you

---

[4] From E. B. White, *The Second Tree from the Corner,* Harper & Brothers. Copyright, 1954, by E. B. White.

[5] From *Wives,* by Gamaliel Bradford. Copyright, 1925, by Harper & Brothers.

mean by alarming the citadel at this time of night consecrated to me? Do you think I am ever caught napping at such an hour, and that I have not got lungs and a larynx as well as yourself? *Boo-hoo, boo-hoo, boo-hoo!* It was one of the most thrilling discords I ever heard. And yet, if you had a discriminating ear, there were in it the elements of a concord such as these plains never saw nor heard.[6]

Expository *details:*

We all appear to ourselves to be thinking all the time during our waking hours, and most of us are aware that we go on thinking while we are asleep, even more foolishly than when awake. When uninterrupted by some practical issue *we are engaged in what is now known as a reverie.* This is our spontaneous and favorite kind of thinking. We allow our ideas to take their own course and this course is determined by our hopes and fears, our spontaneous desires, their fulfillment or frustration; by our likes and dislikes, our loves and hates and resentments. There is nothing else anything like so interesting to ourselves as ourselves. All thought that is not more or less laboriously controlled and directed will inevitably circle about the beloved Ego. It is amusing and pathetic to observe this tendency in ourselves and in others. We learn politely and generously to overlook this truth, but if we dare to think of it, it blazes forth like the noontide sun.[7]

2. Development by *illustration* or *example* uses a series of sentences which furnish an instance representative of the more general statement in the topic sentence. The instance may be semi-specific, like "Consider a man who is overly ambitious"; or, for greater effectiveness, it may be specific and concrete, like "Consider Shakespeare's Macbeth, who was overly ambitious." An example familiar to the reader carries its own explanation and thus aids clearness. Either a longer single example or several shorter instances serve to drive home to the reader the idea expressed in the topic sentence.

Following are two consecutive paragraphs developed by illustration or example. With topic sentences italicized, the first uses numerous illustrations, the second uses three examples:

The story of the Arizona rancher who made out a $500 check on a six-by-three-foot cowhide recalls the *many curious surfaces on which checks have legally been written through the years:* in lipstick on handkerchiefs, on

[6] From Henry David Thoreau, "Winter Animals," *Walden, or Life in the Woods.*
[7] From *The Mind in the Making,* by James Harvey Robinson. Copyright, 1921, by Harper & Brothers.

cigarette paper, on calling cards, fragile valentines, on whisky labels, Christmas cards, envelopes, newspaper, cigar-box tops, paper bags, laundry bills. A check written on a hard-boiled egg was cashed without trouble at the Victoria branch of the Canadian Bank of Commerce. A Midwestern lumberman made out so many checks on his own brand of shingle that his bank had to construct a special type of file cabinet for them. A contractor in Memphis once settled his weekly payroll by drawing on the bank with slabs of wood. A business man eager to pay for a newly arrived television set recently pried off the side of the packing case and wrote his check on it.

The odd ways in which checks have been written are a reflection of the foibles of those who make them out. This was symbolized a few years ago when a check for $1,000, painted on the side of a 134-pound watermelon, was drawn against the account of the Parker County (Texas) Melon Growers Association to pay a contestant on a television show with the appropriate title, "People Are Funny." Then there was the sailor stationed at San Diego who was plagued with requests for money from home. In desperation he engraved a check on a piece of battleship plate with a blow torch and sent it home, confident that the annoying requests would now stop. At the end of the month, though, the steel check came back with his other canceled checks, with a proper endorsement on the back—also made with a blow torch. And recently a Connecticut perfume company drenched its check books with samples of its product, printed the word "scent" instead of "cent," and the words "pay to the odor of" the customer.[8]

In the following, one expanded *example* is the major means of developing the topic, the italicized part of the last sentence:

Many people, especially older people, are inclined to underestimate their talents and to lead lives unworthy of their full abilities. But many more (the younger generation is well represented here) believe they have no limitations; they consider themselves capable of doing everything and anything all at one time. It is a member of this latter group who endangers not only himself, but also those with whom he associates. I once had a grade-school teacher notorious for her personal self-confidence (and public failure) in her ability to handle alone a job really needing three people. She was school principal, teacher of the fifth and sixth grades, and librarian. As a result of her triple task, my classmates and I were never quite certain who discovered the Fountain of Youth, or what eleven times four equaled. To be sure, we were all perfect at the techniques involved in pasting labels in books, but many other parts of our sixth-grade education were sadly neglected because teacher was usually flitting about attending to her various other

[8] From "Topics," *The New York Times,* September 20, 1960.

duties. To make matters worse, nervous strain frequently wrought havoc in her easily upset emotional state. I remember one particularly trying day when nothing seemed to go right for her. Lazy janitors, school board troubles, and several missing encyclopaedias combined to wear her patience thin. A spilled bottle of ink was the final straw. She burst into tears, picked up a three-volume set of *Our Latin American Neighbors,* hurled them blindly at the class, and locked herself into the closet. "Bolivia" hit me; "Mexico" gave another boy a black eye. The class was thereafter in a state of humiliation. On that day I learned a lesson I'll never forget: *Never undertake more than you can handle, and handle well.*[9]

3. A topic may be made clear and effective by the use of *comparison* or *contrast.* Comparison shows the likeness between the topic and some idea or object familiar to the reader; contrast shows differences. Not infrequently both comparison and contrast are used within the same paragraph.

Comparison:

The oblique band of sunlight which followed her through the door became the young wife well. It illuminated her as her presence illuminated the heath. *In her movements, in her gaze, she reminded the beholder of the feathered creatures who lived around her home.* All similes and allegories concerning her began and ended with birds. There was as much variety in her motions as in their flight. When she was musing, she was a kestrel, which hangs in the air by an invisible motion of its wings. When she was in a high wind, her light body was blown against trees and banks like a heron's. When she was frightened, she darted noiselessly like a kingfisher. When she was serene, she skimmed like a swallow, and that is how she was moving now.[10]

The emotion of a mob is like a flooding river. The river is at first quiet and still, but as the rain continues to fall day by day, and the waters rise higher, it begins to build up tremendous pressure. The river is no longer quiet. There is a murmur that grows in volume, grows louder and louder until finally the river breaks loose and surges over its banks, gathering momentum as it goes, rolling over everything in its path, wrecking homes, killing people. When the rampage is over, the river is once more quiet and still, showing no signs of its late turmoil, unmindful of the damage it has

[9] "Know Thyself," one-paragraph theme by Nancy Hieronymus, DePauw University student. From *Indiana English Leaflet,* February, 1955.

[10] Thomas Hardy's description of Thomasin Wildeve, from *The Return of the Native,* Book III, Ch. vi.

caused. So it is with the mob. It is one of the most destructive instruments on earth when aroused. It loses all power of reason and can only follow its leaders, roaring, destroying everything in its path, until the individuality of its members reasserts itself. Then the mob begins to break up, to disperse itself. Each member, going his own way, hardly remembers what the common bond was that had held them together. Even the memory of what has happened finally disappears.[11]

Contrast:

Novelette [is] a form of fiction intermediate between the short story and the novel. (The cumbersome term "long short story" is sometimes used as a synonym.) No exact limits can be set as to length, but the novelette differs from the short story in that it is not only longer but is more elaborate and has greater scope. It is not only shorter and less elaborate than the novel but is designed to be read at a single sitting and to produce a single, concentrated effect. Practically speaking, the novelette can be defined as a piece of prose fiction between 50 and 150 ordinary pages long.[12]

It is a misfortune of the English language in modern times *that the word "disinterested" is commonly confused with the word "uninterested."* The modern lexicographers who work on the principle that whatever is the usage of people is acceptable are beginning to accept the confusion, and perhaps they are very wise in their principle, but in this instance the usage of people—or at least of some people—has deprived us of our only word for a very important virtue. Up until recently the meanings of the two words were kept distinct, and it was a mark of ignorance to confuse them. "Disinterested" meant that one had nothing to gain from the matter at hand, that one was objective in one's judgment, that one had no selfish motive but was impartial and unbiased. "Uninterested" meant that one was bored with the matter at hand, that it did not engage one's attention. The distinction is still in force among almost all careful writers and speakers; they blame, say, a labor arbitrator who is *uninterested* in the case he is hearing, but they praise him for being *disinterested* in the way he decides it.[13]

4. Developing a topic by *division* means that the writer calls attention to two or more parts of the topic and discusses each one briefly

[11] "Mob," an expanded simile in a one-paragraph theme by Phyllis Hahn, DePauw University student. From *Indiana English Leaflet*, February, 1955.

[12] From *The Reader's Companion to World Literature*, Lillian H. Hornstein, ed. Copyright, 1956, by The Dryden Press.

[13] From Lionel Trilling, prefatory note to Matthew Arnold's "The Function of Criticism at the Present Time," *Major British Writers*. Copyright, 1954, by Harcourt, Brace and Company.

within the same paragraph. Of course, if each part is expanded in some detail, separate paragraphs are preferable. The following paragraphs are developed by division:

There are roughly three New Yorks. There is, first, the New York of the man or woman who was born here, who takes the city for granted and accepts its size and its turbulence as natural and inevitable. Second, there is the New York of the commuter—the city that is devoured by locusts each day and spat out each night. Third, there is the New York of the person who was born somewhere else and came to New York in quest of something. Of these three trembling cities the greatest is the last—the city of final destination, the city that is a goal. It is this third city that accounts for New York's high-strung disposition, its poetical deportment, its dedication to the arts, and its incomparable achievements. Commuters give the city its tidal restlessness; natives give it solidity and continuity; but the settlers give it passion. And whether it is a farmer arriving from Italy to set up a small grocery store in a slum, or a young girl arriving from a small town in Mississippi to escape the indignity of being observed by her neighbors, or a boy arriving from the Corn Belt with a manuscript in his suitcase and a pain in his heart, it makes no difference: each embraces New York with the intense excitement of first love, each absorbs New York with the fresh eyes of an adventurer, each generates heat and light to dwarf the Consolidated Edison Company.[14]

The question—*"Which is the happiest season of life?"*—being referred to an aged man, he replied: "When spring comes, and in the soft air the buds are breaking on the trees, and they are covered with blossoms, I think, 'How beautiful is Spring!' And when the summer comes, and covers the trees with its heavy foliage, and singing birds are among the branches, I think, 'How beautiful is Summer!' When autumn loads them with golden fruit, and their leaves bear the gorgeous tint of frost, I think, 'How beautiful is Autumn!' And when it is sere winter, and there is neither foliage nor fruit, then I look up through the leafless branches, as I never could until now, and see the stars shine."[15]

To the fatalism of the Orient and the other-worldliness of the Christian Middle Ages must be added a second idea opposed to the concept of progress—that is, *utopianism. This idea takes two forms.* In the minds of some thinkers it is related to the past; there has been a golden age, in the "good

[14] From E. B. White, *Here Is New York,* Harper & Brothers, New York. Copyright, 1949, by E. B. White and The Curtis Publishing Company.
[15] Author unknown. From *Cheer,* April, 1960.

old days of the fathers" or in some remote period of the early evolution of mankind. In seeking to escape the evils of the present, we must return to the perfection of long ago when people lived in peace, happiness, innocence, and plenty. But, in other minds, utopianism is related to the future: by doing this or that we can establish a static order of bliss—a fixed scheme of things so nearly perfect that they will never have to be changed. A variant on these aspects of dreaming may be called the utopianism of whitewash: the present order is so nearly perfect that it is almost profane to inquire into its evils or to propose modifications, for the possibility of doing harm is always greater than the chances of doing good. Historians, with all their searching, have not been able to find the golden age in the past, and skeptics doubt the perfection of the present. Still the illusion of utopianism shadows all human thought about public and private affairs, challenging the idea of progress.[16]

5. Development by *cause* (*causes*) or *effect* (*effects*) is ordinarily used for topic statements regarded as facts and hence is common in much expository writing. The topic sentence gives the generalized statement or conclusion drawn from the data; these data make up the supporting material of the paragraph, the causes or reasons. Or the supporting material tells what the various results or effects are of the general statement in the topic.

Cause:

The birth of a volcanic island is an event marked by prolonged and violent travail: the forces of the earth striving to create, and all the forces of the sea opposing. The sea floor, where an island begins, is probably nowhere more than fifty miles thick—a thin covering over the vast bulk of the earth. In it are deep cracks and fissures, the results of unequal cooling and shrinkage in past ages. Along such lines of weakness the molten lava from the earth's interior presses up and finally bursts forth into the sea. But a submarine volcano is different from a terrestrial eruption, where the lava, molten rocks, gases, and other ejecta are hurled into the air through an open crater. Here on the bottom of the ocean the volcano has resisting it all the weight of the ocean water above it. Despite the immense pressure of, it may be, two or three miles of sea water, the new volcanic cone builds upward toward the surface, in flow after flow of lava. Once within reach of the waves, its soft ash and tuff are violently attacked, and for a long period the potential island may remain a shoal, unable to emerge. But, eventually, in new

[16] From *A Century of Progress,* by Charles A. Beard. Copyright, 1932, by Harper & Brothers.

eruptions, the cone is pushed up into the air and a rampart against the attacks of the waves is built of hardened lava.[17]

Effect:

To most participating nations, *a modern war brings complex economic results*. Science and industry are occasionally advanced by researches derived from the stimulus and energy of war. Life and property are destroyed; vast sums are consumed in armament; impossible debts accumulate. Repudiation in some form becomes inevitable; currencies are depreciated or annulled, inflation relieves debtor governments and individuals, savings and investments are wiped out, and men patiently begin to save and lend again. Overexpansion in war is followed by a major depression in peace. International trade is disrupted by intensified nationalism, exalted tariffs, and the desire to develop at home all industries requisite in war. The vanquished are enslaved—physically, as in antiquity, financially and by due process of law today. The victorious masses gain little except in self-conceit; the ruling minority among the victors may gain much in conquered lands, markets, spheres of influence, supplies, and taxable population.[18]

6. Development by *reason* or *inferences* is a method usually used for topic statements regarded as opinions and hence is common in exposition of ideas and argumentative writing. Supporting material gives the reasons used in establishing the opinion, or it gives the data from which the statement of the topic sentence was inferred.

Has electricity lightened the housewife's work? No, *it [electricity] has only altered the type of work*. Although modern appliances have supposedly removed the pioneer drudgery from tending a home, the wife of today not only must be a cook, baby sitter, mother, cleaning woman, gardener, laundress, mechanic, diplomat, tutor, seamstress, interior decorator, and caterer; she must also be an electrician. Narcissa Whitman did not have to worry about pennies in the fuse box or an electric dryer which got rust spots on her wash. However, she is a heroine in our history while the contemporary housekeeper is classified as a sluggard. Men wonder why women are taking over their jobs in the business world. If they had a centigram of sense and would do a minute bit of repair work at home, their overworked wives would not seek a career for a release from the sweat-shop domiciles. Edison's tinkering was theoretically fine and dandy, but he failed to consider that woman might destroy herself by fixing her iron with a hairpin. Men,

[17] From Rachel L. Carson, *The Sea Around Us*. Copyright, 1950, 1951, by Oxford University Press, Inc.

[18] From Will Durant, "Why Men Fight," *The Saturday Evening Post,* July 10, 1937.

this is an open letter to you suggesting that "the little woman" may not have the "lead-pipe" cinch you think she has—electricity or no electricity.[19]

7. Development of a topic by *definition* (see Section 16c2a) involves the use of content which answers the implied question of the reader, "What do you mean by this?" To be clear and effective, the paragraph developed by this method also uses some of the foregoing methods: details and particulars, illustration and example, comparison or contrast, cause or effect. A straightforward definition is the following:

Science is a method of knowledge that arose and first proved its usefulness within the realms of mechanics, physics, and chemistry. In essence it is remarkably simple. The first step is to discover the pertinent facts. Next, you make a guess as to the law which accounts for these facts. And finally, you test the correctness of this guess by experiment. If your experiments do not verify the first guess, you admit that you were wrong, and make another guess. And so on, until you have found a piece of demonstrable knowledge, or demonstrated that the truth with regard to that particular matter is so far unknown.[20]

24c. Combine various methods of developing the topic sentence when they are necessary and appropriate.

You can write clear and effective paragraphs by developing topics according to one of the methods described above. On the other hand, frequently not only is it impossible to eliminate the overlapping of some of the methods, but doing so would be illogical and undesirable. As seen in some of the illustrations, the use of several methods is effective; in fact, a few of the methods virtually require the use of others. An analysis of many well-written paragraphs, therefore, shows that the method of development cannot be rigidly exclusive; the important point is not to be limited to any particular method but to achieve adequate development of the topic.

The following student-written paragraph has elements of contrast, descriptive details, and example:

Nature is a true artist. To have the skill of an artist is surely worthy of esteem, but in my opinion no person will ever be the artist that Nature is.

[19] "Has Electricity Lightened the Housewife's Work?" A one-paragraph theme by Diane Bosse, Purdue University student. From *Indiana English Leaflet,* February, 1955.
[20] From Hugh Stevenson Tigner, "The Pretensions of Science," *The Christian Century,* September 14, 1938.

Nature has the advantage of possessing skill and originality, whereas people can do nothing but copy the works of Nature. The four seasons of the year provide a variety of subjects for the artist to work with: the fresh, bright greens of the grass, buds, and leaves in spring, the lavish multi-varied colors of the flowers in summer, the gorgeous red, yellow, and brown leaves of the autumn season, and the delicate lacework etchings of Jack Frost on the window panes in winter. These are all among the subject-models which Nature gives the human artist to choose from. When such an artist attempts to duplicate the colors and designs of Nature's subjects, he finds it impossible to duplicate them exactly. True, he may come close, but it seems that some slight or even major difference is always evident between the original works of Nature and the copies made by the human hand.

Not infrequently a single topic is developed in a series of paragraphs. To establish a certain statement, several expanded illustrations may be given, each in a separate paragraph. Similarly, a series of paragraphs may support the truth of a major division or topic; one may give the causes; one may give the effects. Such a series usually results from the writer's desire to make materials convenient to the reader, as opposed to one long, complicated paragraph, and to attain clearness and effectiveness.

After practice you will find choice and use of the various methods of paragraph development to be easy. Since the purpose in writing paragraphs is to develop paragraphs adequately and to let the reader see exactly and fully the developed ideas contained in expressed or implied topic sentences, the names of development methods are of little importance. The test of the content of a paragraph is clear and effective communication.

24d. Avoid developing paragraphs with hazy generalizations.

Adequate content consists of definite, concrete ideas, impressions, reflections, and observations. Generalizations are frequently trite, vague, and ineffective. Note the lack of worth-while content in this student-written paragraph:

Cheating never pays. After all, "honesty is the best policy"; also when one gets something for nothing he does not appreciate it. I think that every student should be on his own, even if his "own" is not good enough for him to pass his course. One should be honest, no matter what the cost. The student who thinks cheating is a sin only when it is detected is fooling nobody but himself. Sooner or later, his sins will find him out, and he will have nobody but himself to blame.

After revision the paragraph attained greater effectiveness through the use of specific illustration:

Cheating does not pay. A friend of mine, whose identity I shall conceal by merely calling him J., thought that it did. He frequently said to me in high school: "Why should I study when it is so easy to get the desired results without work? The only sin in cheating is being caught." And so J. was dishonest all through his four years at school. But when he took the college board examinations, he could not cheat because of the nature of the questions and the efficiency of the proctors. He failed, and was bitterly disappointed, since he wanted very badly to enter — University. As he read his letter of failure, he was convinced that cheating does not pay, that it is not a substitute for honest hard work.

24e. Avoid meaningless, ineffective repetition of the topic sentence.

Repeating the topic sentence in different words is a device auxiliary to other methods of paragraph development, but no matter how varied the words, it is rarely used as the major method. Repetition which adds nothing new is merely thought going round in circles. Note the inadequacy of this repetitious paragraph:

Some people pay too much attention to their diet. They spend hours every day wondering if they should eat this or that. They are too concerned about their digestive processes. One would think their greatest concern was low-calorie food, and their talk shows that it is. Diet is not nearly so important as these people think it is; it's the amount they eat. Paying so much attention to diet does not warrant so much concern. They just pay too much attention to it.

Repetition, to be effective, should add clearness and should expand and develop the idea by specific details or other methods. Note the effective use of repetition in the following student-written example:

The residents of our town can look toward the future and say that they are proud to live here. Why can they be proud? Why are they proud now? They are proud because there are no large industries in Scotch Plains! They are proud because there are no cheap housing developments in Scotch Plains! They are proud because there are no dirty railroads in Scotch Plains! They are proud because there are no degrading slums in Scotch Plains! The town is more than a town of houses. It is a town of homes!

24

EXERCISES

A. Write 14 sentences which you would like to develop into paragraphs. Compose these topic sentences so that you could develop two paragraphs using (1) particulars and details, (2) illustration or example, (3) comparison or contrast, (4) division, (5) causes or effects, (6) reasons and inferences, (7) definition.

B. Choose seven of the topic sentences (Exercise A) and write seven paragraphs, one illustrating each of the methods listed.

C. From your reading, select two paragraphs which illustrate each of the methods of development discussed in Section 24b.

D. Develop each of the following topic sentences, each paragraph to illustrate a method of development listed in Exercise A:

1. Saturday night is a busy time in our town.
2. Driving on icy roads is dangerous.
3. My favorite spectator sport (activity sport) is ___.
4. Smoking cigarettes is a harmful habit.
5. Is courtesy to women a custom of the past?
6. Living in a dormitory (fraternity, sorority) is preferable to living in a private home (fraternity, sorority).
7. I have had an embarrassing encounter with the police.
8. Girls seem to be better students in English than boys.
9. What is a good student?
10. My grandfather (or someone else) is a "character."
11. Several aids to correct spelling are ___.
12. I admire (dislike) my roommate for his (her) ___.
13. There are numerous ways to earn money at college.
14. A large college has more advantages (disadvantages) than a small college.
15. The greatest need of my home town is ___.
16. We need longer (shorter) vacations.
17. An engineer and a mechanic are not exactly the same.
18. Many mistakes are made because of ignorance (or carelessness).
19. "A practical joke" and "a mean trick" are different.
20. Experience is a good but an expensive teacher.

E. Directions given in D.

1. Most lectures are forgotten in a day or so.
2. Grandfather's generation lived a happier life than ours does.
3. A telephone contributes to the conveniences (inconveniences) of living.

4. The future of America depends upon the proper use of atomic energy (or the proper conservation of its oil, soil, water, manpower, inventive ingenuity, etc.).
5. The era of the small independent farmer is (is not) passing.
6. A vast difference exists (does not exist) between sports and athletics (or between amateur and professional athletics).
7. Television and radio are distinctly 20th-century forms of entertainment.
8. An effective use of connectives reveals more clearly than anything else a writer's mastery of his material.
9. I believe that ___ is the most interesting magazine published in America today.
10. A man's best friend is his ___.
11. College is a poor (good) place in which to get an education.
12. I offer three solutions to the problem of the increase in traffic fatalities.
13. My last summer vacation was one that I shall long remember.
14. Here are directions for ___.
15. Atomic energy will change our daily life in many ways.
16. The view from the top of ___ is one of sheer beauty (fascinating interest).
17. What is an honor system in campus life?
18. A good theme is characterized by ___.
19. Getting involved in campus activities (politics) brings complex results.
20. The end of the week is a pleasant (unpleasant) time for the college student.

F. Study the following paragraphs. Choose the topic sentence or topic statement of each, or phrase the topic if it is merely implied. Identify the dominant method of paragraph development. What other methods are used in addition to the main method? Is a combination of methods used, with no one method outstanding?

1. His daily life was of a curious microscopic sort, his whole world being limited to a circuit of a few feet from his person. His familiars were creeping and winged things, and they seemed to enroll him in their band. Bees hummed around his ears with an intimate air, and tugged at the heath and furze-flowers at his side in such numbers as to weigh them down to the sod. The strange amber-coloured butterflies which Egdon produced, and which were never seen elsewhere, quivered in the breath of his lips, alighted upon his bowed back, and sported with the glittering point of his hook as he flourished it up and down. Tribes of emerald-green grasshoppers leaped over his feet, falling awkwardly on their backs, heads, or hips, like unskilful acrobats, as chance might rule, or engaged themselves in noisy flirtations

under the fern-fronds with silent ones of homely hue. Huge flies, ignorant of larders and wire-netting, and quite in a savage state, buzzed about him without knowing that he was a man. In and out of the fern-dells snakes glided in their most brilliant blue and yellow guise, it being the season immediately following the shedding of their old skins, when their colours are brightest. Litters of young rabbits came out from their forms to sun themselves upon hillocks, the hot beams blazing through the delicate tissue of each thin-fleshed ear, and firing it to a blood-red transparency in which the veins could be seen.[21]

2. The first requirement for logical discourse is knowing what the words you use actually mean. Words are not like paper money or counters in a game. Except for technical terms in some of the sciences, they do not have a fixed face value. Their meanings are fluid and changing, influenced by many considerations of context and reference, circumstance and association. This is just as true of common words such as *fast* as it is of literary terms such as *romantic*. Moreover, if there is to be communication, words must have approximately the same meaning for the reader that they have for the writer. A speech in an unknown language means nothing to the hearer. When an adult speaks to a small child or an expert to a layman, communication may be seriously limited by lack of a mature vocabulary or ignorance of technical terms. Many arguments are meaningless because the speakers are using important words in quite different senses.[22]

3. In many circles the notion of death seems to be more tolerable to the human consciousness if the verb *to die* is not spoken in reference to this most unpleasant and most unaesthetic of all the phenomena of life. Miss [Louise] Pound has collected an impressive list of substitutions in her "American Euphemisms for Dying, Death, and Burial," published in *American Speech* for October, 1936, among them such fine growths as "laid down his burden," "the golden cord is severed," "breathed his last," "called to his reward," "gathered to his fathers," "the Angel of Death claimed him," "her frail tabernacle drifted away," "called to Jesus," "he has left a vacant chair," "his clock has run down," "slipped into the great democracy of the dead," "safe in the arms of Jesus," "passed within the pearly gates," "gone to the Great Adventure," "the bell rang and he went," and "at five o'clock in the morning she plumed the wings of her soul and took her flight to glory." Miss Pound concludes that "one of mankind's gravest problems is to avoid a straightforward mention of dying or burial."[23]

[21] From *The Return of the Native*, by Thomas Hardy.

[22] From Robert Gorham Davis, "Logic and Logical Fallacies," *Handbook for English.*

[23] From *Words and Ways of American English*, by Thomas Pyles. Copyright, 1952, by Random House, Inc.

4. A somewhat more subtle kind of personal attack is the *innuendo,* which differs from the direct accusation roughly as a hint differs from a plain statement. It is chiefly useful where there are no facts to give even a semblance of support to a forthright charge. The writer or speaker therefore slyly plants seeds of doubt or suspicion in the reader's or listener's mind without saying anything that he could be forced to retract later. Innuendo is a trick that is safe, effective, and dirty. It is a favorite weapon of the gossip. "They were parked for an hour with the lights out." The statement, in itself, may be entirely true; but what counts is the implication it is meant to convey. The unfairness is compounded when the doubts that the innuendo raises concern matters that have nothing to do with the issue anyway. An example of the irrelevant innuendo is found in the writings of the historian Charles A. Beard. In assailing the ideas of another historian, Admiral Alfred T. Mahan, Beard referred to him as "the son of a professor and swivel chair tactician at West Point" who " served respectably, but without distinction, for a time in the navy," and "found an easy berth at the Naval War College." Actually, the occupation of Mahan's father has nothing to do with the validity of the son's arguments; but observe the sneer—which is meant to be transferred from father to son—in "professor" and "swivel chair tactician." Beard's reference to Mahan's naval record is a good elementary instance of damning with faint praise. And whether or not Mahan's was "an easy berth" at the Naval War College (that is a matter of opinion), it too has no place in a discussion of the man's ideas.[24]

5. The real attraction of skiing is probably the fact that it is a magnificent form of escape. For those great numbers of Americans who are too deeply mired in the complexities of present-day society to attempt permanent simplification of their lives, skiing offers a brief, uninhibited respite. The sensation of complete freedom, both physical and mental, that overcomes a skier while flying down a mountainside can be almost miraculous. For a short space of time his life is his private property, dependent on no time schedules, restricted not one whit by his own intellectual limitations or by those of others. His whole being is absorbed in what he is doing and in where he is doing it, and both considerations are physical. In the concentration essential to the moment, the past of desk calendars, time clocks, phone calls, social forms, train schedules, personal relationships, self-examinations, and world idiocies is blotted out; and the only perceivable future is involved with the pine tree that marks the turn ahead. The sensation of grace and speed, independent of devices, that a skier feels while competing with nature and with

[24] From *Preface to Critical Reading,* 4th ed., by Richard D. Altick. Copyright, 1960, by Holt, Rinehart and Winston, Inc.

himself may be elusive, and it may end abruptly with a crash into the under-brush, but once felt it gains a grip which again and again brings him out of his cave and up to the timberline in winter.[25]

UNITY (ONENESS)

25. Unity, defined in Section 10, applies to the theme (Section 10), the paragraph, and the sentence (Section 34). A paragraph, consisting of a series of related sentences, should develop consistently the larger idea, the topic, binding these sentences together. If a paragraph contains substance, no matter how excellent, which is irrelevant to the central thought, it is not unified. Two standard tests for unity, whether the writing be a theme, a paragraph, or a sentence: (1) *omit* all material which is not an essential, logical part; (2) *include* all material which is an essential, logical part.

25a. Omit material not related to the main thought of the paragraph.

Material unrelated to the topic which is the subject of the paragraph should be omitted or placed in another paragraph where it does belong. In planning and writing, you will find that your mind does not always work logically and that frequently unrelated ideas will occur to you, or you may inadvertently shift to related materials which may be interesting and necessary but which should be placed in a separate paragraph. Test each idea by asking, Does this material refer to the thought contained in the expressed or implied topic sentence? If it does not, exclude the material from your paragraph; its inclusion will both confuse and irritate your reader in his attempt to see what the relationship is. Let each paragraph develop and convey one idea, its own idea—and no other.

The italicized sentences in the following violate paragraph unity:

Lake-of-the-Woods is an excellent place for the sportsman to spend the summer. If you like to fish, there are all kinds of fresh-water fish to be found, the most common of which is the pike. A few miles away, up in the mountains, the streams are filled with brook trout. *For people who like to winter-fish, there is ice-fishing nearly every day.* People who are fishing there for the first time can obtain guides, leaving the town early in the

[25] From Eric Swenson, "Let Fly Downhill," *Harper's Magazine,* January, 1948.

morning before the weather gets hot and returning in the cool of the evening.

Thanksgiving is always a happy time at my home. *This is the time of year to be thankful for all the things we have in this country. Thanksgiving was first started by the Pilgrims during the time of the foundation of our country. The Pilgrims left England in September, 1620, and arrived at Plymouth in November. They had a long, hard winter; many died. But the following year was prosperous, and in gratitude to God they celebrated the first Thanksgiving with prayers and a bountiful feast. They invited many Indians to the feast.* At Thanksgiving our family is always together for at least one time during the year. Sometimes we have friends in for dinner; at other times we have a large family reunion. When all of the relatives are present, everyone has a wonderful time.

25b.   Include all material necessary for adequate development of the topic sentence.

Lacking adequate thought and careful consideration, a paragraph may be brief and underdeveloped (see "Revision," Section 30). Two or three sentences, at the most, supposedly give full development to the topic. Obviously, such paragraphs lack unity; being too short and underdeveloped, they omit a number of important ideas and details necessary to clear, adequate treatment of the topic of the paragraph (Section 24b).

The following paragraph is representative of this kind. The writer omitted material with which, presumably, he wanted to prove the statement in the second sentence:

When you do your own freezing at home and grow your own fruits and vegetables, the cost is very little as compared to the frozen food in the stores. It's no wonder why the 4-H clubs in Ohio are the largest in the United States.

The paragraph might have been revised and expanded:

When you grow your own fruits and vegetables and do your own freezing at home, the cost is very little compared to the cost of frozen food in the stores. More and more Ohio families have learned the truth of this statement, and not only on farms but in many small towns and on vacant lots in cities, people are setting out vegetable gardens and fruit trees. The younger generation is in large part responsible; they are learning through 4-H clubs how to grow fruits and vegetables and how to freeze them. And this is only one of many 4-H activities. It's no wonder that the 4-H clubs in Ohio are the largest in the United States.

In the following, one of the two ideas forming part of the topic statement, the man's education, has not been discussed:

When chosen for the position of City Sanitary Engineer, John Harris was qualified by both education and experience. He had been assistant to the City Sanitary Engineer of Indianapolis for five years; during one of those years, when his superior was ill, he had been in sole charge. He then became a consultant for the Indiana State Conservation Commission, which was making a survey of stream pollution. Two years of private practice in Louisville followed. When our city decided that it had grown large enough to need a sanitary engineer, our City Council looked over the field of applicants carefully, and felt fortunate in obtaining the services of Mr. Harris.

In revision, this writer has three choices: omit mention of "education" as part of the topic; include in the paragraph materials developing "education"; or write a separate paragraph on "education."

25c.   **Include only enough related materials to develop and unify the paragraph.**

In contrast to the underdeveloped paragraph is the overdeveloped one. Frequently you may be tempted to expand a single paragraph to greater length than you should by including too much material, even though pertinent, suggested by the method or methods of development that you are using. Skillful use of one method or of a combination of two or more methods can guide you in including, expanding, or excluding material so as to produce a well-rounded, unified paragraph. In choosing content to achieve this purpose, check carefully to see that you have included *all* essential information, that you have left no unanswered questions to puzzle your reader, and that you have included *only* material which makes complete the discussion of your topic sentence. If you have too much additional pertinent material, consider including it in a separate paragraph.

EXERCISES

A. Show why the following paragraphs do not possess unity.

1. My name is Herbert E. Brook, Jr. I live on a small dairy farm near Colvair, Ohio. Colvair is located about 85 miles northeast of Collegeville. I

am enrolled in the School of Agriculture. I have one brother and two sisters. My older sister lives in Tucson, Arizona. My other sister is fourteen and my brother is ten. Dad is in charge of the cheese department in a dairy plant in Plymouth, Ohio. Plymouth is 12 miles from my home and has a population of 6,000. I graduated from West Township Consolidated High School, a small country school. We attend the United Church in Burr Oak, a small town between Colvair and Plymouth.

2. Greater New York City contains several main divisions. Originally, the city was confined to Manhattan Island, but it has enlarged through consolidation of other divisions. The city consists of five boroughs, Manhattan, Brooklyn, Queens, Richmond, and the Bronx. Manhattan is the heart of New York and contains its great commercial, financial, and mercantile institutions, and also its famous museums, libraries, cathedrals, railway stations, and imposing apartment houses. Brooklyn is a residential district with a large number of industrial establishments. Staten Island is mainly residential, while Queens, containing more than a third of the total area of Greater New York, is the "home" borough. Running through some of these divisions are many famous thoroughfares. The most well-known is Broadway, which is lined with fashionable shops, beautiful churches, elegant clubs, and immense hotels. Most of the great trans-Atlantic lines have their piers in the Hudson River.

3. The island of Malta lies almost in the middle of the Mediterranean Sea—55 miles from Sicily and about 150 miles from Africa. Its area is less than one hundred square miles. The island was originally all rock, no soil whatever. Legend has it that all the soil was shipped in from Sicily years ago. The island is under the control of the British. The highest point on the island is the small town of Rabat, 700 feet above sea level. Malta's strategic location made possible raids on Italian and German shipping to Africa, when General Rommel's German forces were in Egypt and Tunisia. This was during World War II. The population is mainly Italian. They remained loyal to the British during the war. The poet Samuel Taylor Coleridge was for a time the Secretary to the Governor of Malta. He wrote the famous poem, "The Rime of the Ancient Mariner," about how a sailor was accursed because he killed an albatross. Coleridge planned to come to America and establish a happy colony on the banks of the Susquehanna River. He died in 1834.

B. Write constructive advice for the student authors of the following paragraphs. Show them why their paragraphs lack unity and give suggestions for unifying and developing each.

1. There are many superstitions all over the world. In some foreign countries like New Guinea, superstitions have more meaning to the people than they do here in the United States. Many people believe in superstitions to the extent that they would stake their lives on them. However, the other group of people disbelieve in superstitions. I am one of these people who disbelieve them, and I am proceeding to tell why I do.

2. My first horse was a beautiful animal that I liked and had a lot of fun with. I bought her from a man who was tired of taking care of her. She was named Nancy and was a three-year-old thoroughbred. She was reddish-brown in color and had a black mane and tail. Nancy did not know how to do any tricks, but she did obey me all the time. She was a fast horse and could run for a long distance without becoming tired.

3. Living on a farm has encouraged my interest in 4-H. During my nine years of 4-H work, I have taken nearly every project offered. Through 4-H I have met many wonderful friends; 4-H members are considered as top quality future leaders. In our county it is very seldom that a 4-H member is found guilty of robbing the local drug store or knocking over stop signs.

4. Aunt Allie was an eccentric person. She kept honey bees and was never stung. She used oil lamps when everyone else used electricity. She was afraid of automobiles. She never married, but lived with her brother for many years. He was also unmarried, and like Aunt Allie had peculiar ways. He started going with a girl many years ago, and they are still going together. He had a large bank account, and yet he never hired anyone to help him with his chores. All in all, Aunt Allie really was eccentric.

5. One of the signs of spring is the return of the birds. They begin to fly and flutter about with the happiness of a little boy who is seeing a circus for the first time. He dreams of its coming for weeks, and the night before it arrives, he cannot sleep a wink. He arouses the rest of the family at daybreak and wants to arrive at the circus before there are any signs of life there. Their mating and courting calls fill the air with the harmonious sounds which they only know how to make. Soon they are busily building their nests and preparing for their families of the future.

ORDER

26. With full, interesting, unified material, an important problem is *arrangement,* since excellent content will lose effectiveness if paragraph sentences are incorrectly and illogically arranged.

26a.   Arrange sentences in a paragraph in clear sequence.

Hasty and inaccurate thinking causes a lack of paragraph unity and may also result in a disorderly arrangement of sentences. Because your mind does not always work logically, you may write ideas as they occur to you, as they flow or drift into your stream of consciousness; you may illogically place ideas ahead of the place where they belong, or forget them and add them later in the paragraph. Anyone who has attempted to tell a long story or who has heard one told ("Oh, I should have said" or "I forgot to say") knows how easy it is to get ideas arranged in the wrong order. Give each idea and each sentence a definite position in the arrangement; make each sentence lead clearly to the one that follows. Keep related parts together; finish one part of the thought before you begin another.

26b.   Make the arrangement of sentences show clear progress or a clear forward movement.

Arrangement of sentences requires progress, a forward movement of some sort. The thought must go from some place to some other place. For such forward movement, sentences may be arranged according to certain kinds of order:

1. *Chronological* (time) *order,* as in much narrative writing, expository processes, and some descriptions—all of which progress as the writer changes his temporal point of view. That is, one sentence follows another in the order that the events discussed followed one another in time. (See Section 16a.)

2. *Space order,* as in some descriptions, in which details are arranged according to the position they have in space: from near to remote, or remote to near; from outside to inside, or from inside to outside; from left to right, or from right to left. (See Section 16b.)

3. *Order of logic,* as in some exposition and argument, in which the writer makes a general statement and then supplies details to support it; or he presents a series of details for particular statements, all of which lead up to a generalized statement at the end of the paragraph (inductive method); or he makes a general statement or conclusion and then applies it in the succeeding sentences to a particular instance or example (deductive method); or he states a cause and shows what its results or effects are; or he states an effect or result and shows what its causes or origins are. For examples, see Section 24b5.

26c. Arrange sentences in a paragraph in effective order.

Order in the paragraph involves not only clearness but effectiveness. Among many others which you can discover from your own reading, three effective methods of arranging sentences within the paragraph are the following:

1. *Beginning and ending as effective positions.* Ordinarily, sentences developing the most important idea of the paragraph should be placed at the beginning or the end. The most trenchant statement of the paragraph should not be embedded somewhere in the middle. First and last impressions of paragraphs, as of sentences and of people, are genuinely important.

2. *Order of climax.* When various ideas are arranged in an ascending order of importance or strength, with the most important thought placed at the end, the arrangement is called order of climax. The reader reads on, lured by the prospect of a concluding, climactic statement.

Study the following examples for their use of climax. The first contains three ideas or "adjustments," moving from the least important to the most important. The second, a 121-word one-sentence paragraph, contains a series of important statements building up to a decisive conclusion.

My first week on the campus I had three adjustments to make. The first and most minor was being away from home. Previously I had never been away from home for any period longer than a week. Not having any brothers and sisters, I was always very close to Mother and Father, and here I had to overcome any fear of homesickness. My second adjustment was learning to be on my own. In the past Mother and Father had always helped me with all my decisions. Now that I was 200 miles away from home, I had no way of asking them about every little problem that came up; I had to solve each for myself. The third and greatest adjustment I had to make was living with someone else. After meeting my roommate, I discovered that we were nothing alike. Our sleeping, eating, and studying habits were completely different. By consideration and cooperation, we have solved this problem reasonably well, but it has been the hardest of the three adjustments for me to make.

—Student theme

So, after four years of seeing everything there is to see in big-time college football—victories, defeats, publicity, hospitals, championships, and bowls—of being known as a "football player" rather than a human being, of seeing myself and my teammates misrepresented and misquoted by sportswriters who seldom attempted to know the players personally, of playing in a 97,000-seat stadium in which my nonpaying student friends were forced to sit in the end zone, of having my natural desire for physical exercise corrupted and commercialized, of giving up pleasant afternoons in favor of kicking and rolling in the dust and muck of the practice field— I have decided that big-time football is a poor bargain for the boys who play the game.[26]

—ALLEN JACKSON, "Too Much Football"

If you fail to keep something in reserve, if you fully inform your reader in advance what your statement implies, appropriate as that method is for certain kinds of writing, you lose the effectiveness that climactic arrangement affords.

3. *Order of choice.* When several ideas, related and coordinate, are presented in one paragraph, and when neither of the preceding methods applies, choose the order of arrangement which you believe your designated reader will find interesting and attractive. For example, on subjects like "three ways to study," or "three places to eat," or "three reasons for joining *x* organization"—whether developed in one paragraph or in three paragraphs—the ideas, if of equal importance, can be presented in an order which you believe is best. Such order could be called the order of psychological interest; that is, material is so arranged that it is effective and has interest appeal both for you as writer and for your reader or readers.

A clear order is usually an effective order. Any distinction is arbitrary, made here for the purposes of discussion. Most well-developed paragraphs show both clear and effective order.

EXERCISES

A. Write three topic sentences for which the development will emphasize clearness according to the respective methods mentioned in Section,26b. Write the paragraphs.

B. Write three topic sentences, one each for development emphasizing effectiveness according to the respective methods mentioned in Section 26c. Write the paragraphs.

[26] From *The Atlantic Monthly,* October, 1951.

C. Show why the order of sentences in the following paragraph is neither clear nor effective:

Since this is a theme on dictionaries, I have looked up some material on dictionaries and their background. The first dictionary aiming to give a complete collection of English words was published in 1721 by Nathan Bailey, and was called *The Universal Etymological English Dictionary*. This book was also the first in English to trace the derivation of words and to mark the accents as an aid to pronunciation. The greatest American lexicographer was Noah Webster. His dictionary was published in 1828 and has been repeatedly revised. It provided features such as illustrations, synonyms, abbreviations, and other helpful additions. The earliest Greek and Latin dictionaries did not contain all of the words of the language, but instead contained the more difficult words and phrases. Samuel Johnson published a dictionary in London in 1755; he had married a woman some twenty years older than he was. A pronouncing dictionary was prepared by Thomas Sheridan; he was the father of Richard Brinsley Sheridan, who wrote a number of plays and gave some speeches in Parliament. The earliest dictionary was written in the seventh century B.C. and was printed on clay tablets. The dates and specific information about these dictionaries were taken from a reference book I have.

D. In the following paragraph, the sentences have been jumbled. Rewrite the paragraph with the sentences in an order which makes sense.

1. Compounding terms to make new words is the most popular method of enlarging a vocabulary. 2. Two words can also be combined to produce new words such as typewriter, blackbird, and schoolhouse. 3. This method of compounding is more useful as a means of word development because the components of the word are known and the new concept is more easily grasped. 4. As a third example, television is a new development but the components of the word have been in existence for centuries. 5. The resulting word means under the water, but its meaning is restricted to this type of underwater vessel. 6. From the word "intend," which is a French loan word, we are able to make a dozen or more commonly used terms: intended, intentional, intentionally, unintentional, unintended, are only a few possibilities. 7. A second example: When the underwater ship was developed, it was named by taking the word "marine," which pertains to the sea, and attaching the prefix "sub," which means under. 8. The English language has a vast number of prefixes and suffixes that can alter the meanings of a basic word.

PROPORTION

27. Paragraphs having adequate content, unity, and correct order of sentences need right proportion also. One paragraph should not, through its writer's carelessness or thoughtlessness, be made unduly long, another unduly short. Proportion means that the ideas in a paragraph are developed according to their importance and that all paragraphs are planned and written carefully and thoughtfully in relation to one another and to the whole theme.

27a. Make sure that paragraphs are properly proportioned.

In writing a theme of 500 words, a student may compose a long introductory paragraph, follow with a transitional paragraph, and have left only 100 words or so for the final paragraph containing the actual *theme,* the central idea, the purpose for which the paper was written. Such writing, obviously, is badly proportioned.

If a paragraph contains discussion of a proportionately important idea, its length is greater than that of a paragraph which develops a comparatively minor topic. Occasionally, the inclusion of many or important details may need greater space, but readers are likely to attribute importance to ideas according to the length of the paragraphs in which they are discussed.

In general, therefore, do not expand ideas relatively subordinate or treat sketchily ideas of fundamental importance. Between these two extremes of overexpansion and underdevelopment is a golden mean: the writing of paragraphs which adequately deal with their topics and which, added together, give a unified, well-proportioned discussion of the subject.

27b. Achieve proportion through careful planning.

Correct proportion demands careful planning. If you dwell at length upon some part of the theme because you are interested in that part or know it thoroughly, you may not be taking into account its importance in relation to the reader. To achieve correct paragraph proportion, consider the relation of the paragraph to the whole subject, and also your reader's reaction. Study the following suggestions:

→1. Consider the subject as a whole before writing an individual paragraph.

→2. Think of the reader; determine the central purpose which each paragraph is to have in communicating ideas to him.

→3. Assign tentatively the number of words you believe will adequately develop each paragraph (see Section 7b). As you write, you need not be rigidly bound by your allotment; it is only a planning guide.

→4. Shorten paragraphs if they are out of proportion in relation to the subject and the reader, even though they contain favorite ideas and their revision will sacrifice proudly written, precious words.

→5. Lengthen paragraphs if they contain ideas that need amplification, illustration, or repetition, so that their significance may be seen by the reader.

EXERCISES

A. Study one of the articles in your book of readings. Comment upon it as an illustration of paragraph proportion.

B. Choose three to five topics for 500-word themes and estimate the proportionate importance of the several developing paragraphs.

C. Indicate the number of words proportionately correct for each paragraph of a 500-word theme based on a theme subject, "Learning to —." Follow or adapt this plan:

Learning to Swim

1. Correct mental attitude for the beginner.
2. Correct body position.
3. How to handle the arms.
4. How to handle the feet.
5. How to breathe.
6. Errors to be avoided.
7. Summary.

LENGTH

28. Paragraph length, like proportion, is determined by the purpose of the writer and by the relative importance of the thought unit that the paragraph embraces. In present-day writing, paragraphs tend to be short, perhaps because of the influence of advertising materials, news stories, business letters, and the desire to have the reader obtain ideas by a swift eye-sweep of one sentence to three or four sentences. No specific rule, therefore, for paragraph length can be laid down, save the principle of importance and the principle of appropriateness (see Section 29).

28a. Avoid a short, underdeveloped paragraph.

At times short paragraphs are necessary, effective, and appropriate. Aside from such purposes, however, a short paragraph is usually an underdeveloped paragraph—much to the confusion and dissatisfaction of the reader. Too often some students take neither time nor trouble to study the topic and means of development and to expand the paragraph sufficiently. Instead, they are unwisely content to let two or three short sentences serve for what they consider adequate treatment. Each of the following, telling little about the key word or paragraph topic, italicized, is an example of such a short, underdeveloped paragraph:

The *curriculum* in the School of Home Economics is largely basic, for students follow the same plan of study for the first two years. At the beginning of the third year, you have the opportunity to choose the option in which you are most interested.

We met *several interesting people* as we walked up and down the Miami beach. Often we would meet someone from home. Once we met the daughter of the mayor of Caracas.

28b. Avoid a series of short, choppy paragraphs.

A series of short, choppy paragraphs is usually a sign that a writer has not thought carefully about analyzing his topic sentence and has not developed fully and clearly the central idea of each paragraph, or that he has failed to see the relationship of ideas and has divided into several paragraphs what should have been united into one of greater length.

Note the choppy, disconcerting effect of the following short paragraphs:

I admit 10 acres are big for a garden, but I had grandiose ideas about getting money to help me on my college career.

As my various vegetables came on, I was happy. Every morning at an early hour I arose and set out for Louisville.

Louisville has a large farmers' market, and I wanted to be among the first traders there.

I arrived there before most people were awake and had my produce neatly arranged before the housewives set out to market.

Because my vegetables were fresh and attractively displayed, I usually had little difficulty in selling them.

Sometimes on rainy days people were slower in arriving and buying. By noon of each day, however, on the average, I had completed my sales and returned to my gardens.

Then I worked in the fields until sunset, and spent the rest of the evening preparing for the next day's market.

Thanks to the long hard days and nights I put in, I am able to finance my first two years in college.

To correct such short paragraphs, a writer should follow one of two suggestions: (1) review and apply the methods of analysis and expansion discussed in Section 24, or (2) examine his paragraphs which precede or follow; perhaps with minor revisions these can be combined into a paragraph of adequate length.

Short paragraphs and series of short paragraphs are not always to be avoided. They may be correctly used for emphasis and they have other appropriate uses. In description or narration, short paragraphs often aid in achieving a vigorous, emphatic style; they are necessary in dialogue to indicate change of speakers; they are appropriate in business letters. But very short paragraphs should not be written except for definite purposes or effects.

28c. Avoid a group of long, uninteresting-looking paragraphs.

A series of very long paragraphs is likely to strain your reader's attention. It is better to furnish him with an occasional paragraph break which will afford an opportunity to catch his breath and summarize the thought. Moreover, very long paragraphs may contain material which does not properly belong in them; they thus violate the principle of unity (see Section 25). Usually it is difficult to write an effectively unified paragraph of over 250 or 300 words.

When paragraphs are unduly long, it is often possible to break each one, at logical dividing places, into two or more shorter paragraphs without violation of unity, provided that appropriate transitional words or phrases are used.

28d. **Choose long or short paragraphs in accordance with your central purpose.**

Do not avoid either long or short paragraphs, but use them according to the proportionate value of the thought units they express. It is only a *series* of either that may prove ineffective. Writers today tend to use shorter paragraphs than formerly, but in scholarly or technical papers paragraphs still run to considerable length. In popular magazines and newspapers the average length is about 100 words or even fewer. The use of long or short paragraphs, or a compromise between the two, is often a matter of convention and appropriateness. (See Section 29.)

You might well give consideration, therefore, to this advice from the Modern Language Association *Style Sheet:* "For the sake of both appearance and emphasis, avoid writing many very short or very long paragraphs, especially in sequence. Remember that brief paragraphs on your typed page will usually look even briefer in print." Also, brief paragraphs in longhand look even shorter when typewritten.

EXERCISES

A. Compare the average length of paragraphs in an article in *The Atlantic Monthly* or *Harper's Magazine* with the average length of those in an article in *The Saturday Evening Post.*

B. Read some of the articles in an issue of *The National Geographic Magazine.* Count or estimate the average number of words in the paragraphs. Can you account for the appropriateness of paragraphs of such brevity?

C. In your book of readings or in a magazine or two magazines, choose two articles: one using very short paragraphs and one using paragraphs averaging at least four or five sentences. Prepare a paper comparing the clearness, effectiveness, and appropriateness of the paragraphing in the two articles.

D. Count the number of words in five consecutive paragraphs of some article in your book of readings. How many words in the longest paragraph? In the shortest? What is the average? Repeat this exercise for another article by a different writer. Make a comparison of the two.

E. Compare the number of words in the opening three or four paragraphs of several articles in your book of readings.

F. Compare the number of words in the closing three or four paragraphs of several articles in your book of readings.

G. Ascertain the average length of the paragraphs in a newspaper news

28

story. What effects are achieved by the brief paragraphs? Repeat this exercise with another newspaper, and make a comparison.

H. What written advice concerning paragraphing would you give to students who write themes like the following:

(1)   My Plans for Christmas Vacation

The trip from the University to my home in Sierra Bay, California, takes about one day by airplane; therefore, I will have to leave the University about a day early in order to reach home by Christmas Eve.

You might be wondering why I live in Sierra Bay, California.

That is a good question.

The reason I live in Sierra Bay is that my father is an assistant professor of mathematics at a technical college there.

After my vacation is over, I will return to the University about the same way I went home, except that I will take the train.

I hope this will be a very enjoyable vacation.

I am looking forward to it.

(2)   A Scenic Trip to Blue Mountain State Park

A trip to Blue Mountain State Park had been planned for the Young People's Club of our community. We awaited the day.

Finally the day arrived, beautiful and sunny. Our last-minute tasks were to prepare the lunches for everyone. We prepared much extra food, and we enjoyed it.

We packed all the food into the cars and started. We laughed, enjoyed the scenery, and were sure of a very good time.

We found a very nice cabin in which to eat, and we soon had the food on the tables. After we had eaten what we desired, we rested before ascending the hills and pacing down the trails.

We climbed many hills and walked on a few trails. We had plenty of excitement on this hike because someone was always falling into a mud hole or stumbling down a hill.

Soon it was time for our return trip, and we had to say good-by to this happy day at Blue Mountain State Park.

(3)   Where I Live

The town in which I live is named Mooseheart. It was named Mooseheart because it was built in the shape of a moose's heart.

This year Mooseheart celebrates its one hundredth birthday.

In Mooseheart we have one high school, three junior high schools, and numerous grade schools. We also have five recreational parks.

Another thing which we have in Mooseheart is a large number of factories. These factories provide a large amount of the employment for the city's population of 40,000.

The one thing that Mooseheart is probably the most famous for is its medicine laboratory. This is where vitamin pills and many other pharmaceutical products are made.

Another thing that Mooseheart is famous for is that it has the largest high school gym in the world.

And still another thing for which Mooseheart is famous is that it has one of the biggest switching railroad yards in the United States.

One thing that makes up Mooseheart's beauty is its many rivers which surround the city on all sides. They wind and join in the shape of a moose's heart.

All the aforementioned things are the good and beautiful aspects of our town. But like all towns there are a few skeletons in its closet. Some of these I will try to expose.

For instance, Mooseheart has a bad slum area on the east side of the city.

Another is the high rate of juvenile crimes. Which I think connects with the third fault of the city.

The third fault is that there is not enough supervised recreation for the teen-agers.

In this paper I have tried to paint a picture of Mooseheart by telling of its good points and some of its bad points.

APPROPRIATENESS

29. The normal paragraph or series of paragraphs develops the various phases or divisions of a subject, and each is unified by being built around a specific topic, especially in description, exposition, and argumentation; other paragraphs—having brevity or length, or consisting of loosely related or even single statements—perform special functions. The following suggestions concern the appropriateness of such paragraphs.

29a. Use short paragraphs in writing dialogue or recording conversations.

In *writing dialogue* or *recording conversations,* use a separate paragraph for each speaker's words. Most of these paragraphs will be short, some very short. Such is conventional practice, although you may find several separate speeches included in one paragraph—to the possible confusion of the reader.

The following illustrates short speeches of dialogue:

Larry spooned a generous portion onto his plate, speared a piece of beef, and lifted it to his mouth.

"How is it?" asked Polly.

"Pretty good," said Larry.

"Only pretty good?"

"I mean it's wonderful."

"How wonderful?"

"If you served it to a maharajah, he'd probably send you around a trunkful of rubies in the morning."[27]

—LEE ROGOW, "That Certain Flavor"

In the following example, a dialogue between a girl and a policeman, three particulars may be observed: correct paragraphing of conversation, correct paragraphing of explanatory material, and correct form for introductory and explanatory words within paragraphs which contain dialogue:

"Oh, I'm not a bad driver, really. I do like to go fast, but I'm careful. In Buffalo, where we lived before, the policemen all knew I was careful and they generally let me go as fast as I wanted to."

"This ain't Buffalo. And this ain't no speedway. If you want to go fast, stay off Fifth Avenue."

The girl looked him right in the eye. "Would you like that?"

"No," said Ben.

She smiled at him again. "What time are you through?"

"Four o'clock," said Ben.

"Well," said the girl, "some afternoon I may be going home about then—"

"I told you I wasn't ready to die."

"I'd be extra careful."

Ben suddenly realized that they were playing to a large staring audience and that, for once, he was not the star.

"Drive on!" he said in his gruffest tone. "I'm letting you go because you're a stranger, but you won't get off so easy next time."

[27] From *This Week,* April 10, 1949.

"I'm very, very grateful," said the girl. "Just the same I don't like being a stranger and I hope you won't excuse me on that ground again."[28]

—Ring Lardner, "There are Smiles"

29b. Use short paragraphs for introductory, concluding, and transitional paragraphs.

For long or fairly long papers, or long sections, a brief *introductory* paragraph is sometimes desirable, especially of the outline-beginning kind (Section 8e4). The following is an introductory paragraph listing the topics to be expanded in subsequent paragraphs:

The causes of war are psychological, biological, economic, and political —that is, they lie in the impulses of men, the competition of groups, the material needs of societies, and fluctuations of national power.[29]

Similarly, for long or fairly long papers, a brief *concluding* paragraph is sometimes desirable. For the material introduced by the example above and discussed in detail in the article, the following serves as a summary and conclusion:

These, then, are the causes of war. How natural it seems now, in the perspective of science and history; how ancient its sources and how inscrutable its destiny.[30]

For a discussion of transitional paragraphs, see Section 11.

29c. Use short paragraphs in business letters.

Paragraphs in *business letters* vary from one or two to six lines. Longer paragraphs are seldom used; short paragraphs permit the reader to get the message at a single glance, a major purpose of most business letter paragraphs. (For examples, see pp. 731–732. On 8½-x-11 business stationery, the paragraphs of the sample letters would take even fewer lines.)

29d. Use a single, complete-in-itself paragraph to develop a simple subject or a single topic.

In treating briefly *a single topic* or *a simple subject,* use only one paragraph. Such a paragraph is of course independent and complete; it is a short theme or a theme in miniature. Many newspaper editorial writers, columnists, advertising writers, magazine editors, and text-

[28] From *Roundup,* copyright, 1929, Charles Scribner's Sons.
[29] From Will Durant, "Why Men Fight," *The Saturday Evening Post,* July 10, 1937.
[30] *Ibid.*

book editors, among others, make frequent use of independent paragraphs. Examples are common in the editorial columns of newspapers; news items in newspapers; editorial or commentary paragraphs in magazines, especially the news weeklies; brief introductory notes or biographical sketches in books of readings; brief articles in encyclopedias; and narrative or expository material in semitechnical or popular science magazines.

At the beginning of the term especially, freshman English students are often required to write independent paragraphs. Later they are required to write on larger topics, and their paragraphs become units of longer compositions. Following are two examples of the independent paragraph: the first develops its topic, "free verse," by definition; the second develops its topic, "crab grass," by details.

Free verse is a type of poetry in which the line is based on the natural cadence of the voice, following the phrasing of the language, rather than a repeating metrical pattern. The rhythm of a free-verse line is marked by the grammatical and rhetorical patterns of normal speech and by the "sequence of musical phrase" (Ezra Pound). A single line of free verse will normally contain varied types of feet, and a single poem will contain lines with varying numbers of feet. Hence the poem is unconfined, "free" of the traditional repeated metrical patterns of foot and line. Free verse is never so free as prose, never really free in the sense of being formless or unrhythmical. Rather its rhythms follow a pattern more varied than that of traditional verse, moving away from and returning to certain rhythmical norms and regularities. Although most people associate free verse with modern poetry, the type is found throughout literature [beginning with] Hebrew poetry (Psalms and Song of Songs).[31]

With lawnmowing just about over for the year, it was a pleasure the other morning to find a letter in the *Tribune* in defense of crab grass. The letter was from Mr. Gilbert G. Brinckerhoff, a retired schoolteacher living in Radburn, New Jersey, and it was the first piece of original thinking we had come across in weeks. Mr. Brinckerhoff, probably alone among homeowners in the United States, has taken the pressure off crab grass and off himself: he has come up with the discovery that you can just leave the stuff alone and survive; you don't have to fight it. Brinckerhoff has developed a lawn that is one hundred per cent crab grass; not a spear of anything else mars its lovely green surface. It makes, he says, a very pre-

[31] From *The Reader's Companion to World Literature*, Lillian H. Hornstein, ed. Copyright, 1956, by The Dryden Press.

sentable lawn. What this discovery will do to the Scott Lawn Company, what steps against Brinckerhoff will be taken by an aroused citizenry of Radburn—these are subjects for conjecture. But at least there is one man in America whose energies are not flowing into silly channels and who can stand erect and look something in the face. We admire Brinckerhoff and wish him a long, indolent retirement, much of which can be spent in a rocker on the porch overlooking the weedy plain.[32]

Other examples are among the quoted paragraphs in Section 24.

29e. Use a paragraph of not too closely related sentences for a summary, conclusions, recommendations, or directions.

Many longer papers require for their rounding out and for effective endings a paragraph giving a *summary, conclusions,* or *recommendations.* Such a paragraph consists of sentences which are not too closely related; that is, as the paragraph develops, the last sentence is somewhat or even far removed from the thought of the first sentence. The same kind of paragraph is used in writing which gives certain kinds of *directions*—for example, short "how to" articles. The unifying topic of such paragraphs, usually implied, is one of the foregoing italicized words.

The following is a concluding paragraph of a student theme in which advantages and disadvantages were discussed:

Let me now summarize both sides of the problem. Phonograph records show us how poetry should be read; they help us in our comprehension of poetry; and they make class meetings more interesting. The chief disadvantage is that use of even one long-playing record allows little time for a lecture or class discussion. My conclusion is that using records in our English literature class is more beneficial and advantageous than detrimental and disadvantageous; in other words, the advantages outweigh the disadvantages.

As a good example of the summary of an entire book, study the following:

Robert Gunning, the author of *The Technique of Clear Writing,* accomplishes what he sets out to preach. This whole book is one of the best examples of clear writing written about the subject. The opening chapters tell what has been learned about the habits and preferences of readers. The

[32] From E. B. White, *The Second Tree from the Corner;* Harper & Brothers. Copyright, 1954, by E. B. White.

closing chapters review causes and cures for foggy writing in business, journalism, law, and the technical fields. The main body of the book consists of Ten Principles of Clear Writing: (1) Keep sentences short; (2) Prefer the simple to the complex; (3) Prefer the familiar words; (4) Avoid unnecessary words; (5) Put action in your verbs; (6) Write like you talk; (7) Use terms your reader can picture; (8) Tie in with your reader's experience; (9) Make full use of variety; (10) Write to express, not impress.[33]

The following is an example of a paragraph *giving directions*. The general subject was "preparing reports"; paragraphs of advice concerned selecting a topic, building a bibliography, keeping an idea page, outlining the paper in detail, and then this on the actual writing:

Write the paper; dash it off from the outline and polish it later. It is difficult to keep many things in mind as you write. Devote your initial writing efforts to getting your ideas stated; this initial draft can be gone over later in order to correct English mistakes and to put in headings, references, and footnotes. Dashing this first version off helps a writer keep his attention on his theme rather than getting lost in details, and the sentence ideas tend to flow into each other much better. Usually all needed corrections can be inserted in this first draft, but if necessary, parts can be cut out and pasted in order.[34]

29f. Use paragraphs of isolated statements to emphasize summaries, conclusions, recommendations, directions, or important statements.

For effectiveness in writing *summaries, conclusions, recommendations,* certain kinds of *directions,* or *important statements,* use paragraphs of isolated statements; that is, paragraphs consisting of single sentences or parts of sentences. Such paragraphs are frequently numbered. Their position in a theme or an article may vary: summaries may come at the beginning or end, conclusions and recommendations at the end, directions and important statements anywhere in the paper where they are most effective. Here is an example:

As a result of this investigation, our conclusions are as follows:
1. Weather conditions that morning were not suitable for flying.

---

[33] From "Reading about Writing," *Effective Letters Bulletin*, New York Life Insurance Company.

[34] From Francis P. Robinson, *Effective Study*, Harper & Brothers. Copyright, 1941, 1946.

2. The engine of this plane had mechanical defects that should have been corrected before the take-off.

3. The pilot, and owner, of the plane was comparatively inexperienced in flying under unfavorable weather conditions.

4. The Brooktown Municipal Airport authorities, since their advice and commands were ignored, should be absolved of responsibility for the accident.

Paragraphs of isolated statements sometimes come within the body of a paper or article. For example, concerning the new students who attend Freshman Week:

They are breezed through a very pleasant week—dizzying, perhaps, but new and different. They don't even have time to get homesick. That comes about two weeks later. Now, during this week, deans and advisers say many things which freshmen may, to their sorrow, ignore:

Start studying at once.

Get to know the library immediately.

Set up a schedule for yourself—revise it later if necessary—to include both social and academic activities.

Join one or two extracurricular activities, but not every one in sight.

Get enough sleep.

Don't forget chapel.

Don't cut classes.

You're on your own; make the most of your independence. But, if you get into trouble, see your adviser right away.[35]

EXERCISES

A. From a magazine or your book of readings choose a short story and examine the paragraphing of dialogue. Note how much, if any, explanatory material is included in the paragraphs giving quoted speeches.

B. Write a short paper to illustrate paragraphing and use of quotation marks (see Section 95) on the subject "A Dialogue Between — and —."

C. In an article in a magazine or in your book of readings mark all the short paragraphs (two to six lines). Determine what purpose they serve: introductory, concluding, transitional, etc.

D. Look through such magazines as *The New Yorker, Time, Newsweek, U.S. News & World Report,* or *The Reader's Digest,* for one-para-

[35] From Robert U. Jameson, "How to Stay in College," *The Saturday Evening Post,* October 2, 1954.

graph articles or discussions. Estimate their length. Find the topic sentence or statement and discuss the method or methods of paragraph development used.

E. Look for one-paragraph editorials in several newspapers. Estimate their length. Find the topic sentence or statement, and discuss the method or methods of paragraph development used.

F. Comment on the length and purpose of the paragraphs in several business letters written to you or to relatives and friends.

REVISION
30. Give time and thought to careful revision of every paragraph.

Although the preceding sections have discussed the paragraph as something separate from a theme or a longer paper, the distinction is artificial. A paragraph may be a theme, or a theme may consist of one paragraph, or two paragraphs, or many paragraphs.

The clearness and effectiveness of a theme depend upon the clearness and effectiveness of its paragraphs. Using the work-sheet method suggested on page 24, and also in Section **24a,** anyone can put on paper the words and sentences that constitute a paragraph. The real work then begins, *revision*. Every paragraph should be carefully considered in the light of the preceding sections: characteristics, mechanics, topic statements, analysis, content, unity, order, proportion, length, and appropriateness. In addition, every sentence, even every word, should be checked with the handbook advice given about sentences, diction, grammar, and punctuation.

Revision is important. Your own writing of paragraphs can be improved through study of the following illustration of revision. It consists of two versions of the same theme, revised paragraph by paragraph by the student himself in the light of constructive criticisms given by the instructor in conference with the student.[36] The two versions show how much improvement is possible when careful attention is given to paragraph detail, organization, and transitions.

As you study these revisions, keep in mind the instructor's constructive comments concerning the unrevised paper:

[36] For permission to use this material, the authors gratefully acknowledge their indebtedness to the student-author, Ronald Van Putte, his instructor, Professor William Stafford of Purdue University, and the *Indiana English Leaflet,* where this material first appeared in print.

1. On any cont.oversial subject, it is good psychology to take into account, or at least show an awareness of, what an opponent would claim for the subject.

2. Use of detail is inconsistent. Although the three main arguments are concretely illustrated, opportunities to be more convincing are lost because of vague generalities instead of facts, as in paragraphs one and three.

3. The original and most compelling of the arguments should be chosen and pointed up with the most effective composition devices possible.

4. Each paragraph should be examined and revised in the light of the foregoing and with the thought in mind that while a paragraph has a beginning, a middle, and an end much as a theme has, each paragraph here is also a part of a larger whole.

I Didn't Pledge a Fraternity

Original

I have learned from various sources about fraternities and I don't think that I should join one.

Revised

I have talked to many fraternity men and independents about fraternities. I listened to what they had to say and decided that I shouldn't join a fraternity. It is true that fraternity life has some benefits, such as living in a close-knit group, getting a feeling of responsibility, and learning the social graces. Since the disadvantages offset the advantages, however, I don't think that I should join one.

Original

Fraternity life takes up too much time. Everyone, especially the freshmen, has special jobs to do. These jobs may range from serving dinner to cutting the lawn. All of these jobs take time away from studying. The bad part about Hell-week and initiation is that it takes up the time a student should be using to build a firm foundation of studies. Although it is not supposed to, initiation takes preference over studies during Hell-week. The members of a fraternity are required to go to the various social events whether or not they desire to.

Revised

One of the disadvantages of living in a fraternity is that the extracurricular activities take up too much time. Everyone, especially the freshmen, has special jobs to do. These jobs may vary from serving dinner to cutting the lawn. All of these jobs take time away from studying. Another time-consumer is the various social functions that a member must attend, many of them whether he wants to or not. Hell-week and initiation also take valuable time—and from that crucial part of the semester when the new student should be acquiring good study habits. Little free time, then, is available to the fraternity member when he is pledging.

Original

Another one of the sore spots of fraternity life is the money problem. The cost of a fraternity is usually above that of a university-sponsored dormitory. The cost usually doesn't include the price of parties, picnics, dances, trade functions, or displays for the fraternity lawn. Fraternity life is fine for the person who has a lot of money to throw away, but a student with a limited amount of money has a tough time. He will usually break his budget and the back of his bank account.

Revised

Another one of the sore spots of fraternity life is the money problem. According to the Inter-fraternity Council, the average cost per year at a Purdue fraternity is $675. The cost of living at a university-sponsored dormitory is $630. Although $45 is not much money, it does become a major factor when the cost of parties, picnics, dances, trade functions, and lawn displays is added to it. Fraternity life is fine for the student who has a great deal of money to spend, but a student with a limited amount of money has a difficult time. He will usually break his budget and the back of his bank account if he joins a fraternity.

Original

Living in a clique may lead to prejudiced thinking. The fraternity may not allow foreign students, colored students, or students having a certain religion to pledge the fraternity. The fraternity member will not get a chance to meet these students and may get the wrong ideas about them. These rejected students will tend to cling together and worsen the problem by getting false ideas.

Revised

The most important disadvantage of living in a fraternity, however, is the effect that it may have on a person's mind. Living in a clique may lead to prejudiced thinking. The fraternity may not allow foreign students, colored students, or students having a certain religion to pledge the fraternity. The member will not get a chance to be in close contact with these people and may misinterpret their ideas and beliefs. The rejection of some students may lead to rejection of others of the same race, nationality, or religion and thus instill in the student an intolerant attitude for the rest of his life.

Original

In general, I can't see that a fraternity can do a person much good, but I can see where it is possible to do him harm. The fraternity may provide a person with the social graces, but if his thinking is prejudiced and narrow-minded, what good can they possibly do?

Revised

In general, I can't see that a fraternity can do a person much good, but I can see how it is possible to do him harm. The fraternity may provide a person with the social graces, but if his studies suffer from lack of time, if his money is wasted, and if his thinking is prejudiced and narrow-minded, what good can it possibly do?

THE SENTENCE

Good themes, good articles, good papers are built with good paragraphs, which, in turn, are built from good sentences. Clearly, good themes cannot be made from faulty paragraphs, nor can good paragraphs be built from awkward, incomplete, rambling, or choppy sentences. The paragraph can be only as good as its component parts, its sentences, i.e., units of complete expression. To be a successful writer, therefore, you must achieve unity, clearness, effectiveness, and appropriateness in your sentences.

Obtaining such characteristics in sentence structure requires a solid foundation, a substantial framework. You must first know what a sentence is; you must understand grammatical structures and functions and upon that foundation and framework construct sentences that are correct, clear, effective, and appropriate.

A fairly satisfactory definition of a sentence is that it is a word or group of words conveying a sense of complete meaning to the reader. Although exceptions occur, the word or group of words conveying complete meaning *usually* has a subject and a predicate. The subject may be expressed or it may be understood; either subject or predicate may also be understood from the context. (See Section 74.)

The foregoing statements refer to *grammatical* completeness. In one sense you do not have a complete thought until you have read or written a whole series of sentences, perhaps an entire paragraph or theme. A pronoun in one sentence may take its meaning from an antecedent in another. Such words as *Thus, these, another,* and *again,* and such phrases as *for example* and *on the other hand* frequently show that

The Sentence

the thought presented in a new sentence is intimately related to the thought in a preceding sentence or paragraph.

When we say, then, that a sentence conveys a sense of complete meaning to the reader, we do not mean that we can dispense with its context. We mean only that we have a group of words so ordered as to be *grammatically* self-sufficient. For example, the statement "He entered that profession when he was only 23 years old" is grammatically complete. It has a subject, the pronoun *he,* and it has a main predicate verb, *entered;* moreover, the dependent clause, "when he was only 23 years old," is properly integrated into the sentence by the subordinating conjunction *when.* In this sense the entire statement is complete; it begins with a capital and is followed by a period. So far as total meaning is concerned, however, we need other sentences to tell us that *he* refers to a specific man, Henry Brown, and *that profession* refers to the profession of law.

Because punctuation and capitalization are governed in part by grammatical rather than logical completeness, understanding the grammar of the sentence is basic for clear and effective writing. Sentence clearness and effectiveness, however, are more than matters of punctuation and capitalization; they depend also upon forms and patterns of sentences, discussion of which is given in Section 74. A review of this material may be helpful before you study the following sections, which deal with errors frequently made in writing the sentence and which suggest definite ways of avoiding them.

Like the problems dealing with themes, paragraphs, and words, the problems of writing sentences may be classed under four main heads: *correctness, clearness, effectiveness,* and *appropriateness.* Sections 31–50 deal with these four divisions as follows:

Correctness
   Sentence fragment and incompleteness of meaning—Section 31
   Comma splice—Section 32
   Fused sentences—Section 33

Clearness
   Sentence unity (oneness)—Section 34
   Mixed and illogical constructions—Section 35
   Faulty coordination—Section 36
   Faulty subordination—Section 37

Illogical dependent clauses—Section 38
Misplaced modifiers—Section 39
Dangling modifiers—Section 40
Split constructions—Section 41
Transition—Section 42

Effectiveness

Conciseness—Section 43
Parallelism—Section 44
Consistency—Section 45
Choppy sentences and clauses—Section 46
Position and arrangement—Section 47
Variety—Section 48

Appropriateness—Section 49

Such a listing may help you keep in mind the four qualities of good writing. Note, however, that these topics are not mutually exclusive. Correctness and clearness depend upon sentences complete in grammar, structure, and meaning; effective sentences result from correctness and clearness; sentence unity is probably as much a problem of correctness as of clearness and could have been placed under either heading. Or, for another illustration, both proper coordination and proper subordination are necessary for clearness and effectiveness. As you study the following sections, focus your attention on the larger problem: how to make sentence *correctness,* sentence *clearness,* sentence *effectiveness,* and sentence *appropriateness* contribute to the correctness, clearness, effectiveness, and appropriateness of the longer units (paragraphs, themes, papers) which you write.

As a supplementary aid, "Glossary of Sentence Errors" (Section 50) contains an alphabetical list of sentence errors, a brief discussion, and cross references to more detailed discussion and suggestions.

SENTENCE FRAGMENT AND INCOMPLETENESS OF MEANING

31a. Use justifiable sentence fragments for clear and effective writing.

Grammatically defined, a sentence consists of a subject and predicate and expresses a complete thought. Yet various kinds of statements express a complete thought without a stated or implied subject or predicate.

1. Some non-subject-and-predicate words or word groups are sentence fragments only grammatically; otherwise, they are clear, effective statements, such as the following:

Interjections: *Hush! Ouch! Indeed! Ah! Oh! Oh, oh! Pshaw!*

Greetings: *Hello. Good morning. Good evening. Good night. Good-by.*

Expressive or exclamatory statements: *Fine! Sure! Never, never, never! What a day! Never again! Oh, for another vacation!*

Transitional statements: *But to continue. Enough for the actual story and its characters. Now another advantage. One other important matter. Now for the opposite point of view. To summarize. Now in conclusion.*

2. Considered as sentence fragments but justifiable and effective are elliptical sentences. An elliptical sentence is a grammatically incomplete group, a part of a sentence without a subject or predicate, or both, but the omitted parts are understood from the context, from what precedes or follows. Ellipsis is common in recording dialogue or giving answers to questions, or even in some of the exclamatory and transitional statements in (1) above: *What a day (that was)! Never again (will I do that)! Now (here is) another advantage.*

Context is frequently important, as in answers to questions or in giving details after an assertion, using words like *yes, no, never, always, of course,* or statements such as the following (combinations of conversation and questions-answers):

"Where have you been?"
"In the library."
"Were you studying?"
"No."
"When did you leave?"
"At four o'clock."
"Why are you so late?"
"Because I was delayed in traffic."

NOTE: Frequently, of course, the word or group of words standing as a complete statement has a subject and predicate. If the single word is a verb, or a phrase consisting of a verb with object or modifiers, "you" is very probably the understood subject, as in commands and requests:

Come here (cf. *You come here*).
Bring a friend.
Stop! Proceed with caution. *Obey* traffic signs.

3. For certain kinds of writing—not sustained formal or informal prose—sentence fragments are peculiarly appropriate, as in descriptive notes on books in a bibliography or reading list:

Charles Major, *When Knighthood Was in Flower.* A romantic novel dealing with Renaissance England. Of interest to the older teen-age group. Especially valuable for its vivid life and swift movement.

Such justifiable sentence fragments are used in this book, as in "Glossary of Sentence Errors" (Section 50), "Glossary of Faulty Diction" (Section 70), "Grammatical Terms Defined" (Section 85), and in comment on periodical indexes, pages 163–164.

31b.   Avoid using unjustifiable sentence fragments.

An unjustifiable sentence fragment is a word or group of words (1) which does not make sense to the reader, or (2) which is not clear or effective because it is set apart from other words with which the reader expects it to be associated. The error is also called the "period fault," since it can be considered an error in punctuation, but it is more commonly considered an error in sentence construction. (Review the correct uses of the period, Section 86.)

Common kinds of unjustifiable sentence fragments are dependent clauses and phrases. (See "Phrases" and "Clauses," Sections 72, 73.) Each kind is given discussion in Sections 31c and 31d. Unjustifiable sentence fragments can be eliminated by several methods:

→1. Attach each fragment to an independent statement or to a statement making sense, if the fragment naturally and logically belongs with that statement.

→2. Revise so that the fragment becomes included as part of a complete statement (compound subject, compound predicate, compound sentence, complex sentence, etc.).

→3. Make each fragment complete by providing it with a subject and predicate so that it fulfills the grammatical definition of a sentence.

NOTE: Using a semicolon ("semicolon fault," Section 89d) instead of a period does not correct the sentence-fragment error, since the semicolon, also, conventionally sets off complete statements.

31c. Avoid setting off a dependent clause as a sentence.

Dependent clauses frequently mistaken for sentences are adverbial and adjective clauses. The adverbial clause may be wrongly set off when it logically should be at the beginning or end of an independent clause. The adjective clause may be wrongly set off when it logically should be at the end of an independent clause.

Wrong: I had no money for a trip to Europe. *When suddenly I was left a small fortune.* (Adverbial clause)
Unless you can't find anything else. We don't advise you to take this job. (Adverbial clause)
The governor decided not to veto the bill. *Even though there were parts of it that he did not like.* (Adverbial clause)
I was a student for four years at Oriole High School. *From which I was graduated in June, 1961.* (Adjective clause)
I have talked with a businessman. *Who thinks that the prospects for the next 12 months are excellent.* (Adjective clause)

Correction of the dependent-clause sentence fragment usually involves no change in the wording. A change in capitalization, from a capital to a small letter, and in punctuation, from a period to a comma or no mark (see Sections **88f, 88m**), is enough. Or the dependent clause may be made independent by omitting the subordinating conjunction from the adverbial clause, or by changing the relative pronoun to a personal pronoun in the adjective clause.

Correct: I had no money for a trip to Europe. Suddenly I was left a small fortune.
Unless you can't find anything else, we don't advise you to take this job.
The governor decided not to veto the bill. There were parts of it, however, that he did not like.
The governor decided not to veto the bill, even though there were parts of it he did not like.
I was a student for four years at Oriole High School, from which I was graduated in June, 1961.
I have talked with a businessman who thinks that the prospects for the next 12 months are excellent.
I have talked with a businessman. He thinks that . . .

31d. Avoid setting off a phrase as a sentence.

The phrases that cause trouble as sentence fragments are usually

the following: participial, infinitive, absolute, prepositional, prepositional-gerund, appositional, subject (noun with modifiers), and verb
(as the second member of a compound predicate).

To correct such sentence fragments, (1) attach the phrase to or in-
corporate it in the sentence with which it belongs, or (2) make the
phrase a sentence by adding subject and predicate, for completeness.

In the following illustrations, each has at least two parts: the first
contains a sentence fragment with a label as to its kind; a corrected
version follows, achieved by use of one or both of the methods just
suggested.

Incorrect: *Having worked in a garage for four summers.* John thinks he is
an experienced mechanic. (Participial phrase)

Correct: Having worked in a garage for four summers, John thinks he is
an experienced mechanic.

Incorrect: I studied for hours every night. *Preparing myself to take and
pass the College Entrance Board examinations.* (Participial
phrase)

Correct: I studied for hours every night, preparing to take and pass the
College Entrance Board examinations.

Incorrect: Harry has now two goals in life. *To graduate from college and
to establish himself in business.* (Infinitive phrase)

Correct: Harry has now two goals in life. He wishes to graduate from
college and to establish himself in business.
Harry has now two goals in life: to graduate from college and
to establish himself in business.

Incorrect: *Winter having come early that year.* The mountain passes were
soon blocked by the snow. (Absolute phrase)

Correct: Winter having come early that year, the mountain passes were
soon blocked by the snow.
Winter came early that year, and the mountain passes were soon
blocked by the snow.

Incorrect: *After a long hard day of classes and studying.* A student is
ready to tumble into bed early. (Prepositional phrase)

Correct: After a long hard day of classes and studying, a student is ready
to tumble into bed early.

Incorrect: Some people constantly discuss politics. *Without really knowing
what they are talking about.* (Prepositional-gerund phrase)

Correct: Some people constantly discuss politics without really knowing what they are talking about.

Incorrect: My mother spent her girlhood on a farm near Wildwood. *A small town in southeastern Ohio.* (Appositional phrase)

Correct: My mother spent her girlhood on a farm near Wildwood, a small town in southeastern Ohio.

Incorrect: We were fascinated by the scene at timberline. *Especially the stunted, twisted trees.* (Appositional phrase)

Correct: We were fascinated by the scene at timberline, especially the stunted, twisted trees.

Incorrect: *One of my neighbors, who killed all the weeds in his lawn by spraying them with a weed killer.* (Subject phrase)

Correct: One of my neighbors killed all the weeds in his lawn by spraying them with a weed killer.

One of my neighbors, who killed all the weeds in his lawn by spraying them with a weed killer, now has the most beautiful lawn in town.

Incorrect: *Even the winters, which are very long and severe in that climate.* (Subject phrase)

Correct: Even the winters are very long and severe in that climate.

Even the winters, which are very long and severe in that climate, cannot compare with the winters I remember as a boy.

Incorrect: That night the river overflowed its banks. *And flooded the lowlands.* (Verb phrase)

Correct: That night the river overflowed its banks and flooded the lowlands.

Admittedly, sentence fragments are frequently used by skilled writers for stylistic purposes. For example: "He walked as though he were dreaming. Dreaming? Hardly. He was more detached than that. He was hypnotized! Far away. Lost in another world."

Students frequently complain that their instructors mark all fragmentary sentences as incorrect, even those they deliberately write for stylistic effect. The truth is that most teachers wish their students to use fragments for such purposes only after they demonstrate their knowledge of sentence completeness. After you have shown that you know what a sentence is, you may be allowed to experiment.

31e. Do not start a statement with one construction and then stop, or shift to another, leaving one or more sentence elements incomplete.

The sentence-fragment error includes two other varieties:

1. *An incomplete and unfinished construction.* Sometimes a writer begins a statement, changes his construction and direction, forgets where he is, keeps adding words while moving in a different direction, and then stops before he has given meaning to the words with which he started. Such unfinished constructions result in the following:

Wrong: A high school friend of mine, who, because he ran out of funds, had to leave college at the beginning of his sophomore year and go to work in a local factory.

Our college band, not being accustomed to the new conductor and resenting his extremely critical manner.

Such unfinished constructions may be made complete by the addition of pertinent material expressed in proper grammatical elements:

Right: A high school friend of mine who, because he ran out of funds, had to leave college at the beginning of his sophomore year and go to work in a local factory, saved enough money in three years to return to college and finish his education.

Our college band, not being accustomed to the new conductor and resenting his extremely critical manner, soon lost its morale and its high standing.

2. *A paradoxically complete-and-incomplete construction.* Sometimes a writer does begin with an independent clause, but he adds an unfinished statement and forgets to include material to coordinate with his first independent statement.

Not clear: I thought I would have an easy time in college, but when I arrived on the campus and learned how many classes I would have, how little free time for study, and how keen the scholarly competition.

Improved: I thought I would have an easy time in college, but when I arrived on the campus and learned how many classes I would have, how little free time there would be for study, and how keen the scholarly competition was, I immediately changed my mind about college being mostly fun and little work.

31f. Do not use punctuation marks to replace necessary words.

Sometimes a careless writer lets a mark of punctuation, usually a comma, replace a needed subordinating conjunction like *that* or a relative pronoun.

Incomplete: We asked, she should consider being our candidate for Prom Queen.
Henry always believed, he could become an honor student.
The man, I wrote to was the Registrar.
People in Fayville are so friendly, I could live here forever.

Improved (by omitting the commas and inserting any words necessary for clearness):
We asked that she should consider being our candidate for Prom Queen.
Henry always believed that he could become an honor student.
The man I wrote to (or, The man that I wrote to) was the Registrar.
People in Fayville are so friendly that I could live here forever.

31g. Avoid a telegraphic style in formal and informal writing.

Because every word telegraphed, cabled, or radioed costs money, a telegraphic style is used for such messages. By omitting subjects or main verbs or auxiliary verbs or adjectives or adverbs or conjunctions or prepositions or pronouns, senders try to make themselves understood with the least possible number of words and at lowest cost.

Such writing can be understood even when important words are omitted. Otherwise, many important telegrams would be misinterpreted. The following message serves its purpose:

Letter received. Leaving tomorrow noon. Reserve room Carter Hotel. Arrive early evening. Get theater tickets Saturday matinee, night.

Appropriate for telegrams, day letters, night letters, cablegrams, and radiograms, such a style is inappropriate and ineffective in formal or informal writing, even for friendly letters.

EXERCISES

A. Read carefully an article in your book of readings or in a recent magazine. Underline any sentence fragments that you find. Do you think they are justifiable? Do you think they, or some of them, would be more effective if they were sentences?

B. Correct the unjustifiable sentence fragments in the following by attaching them logically to materials with which they belong:

1. During my last year in school I did some work on the school paper. And took care of the sports department in our yearbook.
2. Last spring I took the most thrilling trip of my life. A trip to our nation's capital.
3. Winter does something to me. When the snow leaves a white blanket over the ground.
4. I asked Father what he wanted me to do. Hoping that he would say, "Go hunting."
5. The next experience that I recall happened to my mother and me. Mother being the driver, of course.
6. Senior week we shall never forget. The magnificent prom, a great picnic, and much fun.
7. In the city the people rush from place to place. Always in a hurry to be somewhere else.
8. Since school afforded few extracurricular activities of any kind. I participated in all those that were offered.
9. The complimentary close is "Sincerely yours." A good close for friendly business letters.
10. And now once again I've moved. This time to Atwood University.
11. After that trip I reached home with only a few pennies in my pocket. But with many fond memories.
12. Don't walk under a ladder. Not just because it is a superstition, but it is dangerous.
13. I slid through high school as an otter slides down a snowy hill. Free and easy without a care in the world. Not caring about anything.
14. The plane rose higher and higher. Its wings swept back and its nose piercing the air.
15. There are many words that I use incorrectly. Such as *have went* for *have gone, I seen* instead of *I saw,* and many, many others.
16. I have yet to live down that embarrassing incident. As my friends love to remind me of it from time to time.
17. At the ball park we each had a hot dog and coke. The moment we reached our seats. The umpire yelled, "Play ball!"
18. Such is the equipment you will need for an overnight camping trip. Good luck on your outing.
19. My clothing bill for this summer was $375. This being more than double what I expected to spend.

20. Then Mother begins preparing Thanksgiving dinner. Roast turkey and dressing, mashed potatoes and gravy, baked beans, coleslaw, pickles, radishes, and carrots.

C. Correct the unjustifiable sentence fragments in the following by expanding them into sentences:

1. Football is not the only sport I like, as there are baseball and basketball. The other two outstanding sports in America.
2. In the School of Pharmacy a total number of 142 credit hours is required to graduate. Also an average grade of C or higher.
3. The card catalog has three divisions. The first of which contains the author cards.
4. In college there is nobody to tell you to get up in the morning. Nobody to make you study.
5. A man of average height and rugged build, with silvery gray hair, his hair indicating that he was in his fifties.
6. When I first came to this campus, I was scared. Scared to death.
7. There are memorable joys in Nature to be experienced. The joys of a sunrise, of a sunset, of starlight, and of star-gazing.
8. In college, there has to be quality with quantity. Because college instructors will not accept inferior work for a passing grade.
9. Fraternities want you to be a "big activities" man on the campus. Get you into all the activities they can load you down with and then they wonder why your grades in school are so low.
10. I wish I could go back to the time I was a freshman in high school. With the knowledge I have now about how important study is and the importance of good study habits.
11. The name of our farm is The Hedges. Named thus because of the abundant growth of trees and shrubs.
12. New York City—a place everyone would like to visit.
13. My roommate lives in a small town in central Missouri. A quiet town, the kind of town I would like to live in myself.
14. The whine continued and the old man got more and more nervous. If only he could stop the noise.
15. There are many important reasons for going to college. The first being the furthering of one's education.
16. Some thoughtless, self-centered driver can cause an accident. Where if he had yielded the right of way, a life could have been saved.
17. Experience is a good but expensive teacher. Although after having a costly experience, one usually never lets it take place again.
18. My parents let me drive the car on certain conditions. One of these

being that I would not go more than five miles from home and the other that I would be in by 10:30 P.M.

19. Magazine rates for three-year subscriptions are cheaper. Thereby saving the subscriber a considerable sum of money.

20. With the new motels, a family can sleep along the highway, not in some dirty town. No more traffic jams as you enter a city seeking a place to stay.

D. Make complete the sense of the following by substituting or adding necessary words, by revision, or by rewriting.

1. Our supply of drinking water is dwindling, and if we continue to pollute our streams as we are now.

2. The route was finally decided upon and when all preparations for the trip had been made.

3. Previous to this, my father told me that when he was sitting in an airplane, waiting for engines to start, but they didn't start.

4. For the summer between my junior and senior years will be spent on cruise with the Navy.

5. Was surely glad to hear from you again. Wish you all the success in your new business. Your city in need of a good civil engineer like you.

6. You soon learn, and after these simple instructions about borrowing books from the library.

7. Since the early 1900's, automobiles have greatly improved as far as economy, dependability, size, shape, and style.

8. By this, I mean that by the time I realized that one gets out of something only what one puts into it.

9. You may have the kind of trouble I had last night, and when you wake up one hour late the next morning. What can you expect?

10. The plans have all failed, and some plans promising to put an end to our difficulties.

11. The will stated that if our uncle died suddenly. My brother was to take over the business immediately.

12. Would appreciate an early reply. Anxiously awaiting to meet you then.

13. I have come to the conclusion that since literature takes up time that high school teachers could spend in teaching writing.

14. Seems to me the Union Building is the most beautiful building on the campus.

15. My name is Paul Jenkins, and coming, as I do, from a very small rural high school and not much variety of courses.

COMMA SPLICE

32. Like the sentence fragment, the comma splice may be considered an error in punctuation or an error in sentence construction. With either label, the unjustifiable comma splice is a serious error which causes confusion to the reader, since the writer does not show him where one sentence ends and another begins.

The comma splice, also called the "comma fault" or "illiterate comma," is not an ordinary misuse of the comma. Instead, it is the error of using a comma to join two sentences; literally, the comma "splices" or links the sentences. In grammatical terms, the comma splice is the error of using a comma between two independent clauses not joined by one of the pure or simple coordinating conjunctions, *and, but, or, nor, neither, yet.* (See Section **88d.**)

32a. Avoid unjustifiable comma splices.

The unjustifiable comma splice, as defined above, appears in several specific forms:

1. *Two statements which have no grammatical relationship but which are related by content.*

Incorrect: A meeting of the Botany Club will be held on Friday evening, several important matters are to be discussed.

2. *Two related statements, the second of which begins with a personal pronoun whose antecedent is in the first.* Personal pronouns, though they often refer to antecedents in other sentences, do not make grammatical connections between clauses; only relative pronouns perform that function.

Incorrect: Father's office is on the 35th floor, it overlooks the Hudson River.
The trees on the campus are old and sturdy, they were planted over 100 years ago.
The dean considered a few minutes and then shook his head, he did not say a word.

3. *Two related statements, the second of which begins with a demonstrative pronoun or adjective (this, that, these, those, such).* Like

275

the personal pronouns, demonstrative pronouns and adjectives do not make grammatical connections between clauses.

Incorrect: Go south until you come to the corner of State and Madison Streets, this is one of the busiest intersections in the world.

4. *Two statements, the second of which begins with or contains a conjunctive adverb* (see list of conjunctive adverbs in Section **89b** and on pp. 605–607). Despite the word *conjunctive,* such adverbs (*however, accordingly, then, nevertheless,* etc.) do not make the close grammatical connections between independent clauses that are made by the pure conjunctions. Conjunctive adverbs show only a logical relationship; hence, the comma is not a strong enough mark of punctuation to stand between the clauses.

Incorrect: We had taken a wrong turning near Northville, thus we found ourselves traveling miles out of our way.
The spring vacation ended on Thursday morning, however, I did not return from the South until Sunday evening.
The University imposes no penalties for absences, you are, however, expected to make up all work that you miss.

The comma-splice error can be corrected in several ways:

1. Use a period after the first statement and a capital at the beginning of the second. This method may be objectionable if short, choppy, jerky sentences result (see Section **46**). It is effective, however, if the ideas are not too closely related and if a series of short, choppy, jerky sentences is avoided.

Incorrect: My parents cannot come for Homecoming, they have other plans.
Correct: My parents cannot come for Homecoming. They have other plans.
A meeting of the Botany Club will be held on Friday evening. Several important matters are to be discussed.

2. Use a semicolon between the statements (see Section **89a** and **b**). This method is preferable when a conjunctive adverb is used to make clear a close or fairly close relationship between the two statements.

Incorrect: My roommate spent money faster than he anticipated, therefore he had to drop out of school at the end of the first semester.

I was able to borrow money to complete my first year, otherwise I should have had to leave at the end of the first semester.

Correct: My roommate spent money faster than he anticipated; therefore he had to drop out of school at the end of the first semester.

I was able to borrow money to complete my first year; otherwise I should have had to leave at the end of the first semester.

The University imposes no penalties for absences; you are, however, expected to make up all work that you miss.

3. Insert a pure conjunction between statements, or as a substitute for the conjunctive adverb, and retain the comma (see Section **88d**). If ideas are closely related, this is an effective method, for the pure conjunction makes the close relationship evident. Sometimes, of course, the needed pure conjunction is not appropriate.

Incorrect: Classes will begin on September 20, freshmen should be on the campus for orientation the preceding week.

Correct: Classes will begin on September 20, and freshmen should be on the campus for orientation the preceding week.

The spring vacation ended on Thursday morning, but I did not return from the South until Sunday evening.

4. Subordinate one of the statements and retain the comma. This is usually the most effective method if the thought expressed is not radically changed by the subordination. In fact, the comma-splice error is often the result of an attempt to show a causal relationship without proper subordination. One of the statements can be reduced to a dependent clause or to a phrase.

Corrected by using dependent clauses:

Although the University imposes no penalties for absences, you are expected to make up all work that you miss.

My parents cannot come for Homecoming, since they have other plans.

If I had not been able to borrow money to complete my first year, I should have had to leave at the end of the first semester.

Go south until you come to the corner of State and Madison Streets, where the intersection is one of the busiest in the world.

Corrected by using phrases:

On Friday evening a meeting of the Botany Club will be held, in order to discuss several matters. (Adverbial phrase)

Father's office is on the 35th floor and overlooks the Hudson River. (Verb phrase)

277

Having taken a wrong turning near Northville, we found ourselves traveling miles out of our way. (Participial phrase)

Go south until you come to the corner of State and Madison Streets, one of the busiest intersections in the world. (Appositional phrase)

In correcting the comma splace, do not make a "frying pan" error, an error worse than the one already made. Omitting the comma does not correct the comma splice; it replaces it by the more serious error of fused or blended sentences (see Section 33).

32b. Use a justifiable comma splice when it is appropriate and effective.

The foregoing discussion has dealt with the unjustifiable comma splice. Although occasional examples may be found in print, many writers and editors are careful to avoid the error, using instead the punctuation suggested above.

Certain kinds of comma splice are appropriate and effective, but be sure that they are justifiable:

1. *When the independent clauses are very short, with the subjects usually the same.*

> I came, I saw, I conquered. (Julius Caesar's famous sentence)
> You do work hard, you should work even harder.
> Mother obeys signs, she is a careful driver.

If a conjunctive adverb joins even such short independent clauses, use a semicolon.

> You do work hard; however, you should work even harder.
> Mother obeys signs; therefore, she is a careful driver.

2. *When the independent clauses, neither one very long, express contrast.* Sometimes the first clause makes a negative statement, the second an affirmative one, or, as in one form of question, the first statement is affirmative, the second negative (see Section 88j).

> This is Henry, that is George.
> *Biology* comes from two Greek words: *bios* means "life," *logos* means "study."
> We are not spending the summer in Maine, we are spending it in Wisconsin.

Some students like mathematics, others do not.
You have a copy of the assignment, haven't you?
The weather looks very stormy, doesn't it?

EXERCISES

A. Study an article in your book of readings or in a magazine such as *The Atlantic Monthly, Harper's, The Saturday Evening Post, Time,* or *Newsweek.* Encircle any comma splices. Are they justifiable or unjustifiable? Comment on kinds of clauses spliced, perhaps as follows: "short independent clauses," "first clause is negative, second is positive," "conjunctive adverb seems to relate clauses closely enough for the comma." Which of the sentences containing comma splices would be clearer or more effective if the comma were changed to a stronger mark of punctuation?

B. Correct any unjustifiable comma splices in the following sentences. If possible, correct each by all the methods suggested in Section 32a. Arrange your corrected versions in order of most to least effective.

1. The people in my home town are almost all alike, most of them are not socially ambitious.
2. The College Union party was a big one, thousands of students attended it.
3. Now we all know that this is a lot of nonsense, Friday the 13th is just like any other day in the year.
4. "Well, you see, it is this way, Harry," I said, "I have a date tonight, and I have only $1.50."
5. Our outlines were not made to further our knowledge of English or literature, they were made just for the sake of outlining.
6. My new school was also small, it had only 200 boys in it.
7. The turkey is then put in the oven, the pumpkin pies, cranberry sauce and other foods are prepared for Thanksgiving dinner.
8. From the time a driver enters a car until he leaves it, he must be careful, a moment's carelessness may be his last.
9. We are always trying to improve the appearance of our town, for instance, two years ago we completed a beautiful new library to replace the old one.
10. A report may be written to someone with more or less general knowledge about the subject than the writer, such knowledge determines the amount and type of detail in the report.
11. There is only one water sport that I have not tried, that is skin-diving.
12. Little did I care what the illness was, all I knew was that I felt terrible.

32

13. The library card catalog proves to be a great convenience, as you can see, it is necessary for you only to look through this catalog to find where the books are located.
14. Each man wrestles in a different weight division, these divisions range from a 98-pound weight division to a 225-pound weight division.
15. My uncle and aunt raise chickens and ducks, some they sell and some they keep for their own consumption.
16. On our campus are five dormitories, three of them are for freshmen only and the other two are for upperclassmen.
17. One of my errors is incorrect spelling, another is the occasional use of faulty diction.
18. Occasionally let a friend proofread for you, he may not overlook the mistakes that you overlook.
19. My parents have both made many trips by plane, now they are eager for me to travel by air.
20. Edward did not want to listen to my story, all he wanted was to borrow some money.

    C. Directions given in B.

1. Anarchy can only represent that which is corrupt and evil, therefore people throughout the world must be educated against it.
2. In high school I spent very little time studying, as a matter of fact I never so much as took a book home, now I am sorry.
3. We practiced for a short time, then we played several games.
4. I do not think a conference is necessary at this time, however, I believe I will desire one in a few weeks.
5. Parents complain if their children are worked too hard, thus the teacher's power is limited.
6. Luckily the seniors didn't have final examinations, consequently the amount of studying I did was small.
7. I didn't believe in superstitions, therefore I decided to wear the number 13.
8. The average freshman does not find college courses too hard, instead he finds it difficult to adjust himself to the new way of college life.
9. Saturday is my only day for fun and relaxation, consequently, the local golf course is usually my playground.
10. My home town is a north-side suburb of Chicago, nevertheless, fame has not been its fortune.

    D. Which of the following sentences contain justifiable comma splices and which do not?

1. An ambitious student is forward-bound, his distinguishing cry is "onward and upward."
2. I did as many other young men and women have done, I decided to obtain a college education.
3. The first reason is important, the second is of no consequence.
4. I have grown up with dancing, I am still dancing, I hope to continue dancing for my own enjoyment.
5. In spanking me, the teacher didn't try to hurt me, she just tried to scare me.
6. As soon as dinner was over, we left to go to a show, it was a special show for Thanksgiving at a local theater.
7. Uncle Willie isn't really a relative at all, he merely lives at my uncle's hotel on 64th Street.
8. I think that worrying is nonsense, thus I try to live my life only from day to day.
9. So it isn't the number 13 that causes all the trouble, it is just the thought processes of people who worry about that number.
10. My college education isn't the only thing my parents had to "penny-pinch" for, there were the car, remodeling the kitchen, and business college for my sister.

FUSED SENTENCES

33. *Fused* sentences are two grammatically complete sentences which are joined or run together with *no* mark of punctuation between. The reader is confused because the writer has not indicated where one complete thought ends and another complete thought begins.

33a. Do not write two sentences with no punctuation between them. Use a terminal mark (period, question mark, exclamation point) or a semicolon.

Fused sentences are a serious grammatical error, an error in punctuation, and a violation of the principle of unity. The error is an even more flagrant violation of correctness than the comma splice, for the writer of a comma splice shows that he senses the need for punctuation of some sort.

A sentence is a complete and meaningful statement and should always be followed by a full stop, that is, by a terminal mark of punctuation (see Sections **86, 87**).

Incorrect: That night the river overflowed its banks and spread over the lowlands thousands of people were left homeless by the time the waters receded.

Judged by grammatical form, this "sentence" contains two independent statements. Each may be written as a separate sentence; or, if the writer thinks that the statements are sufficiently related in thought, a semicolon may be used, and the result is a compound sentence.

Correct: That night the river overflowed its banks and spread over the lowlands. Thousands of people were left homeless by the time the waters receded.

That night the river overflowed its banks and spread over the lowlands; thousands of people were left homeless by the time the waters receded.

33b.   Never correct fused sentences by placing a comma between them.

If you correct the fused-sentences error by using a comma, your error is the comma splice (see Section 32). The four methods, therefore, for the correction of the comma splice should be carefully studied for similar correction of fused sentences.

EXERCISES

Copy the following sentences and use capital letters (see Section 97), periods, question marks, exclamation marks, or semicolons where they are needed.

1. Rain, rain, rain that's all it ever does.
2. I attended Highland High School in Millville during my freshman year then I was transferred to the new Forest Heights High School.
3. There are many different things that the veterinarian must be able to do successfully among these are the following tasks.
4. No one had any time to eat everyone wanted to start for the game.
5. I was much too tired to study therefore I went to bed to try to rest up after the week end.
6. There are two places to swim in our town one of them is at an artificial lake with a sand bottom and the other is at the pool in the park.
7. This trait I know about my roommate's father he is a very patient man with his family.
8. On Christmas morning Mother has breakfast ready early after we eat it we go into the living room to open our gifts.

9. One of the most scenic national parks in the United States is Yosemite Valley National Park it is located in Mariposa County, California, on the slope of the Sierra Nevada mountains.

10. The last three years in baseball I played center field the first year I played on the bench.

11. But we were not yet settled down for the whole night about 2 A.M. we were awakened by noises just outside our tent.

12. My English errors were let go until my last year in high school for that reason I am now having so much trouble here in college.

13. There is more to college than just the choosing of subjects let's see what else is necessary.

14. At Annapolis we made a tour through the students' living quarters next we proceeded to the chapel.

15. To improve in your writing, read each theme once then lay it aside for a while and proofread it again.

SENTENCE UNITY (ONENESS)

34. Unity, defined in Section 10, applies not only to the theme but also to the paragraph (Section 25) and the sentence. Clearness requires complete meaning from every sentence, but sentence unity is more than one simple idea or use of one short simple sentence.

A unified sentence may refer to several people, places, objects, or ideas and may extend to considerable length. For example, this is a unified sentence: "Although the weather had turned warmer during the night, Jim and I decided to pack our provisions and sharpen our skates in the hope that our guides would decide the ice was still safe for skating." The sentence is long and refers to several things and people, but it is unified because it has a singleness, a oneness of purpose and of content. The ideas are closely related and form a unit of thought.

Another sentence could be one-fourth as long, refer to only one person, and yet violate the principle of unity: "Joe was a good student, and he owned a TV set" or "Having been born in California, Father was graduated from the University of Wisconsin." The ideas in each of these sentences are not related; the sentences lack unity.

Unity in the sentence, essential to clear writing, is violated by (1) introducing too many details and (2) combining unrelated ideas. (Also, see Section 36.)

34a-b

34a. **Avoid rambling sentences which introduce too many details.**

Wrong: We accepted the invitation to have the State High School Golf Tournament at Moose Junction, a small town in Minnesota, which has only 5,000 inhabitants, but which contains several supermarkets, a number of churches, two good hotels, a number of motels, being on the junction of one United States highway and two state roads, and, since 1956, a drive-in restaurant as well as a golf course owned by a wealthy man named Putt.

In revision, long rambling sentences should be shortened, unrelated materials or ideas omitted, and some evidence of transition (Section 42) used between sentences.

At least approaching unity, because of an attempt to keep the golf tournament as the central or single idea, a revision of the sentence above might read:

Revised: We have accepted the invitation to have the State High School Golf Tournament at Moose Junction, Minnesota, because of the facilities it offers. It is easily accessible by railroad and by several highways, United States Route 39 and two state roads, 138 and 139, which intersect there. The city has two good hotels and several motels; in addition, quite a number of the city's 5,000 inhabitants have agreed to open their homes to the high school students. Restaurants are adequate, including a new large drive-in near the golf course. Naturally, the deciding factor in choosing Moose Junction has been this golf course. One of the best, in every sense, in the Midwest, it is owned and maintained by a golf enthusiast and wealthy man named, appropriately, Mr. Putt. He has guaranteed that the course will be in excellent condition for the high school tournament.

34b. **Avoid placing unrelated ideas in the same sentence.**

Unrelated ideas can occur not only in the same sentence but in different sentences, in the same paragraph, or even in the same theme. When such ideas occur in the same sentence, unity can sometimes be attained by subordinating one idea to another or otherwise showing some evidence of relationship. If the ideas are not closely related, they might be placed in separate sentences; if no relationship is evident, one of the ideas should be omitted.

Wrong: Mary wore a white dress, and she had a good time at the dance.
Improved: Wearing a white satin dress and a purple orchid, Mary was the

most popular girl at the dance, where she naturally had a wonderful time.

Joe was a good student; since his grades were high, he felt justified in buying a TV set to use as recreation.

Having been born in California, Father received his elementary and high school education there. But for college, he chose the University of Wisconsin, from which he was graduated in 1940.

EXERCISES

Revise the following sentences to give them unity:

1. I enjoyed our Halloween party very much, but it was a cold night.
2. Jim is a very fine dancer and plays the clarinet well.
3. All my brothers are married, and they are all college graduates.
4. My oldest brother, James, is 25 years old, and he is married to an English teacher.
5. The town of Aurora has a population of 7,000, and no farmers live in the town.
6. One hundred years ago John E. Sherman was elected mayor of our city; however, the present mayor is Wendell G. Orson.
7. We feel that our fraternity is the best at State College, which was founded in 1899 by two brothers, George and Daniel Slate; they founded the fraternity, not the college, which was established by an act of the State Legislature in 1870, and the moving spirit there was Morton Dowhill, the Speaker of the Senate.
8. For our evening meal we have to wear a dress shirt, tie, suitable trousers, and shoes, but the food is really special: roast lamb, beefsteak, roast beef, and pork chops are some of the main dishes that we have.
9. As I grew older, my desire to play basketball grew also, and when I entered high school I was too small to play my first two years of school, being only five feet tall, so I had to sit on the bench, but later in high school I began to grow, and before I graduated my senior year I was playing center on the first team, for I had grown 13 inches in two years.
10. "If I had a million dollars, I would buy me a new car and a new suit and a new pair of shoes and go all around the world and see it all and when the car got something wrong I would not wait to get it fixed, I would buy me another new car and give the old one to some kids and keep going and if it was water I would buy me an airplane and just keep going." (Schoolboy's theme on "What I Would Do with a Million Dollars," in *This Week*, July 3, 1949.)

MIXED AND ILLOGICAL CONSTRUCTIONS

35. In addition to unjustifiable sentence fragments (Section 31b, c, d, e), unjustifiable comma splices (Section 32a), and fused sentences (Section 33), other hindrances to clear writing are mixed and illogical constructions.

Construction in sentence formation means the grouping of words with other words or word combinations. A *mixed and illogical construction* is a grouping of words which (1) is contrary to reason; (2) does not make good sense; (3) violates some principle of regularity; (4) omits an important and necessary word or words that would give proper grammatical relationship within the sentence; or (5) adds a word or sentence element that has no grammatical function to fulfill. Sentence structure should make sense to a reader; if it does not, the reason is frequently ignorance of grammar or slovenly thinking, or both.

You may expect your reader to give attention to your writing, but you cannot expect him to supply omitted words, spend time untangling involved and mixed constructions, or correct mistakes in thinking. He may make the necessary corrections as he reads, but his attention is unwillingly attracted to the errors and away from important communication of ideas.

35a. Do not omit a necessary main verb or an auxiliary verb.

Both formal and informal usage sanctions omission of words in writing and speaking. Such sentences as "He made such a speech as only a politician can [make]" and "I play a better game of tennis than my roommate [does]" are complete and correct without the added *make* and *does*. The following sentences, however, involve more serious breaches of clearness and correctness; in each there are two clauses or a compound predicate, but the auxiliary verb (Section 78) or the main verb (Section 79) is improperly understood to be correct:

Doubtful: The lawn *was* mowed and the hedges neatly trimmed.
Improved: The lawn *was* mowed and the hedges *were* neatly trimmed.

Doubtful: I never *have* and probably never *will write* excellent themes.
Improved: I never have *written* and probably never *will write* excellent themes.

Doubtful: My roommate *has* and always *will study* hard to be an honor student.

Improved: My roommate has *studied* and always *will study* hard to be an honor student.

35b. Include all words essential for the clear expression of meaning.

If a necessary article, pronoun, preposition, or conjunction is omitted, your meaning is not clear; worse, it may be misinterpreted.

Doubtful: The president and chairman of the committee accepted my petition.
(This sentence means that one man is both president and chairman.)

Improved: The president and *the* chairman of the committee both accepted my petition.

Wrong: My father's name is Martin and has been a lifelong resident of Highland Park.

Clear: My father's name is Martin, and *he* has been a lifelong resident of Highland Park.

Doubtful: I have great interest and high regard for your work.

Improved: I have great interest *in* and high regard for your work.

Doubtful: I am asking that statement be made clearer.

Improved: I am asking *that* that statement be made clearer.

In addition to including necessary articles, pronouns, prepositions, and conjunctions, revise any statement not clear because other essential words are omitted.

Not clear: As far as that, we students would not be in favor.

Clear: As far as that proposal is concerned, we students are not in favor of having tuition fees increased.

Not clear: The girl across the hall wears the clothes my sister in Chicago wears.

Clear: The girl across the hall wears clothes like those my sister in Chicago wears.

Not clear: Like all the rest of the Home Economics students, my first two years of study are already planned.

Clear: Like the curriculum of the other Home Economics students, my curriculum for the first two years is already planned.

35c. Avoid mixed, confusing "blends."

Sometimes certain "blends" creep into thinking and writing: words (or even phrases and sentences) may be wrongly blended. In "Irregardless of advice, he decided to stay," *regardless* and *irrespective* are carelessly blended, and in "*Despite of* what you say, I think you are wrong," *in spite of* and *despite* are blended. In the sentence "He had no automobile in which to ride in," the blend contains *in which to ride* and *to ride in*. Similarly, blending *where* (*at* or *in which*) with *at which* results in a statement such as "Where do you live *at*"? or "The room where I live *in*. . . ." Such constructions are mainly errors in diction (see Sections **56, 57, 67b**); other constructions involving longer sentence-elements are as much a result of careless thinking as of grammatical ignorance.

A confusing blend occurs when a noun followed by an adjective-clause modifier or a parenthetic adverbial clause becomes blended with an independent clause.

Wrong: Anyone who can be really happy, most people would look upon him with envy.

Clear: Anyone who can be really happy is looked upon with envy by most people.

Most people would envy anyone who can be really happy.

Not clear: An automobile, unless you take good care of it, you will soon have to have it repaired.

Improved: Your automobile will soon have to be repaired unless you give it proper care.

Not clear: With these 11 men functioning as a team is the reason for our successful season.

Improved: With these 11 men functioning as a team, we had a successful season.

Because these 11 men functioned as a team, we had a successful season.

Unfinished construction and a blend of confused ideas:

To me this is truly a book that, after read, you will never be the same again.

Improved: To me this is truly a great book; I believe that, after you have read it, you will never be the same person again.

Another confusing blend is that in which the writer begins with an indirect question and blends the direct question into the statement (see also Section 95k):

Confused: If I had to do it over again, sometimes I wonder would I come to this college or go to work.

Improved: If I had to do it over again, sometimes I wonder whether I would come to this college or go to work.

Similarly, a blend may confuse a direct and indirect quotation (see also Section 95k):

Confused: Henry frankly admitted "that he was not studying as he should study."
Henry frankly admitted "that I am not studying as I should study."

Improved: Henry frankly admitted that he was not studying as he should study.
Henry frankly admitted, "I am not studying as I should study."

35d. Avoid a mixed or double comparison.

A frequent example of the mixed and confused blend occurs when a writer tries to include two comparisons in the same statement: (1) the grammatical positive and comparative degree of an adjective or an adverb (first set of examples below) or (2) the use of the superlative degree to include both a singular and a plural (second set of examples below). Good use sanctions the double comparison in the same sentence, but, for clearness and effectiveness, it demands that the second come after the first has been completed. (For omissions of necessary words in comparisons, see Section 35f.)

Wrong: He is *as* strong, if not stronger, *than* Fred.
For a short distance a man can run *as* fast, if not faster, *than* a horse.

Improved: He is *as* strong *as*, if not stronger *than*, Fred.
For a short distance a man can run *as* fast *as*, if not faster *than*, a horse. (These are improved but awkward.)

Preferable: He is *as* strong *as* Fred, if not stronger.
For a short distance a man can run *as* fast *as* a horse, if not faster.

Wrong: My father is *one of the tallest, if not the tallest man* in town.
The Battle of Waterloo was *one of the greatest if not the greatest battle* in all history.

Preferable: My father is *one of the tallest men in town, if not the tallest*.
The Battle of Waterloo was *one of the greatest battles in all history, if not the greatest*.

35e. Make clear whether an object or term being compared is or is not part of a class or group.

Another mixed and confusing blend involving comparison occurs when a member or object of a class or group is also treated as a unique member. Avoid including within the class or group the object or term being compared, if it is part of the class or group. The excluding word *other* is needed.

Inaccurate: Straziboski is older than any man on the football team.
Clear: Straziboski is older than any *other* man on the football team.

Inaccurate: Henry has a higher scholastic average than any student in the College of Arts.
Clear: Henry has a higher scholastic average than any *other* student in the College of Arts.

Also, a member or object of a class or group may illogically be excluded from a group or class to which it belongs. Do not use the word *other* when the superlative degree indicates that the object or term compared is included within the group or class.

Inaccurate: Straziboski is the oldest of all the *other* men on the football team.
Clear: Straziboski is the oldest of all the men on the football team.

Inaccurate: Henry has the highest scholastic average of all the *other* students in the College of Arts.
Clear: Henry has the highest scholastic average of all the students in the College of Arts.

35f. Do not omit words necessary in a comparison.

When a comparison is begun or implied, use the words necessary to complete it and to make it clear; also, do not omit the standard of comparison.

Doubtful: He is so sick.
Improved: He is so sick that he cannot attend class today.
            He is really sick.

Doubtful: Country life is so friendly and peaceful.
Improved: Country life is so friendly and peaceful that many people will
            not live anywhere else.

Doubtful: Your speech has been the greatest success.
Improved: Your speech has been the greatest success of any given thus far.
            Your speech has been a great success.

Doubtful: Mathematics interested Henry more than Nora.
Improved: Mathematics interested Henry more than it did Nora.
            Mathematics interested Henry more than Nora did.

Doubtful: His hands are bigger than any man I know.
Improved: His hands are bigger than those of any other man I know.

35g. Avoid confusing double negatives.

A violation of clear phrasing is the unjustifiable double negative.
Illiterate speech abounds with such expressions as "can't hardly,"
"can't scarcely," "haven't scarcely." In good English, however, they
should be avoided.

Although rigid double negatives have been allowable in past centuries, they are now out of style and unacceptable. You are not likely
to say or write "I didn't get no food" or "I didn't see nobody" or
"Nobody isn't going to tell me anything," but avoid using *not* with
such "negative words" as *no, but, nor, only, hardly, scarcely,* and
except.

Questionable: I did not have *but* four hours' sleep last night.
                You *can't help but* admire the man's courage.
                Some students have *not scarcely* enough money to pay for
                their bare necessities.
Improved: I had *but* four hours' sleep last night.
                You *can't help* admiring the man's courage.
                Some students have *scarcely* enough money to pay for their
                bare necessities.

Allowable and occasionally effective, however, are certain double
negatives expressing a weak positive: using *not* with an adjective or
adverb having a negative prefix or suffix.

291

Dealing with uninteresting subjects is a *not uncommon* experience of writers and speakers.

A flashlight is a *not unnecessary* piece of equipment.

Our chances of winning are *not entirely hopeless*.

Sentences may of course contain more than one negative when the sense justifies the use:

That I was *not* present in class today is *not* true.

I can*not* tell why I was *not* able to concentrate in that test.

You *wouldn't* have known that I was *not* present if you had *not* been present yourself.

EXERCISES

A. Words necessary for correctness or clearness are omitted in the following sentences; supply them.

1. After supper is over and the dishes washed, we play games.
2. You may very easily incriminated if you say the wrong thing.
3. The Declaration of Independence stated men are created equal.
4. In the country the air is fresh, the water clear and pure, and the people friendly.
5. John has and always will be Mary's only true love.
6. Belonging and working in a 4-H Club improves a person's personality.
7. I think I know my two sisters better than my parents because I grew up with them.
8. Paul Bunyan always has and always will stand for the symbol of American legendry.
9. Whether or not he follows this plan through depends on much more he learns in the next four years.
10. At half-time five finalists were escorted onto the field and the queen announced.
11. Next semester I plan to study hard and to make better grades than I am this semester.
12. Its main purpose is to appeal and inform the reader.
13. A military officer lives and works in a position comparable and closely resembling that of a manager or supervisor in a civilian job.
14. In my opinion and in many others, she is the best cook in the state.
15. No matter how many times a field was plowed and the stones removed, there were always just as many stones to pick the next time.

B. Correct the mixed or illogical constructions in the following sentences:

1. Ray is the kind of person that if you are in trouble and need help, he is the first person there.
2. Special courses are set up, in many instances, if the college notices a need for the courses as to the general need of the students enrolled.
3. The mature trees are sold for timber, the diseased and dead sawed into short lengths and used for fuel, and last the places where these trees come out, small ones will grow.
4. I don't believe I have eaten that good of food in my three months at college.
5. The raindrop does not hit the ground directly and quickly runs off to form deep erosion ditches and cause flash floods.
6. Football is an outdoor sport which in order to watch one has to be outdoors soaking up the sunshine or defying the elements.
7. Here across the table from her is a man who expresses no desire to talk to her, no longer stares at her beauty, but most of all no attempt to impress her with himself.
8. With the heading of the letter in the upper right-hand corner, the reader can immediately see the address and can easily be copied.
9. Superstitions are numerous, and although sometimes seem illogical, actually, were, at one time, probably very logical.
10. The Wright brothers' father was elected editor of a church magazine and made it necessary for the family to move to Dayton.
11. A courteous driver is not only a good driver as to whether or not the person can keep control of the car, but also watches out for other drivers.
12. On the farm we have many freedoms over the people that are living in the city do not have.
13. Her face was coated with about a quarter-inch of powder and still unbearable at which to look.
14. Sometimes death or serious illness occurs in a family, and a bedfast, aging person is not told, as not to worry him, thereby making them sicker.
15. I'm sure that after these few excerpts about my life will give you a few ideas about what kind of a person I might be.

C. Correct any errors in comparison in the following sentences:

1. He is one of the most talked about, but the public knows less about, than anyone else.
2. The more the teachers talked to us, the more my fears of them became fewer.
3. Lately, there have been reports that starting wages for engineers are more likely to increase in the near future than ever before.

4. Our university has one of the best pharmacy schools.
5. It is impossible to tell whether the hero of the story is more faithful to his parents or his sweetheart.
6. The atmosphere in that teacher's classes was different from any of the other classes.
7. Our city is one of the largest, if not the largest, inland city in America.
8. Christmas in my family probably differs little from the many other families in our land.
9. Automobiles in the future will be safer and more advanced in their performance and engineering.
10. By mid-October there are as many if not more leaves on the ground as there are on the trees.
11. He is one of my favorite and definitely my most wealthy uncle.
12. The alumni cheer as loud, if not louder, than the rest of the student body.
13. Our educational system is very good in comparison with other nations.
14. I enjoyed this kind of relationship with my dog, and even wondered whether he was more intelligent.
15. She was more concerned with this sincerity instead of his social standing.
16. A chart is worth just as much and even a little more than numerous words.
17. English is one of the most, if not the most, important subject taught in high school.
18. Dorothy was the greatest influence on her brother than any other person.
19. A collector of dolls finds that every country has dolls that are different from any other country.
20. Our town is small, and the people, therefore, are more dependent upon one another.

D. Correct the confusing double negatives in the following sentences:

1. I wasn't in bed but a few hours when Dad woke me up to go fishing.
2. This record could have been broken, but none of the American cars had never run a course measured in kilometers.
3. For generations no member of our family has never voted a straight ticket.
4. When I tried to make my first speech, I discovered that I couldn't hardly make a sound.
5. It is almost useless for parents to go to bed on Christmas eve, for it isn't but a matter of a couple of hours until they are pulled out of bed by eager children.

FAULTY COORDINATION

36. To be clear and effective, sentences must be so constructed that the relative importance of their elements is fully apparent. Are these elements coordinate, of equal rank? Are some of them subordinate? In clear and effective sentences, appropriate coordination and subordination are observed.

The immature writer phrases his sentences as a child speaks: he will construct a series of independent clauses loosely held together by coordinating conjunctions. A child very naturally might say, "We went to the circus, and we saw all the freaks, and we drank pink lemonade, and we had a grand time." A careful writer avoids such running-on sentences. If he thinks carefully, he expresses ideas in constructions which show their varying importance. He coordinates equal ideas and subordinates minor ideas so that the important statement may be more emphatic.

Avoid excessive coordination, then, because it is childish, monotonous, and ineffective. Avoid inaccurate and illogical coordination because it reveals that you have not thought through the relationship of ideas, and you thereby give the reader hazy, incorrect impressions of the thoughts presented to him.

36a.   Avoid stringy, running-on sentences.

Obviously, a stringy, running-on sentence goes on and on. Do not overwork the possibilities of the compound sentence. Avoid excessive use of a series of short independent clauses and of coordinating conjunctions between independent clauses. Reduce predication: change an independent into a dependent clause, a dependent clause into a phrase, a phrase into a single word (see Section 43a).

Immature: George bought a new automobile; it had free wheeling; it had
            a heater; it had automatic transmission; it had no radio; and it
            had no seat covers.
            George bought a new automobile, and it had free wheeling, and
            it had a heater, and it had automatic transmission, but it had
            no radio and it had no seat covers.
Improved: George's new automobile has free wheeling, a heater, and auto-
            matic transmission, but it has neither radio nor seat covers.

36b. Avoid "seesaw" sentences.

"Seesaw" sentences are compound sentences with two independent clauses of approximately equal length, whether joined by conjunctions or not. Alone or used occasionally, such a balanced sentence is effective; a succession of sentences of this kind is monotonous and ineffective. Usually one of the clauses can be subordinated.

Ineffective: I did not find too much to do between Christmas and New Year's, but I managed to attend a few good movies during this time. New Year's Eve wasn't too exciting either, and there were only the same old things to do. The "old gang" was together, more or less, and we had a fairly good time. Most of my old friends who were not attending college seemed immature, but I guess they will improve with time. All in all, it was nice to go home, but I certainly enjoyed seeing the campus again.

36c. Avoid the overuse of <u>so</u> as a conjunction.

Even though *so* is correctly used as a conjunctive adverb with a semicolon preceding, and even though it is frequently used between independent clauses with only a comma before it, one objection to *so* in such constructions is simply overuse, and overuse of any word makes it ineffective; another objection is that use of *so* as a conjunction frequently gives a juvenile effect; and still another is that *so* commonly is inappropriate in formal use. In constructions like those below, *so* can often be replaced by *therefore, thus, accordingly,* and the like, or predication may be reduced.

Ineffective: He had to study, *so* he did not attend the game.
The bridge was out on Highway 40, *so* we had to make a long detour on Route 28.
Improved: He had to study; therefore he did not attend the game.
Having to study, he did not attend the game.
Since the bridge was out on Highway 40, we had to make a long detour on Route 28.

In correcting the overuse of *so,* guard against a worse error, the "frying pan" error: using another conjunctive adverb with a comma before it and thus writing an unjustifiable comma splice (see Section 32).

Wrong: The bridge was out on Highway 40, therefore we had to make a long detour on Route 28.

Sometimes *so* is misused when the writer means *so that* or *in order that*:

Ineffective: Shorter assignments are given *so* more students can master them.

Do people want the government to spend more money *so* they can pay higher taxes?

Improved: Shorter assignments are given *so that* more students can master them.

Do people want the government to spend more money *in order that* they can pay higher taxes?

36d. Avoid false coordination: do not join a relative clause to its principal clause by <u>and</u>, <u>but</u>, or <u>or</u>.

Remember that *coordinate* means "of equal rank." An independent clause, therefore, cannot be joined to a dependent clause by a coordinating conjunction. *And, but, or,* and other coordinating conjunctions connect only elements that are equal in rank.

The most frequent violation of this principle is the so-called "and which" construction. Do not use *and which, but which, and who, but who,* etc., unless a preceding "which clause" or "who clause" is coordinate with it.

Wrong: He showed much energy at first, *but which* soon vanished.

Tompson is a man of intelligence, *and who* is an industrious worker.

I do not trust Henry, *or whom* I should like to have as a close friend.

This is a beautiful golf course, *and which* you will enjoy playing on during your college years.

The simplest method of correcting these sentences is to omit the conjunctions, but remember to apply the principle of punctuation regarding restrictive and nonrestrictive clauses (Section **88m**).

Revised: He at first showed much energy, which soon vanished.

Tompson is a man of intelligence who is also an industrious worker.

I do not trust Henry, whom I should not like to have as a close friend.

This is a beautiful golf course on which you will enjoy playing during your college years.

Another method of correcting this error is the use of parallelism (Section 44), by adding a "who clause" or "which clause" to be appropriately coordinate.

Revised: I do not trust Henry, whom I have come to know well and whom I should not like to have for a close friend.

This is a beautiful golf course which is open only to students and on which you will enjoy playing during your college years.

Tompson is a man who is intelligent and who is an industrious worker.

Sometimes such revision is wordy and ineffective, as in the last revised example. Made more concise, the sentence might read:

A man of intelligence, Tompson is an industrious worker.
or
Tompson is intelligent and industrious.

EXERCISES

A. Rewrite the following sentences in order to eliminate improper coordination:

1. I have a sister who is 22 years old and she is married.
2. It was very hot that day, and I soon became pretty tired.
3. I met my brother and he asked me how my first day of school had been.
4. I went on a tour of our library and it proved to be very interesting.
5. In Cleveland I completed kindergarten, first, second, and third grades.
6. I would like to teach in a small country school, but I am also taking speech therapy as a minor.
7. I ran into the kitchen where my sister was phoning the doctor and saw my brother.
8. I was born on a farm in Kentucky, late in the month of May, but it snowed that day.
9. Sleeping in class is caused by insufficient sleep at night, by boredom, and by the students.
10. My teacher was a benevolent sort of person, but she would always help in any way possible.
11. My history teacher became ill for a short time and there was no substitute teacher to replace him.
12. I finished the paint job around noon, and Mother said we would stop and have something to eat.

13. Mr. Burnett had been in the Army and he sometimes taught as if he still were an Army instructor.

14. She told her mother that she had a wonderful time, but she was tired and her feet hurt, and she said she would tell her all about it in the morning.

15. This 500-mile race is always exciting, and so, with all its interesting features, May holds more excitement for me than any other month of the year.

16. The barbecue turned out to be a success even though it was burned a little, and the camping session ended the day after the barbecue supper.

17. After six lessons I was at the place that I could drive through town in the deepest traffic and also I was beginning to learn how to park the car.

18. In the drug store that night we thought we did a pretty good job, until the next morning, when we came to work and smelled that a bottle of cod-liver oil had fallen off the shelf, broken, and splattered all over the elevator shaft—it was a job to clean up.

19. Although, at times, a roommate may seem to have only faults, you must remember when she has left when there was an hourly to study for, the many trips into the village when she has gotten supplies for your use, and the many times she has cleaned the room when you just couldn't find time.

20. The game began with Tech winning the toss and their fullback kicked off. We received the ball on our 20-yard line, and our halfback ran it up to the forty. We ran a series of plays, but we didn't advance. We punted the ball to Tech, and they returned it to their own thirty. They also ran a series of plays, but they didn't gain either. It seemed as though the two teams were very evenly matched.

B. Rewrite the following sentences in order to eliminate the overuse of *so*. Use different methods.

1. Fishing season opened Friday so we had to try our luck.

2. My grades in high school were good enough to satisfy me, so I saw no point in studying any harder.

3. In high school I did not believe in being a bookworm, so I went out for activities.

4. There was no one my age with whom I could play, so I learned to amuse myself.

5. We didn't know what was planned for the week end, so we had to come prepared for anything.

6. We went to bed early so we could get a good long night's sleep.

7. I had slept only three hours the night before, so I was very sleepy when I went to class.

8. Every social activity is planned so carefully so each student may have a good time.
9. I woke up too late to go to church, so my roommate and I listened to a church service on the radio.
10. My parents are living the way they are so I can have the things they never had.
11. A few girls were sitting in one of the rooms conversing, so I went in to find out what was going on.
12. I realized that I was alone too much, so I decided that I would get to know people.
13. People must be able to speak English correctly so they can transmit their ideas to others.
14. The building and surrounding lawns occupy nearly one acre of ground, so you can imagine how spacious it is.
15. My father plans to take a week of his vacation during the holidays, so all of us plan to leave Christmas Day for Florida.

FAULTY SUBORDINATION

37. Like appropriate coordination, appropriate subordination contributes to clear and effective writing by showing the relationship of less important to more important ideas.

Careful, thoughtful writing contains much subordination. A good writer, recognizing that not all his ideas deserve equal rank, judiciously places them in constructions corresponding to their importance. Thus he writes unified and effective sentences. His thoughts are clearly communicated to his readers, for they see what the relationship of the sentence elements actually is.

The careful writer, in avoiding excessive and faulty coordination (see Section 36), also avoids excessive and faulty subordination. Reducing predication (Section 43a) requires thought; you must be certain that you know exactly the relationships of your ideas so that your reader is also made aware of exactly the same relationships.

37a. Avoid putting a coordinate idea in a subordinate form.

Inaccurate: My older brother was heavy and slow, *while* my sister was lithe and active.
Born and reared in Canada, he became an American citizen at the age of 25.
I called to my pouting sister, *though* she refused to answer.

To make these sentences and others like them more effective, change the subordinating conjunction to a coordinating conjunction, or otherwise coordinate the ideas:

More effective: My older brother was heavy and slow, *but* my sister was lithe and active.

He was born and reared in Canada, *but* he became an American citizen at the age of 25.

I called to my pouting sister, *but* she refused to answer.

37b. Avoid putting the main idea of a sentence in a subordinate construction, or a subordinate idea in a main clause.

Upside-down subordination exists when an idea of less importance is put in an independent clause, and the important idea is put in a dependent clause or phrase. Such a sentence is correct and usually clear, but it is not so effective as a sentence using the principle of important ideas in independent clauses, less important ideas in dependent clauses. Careful consideration of content reveals that often the most dramatic incident and the effect, rather than the cause, are major ideas; preliminaries, such as time, place, and attendant circumstances, are minor and subordinate ideas. Also, even when proper subordination is used, putting the dependent clause and the independent clause in the form of a periodic sentence adds to effectiveness (Section 74c).

Ineffective: We were getting tired of walking when we decided to hail a taxicab.

I was halfway across the street when I saw a truck heading straight toward me.

Improved: Since we were getting tired of walking, we decided to hail a taxicab.

When I was halfway across the street, I saw a truck heading straight toward me.

37c. Avoid excessive subordination.

Sentences containing overlapping subordinate statements are not effective. In such series, each clause or phrase depends upon a preceding clause or phrase. Sentence elements should be linked, but they should not be built like an accordion, or, to vary the simile, like stairs, where each step is attached to the one just above.

Ineffective: These are inexpensive toys which have been made in Japan where there is cheap labor which depends upon American trade.

301

I loved to watch the children who fed the squirrels the nuts which were on sale at the corner stand that was near the park entrance.

Improved: These are inexpensive toys which have been made in Japan. There labor is cheap, and laborers' wages depend upon American trade.

I loved to watch the children feeding nuts to the squirrels in the park. These nuts were on sale at the corner stand near the park entrance.

EXERCISES

Rewrite the following sentences, correcting the faulty subordination:

1. I was 14 years old when I took my first airplane ride.
2. We had just started for the car, when a cloudburst halted us in our tracks.
3. We were almost home before our car skidded into another car and caused a wreck.
4. As the lightning struck the house, Mother was talking on the telephone.
5. We lost the last game by a close score in the last few seconds, when the coach rose from the bench, shaking his fist at the referee.
6. Whitefish Bay is eight miles north of Milwaukee, having a population of about 12,000 people.
7. Another of my fond memories is the old jalopy which I bought for $25.00 from the man who has a gas station near Tilton where I took the bus that took me to high school.
8. During my freshman year I am living in a rooming house which is owned by an elderly lady whose father was a college professor for some 50 years at Marion, which is the other teachers' college in the state supported by public funds.
9. It was so dark that I had to turn on a light to read the clock in the kitchen that is directly opposite a large window which is on the east side of the house that is hidden from the street light by a large oak tree.
10. In order to cover up for themselves these notorious few decided to start this teen-age drivers' club, enabling them to hide behind the backs of those members, of which none of them ever drove over 30 miles per hour in his life, who were completely innocent but drawn into the club, nevertheless.

ILLOGICAL DEPENDENT CLAUSES

38.   Sentence clearness and emphasis require the use of dependent clauses. Proper subordination through the use of such clauses calls for careful thinking. Therefore, in order to avoid confusion and ineffectiveness due in part to grammatical incorrectness, use dependent clauses correctly and clearly.

All dependent clauses have the functions of separate parts of speech—noun, adjective, adverb. To use one of them for another is like misusing the single-word parts of speech. Specifically, common errors include the following: adverbial clause used for noun clause, adverbial clause used as a substitute for a noun, and a complete sentence used for a noun clause or a noun.

38a.   Do not use an adverbial clause as a noun clause.

When a noun clause is grammatically needed as the subject of a verb, the object of a verb, or a predicate nominative noun clause, do not use an adverbial clause in its place. *When, where, because* clauses are frequent offenders. The obvious correction: substitute a noun clause for the adverbial clause, or give the adverbial clause a verb to modify.

Dubious: *Because he had no money* was the reason Henry dropped out of school.

I see *where the paper says that colder weather is coming.*

The reason the airplane crashed was *because it had run out of gasoline.*

Correct: *That he had no money* was the reason Henry dropped out of school.

Henry dropped out of school *because he had no money.*

I see *that the paper says that colder weather is coming.*

The reason the airplane crashed was *that it had run out of gasoline.*

The airplane crashed *because it had run out of gasoline.*

For a discussion of the illogical "The reason is because . . ." error, see Section 70, "Glossary of Faulty Diction," Item 116.

38b.   Do not use an adverbial clause in place of a single noun or noun phrase.

Similar to errors mentioned in Section 38a is the use of adverbial

303

clauses for single nouns or noun phrases. Again, *when, where, because* clauses are the chief offenders in this type of incorrect subordination, especially in explanations or definitions.

To correct, substitute a single noun or a noun with modifiers for the adverbial clause, or change the construction to make the adverbial clause grammatically correct.

Dubious: Plagiarism is *where* you take the work of another and pass it off as your own.

Anemia is *when* the blood has certain deficiencies.

When you graduate from college is the time to take life seriously.

My low grade on the test was *because* I had not studied for it.

Correct: Plagiarism is taking another's work and passing it off as your own.

Plagiarism occurs when you take the work of another and pass it off as your own.

Anemia is a disease in which there are certain deficiencies in the blood.

When you graduate from college, you should take life seriously.

My failure to study for the test caused my low grade.

38c.   Use a noun clause, not a sentence, as the subject or complement of is and was.

A sentence rarely can be used effectively as a grammatical subject or complement. Make the sentence (independent clause) into a dependent clause by using the proper subordinating conjunction, usually *that,* or change the sentence into a correctly used adverbial clause, or reduce the independent clause to a phrase.

Dubious: I had sprained my ankle was the reason I could not go to the dance.

Mary's only fault is she has a bad temper.

Correct: The reason I could not go to the dance was that I had sprained my ankle.

I could not go to the dance because I had sprained my ankle.

Mary's only fault is that she has a bad temper.

Mary has only one fault: a bad temper.

A quoted sentence, however, may be used as a noun.

Correct: "Fools rush in where angels fear to tread" is a well-known quotation from Alexander Pope's "An Essay on Criticism."

EXERCISES

A. Compose 12 original sentences, four each of which illustrate, respectively, noun clauses, adjective clauses, and adverbial clauses.

B. Rewrite the following sentences, correcting the misuse of dependent clauses:

1. With the Three Wise Men was where the idea of giving gifts at Christmas originated.
2. If someone was hurt or even killed and a person knew it was his fault would be enough punishment for him.
3. The reason I wanted to begin school was because all of my neighborhood friends were in school.
4. Perhaps the best indication of boredom is when the entire class falls asleep.
5. How I came to hate rainy weather was after joining the Army and being stationed at Fort Lewis, Washington.
6. One of the main reasons students do not know how to study is because they do not know how to use their time to the best advantage.
7. When the weather is warm and mild is a good time to play golf.
8. Traveling so far would change your life so much is why a situation of this type is difficult to understand.
9. I read in a magazine where eight Westerns rated in the top television pictures of the week.
10. The spring, the happiest season of all, is when everything starts growing after the long winter.
11. Because it is an adult who is smoking does not change the harmfulness of smoking.
12. College is where a girl becomes a woman and a boy becomes a man.
13. Just because someone might have had a little bad luck on Friday the 13th does not mean that everybody is going to be unlucky.
14. Where we witnessed a serious accident was on a curve two miles northwest of Jasonville.
15. When I learned that my girl friend had come in one day early from San Antonio, and had called me up, was when I really got embarrassed.

MISPLACED MODIFIERS

39. In highly inflected languages nouns, adjectives, adverbs, and verbs have varied and identifying endings, by which relationships of words are usually shown. The English language is not highly inflected.

Consequently, clearness often depends in part or solely upon the position of words in a sentence.

You should correctly place related words together so that the reader sees their connection and is not misled. It is especially important to place each modifier close to the word it modifies.

39a. Place clearly such words as <u>only</u>, <u>not</u>, <u>even</u>, <u>hardly</u>, <u>scarcely</u>, etc.

Words like *only, not, even, hardly, scarcely, today, tomorrow,* as well as other words like correlative conjunctions, *both—and, neither—nor, either—or, not only—but also,* should be placed in a sentence so that they convey precisely the meaning you intend.

Consider the difference in meaning of the following:

> I was invited to a luncheon today.
> I was today invited to a luncheon.

> My first teacher's name was Rosemary.
> My teacher's first name was Rosemary.

Or consider how the position of *only* changes meaning in a sentence:

> *Only* the teacher told me to write a theme of 300 words.
> The *only* teacher told me to write a theme of 300 words.
> The teacher *only* told me to write a theme of 300 words.
> The teacher told *only* me to write a theme of 300 words.
> The teacher told me *only* to write a theme of 300 words.
> The teacher told me to write *only* a theme of 300 words.
> The teacher told me to write a theme *only* of 300 words.
> The teacher told me to write a theme of *only* 300 words.
> The teacher told me to write a theme of 300 words *only*.

Words like *only* are associated with the word or phrase immediately preceding or following. Even when no confusion results, effectiveness is better served when *only* is placed in its proper place:

Less effective: Henry *only* wanted to borrow a few dollars.
                  I *only* have two days left to finish my packing.
More effective: Henry wanted to borrow *only* a few dollars.
                  I have *only* two days left to finish my packing.

39b. Place clearly phrases and clauses.

The suggestions about clearly placing words (see Section **39a**) apply also to phrases and clauses. In general, place phrases and clauses near or next to the words they modify if there is the slightest chance of confusion. A dangling modifier (Section **40a**) may sometimes be only a misplaced phrase. In the following, the writers obviously did not mean what their sentences say:

> A few years ago the White House in Washington was closed for alterations to visitors.
> I decorated our Christmas tree with our family.
> We all put our presents under the tree, which we had wrapped up the night before.

Nor did these newspaper advertisers really mean what their printed words conveyed:

> LOST—A green lady's purse on Main Street last Friday.
> WANTED—An apartment by a young couple freshly painted and newly plastered.

Sometimes rephrasing is necessary:

> A few years ago the White House in Washington was closed to visitors while alterations were being made.
> We all put our presents, which we had wrapped up the night before, under our Christmas tree.

39c. Avoid a "squinting modifier."

"Squinting," in one sense, means "looking in two directions at once." A modifier is *squinting* when it refers to either of two parts of a sentence: what has gone before or what has followed. The inevitable result is ambiguity; just which of two possible meanings did the writer want his reader to accept?

For clearness, move the modifier and include it with the material it qualifies. If the sentence is still awkward, rewrite it. Punctuation may also help (see Section **88k**), but it is not a safe guide.

Ambiguous:	Most boys who have the name John *somewhere along the line* get a nickname.
	All the family sat still *momentarily* with a surprised look on their faces.
Clear:	Most boys who have the name John get a nickname somewhere along the line.
	All the family momentarily sat still, with a surprised look on their faces.
	All the family sat still, with a surprised look, momentarily, on their faces.

EXERCISES

Revise the following sentences so as to remove any lack of clearness or effectiveness due to misplaced modifiers:

1. Be sure you have only the right-sized shells for the shotgun you are carrying in your hunting coat.
2. Before each vacation I tackle the problem of how to go home enthusiastically and hopefully.
3. Friday the 13th only comes a few times each year.
4. I do not think that we will be able to overcome these difficulties.
5. Surely no one has a desire to injure or kill those whom he loves by carelessness.
6. The band I am in now practices every day.
7. The surface of the lake was calm except for the air bubbles from the fish which formed ringlets on the surface.
8. All the way home I tried to think of a way to tell my mother of the accident in a smooth manner.
9. I am not speaking for all our students, but for quite a few.
10. I would like to schedule a conference to discuss my theme writing on the 10th of October.
11. Some paper companies write letters pointing out the advantages of buying paper in groups of sentences separated by double spacing.
12. The car we bought had only been driven a total distance of 3,000 miles.
13. During their courtship Father asked Mother to marry him many times.
14. I usually spend a week with my relatives in Colorado a year.
15. Sometimes concentrating is easier if I study the subject I like least at the beginning of the study period.
16. The coach said he wanted to see all boys who desire to play football at 10 A.M. Thursday in the high school cafeteria.
17. In astronomy I still plan to pick up where I left off next summer.
18. I am returning the completed file with authorized bills attached to you.
19. Although she is a natural practical joker, in my opinion, my little sister is liked by everyone.
20. On our way home the car we were driving slowly puttered to a stop.

DANGLING MODIFIERS

40. Dangling modifiers, those which do not properly or clearly depend upon the right words, are of two kinds: dangling verbal phrases and dangling elliptical clauses. Ambiguity and even ludicrousness frequently result from their use.

40a. Avoid dangling verbal phrases at the beginning of a sentence or independent clause.

Dangling verbal phrases consist of participial, prepositional-gerund, and infinitive phrases. Such a phrase dangles when (1) it has no substantive (i.e., noun or pronoun) to modify, or (2) the substantive is the wrong one. Usually the phrase begins the sentence or the independent clause and should therefore logically modify the subject of the sentence or the clause. The most ludicrous examples are those in which a phrase expressing motion modifies a subject which is stationary, or a phrase expressing fixity modifies a moving subject.

Ludicrous: Walking through the main gate of the park, the swimming pool is just ahead. (Dangling participle)

Turning the corner, the Post Office Building is seen. (Dangling participle)

Standing at the intersection, the Greyhound bus roared by. (Dangling participle)

Having been soaked all night in diluted acid, I hung the specimen up to dry. (Dangling participle)

Smelling of liquor, the policeman arrested the driver. (Dangling participle)

Sometimes the dangling phrase is merely a misplaced modifier (see Section 39b), as in the two incongruous examples below.

Incongruous: Hanging from the very top of the tree, Grandfather saw a robin's nest.

Buried several inches under ground, our dog tried to locate the bone.

Improved: Grandfather saw a robin's nest hanging from the very top of the tree.

Our dog tried to locate the bone buried several inches under ground.

Not so serious but still to be avoided are less ludicrous and incongruous modifiers.

In preparing for a test, it is advisable to review thoroughly. (Dangling prepositional-gerund phrase)

In business letters, the dangling *enclosed you* phrase is common—
does it mean that *you* are enclosed?

Dangling: Enclosed with this letter you will find your membership card.
Enclosed you will find an order blank.
Enclosed please find a check for $7.85.
Improved: Enclosed with this letter is your membership card.
You will find an order blank enclosed.
A check for $7.85 is enclosed.
I am enclosing a check for $7.85.

The dangling infinitive phrase is less frequent and incongruous,
partly because a writer usually uses, or has in mind, an adverbial *in
order to* phrase. Many introductory infinitive phrases state or suggest
purpose. Clearness and effectiveness are best served when such infinitive
phrases depend upon the noun or pronoun indicating the one who has
the purpose in mind.

Questionable: To succeed in life, ambition is necessary.
To play golf well, a good set of clubs is needed.
Improved: To succeed in life, a man must have some ambition.
To play golf well, you need a good set of clubs.

Sentences containing dangling verbal phrases may be corrected in
several ways: (1) expand the verbal phrase to a dependent clause; (2)
supply the noun or pronoun which the phrase should modify; (3) place
the phrase so near the proper substantive that there can be no confusion. Such corrections eliminate the dangling modifier, but some of
them are awkward and inconsistent, and the sentence may need rephrasing.

Correct and Walking through the main gate of the park, I saw the swim-
clear: ming pool just ahead.
After you walk through the main gate of the park, the swim-
ming pool is just ahead. (Better: . . ., you see the swimming
pool just ahead.)
Turning the corner, you will see the Post Office Building.
Just as you turn the corner, the Post Office Building is seen.
(Better: . . ., you will see the Post Office Building.)
Standing at the intersection, we saw the Greyhound bus roar
by.

As we stood at the intersection, the Greyhound bus roared by.

After being soaked all night in diluted acid, the specimen was hung up to dry.

Smelling of liquor, the driver of the car was arrested by the policeman.

In preparing for a test, a student should review thoroughly.

When a student is preparing for a test, it is advisable to review thoroughly.

Occasionally, even an introductory prepositional phrase is dangling:

After graduation from high school, my father asked about my future plans.

Better: After I graduated from high school, my father asked about my future plans.

After graduation from high school, I was asked by my father about my future plans.

40b. Avoid dangling verbal phrases tacked on at the end of a sentence or independent clause.

Participial phrases tacked on to the end of a statement with *thus, thereby,* and *therefore* are also dangling because they have no noun or pronoun to modify. Clearness is served if these dangling modifiers are removed by (1) making the participle a member of a compound predicate or (2) rephrasing the sentence.

Questionable: I was ill for several weeks, thus causing me to fall behind in my work.

We lost the last game of the season, thereby preventing us from going to the Rose Bowl.

Improved: I was ill for several weeks and thus fell behind in my work.

We lost the last game of the season and were thereby prevented from going to the Rose Bowl.

My several weeks' illness caused me to fall behind in my work.

Our loss in the last game of the season prevented us from going to the Rose Bowl.

When a verbal phrase is used to specify a general action, it is not considered a dangling modifier:

Approved: Generally speaking, tuition fees should not be increased.

Such words or phrases as *considering, concerning, according to, owing to,* etc., are used prepositionally, not as verbals. Thus, "*Considering* everything, the proposal was fair" is a correct and clear sentence.

40c. Avoid dangling elliptical clauses.

Ellipsis means an omission. An elliptical clause, usually a dependent clause, is one from which the subject or verb, or both, have been left out. The reader understands what they are, for presumably they are the same as those in the independent clause.

Clear: When [. . .] in New York last month, we visited the United Nations Building.

       When [we were] in New York last month, we visited the United Nations Building.

The *dangling* elliptical clause is one in which the understood subject and predicate are not the same as those of the main clause. The usual offenders are clauses introduced by *before, after, while, when, though,* and *if.*

As from dangling verbal phrases, ambiguity and ludicrousness result from dangling elliptical clauses:

> Before warmed up, you should never race a motor.
> While studying last evening, the lights went out.
> When six years old, my grandmother died.
> Though failing the course, my instructor kept giving me encouragement.

Two ways of correcting dangling elliptical clauses are the following: (1) insert in the dependent clause the subject and verb or verb part needed to make the sentence clear, or (2) change the subject or subject-verb in the independent clause so that it, or they, would be clear logically if they were also expressed in the dependent clause.

Clear: Before it is warmed up, you should never race a motor.

       Before being warmed up, a motor should never be raced.

       While I was studying last evening, the lights went out.

       While studying last evening, I found myself suddenly in darkness; the lights had gone out.

       When I was six years old, my grandmother died.

       When six years old, I grieved because my grandmother had died.

       Though I was failing the course, my instructor kept giving me encouragement.

Though failing the course, I was given constant encouragement by my instructor.

EXERCISES

A. Each of the following sentences contains a dangling phrase at or near the beginning. Correct each sentence twice, by using two of the three methods suggested in Section **40a**.

1. After twenty minutes of riding, the lights of the football field appeared before us.
2. Looking to the future, it appears that more and more engineers will be needed in the atomic-energy field.
3. After seeing that fish for the first time, my heart skipped a few beats.
4. Upon entering my room, my tired mind reminisced over the events of the day.
5. Speaking for myself, one day at the State Fair is often too much.
6. After three hours of performing, the judges announced the winners.
7. Traveling toward the Oregon boundary, the hills become rugged.
8. Cooked on her eight-burner cob-burning stove, Grandma would have slabs of bacon, dozens of eggs, hot cereal, stacks of pancakes, honey, and a bowl of melted butter.
9. By sending me to my father's school, other students thought I was given special consideration.
10. Upon entering the driveway of my home, lights were turned on all over the house.
11. Living on Long Island Sound, swimming and boating facilities are almost limitless.
12. In reviewing my errors in writing, it appears that misspellings are the most common.
13. After living in Philadelphia for three years, my father's occupation took him to Cleveland.
14. Sitting here, my thoughts wander to the past.
15. Upon graduation from high school, my parents promised me that I could buy a car.
16. Being a fraternal organization, the boys are glad to go to camp at the expense of the Rotarians.
17. In trying to do a few last-minute things, the plane was missed.
18. Looking from the tower. many churches are noticed.
19. To enjoy poetry, it should be read slowly and carefully.
20. After walking around the station for an hour, my train was by then ready to leave.

B. Each of the following sentences contains a dangling phrase at or near the end. Correct each.

1. As I have pointed out, pharmacy is growing, thus making immense the opportunities for a person entering the field.
2. Someday you may be able to help others with your success, thereby repaying the help you received.
3. Study habits are developed by sitting down and reading the material carefully.
4. Some things cannot be completely understood before coming to college.
5. He became old, wrinkled, and ugly, resulting from the evil he had done.
6. A drowning person becomes panicky and incoherent, thus lessening his chances for being rescued.
7. It was really a pleasure to see my friends again, after being away for over two months.
8. The letter was inexactly addressed, thereby causing delay in its delivery.
9. "Welcome" is the first sign noticed upon entering our city limits.
10. Snow fell most of the night, causing the plane to be delayed for three hours.

C. Correct each of the dangling elliptical clauses in the following sentences by using for each the two methods suggested in Section **40c.**

1. While still a child, Father started to discipline me.
2. If applied too suddenly, the wheels will lock.
3. Before writing a theme, it is wise to follow an outline.
4. When speaking of orange juice, Florida will always enter the mind first.
5. Before you know it, a fight has started under the goal while trying to rebound.
6. While walking to classes, the heel of one of my shoes came off.
7. Many problems arise when owning a car.
8. Though fried in deep fat, Mother still served half-raw potatoes.
9. When driving along this beautiful highway, massive cliffs loom ahead.
10. Sign in a butcher shop: Meat may be watched by the customer while being chopped.

SPLIT CONSTRUCTIONS

41. Nothing is actually incorrect about separating or splitting closely related materials. From the point of view of the reader, the objection to splitting involves clearness and, even more, effectiveness.

Since English is not a highly inflected language (Section 39), and since many English words show little if any inflectional change, it is important to keep related elements together. Writers sometimes unnecessarily separate closely related elements, and the result is awkwardness and ambiguity, not clearness and effectiveness.

Closely related parts in a sentence are verbs in a verb phrase, coordinate sentence elements, subject and predicate, verb and object, verb and complement, preposition and object, the two parts of an infinitive, and other word combinations logically belonging together.

41a. Do not needlessly separate the parts of a verb phrase.

When more than one verb word is involved, the normal verb phrase in English consists of the auxiliary verb and the main verb. Apply the tests of smoothness and logic, clearness and effectiveness in separating these verb forms; single adverbs splitting a verb phrase are usually effective and rarely awkward:

Awkward: I *shall see* never his like again.
             I *shall see* his like never again.
Effective: I never *shall see* his like again.
             I *shall never see* his like again.

When long phrases or clauses do the splitting, however, keep the parts of a verb phrase together.

Awkward: This tree *has,* although you would not think so, *been* here for 80 years.
Improved: Although you would not think so, this tree *has been* here for 80 years.

Awkward: He *is,* despite many objections from his parents, *going* to study music and painting.
Improved: He *is going* to study music and painting despite many objections from his parents.
             Despite many objections from his parents, he *is going* to study music and painting.

41b. Avoid a widely split infinitive.

In some verb constructions the infinitive is used without its accompanying sign *to;* in other verb constructions the sign of the infinitive *to* is necessary. When words, phrases, or even clauses come between *to* and the verb, the construction is called a *split infinitive.*

Split infinitives have been used by many reputable writers, but a study of these examples shows that in effective writing rarely is more than a single word, usually an adverb, used between *to* and the verb. In "He failed to *entirely* pay for it," *entirely* is properly and effectively placed next to the verb *pay,* which it modifies.

Let clearness, naturalness, and effectiveness be the tests for split infinitives. The use of a phrase or a clause as a separating element is rarely clear, or natural, or effective.

Ineffective: Our family physician telegraphed us *to* as soon as possible *come.*
Improved: Our family physician telegraphed us *to come* as soon as possible.

41c.   Avoid unnecessary separation of subject and predicate, verb and object, verb and complement, preposition and object, or other closely related sentence elements.

Awkward and My brother, as soon as he received a favorable reply to his
ineffective: application, left for New York for an interview.
                 Mary asked, even before my sentence was completed, the exact meaning of my statement.
                 His remark was, despite its seemingly apparent innocence, both impolite and unkind.
                 With, and no one hopes for any other kind, good weather, we should arrive early in the afternoon.
Improved: As soon as he received a favorable reply to his application, my brother left for New York for an interview.
                 Even before my sentence was completed, Mary asked the exact meaning of my statement.
                 Despite its seemingly apparent innocence, his remark was both impolite and unkind.
                 With good weather, and no one hopes for any other kind, we should arrive early in the afternoon.

On occasion, greater clearness may be achieved by separation, as suggested in "Misplaced Modifiers" (Section 39), or both greater clearness and smoothness, as in this sentence, where verb and object are split in the improved version:

Vague: In his remarks the psychologist discussed everyday matters and people whom you and I know *as simply as a child.*
Improved: In his remarks the psychologist discussed, *as simply as a child,* everyday matters and people whom you and I know.

Such separation of closely related elements should be made for appropriate and specific purposes, never aimlessly.

41d.　Place coordinate sentence elements together.

When two coordinate phrases or two coordinate dependent clauses are used in a sentence, one should not come at the beginning and the other at the end. For effectiveness keep them together and indicate their relationship by the appropriate coordinating conjunction.

Ineffective:　*Although he was a good tennis player,* he was not able to make the varsity squad, *although he practiced daily.*

Effective:　*Although he was a good tennis player* and *although he practiced daily,* he was not able to make the varsity squad.

Ineffective:　*With fair weather,* we should have an enjoyable fishing trip, *with good luck.*

Effective:　*With fair weather* and *good luck,* we should have an enjoyable fishing trip.

EXERCISES

Point out and correct all faulty split constructions in the following sentences:

1. I, during the last three summers, have worked for my father.
2. Plant improvement has made larger yields, from a better adapted grain variety, possible.
3. If the coach gives his permission, we can play 36 holes of golf this afternoon, if it does not rain.
4. My resolution had not been made an hour until a very good friend of mine, who had just arrived home for the holidays, called.
5. Almost everyone has, at one time or another, let his mind wander during the class hour.
6. I hope to eventually and completely eliminate all errors in spelling from my writing.
7. Uncle Bob attempted to start the engine, but it would just not start.
8. Because it was raining, I did not like to go fishing, because the fish would not bite well.
9. This dog could do almost everything required of a retriever perfectly.
10. Then the glorious task of cleaning up the mess of papers which have accumulated in the middle of the floor and the boxes which were thrown in every direction begins.

TRANSITION

42.   Individual sentences may be correct, clear, effective, and appropriate, and yet be neither clear nor effective when they are put together in a paragraph. If the order of sentences within a paragraph is fully logical, any lack of clearness probably is due to faulty *transition*. Remember that *transition* means passing from one place, state, or position to another, and that *evidence of transition* consists of linking or bridging devices.

Three kinds of transition apply to writing: between paragraphs (Section 11), within the sentence, and between sentences. When used within the sentence, transitional devices usually come between clauses; when used between sentences, they come near or at the beginning or end of the sentences they link. Not only must your thoughts progress logically; your reader also must readily grasp both them and their interrelations. Only thus can effective communication be achieved.

42a. Make sentence transitions clear by using transitional words and phrases.

Transitional words and phrases are not needed within or between all sentences, and your best guide is consideration for your reader: have you made the relationship between ideas evident to him?

1. Between dependent and independent clauses evidence of relationship is expressed by

subordinating conjunctions: *after, as soon as, because, before, for, if, in order that, lest, since, unless, until, when, where, whereupon, whither,* etc. (For fuller list, see pp. 605–607.)
relative pronouns: *who, whose, whom, which, that*

2. Between independent clauses or between sentences, evidence of relationship is expressed by

personal pronouns: *I, my, mine, me, we, our, ours, us, you, your, yours, he, his, him, she, her, hers, it, its, they, their, theirs, them*
demonstrative pronouns: *this, that, these, those, such*
simple or pure conjunctions: *and, but, or, nor, neither, yet*
correlative conjunctions: *both . . . and, neither . . . nor, either . . . or, not only . . . but also*
conjunctive or parenthetic adverbs: *accordingly, besides, consequently,*

furthermore, hence, however, instead, meanwhile, moreover, nevertheless, otherwise, still, then, therefore, thus, etc. (For fuller list see pp. 605–607.)

3. Other words and phrases for sentence transition include the following: *afterward, again, as a result, as an illustration, as I said, for example, fortunately, from what has been said, here, in addition, in contrast, in fact, in short, in the next place, indeed, more than, most of all, namely, naturally, now, of course, on the contrary, soon, temporarily, too, truly, well.*

In using these transitional words and phrases, remember that the beginnings and endings of sentences are emphatic positions. Pure conjunctions must, of course, come at the beginning of sentences or clauses, subordinate conjunctions and relative pronouns at the beginning of dependent clauses; conjunctive adverbs and parenthetic phrases may come at the beginning of independent clauses, but here and in sentences they add effectiveness by being placed as second or third words.

Special care should be taken when you move from your own writing to quoting or phrasing others' materials. Examples:

. . . As Abraham Lincoln said, in his "Address at Gettysburg," ". . . ." The result is that . . .

Certain lines from Shakespeare's *Julius Caesar* well summarize this philosophy:

In considering ideals over and beyond our vocational activities, let us remember the Bible verse concerning man's need to live by more than bread alone.

. . . This point is well illustrated in the following sentence from Matthew Arnold's essay, "Literature and Science": . . . As a result, we can apply . . .

42b. Make sentence transitions clear by repetition of nouns and by use of pronouns.

The most effective kind of repetition for sentence transitions is the use of pronouns referring to preceding nouns and pronouns. Synonyms are also effective. Occasionally, too, key or important words can be repeated in several sentences, but this kind of repetition (see Section **67e, f**) for sentence transition is not nearly so effective as it is for paragraph transition.

In the following sentences, from the first two paragraphs of Thomas

319

Henry Huxley's "The Method of Scientific Investigation," the italicized words illustrate the various devices for sentence transition, discussed above.

The method of scientific investigation is nothing but the expression of the necessary mode of working of the human mind. *It* is *simply* the *mode* at which all phenomena are reasoned about, rendered precise and exact. . . .
You will understand *this better, perhaps, if* I give *you* some familiar example. *You* have all heard it repeated, *I* dare say, that *men of science* work by means of *induction and deduction, and* that by the help of *these operations, they,* in a sort of sense, wring from nature certain *other* things which are called natural laws and causes, and that out of *these,* by some cunning skill of *their* own, *they* build up hypotheses and theories. *And* it is imagined by many that the operations of the common mind can be *by no means* compared with *these processes, and* that *they* have to be acquired by a sort of special apprenticeship to the craft. To hear *all these* large words *you* would think that the *mind* of *a man of science* must be constituted differently from *that* of *his* fellow men; *but if you* will not be frightened by terms, *you* will discover that *you* are quite wrong, *and* that *all these* terrible apparatus are being used by *yourselves* everyday and every hour of *your* lives.

42c. Avoid inexact transition.

Use transitional words and phrases as necessary, but use them correctly. Inexact transitional words are the equivalent of inexact diction. (See Section 61.)

Inexact: He did not get the telegram before he left *whereas* it was delivered late.

I wanted to study architecture, *and* my father wanted me to become a lawyer.

I know I forgot to pay the bill *whereupon* I have the money in my pocket.

My roommate wished to spend Christmas vacation in Florida; *on the other hand,* his parents also wanted him to go.

Improved: He did not get the telegram before he left *because* it was delivered late.

I wanted to study architecture, *but* my father wanted me to become a lawyer.

I know I forgot to pay the bill, *for* I *still* have the money in my pocket.

My roommate wished to spend Christmas vacation in Florida; *fortunately,* his parents also wanted him to go.

42d. Avoid labored and artificial transition in sentences.

The major purpose of transitions is to show relationship and the direction of relationship; a secondary but not unimportant aim is to make evident this relationship smoothly, skillfully, and unobtrusively.

In the first example transitions are needed between short choppy sentences and clauses:

Baseball is said to be the national game; I do not like it. If it is the national game, thousands must enjoy watching it, or playing it. I know people who do not ever attend a game; I know people who see as many as 50 games a year. I should not make a dogmatic statement about the appeal of the sport; I have never witnessed a game.

In a first revision, the student conspicuously inserted transitional words and phrases, here italicized, at the beginning of each sentence or independent clause, as follows:

Baseball is said to be the national game; *however,* I do not like it. *Yet* if it is the national game, thousands must enjoy watching it, or playing it. *To be sure,* I know people who do not ever attend a game; *on the other hand,* I know people who see as many as 50 games a year. *Perhaps* I should not make a dogmatic statement about the appeal of the sport; *you see,* I have never witnessed a game.

After considering Section 47, "Position and Arrangement," and Section 48, "Variety," and letting pronouns and repetition serve as part of the transitional devices, the student produced this more acceptable revision. Greater clearness and smoothness are gained with the italicized words:

Although baseball is said to be America's national game, I do not like *it.* *Yet* if *it* is the *national game,* hundreds must enjoy playing the *game* and thousands must enjoy watching *it.* I know people who see as many as 50 or 60 *games* a season and who drive many miles to see *them;* on the other hand, I know people who never attend a *game* and who wouldn't walk across the street to see *one. Perhaps* it is all a matter of *sporting* taste, *and perhaps* I should not make a dogmatic statement about the appeal of *baseball. You see,* I have never seen a *game, and* I prefer a *sport* that I can take part in, peacefully, quietly, badly perhaps, and without "fan"-fare. *I prefer* golf.

EXERCISES

A. Mark all the transitional words and phrases used in the sentences in five paragraphs of an article in your book of readings. Try to read the sentences, omitting the transitional devices. Then discuss these transitional words and phrases by indicating their meaning and the purposes that they serve.

B. Repeat Exercise A, but apply the directions to an article in a current magazine.

CONCISENESS

43.   *Conciseness* literally means "expressing much in a few words; brief and to the point." Logically, therefore, conciseness is primarily a problem in diction, and as such it is discussed in Section 67. There the discussion concerns words and word combinations in phrases, such as avoidance of superfluous words, unnecessary repetition, reduction of wordy phrases, circumlocutions and euphemisms, and overuse of modifiers. Conciseness is also a problem in writing sentences.

A sentence may be complete and unified and yet be ineffective because it is wordy. A sentence of 100 words may be concise, and one of 20 may be wordy. No sentence can be effective when it contains too many words or ideas—or too few. Francis Bacon was probably the most concise of English writers (see pp. 106, 331) and somewhat difficult to understand because of his conciseness.

In the clear and effective use of "how many words?" the golden mean of word number applies to parts of sentences, to sentences, to paragraphs, to themes. Its guiding suggestion: Do not use so many words that meaning is lost in a forest of verbiage and so few that meaning is obscured through brevity. The problem is one of effectiveness. Wordiness, like long-windedness in speech, is never effective.

In addition to the advice concerning conciseness in word use (Section 67), three suggestions apply specifically to sentences.

43a. Reduce predication.

At various places—in this handbook and by your instructor—you are advised to *reduce predication*.

Reducing predication means reducing the number of words to make an assertion, cutting out all unnecessary words by making one word serve the purpose of two or three or more. For example, one synonym can replace several words without jeopardizing in any way the intended meaning. For clearness and effectiveness, a writer will

1. Combine two short sentences into one (see also Section **46**):

From: I am a freshman in the School of Home Economics. I am specializing in Applied Design.

To: I am a freshman in the School of Home Economics, specializing in Applied Design.

2. Reduce a compound sentence to a complex or simple sentence:

From: Joe E. Brown has for years been an excellent comedian, and there isn't anyone who doesn't like Joe E. Brown.

To: Everyone likes Joe E. Brown, who has for years been an excellent comedian.

3. Reduce a complex sentence to a simple sentence:

From: Everyone likes Joe E. Brown, who has for years been an excellent comedian.

To: Everyone likes Joe E. Brown, for years an excellent comedian.

4. Reduce clauses to phrases (see preceding example also):

From: . . . a haze which resembled the color of smoke.

To: . . . a haze like the color of smoke.

5. Reduce clauses and phrases to single words:

From: . . . waiting until I became frantic.

To: . . . waiting frantically.

From: . . . a haze like the color of smoke.

To: . . . a smoke-colored haze.

6. Reduce two or more words to one:

From: . . . a member of a fraternity.

To: . . . a fraternity member.

From: . . . an instructor in the Department of Mathematics.

To: . . . a mathematics instructor.

From: . . . are going to attend.

To: . . . will attend.

Study the following series of reductions. In the first statement are 19 words. In the last statement are seven words. Has the last omitted any essential information not included in the first?

1. In the distance we could see the tops of the Rocky Mountains. These mountain tops were covered with snow.

2. In the distance we could see the tops of the Rocky Mountains, which were covered with snow.
3. In the distance we could see the Rocky Mountains, which were covered with snow.
4. In the distance we could see the Rocky Mountains, covered with snow.
5. In the distance we could see the snow-covered Rocky Mountains.
6. In the distance we saw the snow-covered Rocky Mountains.
7. We saw the distant, snow-covered Rocky Mountains.

An ancient Eastern king commissioned his wise men to condense all the wisdom of the world. Through the years they successively produced 500 volumes, then 50 volumes, then one volume, because through the years the king, becoming older, had less and less time for extended reading. With old age and death upon him, the king asked for one paragraph, then one sentence, finally one word. The word: *Perhaps!*

43b. Avoid sentences containing unnecessary details.

Sentences containing unnecessary details illustrate the fault of *prolixity*. A prolix sentence is long-winded and tiresomely wordy; it extends to tedious length; it is therefore ineffective because its details obscure or weaken the point of the main idea.

> Last summer the local junior golf tournament was won by my brother Harry with a set of golf clubs that he had purchased two years before from a friend of mine who had bought a new set and who sold the boy his old clubs at a bargain price.
> "Pursuant to your recent telephone request, we have noted our records to the effect that receipts are to be sent to you each time a premium is paid by you on your policy." (From a life insurance letter)

Freed of unnecessary details, these sentences say:

> Last summer my brother Harry won the local junior golf tournament with a second-hand set of clubs.
> "We will be glad to send you a receipt each time you pay a premium on your policy." (Life insurance company's revision)

43c. Avoid the useless repetition of an idea.

Useless repetition of an idea in a different word, phrase, or sentence is called *tautology*. Applied to the sentence, tautology is illustrated by the following:

I was very anxious for my friend to succeed, eager that he do so, and zealous that he achieve the self-satisfaction of being a success.

This absolutely new and novel innovation will please our customers; it has just been introduced for the first time and will cause pleasure to many people.

We climbed steadily all morning and finally ascended up to the very top of the mountain; then, after a short rest, we started the return journey, continued steadily toward lower levels, and soon had descended down in half the time it had taken us to ascend up.

EXERCISES

A. Look up in a good dictionary the following nouns: *brevity, circumlocution, curtness, diffuseness, periphrasis, pleonasm, prolixity, redundancy, sententiousness, succinctness, tautology, terseness, verbiage, verbosity*. Write expanded definitions of any five (see Sections **16c**2a and **24b**7).

B. Look up in a good dictionary the following adjectives: *compendious, concise, diffuse, laconic, pithy, prolix, redundant, succinct, summary, terse*. Write expanded definitions of any five (see Sections **16c**2a and **24b**7).

C. Make more concise the following sentences:

1. There are two basic forms of communication which man uses. These two forms of communication are writing and speaking.
2. Last summer I took a week-end trip to Kentucky Lake. Kentucky Lake is located near Benton, Kentucky.
3. I come from Fountain City, Tennessee. It is a small town located on U.S. 29, just nine miles south of Richmond, Tennessee.
4. Pictures of our city's industries were compiled into colorful booklets. These booklets were printed in many languages and distributed throughout the world.
5. My favorite sport is baseball. That is a wonderful sport for boys and a sport that keeps an athlete on his toes.
6. We now have a park that was opened not long ago. The land, not long ago, on which the park is now located, was once just a piece of wasteland and swamp that has since been drained.
7. She was a great talker who spoke well and who often had a great deal to say on each and every possible occasion.
8. Anyone who knows anything about the young people of this day and age knows that the more tactfully and diplomatically they are handled, the better their social behavior will be as far as the other sex is concerned.

9. That side of the structure receives the morning sun but during the time that the sun is in the west and afternoon shadows begin to fall, it is dreary and cheerless.

10. I waited for the signal which would indicate that the hunt had begun, but the dogs with their barking and the horses with their stamping drowned out all other sounds and noises.

PARALLELISM

44. *Parallel,* a word from the field of mathematics, in its usual sense and referring to two lines, means extending in the same direction and at the same distance apart at every point. Teachers of writing have adopted the words *parallelism* and *parallel* to mean "close resemblance, similarity"; that is, when two or more ideas in a sentence are related and serve a similar purpose, they can be phrased in the same grammatical form.

When not overused, parallel construction is an excellent device for correctness, clearness, and effectiveness. It shows immediately what ideas are of equal importance; it helps to make sentences grammatically correct; and, appropriately used, it is one means of attaining or contributing to an emphatic, vigorous style.

The simplest form of parallelism is two or more words in a series. Using more complex forms, the writer can make two or more phrases parallel, or two or more dependent clauses, or two or more independent clauses, or two or more sentences, or even two or more paragraphs.

Words:	Henry is *slow* but *thorough.*
	The American colors are *red, white,* and *blue.*
	My favorite boyhood activities were *hunting, fishing,* and *trapping.*
Phrases:	Both *at home* and *at school* Joe has his mind only on basketball.
	Every afternoon my grandfather is at the barber shop *telling yarns about his youth* or *hearing the yarns that his cronies tell.*
Dependent clauses:	I was desperate *when I arrived late on the campus* and *when I found that no desirable rooms were available.*
Independent clauses:	Julius Caesar's most famous statement was this: *"I came, I saw, I conquered."*

Sentences: Alfred Lord Tennyson was the British poet who wrote lyrics in his early life and dramas in his closing years. Robert Browning was the British poet who wrote dramas in his early career and other forms of poetry in his later life.

As an effective test for true parallelism, draw lines under the parallel elements. Then draw a corresponding number of lines in parallel form and write the underlined words on them. Examples from the illustrations above:

Every afternoon Grandfather is at the barber shop

<u>telling yarns about his youth</u>

or

<u>hearing the yarns that his cronies tell.</u>

Julius Caesar's most famous statement was this: <u>I came</u>

<u>I saw</u>

<u>I conquered</u>

For clear and effective parallelism, apply the following principles:

44a. Sentence elements that are coordinate in rank should be parallel in structure.

An infinitive phrase should be coordinate with an infinitive phrase, a prepositional phrase with a prepositional phrase, a participial phrase with a participial phrase, a dependent clause with a similar dependent clause, an independent clause with an independent clause. The same general principle applies to other kinds of phrases and to similar kinds of words.

Wrong: He liked to row and playing tennis.
Right: He liked to row and to play tennis.
   or
   He liked rowing and playing tennis.

Wrong: Our Glee Club sings at many school functions, engagements in nearby towns, and concert tours.
Right: Our Glee Club sings at many school functions, has engagements in near-by towns, and makes other concert tours.

Wrong: An all-round student would like to make Phi Beta Kappa and that he might earn a varsity letter.

Right: An all-round student would like to make Phi Beta Kappa and to earn a varsity letter.
or
An all-round student has two ambitions: a Phi Beta Kappa key and a varsity letter.

Observe how a parallelism diagram helps to distinguish faulty parallelism from true parallelism:

He liked   to row   to row
            and   and
            playing tennis to play tennis

Our Glee Club sings at many school   sings at many school functions
                        functions   has engagements in near-by
                        engagements in   towns
                        near-by towns   and
                        and   makes other concert tours
                        concert tours

An all-round student
    would like   to make Phi Beta Kappa   to make Phi Beta Kappa
                 and   and
                 that he might earn a varsity letter   to earn a varsity letter

Absolute parallelism is not always required. In the following the form is not parallel, but the functions are. In the first example, parallel elements are adverbial; in the second, three nouns (two proper, and one common noun with modifier) are parallel.

The second speaker talked *slowly* and *with a slight stammer.*
I saw *John, Henry,* and *a man whom I did not know.*

NOTE: For clearness, parallelism is necessary in outlines: in the sentence outline all coordinate divisions should be sentences; in the topic outline all coordinate divisions should be the same kinds of words, phrases, or clauses. (See Section 6e2.)

44b. Sentence elements following correlative conjunctions should be parallel in form.

The four common pairs of correlative conjunctions, *both—and, either—or, neither—nor,* and *not only—but also* (see pp. 602–603, 605–

607), coordinate and correlate similar ideas. Each member of the pair should be followed *immediately* by the same grammatical form, two similar words, two similar phrases, or two similar clauses.

Faulty: I *neither* have the time *nor* the inclination to play basketball.
          Either you can cash your check at the bank *or* at the local bookstore.
          The committee requests that you be *either* seated before the beginning of the concert *or* that you wait outside until the conclusion of the first number.

Improved: I have *neither* the time *nor* the inclination to play basketball.
          You can cash your check *either* at the bank *or* at the local bookstore.
          The committee requests *either* that you be seated before the beginning of the concert *or* that you wait outside until the conclusion of the first number.

Parallelism diagram:

I have <u>neither</u> the time
       <u>nor</u>   the inclination to play basketball
You can cash your check <u>either</u> at the bank
             <u>or</u>   at the local bookstore
The committee requests <u>either</u> that you be seated before the beginning of the concert
             <u>or</u>   that you wait outside until the conclusion of the first number

44c.   Avoid ineffective partial parallelism.

In using the formula A, B, and C for a series of elements, make certain that the sentence elements are similar in idea and parallel in form. If they are not, a faulty and unemphatic series will result.

Undesirable: The story is *vivid, interesting,* and *has a simple plot.*
Improved: The story is *vivid, interesting, simple in plot.*
             or
             The story is *simple, interesting,* and *vivid.*
Undesirable: Uncle James has worked *in the steel mills, ordnance plant, a factory,* and *kept a filling station.*
Improved: Uncle James has worked in *the steel mills, an ordnance plant,* and *a factory;* he has also kept a filling station.

Parallelism diagrams:

(Showing error)   The story is <u>vivid</u>
                              <u>interesting</u>
                              and
                              <u>has a simple plot</u>

(Showing corrections) <u>Uncle James has worked in the steel mills</u>
                                          <u>an ordnance plant</u>
                                          and
                                          <u>a factory</u>
                    <u>he has also kept a filling station</u>

44d. Avoid misleading parallelism.

Use the same structural form only for sentence elements of equal value. Apparent parallelism misleads in two ways:

1. Certain ideas are arranged in parallel form, but study shows that they are neither parallel nor coordinate in content, that there is little logical relationship in the ideas expressed. Example (second idea not related to first):

> We recently bought a TV from a local dealer and with a beautiful mahogany finish.

Example (third idea not parallel in thought with the first two ideas):

> The speaker pointed out that college graduates have more earning power, enjoy a higher social status, and can be more accurately sampled in a survey of this kind than manual workers.

2. A series of elements may appear to modify the same element when really not parallel. Two phrases or two clauses may begin with the same words, but they do not introduce parallel elements or ideas. Apply the parallelism diagram as a test.

Wrong: *For your sake for $50* I will help you.
         It is important *that each of you bring along a prospective new member that you can wholeheartedly recommend.*
Clear: For your sake I will help you to the extent of $50.
         It is important that each of you bring along a prospective new member whom you can wholeheartedly recommend.

EXERCISES

A. Make parallelism diagrams for all parallel elements in the following passages, each of which is from the work of a master of English prose:

1. The world will little note nor long remember what we say here, but it can never forget what they did here. It is for us, the living, rather, to be dedicated here to the unfinished work which they who fought here have thus far so nobly advanced. It is rather for us to be here dedicated to the great task remaining before us; that from these honored dead we take increased devotion to that cause for which they gave the last full measure of devotion; that we here highly resolve that these dead shall not have died in vain; that this nation, under God, shall have a new birth of freedom; and that government of the people, by the people, for the people, shall not perish from the earth.

—ABRAHAM LINCOLN, "Address at Gettysburg"

2. Studies serve for delight, for ornament, and for ability. Their chief use for delight, is in privateness and retiring; for ornament, is in discourse; and for ability, is in the judgment and disposition of business. For expert men can execute, and perhaps judge of particulars, one by one; but the general counsels, and the plots and marshalling of affairs, come best from those that are learned. To spend too much time in studies is sloth; to use them too much for ornament, is affectation; to make judgment wholly by their rules, is the humour of a scholar.

—FRANCIS BACON, "Of Studies"

3. It is the fate of those who toil at the lower employments of life to be rather driven by the fear of evil than attracted by the prospect of good; to be exposed to censure, without hope of praise; to be disgraced by miscarriage, or punished for neglect, where success would have been without applause, and diligence without reward. . . .

In this work, when it shall be found that much is omitted, let it not be forgotten that much likewise is performed, and, though no book was ever spared out of tenderness to the author, and the world is little solicitous to know whence proceeded the faults of that which it condemns, yet it may gratify curiosity to inform it, that the *English Dictionary* was written with little assistance of the learned, and without any patronage of the great; not in the soft obscurities of retirement, or under the shelter of academic bowers, but amidst inconvenience and distraction, in sickness and in sorrow. . . .

I have protracted my work till most of those whom I wished to please have sunk into the grave, and success and miscarriage are empty sounds; I therefore dismiss it with frigid tranquillity, having little to fear or hope from censure or from praise.

—SAMUEL JOHNSON, "Preface to *A Dictionary of the English Language*"

B. Correct all errors in faulty parallelism in the following sentences by (1) changing the structure of the first element to agree with that of later ones, and then (2) changing the structure of later elements to agree with that of the first.

1. I have brown hair, brown eyes, stand about six feet high, and I am 18 years of age.
2. The prerequisites for joining our glee club are an interest in music, a male, and having a voice with which to sing.
3. Mother knew his family and also that he had been brought up properly by his parents.
4. Other activities I took part in were girls' chorus, junior play, Latin Club, and a typist for our annual yearbook.
5. I have now reached my first goal—to be enrolled in college and supporting myself.
6. Three common superstitions are: (1) third man on a match; (2) avoid walking on cracks in the sidewalk, and (3) don't let a black cat walk in front of you.
7. Since the two were good friends and also that my father was one of the best sales engineers in the business, my father was offered the job.
8. Basketball is fast moving, fun to play, enjoyable to watch, and requires team play.
9. The best way to spend money is a combination of two ways: not spending too much and not to spend too little.
10. I found out his name; Chuck Brown, and that he was from Abilene, Kansas.
11. An American is never happy until he can buy food, appliances, and spend his money on entertainment.
12. From reading books, a person can put himself in a hurricane, picture himself in battle, fighting along with the hero, or see himself stranded on a desert island.
13. Monday I went into the city to apply for a summer job, get a physical examination, and a driver's license.
14. All of the opportunities which are available to those who live in Chicago, such as shopping, being able to see plays, shows, and concerts, are within easy reach of us who live in Flossmoor.
15. I read because I was taught to, my family did, feeling among the

students in my high school, entertainment, curiosity, and since coming
to college, I read because it is compulsory toward obtaining an education.

  C. Correct all faulty parallelism in the construction of the sentence elements following the correlative conjunctions:

1. Some people say that you either want to go to college or you do not
want to go to college.
2. She both taught us how to make a speech and to have confidence in
ourselves.
3. So I enrolled in Purdue University, not only because of college life, but
also mainly I wanted to become an engineer.
4. Living things on the earth will neither be destroyed nor radically
changed.
5. I agree with the author not only because she explained it so under-
standingly, but also that she had the courage to say so to her daughter.
6. In that game I knew I either had to do well or I would be benched.
7. A well-written letter is both a joy to read and makes the reader think
well of you.
8. I persisted in trying to neither enter nor to depart by the wrong door.
9. Not only have there been improvements made in construction, but in
mechanics as well.
10. I believe you should either attend the next meeting and pay your dues
in person, or you should send a check prior to the meeting.

CONSISTENCY

45.   *Consistency* in a sentence or in a series of sentences means that
two or more elements agree and remain similar unless a good reason
exists for shifting. To write appropriately and effectively, be consistent
in tense, voice, mood, and pronoun reference (number and person).

45a.   Be consistent in the use of tense.

  Tense (see Section 80) is a grammatical term meaning the time of
the verb: present, past, future, present perfect, past perfect, future
perfect. Do not shift unnecessarily from one tense to another, an error
frequent in amateur narrative and narrative exposition, the writer
shifting from past to present or from present to past, or back and forth
between the two.

Inconsistent: My nearest approach to death came last summer. I was walking slowly down a little-traveled country road when an automobile came suddenly over the rise in the road. It dashes wildly down the road, careening and twisting as if its driver is crazy. I think he is going to strike me, and I jump across the ditch and over the fence. Thus, I saved my life.

Consistent: My nearest approach to death came last summer. I was walking slowly down a little-traveled country road when an automobile came suddenly over the rise in the road. It *dashed* wildly down the road, careening and twisting as if its driver *were* crazy. I *thought* he *was* going to strike me, and I *jumped* across the ditch and over the fence. Thus, I saved my life.

45b. Be consistent in the use of subject and voice in a sentence.

Voice (see Section 81) is a grammatical term telling whether the subject of the sentence is acting (active voice) or is acted upon (passive voice). Writing is more effective if one voice, active or passive, is consistently used unless a writer has excellent reason for a shift; in general, too, active voice is more effective than passive. Consistency in voice also eliminates a major reason for shifting from one subject to another in a compound or complex sentence.

Faulty: You should follow a budget, and much money will be saved.
When a person approaches the Great Smoky Mountains, a blue haze can be seen in the distance.
Join the Navy and the world will be seen—through a porthole!
I asked a question but he made no reply.

Improved: You should follow a budget, and you will save much money.
If you follow a budget, you will save much money.
When a person approaches the Great Smoky Mountains, he can see a blue haze in the distance.
Join the Navy and see the world—through a porthole!
I asked a question but received no reply.

45c. Be consistent in the use of mood or mode.

Mood or *mode* (see Section 82) is a grammatical term telling the "style" or "fashion" of the verb. Do not needlessly shift from indicative to imperative or subjunctive or mix their use.

Faulty: Last summer I would play golf every morning and swam every afternoon.

Improved: Last summer I would play golf every morning and would swim every afternoon.

Last summer I played golf every morning and swam every afternoon.

45d. Be consistent in the use of number.

Frequent errors in inconsistent use of number are shifts from singular nouns to plural nouns, or plural nouns to singular, or failure to make pronouns and antecedents agree in number (see Section 77).

Faulty: If a *college man* really works hard, *they* are bound to succeed.
Correct: If *a college man* really works hard, *he* is bound to succeed.

If *college men* really work hard, *they* are bound to succeed.

45e. Be consistent in the use of the class or person of pronouns.

A shift in pronoun reference violates the general principle that pronouns and antecedents agree in person (see Section 77). The most frequent occurrence of the error is in shifting from the third person to the inappropriate second person *you*. (See also Section 13a.)

Faulty: If *one* studies hard enough in high school, *you* will have no trouble with college subjects.
Correct: If *one* studies hard enough in high school, *he* will have no trouble with college subjects.

EXERCISES

Rewrite the following sentences, making them conform to principles of consistency:

1. This is how you find material in bound magazines. First, one must have a subject on which to expand.
2. We boarded the plane with thoughts of home in our minds, but the fabulous trip to Alaska will never be forgotten.
3. A coach has to work only nine months of the year, and the other three months can be spent fishing, hunting, or working in a boys' camp.
4. In Canada I hired a guide. They could neither read nor write.
5. When you don't have these distractions, one can concentrate on his studies.
6. Our team has played nine games this season and have won only three.
7. A girl should keep her hair well groomed; oily hair makes necessary for you to wash it more often.
8. We wish to advise that we feel these chairs are quite wonderful. The writer is one of those who are blessed with an injured back and while

other chairs have sent me home many times with a backache, we feel this model is the most comfortable chair that one has used. (From a testimonial letter)

9. A student must learn to take his adviser's advice. They will save both time and energy if they do.

10. The cabin was not elaborate, but it did serve its purpose, which was making one feel at home, and putting a roof over your head.

11. Finding material in the Memorial Center Library will be a problem for many students; but after he finds out how to use the library, it will be of great value to the student.

12. There are other reasons why I liked spring vacation: it gave one time to sit back and enjoy himself, and it gave you time to catch up on your assignments.

13. The lecturer talked and talked until the bell rings and it is time for a change in classes.

14. In remembering my goal here in college, you must realize that you are here to study, and I must do my best.

15. If a student tries to engage in too many extracurricular activities, his assignments will be neglected.

16. If the reader has ever baked a cake, she will know that you must know some mathematics to follow the directions of the recipe.

17. Be careful to remove all rubbish from the cellar near the furnace, and the risk of fire will be greatly reduced.

18. I like to go outdoors of a morning and feel the fresh air as I take a deep breath. It makes you feel as if you were on top of the world.

19. When you are by yourself and very quiet, it is surprising the many little creatures of nature one can see. You have the feeling of closeness to nature, and I am very glad to be so close to nature.

20. There are many things that make a duck-hunting trip very risky. A typical trip starts before dawn on a cold, icy December day. The hunting party piles in the car and drives 30 miles to the river, where we put our boat in the river. There one must back his car near the muddy river and there is danger of the car getting stuck. When you are in the boat going up the river, the real trouble starts. I have to watch constantly for snags in the river.

CHOPPY SENTENCES AND CLAUSES

46a. Avoid writing a series of short, jerky sentences.

An occasional short sentence is effective. A series of short sentences, however, conveys a sense of choppiness and jerkiness and violates unity, clearness, effectiveness, and even appropriateness. Such a series is monotonous; it gives undue emphasis to relatively unimportant ideas. Give thought to the relationship of ideas and then coordinate or subordinate them properly in one longer, unified sentence (see Sections 36, 37).

Faulty: As a boy I once found a pocketbook. I saw that it contained a large sum of money. Naturally I wanted to keep it.

Improved: When I was a small boy, I found a pocketbook which contained a large sum of money and which, naturally, I wanted to keep.

Faulty: Mulberry is a small town in Clinton County. It is in the northwestern part of Indiana. It is located 10 miles west of Frankfort and 15 miles east of Lafayette on State Road 38. It has a population of about 1,050. It is an incorporated town and is governed by a local town board. It boasts a city water works, a volunteer fire department, and a public library. It has its own newspaper, *The Reporter,* published weekly.

Improved: Mulberry, a small town in Clinton County in northwestern Indiana, is located 10 miles west of Frankfort and 15 miles east of Lafayette on State Road 38. With a population of about 1,050, it is an incorporated town, governed by a local town board. It boasts a city water works, a volunteer fire department, a public library, and its own newspaper, *The Reporter,* which is published weekly.

46b. Avoid writing a series of sentences containing short, jerky independent clauses.

You cannot eliminate a series of short, jerky sentences by combining them into compound sentences with independent clauses joined by pure conjunctions and conjunctive adverbs or separated by semicolons. As a writer mindful of your reader, you should apply to such choppy clauses the principles of coordination and subordination. (See Sections 36, 37.)

Faulty: There were two ways to reach the cone: one was by cable car, the other was by car and foot. Mother and I chose the latter. The road was under construction; once we had to wait for a load of stone to be unloaded before we could pass.
We finally reached the end of the road. Here we hired a guide to take us to the cone. The path we followed was very narrow and steep; in fact it was so steep that the guide put a belt over his shoulder for Mother to hold to as we climbed.

From the cone, looking down the side of the mountain, we could see the black lava from the last eruption; it had destroyed many houses. The strange thing was that the people had rebuilt their houses on the lava. This kind of reasoning I can not understand.

Mother was much too scared to enjoy the scenery from the cone, but I thoroughly enjoyed it, and she remembers the trip as a great experience.

— Student theme, "To the Top of Mt. Vesuvius"

Improved: Of the two ways to reach the cone, one by cable car and the other by car and foot, Mother and I chose the latter. The road was under construction, and once we had to wait for a load of stone to be unloaded before we could pass. When we reached the end of the road, we hired a guide to take us to the cone. The path we followed was very narrow and steep, so steep, in fact, that the guide put a belt over his shoulder for Mother to hold to as we climbed.

From the cone, looking down the side of the mountain, we could see the black lava from the last eruption, which had destroyed many houses. The strange thing was that the people had rebuilt their houses on the lava, because of a process of reasoning that I could not understand.

Mother was much too scared to enjoy the scenery from the cone, but I thoroughly enjoyed it. We both remember the trip as a great experience.

EXERCISES

A. Combine the following groups of sentences into complex, compound, or compound-complex sentences:

1. I am Donald Jones. I was born in Columbus, Ohio, on August 1, 1945. Dr. and Mrs. Frank P. Jones are my parents.
2. My father wanted to teach me to swim in the way he learned. He said his father took him out in the middle of the lake and threw him in. He had to either swim or drown.
3. The ice broke up in the spring. We boys used to "hop cakes." We would ride downstream on the cakes. This kind of play was dangerous. We might have fallen off and drowned. The river was deep there. We received dire threats and warnings from our parents.
4. We loaded the car and started for the campus. It was still dark out. We drove for almost an hour before it started to get light. It then started to

rain. It was a freezing rain. This made the roads slippery. This made for slow driving.

5. I like sports very much. I try to participate in certain sports: basketball, track, swimming, and golfing. If I have time, I will take part in other sports. I think that taking part in sports activities will tend to keep a man feeling fit.

B. Rewrite the following paragraphs in order to eliminate the short, choppy, jerky sentences. Paragraph unity may also need attention.

1. We reached Cleveland about dusk. In the center of the city stood the Terminal Tower. It rose high above the other buildings of Cleveland. The Terminal Tower had spotlights trained on it. It stood like a king of this great city. The public square was decorated for the coming Christmas season. It seemed strange to be in such a large city. Already I liked Cleveland.

2. My roommate is John Adams. He is from Springfield, Ohio. He is a freshman. John is very friendly; he has a good disposition. He quickly made friends with everyone in the dormitory; he is therefore well liked by everyone. John is very considerate of others. He seldom studies when I study. But he is quiet and does not disturb me. He keeps his half of the room neat; he does not leave his clothes or other personal belongings scattered about the room.

3. The first real exciting adventure took place while we were on our way to camp. Gary and I had both been driving. We were tired. We decided to stop along the road. We wanted some rest. The two of us had just got settled down. Then we heard a knock at the car window. There was a policeman staring in the window at us. He wanted to know what we were doing. He also asked why we were doing it. I tried to explain. I said the long trip had made us sleepy. We were trying to get some rest. He told us to move on. Otherwise, he would have to take us before the judge.

4. I have made my first visit to our library. I toured the library with the rest of my English class. We were taken through the different parts of the building by one of the librarians. She was a very nice lady. She met us in the lounge; then she took us to the second floor. There she passed out some folders and a pamphlet. These told some of the important data about the library. She then took us on the tour. It was a great deal of walking; however, it proved worth while to most of us. I had never been in the library before; so I was very attentive to what she had to say. The tour actually started on the third floor. We had had our meeting on the second floor, so we had to walk up another flight of stairs before we actually got started.

5. The library has a main reading room. I have been in this room many times. Many chairs are placed conveniently in the room. It is a pleasant place to go between classes. It is nice to read and study there. I walked out of this room about a week ago. The librarian stopped me. She wanted to search my brief case. This searching was a surprise to me. I found out about it later. Everyone is searched as they leave the reading room. I never used reading rooms very much before I came here. I am getting the habit now. I am learning to use all of the library. I believe using the library will help me in my studies; I hope to become an engineer.

POSITION AND ARRANGEMENT

47. In addition to applying the suggestions for emphatic diction (Section 64), for correct, clear, and effective word arrangement (Sections 39–42, and 44), and for proper coordination and subordination (Sections 36, 37), give careful attention to the position and arrangement of words in sentences since effectiveness can also be attained by arrangement for maximum impressiveness. Naturally, not all words or ideas in a sentence are of equal importance; consequently, place the elements of your thought so that relatively unimportant items will remain in the background and important ones will achieve prominence.

47a. Place strong and relatively important words and ideas at the beginning or end of a sentence.

The conspicuous and emphatic parts of a sentence, and of independent clauses, are the beginning and end. Like other first and last impressions, they are remembered. Sentences should usually be built with the most important idea at the beginning or end, places where the attention of the reader is most keen. Remember, also, that transitional words and phrases, although seemingly colorless, are important and frequently deserve near-beginning positions (see Section 42). On the other hand, prepositions, pure conjunctions, and many other parenthetical expressions are usually not pivotal or important words and should usually not begin a sentence.

Ineffective: These are the dormitories which the women students live in. Mrs. Browne is the only person here whom we haven't spoken to.

The operation was a long and delicate one. However, Mother will recover, the physician says.

Improved: These are the dormitories in which the women students live.
Mrs. Browne is the only person here to whom we haven't spoken.
The operation was a long and delicate one; however, the physician says that Mother will recover.

Placing prepositions at the end of sentences is not grammatically wrong, nor is there any question of clearness. The problem is solely one of effectiveness—a weak word in a strong, emphatic sentence position. Hence, the joking rule which violates its suggestion:

A preposition is a weak word to end a sentence with.
Improved: A preposition is a weak word with which to end a sentence.

Remember, however, Sir Winston Churchill's famous reply to those who objected to his use of prepositions at the end of sentences:

This is the kind of thing up with which I don't intend to put.

A newspaper columnist once wrote to one who had criticized his ending a sentence with a preposition (from *Word Study,* April, 1949); perhaps inadvertently, he also illustrated the weakness of such sentence endings:

What do you take me for? A chap who doesn't know how to make full use of all the easy variety the English language is capable of? Don't you know that ending a sentence with a preposition is an idiom many famous writers are very fond of? They realize it's a colloquialism a skillful writer can do a great deal with. Certainly it's a linguistic device you ought to read about.

47b. Use periodic sentences to secure emphasis.

A *periodic sentence* is so constructed that full meaning is not apparent until the end; that is, the independent clause, the main verb, the direct object, the complement, or some other completion word or group of words is placed at or very near the end of the sentence. Such a sentence creates suspense; something is held back and the reader continues in a state of expectation. Frequent use of periodic sentences is awkward and artificial, but occasional use is justified by the suspense they achieve. Note the following:

Tired, dirty, footsore, and hungry, the hikers climbed the last mile to the warm and brightly lit restaurant. At first slowly, then eagerly, then almost fiercely, each seized and drank a cupful of steaming coffee.

To students in despair about their prospects of success in college, words of encouragement from a teacher mean a great deal.

When we are young and concerned with the overriding importance of the approaching football game, the class dance, the long summer vacation, with making an impression on the new employer, passing the C.P.A. or the Bar examinations, getting married—the importance of knowing a great deal fails to disturb us.

—DEAN PAUL A. McGHEE

As these examples show, sentences introduced by phrases or by dependent clauses are periodic; they are effective. In loose sentences— usually compound sentences or complex sentences with the dependent clause following the independent clause—complete meaning is possible before the end of the sentence. Nothing is wrong with loose sentences; they predominate in most writing. Because of this predominance, an occasional periodic sentence is effective.

47c. Arrange ideas in the order of their importance so as to secure climax.

Climax means arranging a series of ideas in a sentence so that each succeeding idea has greater force than its predecessor. The idea implied or expressed by the phrase "last and most important" is a fair statement of the order of climax. Consider the following:

Unemphatic: In this wreck, some died horrible deaths, some received serious injuries, and a few were barely scratched.

Better: A few were barely scratched in this wreck; but some received serious injuries; and some died horrible deaths.

Unemphatic: We were frightened by the noises: the crashing of the thunder, the pouring of the rain, and the steady blowing of the wind.

Better: We were frightened by the noises: the steady blowing of the wind, the pouring of the rain, and the crashing of the thunder.

Unemphatic: Some of my teachers have been bad, some excellent, some indifferent, some fair.

Improved: Some of my teachers have been bad, some indifferent, some fair, and some excellent.

47d. Use words out of their natural order, occasionally, as a method of emphasis.

The usual English word order is subject and modifiers, predicate and modifiers, object or complement and modifiers. Since the reader expects this usual word order, it is clear, but it does not strike his attention. Putting the predicate or the object or the complement or an adverbial modifier first is unusual; if not overdone and made monotonous, it is emphatic.

Normal:	Thirty men have sleeping quarters in the dormitory of our fraternity.
	The days of our life are swift and fleeting.
	If any, speak; for I have offended him.
Inverted and effective:	In the dormitory of our fraternity 30 men have sleeping quarters.
	Swift and fleeting are the days of our life.
	If any, speak; for him I have offended. (SHAKESPEARE, *Julius Caesar*)

47e. Repeat important words to gain sentence emphasis.

Faulty repetition should be avoided (see Section **67e, f**), but the effectiveness of many sentences can be increased by repetition of pivotal words. Thus the ideas are driven home. Notice, however, that effective repetition does not occur in one sentence but in a series of sentences.

Study the effect of repetition in the following:

Give! Give money when you see that women and children are hungry. *Give* sympathy when you can cheer a beaten man. *Give* time to study conditions in your own community. *Give* your whole self in an attempt to change and better the life of all humanity.

EXERCISES

A. Study sentence beginnings in any five paragraphs in your book of readings or in a current magazine. How many begin with ineffective words or phrases? How can the sentences be improved?

B. Study sentence endings in any five paragraphs in your book of readings or in a current magazine. How many end with ineffective words or phrases? How can the sentences be improved?

C. Rewrite the following sentences, arranging the ideas in the order of climax:

1. My mother is not only a wonderful mother but she is also a very good friend and a pleasant person.
2. According to one's point of view, an election may be a sweep, a straw in the wind, a landslide, or a general trend.
3. For popular sports events scalpers sell tickets for $75, $25, $50, and even $5.
4. When I received my semester grades, I was shocked and devastated; I was also disappointed.
5. Some people are afraid of elephants, some are afraid of worms, some are afraid of mice, and some are afraid of dogs.
6. Grandfather always claimed that he was a citizen of the world, or at least of Fairfield Township, South Dakota.
7. At first she did not love him, but as time went on she began to admire him very much and then to like him.
8. My brother has had several operations: one for appendicitis, one for adenoids, and once he had a wart removed from his little finger.
9. My father has normal interests such as his family, the family car, the law, the financial committee at church, hobbies, and his hunting dog.
10. The basic thing that is needed in the world is love: love of parents, love of God, love of all things good, love of country, love of mankind, and love of animals.

VARIETY

48.   A series of sentences monotonous in structure is not effective. Your reader tires of a long succession of identical sentences, or nearly identical ones, just as he tires of sameness in anything. Variety is more than the spice of writing; it is a quality which accurately reflects the mature or immature processes of a mind.

Monotony may be caused by a series of short, simple sentences (see Section 46); by a series of compound "seesaw" sentences (Section 36b); by a series of sentences beginning with the same word or same kind of phrase, or same kind of dependent clause (Section 48a); by a series of similarly constructed complex sentences; or by a series of sentences of approximately the same length (Section 48c).

Revise sentences to make sure that they have variety. Vary their length, and, occasionally, their normal word order. Use declarative, imperative, interrogative, and exclamatory sentences (see Section 49b), and use periodic sentences as well as loose sentences (see Sections 47b and 49c). Subordinate ideas and thus construct complex sentences (see Section 37) to take the place of too many simple and compound sentences. You can give variety to a series of even simple sentences by using various kinds of words, phrases, and clauses as beginnings or endings. Such variety could include beginning or ending with subject, predicate, adjective, adverb, correlative conjunctions, phrase (absolute, gerund, infinitive, participial, prepositional), dependent clause.

48a. Do not begin successive sentences with the same word or phrase or dependent clause.

Avoid, whenever possible, outworn beginnings such as *there is, there are, it, this, that, the, he, I,* and *we,* or beginning a sentence with the same words that end the previous sentence (Section 67f).

Awkward: It was just the kind of trip our high school class had planned. It was just the time of year for the trip. It was the consummation of our four years of planning.

Improved: It was just the kind of trip our high school class had planned and just the right time of year for the trip, the consummation of our four years of planning.

Awkward: Electronics is a very large and difficult field. Electronics takes in all kinds of electrical behavior and equipment. Electronics was originally just a branch of the communications field but is now a field of its own. Electronics has to do with the conduction of electricity in gases and in certain solid materials.

Improved: Electronics, a large and difficult field, takes in all kinds of electrical behavior and equipment. Originally just a branch of the communications field but now a field of its own, it has to do with the conduction of electricity in gases and in certain solid materials.

Do not begin every sentence with a phrase and do not overuse the same kind of phrases (prepositional, participial, prepositional-gerund, absolute, adverbial) as a beginning. Note the monotony of the following:

Having considered going to college, I wrote to various colleges about admission. Receiving their catalogues, I gave them careful study. Deciding that engineering was my major field of interest, I applied for admission at Kansas Tech. Being accepted, I made plans to be on the campus by mid-September. Having carried out these plans, I am now here, writing this orientation theme.

Do not begin every sentence with a dependent clause (a *when, while, if, since, because* clause, etc.). To begin with a series of dependent clauses is monotonous; to begin these clauses with the same subordinating conjunction is deadly.

Changing the phrases in the faulty example above to dependent clauses is merely changing the grammatical form of the monotony:

When I considered going to college, I wrote to various colleges about admission. After I received their catalogues, I gave them careful study. As soon as I had decided that engineering was my major field of interest, I applied for admission at Kansas Tech. After I was accepted, I made plans to be on the campus by mid-September. Since I have carried out these plans, I am now here, writing this orientation theme.

48b.   Do not place the subject at the beginning of every sentence.

Occasionally change the word order of subject + verb + complement (direct object, object complement, predicate noun, or predicate adjective). Deviation from this order avoids monotony, attracts attention, and is emphatic (see Section 48d).

Usual order:	I saw that musical comedy when I was in New York.
	Those who can study with people about them are fortunate.
Position changed:	That musical comedy I saw when I was in New York.
	Fortunate are those who can study with people about them.

48c.   Vary the length of successive sentences.

Monotony results when every sentence is of approximately the same length. If the sentences are all short, they resemble the writing of a childish or immature person; at best, they give a choppy, jerky effect (Section 46). The same number of words in a series of medium-long or long sentences is likewise undesirable. Vary the length of your sentences. Twelve to 20 words is a good average. For variety, use an occasional sentence of 3 or 4 words, one of 30 or 40. (See also "Guideposts to More Effective Writing," p. 114.)

48d.   Vary the form of successive sentences.

Not every successive sentence should be simple, complex, compound, compound-complex, periodic, or loose. Sentences of the immature person are likely to be predominantly simple or compound, whereas the work of an effective writer will abound in variety, a judicious mixture of sentences with ideas effectively coordinated and subordinated (see Sections 36 and 37).

EXERCISES

A. Make a study of any five paragraphs in five articles in your book of readings or in a current magazine. Prepare a summary report for each five paragraphs, giving the following kinds of information:

1. Number of simple sentences.
   Number of complex sentences.
   Number of compound sentences.
   Number of compound-complex sentences.

2. Number of sentences.
   Number of words in each sentence.
   Average length of sentences.
   Number of words in longest sentence.
   Number of words in shortest sentence.

3. Number of sentences beginning with subject or subject and modifiers.
   Number of sentences beginning with inverted order (adverbial phrase, predicate, object, etc.).
   Number of sentences beginning with phrases.
   Number of sentences beginning with adverbial clauses.

4. Number of periodic sentences.
   Number of loose sentences.

Write a paragraph of comment on each author's use of sentence variety.

B. Apply the methods of A to one of your recent themes. What are your conclusions?

C. Rewrite the following paragraphs, improving and varying the sentence beginnings:

1. It was a beautiful corsage. It was made of carnations, ferns, and ribbon. It was very beautiful. It was, in fact, just the kind of corsage that Mother liked for Easter.
2. After I had finished cleaning, I went into my room in order to wrap the gifts which I had bought for the members of my family. After I had completed this task, I went into the kitchen to help my Mom prepare dinner. After eating dinner and doing the dishes, I relaxed for an hour before getting ready to go to church.

3. I shall long remember my last summer vacation. I began my working career then. I had never had a job before; therefore it was quite an experience to start my first job. I found that my bosses were human and wanted to help me in every way they could. I worked at the Ohio Bell Telephone Company at Dayton, Ohio. I learned to accept responsibility and also learned a good lesson in psychology. I learned to coordinate my voice and my temper. I talked to almost every type of person every day. I found that some were "nasty" and some were just as nice to me as I was to them.

4. I.A.S. stands for the Institute of the Aeronautical Sciences, Inc. It was founded in 1932 to advance the scientific knowledge and prestige of the aeronautical profession. I.A.S. is a nation-wide organization bound together to further aviation. I.A.S. has a local chapter here on the campus. It has about 250 active members. The head chapter for Indiana is located in Indianapolis. The main headquarters are located at New York and Los Angeles. The I.A.S. meets once every other week on Thursday at 7 P.M. in the Chemistry Building. Each I.A.S. meeting has a speaker. He talks on a topic of interest in the field of aviation. Each speaker is usually an important man in the aviation field. He talks for about an hour. He has a question-and-answer period afterwards. The talks are given on a technical level and get rather involved at times.

5. I left the campus Saturday afternoon and arrived in Chicago three hours later. I then took a taxi to the hotel where my father and I were going to stay. I spent the next two or three hours talking to Dad about school and other things. At 6:30 we went to a good restaurant for a good dinner. We had a delicious dinner consisting primarily of Oriental food. We finished eating about 8:30 and decided to go to one of the downtown movie theaters. We wanted to see *Ben Hur,* but it was sold out. We then went to a theater with the shortest line and saw a full-length feature cartoon. After the show we went to a bowling alley, where we bowled three games. We then retired to our hotel room and got some sleep.

APPROPRIATENESS

49. Appropriateness involves using the most suitable kinds of sentences to convey purpose and meaning correctly, clearly, and effectively. Sentences differ in grammatical classification, in meaning and purpose, in word order and arrangement of ideas, and in length. A judicious mixture of varying sentences results in a clear and effective style.

**49a. Use the appropriate kind of sentences according to gram-
matical classification.**

Sentences are classified grammatically as simple, compound, complex,
and compound-complex (see Section 74a).

1. Are your ideas best expressed in two sentences?

2. Are your ideas best expressed in a simple sentence? With numerous phrases and word modifiers? With a minimum of modifiers?

3. Are your ideas best expressed in a compound sentence?

4. Are your ideas best expressed in a complex sentence?

5. Are your ideas best expressed in a compound-complex sentence?

**49b. Use sentences appropriate for the expression of meaning
and purpose.**

Declarative, imperative, interrogative, and exclamatory sentences (see
Section 74b) serve specific purposes.

1. Use declarative sentences for statements of fact or condition. They
are appropriate for all kinds of narration, description, exposition, and
argument.

2. Use imperative sentences for giving directions, giving advice, or
addressing someone directly. When you are writing completely from
the reader's point of view, and using, as in this sentence, the second
person *you,* meaning specifically and directly *your* reader, use imperative sentences.

3. Use interrogative sentences when asking direct questions or rhetorical questions (asked, for effect, of one person or group, but without
the expectation of direct answers). A paragraph of such questions can
be monotonous, but one or two direct questions in a paragraph of
declarative or imperative sentences can be appropriate and effective.

4. Use exclamatory sentences—such as "What a day!"—when they
serve interest, emphasis, and effectiveness. Like a series of interrogative
sentences, a series of exclamatory sentences is monotonous and ineffective, but an occasional exclamatory sentence, appropriately used, is an
excellent means of achieving clearness, interest, and effectiveness.

**49c. Use the appropriate kind of sentences for clear and effective
arrangement of ideas in sentences.**

Loose, periodic, and balanced sentences (Sections 47b and 74c)
serve purposes of appropriate arrangement of ideas.

1. Use loose sentences when important statements or statements

making sense come first, followed by less important statements or dependent sentence-elements.

2. Use periodic sentences, not too frequently, when you reserve or suspend the important ideas and independent sentence-element until near the end of the sentence.

3. Use a balanced sentence usually for contrast or comparison of important ideas.

Within the sentence, also, for clear and effective arrangement of ideas, consider the appropriateness of word order (Section 39), parallelism (Section 44), position and arrangement (Section 47), and variety (Section 48).

49d. Use the most appropriate kind of sentences according to length.

Sentences vary in length from long and medium-long sentences to short sentences of one word or of a few words only. A judicious mixture makes for clearness, interest, emphasis, and effectiveness (see Section 48c and "The Writing Yardstick," pp. 112–114).

As a concluding guide to your appropriate use of sentences, consider the following:

1. Write concisely but coherently, not cryptically.

2. Make the direct statement your first choice.

3. Phrase your sentences in the active voice.

4. Prefer positive to negative statements, except in warnings and some direction-giving.

5. Vary sentence and paragraph structure, but retain naturalness of expression.

6. The beginnings of sentences and paragraphs must be varied, vivid, and clear.

EXERCISES

A. In three paragraphs of an essay in your book of readings or in a current magazine, analyze each sentence according to its appropriateness for both subject and reader. Apply the tests suggested above for appropriateness.

B. Apply the directions given in A to one of your recent themes.

GLOSSARY OF SENTENCE ERRORS

50. A survey of the following errors, alphabetically arranged, may aid in checking flaws in your writing and in referring you to more detailed discussion and suggestions for avoiding such errors.

1. **"And which, but which, and who, but who."** Joining relative clauses to independent clauses by using a pure conjunction; i.e., making dependent clauses coordinate with independent clauses—an impossibility. (Section 36d.)
2. **Appropriateness, lack of.** Failure to use, for clear and effective expression, the appropriate kinds of sentences according to grammatical classification (simple, compound, complex, compound-complex), kinds of meaning and purpose (declarative, imperative, interrogative, exclamatory), kinds of arrangement (loose, periodic, balanced), and length. (Section 49a, b, c, d.)
3. **Arrangement.** See **Position and arrangement,** Item 29.
4. **Blended sentences.** See **Fused sentences,** Item 19.
5. **Blends, confusing.** A mixing of the meaning of overlapping words or phrases, or a blending of a direct and indirect question or a direct and indirect quotation. (Section 35c.)
6. **Choppy sentences.** See **Sentences, choppy,** Item 35.
7. **Climax, faulty order of.** Failure, in a series of ideas, to arrange the order so that the weakest is put first; next stronger, next; and so on; the strongest last. (Section 47c.)
8. **Comma splice or comma fault or illiterate comma.** Using a comma between two independent clauses not joined by a pure conjunction, or, meaning almost the same, "splicing" two complete sentences with a comma if the second sentence does not begin with a pure conjunction. (Section 32.)
9. **Comparisons, mixed, double.** Using illogically the grammatical positive and comparative degree of adjectives or adverbs in one single statement, or including a member in a group or class and yet as a single member, or excluding a member from a group or class in which it belongs. (Section 35d, e, f.)
10. **Conciseness, lack of.** Using unnecessary or too many words to

351

express ideas clearly, effectively, appropriately—through failure, chiefly, to reduce predication. (Section 43).

11. **Consistency, lack of.** Unjustifiable shifting, in a sentence or sentences, of tense, voice, mood, number, or the class or person of pronouns. (Section 45a, b, c, d, e.)

12. **Constructions, mixed and illogical.** Starting a sentence and shifting to a different construction; adding to already complete statements other statements incomplete and leading nowhere; using mixed and confusing "blends," mixed or double or illogical comparisons, and double negatives. (Section 35a, b, c, d, e, f, g.)

13. **Coordination, false, inaccurate.** Ineffective use of independent clauses in compound sentences: stringy running-on sentences, Item 38; using seesaw sentences, Item 32; joining relative clauses to independent clauses by using pure conjunctions, Item 1; and coordinating clauses with inexact conjunctions (Section 84a).

14. **Dangling elliptical clauses.** A dependent clause with its subject and/or predicate omitted because understood from the subject and/or predicate of the independent clause. However, the omitted parts are not the same as those expressed in the independent clause —hence, a dangling elliptical clause. (Section 40c.)

15. **Dangling verbal phrases.** An introductory participial, prepositional-gerund, or infinitive phrase which should modify the subject of the sentence; if the subject is not the noun or pronoun logically and clearly modified, the effect is ludicrous. (Section 40a.) Sometimes a participial phrase is tacked on the end of a sentence with *thus, therefore,* or *thereby,* and it dangles without any noun to modify. (Section 40b.)

16. **Dependent clauses, illogical.** The use of noun clauses or adverbial clauses to serve as grammatical parts of speech which they cannot correctly or effectively serve: that is, an adverbial clause used for a single noun, noun phrase, or noun clause; or use of a sentence, instead of a noun clause, to serve as subject of a verb or as predicate complement. (Section 38a, b, c.)

17. **Double negatives.** Using two or more negative words—adverbs, adjectives, nouns—to express a single negative. (Section 35g.)

18. **Frying pan errors,** from "out of the frying pan into the fire." The correction of one error, like the "comma splice" or the "*so* fault," by making a worse error. (Sections 32a, 36c, 77f.)

19. **Fused sentences.** Two sentences in succession with no mark of punctuation between and with no capital to indicate the beginning of the second sentence. (Section **33.**)

20. **Illiterate comma.** See "**Comma splice,**" Item 8.

21. **Incompleteness of meaning.** Grammatically complete sentences which are incomplete or vague in meaning because of omission of needed main verbs, auxiliary verbs, articles, pronouns, prepositions, conjunctions, or words in comparisons; or because of substitution of punctuation marks for necessary words; or because of a telegraphic style. (Section **31e, f, g.**)

22. **Modifier, misplaced.** A word, phrase, or sometimes a dependent clause so placed in a sentence that it modifies words other than the one it should clearly modify. (Section **39a, b.**)

23. **Modifier, squinting.** A word, phrase, or sometimes a dependent clause used between two parts of a sentence, so that it could modify either, i.e., squinting or looking in two directions at once. (Section **39c.**)

24. **Negatives, double.** See **Double negatives,** Item 17.

25. **Omissions of necessary words.** See **Incompleteness of meaning,** Item 21.

26. **Oneness, lack of.** See **Unity, lack of,** Item 47.

27. **Parallelism, faulty.** Not using the same grammatical constructions for sentence elements coordinate in rank, such as coordinate words or phrases or clauses. Faulty parallelism frequently occurs after correlative conjunctions, or in a series of several sentence elements when one or more are not parallel grammatically with the others. (Section **44a, b, c, d.**)

28. **Period fault.** See **Sentence fragment,** Item 34.

29. **Position and arrangement, ineffective.** Failure to use the following: sentence beginnings and endings for important words and ideas (Section **47a**); occasional periodic sentences (Section **47b**); order of climax (Section **47c**); words out of natural order (Section **47d**); repetition of important words (Section **47e**); and active voice instead of passive voice (Section **81e**).

30. **Prolixity.** A sentence or sentences containing unnecessary words or unnecessary details (Section **43b, c.**) See also **Conciseness, lack of,** Item 10.

31. **Punctuation marks vs. words.** Omitting words like subordinat-

ing conjunctions and relative pronouns and replacing them by a punctuation mark, usually a comma. (Section **31f**.)

32. **Seesaw sentences.** An ineffective series of compound sentences, each containing two independent clauses of approximately the same length, whether joined or not by pure conjunctions or conjunctive adverbs. (Section **36b**.)

33. **Semicolon fault.** Use of a semicolon to separate a dependent clause or a phrase from the complete statement on which each depends for clear meaning. (Sections **31b, 89d**.)

34. **Sentence fragment, unjustifiable.** A word or group of words not conveying complete sense to the reader and usually not containing a subject and predicate. The error may consist of a dependent clause or one of several kinds of phrases: absolute, appositional, infinitive, participial, prepositional, prepositional-gerund, subject, verb. (Section **31b, c, d**.)

35. **Sentences, choppy.** A series of short, perhaps simple, sentences, the result being monotonous and jerky reading—analogous to riding a boat on short, choppy waves. (Section **46**.)

36. **Sentences, rambling.** Sentences having grammatical completeness but violating unity by containing too many details. (Section **34a**.)

37. **Sentences, running-on.** A form of rambling sentences (see Item 36), consisting usually of a series of short independent clauses separated by semicolons or joined by pure conjunctions or conjunctive adverbs. (Section **36a**.)

38. **Sentences, stringy.** A series of short independent clauses as if combined or knotted into a string. See **Sentences, rambling,** Item 36, and **Sentences, running-on,** Item 37.

39. **Separation of parts, needless.** Unnecessary, unclear, or ineffective separation of the following: parts of a verb phrase; subject and predicate; verb and object; verb and complement; preposition and object; coordinate sentence elements; *to* and the infinitive verb. (Section **41a, b, c, d**.)

40. **"So" overused.** Monotonous, overfrequent, and therefore ineffective joining of two independent clauses by the conjunctive adverb *so*. (Section **36c**.)

41. **Split infinitive.** Separating widely and unnecessarily, by adverbs or adverbial phrases, the sign of the infinitive *to* and the infinitive verb. (Section **41b**.)

42. **Stair-step construction.** An independent clause followed by a series of dependent clauses or phrases, each dependent on the one just preceding—somewhat analogous to stairs, where each step is attached to the one just above. (Section **37c.**)

43. **Subordination, excessive.** Putting a coordinate idea in subordinate form, putting a subordinate idea in a main clause, or writing a series of dependent clauses and phrases with each depending, respectively, on the material just preceding (**Stair-step construction,** Item 42). (Section **37a, b, c.**)

44. **Tautology.** Sentences containing useless or unnecessary repetition of an idea or ideas. (Section **43c.**) See also **Conciseness, lack of,** Item 10.

45. **Telegraphic style.** A style omitting as many words as possible and yet conveying an understandable message. Not appropriate for formal and informal writing. (Section **31g.**)

46. **Transition, lack of, or faulty.** Failure to make evident, unobtrusively, the relationship—or bridges, crossings-over—between sentences or clauses by means of transitional words and phrases, use of pronouns, and repetition of key nouns. (Section **42a, b, c, d.**)

47. **Unity, lack of.** Inclusion of too many details or several unrelated and incongruous ideas in a sentence. (Section **34.**)

48. **Upside-down subordination.** A somewhat ineffective complex sentence in which the more important idea is in the dependent clause, the less important in the independent clause. (Section **37b.**)

49. **Variety, lack of.** An ineffective series of sentences monotonous in structure because of the following: similar beginnings of successive sentences; unvarying position of subject at beginning; same length of sentences; same form of sentences; overuse of short sentences; "seesaw" sentences. (Section **48a, b, c, d.**)

50. **Word order.** See **Modifier, misplaced,** Item 22, and **Position and arrangement, ineffective,** Item 29.

THE
WORD

The word is the smallest unit of speech or writing which has meaning by itself. In length, it may vary from one letter (*a, I, T*) to many letters and syllables (e.g., *antidisestablishmentarianism*). Problems with words involve spelling and diction; each is important and difficult.

Correct spelling is mandatory in all printed materials; even errors due only to faulty proofreading are inexcusable. Correct spelling should also be the aim in all longhand writing and typescript, for two or three misspelled words in an otherwise well-written paper are irritating and distracting to a reader. Misspelling is therefore looked upon by teachers, employers, business and professional associates, and friends as a serious fault.

Diction is the choice of a word, or words, or groups of words, for the expression of ideas. As thus defined, diction applies to both writing and speaking, although "diction" has additional meaning when applied to speech, since it involves enunciation, voice control, and voice expression. From the Latin *dictio,* meaning "saying, word," consider how the root *dict* adds meaning to words like *dictaphone, dictate, dictator, dictionary, dictograph,* and *dictum.*

Words are the most important medium for communicating thought from one person to another. Compare, for example, word use with other communication media like painting, sculpture, architecture, music, and dancing. Because there are many different ideas to express in many different shades of meaning and emphasis, with many words to choose from, and because there are many errors in word choice to be avoided, students frequently maintain that diction is the most difficult part of composition to master.

356

The Word

Since diction is basic in all writing, and since it is clearly indicative of what we are and what we wish to express, everyone who puts words on paper, who even opens his mouth to speak, should make earnest effort to improve his choice and use of words, the basic materials he puts into his themes. Improvement in diction is a constant challenge; you, as a college student, have an unusual opportunity to meet it.

Diction should be *correct, clear,* and *effective.* Since no standards of diction, however, can be absolute, another worth-while test is *appropriateness* (according to time, place, occasion, and circumstances). Language used in a discussion in your home is not precisely the language used in a classroom or church discussion group. Words used casually with your roommate are hardly the words you would use in an interview with your dean or a prospective employer. Following the principles of the process of communication, you, as the writer or speaker, should adapt your language to your subject, your reader or listener, and the occasion.

Any rule or prescription concerning word usage *must* be modified by considerations of time, place, occasion, and circumstances. Word choice is not inflexibly "good" or "standard." A word or expression in correct or clear usage a generation or two ago may now be outmoded. A word appropriate in one section of the country ("localisms") or used before a particular group of hearers (technical expressions, for example) may not be correct, clear, or effective elsewhere.

Nor can the use of a certain word be justified because it is seen frequently in print. Advertisements, newspapers, magazines, and even well-considered books may have occasional examples of poor diction. Several examples in print, several misuses by a famous speaker or writer, several mispronunciations in a national radio broadcast do not make a word, an expression, a pronunciation generally or universally acceptable. If your purpose is *general* acceptance, use words that are understandable in all sections of the country at the present time, words that are used generally by reputable writers and speakers of the past and present. Correct, clear, effective English, therefore, is that which is in *present, national,* and *reputable* use, and the use of such English is, in general, our safest practice. In the following pages, present usage is discussed in Section 53, national usage in Section 54, and reputable usage in Sections 55–59, inclusive.

The best guide concerning words in present, national, and reputable usage is an adequate dictionary, since it records, not dictates, and labels words and expressions for its users; by observing carefully the information that a dictionary provides (see Section 51), you learn what current practice is and can be guided accordingly.

Avoid *substandard* words and expressions, such as narrowly local dialect, ungrammatical expressions, illiterate words, mispronunciations, misspellings, excessive and unskillful use of slang, archaic and obsolete words, and unauthorized newly coined words. Use all available means to assure yourself that your diction is *standard* and is understood by cultivated people over a wide area.

Standard diction may be *formal*, i.e., used when you are on your "very best behavior," as in letters of application, platform speaking, technical and scientific papers and speeches, serious friendly letters (like condolence), petitions, research papers, and some of your themes. Or such

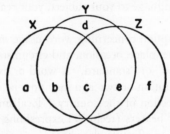

The three circles X, Y, Z represent the three sets of language habits indicated above.

X—formal literary English, the words, the expressions, and the structures one finds in serious books.

Y—colloquial English, the words, expressions, and the structures of the informal but polite conversation of cultivated people.

Z—illiterate English, the words, the expressions, and the structures of the language of the uneducated.

b, c, and e represent the overlappings of the three types of English.

c—that which is common to all three: formal literary English, colloquial English, and illiterate English.

b—that which is common to both formal literary English and colloquial English.

e—that which is common to both colloquial English and illiterate English.

a, d, and f represent those portions of each type of English that are peculiar to that particular set of language habits.

From Charles C. Fries, "Usage Levels and Dialect Distribution," *The American College Dictionary,* p. xxvi. Reprinted by courtesy of the publishers. Copyright, 1947–1960, by Random House, Inc.

The Word

diction may be *informal,* frequently termed *colloquial,* i.e., friendly, familiar, conversational, the usual writing and speaking of most educated people, as in friendly letters, letters home, friendly exchange of ideas, some forms of discussion, much of your speaking, familiar essays, and some of your themes. Note that *formal* and *informal* apply to both writing and speaking; note further that, depending upon the occasion, degrees of *formality* and *informality* exist in language as in dress, but no rigid lines separate these degrees.

Further subdivisions of language use could be made, but for practical purposes three are sufficient. By way of summary, substandard, formal, and informal English are made graphic in the above diagram. Notice that many words and expressions are in general use in two of these groups and even all three.

The following sections will help you improve your diction. Section 51 introduces you to the dictionary and supplements your knowledge of it. Section 70, "Glossary of Faulty Diction," with perhaps more discussion and illustration than your dictionary gives, contains a list of common errors in the use of specific words. The other sections, between 51 and 70, deal with correctness, clearness, effectiveness, and appropriateness.

Correctness in the use of words
Spelling—Section 52
Obsolete, archaic, and poetic words—Section 53
Localisms and nationalisms—Section 54
Colloquialisms—Section 55
Idiomatic English—Section 56
Illiteracies—Section 57
Improprieties—Section 58
Slang—Section 59
Neologisms—Section 60

Clearness in word choice
Exact and precise diction—Section 61
Technical words—Section 62

Effectiveness in word choice
Figurative language—Section 63
Emphatic diction—Section 64
Triteness—Section 65

"Fine writing"—Section **66**
Conciseness—Section **67**
Euphony—Section **68**

Appropriateness in the use of words—Section **69**

Some of these sections simultaneously deal with correctness, clearness, effectiveness, and appropriateness. For example, incorrect idiomatic usage can be neither clear nor effective; figurative language is clear and effective, but mixed figures are incorrect, ineffective, and vague in meaning; localisms, incorrect in some writing, may be appropriate in others. The outline above, therefore, may be useful in keeping your attention focused on important principles.

USING THE DICTIONARY

51. To write and speak competently, you need as an indispensable guide a reliable dictionary. If you have not done so yet, make the acquaintance of your dictionary *now*. Better still, make it your friend; best of all, make it your constant companion. To paraphrase the advice of Samuel Johnson, the great lexicographer, about learning to write well: "Give your days and nights to wise study of your dictionary."[1]

51a. Choose a reliable dictionary.

An appeal to "*the* dictionary" as an authority is as illogical as saying, "Don't buy me a book; I already have one," or "It must be so; I saw it in print." Dictionaries may be good, mediocre, or bad. Some, like a pocket dictionary, are so small that they are virtually worthless except as a limited guide to spelling, one simple meaning, and perhaps pronunciation. Others, of fair size, may be so hastily and carelessly produced that they are unreliable. Even the name "Webster," no longer copyrighted, appears alike in both reliable and unreliable dictionaries.

Choose and *buy* a dictionary which you, your bookstore, and your teachers can trust to give satisfactory answers to the following test questions:

---

[1] "Whoever wishes to attain an English style, familiar but not coarse, and elegant but not ostentatious, must give his days and nights to the volumes of Addison."—Samuel Johnson, "Addison," in *Lives of the English Poets,* World's Classics Ed. (London, New York, and Toronto: Oxford University Press, 1906), I, 466.

→1. Has this dictionary been recently published or recently revised?
→2. Is it kept up-to-date?
→3. What are the qualifications of those who compiled and edited it?
→4. What is the reputation of the company that publishes it?
→5. Is it sufficiently large (approximately 100,000 or more entries)?
→6. Is the information concerning words adequate and satisfactory? (See Section 51c.)
→7. Is the other information in prefatory and supplementary pages useful and satisfactory? (See Section 51d.)

Other desirable features or tests are attractive covers, clear type, printing on readable paper, convenience in handling, and favorable judgment of competent critics.

Three reliable dictionaries, comparable in quality, size, and price, are

The American College Dictionary (New York: Random House)
Webster's New Collegiate Dictionary (Springfield, Mass.: G. &. C. Merriam Co.)
Webster's New World Dictionary of the American Language, College Edition (Cleveland and New York: The World Publishing Company)

Excellent larger dictionaries provide much more information but are bulky and expensive: *Webster's New International Dictionary, The Shorter Oxford Dictionary* (2 vols.), Funk and Wagnalls' *New Standard Dictionary,* and the monumental 20-volume *New English (Oxford) Dictionary.* These are usually placed in libraries, classrooms, and offices for reference.

51b.   Learn the general use of your dictionary.

A reliable dictionary is a guide to use of English. It tells much about "standard English—the practice of the socially accepted, those who are carrying on the important affairs of English-speaking people."[2] It is an "authority" in the sense that it *records* and *interprets* English words and phrases. But it does not dictate or prescribe, except in a deductive sense. It indicates what is *general* language practice. When you have specific or particular problems about usage, apply in your own writing and speaking the general information which the dictionary has recorded and interpreted.

[2] Charles C. Fries, "Usage Levels and Dialect Distribution," *The American College Dictionary,* p. xxv.

In initiating and developing friendship with your dictionary, turn first to the table of contents to see what kinds of information and materials the editors have included. Examine the inside of the front and back covers. At least skim the prefatory pages as well as any supplementary materials at the back. Next read carefully any editorial sections that enable you to use the book more effectively.[3] These sections may have headings such as "General Introduction," "Guide to the Use of the Dictionary," "Guide to Pronunciation" or "Pronunciation Key," "Etymology Key," "Explanatory Notes," "Symbols and Abbreviations Used in the Work."

Each page in the body proper of your dictionary contains a wealth and variety of useful, valuable information. Examine the reproduction on pages 364–365 for tangible guides to this wealth and variety. Whichever of the three dictionaries, recommended on page 361, you own, you will find such a concrete presentation of its resources, or a "composite page" either on the inside of the paper jacket attached to the cover or available from the publisher of your dictionary.

51c.   Master the variety of information given for word entries.

Many students use a dictionary merely to learn the spelling, pronunciation, or one definition of certain words. As an attentive writer, you will *study* each word you look up; you will read carefully the entire entry and thus make the word a real part of your vocabulary. Time spent in thoroughly studying words will save time and errors later. You will not need to return again and again to the dictionary for information about words or expressions that you have already met in your reading and listening.

Study the material concerning the words *begin, bottle,* and *brass* on pages 364–365. From such examples you will learn much of the following information:

1. Vocabulary entry.
2. Spelling.
3. Syllabication.
4. Pronunciation.
5. Part(s) of speech.
6. Meanings.
7. Level(s) of usage.
8. Derivation (Origin).
9. List of synonyms and, frequently, definition of synonyms.
10. Antonyms.
11. Other information.

[3] For example, somewhere you will be told that if plurals of nouns are formed by adding *s* or *es,* these plural forms will not be entered after each noun, nor will principal parts of verbs be entered when *ed* is added to the present-tense form.

1. Vocabulary entry.

Ordinarily, the basic or "entry" word is given in black type. Associated with the main entry may be other words in black type indicating run-on entries (endings such as *er, like* added: *beginner, bottlelike*) and alternative entries or variant forms (*brigandage, brigandism*).

2. Spelling.

As indicated, the basic or "entry" word is ordinarily given in black type, this same form serving for the spelling. Also, in attention-attracting type (blackface or capitals), spellings of the word with various endings may be given. Note especially that

a. The plurals of nouns are given if a noun forms its plural other than by adding *s* or *es*.

b. The comparative and superlative degrees of adjectives and adverbs are given if a spelling change is made in the addition of *er, est*.

c. The past tense, past participle, and present participle of verbs are given if these forms differ from the present-tense form or if the spelling changes in the addition of an ending.

d. Many compound words spelled with a hyphen or as one word or as two words are so indicated.

When a word has two or more spellings, the preferred spelling form is usually given first. Sometimes the variant spelling is also placed separately as a vocabulary entry.

The spelling of proper names (people, places, etc.) is given either in the regular place in the alphabetical listing or in a special section or sections at the back of the dictionary, depending upon the dictionary.

3. Syllabication.

Learn to distinguish between the light mark or dot (·) used to separate syllables (e·ja·cu·late—so labeled in the dictionary but in use written solid) and the hyphen (-) used to show that the word is a compound (*well-known*). All reliable dictionaries use the dot system of indicating syllabication; some replace the dot in the vocabulary entry by an accent mark after the stressed syllable.

Knowledge of syllabication is important for two reasons: it helps in pronunciation of words, which in turn helps in correct spelling, and it indicates where to divide words, between syllables, if division is needed at ends of lines (Section 93c).

Running Head	**beauty**
Vocabulary Entry	**beau·ty** (bū′tĭ), *n.*, *pl.* **-ties.** **1.** that quality of any object of sense or thought whereby it excites an admiring pleasure; qualification of a high order for delighting the eye or the aesthetic, intellectual, or moral sense. **2.** something beautiful, esp. a woman. **3.** a grace, charm, or pleasing excellence. [ME *beute*, t. OF: m. *beaute*, der. *beau*. See BEAU] **—Syn. 1.** loveliness, pulchritude.
Idiomatic Phrases	**beck**[1] (bĕk), *n.* **1.** a beckoning gesture. **2.** *Scot.* a bow or curtsy of greeting. **3. at one's beck and call**, ready to obey one immediately; subject to one's slightest wish. **—v.t., v.i. 4.** to beckon. [short for BECKON]
Syllabication Dots	
Pronunciation	**be·di·zen** (bĭ dī′zən, -dĭz′ən), *v.t.* to dress or adorn gaudily. [f. BE- + DIZEN] **—be·di′zen·ment,** *n.*
Example Contexts	**be·fore** (bĭ fōr′), *adv.* **1.** in front; in advance; ahead. **2.** in time preceding; previously. **3.** earlier or sooner: *begin at noon, not before.* **—prep. 4.** in front of; ahead of; in advance of: *before the house.* **5.** previously to; earlier than: *before the war.* **6.** ahead of; in the future of; awaiting: *the golden age is before us.* **7.** in preference to; rather than: *they would die before yielding.* **8.** in precedence of, as in order or rank: *we put freedom before love.* **9.** in the presence or sight of: *before an audience.* **10.** under the jurisdiction or consideration of: *before a magistrate.* **—conj. 11.** previously to the time when *before we go.* **12.** sooner than; rather than: *I will die before I submit.* [ME *before*(n), OE *beforan*, f. *be* by + *foran* before] **—Ant. 1.** behind. **2.** afterward. **3.** later.
Antonyms	
Part of Speech and Inflected Forms	**be·gin** (bĭ gĭn′), *v.*, **began, begun, beginning.** **—v.i. 1.** to enter upon an action; take the first step; commence; start. **2.** to come into existence; arise; originate. **—v.t. 3.** to take the first step in; set about; start; commence. **4.** to originate; be the originator of. [ME *beginne*(n), OE *beginnan*] **—be·gin′ner,** *n.*
Synonym Study	**—Syn. 3.** BEGIN, COMMENCE, INITIATE, START (when followed by noun or gerund) refer to setting into motion or progress something which continues for some time. BEGIN is the common term: *to begin knitting a sweater.* COMMENCE is a more formal word, often suggesting a more prolonged or elaborate beginning: *to commence proceedings in court.* INITIATE implies an active and often ingenious first act in a new field: *to initiate a new procedure.* START means to make a first move or to set out on a course of action: *to start paving a street.* **4.** institute, inaugurate, initiate. **—Ant. 1.** end.
Variant Principal Parts	**be·jew·el** (bĭ jōō′əl), *v.t.*, **-eled, -eling** or (*esp. Brit.*) **-elled, -elling,** to adorn with or as with jewels.
Variant Spelling	**be·la·bor** (bĭ lā′bər), *v.t.* **1.** to beat vigorously; ply with heavy blows. **2.** to assail persistently, as with ridicule. **3.** *Obs.* to labor at. Also, *Brit.*, **be·la′bour.**
Hyphenated Entry	**belles-let·tres** (bĕl′lĕt′r), *n.pl.* the finer or higher forms of literature; literature regarded as a fine art. [F] **—bel·let·rist** (bĕl lĕt′rĭst), *n.* **—bel·le·tris·tic** (bĕl′lĕ trĭs′tĭk), *adj.* **—Syn.** See **literature.**
Word Element	**bene-,** a word element meaning "well", as in *benediction.* [t. L, comb. form of *bene*, adv.]
Consecutive Definition Numbers	**be·neath** (bĭ nēth′, -nēth′), *adv.* ① below; in a lower place, position, state, etc. ② underneath: *the heaven above and the earth beneath.* ③ below; under; *beneath the same roof.* ④ further down than; underneath; lower in place than. ⑤ lower down on a slope than: *beneath the crest of a hill.* ⑥ inferior in position, power, etc., to: *a captain is beneath a major.* ⑦ unworthy of; below the level or dignity of: *beneath contempt.* [ME *nethe*, OE *beneothan*, f. *be* by + *neothan* below] **—Syn. 3.** See **below. —Ant. 1.** above.
Etymology	
Usage Note	**bent**[1] (bĕnt), *adj.* **1.** curved; crooked: *a bent stick. bow, etc.* **2.** determined; set; resolved (*fol. by on*). **—n. 3.** bent state or form. **4.** direction taken (usually figurative); inclination; leaning; bias: *a bent for painting.* **5.** capacity of endurance. **6.** *Civ. Eng.* a transverse frame of a bridge or a building, designed to support either vertical or horizontal loads. [pp. of BEND[1]]
Synonym List	**—Syn. 4.** tendency, propensity, proclivity, predilection.
	bent[2] (bĕnt), *n.* **1.** bent grass. **2.** a stalk of such grass. **3.** (formerly) any stiff grass or sedge. **4.** *Scot. and N. Eng.* a grassy tract, a moor, or a hillside. [ME; OE *beonet*, c. G *binse* rush]

Illustrations of the Resources of a Dictionary. From *Using the Dictionary: A Study Guide for Use with The American College Dictionary.* Copyright, 1947, 1961. *The American College Dictionary,*

brunch

bi-, a prefix meaning: **1.** twice, doubly, two, as in *bilateral, binocular, biweekly.* **2.** (in science) denoting in general two, as in *bicarbonate.* Also, **bin-.** [t. L, comb. form of *bis* twice; doubly, der. L *duo* two] — **Prefix**

Bi, *Chem.* bismuth. — **Abbreviation**

B.I., British India.

bi·son (bī'sən, -zən), *n., pl.* **-son.** *Zool.* a large North American bovine ruminant, *Bison bison* (**American bison,** or buffalo), with high, well-haired shoulders. [t. L. t. Gmc.; cf. G *wisent*] — **Illustration**

American bison. *Bison bison*
(10 to 12 ft. long,
ab. 6 ft. high at the shoulder) — **Caption**

blood·mo·bile (blŭd'mə bēl'), *n.* a small truck with medical equipment for receiving blood donations. — **Geographical Entry**

Bos·ton (bôs'tən, bŏs'tən), *n.* **1.** the capital of Massachusetts, in the E part: the largest city and seaport in New England. 801,444; with suburbs, 2,354,507 (1950). **2.** (*l.c.*) a game of cards, played by four persons with two packs of cards. **3.** (*l.c.*) a social dance, a modification of the waltz. —**Bos·to·ni·an** (bôs tō'nĭ ən, bōs tō'-), *adj., n.* — **Run-on Entry**

bot·tle[1] (bŏt'əl), *n., v.* **-tled, -tling.** —*n.* **1.** a portable vessel with a neck or mouth, now commonly made of glass, used for holding liquids. **2.** the contents of a bottle; as much as a bottle contains: *a bottle of wine.* **3. the bottle,** intoxicating liquor. **4.** bottled milk for babies: *raised on the bottle.* —*v.t.* **5.** to put into or seal in a bottle; esp. in England, to can or put up fruit or vegetables. **6. bottle up,** to shut in or restrain closely: *to bottle up one's feelings.* [ME *botel,* t. OF: *m. botele,* g. LL *butticula,* dim. of *buttis* BUTT[4]] —**bot'tle·like'**, *adj.* —**bot'tler,** *n.* — **Homograph Numbers**

bot·tle[2] (bŏt'əl), *n. Brit. Dial.* a bundle, esp. of hay. [ME *botel,* t. OF, dim. of *botte* bundle] — **Foreign Word Label**

bouf·fant (bōō fäɴ'), *adj.* French. puffed out; full, as sleeves or draperies. —**bouf·fante** (bōō fäɴt'), *adj. fem.* — **Two Word Entry**

brain washing, systematic indoctrination that changes or undermines one's political convictions. —**brain-wash,** *v.*

brain wave, 1. (*pl.*) *Med.* electroencephalogram. **2.** *Colloq.* a sudden idea or inspiration.

brass (brăs, bräs), *n.* **1.** a durable, malleable, and ductile yellow alloy, consisting essentially of copper and zinc. **2.** a utensil, ornament, or other article made of brass. **3.** *Mach.* a bearing, bush, or the like. **4.** Music. **a.** a musical instrument of the trumpet or horn families. **b.** such instruments collectively in a band or orchestra. **5.** Brit. a memorial tablet incised with an effigy, coat of arms or the like. **6.** metallic yellow; lemon, amber, or reddish yellow. **7.** *U.S. Slang.* **a.** high-ranking military officers. **b.** any important officials. **8.** Colloq. excessive assurance; impudence; effrontery. **9.** *Brit. Slang.* money. —*adj.* **10.** of brass. **11.** using musical instruments made of brass. [ME *bras,* OE *bræs*] —**brass'·like'**, *adj.* — **Subject Label / Geographic Label / Usage Label**

brig·and·age (brĭg'ən dĭj), *n.* the practice of brigands; plundering. Also, **brig'and·ism.** — **Variant Form**

Bron·të (brŏn'tĭ), *n.* **1. Anne,** (*Acton Bell*) 1820–49, British novelist. **2.** her sister, **Charlotte,** (*Currer Bell*) 1816–55, British novelist. **3.** her sister, **Emily Jane,** (*Ellis Bell*) 1818–48, British novelist. — **Biographical Entry**

brown·ie (brou'nĭ), *n.* **1.** (in folklore) a little brown goblin, esp. one who helps secretly in household work. **2.** *U.S.* a small, highly shortened chocolate cake, often containing nuts. **3.** (*cap.*) a trademark for a type of inexpensive box camera. **4.** any inexpensive box camera. **5.** (*cap.*) a member of the junior division (ages 8–11) of the Girl Scouts or (*Brit.*) the Girl Guides. —**Syn. 1.** See **fairy.** — **Capitalization**

Brum·mel (brŭm'əl), *n.* See **Beau Brummell.** — **Cross Reference**

brunch (brŭnch), *n.* a mid-morning meal that serves both as breakfast and lunch. [b. BREAKFAST and LUNCH]

4. Pronunciation.

Pronunciation depends upon accent or emphasized syllables and upon the sound given to alphabetical letters or letter combinations.

Some dictionaries include both accent marks and syllabication dots in the entry word; other dictionaries include only the syllabication dots in the entry word and include the accent marks in the "pronunciation" word.

Learn to distinguish the accent marks: primary or heavy stress is indicated by a heavy mark (′) and secondary or less heavy stress by a light (′) or double (″) mark: *search′light′, search′light″*.

Pronunciation of sounds is more complicated than accent. That you need considerable help is evident from the fact that the 26 alphabetical letters are used in 250 common spellings of sounds. Linguists have successfully devised systems whereby 40 to 60 symbols, depending upon the dictionary, are adequate to solve most pronunciation problems. The general method is the use of a "pronunciation" word, which is usually included in parentheses just after the entry word. It is a respelling of the word, giving the sounds of vowels and consonants by syllables and according to the pronouncing key which the dictionary has adopted. Look for and become acquainted with this pronouncing key in your dictionary; it may be inside the front or back cover or both, or it may be included at the bottom of each page or alternate pages.

Learn to interpret diacritical marks. These marks (¨) placed above the second of two consecutive vowels are used when each vowel is separately pronounced. Sometimes or as a variant method hyphens are used instead. Examples: *naïve, coöperation* or *co-operation, coördination* or *co-ordination*. As such words become common, diacritical marks or the hyphen may be omitted, as in *cooperation*.

For foreign words or those recently adapted from a foreign language, your dictionary may contain a separate "foreign sounds" key.

When two or more pronunciations of a word are given, the more commonly used pronunciation is usually shown first. Occasionally, a variant pronunciation may be labeled *British* or *Chiefly British, Brit.* or *Chiefly Brit.*, indicating that this pronunciation is the common one in Great Britain.

5. Part(s) of speech.

Since every word in English is a "part of speech," the part of speech of every entry is usually given. If the word is used as more than one part of speech, such information is provided, with the particular meaning or meanings under each explained. Also indicated are singular or plural of many nouns, comparative and superlative degrees of many adjectives and adverbs, and correct use of verbs as transitive or intransitive, or both.

Learn from the table of abbreviations or elsewhere in your dictionary the more common abbreviations: *act.* for *active, adj.* for *adjective, adv.* for *adverb, art.* for *article, auxil.* for *auxiliary, compar.* for *comparative, conj.* for *conjunction, def.* for *definite, fem.* for *feminine, fut.* for *future, indef.* for *indefinite, indic.* for *indicative, inf.* for *infinitive, intens.* for *intensive, interj.* for *interjection, masc.* for *masculine, n.* for *noun, neut.* for *neuter, nom.* for *nominative, obj.* for *objective, part.* for *participle, pass.* for *passive, perf.* for *perfect, pers.* for *person or personal, pl.* for *plural, poss.* for *possessive, pp.* for *past participle, pred.* for *predicate, prep.* for *preposition, pres.* for *present, prin. pts.* for *principal parts, pron.* for *pronoun, refl.* for *reflexive, rel.* for *relative, sing.* for *singular, subj.* for *subjunctive, superl.* for *superlative, v.* for *verb, v. i.* for *verb intransitive, v. imp.* for *verb impersonal, v. t.* for *verb transitive*.

Such a list is a reminder that some knowledge of grammar and grammatical terms is necessary for intelligent and effective use of the dictionary (see sections in this handbook on "Grammar," especially Section 85, pp. 608–629).

6. Meanings.

Words may have one or more of the following meanings: a historical meaning, a traditional meaning, a figurative meaning, a special meaning, or a new meaning. Note the various definitions giving both usual and specialized meanings. Learn the method used in the order of definitions—by parts of speech, for example, or by historical development of meanings, by frequency of occurrence, or by general to specialized meanings. Learn also the significance of definitions preceded by Arabic numbers (1, 2, 3, etc.) or by letters of the alphabet (a, b, c, etc.). Observe the method of entry for capitalized and small-letter words, for words known as homographs and homonyms, and for words having a superficial resemblance. Although all these may be spelled nearly alike, or pronounced alike, their meanings are quite different. Fit the meaning into the context where you have met the word in your reading and listening.

Hyphenated words and two or more words forming phrases which have idiomatic, specialized, or figurative meaning are explained in the regular alphabetical listing, either entered separately or put under the main word. Most dictionaries include abbreviations and foreign words or phrases in their alphabetical position.

Here, for example, is part of the entry for the word *lock,* giving the word as used in several phrases with the phrases explained:

> **lock away,** to store or safeguard in a locked box, container, etc.
> **lock out,** 1. to shut out by or as by locking the door against. 2. to keep (workers) from a place of employment in an attempt to make them accept the employer's terms.
> **lock, stock, and barrel,** [Colloq.], completely.
> **lock up,** 1. to fasten the doors of (a house, etc.) by means of locks. 2. to enclose or store in a locked container. 3. to put in jail.
> **under lock and key,** locked up; safely put away.

From Webster's *New World Dictionary* of the American Language, College Edition, copyright 1962 by The World Publishing Company.

7. Level(s) and labels of usage.

Mere entry in a dictionary does not guarantee that a word is in good use or that special meanings of the word are appropriate in current English. Your dictionary enables you to judge the acceptability of a word by the absence or presence of a "restrictive label." Some words have no labels, and others have labels for certain meanings or for use as a certain part of speech. Any word not accompanied by a restrictive label is appropriate in formal and informal English. Any word labeled "colloquial" is generally acceptable in *all* informal speech and writing. All other labels are guides to special appropriateness of word use.

Four classifications of restrictive labels are common:

a. *Geographical,* indicating a country or section of a country where the word is common: *Chiefly U.S., British, Scotch, New England, Southern, Southwest, Western U.S., dialect,* etc. It is not surprising that geographical labels are necessary, for English is the native language of 300,000,000 people in various parts of the world, and it is a second language for even more.

b. *Time,* indicating that the word is no longer used, is disappearing from use, or is still used but has a quaint form or meaning: *obsolete, obsolescent, archaic.* However, when words are no longer used, dictionaries rarely record them, and words with these labels are not common. Words bearing no "time" label are in current use.

c. *Subject,* indicating that a specialized word or a specialized meaning belongs to a restricted department of knowledge like science, technology, trade, profession, sport, and the like. As many as 100 such labels are in use, including astronomy, biology, electrical engineering, carpentry, dentistry, painting, baseball.

d. *Cultural,* indicating whether the word or a special use is substandard or acceptable as informal English: *illiterate, slang, dialect* (may be geographical also), *colloquial, poetic, literary.* Absence of any such label indicates that the word is suitable for use in formal and informal writing and speaking.

NOTE: No Supreme Court in language exists to which final appeal can be made. Lexicographers can only use their best judgment in compiling and interpreting language data. Dictionaries may differ, therefore, in the labels they attach to certain words or certain meanings. For example, the same word in several dictionaries may have the label "obsolete," "archaic," "dialect," or even no qualifying label at all.

8. Origin.

The origin of a word—linguistically speaking, its etymology—may be twofold: (a) less commonly, a narrative account of how a word was formed or received its meaning (see in your dictionary, for example, *derrick, burke, macadam, radar*), or (b) whenever known, the ancestral or foreign languages from or through which the word attained its English form. Old English, Latin, Greek, German, and French have been heavy contributors, but a number of other languages have had a part: Italian, Spanish, Scandinavian, etc.

These derivations, usually entered between brackets, may come near the beginning or at the end of the vocabulary entry. They are of value in helping to fix the meaning and spelling of words in your mind. Learn the more common abbreviations used by your dictionary to indicate them: *OE* (*Old English*), *L.* (*Latin*), *Gk.* (*Greek*), *Sp.* (*Spanish*), etc. Learn also the space-saving short cuts: *b.* (*blended of*), *f.* (*formed from*), *t.* (*taken from*), < *derived from,* etc. Every dictionary contains a table or tables of such abbreviations.

9. Synonyms.

Synonyms are words that in one or more of their definitions have the same or similar meanings. Study synonyms; frequently these approximate equivalents have significant differences in meaning which enable you to choose precise and emphatic words (see Sections **61, 64**). So necessary is this study that entire volumes have been compiled to aid speakers and writers: *Webster's Dictionary of Synonyms, Crabb's English Synonyms,* and *Roget's International Thesaurus of English Words.*

Your dictionary includes the listing and frequently a brief discussion of hundreds of synonyms, showing the differences in meaning of apparently similar words and indicating by a number which usage is part of synonymous meaning. For example, study this treatment of synonyms of the word *silent:*

> **si′lent** (sī′lĕnt), *adj.* [L. *silens, -entis,* pres. part. of *silere* to be silent.] **1.** Making no utterance: **a** Speechless; mute. **b** Taciturn; not loquacious. **2.** Free from noise; still. **3.** Performed or borne without utterance; as, *silent* prayer, grief. **4.** Making no mention; as, history is *silent* as to this; also, unmentioned. **5.** Performed without sound; as, the *silent* drama. **6.** Maintaining a state of inactivity; as, a *silent* volcano. — **si′lent‑ly,** *adv.* — **si′lent‑ness,** *n.*
> **Syn.** **Silent, taciturn, reticent, reserved, secretive** mean showing restraint in speaking to others. **Silent** implies a habit of saying no more than is absolutely necessary; **taciturn,** a temperamental disinclination to speech; **reticent,** a disposition to keep one's own counsel or to withhold much that could be said; **reserved,** a temperamental indisposition to the give and take of familiar intercourse; **secretive,** a displeasing reticence that gives the impression of concealing something. — **Ant.** Talkative.

By permission. From *Webster's New Collegiate Dictionary,* copyright 1960 by G. & C. Merriam Co., Publishers of the Merriam-Webster Dictionaries.

10. Antonyms.

Antonyms are pairs of words that have opposite or negative meanings: *man—woman, man—boy, man—beast, man—God, holy—unholy,* etc. These opposite meanings are not all-inclusive: a word may be an antonym of another only in a certain limited meaning. One antonym of *man* concerns sex; another, age; another, biology; another, religion. Your dictionary suggests antonyms for many words. For example, see the antonym entry under *silent.*

11. Other information.

Other information as part of an entry or as separate entries in the main part of your dictionary includes abbreviations; biographical names; capitalized words and words spelled with both capitals and small letters; cross references to words listed elsewhere; examples of word use in phrases and sentences; foreign words and phrases (usually so labeled or given a special symbol); geographical names; homographs and homonyms (respectively, words spelled alike but having different meanings, and words spelled differently but pronounced alike); meaning of idiomatic phrases; prefixes, suffixes, and other combining word-elements; and, for appropriate words, pictorial or graphic illustrations.

51d. Become familiar with additional miscellaneous information in your dictionary.

With the wealth of information included under each vocabulary entry (see Section 51c and pp. 364–365) reliable dictionaries contain other materials in the front or back pages. Become familiar with this material. In addition to a discussion of spelling (orthography), pronunciation, usage levels, etc., sections may give guidance on punctuation, grammar, letter writing, proofreading, and rhyming; a list of American colleges and universities; and other useful and interesting information.

51e. Use your dictionary to improve and increase your vocabulary.

For greater effectiveness in writing, speaking, reading, and listening, you should constantly improve and enlarge your vocabulary. Knowledge of a foreign language, listening to good speakers in person or on radio and television, carefully reading the works of good writers, and giving attention to the meanings of prefixes, suffixes, and root words and to synonyms and antonyms are effective aids.

Building an adequate vocabulary is not the work of a week, month, or even year, but intelligent use of a dictionary will accomplish much for you in a comparatively short time. Three suggestions:

1. Learn the meaning of as many prefixes and suffixes as you can. When these are attached to a word, notice how either the meaning or the part of speech is changed. Of some 140 prefixes and some 115 suffixes, here are representative examples:

Prefixes		*Suffixes*	
ante- (before)	antedate	*-ful* (characterized by	beautiful
	anteroom	or as much as will	spoonful
anti- (against,	antisocial	fill)	
opposite)	antiwar		
		-hood (state, condition,	childhood
hyper- (beyond the	hypercritical	character)	falsehood
ordinary)	hypersensitive		likelihood

il-, im-, in-, ir- (not)	illiterate illogical impossible immature inaccurate indefinite irreligious irresponsible	*-less* (without)	faultless hopeless
		-ly (like)	saintly womanly
		-meter (measure)	speedometer thermometer
poly- (many)	polygon polysyllable	*-polis* (city or resident of)	Indianapolis metropolis cosmopolitan
post- (after)	postseason postwar	*-ship* (condition, character, skill)	friendship statesmanship
		-some (tendency)	loathsome meddlesome

Other Common Prefixes [4]

a-	*neo-*
audio-	*non-*
auto-	*off-*
bi-	*out-*
bio-	*over-*
co-	*per-*
com-	*peri-*
cross-	*pre-*
de-	*pro-*
dis-	*pseudo-*
en-	*re-*
ex-	*semi-*
extra-	*sub-*
fore-	*super-*
inter-	*syn-*
intra-	*tel-*
micro-	*trans-*
mid-	*un-*
mis-	*under-*
multi-	*up-*

Other Common Suffixes [4]

-age
-al
-er
-est
-fold
-graph
-ine
-ish
-ist
-ity
-let
-like
-logy
-ment
-ness
-phone
-ward
-ways
-wise
-y

[4] For the meaning of these prefixes and suffixes, see your dictionary. Also, an excellent discussion of prefixes, suffixes, and compound-word elements is given in Arthur G. Kennedy's *Current English* (Boston: Ginn and Company, © 1935), pp. 335–350.

For similar study: the combination of two root words (*absent-minded, air-conditioned, masterpiece, playbill, trademark*) and the combination of prefixes and suffixes (*autograph, biography, euphony, geology, homograph, perimeter, telephone*).

2. Either read with a dictionary at hand, examining words about which you need information, or make lists of unfamiliar words and look them up later.

3. List words which you hear in lectures or conversations, study them in a dictionary, and add them to your active vocabulary by using them in your conversation and in your writing.

An effective step toward building an active vocabulary is checking your list of words periodically, perhaps once a week, for words which appear twice or oftener. These are likely to be met repeatedly; they should become part of your speaking and writing vocabulary.

Following are 45 not uncommon words which any student, adopting this plan, can add to his vocabulary:

1. adversity	16. hilarity	31. precocious
2. anachronism	17. inexorable	32. procrastinate
3. arduous	18. inimical	33. prolixity
4. articulate	19. irascible	34. quintessence
5. assiduously	20. loquacious	35. recalcitrant
6. authentic	21. mellifluent	36. relevant
7. belligerent	22. meticulous	37. sophistication
8. crucial	23. nostalgic	38. sordidness
9. efflorescence	24. ostensible	39. succinct
10. enigmatic	25. ostentatious	40. transient
11. exotic	26. paradox	41. trenchant
12. extraneous	27. pedantic	42. utilitarian
13. fortuitous	28. phlegmatic	43. vacillate
14. garrulity	29. platitudinous	44. versatility
15. heterogeneous	30. polemical	45. vivacious

EXERCISES: THE DICTIONARY

The purpose of the following exercises is to make you completely familiar with the resources of your dictionary.

A. Write a 400-word paper to be read by or to the members of your English class, on one of these subjects:

An Introduction to My Dictionary.

The Uses of a Dictionary.

Good and Bad Features of My Dictionary.

How to Use a Dictionary.

Why Everyone Should Own a Desk Dictionary.

How to Pronounce Words.

Special Features of My Dictionary.

Supplementary Information Supplied by My Dictionary.

The Dictionary as a Source for Synonyms and Antonyms.

Usage Labels as Illustrated in My Dictionary.

A Précis of Pages — to — in the Preface of My Dictionary.

What My Dictionary Says About Spelling (Punctuation, Letter Writing).

The Section on American Colleges and Universities in My Dictionary.

What My Dictionary Says About the Names of Days of the Week.

What My Dictionary Says About the Names of Months.

B. Read carefully every word on *one* page of your dictionary. Write a 400-word paper telling some of the interesting items you have found.

C. What does your dictionary say about the letters of the alphabet? For example, write a paper on the information given for two or three of the following (include capitals and small letters): A, I, O, Q, S, V, X, Y.

D. Of the 20 words on this "demon list," which are misspelled? *sargeant, temperment, exhilerate, naphtha, siege, morgage, perseverance, merangue, sieve, sacrilegious, questionaire, weird, mosquitos, rarefy, supercede, diphteria, villian, ecstacy, batallion, liquify.*

E. How should these words be written: as one word, with a hyphen, or as two words? *white wash, boom and bust, under dog, able bodied, pot boiler, will o' the wisp, soldier of fortune, table talk, young blood, cul de sac, twenty one, ante chamber, sell out, boll weevil, well nigh, hand made, court martial, base ball, post office, let up.*

F. Since each of the following words has two pronunciations, what does each pronunciation indicate about the part of speech and the meaning? *record, moderate, produce, subject, compound, appropriate, rebel, present, address, insert, transfer, progress, contest, insult, minute, protest, refuse, object, increase, contrast.*

G. Find out the pronunciation of the following words: *gnome, adult, amateur, egotist, data, beret, imperturbable, maraschino, subtle, superfluous, often, impugn, victuals, valet, advertisement, italics, suite, coupon, forehead, indefatigable.*

H. What is the pronunciation of, and what are, the following geographical names? *Sault Sainte Marie, Attu, Mandalay, Okinawa, Monadnock,*

Dunsinane, Austerlitz, Dolomites, Rotterdam, Oahu, Gibraltar, Cappadocia, Monaco, Assisi, Thames, Pompeii, Thermopylae, Mackinac, Riviera, Eire.

I. For each of the following persons, give (1) the proper pronunciation of the name, (2) the given or Christian names, (3) dates of birth and death, (4) major occupation: *Tschaikovsky, Robespierre, Euripides, Lafayette, Daguerre, Phyfe, Audubon, Cortez, Vinci, Tagore, Oglethorpe, Galileo, Liszt, Tecumseh, Verdi, Puccini, Tennyson, Garibaldi, Lippi, Rousseau.*

J. The following names come from legend, mythology, or folklore. Identify each: *Damocles, Avalon, Bucephalus, Lilith, Oberon, Rosicrucian, lamia, Uther, Valkyrie, Cyclops, Nibelungs, Icarus, Arden, Robin Hood, Eblis, Elysium, Paul Bunyan, Rumpelstiltskin, troll, Lorelei.*

K. According to your dictionary, what are the plural forms of the following nouns: *erratum, moose, automaton, ax, seraph, ultimatum, virtuoso, salmon, cupful, candelabrum, duomo, basis, campus, bateau, ceramics, mongoose, poet laureate, stigma, tenderfoot, stratum.*

L. What are the past tense, the past participle, and the present participle of the following verbs? *Speak, fall, flee, fling, sneak, strive, bear, swear, shake, bite, broadcast, free, grow, hurry, bivouac, drink, forbid, throw, forsake, spring.*

M. Answer the following questions with the aid of your dictionary. If your answer to any question is "yes," explain. Can (1) *cabbage* be used as a verb? (2) *perquisite* be a synonym for *prerequisite?* (3) *how* be used as a noun? a conjunction? (4) *author* be used as a verb? (5) the plural of *money* be spelled *monies?* (6) *daily* be an adjective? adverb? noun? (7) *propeller* be spelled also *propellor?* (8) *buy* be used as a noun? (9) *carry* be used as an intransitive verb? (10) *by* be used as an adjective? an adverb? a noun? (11) *data* be used in the singular? (12) *quahog* be used to refer to pork? (13) the past tense of *fly* be written *flied?* (14) *dieing* ever be a correct spelling? (15) *farewell* be an interjection? noun? adjective? verb? (16) *either* be an adjective? a conjunction? (17) *thank* be used as the past tense of *think?* (18) *loafs* be used correctly in a sentence? (19) *sacred* and *religion* be considered the root words of *sacrilegious?* (20) *merry* be considered an adjective or an adverb in the Christmas carol, "God rest you merry, gentlemen"?

N. The following common, everyday words have many meanings: *appeal, set, spring, point, go, fix, field, about, strike, stay, all, buck, do, sweep, free, up, take, top, work.* Prepare for class an oral or written discussion of five of these words. (1) Which meanings seem to you most common? (2) Which meanings seem most unusual? (3) What idiomatic phrases do these words appear in?

O. Apply the directions of N to *break, send, short, stand, hand, run, fast, off, stock, boot, button, even, get, face, give, way, time, type, turn, style.*

P. From your dictionary give the origin (derivation) of the following words including the languages involved in the history of each word: *interregnum, anthropomorphic, banzai, safari, snorkel, cortisone, hasheesh, voodoo, gammadion, pagoda, coulee, succotash, cameo, chocolate, potato, dinghy, gingham, caravan, alpaca, indigo.*

Q. For each of the following words, give the current meaning and the "narrative" origin, i.e., the story behind the word: *bazooka, marathon, meander, chauvinism, Hobson's choice, gerrymander, quisling, loran, boycott, brummagem, macadam, boondoggle, willy-nilly, robot, strafe, milquetoast, poinsettia, bedlam, guillotine, realtor.*

R. With what is each of the following proper names associated (person, river, mountain, valley, island, etc.)? Also, how is each pronounced? *Antoinette, Axminster, Susquehanna, Waikiki, Colosseum, Simplon, Wimbledon, Balearic, Magellan, Adriatic, Saranac, Pribilof, Micmac, Himalayas, Matterhorn, Esperanto, Frankenstein, Bayeux, Eiffel, Blarney.*

S. When the following words begin with a capital letter, they mean one thing; when they begin with a small letter, they mean another. For each of the following, distinguish both meanings: *derby, ham, revere, scotch, warren, utopia, renaissance, host, laud, meander, polish, chinook, seine, marathon, polo, ruth, sac, battery, husky, maud.*

T. The following words or phrases, of foreign origin, have been "naturalized" into English, i.e., used without underlining or italics. (1) What was their original language? (2) What do they mean? (3) How are they pronounced? *À la carte, carilloneur, chaise longue, potpourri, danseuse, a priori, précis, bête noire, anno Domine, ad infinitum, zwieback, hors d'oeuvre, debris, rendezvous, cañon, grand tour, au gratin, smörgåsbord, blitz, tête-à-tête.*

U. The following foreign words or phrases have not been "naturalized" into English but appear frequently in an English context. (1) What language do they belong to? (2) What do they mean? (3) How are they pronounced? *Amigo, annus mirabilis, risorgimento, entre nous, enfant terrible, auf Wiedersehen, tout le monde, garçon, sub rosa, adios, ad hoc, cum laude, au jus, Zeitgeist, faux pas, flâneur, Deo volente, bouleversement, ex libris, deus ex machina.*

V. Give the meaning of the following prefixes and list at least five common words containing each prefix: *non-, mono-, semi-, pseudo-, over-, micro-, bi-, cross-, auto-, multi-, pre-, sub-, re-, intra-, un-.*

W. Give the meaning of the following suffixes and list at least five common words containing each suffix: *-let, -ness, -fold, -ine, -ward, -wise, -ish, -ment, -like, -ist, -able, -er, -y, -al, -est.*

X. What is the meaning of each of the following abbreviations? Which *must* have periods? Which *may* have periods? *AAA, ad lib, DDS, VFW,*

* kw, ARC, RSVP, Mlle, AWOL, ie, bbls, qv, GOP, blvd, DSC, BPOE, circ, c/o, DNB, SPCA.*

Y. What restrictive label is attached to each of the following? Group these words and their labels under one of these classifications: geography, time, subject, culture (see Section **51c7**): *pesky, rodeo, caboose, dight, baloney, allegro, canny, renege, selectman, sashay, dado, pica, boughten, primp, corn pone, jiffy, rotenone, stymie, chaw, orb, lunkhead, colleen, nohow, pectin, dogie, benison, osmosis, bree, e'er, nubbin.*

Z. Prepare five groups of 10 words each which your dictionary marks with subject labels. After each word, indicate its "subject" and its specialized meaning. (If your dictionary has a list of abbreviations, you can easily compile a subject label list of at least 25 or 30 items from which to choose your five groups.)

EXERCISES: SYNONYMS AND ANTONYMS

A. List all the synonyms given in your dictionary for each of the following words, and prepare for class presentation (oral or written) a brief discussion of the likenesses and differences among the synonyms given for two of the words: *street, defame, trite, yield, opposite, magic, intolerant, know, blunt, avenge, beat, choice, building, colloquial, effort, kindle, grasp, frank, answer, blemish.*

B. Give one antonym for each of the following: *arrive, tempt, affirmative, arrogant, grave, taste, professional, climb, suave, refuse (v.), latent, sophisticated, temporary, repudiate, dark, huge, fine, draw, decrease, solitude.*

EXERCISES: VOCABULARY

A. The following words, although not too uncommon, have only one, two, or three meanings. On 3-x-5 cards to turn in, copy these words; check their spelling; give their syllabication, pronunciation, and meaning; and use each word properly in a sentence: *cacography, hegemony, innuendo, ubiquitous, capitulation, quondam, deify, procrastinate, erubescent, stalactite, nostalgia, lexicographer, fanfaronade, pulchritude, ornithology.*

B. Directions given in A: *apropos, valetudinarian, surreptitious, chiaroscuro, superannuated, cicerone, genuflection, rodomontade, pusillanimous, cosmogony, lugubrious, eleemosynary, culinary, immolate, hypothesis.*

C. In a selection in your book of readings, or in a current magazine article, underline or encircle all the words not in your active speaking or writing vocabulary. Copy 15 of these words on 3-x-5 cards and include with each several additional words to give the context. For each word, give its syllabication, pronunciation, meaning, and origin.

D. Prepare a vocabulary exercise or test, for class use, containing 25 items similar to the vocabulary test given in E, below.

E. Select in each series the word or word group which is closest in meaning to the word italicized in the phrase. Put your list on a separate sheet. Check it with your dictionary.

1. *Propriety* of actions.   property/properness/standard/principle/behavior

2. An ugly *scowl*.   boat/look/nose/statement/skull

3. Your reasoning is *erroneous*.   incorrect/convincing/right/pleasing/learned

4. Never *procrastinate!*   forget/delay/hurry/prophesy/overeat

5. These fruits are *indigenous*.   common/expensive/sweet/native/non-existent

6. An *orthodox* belief.   ordinary/mistaken/religious/approved/pagan

7. Completely *exasperated*.   thoughtful/exalted/pleased/worn-out/angered

8. An *incredulous* person.   insincere/kind/inefficient/unbelieving/skillful

9. To eat *voraciously*.   rapidly/slowly/politely/indifferently/greedily

10. Financial *solvency*.   saving/transaction/debt/soundness/contract

11. Religious *intolerance*.   unwillingness/uneasiness/narrow-mindedness/faith/sincerity

12. *Spontaneous* applause.   unpremeditated/forced/insincere/loud/pleasing

13. An *antiquated* building.   rustic/outdated/magnificent/modern/haunted

14. To *tantalize* a child.   tease/please/titillate/adopt/caress

15. A *boon* to mankind.   legacy/blessing/boost/friend/curse

16. A *somnolent* atmosphere.   sleepy/clear/warm/cloudy/healthful

17. We *subjugated* the natives.   educated/clothed/conquered/harassed/victimized

18. A *potent* medicine.   bitter/pleasant/patented/powerful/expensive

19. The child wept *copiously*.   little/abundantly/often/secretly/openly

20. Reached the *zenith*.   horizon/rim/top/zero point/goal

21. A *peculiarity* of manners.   politeness/quality/genuineness/change/oddity

22. The *limpid* water.   cold/muddy/clear/obscure/purified

23. A *beatific* smile.   silly/flashing/beaming/blissful/sincere
24. To be *arraigned* in court.   invited/acquitted/accused/presented/
                                       sentenced
25. A *colossal* undertaking.   approved/amazing/huge/impossible/
                                       secret

SPELLING

52.   Misspelling is not a problem in word choice, but it does concern word use and is an important part of word study.

Admittedly the spelling of English words *is* difficult. For centuries many words have been spelled "without rime or reason," and through this method, or lack of it, their spelling became fixed. Very likely, in past centuries enough people misspelled certain words so that the misspelled forms came to be considered correct. In fact, the process is still going on.[5] But the possibilities are that only minor changes will be made in English spelling and that the spelling we have now will remain as it is, or will change slowly. English-language spelling is, therefore, much like English-language grammar, which a linguistics scholar has called "as pigheaded and stubborn . . . as the human minds that evolved it—and as illogical."[6] Many words contain silent letters; many are not spelled as they sound; many which sound alike (homophones) are spelled differently; and spelling by analogy, therefore, is not a safe guide. Let us recognize such difficulties.

The first step in correct spelling is to have the *desire* to learn, really to want to become a competent speller. The second is to take the necessary *time* to learn. The third is to use all available *means* to learn. If you are chronically and consistently a poor speller, you should obtain a special book which deals solely with spelling problems and which provides many spelling exercises.[7]

[5] For example, *benefitted* and *benefitting* were considered misspelled until a few years ago; now they appear in *Webster's New Collegiate Dictionary* as an alternate correct spelling.

[6] Harold Whitehall, "The English Language," *Webster's New World Dictionary*, p. xxii.

[7] Among such recent books—inexpensive, too—are the following: Falk S. Johnson, *A Spelling Guide and Workbook* (New York: Rinehart & Co., Inc.); Patrick H. Hodgkin, *It's Easy to Spell* (Culver, Ind.: The Culver Press); Julia N. McCorkle, *Learning to Spell* (Boston: D. C. Heath and Co.); Joseph Mersand, *Spelling Your Way to Success* (Great Neck, N.Y.: Barron's Educational Series, Inc.); Thomas Clark Pollock and William D. Baker, *The University Spelling Book* (Englewood Cliffs, N.J.: Prentice-Hall, Inc.); Harry Shaw, *Spell It Right!* (New York: Barnes & Noble).

As you study, remember these words of a spelling authority: "All the investigations indicate that any *child* of normal intelligence can learn to spell with very little difficulty in a reasonable length of time." Other spelling authorities assert that the common causes of poor spelling are *carelessness* and *laziness!* No poor speller who is conscientious and wants to improve need be either careless or lazy.

Although most college students are not, by birth and constitution, chronic misspellers, many do have trouble with spelling. The three steps—*desire, time,* and *means*—include the following:

→1. Pronounce words correctly.
→2. Watch for variations between spelling and pronunciation.
→3. Mentally *see* words as well as hear them.
→4. Use a dictionary to fix words in the memory.
→5. Watch for unpronounced (i.e., silent) letters.
→6. Use memory devices to help remember troublesome words.
→7. Learn a few simple rules for spelling.
→8. Write words carefully in order to avoid errors due not to ignorance but to carelessness.
→9. *List* the words most frequently misspelled.

52a. Pronounce words correctly.

You should recognize at once that pronunciation is not a safe guide to spelling. It is possible to spell the sound of many simple words and yet not get a single letter right: by sound *coffee* can be spelled K A U P H Y. Another illustration, frequently cited, is that if you use the sound of *f* as in *enough,* of *i* as the *o* in *women,* and of *sh* as the *ti* of *fiction,* you can spell *fish* as *ghoti.*

Aside from many fine distinctions in sound, English pronunciation has between 40 and 50 common sounds. Our 26 vowels and consonants must represent these sounds; to do so the English language uses approximately 250 *spelling combinations!* For example, the simple sound of long *e* is represented, inconsistently, by 12 spellings: *ae* (*Caesar*), *ay* (*quay*), *e* (*evening*), *ea* (*read*), *ee* (*need*), *ei* (*receive*), *eo* (*people*), *ey* (*key*), *i* (*police*), *ie* (*piece*), *oe* (*amoeba*), and *ui* (*suite*). Illogical? Yes. Hopeless? No!

Correct pronunciation may help, but mispronunciation is a definite hindrance. It is responsible for a large number of misspelled words, for it is difficult to spell correctly a mispronounced word. Could anyone spell *Egypt* if it were pronounced *eggpit?* Or *garage* pronounced *gararge?*

1. Do not add vowels or consonants in pronouncing such words as *athletics, disastrous, height, hindrance, remembrance,* and *similar,* and you will not misspell them as ath*a*letics (or ath*e*letics), disast*e*rous, heigh*th,* hind*e*rance, rememb*e*rance, and simil*i*ar.

2. Do not omit necessary consonants in pronouncing such words as *environment, February, government, library.*

3. Do not omit syllables in pronouncing such words as *accidentally, convenience, criticism, interesting, laboratory, miniature, sophomore,* even though, when some of these are said fast, they sound like *int'resting, lab'ratory, soph'more.*

4. Do not mispronounce the prefixes of words, such as *preform* for *perform, prehaps* for *perhaps, perfix* for *prefix, porposal* for *proposal.* Remember the student who said:

When I wrote "preformance" for "performance" five times and "preformer" for "performer" seven times, my instructor commented: "An interesting perper but you percipitate too many prejuries in preversely misusing per and pre!"

5. Carefully examine words that contain silent letters. In a number of English words, the following letters are often silent: *b (doubt, subtle, thumb); c (muscle, scene); ch (schism, yacht); d (handsome, Wednesday); e (bite, come,* see Section **52e5**); *g (gnat, sign); gh (bough, height); h (ghost, honest); k (knife, know); l (calm, would); n (hymn, solemn); p (raspberry, pneumonia); s (aisle, island, demesne); t (listen, mortgage); u (guess, rogue); w (answer, snow, write).*

6. Be suspicious of words containing lightly stressed syllables. The technical name *schwa* (ə) is given to indicate the sound, a kind of "uh"; the vowel used may be any one of the six, *a, e, i, o, u, y: dollar, grammar; corner, model; nadir, peril; professor, sponsor; murmur, sulfur; martyr.* In such words, it may help to exaggerate the "trouble spots": gramm*A*r, sep*A*rate, rep*E*tition, math*E*matics, hum*O*rous, exist*E*nce, d*E*scribe.

7. Cultivate the habit of spelling troublesome words aloud, syllable by syllable, writing them, and then spelling them aloud again in order to relate the sound to the spelling.

52b. Actually see words as well as hear them.

One method of improving spelling is to look at, or repeat, a word until you really *see* it. Correct pronunciation is helpful to an "ear-minded" person in spelling correctly, but to visualize words is also important. Frequently you say of a word you have written, "That doesn't look right." Many students constantly misspell words because they have never learned to observe a printed page; their errors in spelling come from an unwillingness or apparent inability to *see*. Look at the word alone or in its context, pronounce it, study it, write it, see it with your eyes shut, write it again, see whether it is correct, write it again, pronounce it. This method of studying words until you can *see* them anywhere is particularly valuable when dealing with tricky words which for no apparent reason may drop letters; add or transpose letters; change one or two letters for others; or contain unpronounced letters: *curious* but *curiosity; explain* but *explanation; fire* but *fiery; maintain* but *maintenance; proceed* but *procedure; pronounce* but *pronunciation; repeat* but *repetition.*

The most frequent error in visualizing words is mistaking one for another similar to it or one pronounced like another but spelled differently (homonyms). Observe the pairs or triplets in the following list. Those marked with an * are among the words frequently misspelled in written work, although every student could probably spell such words correctly in a spelling test. Understand the meaning of each word and do not use one when you mean the other. (See also Section 61a.)

*accept, except	counsel, council, consul
*advice, advise	dairy, diary
*affect, effect	decent, descent
an, and	desert, dessert
angel, angle	dining, dinning
are, our, or	due, do
biding, bidding	ever, every
breath, breathe	formally, formerly
capital, capitol	*forth, fourth
*choose, chose, choice	freshman, freshmen
cite, sight, site	*hear, here
clothes, cloths	hoping, hopping
*coarse, course	human, humane
conscience, conscious	*its, it's (never *its'*)

know, no
*later, latter
*lead, led
least, lest
lightening, lightning
*loose, lose
*lose, loss
medal, metal
of, off
on, one
passed, past
peace, piece
*personal, personnel
*precede, proceed
*principal, principle
*quiet, quite, quit

shone, shown
shudder, shutter
stationary, stationery
*than, then
*their, there, they're
therefor, therefore
*thorough, through
though, thought, through
*to, too, two
*want, wont, won't
weak, week
*weather, whether
*were, where
whose, who's
woman, women
*your, you're

Illustrations of correct use:

I can only *advise* you; you do not have to follow my *advice*.

The *effect* of the damp weather is that my sinuses are *affected*.

Breathe deeply before you dive, and then hold your *breath*.

When some of Mother's *clothes* wear out, she uses them as *cloths* for dusting.

This laboratory *course* makes use of fine and *coarse* rocks.

He's a *decent* old gentleman of French *descent*.

Our high school *principal* is a man of high *principle*.

My talkative roommate has been unusually *quiet* for *quite* a time now.

There go the runners; *they're* on *their* last two laps now.

I was *then* a smaller boy *than* my playmate.

Two people are not *too* many *to* share a room of this size, especially since there are *two* doors leading *to* the hallway, *too*.

I *want* to buy a record-player, but I *won't* spend the money.

With such *weather,* we don't know *whether* to wear overcoats or not.

The handkerchiefs *were* in the bottom drawer, *where* I did not think of looking.

When *you're* downtown tomorrow, you can buy *your* ticket.

52c.   Use the dictionary to help in your spelling.

When you are suspicious of the spelling of any word, check its spelling immediately in the dictionary. If you cannot find it, look up and down the column, since a silent letter may be causing the trouble:

aghast will be there, but not *agast*. If the initial letters confuse you, ask someone for suggestions: you will never find *mnemonics* under *n*, *philosophy* under *f*, *pneumonia* under *n*, *psychology* under *s*.

Knowledge of the etymology (origin, derivation) of a word also helps you to spell correctly. For example, if you know that *preparation* is derived from the prefix *prae* plus *parare* (to make ready), you will not spell the word *prepEration*. If you know that *dormir* is the French word for *sleep* (from Latin *dormitorium*), you will not spell *dormitory* with an *a* for the *i*. Sometimes, too, spelling the simpler or root form of the word helps: *contribute, contribution*, not *contrabution; finite, definite, infinite*, not *definate, infinate; please, pleasing, pleasant*, not *plesant; prepare, preparation*, not *preperation; relate, relative*, not *relitive; ridicule, ridiculous*, not *rediculous*. But watch the tricky words that vary from theirs roots: *curiosity, explanation, fiery, maintenance, procedure, pronunciation, repetition* (Section **52b**).

Similarly a study of prefixes and suffixes—noting their meaning and spelling, and of course using them to help in vocabulary study—enables you to spell correctly by grouping similar forms in a way which emphasizes their resemblance. See Section **51e** for a list of common prefixes and suffixes.

In using prefix and suffix words, you can avoid many misspellings by applying the one-plus-one rule (see Section **52e4**).

Further assistance in the use of your dictionary for spelling is available if your dictionary has among its supplementary aids an article on orthography or correct spelling. Read carefully any such article.

52d. Use memory devices to help you remember troublesome words.

Some memory devices apply to groups of words, such as the common spelling rules (Section **52e**) and the rhyme for the *ei-ie* words (Section **52e1**). Others apply to specific words, such as the root-word plan illustrated just above, in Section **52c**. Other examples:

> *I* am (is) always in *busIness*.
> I like the *i* in *complIment;* otherwise, I look for *e*'s—*complEment*.
> In *exisTENce* you find *TEN;* in *mainTENance* you need *TEN*.
> *Grammar:* spell the first syllable, *gram*, and add its last three letters in reverse order, *mar*.
> *Omitted, omitting*, and *omission* OMIT an extra *m*.
> *Necessary*—pronounce *NEcessity* first.

Possess, possesses, possessing, possession—put in as many *s*'s as you can
PotaTOES and *tomaTOES* have TOES.
PrincipLE means a *ruLE*, a theory, a standard; otherwise, *principAL*
is used.
SePARate means to keep *aPARt*.

52e. Learn a few simple rules for spelling.

Numerous rules for spelling cover certain words and classes of words,
but remember that the words came *first*, the rules *second*. These rules
are generalized statements applicable to a fairly large number of words,
but not all; consequently, every rule has its exceptions.

For words ending in *able* or *ible, ant* or *ent, ance* or *ence, ise, ize,* or
yze, tion or *sion,* and for the addition of *s* or *es* to words ending in *o*
(see Section 71c4) no safe guide exists except memory or constant
reference to the dictionary.

The eight rules which follow, with their corollaries, are easily learned;
mastering them will eliminate many recurring errors. Memorizing a
simple key word or a common example of each rule can help you both
to memorize the rule and to recite it from your example.

1. Words containing ei or ie.

> Write *i* before *e*
> Except after *c,*
> Or when sounded like *a*
> As in *neighbor* and *weigh.*
> *Either, neither, leisure, seize*
> Are exceptions; watch for these.

This rule or principle applies *only* when the pronunciation of *ei* or
ie is a long *e* as in *he* or the *a* sound as in *pale: believe, chief, conceive,
deceive, field, niece, piece, relieve, siege, yield, view; eight, freight,
reign, veil.*

A memory device for remembering whether the *e* or *i* comes after
the *c* or *l* is the key word *Celia* (or *Alice,* or *police,* or *lice*). Another
memory device: *ie* is the usual spelling when an *r* follows: *brigadier,
cashier, cavalier, fierce, financier, frontier, pier.*

If the sound of *ei* or *ie* is other than long *e* or *a,* the principle does
not apply: *conscience, conscientious, foreign, forfeit, height, omniscient,
raciest, science, their, weird.*

52e

2. **Final y.**

The "final *y*" rule, the most commonly illustrated spelling principle, is especially helpful in forming plurals of nouns ending in *y* or in forming the third person singular present tense, past tense, and past participle of verbs ending in *y*.

a. Words ending in *y* preceded by a consonant usually change *y* to *i* before any suffix except one beginning with *i* (such as *ing, ish, ist*).

Nouns	*Verbs*
activity, activities	carry, carries, carried, carrying
lady, ladies	modify, modifies, modified, modifying
library, libraries	try, tries, tried, trying
strawberry, strawberries	

Nouns or Verbs

copy, copies, copyist, copied, copying
study, studies, studied, studying

Other Words

beauty, beautiful	lively, livelihood
easy, easier	lucky, luckily
empty, emptiness	merry, merriment

Proper-name exceptions: Proper names ending in *y,* especially family names, simply add *s* to form their plurals, regardless of whether a vowel or a consonant precedes the final *y:*

> The *Murphys* and the *Kellys* will hold their annual reunion at Hudson River State Park.
>
> Portraits of the three *Marys* appear in some paintings.

Important common-word exceptions: one-syllable adjectives adding *ly* or *ness: shy, shyly, shyness; wry, wryly, wryness* (but *dryly, drily, slyly, slily* are commonly used); and a few polysyllables adding *ship, like, hood: ladyship, citylike, babyhood*. Note also *busyness* (state of being busy).

b. Words ending in *y* preceded by a vowel do not change *y* to *i* before suffixes or other endings.

day, days	annoy, annoyed, annoying
turkey, turkeys	array, arrayed, arraying
valley, valleys	obey, obeyed, obeying

Important exceptions: *day, daily, lay, laid* (but *allay, allayed*); *pay paid, say, said; slay, slain.* But in good use are *gayly, gaily, gayety, gaiety.* Note also *soliloquy, soliloquies.*

3. Doubling final consonant.

a. One-syllable words and words of more than one syllable accented on the last syllable, when ending in a single consonant (except *x* equal to *ks*) preceded by a single vowel, double the consonant before adding an ending which begins with a vowel.

This rule is valuable in forming the past tense, past participle, and present participle of many regular verbs and in forming the comparative and superlative degrees of adjectives. Common endings beginning with a vowel are the following: *ed, es, ing, er, est, able, ible, ance, ence, ish,* and *y.*

acquit (*qu* equals *kw*), acquitted, acquitting, acquittal

admit, admitted, admitting, admittance

drop, dropped, dropping

overlap, overlapped, overlapping

plan, planned, planning

refer, referred, referring

clan, clannish

forget, forgettable, unforgettable

man, mannish

red, redder, reddish, redden

run, running, runner

tax, taxes, taxable

tin, tinny

Important exceptions: *transferable, transference, gases, gaseous, humbugged, humbugging.*

b. If the accent is shifted to an *earlier* syllable when the ending is added, the final consonant is not doubled.

refer, referred, referring, *but* reference
prefer, preferred, preferring, *but* preference

Exception: *excellent, excellence.*

c. Derivatives from basic words that change pronunciation from a long vowel to a short vowel follow the doubling rule:

bite, biting, *but* bit, bitten
flame, inflame, inflamed, *but* flammable, inflammable
write, writing, *but* writ, written

d. Words ending in a final consonant preceded by two vowels do not double the final consonant:

387

appear, appeared, appearing, appearance
need, needed, needing, needy
train, trained, training, trainee

e. Words ending in *two* consonants do not double the final consonant:

bend, bending (*not* bendding)
insert, inserted, inserting (*not* insertted, insertting)
turn, turned, turning (*not* turnned, turnning)

f. Words not accented on the *final* syllable do not ordinarily double the final consonant:

happen, happened, happening
murmur, murmured, murmuring

A good two-syllable key word is *combat*. It can be pronounced with the accent on either syllable, but note the spelling:

combat′   combat′ted   combat′ting
com′bat   com′bated   com′bating

A few words usually ending in *l*, not accented on the last syllable, violate the rule by having alternate spellings: *marvel, marveled, marvelled, marveling, marvelling, marvelous, marvellous; tranquil, tranquilize, tranquillize, tranquility, tranquillity.*

4. The "one-plus-one" rule.

When the prefix of a word ends in the same letter with which the main part of the word begins, or when the main part of the word ends in the same letter with which the suffix begins, be sure that both letters are included. Otherwise, do not double the letters.

The same rule applies when two main words are combined, the first ending with the same letter with which the second begins: *roommate, bookkeeping, glowworm, bathhouse.*

In your study of spelling, note how words are spelled when word bases have prefixes like *dis, il, ir, mis, over, un,* and *under,* or suffixes like *less, ly, ment, ness,* and *ship.*

dissatisfied	overrun	discolor	undertake
dissimilar	unnoticed	incomplete	accidentally
illiterate	underrate	misfit	soulless
irresponsible	disappear	overdo	coolly
misspell	disappoint	undecided	cruelly

occasiona*ll*y	sudde*nn*ess	severely	greatness
brow*nn*ess	reckless	suddenly	contentment
mean*nn*ess	sadly	sadness	wonderment

Exception: *eighteen,* not *eightteen.*

Naturally, three identical consonants or vowels are never written solidly together: cliff-face, not cli*fff*ace; shell-like, not she*lll*ike; still-life, not sti*lll*ife; cross-stitch, not cro*ss*stitch; sight-seer, not sight-se*ee*r.

5. Final silent e.

A final silent *e* is an *e* ending a word but not pronounced; its function is to make the vowel of the syllable long; *rate* (but *rat*); *mete* (but *met*); *bite* (but *bit*); *note* (but *not*); *cute* (but *cut*).

a. Most words ending in silent *e* drop the *e* before a suffix beginning with a vowel but keep the *e* before a suffix beginning with a consonant.

argue, arguing	amuse, amusement
arrive, arrival	bare, bareness
believe, believing	hope, hopeless
come, coming	safe, safety
guide, guidance	sincere, sincerely
ice, icy	sure, surely
live, livable	tire, tiresome
true, truism	use, useful

Exceptions: when final silent *e* is preceded by another vowel—except *e*—the final *e* is not retained before a suffix beginning with a consonant: *argue, argument; due, duly; true, truly; agree, agreement.*

b. Words which end in *ce* or *ge* retain the *e* when *able* and *ous* are added, in order to prevent giving a hard sound (*k* or *ga*) to the *c* or *g*:

marriage, marriageable	change, changeable
notice, noticeable	courage, courageous
service, serviceable	outrage, outrageous

Compare the pronunciations of *cable* and *serviceable, gable* and *changeable.*

c. The few words ending in *ie* (pronounced like long *i*), in which the *e* is also silent, change *ie* to *y* before *ing,* perhaps to prevent two *i*'s from coming together:

die, dying	hie, hying (*but also* hieing)
lie, lying	tie, tying (*but also* tieing)
vie, vying	

d. The silent *e* is retained in the *ing* forms of *dye, singe, swinge,* and *tinge* (*dyeing, singeing, swingeing, tingeing*) to distinguish these words from *dying, singing, swinging,* and *tinging.*

6. The inserted -k- rule.

In the few words ending in *c* to which a suffix is added beginning with *e, i,* or *y,* the letter *k* is usually inserted before the suffix in order to prevent mispronunciation. Note the different pronunciation, for example, between *picnicking* and *icing.*

picnic, picnicked, picnicking	shellac, shellacked, shellacking
panic, panicky	frolic, frolicked, frolicking
traffic, trafficked, trafficking	

7. The -ceed, -cede rule.

For words ending in a *ceed* sound, memorize the three words spelled with a *ceed* ending and the one ending in *sede;* all other words in this group end in *cede:*

exceed	supersede	accede
proceed		antecede
succeed		concede
		intercede
		precede
		recede
		retrocede
		secede

Memory devices:

> *S* begins the first and last syllable of *supersede.*
> To succ*eed* as a safe driver, proc*eed* carefully and do not exc*eed* the sp*eed* limit.

8. -s and -es endings.

When nouns end in an *s* sound (*ch, sh, j, s, x,* or *z*) and the plural requires an extra syllable to pronounce, *es* is added. If no extra syllable is pronounced or if the noun ends in silent *e,* only *s* is added. (See also Section 71c.)

es	s	s
adz, adzes	book, books	ache, aches
ax, axes	boy, boys	advice, advices
box, boxes	delight, delights	edge, edges
bush, bushes	room, rooms	noise, noises
church, churches	street, streets	table, tables

When verbs end in an *s* sound (*ch, sh, j, s, x,* or *z*) and the third person singular requires an extra syllable to pronounce, *es* is added. If no extra syllable is pronounced or if the verb ends in silent *e,* only *s* is added.

es	s	s
filch, filches	buy, buys	advise, advises
finish, finishes	encounter, encounters	argue, argues
polish, polishes	mock, mocks	move, moves
rush, rushes	rain, rains	notice, notices
tax, taxes	walk, walks	raise, raises

52f. Do not carelessly misspell words.

Many spelling errors are caused by carelessness, not ignorance. Studies of long lists of misspelled words from students' themes reveal the following percentages concerning reasons for misspellings: failure to spell easy words by pronunciation and syllable, 6 percent; failure to apply spelling rules, 9 percent; tricky words (silent letters, exceptions to rules, words not spelled as pronounced, etc.), 19 percent; sheer carelessness and failure to proofread, 66 percent. The careful student, realizing these facts, will proofread his written work once or twice solely for the purpose of finding misspelled words.

The simple, easy words, not the difficult ones, cause most trouble in careless misspelling. The following words, which probably everyone could spell correctly in a test, are among others frequently misspelled in student papers (see also Section **52b**):

> *acquaint, against, all right, amount, appear, arise, around, basis, before, begin, careless, clothes, coming, consider, decide, extremely, field, finish, laid, likely, lonely, mere, noble, paid, passed, past, piece, prefer, prepare, sense, simple, stories, strict, therefore, those, tries, truly, until, whose, woman*

Do not omit letters, or carelessly transpose letters of words, or write two words as one when they should be written separately.

a lot, *not* alot

Britain, *not* Britian

collapse, *not* collaspe

curl, *not* crul

doesn't, *not* does'nt

first, *not* frist

frolic, *not* floric

high school, *not* highschool

in fact, *not* infact

in spite, *not* inspite

piano, *not* panio

radio, *not* raido

research, *not* reaserch

religion, *not* regilion

third, *not* thrid

thirty, *not* thrity

thoroughly, *not* throughly

wouldn't, *not* would'nt, etc.

52g. Keep a list of the words you most frequently misspell.

Learning to spell correctly seems a hopeless task because so many thousands of words must be mastered. But no one is expected to be able to spell all words, on demand, and only a comparatively few words are the most persistent troublemakers. Curiously enough, words like *Mississippi, Tennessee, literature,* and *extracurricular* are not frequently misspelled, even when frequently used; rather, words like *too, all right, it's, its, there, their* most often are the offenders (see Section 52b and 52f).

Keep a list of words which you misspell and study them, perhaps according to Section 52a, b, c, d, e, until you thoroughly learn their spelling.

According to one estimate, a basic list of only 1,000 words appears in 90 percent of all writing, a basic list of only 2,000 words in 95 percent of all writing. Many of these words appear in the following group. About 10 percent of this list are the words most frequently used in English; about 75 percent are among the words most frequently misspelled;[8]

[8] The list given has been checked against some of the major studies of frequency word use and frequency misspellings of the last 40 years, as follows:

William Niclaus Andersen, *Determination of a Spelling Vocabulary Based upon Written Correspondence,* University of Iowa Studies in Education, Vol. II (1917), No. 1.

Leonard P. Ayres, *A Measuring Scale for Ability in Spelling* (New York: Russell Sage Foundation, 1915).

Alfred Farrell, "Spelling as a College Subject," *Journal of Education,* 122 (January, 1939), 20, 21.

Arthur I. Gates, *Spelling Difficulties in 3876 Words.* (New York: Bureau of Publications, Teachers College, Columbia University, 1937).

John G. Gilmartin, *Gilmartin's Word Study,* rev. ed. (New York: Prentice-Hall, 1936).

Harry V. Masters, *A Study of Spelling Errors,* University of Iowa Studies in Education, Vol. IV (1927–1929), No. 4.

Thomas Glark Pollock, "Spelling Report," *College English,* 16 (November, 1954), 102–109.

Edward L. Thorndike and Irving Lorge, *The Teacher's Word Book of 30,000 Words* (New York: Bureau of Publications, Teachers College, Columbia University, 1944).

the others appear here because they have been misspelled frequently by college students.

Your own list will contain words not given here, but try to see that none of the following appears on your list or remains there very long. Master the spelling of these words, but do not try to do so all at once; rather, try to master five words a day. They are numbered and spaced for such study.

1. absence	31. altogether	61. attendance
2. absolutely	32. amateur	62. attitude
3. academic	33. ambitious	63. attractiveness
4. accidentally	34. American	64. authority
5. accommodation	35. amusement	65. autobiography
6. accompanying	36. analysis	66. auxiliary
7. accomplishment	37. announcement	67. available
8. according	38. answer	68. awkward
9. accumulation	39. antecedent	69. bachelor
10. accustomed	40. anticipation	70. basically
11. achievement	41. anxiety	71. beautiful
12. acknowledge	42. apology	72. becoming
13. acquaintance	43. apparatus	73. beginning
14. across	44. apparently	74. believing
15. activities	45. appearance	75. benefit
16. actually	46. applied	76. boundary
17. address	47. appointment	77. business
18. adequate	48. appreciation	78. calendar
19. admiration	49. approach	79. campaign
20. adolescent	50. appropriate	80. candidate
21. advantages	51. approval	81. capital
22. advertisement	52. approximately	82. carrying
23. advisable	53. argument	83. category
24. afraid	54. aroused	84. celebrate
25. aggressive	55. arrangement	85. century
26. allotting	56. article	86. certain
27. allowance	57. assistance	87. challenge
28. almost	58. association	88. changeable
29. already	59. athletic	89. characteristic
30. although	60. attack	90. cheerfulness

91. chiefly
92. chosen
93. circumstance
94. clothes
95. coincidence

96. comfortably
97. commission
98. committee
99. communication
100. community

101. companies
102. comparatively
103. comparison
104. compelled
105. competence

106. competition
107. completely
108. complexion
109. compliment
110. composition

111. comprehension
112. conceivable
113. concentrated
114. condemn
115. confidence

116. congratulations
117. conscientious
118. conscious
119. consequently
120. considerable

121. consistent
122. consolation
123. contemporary
124. contemptuous
125. continually

126. continuous
127. contribution
128. controlled
129. controversy
130. convenience

131. correspondence
132. counsellor
133. countries
134. courageous
135. courtesy

136. criticism
137. curiosity
138. curriculum
139. customer
140. dangerous

141. dealt
142. deceive
143. decidedly
144. decision
145. defenseless

146. deficient
147. definitely
148. definition
149. delinquent
150. demonstrated

151. depression
152. descendant
153. descent
154. description
155. desirability

156. despair
157. desperate
158. destruction
159. determination
160. devices

161. difference
162. difficulty
163. diminish
164. dining room
165. disappear

166. disappoint
167. disastrous
168. discipline
169. discoveries
170. disease

171. dissatisfied
172. distinguished
173. divide
174. divine
175. dominant

176. dormitories
177. edition
178. education
179. efficient
180. eighth

181. either
182. elementary
183. eligible
184. eliminate
185. eloquently

186. embarrass
187. emergency
188. emphasize
189. emptiness
190. encouragement

191. enemies
192. English
193. enormous
194. enough
195. entertainment

196. enthusiasm
197. entrance
198. environment
199. equally
200. equipment

201. equipped
202. escape
203. especially
204. essential
205. eventually

206. everybody
207. evidently
208. exaggerating
209. excellent
210. exceptionally

211. excitable
212. exercise
213. exhausted
214. exhibit
215. existence

216. expectation
217. expenses
218. experience
219. experiment
220. explanation

221. extravagant
222. facilities
223. faithfulness
224. fallacy
225. familiar

226. fascinating
227. favorite
228. February
229. fictitious
230. finally

231. financially
232. foreign
233. forty
234. forward
235. fourth

236. fraternity
237. friendliness
238. fundamental
239. further
240. genius

241. gentleman
242. glorious
243. government
244. grammar
245. guarantee

246. guidance
247. handicapped
248. happening
249. happiness
250. haughtiness

251. healthy
252. heartily
253. heavier
254. height
255. helpful

256. heroes
257. hindrance
258. hopelessness
259. hoping
260. hospitality

261. humiliate
262. humorous
263. hungry
264. hurriedly
265. hypocrisy

266. ignorance
267. imaginary
268. immediately
269. important
270. impossible

271. inadequate
272. incidentally
273. indefinitely
274. independent
275. indispensable

276. individual
277. industrial
278. influential
279. initiative
280. innocence

281. insistence
282. installation
283. instructor
284. instrument
285. intellectual

286. intelligent
287. interesting
288. interference
289. interpretation
290. interruption

291. intolerance
292. introductory
293. invariable
294. involved
295. irrelevant

296. island
297. knowledge
298. labeled
299. laboratory
300. laboriously

301. language
302. leisurely
303. lengthening
304. libraries
305. license

306. lightning
307. likelihood
308. literature
309. livelihood
310. liveliness

311. loneliness
312. lovable
313. loyalty
314. luxuries
315. magazine

316. magnificent
317. maintenance
318. managing
319. manufacturing
320. marriageable

321. mathematics
322. meanness
323. meant
324. mechanics
325. medicine

326. mentality
327. merchandise
328. metropolitan
329. millionaire
330. miniature

331. miscellaneous
332. misspelled
333. modified
334. monotonous
335. month

336. morale
337. multiplication
338. mysterious
339. narrative
340. nationalities

341. naturally
342. necessary
343. negative
344. neighbor
345. neither

346. niece
347. nineteen
348. ninety
349. ninth
350. noticeable

351. numerous
352. obstacle
353. occasionally
354. occupying
355. occurred

356. occurrence
357. o'clock
358. omission
359. omitted
360. operation

361. opinion
362. opponent
363. opportunities
364. optimistic
365. organization

366. originally
367. overwhelming
368. pamphlet
369. parallel
370. paralyze

371. participated
372. particularly
373. pastime
374. peaceable
375. peculiarities

376. penniless
377. perceive
378. performance
379. permanent
380. permissible

381. perseverance
382. persistent
383. personalities
384. persuade
385. pertain

386. phase
387. philosophy
388. physical
389. physician
390. picnicking

391. planned
392. planning
393. pleasant
394. politician
395. portrayed

396. possessions
397. possibility
398. poverty
399. practically
400. precedent

401. preceding
402. predominant
403. preferable
404. preference
405. preferred

406. prejudice
407. preparation
408. prevalence
409. previous
410. primitive

411. privilege
412. probably
413. procedure
414. proceed
415. process

416. professor
417. prominent
418. pronunciation
419. propaganda
420. provisions

421. psychology
422. punctuation
423. pursue
424. qualities
425. quantity

426. quarter
427. questionnaire
428. realize
429. really
430. receipt

431. receive
432. recognition
433. recognize
434. recollection
435. recommendation

436. reference
437. referred
438. refrigerator
439. regard
440. regrettable

441. relative
442. relieve
443. religious
444. remembrance
445. reminisce

446. renowned
447. repentance
448. repetition
449. representative
450. requirements

451. research
452. resources
453. response
454. responsibility
455. restaurant

456. reverent
457. reviewing
458. rhythm
459. ridiculous
460. righteous

461. rivalry
462. roommate
463. sacrifice
464. safety
465. sandwich

466. satirical
467. satisfaction
468. satisfied
469. Saturday
470. scarcity

471. scenery
472. schedule
473. scholarship
474. scientific
475. secretary

476. seize
477. selection
478. semester
479. sentences
480. separation

481. seriousness
482. several
483. severely
484. shining
485. shoulder

486. siege
487. significance
488. similar
489. sincerely
490. situation

491. solution
492. sophomore
493. sorrowful
494. source
495. sovereignty

496. specialization
497. specifically
498. specimen
499. spectacle
500. speech

501. sponsor
502. statement
503. stationary
504. stopping
505. straighten

506. strength
507. strenuous
508. studied
509. studying
510. subscription

511. substantiate	541. thirtieth	571. usage
512. substitute	542. thirty	572. useful
513. subtle	543. thoroughly	573. usually
514. succeeding	544. thought	574. vacuum
515. successful	545. thousand	575. varieties
516. sufficient	546. together	576. various
517. summarize	547. tomorrow	577. vengeance
518. superintendent	548. tradition	578. versatile
519. supersede	549. tragedy	579. veteran
520. superstitious	550. transferred	580. vicinity
521. suppose	551. transportation	581. victim
522. suppress	552. tremendously	582. view
523. surprised	553. truly	583. village
524. surrounded	554. Tuesday	584. villainous
525. suspense	555. twelfth	585. virtuous
526. suspicious	556. typical	586. visible
527. swimming	557. unbelievable	587. volume
528. symbol	558. uncivilized	588. warranted
529. synonymous	559. unconscious	589. wealthiest
530. system	560. uncontrollable	590. weather
531. tactfulness	561. undesirable	591. Wednesday
532. technical	562. undoubtedly	592. weird
533. technique	563. uneasiness	593. wherever
534. temperament	564. unforgettable	594. whether
535. temperate	565. universities	595. wholly
536. temperature	566. unmanageable	596. witnessed
537. temporarily	567. unnecessary	597. wonderful
538. tendency	568. unsuccessful	598. writing
539. territory	569. until	599. written
540. theories	570. unusual	600. yield

EXERCISES

A. Pronunciation: Copy on a sheet of paper the following words with their pronunciation "re-spelling." Carefully pronounce them, and then mark the division into syllables (see Syllabication, Section 51c3): *environ-*

*ment, government, incidentally, emperor, frantically, temperament, labo-
ratory, mischievous, metropolitan, pronunciation, misspell, secretary, maintenance, villain, delicatessen, kindergarten, accommodate, extraordinary,
conspicuous, opportunity.*

B. Rules:

1. Insert *ie* or *ei* in the following:

ach--ve	fr--ght	p--ces	gr--vance
br--f	c--ling	s--ge	n--ce
dec--ve	r--gn	n--ther	f--rce
s--ze	y--ld	w--rd	n--ghbor
rev--w	misch--f	bel--f	w--ld

2. Write the present participle (i.e., the *ing* ending) of each of the following verbs: *strive, force, free, argue, singe, die, refuse, change, dye, string.*
3. *Study—studies—studied—studying.* Supply the same verb forms for
the following: *carry, allay, cry, pray, reply, bury, modify, enjoy, envy,
marry.*
4. Add suffixes beginning with vowels to the following words: *clan, gas,
defer, bag, begin, hot, swim, split, concur, commit.*

C. Dictionary study: See whether a study of the derivations of the following words will aid you in spelling them correctly: *atonement, bilingual,
assignee, nasturtium, precedence, nickname, saxophone, coexist, bungalow,
senile, precancel, necrology, orthography, ridiculous, sacrilegious.*

D. Some of the following words are misspelled; correct the misspellings:
*beachead, ecstacy, excellent, retreive, irrelavant, transship, transfered, inter-
rupted, unoticed, approximately, cleptomania, meddle-some, murmered,
suddeness, roommate, existence, accomodation, independant, electrofy,
grievious.*

E. Some of the following proper names are misspelled. Correct the
errors:

Britian	Febuary	Saterday
Britannica	Floridia	Southren
Christain	Hawaiian	Tennessee
Cincinnati	Louisiana	Wendesday
Conneticut	Pennsylvania	Wisconson

F. Consult your dictionary to find the preferred or the variant spellings of
*theatre, traveler, defense, esthetic, acknowledgment, enclose, fulfil, medieval,
judgment, tranquillity, sextet, catalog, instalment, sulfur, canyon;* the preferred plurals of *appendix, stratum, index, medium, cherub.*

G. Find any carelessly misspelled words in the following sentences:

1. He was trying to protray the part of a leading TV comedian.
2. Even basketball in this state has its femine devotees.
3. I have many flauts in English, but one flaut I don't have much of is misspelling.
4. A stern of the ship was New York City.
5. We stayed in front of the fire until our cloths were dry.
6. On cold mornings I breath deeply and start out.
7. Dad is now manger of the entire factory.
8. I found it hard to chose a career from such a large variety of fields.
9. Carless driving contributes to many accidents.
10. I check each of my themes throughly for errors in spelling.
11. One of the high lights of the day is the crowing of the Homecoming queen.
12. Many business letters say that you should reply at your earliest convience.
13. Tribute was payed to my father by many friends.
14. If one method of studying dosen't work, try another method.
15. Today I parted with alot of money, infact, more than I actually had planned to spend.

H. Correct any errors in spelling in the following sentences, errors caused by confusing two words of the same sound or of similar meaning (Section 52b).

1. A college education will have a great affect on a person's career.
2. Too many activities cause a student to loose sleep.
3. After a few years of smoking, many people develop a tell-tail cough.
4. The word of the parents was always excepted.
5. I went to an elementary school where my father was assistant principle.
6. The average person has more money to spend then a person 30 years ago had.
7. Our house was the place where all the children in the neighborhood spent there free time.
8. With that decision I finally acquired piece of mind.
9. In high school our misspellings did not effect our final grade.
10. In such a situation you don't know what to due first.
11. If this plan were tried, their would be many more careful drivers.
12. The number 13 makes many people shutter.
13. This election brought more voters to the poles than ever before.
14. This fall our freshmen class has about 800 students.
15. I had a difficult time deciding weather to get a job or to come to college.

I. In the following, 50 words are incorrectly spelled. List these words on a separate sheet of paper and opposite each give the correct spelling. If a word is incorrectly spelled more than once, list it only once.

After I had been admitted to Atwood University and had completed my registeration, I was very much surprised to recieve a letter from my grandfather. Now, Grandfather was never very much of a man for writting letters, but approximatly every week or so his communications continued to arrive. I am sure that at times it was not convient for him to write (he as much as said so frequently), but he had the urge, so he said, to tell me of his own experiences at Atwood.

Grandfather early wrote about my making friends. He had made the aquaintance, he said, of many people during his first weeks at Atwood, from whom he chose a few intimates. These people he had met in the classroom, at some of the fraternities, in the Union, in resturants, and on the atheletic field. He treated every one in a courtious manner and never cracked jokes at their expense; so doing, he had learned, was a sure way to forfiet their respect.

One of Grandfather's closest associates was Bill Jones, whom he had met at one of the dormatories. Bill was a very tem퍼mental person, but all in all he had a genius for getting along with people, and Grandfather benefited greatly from his comradship. About the middle of the first semester they became roomates.

From Bill Jones Grandfather learned much about the art of studying. Up to the time of their rooming togeather, Grandfather was much disatisfied with his scholastic record, and even though he tried to learn to study, he sometimes was so poorly prepared, usually in mathmatics and English, that he was almost too much embarassed to go to class. Bill made a begining of his work on Grandfather's scholarship by giving him simple explainations of his more difficult assignments, but he was more interested in teaching the methods and dicipline of study. Once Grandfather had mastered these, the maintainance of high marks became for him an easy task.

One of Bill's secrets was concentration; if you divide your attention, you get nowhere. Another was not postponing getting to work. Grandfather admitted, for example, that the night before his grammar test, he spent the evening playing pool at the Union. He had alloted two hours for his review, but the evening just seemed to dissappear, and when Grandfather got to his room, he was too tired to worry about his lack of knowlege, and went immediatly to bed. He was not much mistified when he failed the test, and he even thought of quiting school. But about that time he met Bill, and aquired valuble study habits. No longer was he an irresponsable student, handicaped by a lack of study method. Study was now his first neccessary task. When the next grammar test came, he was so good that he could spot an independant clause a paragraph away; and by the time of the punctuation test, he had mastered the comma, had good control of the semicoln, and was even using recklessly but correctly quite a number of appostrophes.

In high school Grandfather had been a notorously poor speller. The adolescent love notes that Grandfather wrote to the girl accross the aisle contained so many wrongly spelled words that the young lady broke off the correspondance. Love couldn't erradicate Grandfather's spelling disease, and after this disasterous adventure he swore that he would overcome his trouble; but he didn't. It was method, not love, that Grandfather needed, and Bill Jones supplied the answer. Grandfather still spelled a word wrong occassionally, but he became so persistent in his study of the words spelled by rule, the tricky words, and the words spelled according to sylable that when he took the spelling test for the first time, he had only one mispelled word.

I could go on and on telling of the referrences to college life made in Grandfather's letters, and of the many occurences of which he wrote. But I don't want to be accused of wordyness, and, anyway, I've given you a general idea of the content of these letters.

Long before the end of the year I became conscious of the fact that Grandfather was trying to decieve me in a polite way; he was really giving me advice by means of his letters, but whenever I accused him of this fact, he swore to his innocense and vowed that his only object was to entertain me and, perhaps, keep me from becoming homesick. I never did quite beleive him.

OBSOLETE, ARCHAIC, AND POETIC WORDS

53. One requirement of good usage is that words must be intelligible to readers and hearers of the present time. Words are constantly going out of use or being less frequently used because language is constantly changing. New words and phrases take the place of old. Except for somewhat doubtful purposes of humor, therefore, guard against using expressions which, though antiquated, may persist in your vocabulary because of your seeing them in books or reprints of books written centuries ago.

Out-of-date expressions are of two kinds: the actual words themselves which have disappeared from current English, and, more commonly, certain meanings of words which in other meanings are frequently and acceptably used.

53a.   Do not use obsolete words.

An *obsolete* word is one which has completely passed out of use—either in its form or in one or more of its meanings. An *obsolescent* word is one which is becoming obsolete. The status of such words is difficult to be sure of, and compilers of dictionaries usually label many seemingly obsolete or obsolescent words "rare" or "archaic." Indeed, dictionaries differ, in that one may label a word "obsolete," another will label the same word "archaic," and a third may use no label at all, indicating that the word is currently used. (Look up *loblolly boy* and *murther* in several dictionaries.) Consequently, the number of words or word meanings labeled "obsolete" in a dictionary is surprisingly small. Examples:

In form: *egal* for *equal; gaol* for *jail; infortune* for *misfortune; twi-*
              fallow (to plow a second time).
In meaning: *anon* for *coming; and* for *if; garb* for *personal bearing; hold*
              for *bear, endure; permit* for *give over, commit; prevent* for
              precede.

53b.   Avoid the use of archaic words.

An *archaic* word is old-fashioned, a word common in earlier speaking and writing. It may be retained in special contexts, such as legal and Biblical expressions, but has almost entirely passed from ordinary language. Like obsolete words, many so-called archaic words are archaic in only one or two meanings, and in current use in others.

Do not use archaic words except to achieve some particular effect. Even then, be certain that this effect can be secured in no other way. Because archaic words are easier to recognize, a larger number of words bear the dictionary label "archaic" than that of "obsolete." Examples: *enow* for *enough; eftsoon* (*eftsoons*) for *again;* to *glister* for to *glisten; gramercy* for *thank you; methinks* for *it seems to me;* to *jape* for to *jest* (*joke*); *lief* for *willing; whilom* for *formerly; wight* for *person; wot* for *know; y-clad* for *clothed; y-clept* for *named* or *called; silvern* for *like silver.*

53c.   Avoid the use of poetic words in prose.

Poetic diction is the term used for words which have been usually (or are still occasionally) used in poetry but not in prose. For over a century and a half, much poetic diction has consisted of imaginative combinations of words rather than of particular isolated words themselves.

"Poetic" words, sometimes so labeled in dictionaries, are usually archaic words found in poetry written in or designed to create the atmosphere of a somewhat remote past. Examples are certain contractions such as *'tis, 'twas;* the use of *st, est, th, eth* endings on present-tense verbs: *dost, would'st, doth, leadeth;* and words like *'neath, oft, ofttimes,* and *ope.*

EXERCISES

A. Glance through several pages of your dictionary. Compile three short lists of words labeled "obsolete," "archaic," and "poetic."

B. Read several of the older English or Scottish popular ballads or Samuel Taylor Coleridge's "The Rime of the Ancient Mariner." Compile and explain a list of the archaic words.

C. Read one or more of the familiar essays by Charles Lamb. Compile and explain a list of the archaic words.

D. Read or reread one of Shakespeare's plays. From it can you compile a list of 20 archaic words? Of 20 obsolete words?

LOCALISMS AND NATIONALISMS

54a.   Avoid inappropriate localisms.

A *localism* is a word or phrase used and understood in a particular section or region. It may therefore be called also a *regionalism* or a *provincialism* (apparently because, formerly, English used in London was "good English"; English used outside London in the "provinces" was not good English but "provincial").

The northeastern, southern, southwestern, and western areas[9] of the United States are especially rich in colorful localisms which add flavor to speech but which may not be immediately intelligible in other areas. For a resident of one of these areas, such expressions are difficult to detect, for as writer or speaker he accepts them as reputable and

---

[9] For illustrating localisms and regionalisms, these major divisions will serve. Linguistic scholars, considering both word occurrence and pronunciation, make finer distinctions than the four areas mentioned in this paragraph; for example, the eastern part of the United States is divided into North, North Midland, West Midland, South Midland, and South.

assumes that they are generally understood since he himself has known and used them from childhood. Although words and combinations of words used locally may not be explained in print anywhere, dictionaries do label or define many words according to the geographical area where they are common.

Examples: Northeastern: *down-Easter* (a native of New England, especially of Maine), *moosewood* (striped maple), *selectman* (a town official), *skunk cabbage, sugar maple.* South: *butternuts* (a kind of brown overalls), *corn pone* (corn bread), *granny* (a nurse), *hoecake* (a cake of Indian meal), *lightwood* (pitchy pine wood). Southwest: *longhorn* (formerly a variety of cattle), *maverick* (an unbranded animal), *mesa* (flat-topped rocky hill with steeply sloping sides), *mesquite* (spiny tree or shrub), *mustang* (small, hardy, half-wild horse). Western: *coulee* (narrow, steep-walled valley), *dogie, dogy* (motherless calf), *grubstake* (supplies or funds furnished a prospector), *rustler* (cattle thief), *sagebrush* (a flower of the aster family).

Should localisms be used? The only satisfactory answer is appropriateness. If you live in an area or address people in an area where localisms are easily understood, they are appropriate in speaking and in informal writing. But in formal writing for such a geographical area, and in formal and informal speaking and writing to be understandable in other sections, avoid localisms in the interests of clearness. To be generally understood, words and phrases must be in national, not merely sectional, use. For example, it is doubtful that many readers, except in a certain locality, know the meaning of *crick, fress, nibby, a scrounge, spritz,* or *any more* (as in "I get tired any more").

Localisms can also include *dialect*—written or spoken expression used in a limited geographical area, or used by a certain social group in a limited area (like Pennsylvania Dutch), or used by a certain social group on a more extensive geographical scale, like Scotch dialect.

54b. Avoid inappropriate nationalisms.

A further extension of localism is *nationalism,* a term here describing expressions common in or limited to English used by one of the English-speaking nations. *Americanism* and *Briticism* refer to words or word meanings common, respectively, in the United States and in the British Isles; logically, other labels might be, and undoubtedly are,

Canadianisms, Australianisms, New-Zealandisms, and *South-African-isms.* A two-volume reference work, *A Dictionary of Americanisms on Historical Principles,* records only American usage—words of American origin and words with a distinctively American meaning, *American* here referring only to the United States. All reliable dictionaries, however, label many expressions *U.S., Chiefly U.S., British, Chiefly British,* or *Scotch.* Examples:

Americanisms: *calaboose* (prison, jail); *catchup* (tomato sauce); *levee* (an embankment); *stump* (travel to electioneer); *tote* (carry, or a load); *bellhop; caboose; gangster; gusher; haberdasher.*

Briticisms: *accumulator* (storage battery); *croft* (small enclosed field); *gaol* (jail); *petrol* (gasoline); *tube* (subway).

Scotch dialect: *auld* (old); *awee* (a little while); *bairn* (child); *bree* (broth); *canty* (cheerful).

Naturally, the advice to avoid inappropriate nationalisms does not apply to American words and phrases but to those of other English-speaking countries when such words and phrases would not be readily understood in your writing.

EXERCISES

A. Make a list of 10 localisms heard in your neighborhood or vicinity.

B. Select 20 localisms from your dictionary. What is the label attached to each? Do you recall any of them from your reading?

C. What are the American equivalents for the following Briticisms? *Barrister, bobby, caravan, chemist, circus, lift, queue, suspender, tram, treacle.*

D. Read several of Robert Burns's poems. Compile a list of 20 Scotch dialect words, with their meanings.

COLLOQUIALISMS

55.   A *colloquialism* is a word or phrase used in conversation and indispensable to an easy informal style of writing and speaking. The origin of the word is Latin *colloquium,* for "conversation," from Latin *col* plus *loqui,* "to speak." The word *colloquy* means "speaking together, a conversation, a conference," and *loquacious* means "given to talking, fond of talking." Coined words like "speakism" or "speechism" might well be synonyms for *colloquialism.*

Remember two important statements about colloquialisms. First, a colloquialism is never a localism; that is, it is not a provincialism or regionalism (see Section 54). Second, no stigma attaches to any word labeled "colloquial." Such words are *not* vulgar, bad, incorrect, substandard, or illiterate.

Dictionaries mark words and phrases as colloquial (*Colloq.*) when in the judgment of the editors they are more common in speech than in writing or more appropriate in informal than formal discourse. The number of words and phrases so labeled is, naturally, quite large. Because editors differ in interpretations of their findings and because informal English has a wide range, this label applies to many expressions. Some contractions—for example, *don't, shouldn't, won't*—are respectable colloquialisms, whereas others—*'tis, 'twas, 'twere*—should be guarded against in even very informal writing.

In other words, degrees or ranks of colloquialisms range from a high, just below formal written English, to a low of just above dialect, slang, and illiterate English. Dictionary editors, content with one general label, "colloquial," do not try to indicate differences. Experimentally, you might think of "high level," "middle level," and "low level" as differentiating descriptions.

55a. Use colloquialisms appropriately and effectively.

In view of the wide range within which colloquial expressions come, the only test for their use is appropriateness and effectiveness. No objective test or exact rule enables you to determine when they may be used. Certainly it is better to employ them and make your writing easy and fluent than to avoid them and make your writing artificial and awkward. In the various kinds of informal English—speaking and informal writing—mentioned on pages 358–359, colloquialisms not only are not objectionable but also are positively desirable for smoothness, ease, clarity, and power of communication. Some words are colloquial in all their meanings; others are colloquial only in one or more of various meanings or combinations.

Examples (avoiding as do dictionaries and linguists any attempt to indicate their comparative ranking): *ad, angel* (financial backer), *brass* (impudence), *cute, enthuse, freeze* (stand motionless), *gumption, jinx, phone, alongside of, brass tacks* (facts), *hasn't got any, show up, take a try at, try and.*

55b.   Avoid colloquialisms in formal writing.

In formal, well-planned writing (see pp. 358–359) avoid colloquialisms unless they are deliberately used to achieve some effect (see Section 69). For guidance consult your dictionary to determine what words and phrases are colloquial. The absence of any label implies, so far as the dictionary authors are concerned, words and phrases acceptable in both formal and informal writing.

EXERCISES

A. From any two pages in your dictionary list all the words or word meanings labeled *Colloquial.* Can you make any general statements about the kinds of expressions on your list?

B. What are the colloquial meanings of the following words? *Primp, bossy, jinx, middy, preachify, highfalutin, burg, fluke, lab, numbskull, buddy, fizzle, type, sleuth, catch* (n.), *grapevine, mum, rambunctious, uppish.*

C. What are the colloquial meanings of the following phrases? *War horse, small potatoes, blue streak, freeze out, salt away, yes man, walking papers, close call, make time, buck fever, yours truly, rubber stamp, play up to, fill the bill, Dutch treat, sweet tooth, pass the buck, cut a figure, square shooter, pitch in.*

D. What do the following colloquialisms mean? *Bobbysocks, bobbysoxer, playboy, soap opera, standee, jiffy, flimflam, doodad, goner, flabbergast, nosy, get, fellows, take it easy, scoot, getaway, grand, frost, kibitzer, pop.*

E. Point out any colloquialisms in the following sentences:

1. Later my mom fixed breakfast for all of us.
2. Proper English is a must in the business and social world.
3. Some teachers get mad if you sleep in their classes.
4. Every afternoon we would hop on our bikes and take off down the road.
5. I guess that black cats are usually associated with witches.
6. All kidding aside, we really had some fun-filled times together.
7. When I enjoyed those games, I was only a little tyke.
8. Many of my relations live in Frankfort, Kentucky.
9. I had never done that kind of work before, but I was willing to give it a try.
10. In high school I became enthused about becoming a doctor.

IDIOMATIC ENGLISH

English *idiom* or *idiomatic* English concerns words used mainly in combination with others. The key word to an explanation of idiom and idiomatic is *particularity* or *peculiarity*. Of Greek origin, the word meant "a private citizen, something belonging to a private citizen, personal," and, by extension, something individual and peculiar. For idiomatic expressions, then, there are no laws or principles describing their formation, comparable for example to principles describing tense formation or uses of punctuation marks. Each idiomatic expression is a law unto itself. It may violate grammar or logic, or both; yet it is an acceptable phrase, familiar, deep-rooted, widely used, easily understandable—for the native-born.

Not English alone but every language has its idioms, its peculiarities. French and German and Spanish idioms are difficult for us to understand and master, and many foreign expressions cannot be translated literally. In literal translation, the French say, "Here one speaks French" and "We have come from eating"; the English equivalent is, "French is spoken here" and "We have just eaten."

Likewise, idiomatic English is difficult not only for foreigners but for all who have not listened closely to the talk of acceptable speakers. For example, foreign students may have considerable trouble with *the,* using it where English-speaking people omit it, and omitting it where we use it, as "When I came to the America, thing that impressed me most was vast distance between the New York and the San Francisco." Or we may tell a foreign student not to misuse number or concord by saying "many man," "many man is," "a students," "10 foot," and then we confuse him by saying, correctly, "many a man is," "a few students," and "a 10-foot pole." Or we have trouble explaining the proper negative prefixes, like *indescribable* but not *undescribable,* or *undesirable* but not *indesirable.*

The many idiomatic expressions in English permit only a few generalized statements. One is that several words combined may lose their literal meaning and indicate something only remotely suggested by any one word: *lay up, heavy hand, toe the line, bed of roses, make out, dark horse, open house, birds of a feather, read between the lines, black list.*

409

An adaptation of the foregoing statement is that the parts of the human body and words expressing activity have suggested many idioms: *fly in the face of, burn one's fingers, stand on one's own feet, keep one's eyes open, keep body and soul together, all thumbs, make believe, do oneself well, let drive*, etc.

A third generalization is that hundreds of idiomatic phrases contain adverbs or prepositions with other parts of speech. No "rule" guides their use; yet certain combinations are allowable and clear while others are not. Here are some examples (see also Section 56, just below):

run down, run in, run off, run out, walk off, walkover, walk-up, get nowhere, get through, get off. Also:

agree
- *to* a proposal
- *on* a plan
- *with* a person

contend
- *for* a principle
- *with* a person
- *against* an obstacle

differ
- *with* a person
- *from* something else
- *about* or *over* a question

impatient
- *for* something desired
- *with* someone else
- *of* restraint
- *at* someone's conduct

rewarded
- *for* something done
- *with* a gift
- *by* a person

56. Use acceptable idiomatic expressions.

Although idiomatic English cannot be explained scientifically, do not avoid using idiomatic expressions. They make writing and speech vigorous, imaginative, and effective. In fact, idioms are the essential material of which language is made: the widespread, everyday usage of people.

Do not assume, however, that you can create or adapt idioms as you please. Your usage should conform to the word links generally acceptable. A good dictionary contains explanations of idiomatic usage following key words which need such explanation, even though dictionaries may differ about some expressions. Be especially careful to consult your dictionary when using certain words, i.e., *prepositions* with nouns, adjectives, or verbs. Examples of idiomatic and unidiomatic expressions containing troublesome prepositions are the following:

Unidiomatic	*Idiomatic*
accord to	accord with
according with	according to
acquaint to	acquaint with
adverse against	adverse to
aim at proving	aim to prove
among one another	among themselves
angry at (a person)	angry with
as regards to	as regards
authority about	authority on
blame it on me	blame me for it
cannot help but talk	cannot help talking
comply to	comply with
conform in	conform to, with
correspond with (a thing)	correspond to
desirous to	desirous of
graduated (high school)	graduated from (high school)
identical to	identical with
in accordance to	in accordance with
in search for	in search of
prefer (one) over (another)	prefer to
prior than	prior to
responsible on	responsible for (to)
superior than	superior to
treat on (a subject)	treat of
unequal for	unequal to

For examples of how dictionaries record idiomatic phrases, see pp. 364–365.

EXERCISES

A. Correct any errors in idiom which occur in the following sentences:

1. The collection of old relics in the Frontier Room of the museum was valued for over one million dollars.
2. For the first time at this university a course is being offered for elementary education.
3. People of almost any age may participate with this sport.
4. Nothing constructive can be done until we are at friendly terms with our neighbors.
5. Miss Millay's classmates were delighted in her poems.
6. Living in a residence hall is far superior than living in a fraternity.

7. The card catalog saves walking all around and through the stacks in quest for a particular book.
8. While in college, I have learned to study between four to seven hours a day.
9. We were surprised on how good the roads were.
10. Extracurricular activities give a person a break to the regular routine of classes and studies.
11. The primary purpose for the high school is the preparation of the student for college.
12. Man will succeed to inhabit the moon in the near future.
13. The budgeting of time in college is advised to every freshman.
14. In my writing I sometimes have trouble to bring across a point.
15. Here in college we are assigned to certain courses in accordance to the results of certain tests.

B. Make the following sentences idiomatically acceptable by listing the prepositions which would properly fill in the blanks:

1. This letter means that he will accede ___ your request.
2. Contrast this idea ___ that one.
3. She does not adhere ___ that theory.
4. Mr. Bullock will compensate you ___ the work.
5. In this instance, the boys don't agree ___ the girls.
6. Sarah was then admitted ___ the theater.
7. Are you really independent ___ your father?
8. Your mother is apprehensive ___ your safety.
9. Surely you can accommodate yourself ___ any plan.
10. What do you infer ___ that proposal?
11. She could not bear to part ___ it.
12. Mrs. Smoak will be ___ home this afternoon.
13. Do you know an antidote ___ this poison?
14. That species is peculiar ___ this vicinity.
15. Please don't meddle ___ affairs not your own.
16. This drug is not a substitute ___ that one.
17. She will prohibit you ___ doing that.
18. Jack is now reconciled ___ living on a small salary.
19. I didn't think him capable ___ doing such a thing.
20. Jane is too careless ___ her appearance.

C. Use correct prepositions with each of the following verbs: *acquaint, acquiesce, center, collide, concentrate, engage, listen, part, sympathize, wait.*

D. Use correct prepositions with each of the following adjectives: *adverse, angry, identical, independent, obedient, peculiar, sick, superior, unmindful, worthy.*

E. In the following, (1) what is the meaning of each word separately? (2) What is the meaning of the phrase? *Oak leaf cluster, gentleman's agreement, scorched earth, second fiddle, far cry, day letter, blue laws, rabbit punch, automatic pilot, square dance, salad days, poor law, pilot plant, pidgin English, oxygen tent, olive branch, king's evil, match play, round robin, petty cash.*

ILLITERACIES

57. Avoid the use of illiterate words and phrases.

Illiteracies are words and phrases not accepted in either colloquial or formal language. Characteristic of uneducated speech, they are to be avoided in writing unless put into the mouths of people you are characterizing or used on exceedingly rare occasions for purposes of humor. Illiteracies are not necessarily coarse and are frequently effective; in fact, examples exist of eloquent writing and speaking by poorly educated persons deeply sincere in what they said. But anyone with a high school education or beyond should not need illiteracies to help him express his ideas.

Illiterate words and phrases are also referred to as *vulgarisms* (the language of the uneducated), or *barbarisms*. The latter word is from the Greek word for "barbarian," once used of foreigners not included in Greek civilization; hence, linguistically, a barbarism is a word or phrase not included in the language.

Dictionary makers apply a label to indicate some illiteracies, but what may be marked *illiterate* in one dictionary may be termed *dialect* or even *colloquial* in another. Not many examples may appear because most dictionaries primarily record "standard" usage. When such examples are recorded, do not assume that you can use them in your writing simply because they are in the dictionary; be sure to read the label attached to them. The following words and phrases are representative of those that should be guarded against: *acrossed, ain't, anywheres, borned, boughten, brung, disremember, drownded, excessible, hisself, irregardless, kepted, losted, mistakened, nohow, nowheres, ourn, snuck* (past of *sneak*), *vacationize, youse.* Note that an *ed* added to past-participle forms of verbs makes a not uncommon illiteracy.

EXERCISES

A. Write a short paper summarizing what your dictionary tells you of these words applied to language: *barbarism, illiteracy, impropriety, solecism, vulgarism*. Use, if possible, dictionary examples of each.

B. From what is the word *vulgarism* derived? What is the difference between *vulgarism* and *vulgarity*?

C. Make a list of 20 illiteracies heard in the conversation of others or reported in books.

D. Below are two selections from narratives which include the speech of uneducated people. From each compile a list of words that are illiterate and another list which includes words common to informal and formal "good" English.

Tom broke in irritably, "Well, you ain't never gonna know. Casy tries to tell ya an' you jest ast the same thing over. I seen fellas like you before. You ain't askin' nothin'; you're jus' singin' a kinda song. 'What we comin' to?' You don't wanta know. Country's movin' aroun', goin' places. They's folks dyin' all aroun'. Maybe you'll die pretty soon, but you won't know nothin'. I seen too many fellas like you. You don't want to know nothin'. Just sing yourself to sleep with a song—'What we comin' to?' . . . I didn't mean to sound off at ya, mister. It's the heat. You ain't got nothin'. Pretty soon you'll be on the road yourse'f. And it ain't tractors'll put you there. It's them pretty yella stations in town. Folks is movin'," he said ashamedly. "An' you'll be movin', mister."

—John Steinbeck, *The Grapes of Wrath*

"It's the onluckiest place ennywhar nigh about," said Nathan White, as he sat one afternoon upon the porch of his log-cabin, on the summit of Old Rocky-Top, and gazed up at the heights of the T'other Mounting across the narrow valley. "I hev hearn tell all my days ez how, ef ye go up thar on the T'other Mounting, suthin' will happen ter ye afore ye kin git away. An' I knows myself ez how—'t war ten year ago an' better—I went up thar, one Jan'ry day, a-lookin' fur my cow, ez hed strayed off through not hevin' enny calf ter our house; an' I fund the cow, but jes' tuk an' slipped on a icy rock, an' bruk my ankle-bone. 'T war sech a job a-gittin' off'n that thar T'other Mounting an' back over hyar, it hev l'arned me ter stay away from thar."

—Charles E. Craddock, "Over on the T'other Mounting,"
In the Tennessee Mountains

E. Find acceptable words to replace the illiteracies in the following sentences:

1. Careless typing in letters is distractful.
2. Everyone was saying to hisself that we had to win this game.
3. I lost track of time because my watch was busted.
4. Most of the materials were boughten at a nearby lumber yard.
5. The next morning my ear had completely swollened shut.
6. I have made many foolhearty mistakes this past year.
7. Some people have alterior motives for what they do.
8. Too many of our high school teachers were just out of college and completely unexperienced.
9. Every day at our cottage we gather the rubbage and burn it.
10. Then we go to the living room, where the splendrous Christmas tree stands.
11. Some authors make a good living because of their masterment of the English language.
12. We all should do our upmost to make the world a better place in which to live.
13. Occasionally my roommate and I misinterpretate what the other has said.
14. Knowing Latin and Greek mythology can lead to highly allusionated writings.
15. Irregardless of present problems, the younger people must have more control in the future.

IMPROPRIETIES

58.   Unlike illiterate words, *improprieties* are recognized English words which are misused in function or meaning. The word constituting an impropriety is acceptable; its misuse causes an error in diction.

58a.   Avoid improprieties in grammatical function.

One classification of improprieties includes words acceptable as one part of speech but unacceptable as another: nouns improperly substituted for verbs, verbs for nouns, adjectives for nouns, adjectives for adverbs, adverbs for adjectives, prepositions for conjunctions; another consists in misuses of principal parts of verbs. Someone has justly called such improprieties "coined grammar."

A word identified as more than one part of speech may be so used without question, but do not transfer a word from one part of speech to another until this new function is sanctioned by good use. Examples of grammatical improprieties:

Verbs used as nouns:	*eats, an invite, a think, advise.*
Nouns used as verbs:	*birthing* an idea, *biographing,* to *host, ambitioned, heired.*
Adjectives used as adverbs:	*real* pretty, *some* tall, etc. (See Section **83**).
Verb forms:	*seen* for *saw; don't* for *doesn't; done* for *did; laying* for *lying; setting* for *sitting; hadn't ought; of* for *have.*
Other combinations:	*this here, that there, them there, being that* or *being as* or *being as how* for *because* or *since, except as* for *unless.*

For guidance, consult your dictionary, which labels every word according to the part or parts of speech that it is. Note also the "usage" label: *colloquial, dialect, slang,* etc., since the same word may be acceptable as one part of speech but not as another.

58b. Avoid improprieties in meaning.

A second classification of improprieties includes words similar or vaguely similar to other words and used inexactly or wrongly for them. Such words include homonyms and homographs. *Homonyms* are two words that have the same or close pronunciation, but are different in meaning, in origin, and, very often, in spelling; for example, *pale* and *pail; sew* and *so; hour, our,* and *are; bough* and *bow. Homographs* are two or more words that have the same spelling but are different in meaning, origin, and perhaps pronunciation. Examples: *row* (a straight line) and *row* (a noisy dispute); *air* (atmosphere) and *air* (melody), *pale* (faintly colored or colorless) and *pale* (enclosure or limit). Homographs cannot cause misspelling, but they can cause ambiguity and confusion. Errors also arise in confusing words which are near-homonyms: *midst* for *mist, medal* for *metal, later* for *latter, latter* for *ladder, shutter* for *shudder.* (See also Section **52b**.)

> A mother with a large family has a difficult time keeping her children in *toe.*
> Some babies very early accomplish the *fete* of learning to walk.
> Children are likely to get distorted *fews* from reading comic books.

Perhaps such confusions are caused by the increasing emphasis put upon listening, upon hearing words (and hearing them inexactly) rather than seeing them in print and associating their meaning with their appearance as well as their sound.

In writing, bear in mind the lack of clarity caused through confusing homonyms, homographs, near-homonyms, and near-homographs. Your aim should be the word that conveys to the reader *exactly* the meaning that you intend, the word that means *precisely* what you want to say (Section 61a, b). If you are in doubt about the meaning of a word, or of two similar words, the usual advice about dictionary use applies.

In addition to the list of homonyms and near-homonyms given under "Spelling" (Section 52b), other pairs or groups of words frequently confused in meaning appear in Section 61a.

EXERCISES

A. Use correctly in sentences 10 of the pairs of words listed in Section 52b.

B. Use correctly in sentences 10 of the pairs of words listed in Section 61a.

C. Use each of the following words correctly in a sentence: *creditable, apt, vocation, consul, can, may, mad, counsellor, capitol, lightening, personnel, wont, exasperate, imply, noteworthy.*

D. From your dictionary, find the answers to the following questions. If the answer is "yes," explain. Can the following words be used as indicated? (1) *Complected* as a variant for *complexioned?* (2) *Contrariwise* as an adjective? (3) *Rose* as a verb? (4) *Conjugate* as an adjective? (5) *Sure* as an adverb? (6) *Ditto* as a verb? (7) *Quarry* as a verb? (8) *Manly* as an adjective? (9) *Stratums* as a plural? (10) *Cool* as a noun? (11) *Appropriate* as an adverb? (12) *Pshaw* as a verb? An interjection? (13) *Throw* as a noun? (14) *Wrought* as a past participle of *work?* (15) *Quail* as a verb? (16) *Mimicry* as a verb? (17) *Holp, holpen* as past tense and past participle, respectively, of *help?* (18) *Hardy* as a noun? (19) *Equal* as a noun? (20) *Corp* as the singular of *corps?*

E. Correct any improprieties in the following sentences:

1. All these misfortunes I contributed to the fact that I had walked under a ladder that morning.
2. A stern punishment for a litterbug would be a fine afflicted upon the offender.
3. A forester who works for the federal government is always insured of a steady job.
4. In our city new editions are being opened and new residences built all the time.
5. In the Southwest, Spanish was once the most predominate language spoken.

6. The bus was so crowded that most of us had to stand in the isles.
7. Such are some of the most oblivious advantages of our college library.
8. Studying engineering curtails a great amount of work, and work is what I enjoy.
9. Let us do more to award the deserving few.
10. Mother and I were left alone to ready me for my trip.
11. I always weight the advantages before acting.
12. Our town's aspects for the future seem to be getting brighter.
13. He has no patience with students who have trouble containing scientific facts.
14. Every dictionary company tries to keep its latest addition as modern as possible.
15. Our library has a quiet, relaxed atmosphere that conduces a student to want to study.
16. High grades are certainly a boost to a student's moral.
17. I had the honor of receiving a metal as the patrol boy of the year.
18. About two hours latter we found that our tent was going to collapse.
19. I have tried never to disregard the religious beliefs which my parents have worked hard to install in me.
20. I learned a great deal about our natural resources last summer when I was employed by the Department of Conversation.

SLANG

Slang is a label for words and phrases ranging from just below acceptable colloquialisms (see Section 55) down to the lowest level of illiteracies (see Section 57). Characteristics of slang include flippant or eccentric humor; forced, fantastic, or grotesque meanings; novelty; attempts to be vivid, fresh, pungent, colorful. Such expressions may appeal to popular fancy or to some segment of it (college slang, military slang, baseball slang), but in general they are substandard. Even so, slang may for a time be used over a wide area, and a considerable number of words and phrases bear the "slang" label in our dictionaries. If such expressions persist, they may eventually receive the respectable label *colloquial*. Of the following examples, some appear in dictionaries with the "slang" label; some may appear there eventually; and some probably never will, because their vogue is too temporary.

Slang expressions appear as one of several forms:

1. Neologisms (newly coined words): *beatnik, goofy, grandiferous, hornswoggle, ixnay, mooch, nix, oops, payola, razz, scram, scrumptious,*

shyster, sockdologer, wacky. Not all newly coined words, however, are slang (see Section **60**).

2. Words formed from others by abbreviation or by adding endings to change the part of speech: *C-note, chintzy, copper, groovy, nervy, phony, prexy, psych out, snafu* (situation *n*ormal, *a*ll *f*ouled *u*p), *VIP* or *V.I.P.* (*V*ery *I*mportant *P*erson).

3. Words in otherwise acceptable use given extended meanings: *bean, blow, buck, chicken, cool, corny, dish, grub, guts, guy, jerk, lousy, sack, square, swell*.

4. Words formed by compounding or coalescing two or more words: *attaboy* (that's the boy), *egghead, hepcat, high-hat, screwball, slanguage* (*sl*ang and *l*anguage) *slithy* (*sli*my and *lithe*), *stash* (*st*ore and *ca*che), *sweedle* (*sw*indle and *wheedle*), *whodunit*.

5. Phrases made up of one or more newly coined words (neologisms) or one or more acceptable ones: *blow one's top, bum steer, conk out, cut a rug, dead beat, get in orbit, goof off, have a ball, in cahoots, jam session, live it up, off one's rocker, on the skids, pork barrel, shoot the bull*.

59.   Avoid slang in formal and informal writing.

Slang, although popular, has little place in formal writing or even in effective informal writing. Sound reasons exist for avoiding it.

First, many slang words and phrases last for a brief time and then pass out of use, becoming unintelligible and violating the principle that words must be in current use (see Section **53**). How many college students can explain clearly what these phrases—college slang of a generation or so ago—meant when applied to coeds: (a) *powderhouse fluff*, (b) *fever frau*, (c) *hothouse bowwow*, (d) *pop-eyed pansy*, (e) *green peas*, (f) *butter-and-egg fly*, (g) *lolleos*, (h) *cloud*, (i) *wows*, (j) *tin pans*.[10] Or how many college students of a generation hence will know that in the early 1960's students referred to easy courses as *guts, snaps, crips, funs,* and *whizzes*? Numerous currently popular slang expressions will be outmoded in a short time.

Second, the use of slang expressions keeps you from searching for the exact words you need to express your meaning. Many slang expressions are only rubber stamps; to refer to a person as a "great guy" or a "lemon" hardly expresses exactly or fully any critical judgment or

---

[10] (a) sorority girl, (b) girl full of life and animation, (c) a dream girl, (d) and (e) young women lacking charm, (f) social queen, (g), (h), (i), and (j), women students.

intelligent description. To argue that such a word conveys precisely the intended meaning is to reveal a poverty of vocabulary, or careless thinking, or laziness. A serious charge against slang is that it becomes a substitute for thinking.

Third, slang does not serve the primary purpose of writing: conveying a clear message from writer to reader. This objection to slang is evident from the characteristics given above.

Finally, slang is not appropriate in most formal or effective informal writing because it is not in keeping with the context. Words should be appropriate to the audience, the occasion, and the subject matter (see Section **69**).

Some good arguments, however, do favor slang and indicate places where it should be used. It does express feeling, although explosively and sometimes grotesquely. It also makes effective short cuts in expression and often prevents artificiality in writing. Furthermore, it should be used in reporting dialogue to give the flavor of the speech actually used. But avoid an excessive or injudicious use of slang expressions, for the reasons already mentioned.[11]

EXERCISES

A. Write a brief paper comparing and contrasting the meanings given by your dictionary for the following: *slang, argot, cant, dialect, jargon, lingo, shoptalk, vernacular.*

B. Look up in your dictionary the meaning of the following slang words and phrases: *cahoot, gimmick, goo, shyster, jittery, nix, mooch, tizzy, kibosh, hooey, get one's goat, pork barrel, sad sack, on the make, long green, stool pigeon, stuffed shirt, sound off, on the loose, high-hat.*

C. Give a slang meaning and an acceptable meaning for each of the following: *applesauce, flame, guy, plug, salted, noodle, pinch, rat, sell, punch, oyster, stall, stuff, pony, ham, grind, yellow, show, sap.*

D. Collect at least 25 examples of slang words and phrases from your dictionary. What does each mean?

E. Collect at least 25 examples of slang words and phrases heard around the campus. From your list write a 400-word theme on the subject, College Slang, 19—.

[11] For those interested in exploring slang words and phrases, see for, respectively, American and British slang the following: Lester V. Berrey and Melvin van den Bark, *The American Thesaurus of Slang,* 2nd ed. (New York: Thomas Y. Crowell Company, c. 1953), and Eric Partridge, *A Dictionary of Slang and Unconventional English,* 4th ed. (New York: The Macmillan Company, 1953).

F. Point out and correct any slang words or phrases in the following sentences:

1. At my first Halloween party the teachers furnished eats and gave prizes to all the kids.
2. As for money, Harold is loaded.
3. Our high school student body is varied, with characters ranging from hoods to highbrows.
4. Before I left for college, I went back to high school to see some of the kids who had been my buddies, all of them nice guys.
5. The guys I hung around with during my junior year in high school were a crazy bunch.
6. In every town some attention must be given to the teens or they will become a problem.
7. Through activities you learn to meet other fellas and to get along with them.
8. Some students are constantly griping about their teachers and the assigned homework.
9. When I have a date, I want him to have something to talk about and not to be a dead pan.
10. In writing a theme, when I think of a good topic, I have it made.
11. This past week end I really had a ball.
12. Some people consider all superstitions hogwash.
13. At times Jim will get mad, begin a blue streak of yapping, and cuss out everyone in sight.
14. Our hitting the books went along swell for about six weeks, and then the goofing around started again.
15. One Friday the 13th a bunch of fellows and I were on a canoe trip in eastern Canada.
16. My parents wanted to know what had been happening at college, and how I was doing and all of that jazz.
17. These boys have formed a safe-driving club in order to get the town off their necks.
18. Some local high school graduates are living it up now, but in years to come, when the going gets rough, they will regret not attending college.
19. My roommate can use faultless diction, but usually she fractures everyone with her carelessness.
20. Some students have the impression that they can goof off and still remain in college.

NEOLOGISMS

60. Use neologisms appropriately.

A *neologism* is either a word newly coined to fill a need or an established word given a new meaning. If the latter characteristic applies, your dictionary probably includes this meaning; if the former, dictionary editors record the frequency of use, and are guided by their findings. Of two recent coinages, *gobbledygook* and *bafflegab* (see Section **66c**), the latter is not in dictionaries, the former is. *Slash* (/), a needed word for a mark of punctuation, is not so defined among other meanings of *slash*, but it is so used in The Modern Language Association *Style Sheet*.

Word coinages are minted in various ways. Some are adaptations of common words: *elephantasy, millionheiress*. Some are combinations of two or more common words, the so-called portmanteau words: *brunch* (*br*eakfast and l*unch*), *mollars* (*m*illions of d*ollars*), *smog* (*sm*oke and f*og*), *slash* (*sl*anting d*ash*). Some are formed from the initial letters of common words: *loran* (*lo*ng *ra*nge *n*avigation), *radar* (*ra*dio *d*etecting *a*nd *r*anging), *tips* (rumored to be from *to* *i*nsure *p*rompt *s*ervice). Some are virtually new formations like *gobbledygook,* modeled on *hobbledehoy* or starting with the meaningless sounds of a turkey's gobble, and *bafflegab* (baffling gab). And some are still comparatively or completely unknown, despite creation by popular or literary speakers and writers: *clouder-puffs* (a sky full of round soft clouds), by Conrad Aiken; *cigarettiquette* (light the lady's first) and *popaganda* (Father's Day), by Edward Anthony; *looklister* or *listlooker* for TV audience-spectators; *globilliterate* (one ignorant of world affairs), by Norman Corbin; *Babbitt* (narrow-minded businessman), by Sinclair Lewis; *elephantasy* (heavy-handed or -footed writing), by Louis Untermeyer; *avoirduprose* (heavy language), *millionheiress,* and *cinemactress,* from *Time* magazine.[12]

Still other new coinages have been in the fields of the sciences and technology—terms needed to describe new inventions, discoveries, applications, and occupations: *A-bomb, H-bomb, cyclotron, klystron, rhombatron, realtor, beautician,* and the like. Perhaps in this classification also are registered tradenames or trademarks: *Kodak, Nylon,*

---

[12] Examples taken from "Who Makes Up the New Words?" in *Word Study*, October, 1948, published by G. & C. Merriam Company, Springfield, Massachusetts.

Dacron, Simonize, Linotype, Technicolor. Sometimes a major change in our national way of living, like a depression or a war, creates many new words; from World War II came these representative examples: *blitz, foxhole, jeep, kamikaze, tank trap, roadblock, flack, bazooka.*

Depending on the dictionary you own, newly coined words which appear there may have no label or be labeled "slang" or "colloquial." See, for example, *lowbrow, highbrow,* and *gobbledygook.* Some neologisms become popular and change to permanent status, like *motel* (*mo*torist's ho*tel*), coined by a Los Angeles architect and now a common word among motoring tourists.

If you use any of these various neologisms in your writing or speaking, be sure they are appropriate, that is, easily understood by the people whom you are addressing (see Section 69). Or perhaps you will want to apply the advice of author Seumas O'Brien: "I had such an extensive vocabulary as a young man I did not need to invent any words. I never read without a dictionary and was richer in words than in anything else."

EXERCISES

A. Read several issues of *Time* magazine and bring to class a representative list of 20 neologisms that appear there.

B. Read the news articles of several newspaper columnists and make a list of any neologisms you find.

EXACT AND PRECISE DICTION

61. Exact and precise diction is essential for clearness and effectiveness. Since the primary purpose of writing is communication, it is important that words express exactly and precisely what you mean to convey.

61a. Use exact words.

Exact diction concerns exact word order (Section 39a), right word vs. wrong word, and double-meaning words. *Exact* words are not misused for, or confused with, words alike or similar in sound and spelling—homonyms, homographs, homophones—nor are they closely enough like others to be improprieties in function or meaning (Sections 52b, 58b). In addition to the homonyms and near-homonyms listed in Section **52b,** other trouble-causers with subtle or not-so-subtle differences in meaning are in the following list (those preceded by * are discussed in "Glossary of Faulty Diction," (Section **70**):

*accept, except
adverse, averse
*advise, inform
*affect, effect
aisle, isle
*all ready, already
*all together, altogether
allude, elude
*allusion, illusion
*almost, most
altar, alter
*amount, number
*anxious, eager
*apt, liable, likely
avenge, revenge
*believe, feel
*beside, besides
casual, causal
climactic, climatic
complement, compliment
*continual, continuous
conversation, conservation
convince, persuade
credible, creditable, credulous
*disinterested, uninterested
expect, suspect
faint, feint

*farther, further
*fewer, less
*formally, formerly
*healthful, healthy
*if, whether
*imply, infer
*ingenious, ingenuous
interest, intrigue (v.)
irrelevant, irreverent
*leave, let
*lie, lay
luxuriant, luxurious
marital, martial
moral, morale
*notorious, noteworthy, notable
official, officious
*party, person, individual
personal, personnel
*practicable, practical
*principal, principle
prophecy, prophesy
*raise, rise
reputed, reputable
*respectfully, respectively
*sit, set
statue, stature, statute
*suspicion, suspect

61b. Use precise words.

Precise words are exact words, but they are more. Any of several words may convey a general meaning (Section **64a**), but even if you have a choice of several words approximating what you wish to say, each idea has a word or phrase which will express your meaning more precisely than all others. It is your task, your obligation, to find this word or phrase and use it. In the search, a thesaurus is an excellent reference book to have available. Frequently, too, your choice is from several words with nearly identical meanings, and study of the synonyms listed for an expression in a dictionary or thesaurus enables you to choose a more precise term. For example, before allowing a word like *cheerful* or *cheery* to stand in one of your themes, find out whether one of the following adjectives will communicate your meaning more precisely: *blithe, gay, jocose, jocular, jocund, jolly, jovial, joyful, joyous, merry, sportive.*

Do not, however, let the use of synonyms lead you into a different kind of error-absurdity: two words may be synonymous in one meaning but not in another. Consider the following ludicrous uses of synonyms for, respectively, *steal, vision,* and *face:*

> The moon is *pilfering* over the mountaintop.
> In her beautiful new evening gown my girl was a *sight* at the Junior Prom.
> In the poem Lancelot says that the Lady of Shalott had a lovely *map.*

Exactness and preciseness in diction require you to think clearly and carefully. Sometimes the first word which comes to mind is the exact word or the most precise one that can be used; more often it is not. As a good writer, remember always that a word means to the reader what the reader thinks it means. Exact and precise diction results only when the reader understands exactly and precisely what the writer intended to communicate.

EXERCISES

A. Distinguish among the meanings of the words in each of these groups:
  argue, debate, discuss, comment.
  dislike, disgust, distaste, nauseate.
  feature, characteristic, peculiarity, quality.
  color, hue, tinge, shade.
  walk, go, totter, stumble.

B. Substitute better words for any weak ones in the following sentences:

1. My brother is a very nice person.
2. Parents are a wonderful thing, and I am grateful for having such understanding parents.
3. It is a little funny to me not to see snow during November.
4. We wanted the house to look nice when my grandparents arrived.
5. Winning that honor was my biggest thrill yet, but an even bigger one was coming.

6. The latest thing in electronics is space technology.
7. As funny as it may seem, I still have that old car.
8. One of the greatest things a fraternity can teach is getting along with others.
9. Having to go to an 8-o'clock class is a ghastly experience.
10. It's just terrible, terrible; my boy friend hasn't called me all afternoon.
11. I always put off doing my horrible old assignments as long as I can.
12. We're going to listen to TV tonight; won't it be thrilling?
13. It's perfectly splendid that you are studying so hard for this test.
14. The way my roommate cuts classes is simply amazing.
15. I had a marvelous time reading the newspaper last evening.
16. I'd say anyone was phenomenal who attends class regularly.
17. One factor has completely changed my way of life here at college.
18. Our high school is one of the prettiest in the state.
19. By cramming, I figured I could pull my grades up.
20. I had a feeling that my freshman year was going to be just awful.

C. In the following sentences, improve any diction that is not precise or exact.

1. My roommate told me about her freshman year and warned me about doing the same.
2. I have also at one time or another entertained a variety of hobbies.
3. We played on the same football, baseball, and swimming teams together.
4. The study of the theories that are attributed to the many auto accidents is very interesting.
5. The college provides a numerous amount of material to guide students in their studies and careers.
6. I shall always remember my teacher informing me to study a little harder.
7. There have been many cars at the track which have used engines from Detroit.
8. Another important characteristic that teachers should contain is the ability to have discipline.
9. The most important happening to our country was its founding in 1492 by Christopher Columbus.
10. During my first month I gained the University Glee Club and the Camera Hobby Group.
11. Information letters can notify the same event to many people.
12. The problem of overdue and lost books is another obstacle that must be accounted for by the college library.

13. I am happy to say that most of the superstitions around home possess very little enthusiasm.
14. It is always pleasant to learn that our faith has not been mislaid.
15. That night I had to sit and watch the game from the audience.
16. At Christmas everyone is obsessed with a wonderful feeling.
17. I have trouble with the proper sequence of subjects in my paragraphs.
18. Some college teachers cannot get their pupils interested in the subject.
19. Saturday night in my town is an affair which most of the teen-agers look forward to.
20. There is a lacking in my English background.

D. In the following sentences, the writers obviously did not say what they intended to say. What did they mean to say?

1. Each fall a football game is played between the alumnae and the undergraduate students.
2. I remember tearing down the stairs in order to get an early breakfast.
3. My father was an officer in the Navy and kept all the enlisted men's money.
4. I think that my father is the biggest man alive.
5. As I look back to my athletic activities, I see that I have always had a basketball on the brain.
6. My grandpa is like grandma an ideal grandpa.
7. For an excellent method of transportation I would like to dwell upon the automobile.
8. In that accident only one person was injured, and she was killed outright.
9. Chicago is second in size in the United States with about four million population and is located in the Midwest at the bottom of Lake Michigan.
10. Franklin D. Roosevelt was the longest President that this country has ever had.

TECHNICAL WORDS

Technical words have special meanings for people in particular fields, professions, or occupations.

To such words approximately 50 special subject labels are attached by dictionaries: Astronomy, Engineering, Entomology, Manufacturing, Marine, Naval, Psychology, etc. Examples of technical words are *lepidopterous* (zoology), *diastrophism* (geology), *broadside* (nautical), *monocotyledon* (botany), *sidereal* (astronomy), *coniferous* (botany), *stratus* (meteorology), *cuprous* (chemistry).

Thousands of technical words are not in general dictionaries, but the number included is sufficiently large for the general reader not to be baffled by seeing them in print. When technical words are widely used or extend their meanings, their subject labels may be dropped. Some examples (made popular by special fields) are *broadcast* (from radio), *telescope* (from astronomy), *weld* (from engineering), *chisel* (from carpentry), *diagnose* (from medicine), *daub* (from painting), *mold* (from sculpture), *starry* (from astronomy), *arch* (from architecture), *virtuoso* (from music and art).

62. Use technical words and phrases appropriately.

A specialist writing for or speaking to other specialists uses many difficult technical terms. If he communicates with others in his general scientific field, he uses terms that are less difficult. If he addresses the nonspecialist, he should avoid all technical terms or use only those generally understood. These three approaches divide the style used into *technical, semitechnical,* and *nontechnical* or *popular.* For example, few of us could understand a technical treatment of a subject in the magazine *Electronics.* More of us could understand its treatment in *Scientific American.* All of us could understand it if it were adapted for one of the general magazines on the newsstands.

As a student you probably plan to specialize in one of the arts, sciences, or professions. In writing about your field, for your English and other courses on the campus, and in later communications, let the kind of reader or listener you are addressing determine your vocabulary in treating technical subjects. In such writing, avoid *jargon,* a term used in one of its meanings when a writer introduces into his nontechnical writing language peculiar to or understood only by members of a certain profession, trade, science, art, sect, or other special group: legal jargon, medical jargon, pedagogic jargon, etc. And as student-writer, do not bring in unexplained jargon words or phrases from your other courses—in biology, economics, education, psychology, or sociology.

EXERCISES

A. Using your dictionary, tell what sports or games the following terms are associated with. Some may refer to more than one sport. *Rabbit punch, spare, fall, javelin, foul, clay pigeon, K.O., dash, half nelson, double dribble, lateral pass, baby split, fast break, mouse trap, double fault, deuce, Texas leaguer, goalie, ace, grand slam, bull's-eye, bank shot, ringer, break, birdie, love, frame, set point, vulnerable, strike.*

B. What do the following words or phrases mean when they are used in literary criticism? *Accent, character, climax, essay, fatal flaw, meter, novel, octave, plot, setting, stress, style, theme, tragic hero, verse.*

FIGURATIVE LANGUAGE

63a. Make occasional use of figurative language when it is appropriate.

Clear and effective language, in prose as well as in poetry, uses appropriate figures of speech. *Literal language* is language that means exactly what it says, in a matter-of-fact and plain-fact way. If you say, "Since it was raining very hard, I hurried up the hill and into my house," you literally tell what has happened. *Figurative language* is language that suggests sense-impressions, exaggerated activity, images, imagination, pictures; i.e., it suggests "figures" to the mind. Although the words are exact, precise, concrete, and picturesque, the language is not literally true; we find it clear and effective if the suggestion or association is appropriate. "Since it was raining like an April flood, I flew up the hill and into my house."

Or, as another illustration, "Atwood's gridiron machine climbed to the top of the heap when it whitewashed Dorchester U. 27 to 0." Literally a football team is not a machine; it does not climb; it neither whitewashes nor is whitewashed; and college football teams do not assemble in a heap. Literally, this is what happened: "Atwood's football team defeated Dorchester U.'s team by a score of 27 to 0."

Found occasionally in prose are the following figures of speech, which, incidentally, like the parts of speech, occur in both speaking and writing:

1. *Simile,* a figure of comparison: an *expressed* comparison using the words *like* or *as:* "She sings like an angel." "In boxing competition he fights like a tiger." "The miniature plane flew as gracefully as a bird."

2. *Metaphor,* a figure of comparison: an *implied* comparison; the reader or listener uses his imagination to see the likeness: "She is an angel when she sings." "In the ring he is a tiger."

3. *Synecdoche,* a figure of association: use of a part or an individual for the whole class or group, or the reverse. Part for whole: "We have fifty head of cattle on our farm." Whole for part: "Atwood defeated Dorchester U. in the championship game"; i.e., the two universities did not play, but their football teams did.

4. *Metonymy,* a figure of association, somewhat like synecdoche: use of the name of one thing for that of another suggested by it. "My friends agree that Mother sets a good table" (i.e., prepares good food).

5. *Personification:* giving nonhuman objects the characteristics of a human being: "The breezes whispered, and the trees sighed and moaned."

6. *Hyperbole* (note suggestion of *effectiveness* in the definition): "exaggeration, or a statement exaggerated imaginatively, for effect; not to be taken literally." Some similes and metaphors express hyperbole: "An ancient man—as old as Methuselah, I'd say—tottered into the village square." "The towering mountain peaks pierced the heavens."

Figurative language, being imaginative and picturesque, adds clearness and effectiveness to writing. But do not consider figurative language as a mere ornament of style; do not use it too frequently; do not shift suddenly from figurative to literal language; and remember that direct, simple statement is usually preferable to a series of figures, always preferable when the figures are elaborate, artificial, or trite. Many worn-out similes are trite phrases (Section **65**): *brave as a lion, brown as a berry, busy as a bee, clear as crystal, cold as ice, mad as a wet hen.*

63b.   Avoid the use of mixed and inappropriate figures of speech.
Mixed figures are those in which the images suggested by the language cannot be clearly related. Similes or metaphors are especially likely to become mixed, through over-elaborateness, inconsistency, and incongruity. Examples of inappropriate or mixed figures:

1. I was a "big wheel" on our high school campus, but I haven't done much trotting around here at college.
2. When I graduate, I hope to become a well-oiled cog in the beehive of industry.
3. Three of us boys were sure the kingpins on the roost in our high school.
4. After football season many a football player who was a tidal wave on the football field has to put his head to the grindstone and study.

5. At any party there is always a rotten apple that throws a monkey wrench in our food and drink.

63c. Avoid exaggeration.

Hyperbole as a figure of speech (Section **63a**) can be used effectively, but exaggeration can be misleading because of its inexactness and possible ludicrousness. "As a boy I used to die laughing at my grandfather's jokes." Do not inexactly use such words as *terrible, ghastly, horrible, thrilling, marvelous, gorgeous, amazing, awful, splendid, phenomenal,* and *out of this world.* Each of these and similar words have their legitimate uses but have been used inexactly so often that they are rarely effective.

Another kind of exaggeration—the exaggerated metaphor (see Section **63a**)—is substituting a "monumental" phrase for a word which a writer may not wish to repeat or to find a synonym for. Joe Louis, when heavyweight boxing champion, was referred to as "The Brown Bomber," "The Detroit Menace," "The Tan Terror"; Babe Ruth, once the New York Yankees' star batter, was "The Home-Run King," "The Sultan of Swat." College athletic teams may be any kind of wild animals; on a given autumn Saturday afternoon the Bruins may claw the Tigers to ribbons or the Wildcats may make mincemeat of the Gophers. A fleet track man or fast football backfield star (note use of *star*) is a "galloping ghost" or "The Dan Patch of the cinder path (or gridiron)"; the football line is "a concrete wall" or "seven blocks of granite"; a girls' swimming team consists of "freshwater mermaids" or "desert pool dolphins"; a golf star is the "king of the fairways"; a popular radio or TV singer is "the nightingale of the air waves."

Such exaggeration in phrasing must receive careful consideration. When inappropriate, it should be avoided; when appropriate, it is picturesque and effective, as was a poet's phrase for the German Obernkirchen Children's Choir, "angels in pigtails."

EXERCISES

A. Improve the wording of the five sentences in Section **63b,** above.

B. Make a list of 20 effective figures of speech which you have found in reading.

C. Each sentence or group of sentences in the following contains a figure of speech either from themes or from published authors. On a separate sheet, number each item and give the name of the figure of speech contained in it.

1. On Christmas morning we children used to jump out of bed and dash downstairs.
2. Eustacia Vye was the raw material of a divinity.—Thomas Hardy
3. At first I liked my dramatic lessons as much as I like vinegar in my scrambled eggs.
4. Can Honour's voice provoke the silent dust, or Flattery sooth the dull cold ear of death?—Thomas Gray
5. We finally finished our Christmas shopping by completely buying out the store.
6. The Lord is my shepherd; I shall not want.—Psalm xxiii
7. Father received his sheepskin from Atwood University in 1940.
8. She walks in beauty, like the night of cloudless climes and starry skies.—Byron
9. At critical times in our history, the White House in Washington, D.C., has announced special radio talks to the nation.
10. There is the New York of the commuter—the city that is devoured by locusts each day and spat out each night.—E. B. White
11. Below us the fields looked like big quilts, and the buildings appeared as toys, with ants as people running in and out.
12. Above me are the Alps, the palaces of Nature, whose vast walls have pinnacled in clouds their snowy scalps.—Byron
13. In winter, the bare but strong branches of the trees support the sky to give free passage to all who pass underneath.
14. The commuter is the queerest bird of all. The suburb he inhabits has no essential vitality of its own and is a mere roost where he comes at day's end to go to sleep.—E. B. White
15. You shall not press down upon the brow of labor this crown of thorns; you shall not crucify mankind upon a cross of gold.—William Jennings Bryan

D. Point out any inconsistent figurative language in the following, and rewrite the sentences containing it.

1. We are going to have to look the problem in the eye with an open mind.
2. There were six of us in the car, and when we got to our hotel that night we were dead.
3. When you drive a foreign car, you have your feet firmly on the ground.
4. Although our Homecoming was not entirely ruined, Illinois put a big dent in our Homecoming spirit.
5. Some day we will make a start on cleaning the house of freedom, but we must hurry, for there are sharks in these waters.
6. When parents discipline their children sensibly, a child has attained a foothold by which he can police himself.

7. The spirit of the student body is keyed to only one goal: to cheer their team on to victory.
8. My father is always on his toes when he is driving a car.
9. I was at that awkward age that whenever I opened my mouth, I put my foot in.
10. As steam table man at the cafeteria, I am literally roasted to death every day by the great quantities of steam from the table and the heat from the broilers and grills.

EMPHATIC DICTION

64. Diction should be effective as well as clear. Contributing to effective diction are emphatic words, which may well include principles already discussed in "Exact and Precise Diction" (Section 61) and "Figurative Language" (Section 63) and principles to be discussed in the next four sections. Three additional suggestions for emphatic words:

64a. Prefer specific to general words.

Emphatic diction uses expressive nouns, adjectives, verbs, and adverbs. A *general* word names a broad concept: class names of nouns (*animal, land, street*), conventional verbs (*go, move, say*), and vague adjectives and adverbs (*good, bad, gladly, fast*). Especially colorless diction results from overuse of the forms of *to be* (*am, is, are, was, were,* etc.).

A *specific* word names a narrow concept—*collie, pasture, boulevard, totter, dash, shout, errorless, excruciating, mile-a-second, triumphantly*—and each of these could be further narrowed. Why is the second sentence following more effective?

> There was a pleasant stream flowing down the mountain.
> Serpentining Chestnut Creek felt its way noisily down Mount Greyrock over smooth, greenish-white stones.

Other general words are so vague and indefinite that they only approximate an idea. You can surely find specific words for any of the following ineffective words and phrases: *asset, case, character, condition, cute, degree, element, factor, feature, fine, instance, item, interesting, job, lot, lovely, nature, nice, personality, persuasion, phase, quality, state, thing, vital, according as to whether, along the line of, in connection with, in respect of, in the case of, with regard to.*

Vague and indefinite: a fine day
a vital game
a good job
thing used for any idea or object, as "another thing to remember"

Specific: a memorable day
a crucial (or championship-deciding) game
a worth-while achievement
another argument to remember

64b. Prefer concrete to abstract words.

An *abstract* word gives no clear picture; it is often a general word like some of those in the preceding section. A *concrete* word expresses something tangible, something usually perceivable by one or more of the senses: *lilacs, crimson, drumbeats, rose-scented, lemony, jagged, incarnadined.* Excellent examples of concrete words are onomatopoetic words, i.e., "make-a-name-for" words or words which express or suggest sounds: *meow, bark, hoot, lowing, rustling, murmuring, thud, crash, slam, ripple, singsong.*

Specific and concrete nouns, therefore, colorful and dynamic adjectives and adverbs, verbs which tell of action (motion) or relate to the senses (emotion), specific and concrete phrases—all help make writing more forceful.

A statement concerning Jonathan Swift might have been worded as follows:

Jonathan Swift, who as a writer kept a journal, composed essays on religion and politics, and wrote a satire, said good words make a good style.

Instead the writer wrote:

Jonathan Swift, whose writing experience carried him all the way from the baby-talk of his *Journal to Stella* through the fire and thunder of his essays on religion and politics to the satire of his *Gulliver's Travels,* said shrewdly that writing style is "proper words in proper places."
—From "On Writing Clearly," *The Royal Bank of Canada Monthly Letter,* July, 1957

The diction of the following passage is so emphatic and exact that the reader, with no further details supplied, can form a satisfactory picture of Ichabod Crane:

The cognomen of Crane was not inapplicable to his person. He was tall, but exceedingly lank, with narrow shoulders, long arms and legs, hands that dangled a mile out of his sleeves, feet that might have served for shovels, and his whole frame most loosely hung together. His head was small, and flat at the top, with huge ears, large green glassy eyes, and a long snip nose, so that it looked like a weathercock perched upon his spindle neck to tell which way the wind blew. To see him striding along the profile of a hill on a windy day, with his clothes bagging and fluttering about him, one might have mistaken him for the genius of Famine descending upon the earth or some scarecrow eloped from a cornfield.

—WASHINGTON IRVING, "The Legend of Sleepy Hollow"

64c. Understand the difference between denotative and connotative words.

If your purpose is writing exposition or argument (see Section 16c, d), you will use words which are as exact and specific as possible. Clearness is a basic guiding principle. Even in such writing, however, as well as in narration and description, search for words which suggest more than they say, which stimulate the imagination.

Denotative words express merely what the definitions of the words say; they are clear and are to be taken in their literal, explicit meaning for neither more nor less than they say: *house, woman, dog, city, San Francisco*.

Connotative words include implied, suggestive, or associated meanings. They stimulate the imagination and are emphatic: *home*—comfort, love, shelter, intimacy, privacy, etc.; *mother*—love, devotion, understanding, sacrifice, etc.; *dog*—affection, care, trouble, loyalty, obedience, etc.; *San Francisco*—"Golden Gate," "The Gateway to the Orient," "Chinatown," "Earthquake City of 1906," etc.

No guiding principle can be given for the choice and use of words rich in connotative meanings. One simple caution is that you do not exaggerate unduly in your word choice; otherwise, you reduce effectiveness (Section 63c).

EXERCISES

A. With the aid of your dictionary, substitute more emphatic words for the following: *building, applause, task, utter* (verb), *sticky, flock* (noun), *loose* (adjective), *writer, vicinity, run* (verb), *say, walk* (noun), *thing, hastily, instrument, comfortable, good, bite* (verb), *tired, careful.*

B. Name several words which have the same general meaning as the word italicized but which are more exact and emphatic: (1) A *tall* building; (2) a *vital* story; (3) your *nice* child; (4) a *talkative* man; (5) his *grave* condition; (6) a *brief* statement; (7) a *kind* person; (8) a *loud* noise; (9) he *worked* hard; (10) on the *boat;* (11) she *walked* in; (12) an angry *speech;* (13) a *leading* merchant; (14) I was *surprised;* (15) it's a *pleasant* room; (16) a *dislike* of war; (17) a good *pattern* to follow; (18) the bird *flew* away; (19) a *good* mind; (20) he *got* on the carousel; (21) he *ran* quickly; (22) a *small* animal; (23) a dilapidated *conveyance;* (24) the doorbell *sounded;* (25) a miserable *house;* (26) Dr. Jonas is a *specialist;* (27) a *warm* day; (28) a *delightful* book; (29) an interesting *trip;* (30) an *intelligent* student.

TRITENESS

Effectiveness is aided by freshness of diction; it is hindered by triteness. Trite or hackneyed expressions, or clichés, are words and phrases which have lost their force through overuse. The origins of the words *triteness, hackneyed,* and *cliché* are illuminating: *triteness* comes from the Latin word *tritus,* the past participle of *terere,* meaning "to rub," "to wear out"; *hackneyed* is derived from the idea of a horse, or carriage, let out for hire, devoted to common use, and thus worn out in service; *cliché* comes from the French word *clicher,* meaning "to stereotype," "to cast from a mold, to use over and over."

Thus trite words and phrases are but rubber stamps or ineffective repetitions of thought and expression. They may be overworked quotations, overworked similes, or outworn phrases from common speech, literature, and newspapers. They save the writer the trouble of thinking exactly what he means, but their use results in stale and ineffective writing. Such words and phrases inevitably seem humorous; they are, indeed, regularly used for humor or irony by fiction writers and columnists. Used seriously, they are signs that the writer or speaker is naïve.

65. Avoid trite language.

Familiarity with trite words and expressions is likely to cause them to occur to us more readily than others more effective. Look, therefore, with suspicion upon each word or phrase which leaps to mind until you are sure that it is exact, fresh, and unhackneyed. Be on your guard especially against overused similes. Remember, also, that words and phrases which do not seem trite to you may be clichés to any reader familiar with overworked expressions.

Examples of overused similes:

blue as indigo	happy as a lark
brave as a lion	happy as the day is long
brown as a berry	like a blundering idiot
busy as a bee	like a duck out of water
clear as crystal	like a newborn babe
clear as mud	mad as a wet hen
cold as ice	pure as new-drifted snow
fight like a tiger (caged lion)	red as a rose
free as the air	roar like a lion
gentle as a lamb	strong as an ox
green as grass	wild as a March hare

Other examples of trite words and phrases: [13]

a must	believe me
adequate income	bigger and better things
all boils down to	bitter end
all hours of . . .	bright and early
all in all	brings to mind
along this (that) line	butterflies in my stomach
and all that	by and large
and things like that	by leaps and bounds
any manner or means	center of attraction
aroused our curiosity	chills (shivers) up and down my
as a matter of fact	spine
as already indicated (mentioned)	college career
battle of life	come to life
beating around the bush	comes into the picture

[13] The authors gratefully acknowledge the help of Purdue University Department of English staff members in compiling this list, and the inadvertent help of their students. For approximately 2,500 other examples, see Eric Partridge, *A Dictionary of Clichés* (New York: The Macmillan Company, 1940).

comfortable living
conspicuous by its absence
dear old (high school, college, fraternity, Alma Mater)
deeply grateful
definitely
depths of despair
doomed to disappointment
dull thud
each and every
every walk of life
fair land of ours
few and far between
fill the shoes of
fine
first and foremost
fond memories
force of circumstances
get (getting) in orbit
get our (their) wires crossed
give it a try
give out (up)
goes without saying
good old . . .
grand and glorious
great (guy, job, thrill, etc.)
green with envy
hang one on
hapless victim
headed for home
honest to goodness
if I had it to do over
important day (time, year) rolled around
in a fix
in dire straits
in glowing terms
in my opinion
in the best of health
in the final (last) analysis
in the long run
in this day and age

interesting and educational
interesting (surprising) to note
intestinal fortitude
irony of fate
job (excellent, fine, good, splendid, etc.)
just around the corner
last but not least
last straw
leaves little to be desired
level (high school, college, adult, etc.)
live it up
mad dash for
main underlying reason
make the world a better place
many and varied
meets the eye
modern world of today (ours)
more than pleased
Mother Nature
much appreciated
Nature in all her splendor
Nature's wonderland (playground)
necessary evil
never a dull moment
nick of time
nipped in the bud
no fooling
no respecter of persons
no thinking man
none the worse for wear
out of this world
outstanding achievement
packed in like sardines
plagued with violence
poor (food, game, show, etc.)
pounding like a hammer
proud possessor
psychological moment
race, creed, or color (substitute: race, belief, or national origin)

raining cats and dogs	that's another story
real challenge	the fact is . . .
really a thrill	the time of my life
remains a problem	the worse for wear
rise majestically	thing of the past
sad to relate	this day and age
sadder but wiser	this old world of ours
safe to say	through thick and thin
setting the scene	tired but happy
sheer beauty	top it off
shout it from the housetops	true sense of the word
sigh of relief	wait with bated breath
sight to see (behold)	wealth of fond memories
sit up and take notice	wee small hours of the morning
something on the mind	wends his way
start anew	wide open spaces
suffice it to say	with a bang
take a back seat for no one	with fear and trembling
take pen in hand	wonderful (time, day, meal, etc.)
takes shape	wonders of Nature
terrible (terribly)	words fail to express
that good old home-cooking	you can't take it with you

EXERCISES

A. Compare and summarize the meanings given in your dictionary for *banal, cliché, commonplace, hackneyed, stereotyped, trite*.

B. Make a list of 20 trite expressions which you have used in recent themes or conversations, or which you have overheard.

C. Copy the following sentences and underline on your paper the trite expressions in each. Substitute more effective expressions for those which you have underlined.

1. First and foremost, let me introduce my parents.
2. In this day and age, one needs a good education to be successful.
3. I have learned that one does not have to stay up to the wee small hours of the morning to finish his studying.
4. From November 1st on I am looking forward to Thanksgiving and that good old home-cooking.
5. When my parents were away, we children would fight like cats and dogs.
6. When I made my appearance on the ice, I must admit that I had butter-flies in my stomach.

7. One should always put money aside for a rainy day. After all, you can't take it with you.
8. The movie ended with the hero and heroine driving down the highway, like a ribbon winding over the hills, and into the reddening glow of the setting sun.
9. Sometimes Grandfather gets blue as indigo and says he is being cast off like an old shoe.
10. Last but not least, our town has three churches.

"FINE WRITING"

66. "Fine writing" is, paradoxically, anything but fine. It is pompous, artificial, affected, insincere, overdignified, and flowery. Its authors mistakenly think it to be free of all impurities because they have attempted to elevate it, bring it to perfection. "Fine writing" is characterized by at least three faults: use of too many modifiers, overuse of foreign words and Briticisms, and overuse of polysyllabic words.

66a. Avoid "fine writing" by not overusing modifiers.

Give your reader a clear, full understanding of your meaning, and use necessary words to accomplish this purpose, but avoid piling on descriptive words for their own sake or for insincere impressiveness. Use adjectives and adverbs intelligently, not lavishly. Descriptive writing is especially likely to be "fine writing":

A penetratingly loud and constantly insistent buzzer sounded, waking me out of a blissfully pleasant and dream-free sleep. I slowly opened my heavily laden and drowsy eyes and became acutely and instantly aware of the cool, almost raw, breeze blowing strongly through my half-opened window. As I rose slowly and regretfully to dress, I could see through the gracefully flowing and swaying open draperies that colorful, Jack-Frost-touched autumn had begun its annual artistic change of dress. The sky was blue and hazy with light soft fluffy white clouds outlined, surrounded, or pierced by flaming rays of deflected sunlight, which kaleidoscopically changed as the clouds lazily and slowly drifted along. The trees with long, yearning, outstretched branches shook violently and fearfully as the caressing gusts of wind nudged their multicolored overcoats of green, brown, red, and yellow. Beneath the trees the new-fallen leaves, immersed in brindled colors of dark maroon, flaming red, golden amber, pale beige, and olive green created a thick heavy blanket over the half-covered, half-frozen ground. The once green grass peering through thinly tattered patches of the blanket had the forlorn and forsaken appearance of a badly worn brown felt mat rolled out to be aired.

66b. Avoid "fine writing" by not overusing foreign words and Briticisms.

An inexperienced writer, attempting to adopt a pretentious style of writing because he is overwhelmed by the seriousness of his purpose, frequently makes the mistake of interlarding his work with foreign expressions or Briticisms (British expressions rather than American). Examples: *chef d'oeuvre, magnum opus, à bon marché, à propos de rien, dum vivimus vivamus, exempli gratia, garçon, morceau, robe-de-chambre, lift* for *elevator, petrol* for *gasoline, barrister* and *solicitor* for *lawyer, perambulator* or *pram* for *baby carriage* (see Section 54).

Do not hesitate to use the foreign word if it has been generally accepted through naturalization or if no exact English equivalent exists. But do not use such words too frequently or merely to convince the reader of your erudition and affected dignity.

66c. Avoid "fine writing" by not overusing polysyllabic words.

Polysyllabic words are words of more than three syllables, including two of the longest words in the language: *pneumonoultramicroscopicsilicovolcanokoniosis* (see *Webster's New International Dictionary*) and *antidisestablishmentarianism.* The words *gobbledygook* and *bafflegab,* coined respectively by ex-Congressman Maury Maverick and Milton A. Smith, Assistant General Counsel of the U.S. Chamber of Commerce, simply mean "overuse of polysyllabic words." Mr. Smith illustrates his definition, satirically, as follows: "Bafflegab—multiloquence characterized by consummate interfusion of circumlocution or periphrasis, inscrutability, incognizability, and other familiar manifestations of abstruse expatiation commonly utilized for promulgations implementing procrustean determinations by governmental bodies." *Bafflegab* as a word has not yet been accepted by dictionaries; *gobbledygook* has, and is thus defined by one dictionary: "talk or writing, especially of officialdom, that is pompous, wordy, involved, and full of long, Latinized words" (*Webster's New World Dictionary*).

To avoid this kind of "fine writing," use the short word instead of the long, if it will serve as well. Short words are usually more understandable, more sincere, and less self-conscious than polysyllabic words.

Someone gave good advice for effective writing when he said, "Short words are words of might." Such advice does not exclude the use of polysyllabic words; it means that they should not be used if they cause writing to be characterized by any of the following adjectives: affected, artificial, high-flown, ostentatious, pretentious, or pedantic. Word and phrase examples are the following: *comestibles* for *food; devouring element* for *fire; emporium* for *store; inebriated, intoxicated* for *drunk; last obsequies* for *funeral; peregrinations* for *travel; prevaricate* for *lie; pulchritudinous* for *beautiful; ratiocinate* for *think; savory repast* for *meal.*

EXERCISES

A. To show how big words create confusion, the editors of *Effective Letters Bulletin* of the New York Life Insurance Company have rewritten simple proverbs in "fine writing." Five such rewritten proverbs follow; what are the proverbs?

1. Feathered bipeds of similar plumage will live gregariously.
2. Too great a number of culinary assistants may impair the flavor of the consommé.
3. The capital of the papal state was not constructed during a diurnal revolution of the globe.
4. It has come to our attention that herbage, when observed in that section of enclosed ground being the property of an individual other than oneself, is ever of a more verdant hue.
5. Seeking a suitable place for the purpose of courting a state of dormant quiescence during the first part of the crepuscular period and forsaking said suitable place during the first part of the matinal period results in myriad benefits to *homo sapiens,* among which benefits may be noted a substantial increase in body soundness, monies, and sagacity.

B. Changed to simple, understandable language, what do the following mean?

1. Aromatic mint enravishes the olfactories of felines.
2. You should manufacture desiccated alfalfa during solarized incandescence.
3. Platitudinous ponderosity should be forsworn in promulgating esoteric cogitations.
4. Eschew all conglomerations of flatulent garrulity.
5. A fact is a statement of an empirically verifiable phenomenon within a conceptual scheme.

C. Following are three statements, as reported by the Associated Press, concerning a promotion refusal. Which is the least and which is the most effective? Why?

1. Verbal contact with Mr. Blank regarding the attached notification of promotion has elicited the attached representations intimating that he prefers to decline the assignment.
2. I have spoken to Mr. Blank about this promotion; he does not wish to accept the post offered.
3. Blank doesn't want the job.

D. Sometimes a renowned writer may be accused of "fine writing." In the following paragraph from *The Return of the Native,* do you think Thomas Hardy should be accused of or defended from the charge of "fine writing"?

That night was an eventful one to Eustacia's brain, and one which she hardly ever forgot. She dreamt a dream; and few human beings, from Nebuchadnezzar to the Swaffham tinker, ever dreamed a more remarkable one. Such an elaborately developed, perplexing, exciting dream was certainly never dreamed by a girl in Eustacia's situation before. It had as many ramifications as the Cretan labyrinth, as many fluctuations as the Northern Lights, as much colour as a parterre in June, and was as crowded with figures as a coronation. To Queen Scheherazade the dream might have seemed not far removed from commonplace; and to a girl just returned from all the courts of Europe it might have seemed not more than interesting. But amid the circumstances of Eustacia's life it was as wonderful as a dream could be.

CONCISENESS

67. Diction, to be effective, must be economical: not that writing should be sketchy or that necessary words may be omitted (see Section **35a, b**), but wordiness weakens the force of expression.

In forceful writing, the ratio of ideas to words is high. In poetry, consisting of "words in their best possible use," "each word must carry 20 other words upon its back," and prose can effectively approach poetry in this technique. Conciseness alone does not achieve effective writing, but it is difficult to write forcefully if two or three or more words convey the idea which one could express. Effective examples of conciseness are Lincoln's Gettysburg Address (267 words) and, from the King James Version of the Bible, the Ten Commandments (75 words) and the Golden Rule (11 words).

Two types of wordiness which apply particularly to sentence structure, the use of unnecessary details (*prolixity*) and the useless repetition of an idea (*tautology*), are discussed in Section 43. You may, however, wish to consider wordiness as a problem of concise diction rather than as a problem in sentence construction. Both specific and general suggestions follow.

67a. Do not repeat a pronoun after a noun used as subject of a sentence; such a pronoun is superfluous.

Wordy: The coach *he* has a difficult job.
Concise: The coach has a difficult job.

Wordy: My mother *she* writes me letters three times a week.
Concise: My mother writes me letters three times a week.

Wordy: The students here in college *they* should spend more time studying.
Concise: The students here in college should spend more time studying.

67b. Do not use again a conjunction or preposition already used for its specific purpose.

Faulty repetition results when a conjunction or a preposition (*that, in,* etc.) already used is repeated. Necessary grammatical relationship needs only the one word, not both.

Bad: I hope *that* after I graduate *that* I will be able to go into business for myself.
Don't think *that* because you have never had an accident *that* you can't easily have one.
Characteristic of my cousin is the high degree of honesty *in* which he believes *in*.
At what place are you living *at* now?
The Reference Room, *in* which we went *through* quickly, seemed to be the most interesting.

67c. Avoid beginning sentences or clauses with there is, there are, there was, there were, there has been, there have been, etc.

Usually such "there" beginnings are superfluous words, adding nothing. Occasionally they may be effective, as in "there are four genders in English," and you will find them used by many writers.

But each time you see such a beginning, see also whether the writer could have used a more effective way of expressing his ideas. (See "Expletive," Item 47, in "Grammatical Terms Defined," Section **85.**)

Wordy: *There were* four students nominated for class president.
Concise: Four students were nominated for class president.

Wordy: In the library *there are* many reference books to help you.
Concise: The library has many reference books to help you.

Wordy: In our little town *there* live 1,300 people.
Concise: In our town live 1,300 people.

67d. **Do not use two, three, or more words where one or two will serve.**

The moral of "few words for many" is in the following: To the simple question of whether rules should be observed, an administrator wrote, "The implementation of sanctions will inevitably eventuate in subsequent repercussions." What he might have said, simply, was "Yes."

Wordy: You will find the reference librarian *in back of* the desk.
Concise: You will find the reference librarian *behind* the desk.

Wordy: Give your directions *very definitely and precisely*.
Concise: Give *definite* directions.

Wordy: My absence was *due to the fact that* I had an attack of influenza.
Concise: My absence was *due to* an attack of influenza.

Other suggestions:

Reduce these	*to these*
a certain length of time	a certain time
am, is, are going to	shall, will
are of the opinion	believe
at the present time	now
before long	soon
I would appreciate it if	please
in accordance with	by
in case	if
in lieu of	instead
in regard to	about
in so far as	because, since, as
in the amount of	for
in the event that	if

Reduce these	*to these*
in the month of June, etc.	in June, etc.
inasmuch as	since
inquired as to	asked
it has come to our attention that	(begin with the word following *that*)
it is interesting to note that	(begin with the word following *that*)
on condition that	if
provided that	if
the length of 5 feet	5 feet (or) 5 feet long
under date of June 6	of June 6

67e. Avoid useless repetition of ideas already expressed by a word or phrase.

When meaning is expressed or implied in a particular word or phrase, repeating the idea by additional words is useless. One word of two or three expresses the idea, and the other words add nothing. Common examples are using *again* with many verbs beginning with *re;* using *more* or *most* with absolute-meaning adjectives; and using *more* or *most* with adjectives and adverbs already ending in *er, est.*

audible to the ear	more better
Christmas Eve evening	more older
complete monopoly	more paramount
completely unanimous	more perfect
connect up with	most perpendicular
consensus of opinion	most unkindest
cooperate together	necessary essential
descend down	necessary need
each and every one	personal friend
endorse on the back	recur again
fellow classmates	repeat again
first beginnings	resume again
four-cornered square	return back
from whence	rise up
individual person	round in form
join together	sunset in the west
long length	this afternoon at 3 P.M.
loquacious talker	this morning at 9 A.M.
many in number	unusually (most) unique
meet up with	visible to the eye

67f. Avoid objectionable repetition of words and phrases.

Unless a word or phrase is repeated for effectiveness or clarity, faulty repetition may be corrected by substituting equivalent expressions (synonyms), by judicious omission, or by recasting the sentence.

Faulty: *Since* several weeks have elapsed *since* you wrote, I have decided not to repeat the offer.

Improved: Several weeks have elapsed since you wrote, and I have decided not to repeat the offer.

Faulty: He *thought* everyone would *think* his act to be generous.

Improved: He was sure that everyone would think his act generous.

Faulty: Each of you must *study* hard in order to finish your *studies* by noon.

Improved: Each of you must study hard in order to finish your assignments by noon.

Faulty: He *said that* you *said that* we should apply promptly.

Improved: He informed us that you have said we should apply promptly.

When a sentence begins with a word or phrase which ends the previous sentence, ordinarily a pronoun or appositional phrase should be used instead.

Dubious: All my life I have lived in Franklinville. Franklinville is a city of some forty thousand people.

Improved: All my life I have lived in Franklinville, which is a city of . . .
           All my life I have lived in Franklinville, a city of . . .

Dubious: A good example of a historical novel is Charles Dickens' *A Tale of Two Cities*. *A Tale of Two Cities* is a story of the French Revolution.

Improved: A good example of a historical novel is Charles Dickens' *A Tale of Two Cities*. This is a story of . . .
           A good example of a historical novel is Charles Dickens' *A Tale of Two Cities,* a story of . . .

NOTE: Repetition, however, even if faulty, is preferable to artificial and awkward avoidance of it.

Artificial: Some newspapers publish news; other organs of the press issue material which frequently has only an approximate degree of timeliness.

Improved: Some newspapers publish news; others publish material which has only an apparent timeliness.

67

67g.   Use direct words instead of circumlocutions and euphemisms.

A *circumlocution* is literally "a roundabout way of speaking": *tame, villatic fowl* for *chicken; lowing herd* for *cattle; watery plain* for *sea.* *Euphemisms* are mild, inoffensive expressions for blunter, less pleasant, and perhaps more effective words: *to pass away* for *die; perspire* for *sweat; prevaricate* for *lie.*

Wordy: He has pursued his course of studies along the lines of mechanical engineering.
Concise: He has studied mechanical engineering.

Wordy: Grandfather was called home and passed to the Great Beyond in 1937.
Concise: Grandfather died in 1937.

Wordy: Students who disobey regulations will be separated from the university.
Concise: Students who disobey regulations will be expelled.

67h.   Avoid too many modifiers, especially a series of adjectives and adverbs, which result in wordiness (see Section 66a).

Example: It was a cold, bleak, gray day. John walked home nimbly and briskly. He felt full of life, keenly alert, and far from sluggish, despite the gloominess and cloudiness of his immediate surroundings.

EXERCISES

A. Apply principles of conciseness to the following sentences:

1. It was during the summer of 1959 that my brother bought himself a 14-foot motor boat.
2. In the event that we get extra vacation, I plan to go to Florida.
3. About 40 miles south of Frankland is a town called Waverly; this is my home town.
4. A check in the amount of $68.99 is enclosed made payable to your order.
5. There were only about one-fourth of our class who passed mathematics.
6. I do not feel the necessity for a conference at the present time.
7. It has been called to my attention by our treasurer that you have not paid this semester's dues.
8. There should be greater emphasis placed on the junior high school courses.
9. The signs were clever, and it was plain to see that the students had put plenty of work into them.

10. It was on a cold Friday night that I had my most memorable experience.
11. Sundays are the only days our family is able to spend together.
12. I would like to take this opportunity to introduce myself.
13. I have always had a deep interest in the field of mathematics.
14. Some students are not happy with regard to the way their themes are graded.
15. We knew Joe was late but we waited for him a little longer length of time.
16. I decided then to become a teacher in the field of biology.
17. When I asked for the car, Father's answer was usually in the negative.
18. There is still a great deal to be done in the area of chemistry.
19. In case I cannot get a summer job, I may go to summer school.
20. Upon arriving at the Washington Airport, we were ushered into buses for a tour of the city.

B. Correct faulty repetition in the following sentences:

1. At the end of a visit to a fair, most people would say they enjoyed themselves very much and would love to go back another time.
2. This information should be sufficient enough to give you an idea of who I am.
3. This was an original project which I devised and worked out by myself.
4. Dr. J. M. Brown, M.D., is the best surgeon in our city.
5. My roommate thinks that since he made good grades in chemistry and mathematics in high school that he does not have to study these subjects in college.
6. I hope to find the person with whom I am going to spend the rest of my life with.
7. In the biographical section the editors are constantly including the death dates of deceased persons.
8. Some students keep their record-players blaring until 2 A.M. in the morning.
9. On large farms now most of the equipment is heavily mechanized machinery.
10. In this year's cars the engines will not be the only new innovations.
11. I have found that, since my parents have been fair with me, that I want to be fair with them.
12. Our family trips recently have been few in number.
13. Until last summer I had never seen the Grand Canyon before.
14. Indianapolis is a crowded city just before the race. The day before the race the people line the streets to watch a parade.
15. Language is important to anyone living in the modern world of today.

16. Reference books are valuable for the useful and informative information they contain.
17. I think that my roommate is a self-centered egotist.
18. High schools should require each and every student to read widely varied books.
19. That spring I happened to attend a high school dance to which I was invited to by my best personal friend.
20. My favorite spectator sport is football. Football is a game that is popular throughout the country. Football is played by grade school boys, by high school students, by college students, and by professional players.

EUPHONY

68. Euphony means "pleasing sound." Its antonym is cacophony, "harsh, ugly sound." Say each word aloud several times, and notice that the words illustrate their definition.

Although most of us obtain meaning from the written or printed page through our eyes, as we read we are forming—subconsciously, semiconsciously, or even consciously—conceptions of how this writing or printing would sound if read aloud. Even in silent reading the sense conveyed is lessened and our attention is distracted by disagreeable combinations of cacophonous words.

Effective writing, of course, symbolizes sounds which please the ear, not the eye. The *sense* of words is more important than their *sound,* but good prose contains words whose sound and sense are harmonious. Reading aloud is a good method of detecting uneuphonious sounds in your writing and in that of others.

68a. Avoid awkward and harsh combinations of sounds.

Euphonious prose rarely contains *rhyme,* overuse of *alliteration,* or frequent repetition of *unpleasant sounds.*

1. *Rhyme* means similarity of sound of vowels and consonants: *sound, found; bubble, trouble; fair, wear.* In poetry, it is an added adornment; in prose, rhyming words are a general source of annoyance to the reader.

> Don't worry about me; I'll hurry to be on time.
> I start studying at 7 so that I can be in bed by 11.
> I'm writing you this letter to tell you that my health is considerably better.

2. *Alliteration* is using in the same sentence two or more words beginning with the same consonant sound, or using in fairly close succession words beginning with the same consonant sound. Again, like rhyme, alliteration is mainly an adornment in poetry; unlike rhyme, it can be used occasionally and effectively in prose: *lean and lithe, meddlesome muddling, misty mountains, stars of summer, ripples of rapture*. Examples of faulty alliteration, including the so-called tongue-twisters, are the following:

> The balmy breezes blew warmly over the bay.
> The statistics of this strange situation surely seem simple.
> Summer swallows, swiftly skimming, sail serenely summer's skies.
> Peter Piper picked to pickle pints of pickling peppers; did Peter Piper pickle the pints of pickling peppers that he picked?

The poet Swinburne was fond of alliteration, usually skillfully used but sometimes purposely overused:

From the depth of the dreamy decline of the dawn through a notable nimbus of nebulous noonshine,
Pallid and pink as the palm of the flag-flower that flickers with fear of the flies as they float
Are the looks of our lovers that lustrously lean from a marvel of mystic, miraculous moonshine,
These that we feel in the blood of our blushes that thicken and threaten with throbs through the throat?

—From "Nephelidia"

3. Unpleasant sounds are conveyed through overuse of words containing, usually, *k, ck* sounds (*flak, clack, black*), hissing sounds of *s* (*hiss, miss*), nasal sounds of *m, n* (*wrangle, climb*), guttural sounds of *g* (*gutter, gaseous, go*). Pleasant sounds are suggested, usually, by words containing, for example, letters like *l, r, z,* or the *z*-sound of *s: lilies, roses, murmuring*.

Harsh: Gregory's a go-getter; backed against the wall and with bleak and black prospects, he'll get going and never let the gutter get him down.

Pleasant: Roses are flinging their perfumes through the air.

Golden bells of welcome rolled
Never forth such notes, nor told

Hours so blithe in tones so bold
As the radiant mouth of gold
  Here that rings forth heaven.
If the golden-crested wren
Were a nightingale—why, then,
Something seen and heard of men
Might be half as sweet as when
  Laughs a child of seven.
   —Swinburne, "A Child's Laughter"

68b. Avoid overuse of the same or similar-sounding words.

Overuse of the same or similar-sounding words distracts a hearer's attention and, subconsciously or half-consciously, also distracts the reader.

1. Overuse, through repetition of the same words.

My coming to college was made possible by some money which was made possible by a job I had last summer.

Crop rotation, used on many farms, is the use of a plan by which various fields vary in their crops each successive year.

Organized charitable organizations carry on charitable work in my community.

2. Overuse of *homographs:* words with the same spelling but of different origin and meaning.

The committee was pleased to see so many fair ladies in attendance at our county fair.

On my date last Saturday evening, my date was an unmitigated bore, but I patiently bore with him for the entire evening.

The sole reason for using these soles to half-sole shoes is their inexpensiveness.

3. Overuse of *homonyms:* words with the same pronunciation but different in origin, meaning, and, very often, spelling.

The bare facts will bear me out in my assertion.
I shall meet you at the butcher's to buy our meat for the picnic.
During Christmas extra male help is needed to deliver the mail.

4. Overuse of a series of words having endings which are alike or nearly alike. Exaggerated example:

Driven oxen aren't seen moving many times ridden by many singing citizens.

5. Ending a sentence with a word or phrase and beginning the next sentence with the same word or phrase or nearly the same phrase (see Section **67f**).

> All my life I have lived in Lafayette. Lafayette is a city of some importance.
>
> During this semester I had to learn to study with people about me. Studying with people about me has many disadvantages.
>
> I am enrolled in the School of Home Economics. A home economics student has a fairly fixed curriculum to follow.

EXERCISES

A. In accordance with principles of euphony, rewrite the following sentences:

1. As for my high school, there are some much needed improvements that need to be made.
2. The most important decision is deciding what should be one's life's work.
3. After paying our fees came another waiting line. This line was formed inside the Health Service for speech, hearing, and skin tests.
4. When I got home, I changed into my hunting clothes and got my equipment and got ready to go hunting.
5. The ducks were flying well and they were decoying to my decoys.
6. I slept through my 8 A.M. class. That was R.O.T.C. class and that means eight demerits.
7. My second resolution relates to a relationship that I have with a relative.
8. The snows of winter like to sting the toes and bite the nose.
9. The library is responsible for retaining a restrained atmosphere.
10. To give you a little better idea of where I live, I will use the use of a national highway.
11. I relate this incident as an example of a relatively unimportant occurrence.
12. I got my chores done and got ready and got started for church.
13. I did not enjoy receiving presents as much as I enjoyed giving them in past years, and I enjoyed watching my little brother unwrap his presents.
14. I had never ridden in an airplane until the summer of 1956. During the summer of 1956, I paid a short visit to an aunt and uncle of mine, and they planned for my ride.

15. On my first day on the campus, we went to Assembly Hall to take placement tests. These placement tests were for the purpose of determining what classes, regular or advanced, we would be placed in.

B. Which of these words are pleasing to your ear? Which are harsh-sounding? *Spinach, tintinnabulation, cacophony, clackety-clack, vermilion, melody, parsnips, jazz, nevermore, diaphanous, luxuriant, lyrical, autocratic, cabbage, cranberry, moonlight, shrimp, sap, cuspidor, roundelay.*

APPROPRIATENESS

69. Choose words which are appropriate.

Diction may be correct, clear, and effective for one purpose but not for another. A word or phrase is wrongly chosen when it is out of harmony with either its context or the circumstances under which it is used.

You are not likely to use illiterate words (Section 57) except, perhaps, in the most informal of informal conversations, and then perhaps only for humorous purposes. Illiterate words do appear, frequently with good reason, in reports of conversation given in narrative and also in certain comic strips and radio or TV programs. If they aptly characterize or serve other purposes, they are appropriate and hence may be said to "belong." Similarly, much slang and shoptalk appear in these communication media, in the conversation of fellow-workers or close friends, and in informal letters.

Informal writing and speech may use localisms (Section 54), colloquialisms (Section 55) and slang (Section 59). Purposefully used, they aid communication of thought from speaker or writer to hearer or reader and are not to be avoided. Not long ago the G. & C. Merriam dictionary staff gave this answer to the question of appropriateness:

Levels of usage always give rise to many questions in the classroom. What function do the usage labels in a dictionary serve? What is meant by *colloquial?* Is slang in bad taste? One of Merriam's editors recently replied to this last question: "If a man appeared at a formal dinner wearing overalls, his clothing would be in bad taste; if he wore overalls to work in his garden, no one would give it a second thought because the costume would be appropriate for the occasion. Most of us make many changes in our vocabulary according to the impression we wish to make and the formality of the situation." [14]

[14] From *Word Study,* April, 1958, p. 3.

For appropriate writing and speaking, restudy the general areas discussed briefly on pages 356–359—present, general, and reputable use, and formal, informal or colloquial, and substandard English. A somewhat similar but slightly more detailed division is made by Professor Paul Roberts in his book *Understanding Grammar:*

Choice Written English: This is the writing found in carefully edited and copy-read books and magazines. These are published for the most part in the larger cities, but the writing of many people in all parts of the country would fall in this category. This is the usage described by most handbooks of English.

General Written English: This is exemplified by the ordinary run of newspapers the country over and by the scripts read by the average radio announcer. Newspaper and radio writing is necessarily hasty and is often produced by people who are ignorant of or unimpressed by the niceties of Choice Written. General Written English is probably the level attained by the average college graduate who takes pen in hand.

Choice Spoken English: This is the language heard in formal and serious speeches and addresses. It is used also, however, in much ordinary conversation, being for many people the native dialect learned in the nursery and for others the result of an effort to apply the precepts of Choice Written to the spoken language. Choice Spoken English is the language of many college graduates and of some others as well.

General Spoken English: This is the level used by most educated people in conversation. It is the level indicated by the label "colloquial" as this term is used in most dictionaries. General Spoken English is more easygoing than Choice Spoken, and it tends to employ newer and shorter forms, but it is not on that account "incorrect." Some people who are able to speak either, prefer General to Choice Spoken English.

Vulgate English: This is the term used for all expressions associated with the uneducated. (Words are powerful and likely to be invidious when they have social implications. It may not be superfluous to say that one who speaks Vulgate English is not necessarily vulgar, any more than one who speaks Choice English is necessarily snobbish or affected. Most of us simply speak the language of our fathers and our friends.)

These distinctions are more or less arbitrary; they are easily distinguishable at their centers, but they run together at the extremes. Indeed, it might be said that there are as many levels of usage as there are speakers of the language. . . .

We may also observe that most expressions in the language are identical on all levels. For example, no dialect deviation is likely in the sentence "I walked home." In this expression Choice Written English and Vulgate English coincide. On the other hand, there are numerous constructions that we recognize as common to some and not to others.[15]

It is often difficult to label a construction apart from the whole context, but the five levels may be roughly illustrated as follows:

Choice Written: I shall not return.
General Written: I will not return.
Choice Spoken: I'll not return.
General Spoken: I'm not coming back.
Vulgate: I ain't comin' back.

Inappropriateness in writing and speaking is often the result of incongruous associations. Remember that illiterate and slangy words and expressions, and some kind of colloquialisms, are as out of place in formal writing as are learned and dignified words in an informal, humorous account of some campus activity, even though such sets of words may express exactly what you mean. It is important that harmony exists between word and tone, between what you say and your attitude toward your material. Is your purpose a serious, whimsical, satiric, or humorous account? Is your aim a plain or an ornamental style? A formal or a conversational style? An informative style only? Words must be appropriate for your purpose, mood, and style.

As you plan, therefore, and as you write or speak, keep constantly in mind (1) your reader or listener, (2) the circumstances or occasion, (3) your purpose, and (4) the possibilities in your subject. Are your words appropriate for each? Included in effective communication is effective adaptation.

EXERCISES

A. Discuss the appropriateness and correctness of

    nonsense, twaddle, buncombe, bunk
    money, financial resources, legal tender, swag
    talk, converse, chatter, gab
    skin, complexion, pelt, hide
    contemptible, shameful, unsatisfactory, lousy
    combat, scuffle, tussle, scrap

[15] *Understanding Grammar* (New York: Harper & Brothers, 1954), pp. 14, 15. The authors gladly acknowledge their indebtedness to Professor Roberts.

osculation, caress, kiss, smack
banquet, dinner, snack, bite
automobile, car, jalopy, hot rod
fascinate, entertain, please, wow

B. Choose some term from one of your science courses, a term that should have a more detailed definition than that given in the dictionary. Write four definitions of the term, one each for an elementary school child, a high school freshman, a classmate not taking the science course, and a "pen pal" in a foreign country.

GLOSSARY OF FAULTY DICTION

70. The following glossary, alphabetically arranged and numbered for easy reference, contains words and expressions often misused. The list, not all-embracing, is a short-cut discussion of some of the most common violations of good usage. If the material given below does not apply to your problem, if you want more detailed information, or if you do not find listed the word or phrase you are seeking, consult your dictionary.

A few of these expressions are always to be avoided, but many are inappropriate only in formal English. Apply the advice of Section **69** as you interpret the comments provided for these words and phrases. Remember especially that no stigma attaches to the label "colloquial"; it indicates that a given expression is generally more appropriate in conversation and in informal discourse than it is in formal writing.

Usage is so constantly changing that expressions now restricted in some way may later be considered standard. Furthermore, because no dictionary or grammar is a final authority, some usages are disputed. Probably no two linguists would agree on all the comments which follow. But this illustrative list of 150 items should be serviceable as a starter; to it you may add from time to time other words and expressions.

1. **A, an.** *An* should be used before an initial vowel sound, *a* before a word beginning with a consonant sound: *an* adult, *a* problem; *an* honor, *a* hopeful sign.
2. **Accept, except.** *Accept* means "to receive," "say yes to"; *except* as verb means to "exclude"; as preposition, "other than."

He *accepted* the invitation.

I agree to the conditions if I may *except* the fourth in the list.

No one *except* me knew the answer.

3. **Accidently.** An illiteracy (see Section 57). Use *accidentally.*

4. **Ad.** Colloquial word for *advertisement.* In formal writing avoid such shortened forms as *ad, auto, exam, lab, phone,* and *prof.*

5. **Advise.** Overused ineffectively in business letters for "inform," "tell."

   I am happy to *tell* (not *advise*) you that your remittance has been received.

   Please *inform* (not *advise*) me whether my order has been shipped.

6. **Affect, effect.** *Affect,* as verb, means "to influence" or "assume"; *effect* as verb means "to cause" and as noun means "result."

   This essay has *affected* student thinking.

   Though nervous, he *affected* nonchalance.

   This testimony *effected* a political scandal.

   What *effect* has low temperature on iron?

7. **Ain't.** A contraction of *am not,* considered illiterate or dialectal; it is cautioned against in standard English, both written and spoken. Virtually every other contraction, although usually avoided in formal English, is in good use in informal English: *isn't, aren't wasn't, weren't, haven't, hasn't, hadn't, doesn't, don't* (see Item 41), *didn't, won't, shan't,* etc.

8. **All ready, already.** *All ready* (two words) means "completely ready" or "everything (or everyone) is ready"; *already* means "previously," "by this time."

   I am *all ready* for final examinations.

   We are *all ready* to start to the game.

   Hurry! It is *already* past 1:15 P.M.

9. **All right, alright.** *All right* is overworked to mean "satisfactory," "very well." *Alright* is not an acceptable word.

10. **All the farther, all the faster.** These and similar expressions are colloquial or dialectal when the meaning is "as far as," "as fast as," etc.

    This is *as far as* we are going (Not "This is *all the farther* we are going.")

    Is this *as fast as* your car will go? (Not "Is this *all the faster* your car will go?")

11. **All together, altogether.** *All together* means "everybody (or everything) in one place"; *altogether* means "wholly," "completely."

> My brothers and sisters were *all together* for the first time this year.
> Are you *altogether* sure of your statement?

12. **Allusion, illusion.** *Allusion* means "an indirect reference," "a hint"; *illusion* means "a misleading image or vision."

> The speaker made an *allusion* to the strike.
> "Your security," he said, "is but an *illusion*."

13. **Almost, most.** *Almost* is an adverb meaning "nearly"; *most* as pronoun or adjective means "the greater part or number," and as adverb is used in forming some superlative degrees of adjectives and adverbs. See Section **83e.**

> The work is *almost* finished.
> *Most* people have to work *most* of their lives.
> Autumn is to me the *most* beautiful season of the year.

14. **Also, then.** Each word is frequently ineffective and improper when used as a conjunction to join words. See Section **84c.**

> Dubious: He asked his question, *then* sat down.
> For dessert we are having apple pie, *also* ice cream.
> Improved: After asking his question, he sat down.
> For dessert we are having apple pie and *also* ice cream.

15. **A.M.** or **a.m.** (midnight to noon); **P.M.** or **p.m.** (noon to midnight). Both are clear indicators of time. Do not add, "in the morning," "in the afternoon," or "o'clock." (See Section **67e.**) Figures, not words, are conventionally used; omit 00 with on-the-hour figures.

> We leave here at 8 *a.m.* and arrive in Detroit at 3:45 *p.m.*

> Make 12 o'clock time clear by saying 12 **noon** or 12 **midnight.**

16. **Among, between.** Both are Anglo-Saxon words; the former literally means "in a crowd"; the latter, "by two." *Among* shows the relation of more than two objects; *between* refers to only two, or to more than two when each object is considered in relation to the others.

> He distributed the prizes *among* the five winners.
> He divided the prize *between* Jack and Joe.
> This water-level route runs *between* New York, Albany, Cleveland, and Chicago.
> Concord *between* nations is desirable.

17. **Amount, number.** *Amount* is used with a unified mass; *number*, with separate units.

> What is the *amount* of your cash?
> I have a *number* of quarters and half-dollars.
> The *amount* of traffic depends upon the *number* of cars on the road.

18. **And etc.** Redundant. *Etc.* is the abbreviation for Latin *et cetera,* meaning "and so forth."

19. **Anxious, eager.** In precise use, *anxious* implies "anxiety," worry," "uneasiness"; *eager* means "keenly desirous," "wanting to," not "worried about." However, one dictionary definition of *anxious* is "earnestly desirous" or "eagerly wishing."

> I am *anxious* about Father's health.
> I am *anxious* about the outcome of the examination.
> I am *eager* to hear all the news from home.

20. **Anywheres, nowheres, somewheres.** Illiteracies or dialectal words. Omit the *s* from these words.

> I cannot find my pen *anywhere*.
> The kitten is *nowhere* to be found.
> I have a class schedule here *somewhere*.

NOTE: *Anyplace, noplace, someplace*—each written as one word—are illiteracies and cannot substitute for *anywhere, nowhere, somewhere*. But as two words these expressions are acceptable:

> Some teachers will gladly help you at *any place* or time.
> There is *no place* like home.
> My books are missing; I must have left them at *some place* or another.

21. **Apt, liable, likely.** *Apt* suggests "fitness," "tendency," "natural bent or inclination"; *liable* implies "openness or exposure to something burdensome or disadvantageous"; *likely* means "expected," "probable." *Apt* and *likely* are sometimes interchangeable but not in the meaning of "probability."

> She is *apt* in mathematics.
> You are *liable* for damages.
> It is *likely* to rain. (Not: "It is *apt* to rain" or "It is *liable* to rain.")

22. **As.** (1) Overused as a conjunction for *since, because, when,* etc.

As it was raining, we decided. . . . (Use *since*.)

(2) Misused as a substitute for *that* or *whether:*

I doubt *as* I can. (Use *that*.)

(3) Used in affirmative comparisons: *as . . . as.*

I am *as* tall *as* my father.

In negative comparison, many writers and authorities prefer *so . . . as*—"I am not *so* tall *as* my brother"—but *Webster's New International Dictionary* reports that *as . . . as* and *so . . . as* are now generally used interchangeably, and in colloquial usage *as . . . as* predominates.

23. **As good as, if not better than.** A mixed comparison, correctly phrased, but awkward. The statement is more effective when the "if not better than" (or similar words in a mixed comparison) is put at the end.

    Awkward: My record is *as good as if not better than* your record.
    Improved: My record is *as good as* yours, *if not better.*

24. **Auto.** See **Ad.**
25. **Awful, awfully, abominable, abominably, terrible, terrific, terribly,** etc. Loose overworked intensives for overworked *very,* etc. (See **Very,** Item 143, below.)
26. **Awhile, a while.** *Awhile* is an adverb; in *a while, while* is a noun.

    Wait *awhile,* and I'll go with you.
    I cannot go for *a while.*

27. **Believe, feel.** Precisely, *believe* suggests "think," "judge," "have convictions about"; *feel* suggests "feeling," "emotions," not "reason." However, one dictionary definition of *feel* is "think, believe, consider."

    I *feel* cheerful when I read your letters, for I *believe* you have the right attitude toward life.

28. **Beside, besides.** *Beside* is usually a preposition meaning "by the side of"; *besides* is a preposition meaning "except," and, more commonly, an adverb meaning "moreover."

    A willow is growing *beside* the brook.
    I have studying to do; *besides,* I want to go to bed early.

29. Can, may, might. *Can* suggests "ability," physical and mental:

> He *can* make good grades if he tries hard enough.

May implies permission or sanction:

> The teacher says that you *may* leave.

In colloquial and informal expression, *can* and *may* are both used in the sense of permission or sanction; formally, the distinction between *can* and *may* ("ability" vs. "permission") is illustrated in this sentence:

> I doubt that you *can,* but you *may* try if you wish.

May also expresses "possibility" and "wish" (desire):

> It *may* rain today. (Possibility)
> *May* you have a pleasant trip! (Wish, desire)

Might is used after a governing verb in the past tense, *may* after a governing verb in the present tense:

> He says that you *may* go.
> He said that you *might* go.

30. Cannot help but. An illogical double negative (*cannot help* + *can but*). Omit *but.*

> Preferable: I *cannot help* writing you about this matter. (See Section **35g.**)

NOTE: One dictionary gives, without a label, the meaning of *cannot help but* as "cannot fail to, be compelled or obliged to."

31. Can't hardly. An illogical double negative. Omit the contraction of *not.*

> I can *hardly* hear you. (See Section **35g.**)

32. Case. Overused as a word having little specific meaning; similar words are *phase, factor, instance, nature, thing,* etc. (See Section **64a.**)

33. Complected. Dialectal or colloquial for "complexioned."

> Preferable: He was *dark-complexioned.*
> He was a man of *dark complexion.*

34. Contact, contacted. Overworked business terms. Possible replacements: *communicate, call, call upon, telephone, get in touch with.*

35. **Continual, continuous.** In some uses, synonymous. A subtle distinction is that *continual* implies "a close recurrence in time, rapid succession"; *continuous* implies "without interruption."

> The *continual* ringing of the telephone annoys me.
> The ticking of the clock was *continuous.*
> Some alarm clocks ring *continually;* others ring *continuously.*

36. **Cute.** An overworked colloquialism for *attractive, pleasing, clever,* etc.

37. **Data.** Plural form of a naturalized Latin word, *datum,* "something known." The intriguing question of whether *data* can be used in the singular is ignored by some dictionaries. According to *Webster's New Collegiate, data* is "often used with a singular verb."

38. **Different than, different to, different from.** *Different than* and *different to* are considered colloquial by some authorities, improper and incorrect by others. These idioms have long literary usage to support them. *Different from* has no objectors to its formal and informal use.

39. **Disinterested, uninterested.** *Disinterested* means "unbiased," "not influenced by personal reasons"; *uninterested* means "having no interest in," "not paying attention." As a colloquialism, *disinterested* means *uninterested, indifferent.* See paragraph development illustrating "contrast" for further discussion of *disinterested* and *uninterested,* page 225.

40. **Disregardless.** See **Irregardless.**

41. **Don't, done.** *Don't* is used incorrectly as a contraction in the third person singular, present tense. The correct form is *doesn't. Done* is incorrectly used as the past tense of *do.* Principal parts: *Do—did—done.*

> It *doesn't* make any difference.
> He *doesn't* know any better.
> We *did* our studying this morning.

42. **Due to.** As compound prepositions, *due to* (from the adjective *due*), *owing to* (from the participle *owing*), and *caused by* (from the participle *caused*) originally were adjective phrases; adverbial meanings were expressed by *because of, on account of. Webster's New Collegiate:* "Prepositional *due to,* meaning 'because of' and introducing an adverbial modifier, though objected to by some, is in common and reputable use." Whatever you and your teacher decide, remember that, in many uses, *due to the fact that* is a wordy way of saying *since.*

43. **Each . . . are.** An error in grammar. *Each*, if not followed by *one*, implies *one*, and any plural words used in modifying phrases do not change the number. (See Section **76c**.)

> Wrong: *Each* of the students *are* expected to be present at each class meeting.
> Right: *Each* of the students *is* expected to be. . . .

> Wrong: *Each one* of you *are* invited.
> Right: *Each one* of you *is* invited.

44. **Each other, one another.** Reciprocal pronouns (Section **71d**8). *Each other* refers to one of two, *one another* to three or more.

> Father and Mother love *each other*.
> Their four children love *one another*.

45. **Eager.** See **Anxious.**

46. **Either . . . or, neither . . . nor.** The former means "one of two"; *neither* means "not one of two." The statements about "each . . . are" (above) apply if "one" is understood:

> *Either* (one) of you is a desirable candidate.

But

> *Neither* New Englanders *nor* Southerners speak like Midwesterners.

Or is used with *either*, *nor* with *neither*. The use of *either . . . or, neither . . . nor,* coordinating more than two words, phrases, or clauses, is sanctioned by some dictionaries but not by others.

47. **Enthuse.** A colloquialism. For formal writing, prefer "be enthusiastic," "become enthusiastic."

48. **Etc.** An abbreviation of the Latin phrase *et cetera*, "and so forth." Preferably, *etc.* should be avoided; too often it is a confession that the writer can think of nothing further to add to a list; if he can, he might justify *etc.* See also **And etc.,** above.

49. **Exam.** See **Ad.**

50. **Except.** See **Accept.**

51. **Farther, further.** Interchangeable, but many writers prefer *farther* to indicate "space," "a measurable distance," and *further* to indicate "greater in degree, quantity, or time," and also "moreover," "in addition to."

> Let us drive 10 miles *farther*.
> Next week we shall discuss this matter *further*.

52. **Feel.** As a linking verb, *feel* is followed by an adjective, as I *feel bad, happy, angry, sure, sorry, warm,* etc. See also **Believe.**

53. **Fellow, fella, feller.** *Fellow* is a word of many meanings, ranging from low to high, socially. Colloquial for "individual," "person," "one," "man," "boy," "student." *Fella* and *feller* are slang, dialectal, or illiteracies.

54. **Fewer, less.** Both imply a comparison with something larger in number or amount. *Fewer* applies only to number:

> *Fewer* houses are now unpainted on this street.

Less is used in various ways: applied to material in bulk in reference to amount (*less* money in the bank); with abstractions (*less* courage); with attributes such as degree and value (a nickel is *less* than a quarter).

> The *less* clay we have, the *fewer* bricks we can make.
> The *fewer* members we have, the *less* our income will be.

55. **Fine.** A much overused word in the general sense of approval. Find a more specific, concrete word. (See Section **64.**)

56. **Fix.** A word of many meanings. Colloquial: as a verb, "to arrange matters," "to get revenge"; as a noun, for "predicament," "difficulty." Dialectal or colloquial: as a verb, "to prepare, get ready." Fill in these meanings:

> I can *fix* a date for Saturday night.
> A tough gangster always *fixes* his enemies.
> With my car locked and the keys inside, I certainly was in a *fix.*
> I was *fixing* to go home.
> Mother *fixed* lunch as soon as we arrived.

57. **Folks.** Colloquial for "relatives," "one's family."

58. **Formally, formerly.** *Formally* means "in a formal or precisely proper manner"; *formerly* means "in the past."

59. **Funny.** An overworked colloquialism for "strange," "queer," "odd," "remarkable."

60. **Get, got, gotten.** These words have numerous precise, colloquial, slang, and idiomatic meanings. See your dictionary. Examples:

> I've *got* to (must, ought to) go home next week.
> I'm sorry, but I don't quite *get* (understand) you.
> When do we *get* (arrive) in Chicago?

61. **Good, well.** *Good* is an adjective: "to have a good time," "to give a good performance." *Well* functions as either adjective or adverb, but with different meanings: as adjective, "in good health," and as adverb, "ably."

> Since my illness, I have felt *well* all summer.
> The team played *well* during the first half.

62. **Had.** An impropriety when used for *have* after auxiliary verbs in such expressions as *would had, could had, might had, should had,* etc.

63. **Had better, had best.** Idiomatic phrases meaning "ought to," "would be wise to."

64. **Healthful, healthy.** Often used interchangeably. Precisely, *healthful* means "conducive to health"; *healthy* means "possessing health."

> He is a *healthy* person.
> We live in a *healthful* climate.

65. **Help but.** See **Cannot help but.**

66. **I, me.** The former is nominative case, the latter objective. Watch especially in a compound phrase after a verb or preposition.

> This matter concerns only *him* and *me*. (Not *him* and *I*.)
> The way he raved in front of *you* and *me* made me ashamed. (Not *you* and *I*.)

67. **If, whether.** In precise use, *if* introduces one condition only; *whether* introduces alternate conditions, usually with "or not" implied or expressed.

> *If* we save enough money, we can prolong our vacation.
> Even the coaches do not know *whether* or not Smith will be able to play.
> I am wondering *whether* I should go to the movies or stay home and study.

68. **Illusion.** See **Allusion.**

69. **Imply, infer.** To *imply* is "to suggest a meaning hinted at, not explicitly stated." To *infer* is "to draw a conclusion from statements, circumstances, or evidence."

> The detective *inferred* from the position of the fingerprints that the man who fired the shot was left-handed.
> What you say *implies* that I am not telling the truth.

70. In, into. After verbs indicating motion to a place, *into* is generally used:

> When he walked *into* the room, he found the meeting in progress.

In is used to indicate motion within relatively narrow limits:

> She paced up and down *in* the classroom for the whole period.

In is used when the place is not mentioned:

> He came *in* after we finished the discussion.
> The train came *in*.

71. In back of. *Back of* is colloquial for *behind;* the *in* is superfluous. *In the back of* and *in front of* are proper in both formal and informal usage.

> *In the back of* the building are seven windows.
> The car is parked *in front of* the house.
> Some people hide money *back of* a mirror. (Colloquial)
> Some people hide money *behind* a mirror. (Formal)

72. Individual. See **Party, person.**

73. Ingenious, ingenuous. *Ingenious* means "talented," "inventive," "resourceful"; *ingenuous* means "frank" or "naïve."

> I thought the solution was *ingenious*.
> She is one of the most *ingenuous* freshmen here.

74. Inside of, off of, outside of. As prepositional phrases, the *of* is superfluous.

> *Inside* the house, the fire is burning brightly.
> The boy fell *off* his bicycle.
> You will need a passport to travel *outside* the United States and its possessions.

Note use of *outside* and *inside* as nouns:

> The *outside* of our house needs a coat of paint.
> We are getting new upholstery for the *inside* of our car.

75. Irregardless, disregardless. Both words are illiteracies, substandard. The prefixes *ir-* and *dis-* are superfluous.

76. Is when, is where. Misuse of adverbial clauses for noun clauses and, more important, inexact phrasing in definitions. (See Section **38.**)

Bad: A "comma splice" *is where* you use a comma between independent clauses with no pure conjunction.

Passive voice *is when* the subject is acted upon.

Better: A "comma splice" is the joining of two independent clauses by only a comma, when no pure conjunction is used.

In the passive voice, the subject is not the actor but is acted upon.

77. **Its, it's, its'.** *Its* is the possessive form of "it"; *it's* is a contraction for "it is"; *its'* is an illiteracy, nonexistent in correct writing. See Section **94i.**)

78. **Job.** Frequently and inexactly used in the sense of achievement. The chief objection to the word is its overuse to cover many general and inexact meanings. Find a more specific, concrete word (see Section **64**).

Dubious: The coach has done a good *job* with his material.

Hemingway does a splendid *job* in his short stories.

My roommate is doing a good *job* in chemistry.

79. **Kind of a, sort of a, type of a.** The *a* is superfluous. Logically, the last word should indicate a class, not one thing.

What *kind of* book is this?

He is the *sort of* person you like to associate with.

What *type of* flower is suitable for this soil?

80. **Kind of, sort of.** Colloquial when used to mean "almost," "rather," "somewhat."

Father looks *kind of* tired.

I am *sort of* disgusted with myself.

81. **Lab.** See **Ad.**

82. **Leave, let.** Each word has various meanings, but *leave* in the sense of "cause to remain" and "go away from" is often confused with *let* in the sense of "allow," "permit," "cause."

If you *leave* me undisturbed, I can get my work done in half an hour.

Let me take your book back to the library.

83. **Less.** See **Fewer.**

84. **Liable, likely.** See **Apt.**

85. **Lie, lay.** *Lie,* meaning "to recline," is intransitive, takes no object. *Lay,* meaning "to place," is transitive, requires an object. Notice especially the principal parts of each verb and do not confuse the past tense, past participle, and present participle of *lie* with the forms of *lay.* (See Section **71g.**)

> *Lie—lay—lain, lying*
> *Lay—laid—laid, laying*

> I shall *lie* down.
> Please *lay* the book on the desk.
> I was *lying* down when you telephoned.
> College freshmen are *laying* the foundations for success in life.

86. **Like.** A word of many meanings and with uses as suffix, adjective, noun, adverb, preposition, transitive verb, intransitive verb, and conjunction. As conjunction, its use is colloquial for *as, as if.* (See Section **84e.**)

> Colloquial: The naval battle turned out *like* the Admiral predicted.
> It seems *like* it might snow all day.
> Formal: The naval battle turned out *as* the Admiral predicted.
> It seems *as if* it might snow all day.

87. **Lots of, a lot of, whole lot.** Colloquial for "many," "much," "great deal." The chief objection is overuse of a vague, general word. Find a more specific, concrete way of saying what you mean. (See Section **64.**)
88. **Mad.** With a number of meanings such as "insane," "frantic," "frenzied," *mad* is colloquial when used to mean "angry," "furious."
89. **May, might.** See **Can.**
90. **Most.** See **Almost.**
91. **Muchly.** An illiteracy. Substitute *much, very, greatly.*
92. **Nice.** A word with various meanings, including "agreeable," "pleasant," "attractive," "pretty," "delightful." Its overuse indicates the need for more specific, concrete substitutes. (See Section **64.**)
93. **Notorious, noteworthy, notable.** *Notorious* means "infamous"; *noteworthy* and *notable* mean "remarkable," "worthy of note."
94. **Nowheres.** See **Anywheres.**
95. **Number.** See **Amount.**
96. **Of.** An impropriety when used for *have* after auxiliary verbs in such expressions as *would of, could of, might of, should of,* etc. These should be *would have, could have,* etc.

97. Off of. See **Inside of.**

98. O, oh. The former is usually part of a vocative, always capitalized, and is rarely followed by a mark of punctuation:

> O Richard! Come here, please.

Oh is an interjection, may be followed by a comma or an exclamation point, and follows the usual rules for capitalization.

> *Oh!* What a pity!
> But, *oh,* what trust we placed in him.

99. Outside of. See **Inside of.**

100. Party, person, individual. Party implies a group, and, except in legal and telephonic language, should not be used to refer to one person except in a slang or colloquial sense. *Individual* refers to a particular or single person. *Individual,* as an adjective, means "single," "separate," "particular"; it is therefore repetitious and unnecessary when used to modify *person,* as "individual person," or when "each" has been used, as "each individual member." As nouns, *individual* and *person* are synonyms.

101. Pass out. Slang in the sense of "faint," "become completely unconscious."

102. Pep, peppy. Slang. Use *zest, vigor, energy, vivacity, animation,* etc., and corresponding adjectives, *zestful, vigorous, energetic,* etc.

103. Phase. See **Case.**

104. Phone. See **Ad.**

105. Plenty. As an adverb, colloquial for "very," "fully."

> The weather is *plenty* hot this summer.

106. Plus. Not effective as a synonym for *and* or *with.*

> Dubious: My roommate and I, *plus* the two boys across the hall, are attending a lecture tonight.
> Improved: The two boys across the hall, my roommate, and I are attending a lecture tonight.

107. Practicable, practical. *Practicable* means "capable of being put into practice"; *practical* means "concerned with practice rather than theory."

> Let's quit dreaming and be *practical* about this.
> The proposal is not *practicable.*

108. Pretty. Overused as an adverb meaning "rather," "moderately," "somewhat."

> This is a *pretty* large assignment.
> I did *pretty* well on the last test.

109. Principal, principle. *Principal* is a noun meaning "sum of money" or "a chief person," and an adjective meaning "chief" or "main." *Principle* is always a noun meaning "a doctrine," "a rule of conduct," "a governing rule or truth."

> My brother is now a high school *principal*.
> My *principal* objection is the time needed.
> Mr. Brown is a man of high *principle*.
> What is the *principle* of this machine?

110. Prof. See **Ad.**

111. Proven. Although an illogical formation (*moved, moved,* but not *moven*) *proven* is accepted as one of the two past participles of *prove.* Principal parts: *prove—proved—proved* or *proven.*

112. Provided, provided that, providing. *Provided* and *providing* are in good use as conjunctions, with the meaning "if," "on condition," "in case," "it being understood." They are often followed by *that,* but *that* seems an unnecessary word.

> *Provided* I am asked, I shall join your organization.
> We are driving home next week, *provided* there is no snow on the roads.
> I plan to pay my tuition next week, *providing* Father sends me the money.

113. Quite a. Colloquial in phrases meaning "more than a," or "to a great extent or degree," as *quite a* few, *quite a* bit, *quite* cold.

114. Raise, rise. *Raise* requires an object, as a transitive verb; *rise,* as an intransitive verb, does not require an object. Keep in mind also the principal parts and present participle:

> *Raise—raised—raised, raising*
> *Rise—rose—risen, rising*

With neither of these verbs is *up* needed. (See **Up,** below.)

> Please *rise* when you recite.
> I *raised* my right hand in greeting.

115. Real. Usually considered an impropriety or dialectal word as an adverb meaning "very" or "really." "Are you *really* sure of what you say?"

116. Reason is because . . . The construction has a long history of usage behind it, and it is found in the writing and speaking of many people, literary and otherwise. Those who object do so because the expression is illogical, although many other acceptable expressions in English are illogical—idioms, for example. Since we do not say "The cause is because . . . ," why say "The reason is because . . ."? Logically we should give, not the *cause for the reason,* but the reason or cause itself, phrased as a noun or noun clause. (See also Section **38.**)

> Illogical: The *reason* for my absence *is because* of illness.
>
> The *reason* why I went *was because* I had no classes that afternoon.

> Logical: The *reason* for my absence *is sickness.*
>
> The *reason* I went *was that* I had no classes that afternoon.

117. Refer back, repeat again. *Refer* means "to direct attention" or "to make reference"; *back* is therefore superfluous. The same kind of faulty diction is evident in *repeat again* and other tautological expressions. *Re-* as a prefix has as one meaning "backward motion," or "back." (See Section **67e.**)

118. Respectfully, respectively. *Respectfully* means "in a respectful manner" and is the proper conventional closing for certain business letters; *respectively* means "severally," "each in the order given."

> Indianapolis, Springfield, and Madison are the capitals, *respectively,* of Indiana, Illinois, and Wisconsin.

119. Right along, right away, right then, etc. Colloquialisms. In formal writing, substitute *directly, immediately,* etc.

120. Seen, saw. The principal parts of *see* are *see—saw—seen. Saw* is improperly used as a past participle; *seen* is improperly used as the past tense.

> Right: I *saw* him yesterday.
> We have *seen* the exhibit.

121. Shall, will. (1) The distinctions in the use of *shall* and *will* to express simple future time have broken down, but some careful speakers and writers still observe them: *shall* in the first person and *will* in the second and third persons—"I (we) shall go," "you (he, she, they) will go." For other ways to express future time, see pp. 575–576.

(2) For expressing determination or command, use *will* in the first person and *shall* in the second and third persons. "I *will* speak, no matter what the result may be." "You *shall* speak" (meaning "you must speak").

(3) To express intention, willingness, promise, use *will* (same verb, different meaning) with all personal pronouns: "I *will* help you." "You *will* be a candidate?"

122. Should, would. In general, use *should* and *would* according to the recommendations for *shall* and *will*, above. These words also have specialized meanings: *should* in the sense of "ought" and "expectation"; *would* in the sense of "habitual action" and "desire." (See pp. 558–559.)

123. Sit, set. *Sit*, predominantly an intransitive verb, not requiring an object, has the meaning of "place oneself"; *set*, predominantly a transitive verb, requiring an object, means to "put" or "place."

Let me *sit* on this bench; come and *sit* beside me.
Please *set* the box under the table.

"Set" used for "sit" in the meaning above is dialectal or an impropriety. But both words have many special meanings, for example, an intransitive use of *set*, as in "The sun *sets*" (moon, stars).

124. So. *So* has various uses as adverb, conjunction, pronoun, interjection, and in combinations like *so as, so that*. Two objectionable uses of *so*, on the basis of ineffectiveness, are

(1) overuse of *so* as a conjunction between independent clauses, sometimes found three or four times on a single page of student writing. Use more exact connectives. If a clause shows purpose, use *so that*; if the relationship is "consequence," use *therefore, consequently, thus*. (See Section **36c.**)

Martha left early *so that* she could be sure of being on time.
I need money for my tuition; *therefore*, I'm going to work this summer.

(2) Overuse of *so* as an intensive—a general substitute for *extremely, indeed, very*; these, too, are overused and might often be omitted. (See **Very**, below.)

    Dubious: You were *so* careless on your last theme.
                   Her gown is *so* beautiful.
    Approved: You were careless on . . .
                   Her gown is beautiful.

125. So . . . as. See **As** (3), above.

126. Somewheres. See **Anywheres.**

127. Sort of a, Sort of. See **Kind of a, Kind of.**

128. Sure. Both adjective and adverb, but colloquial in the latter use for *surely, certainly, indeed.*

129. Suspicion. Used as a verb colloquially or in dialect for *suspect.*

    Approved: I *suspected* that he was lying.

130. Terrible, terrific. See **Awful.**

131. That, this. As adverbs, used with adjectives and adverbs of quantity and extent: *that much, this much, that far, this far.* Colloquial or dialectal with other adjectives and adverbs:

    I didn't realize that you were *that* good.
    The runner was *that* tired he could not finish the race.
    How can any test be *this* difficult?

    More effective:

    I did not realize that you were as good as you say.
    The runner was so tired that he could not finish the race.
    How can any test be as difficult as this one?

132. Then. See **Also.**

133. These kind, those kind, these sort, those sort. *Kind* and *sort* are singular nouns, *these* and *those* are plural modifiers. Use *this kind, this sort, those kinds, those sorts.*

134. This. See **That.**

135. Thusly. An illiteracy for **thus.**

136. To, too, two. Correct usage here is mainly a matter of careful spelling. *To* is a preposition, "*to* the library," or the sign of the infinitive, "*to* study." *Too* is an adverb meaning "also" or "overabundance of." "I, *too,* am going, but John is *too* sick *to* go." *Two* is the number: "*two* girls," "the *two* of us."

137. Too. Overused as an intensive or as a replacement for *very* and consequently ineffective. (See **Very,** below.)

    I suppose I'm just *too* optimistic.
    I haven't read *too* much about this subject.

138. **Try and.** A colloquialism for *try to.*

139. **Type.** Not acceptable as a substitute for *type of.* We do not say "what kind insect," "what sort insect." Why say "what type insect"? For comment on **Type of a,** see **Kind of a,** above.

140. **Uninterested.** See **Disinterested.**

141. **Unique.** *Unique* means "having no like or equal" and expresses absoluteness along with words like *round, square,* etc. Logically, with no comparison possible, these should not be used in the comparative and superlative degrees or with *most,* etc., unless there is a qualifying word like *nearly.*

> Illogical: This is the *most unique* painting on display.
> I've never seen a *rounder* table.
> Logical: Of many strange flowers, this is the *most nearly unique* one we grow.
> This table seems *more nearly square* than that one.

142. **Up.** Redundant when used with verbs which already include the idea, as in *rise up, stand up, end up,* etc. But *up* is needed in many idiomatic expressions, like *bring up, keep up, lay up, move up, sit up, tie up.*

143. **Very.** (1) *Very,* like *so, surely, too, extremely, indeed,* has been so overused that it has lost much of its value as an intensive. Use these words sparingly and thoughtfully; consider whether your meaning is not just as emphatic without them: "You are *very* positive about the matter."

(2) *Very* is used colloquially to qualify participles; formal use adds adverbs like *much* or *greatly:*

> Colloquial: I was *very disgusted* with myself.
> Formal: I was *very much disgusted* with myself.

> Colloquial: I am *very torn* between the desire to go and the desire to stay.
> Formal: I am *greatly torn* between . . .

144. **Well.** See **Good.**

145. **Where at.** As two words, redundant for *where.* Avoid such a statement as "He did not know *where* he was *at.*"

146. **Whether.** See **If.**

147. **While.** As conjunction, *while* means "during or at the same time that," "as long as"; it is colloquial when used in the sense of "although" or "whereas."

While sick, I kept attending classes.

You thought I was lying, *while* I was telling the truth all the time.

148. **Who, whom.** The former is nominative case, the latter objective. When in doubt, try as a memory device the substituting of *he* for *who* and *him* for *whom,* since proper use of these is more easily recognized. (See Section **75i.**)

> I wonder *whom* I should invite ("I should invite *him*," i.e., "I wonder *whom* I should invite.")

149. **Will, would.** See **Shall, should.**
150. **Worst kind, worst sort, worst way.** Slang for *very much, greatly, intensely.*

EXERCISES

A. Point out and correct any errors in diction in the following sentences:

1. I do not plan to write any great amount of letters or reports.
2. My application follow-up letters will help reach an agreement on salary, duties, and etc.
3. I thought that the Homecoming queen was real cute.
4. I thought I had improved, but the teacher did not think I had improved that much.
5. The road was icy for two miles, and there wasn't a safe piece of pavement anyplace.
6. The driving area was located in back of the main building.
7. Once you fall behind in your courses, it is real hard to catch up again.
8. Leave us never forget our parents, who have made it possible for us to attend college.
9. Not many young people realize how they are effected by smoking.
10. I have three golden memories which shall remain with me as long as I live.
11. No more food, please; I am plenty satisfied.
12. I always except any good advice that is given me.
13. John stopped suddenly; he must of forgotten what he was going to say.
14. Every child anxiously waits for Christmas to come.
15. We won the game, and I'm so glad.
16. I accidently attended the wrong class yesterday morning.
17. My roommate is good at fixing people up with blind dates.
18. This letter had the affect of making me change my plans about vacation.

19. I believe that my hobby is very much worthwhile, plus being educational.
20. A brief survey of our town is apt to show that industry is well represented there.

B. Point out and correct any errors in diction in the following sentences:

1. The library has an immense amount of encyclopedias and reference books.
2. I have been very satisfied with the service that my pen has given me.
3. I will contact you in the near future about a meeting.
4. All of my courses are kind of hard for me.
5. I either play bridge, go to the fraternity house, or do something else other than study.
6. The night was so dark that we didn't know if we were still on the road or not.
7. Errors in spelling can't help but catch the reader's eye.
8. We decided to go someplace and get a sandwich.
9. Our dog learned to do many a trick, not as a trick but as a act of devotion.
10. By attention to writing, I mean spelling, grammar, punctuation, and etc.
11. Our guide did a very good job in showing us the sights of the city.
12. The writer of this letter was neither sympathetic or understanding.
13. Our town is very unique in many ways.
14. I never understood how some classmates got by with the little studying they done.
15. With more careful drivers there would be less accidents.
16. For awhile I thought of quitting school and going to work.
17. Each of these study habits have great possibilities for better grades.
18. I feel that the writing laboratory has helped me a lot.
19. I am writing concerning matters in high school that have effected my studies here in college.
20. One of the reasons students flunk out of college is because they do not know how to study.

C. Point out and correct any errors in diction in the following sentences:

1. I hope that you will be able to make some sort of an adjustment.
2. For most everyone, May is the time when summer comes in earnest.
3. If a student works during the summers, he is liable to make better use of his time in college than is one who did not earn his own money.
4. My home is a large farmhouse about 65 yards off the main highway.

5. My roommate and I don't get mad at each other very often.
6. Fraternities offer many advantages to a student, and three of these shall be discussed in this theme.
7. Someplace in the course of history the superstition about the number 13 arose.
8. Anyone on a ladder may drop most anything on the passer-by beneath.
9. The second day of our visit we were taken on a inspection trip of the farm.
10. The reason why one remembers particular incidents is due to the fact that these incidents have made a deep impression.
11. Your plans are alright, but they will never work out.
12. You should never say that anything busted; instead, you should say that it bursted.
13. Grandfather laid there an hour before any one noticed the wreck.
14. For good fishing it is necessary to get up a hour before sunrise.
15. Our college gym is the nicest gym in the East.
16. I can remember so many exciting things we did together.
17. I think there was never a time when Mary didn't have either a cat, a dog, a chicken, or some kind of an animal following her.
18. My parents have always kind of regretted moving away from the farm.
19. The painter had a bucket of paint setting on the top step of the ladder.
20. These other kind of fruits will be better.

D. Point out and correct any errors in diction in the following sentences:

1. If one is too individual and follows his own inclinations too much, he will have less friends.
2. The first week of school the freshmen are kept real busy.
3. The main reason I do poorly in English is because my high school training was poor.
4. In high school I would never leave anything go until the last minute.
5. My sister is dark complected and I am light complected.
6. By your going to college, your salary will be much higher than it would of been.
7. Many people were gathered inside of the auditorium.
8. It takes a lot of time to do a lot of studying, but it's a lot of fun and you get a lot of satisfaction out of it.
9. The Golden Gate Bridge in San Francisco is one of the most unique bridges in the world.
10. Mother has done most of the cooking, housework, etc.
11. The products all ready discovered in chemistry make an amazing number.

12. In such an emergency we done the only thing we could do.
13. If I had of known then that I was going to college, I would of taken different subjects.
14. I hope that I can improve some in English during this semester.
15. You won't learn much copying off of some one else.
16. My baby sister will lay around and cry until she gets the attention she seeks.
17. I have neither a good vocabulary, a good knowledge of grammar, or a talent for arranging my material in an effective manner.
18. I met John over two years ago, although it does not seem that long.
19. Every traveler always collects a certain amount of items for souvenirs and memories.
20. There were less study rooms in the library than I expected to find.

GRAMMAR
A Useful Review

As a college student you are expected to use the language others with your educational and social advantages do. Therefore, in carrying on your affairs, through language, both in college and in later life, you should have pride in knowing and being able to use words and forms of words and word combinations appropriate to English as it is spoken and written by educated people.

Certain grammatical knowledge can help you to write correctly.[1] If you write *correctly,* grammar can help you write *clearly;* if you write correctly and clearly, grammar can help you write *effectively* and even *appropriately.*

A practical reason, therefore, exists for studying grammar. A knowledge of many grammatical terms does not guarantee good writing—it is even possible, although unlikely, that some gifted person may not know a single grammatical term and yet write competently. On the other hand, most of us need some guidance in writing and speaking, and we obtain that guidance most easily and efficiently through some grammatical vocabulary.

What, then, is grammar? *The American College Dictionary* gives this simple definition: "the features of a language (sounds, words, formation and arrangement of words, etc.) considered systematically as a whole, especially with reference to their mutual contrasts and relations."

Even more simply, grammar deals with words and their relationships to each other or one another; it is a descriptive statement of the way a language works. It includes a discussion of the forms of words, their

---

[1] For definition of *correct, correctly, correctness,* as used in this book, see page 23.

use in phrases, clauses, and sentences, their tenses, cases, or other changes in form. It is the scientific record of a series of observed language phenomena but, like any record, it is subject to constant fluctuations. A useful review concentrates on those words, their changes, and their relationships that assist in making writing and speaking correct, clear, effective, and appropriate. By mastering the useful principles of grammar, you make them serve you in your own writing and speaking.

Grammar is *descriptive;* its application is *prescriptive*. It is descriptive in that it records the actual and changing status of words and their relationships, descriptive in showing how words are said or written, not how they should be said or written. It is not properly considered as a list of rules, imposed by authorities, a rigid set of *do's, do not's, avoid's*. Yet there must be a certain amount of prescription if speaking and writing are to conform to principles generalized from description. For example, description shows that pronouns following prepositions are in the objective case. If your own usage is to conform to the description, you follow the prescription: *Use the objective case of pronouns following a preposition.*

Definitions of grammatical terms used are listed alphabetically in the glossary, Section **85**, page 608. Refer to this glossary whenever necessary as you study the following pages.

WORDS

71. A *word* is a letter or a combination of letters, a sound or a combination of sounds, forming a unit of thought capable of being used as an utterance.

71a. Learn to identify each word as a part of speech.

Words are classified according to their use in larger units of thought—in phrases, clauses, and sentences. This functional classification results in *parts of speech,* a descriptive phrase applied to words used in speaking and writing. A part of speech, therefore, is a word—sometimes a combination of words serving the purpose of one word—used to express a definite idea, such use becoming clear only in relation to surrounding words. Every word must be one of the eight parts of speech: *noun, pronoun, adjective, verb, adverb, preposition, conjunction, interjection*. Every word in your dictionary bears at least one such label.

Many words are used as only one part of speech, but since our language is constantly changing and since words also change in meaning, the function of words reflects such change. The word *iron,* at first thought, seems to be a noun only, as in *made of iron;* yet in *an iron bar* it is an adjective and in *to iron a shirt* it is a verb.

Unless your dictionary permits, do not use nouns for verbs, nouns for adjectives, nouns for adverbs, adjectives for nouns, adjectives for adverbs or adverbs for adjectives, adjectives for verbs, verbs for nouns. (See Sections **58, 71f, 83.**) Notice, however, that often a slight change in a word, such as a different ending, can change a word from one part of speech to another: *arrive* (verb), *arrival* (noun). To determine what part of speech a given word is, see how the word is used in the sentence or clause or phrase of which it is a part.

71b. Distinguish carefully the purposes that words serve.

Although words are classified according to one of the eight parts of speech, they can be classified also according to the purpose that they serve:

Naming words:	nouns and pronouns
Asserting words:	verbs
Modifying words:	adjectives and adverbs
Joining words:	prepositions and conjunctions
Exclamatory words:	interjections

NAMING WORDS: NOUNS AND PRONOUNS

A *noun* (from a Latin word, *nomen,* meaning "name") denotes or "names" a person, place, or thing, a quality, idea, or action. Common nouns name or represent all members of a common group: *man, officer, city, building, state.* Proper nouns name particular members of a group and are capitalized: *Mary, Mr. Ward, Benjamin Franklin, Chicago, Florida.* Some common nouns are concrete: *book, candy, hammer*—names of objects which can be perceived by the senses of touch, sight, taste, hearing, or smell. Some are abstract nouns: *honesty, intelligence, grace, strength*—names of abstractions which cannot be perceived by the senses. Some are collective nouns: *crew, family, assembly*—names used for groups considered as units.

Nouns have certain characteristics:

1. Nouns can be, and usually are, preceded by such words as *the, a, an, my, your, his, her, our, their, this, that, some, each.*

2. Certain groups of nouns have typical endings—such as *al, tion, ness, ment, ure*—which distinguish them from corresponding verbs (e.g., *arrive, arrival, determine, determination, argue, argument*) or from corresponding adjectives (e.g., *goodness, good*).

3. Nouns are sometimes distinguished from identically spelled verbs by accent: *sub'ject, subject', proj'ect, project'.*

4. Nouns are marked by their occurrence in a certain set of positions, e.g., usually before the verb in some statements, after the verb in others, and after prepositions.

5. Nouns are, or may be, marked by other characteristics: number, gender, case: *number*—singular (one) or plural (more than one); *gender*—masculine, feminine, neuter, common; and *case,* a common form for both nominative and objective, and a special form for the possessive (genitive).

Memory devices for recognizing nouns: nouns can be preceded by one of the words mentioned in Item 1, above; nouns usually add *s* or *es* to form their plural; nouns usually add *'s* to form the singular possive case.

For diagraming nouns, or pronouns, in a sentence as subject, object of verb, or object of preposition, see pp. 507–516.

71c. Do not carelessly use the singular form of a noun for the plural, or a plural form for the singular.

Wrong: My home town is only 80 mile from here.
A good student has many favorable characteristic.
Becky Sharp is portrayed as a very scheming women.
Over 800 freshman assembled in the chapel.

Plurals of nouns are formed as follows:

1. Most nouns form the plural by adding *s* to the singular: *dog, dogs; house, houses.*

2. Nouns ending in a sibilant or *s* sound (*ch, sh, j, s, x, z*) add *es: church, churches; fox, foxes*—i.e., when the ending is pronounced as an extra syllable (see Section 52e8).

3. Nouns ending in *y* form their plural according to the *y* spelling rule. (See Section 52e2.)

4. Nouns ending in *o* preceded by a vowel add *s: radio, radios.* Some

nouns ending in *o* preceded by a consonant form their plurals with *s:* *photo, photos; piano, pianos;* others with *es: echo, echoes; potato, potatoes;* still others with *s* or *es: motto, mottos, mottoes; zero, zeros, zeroes.*

5. Nouns ending in *f* are so variable that a dictionary should be consulted: *chief, chiefs; loaf, loaves.* Nouns ending in *ff* add *s: sheriff, sheriffs.* Most nouns ending in *fe* change *fe* to *ve* and add *s: wife, wives; knife, knives.*

NOTE: Normal use, *leaf, leaves;* nickname of baseball and hockey teams, Maple *Leafs.*

6. Some irregular plurals occur: change of vowel or vowels: *man, men; mouse, mice;* peculiar ending added: *child, children; ox, oxen;* or no change: *trout, trout; sheep, sheep.*

7. Compound nouns ordinarily form the plural by adding *s* or *es* to the important word in the compound: *sons-in-law, passers-by.* If the word elements are so closely related as to be considered a single word, the end of the word is pluralized: *handfuls.*

8. Certain nouns of foreign origin retain the plural of the language from which they were borrowed: *alumnus, alumni; datum, data; hypothesis, hypotheses.* Some have two plural forms, foreign and Anglicized: *index, indices, indexes; cherub, cherubim, cherubs.* Many borrowed words, however, have gradually assumed plurals with *s* or *es: area, areas; campus, campuses.*

When in doubt concerning the spelling or the specific form of the singular or plural, consult your dictionary.

For plurals of figures, alphabetical letters, and words as words, see Section **94g.**

EXERCISES

Correct all errors in the use of number (singular and plural) in the following sentences:

1. This is a theme of advice to all freshman.
2. The forest are green and beautiful this year.
3. I bought two pair of long woolen stockings for the winter.
4. My heart felt like two ton of lead.
5. When memorandum are enclosed, please mention that fact.
6. We then went to the Fieldhouse, where the freshman were meeting.

7. My girl friend is five foot and six inches tall.
8. These type of people are the ones who get the most out of college life.
9. Numerous state and federal highway and two major railroads pass through our city.
10. In the evening a large group of deers come down to drink at the lake.
11. In this four weeks we shall have to do our preparations for final examinations.
12. Our high school has one of the best staff of high school teachers in the state.
13. It is unusual that three such different type of people can get along so well.
14. I think the use of this criteria will solve the problem.
15. I am now a young women and a freshmen in college.
16. A Boy Scout is supposed to go around doing kind deed for people.
17. We have taken two rather long vacation lasting about a month each.
18. Our state parks are restful places designed for tourist.
19. My first vacation came after I had struggled through 8 long hard week of college life.
20. We all need to use good English, whether we plan to be a scientist, an engineer, a technician, a doctor, a lawyer, or a factory worker.

71d. Distinguish carefully the different kinds and purposes of pronouns.

A *pronoun* (*pro,* literally "for" or "instead of") substitutes for a noun or, sometimes, another pronoun. Every pronoun, except indefinite pronouns, refers directly or by clear implication to a noun or another pronoun—called the *antecedent* of the pronoun—and it agrees with that antecedent in person, number, and gender: "Each *man* in favor will please raise *his* hand." "Does every *girl* here have *her* luncheon ticket?" (See Section 77.)

Pronouns, used in all the grammatical functions of nouns (subjects of sentences or clauses, apposition, direct or indirect objects of verbs, etc.), are of eight kinds: *personal, relative, demonstrative, interrogative, reflexive, intensive, indefinite,* and *reciprocal.*

1. *Personal* pronouns refer to an individual or individuals. Of all the kinds of pronouns, personal pronouns cause the most trouble; they have 30 case forms. Some of these include all genders, and some have special forms for masculine, feminine, or neuter.

Personal pronouns also bear the labels of 1st person, 2nd person, 3rd person: First person pronouns indicate the speaker or writer—as singular or as plural. Second person pronouns indicate the person or persons spoken to or written to, with the same forms for both singular and plural. Gender or sex is the same for all 1st and 2nd person pronouns. Third person pronouns indicate the person or persons spoken or written about—and here sex or gender needs consideration: singular masculine, singular feminine, singular neuter, and plural for all genders. A table of these pronouns is given in Section **75a**.

2. A *relative* pronoun relates or connects an adjective clause to the antecedent. The same forms—*who, whose, whom, which, that*—serve for gender or number; their being singular or plural or having gender depends upon their antecedents. The choice of a relative pronoun is also determined in part by its antecedent: *who, whose,* and *whom* are used to refer only to persons; *which* is used in reference to things (inanimate objects, animals) and may be used for a group of persons; *that* may refer to either things or persons.

> The girl *who* won the Junior Prom beauty contest is now an airline hostess. (Singular)
> The girls *who* served as the Queen's court are also airline hostesses. (Plural)
> This company owns only one small ship, *which* is used for river traffic. (Singular)
> A New York company owns seven large freighters, *which* ply between Europe and America. (Plural)
> The man *that* I mean was named Mortimer Taylor. (Singular)
> The men *that* I like have the same interests as I do. (Plural)

That and *which* have no changes in form (compare with *who, whose, whom*). The possessive case of the pronoun *which* is indicated by *of which.* A possessive, *of that,* is never used.

Who, which, and *that* are the most frequently used relative pronouns; *whoever, whomever, whichever,* and *whatever* are less frequently used relative pronouns; *whosoever, whichsoever,* and *whatsoever* have almost entirely gone out of current use.

3. A *demonstrative* pronoun points out and identifies. It has different forms for number but not for gender or case. The most important demonstrative pronouns are *this* (singular), *that* (singular), *these* (plural), *those* (plural), *such* (singular or plural).

> *This* is the book that I have recommended.
> *That* is the record I have just bought.

These are your books; *those* on the desk are mine.
Such are the magazines that our teacher recommends.

These five words can also be used as adjectives: *this* and *that* modify only singular nouns, *these* and *those* only plural nouns, and *such* either singular or plural.

This magazine is interesting, *that* book is dull.
These magazines are interesting, *those* books are dull.
Such a book and *such* magazines are worth reading.

4. An *interrogative* pronoun (*who, which, what,* occasionally *whoever, whichever, whatever*) introduces a question.

Who will read his book report on Wednesday?
Which is the best road to take to Louisville?
What do you think about extracurricular activities?
For *whom* are you writing this theme?
Whoever would think of playing such a trick?

Whose, as possessive, can of course accompany a noun. *Which* and *what* are frequently used as adjectives also.

Whose tie are you wearing today?
Which book do you recommend as an exciting novel?
What road should I take to Louisville?

5. A *reflexive* pronoun is used for simple reference to the subject; it usually follows a verb or preposition and directs or *reflects* its action back to the subject. Composed of one of the personal pronoun forms with *self* or *selves,* the most frequently employed reflexive pronouns are *myself, yourself, himself, herself, itself, ourselves, yourselves, themselves* (and the indefinite *oneself*).

6. *Intensive* pronouns have the same forms as the reflexive pronouns, but they appear in an appositive position and are used to emphasize or *intensify* a noun or other pronoun. Use of commas depends on whether the apposition is considered close or parenthetical.

Yesterday my roommate hurt *himself* playing basketball. (Reflexive use)
He *himself* decided to go out for basketball. (Intensive use)
Some students consider *themselves* lucky to be here. (Reflexive use)
The seniors *themselves* chose the day for their commencement. (Intensive use)

Mary asked *herself* the question many times. (Reflexive use)
Sometimes she talked aloud to *herself*. (Reflexive use)
She *herself* finally reached a satisfactory decision. (Intensive use)

7. *Indefinite* pronouns are less exact in meaning than other pronouns. They are *pronouns* because they refer to antecedents; they are *indefinite* because the antecedents are not specifically named persons or things. Among the more frequently used indefinite pronouns are the following: *another, any, anybody, anyone, anything, all, everybody, everyone* or *every one,*[2] *everything, few, many, nobody, no one, none, one, oneself* (as indefinite reflexive), *several, some, somebody, someone.* Compound forms built upon the pronoun *one* or the element *body* have a possessive form ending *'s*, like *anyone's, everybody's, one's.* Indefinite pronouns involve grammatical problems of agreement which are discussed in Section **76c** and Section **77a**.

8. A *reciprocal* pronoun indicates an interchange of action suggested by the verb. This interchange may be seen in the following sentences involving the only two reciprocal pronouns in English:

My roommate and I always confide in *each other*. (Two only)
The members of the party exploring the cave shouted to *one another*. (Three or more)

Possessive forms add *'s: each other's, one another's.*

ASSERTING WORDS: VERBS AND VERBALS

71e.   Understand clearly the functions and uses of verbs.

A *verb* is a part of speech that asserts something, says something, expresses action, expresses a state of being or a condition. Alone or with auxiliary verbs, it may make a positive statement, make a conditional statement or statement of probability, give a command, ask a question, make an exclamation.

Today *is* Friday the 13th. (Positive statement)
If you *are* lucky, you *win* first prize. (Condition and positive statement)
Plan to attend Tuesday's meeting. (Command)
You *have* many students here, *haven't* you? (Question)
You *were* really the winner! (Exclamation)

[2] *Everyone* and *every one* are ordinarily interchangeable, but when followed by *of*, the two-word form is used: *Every one* of you should attend.

In addition to helping express the verb functions mentioned above, auxiliary or helping verbs (Section **78**) add particular shades of meaning—usually of time (Section **80**), tone (Section **80**), voice (Section **81**), or mood (Section **82**)—to what is called the main verb (Section **79**). Such combinations are called *verb phrases*.

> Next Friday *will be* Friday the 13th. (Positive statement, and time or tone)
> I *have written* sixteen themes this semester. (Positive statement, and time or tone)
> We *may have* to have another meeting this month. (Probability)
> *Be prepared* to come to this meeting. (Command)
> *Will* you please *let* us *know* your plans? (Question)
> You *were* really *surprised!* (Exclamation)
> I *do believe* in thorough proofreading. (Tone, emphatic)
> This theme *was revised* four times. (Voice)
> If you *had not been* late, you *would have seen* the thrilling touchdown run. (Mood)

Various uses of verbs—the main verb alone or auxiliary and main verb—are the following:

1. To express *time* (tense): present, past, future, present perfect, past perfect, future perfect. See Section **80** for discussion.

2. To express *tone:* simple, progressive, emphatic. See Section **80** for discussion.

3. To express *agreement with subject in number and person.* See Section **76** and Section **80** for discussion.

4. To express *active* or *passive* voice. See Section **81** for discussion.

5. To express *mood* or *mode:* indicative, imperative, subjunctive. See Section **82** for discussion.

For diagraming verbs as predicates in a sentence, see pp. 507–508.

71f. Distinguish between predicate verbs and verbals.

A *predicate verb* is a *verb* or *verb phrase* used in the predicate of a clause or a sentence where it makes a statement about the subject. The italicized verb or verb phrases in the examples in Section **71e** are predicate verbs. Nearly every clause or sentence contains them. Predicate verbs agree (are in concord) with their subjects in number and person (see Section **76**).

Verbals are *verb forms* that cannot serve as predicates; the verbals are *participles, gerunds,* and *infinitives.* Understanding the differences between predicate verbs and verbals helps to avoid a serious error in writing, the use of unjustifiable sentence fragments (see Section 31). Ordinarily, for clearness and effectiveness verbals or verbal phrases should not stand alone. If a group of words contains a verbal, it should include with it or elsewhere in the sentence the kind of verb or verb phrase which serves as the predicate of the clause or sentence.

A *participle* is a word which has the function of both verb and adjective. The *present participle* always ends in *ing* (*speaking, singing*). The *past participle* has various forms (*spoken, sung, walked, sat*). The *perfect participle* consists of *having* or *having been* followed by the past participle (*having sung, having been asked*). (See Section 79.) The participle as verb form can take an object and be modified by an adverb; the participle as adjective can be modified by an adverb and can itself modify a noun or pronoun.

> *Coming* events cast their shadows before. (Adjective)
> Expertly *driving* the car in traffic, Harry has no fear of cities. (As adjective, *driving* modifies *Harry;* as verb, it is modified by the adverb *expertly* and it takes a direct object, *car.*)
> This brightly *polished* silver is beautiful. (As adjective, *polished* modifies *silver,* is modified by the adverb *brightly.*)

The *gerund* is a verbal noun usually ending in *ing* (*speaking, singing*). Because the *ing gerund* has the same spelling as the present participle, be careful to note the difference in use: the participle is a *verbal adjective,* the gerund is a *verbal noun.* The gerund as a verb form can take an object and be modified by an adverb; the gerund as noun can be modified by an adjective and can be the subject or object of a verb or the object of a preposition.

> *Playing* tennis is good exercise. (Gerund is subject of sentence, but as verb form it takes a direct object, *tennis.*)
> Some people enjoy *spending* money generously. (As noun, the gerund is object of the verb *enjoy;* as verb, it in turn has an object, *money,* and is modified by the adverb *generously.*)
> Henry paid for his education by *planning* carefully. (As noun, the gerund is object of the preposition *by;* as verb, it is modified by the adverb *carefully.*)
> Steady *running* won the race for Henry. (As noun, the gerund is subject and is modified by the adjective *steady.*)

An *infinitive* is a word which has the function of both verb and noun and which may also be employed as an adjective or an adverb. The infinitive is often introduced by the "sign" *to* (*to speak, to sing*).

> *To work* intelligently is sometimes difficult. (Infinitive as noun is subject of sentence; as verb form it is modified by an adverb, *intelligently*.)
> *To win* a scholarship means constant study. (Infinitive as noun is subject of sentence; as verb form it has a direct object, *scholarship*.)
> The best time *to study* is early in the morning. (Infinitive serves as adjective.)
> I came *to inquire* about your vacation. (Infinitive serves as adverb.)

71g. **Do not use a transitive verb for an intransitive verb, or an intransitive verb for a transitive verb.**

Verbs are classified as either *transitive* or *intransitive*. *Transitive* literally means *passing over, crossing over, building a bridge across*. A *transitive* verb is followed by a direct object which completes the meaning of the verb. In other words, a transitive verb is a bridge, a means of crossing over from subject to object. "The teacher *accepted* my excuse." An *intransitive verb* requires no direct object to complete its meaning, does no crossing over. It may of course have word, phrase, or clause modifiers. "I *am going;* I *am going* very soon; in fact, I *am going* just as soon as I can."

Determining whether a verb is transitive or intransitive (the same verb frequently may be either and be so labeled in your dictionary) depends upon meaning, upon the idea the writer wishes to show.

> I *obeyed* the traffic officer's instructions. (Transitive)
> Father now *owns* three garages. (Transitive)
> He gave me instructions; I *obeyed*. (Intransitive)
> After his introduction, the speaker *paused*. (Intransitive)

For almost all practical purposes in writing, being able to distinguish transitive and intransitive verbs is useless information. If you must decide, try the following blank-filling memory device:

> Let's ___ it. (A verb is transitive if it can be inserted in this blank.)
> Let's ___. (A verb is intransitive if it can be inserted in this blank.)

Concerning three pairs of verbs, transitive-intransitive information is useful, but if you memorize these verbs, their principal parts, and their meanings, you can forget about the transitive-intransitive distinctions:

Transitive: $\begin{cases} lay, laid, laid, laying \\ lie, lay, lain, lying \end{cases}$
Intransitive:

Transitive: $\begin{cases} raise, raised, raised, raising \\ rise, rose, risen, rising \end{cases}$
Intransitive:

Transitive: $\begin{cases} set, set, set, setting \\ sit, sat, sat, sitting \end{cases}$
Intransitive:

NOTE: *Lie* in the meaning of "tell a falsehood" and *set* in the sense of "go down" (the sun *sets*) are verbs that cause no trouble.

> I *laid* your books on your desk. (From *lay*)
> As I was *laying* your books there, the telephone rang. (From *lay*)
> Harry *lay* down for a short time. (From *lie*)
> The books are now *lying* on your desk. (From *lie*)
> I spent the afternoon *setting* the boxes on the top shelf. (From *set*)
> Then I began to rest and have been *sitting* here for an hour. (From *sit*)
> The speaker *raised* the microphone six inches higher. (From *raise*)
> The preceding speaker had *raised* it only two inches. (From *raise*)
> Tired of resting, I *rose* and went for a walk. (From *rise*)
> The waters have *risen* two feet since yesterday. (From *rise*)

EXERCISES

A. From the following sentences, make a list of verbals and after each write an identifying letter: **P**—participle, **G**—gerund, **I**—infinitive.

1. I try to study and to make high grades, but studying seems to get neglected when someone tempts me with swimming, bowling, or golfing.
2. A smiling face is better than a discontented one; to smile is one way of winning friends.
3. The college has no objection to our cutting classes, but it does object to our complaining about low grades on tests covering the work that we have missed.
4. Having written with more than usual care, I was surprised when the instructor said that my writing was illegible.
5. To know more about a subject than other people know is a worthy ambition; not to make a parade of one's learning is an even more worthy ambition.
6. William liked to swim and dance with me, but I always felt that he would rather read than do either.
7. He is constantly striving to better himself by taking courses in adult education.

8. Bathing, shaving, and dressing are necessary preliminaries to eating breakfast.

9. The man buying his ticket is a local merchant going to Chicago.

10. The game already having been won, we decided to leave soon after the intermission.

11. Joe's tackling and running are excellent, but I don't believe that he will ever learn to punt or catch passes.

12. He was a person who had enjoyed rowing for years—since reaching his sixth birthday, in fact—but now in this moment of peril to move an oar seemed impossible.

13. Spoken words are naturally kept in mind with much more difficulty than those one reads, but a well-trained person can retain amazing amounts of conversation that he has heard.

14. As it flowed down the gray rock wall, the swiftly falling water seemed to have lost its liquid quality; it looked like a smooth and solidified pillar of green.

15. For a skater to fall occasionally is no more of a calamity than occurs to a speeding hurdler when he topples over a hurdle, but I fell times past counting.

B. Make a list of numbers from 1 to 15. Opposite each, write from the following sentences the correct forms of *lay—lie, raise—rise, set—sit* (see Section **71g**):

1. I *laid lay* down for a short time after lunch.

2. At a table behind me *sat set* two men discussing politics.

3. The water retained by the forests is sufficient to *raise rise* the rivers several feet.

4. Who wants to spend half a day *setting sitting* up a machine?

5. Each night I plan for the day that *lays lies* ahead.

6. The walls of the cliff *raise rise* straight up from the bottom of the canyon.

7. Most people like to see autumn leaves *laying lying* in their yards.

8. At about 4 o'clock in the afternoon, the wind began to *raise rise*.

9. The driver picked me up and *sat set* me in the seat of the racer.

10. When the nurse took my temperature, she took one look at me and made me *lay lie* down.

11. All these machines and the desk that they *set sit* on are made especially for speed and ease of operation.

12. With an automatic jack, all you do is press a button and the car will *raise rise*.

13. In front of me was a hen partridge *setting sitting* on her nest of eggs.

14. There *laying lying* on the counter was the most beautiful doll I had ever seen.
15. Since I had to park the trailer on the side of a slope, the front of the trailer was *raised risen* to put some blocks under it.

MODIFYING WORDS: ADJECTIVES AND ADVERBS

71h.   For correct and exact meaning, understand the functions of adjectives.

An *adjective* modifies a noun or pronoun by describing, limiting, or in some other closely related way making meaning more nearly exact. An adjective may indicate quality or quantity, may identify or set limits. Specifically, therefore, adjectives tell *what kind of, how many, which one*. Adjectives are of two general types: *descriptive*: a *black* dress, an *easy* lesson, a *smashed* thumb; *limiting*: the *sixth* period, her *former* home, *several* times. Another classification includes *common* adjectives and *proper* adjectives (from proper nouns), important only because proper adjectives begin with a capital letter: an *American* play; *Italian* olives.

Many adjectives have endings which mark them as adjectives. The more important of these endings include:

able (*ible*):	payable, desirable, likeable, permissible
al:	cordial, promotional, optional, musical
ary:	elementary, visionary, contrary, secondary
en:	rotten, golden, wooden, molten
ful:	beautiful, faithful, hurtful, sinful
ic:	metric, carbonic, Byronic, artistic
ish:	mannish, selfish, Danish, dwarfish
ive:	permissive, constructive, excessive, decisive
less:	faithless, timeless, lawless, guileless
ous:	vigorous, nervous, marvelous, advantageous
some:	lonesome, tiresome, handsome, bothersome
y:	muddy, stony, funny, dreamy, seedy

The words *a, an, the* are classed as adjectives because they always accompany a noun or, infrequently, a pronoun. They certainly have no descriptive power, but in a limited sense they limit. Compare

man	*a* man	*the* man
deer	*a* deer	*the* deer

A and *an* are *indefinite articles; the* is the *definite article: a* physician, *the* physician; *an* orange, *the* orange. The initial sound of the following word determines the choice of *a* or *an: an* is used before words beginning with a vowel sound (including silent *h*) and before initial vowels that have consonant sounds:

an apple   an hour   a hero   a European visitor

An adjective may modify a noun by preceding it, as do usually single adjectives or a series of single adjectives:

A *merry* laugh greeted us.
Red, green, and *yellow* lights are traffic signals.
The *tired, hungry,* and *emaciated* survivors moved feebly toward the ship.

Certain adjectives or adjective combinations may either precede or follow the noun; others, like restrictive adjective phrases and clauses (see Section **88m**), must follow:

Our delegate *alone* will travel to Washington.
Food *enough* has been provided for everyone.
The traffic lights, *red, green,* and *yellow,* were visible for blocks ahead.
The survivors, *tired, hungry,* and *emaciated,* moved feebly toward the ship.
The boy *in the brown suit* is my brother.
The girl *who is rising to speak* is the valedictorian.

Another position of adjectives in sentences is after certain verbs, the so-called linking verbs (Section **78**):

The corn is *green.*
The water felt *warm.*
The children have grown *taller.*

Such adjectives are related to the subject, the word they modify. The verbs are called linking or joining or coupling verbs because they link subject and adjective, and the adjectives in this use are called predicate adjectives or complements. For fuller discussion, see Sections **78a, b, 83c.**

71i.   For correct and exact meaning, understand the functions of adverbs.

An *adverb* modifies a verb, an adjective, or another adverb by describing, limiting, or in some other closely related way making meaning more nearly exact. Adverbs usually tell *how, how much, how often, when, where, why.*

> A distant bugle sang *faintly.* (Adverb modifies verb *sang.*)
> We heard it *only once.* (Adverb *once* modifies verb *heard;* adverb *only* modifies adverb *once.*)
> *Then* the bugle sang *again.* (Both adverbs, *then* and *again,* modify verb *sang.*)
> I do *not* see my hat *anywhere.* (Both adverbs, *not* and *anywhere,* modify verb *see.*)
> We were *almost* ready to start. (Adverb modifies the adjective *ready.*)
> Close the door *very slowly.* (Adverb *very* modifies the adverb *slowly,* which modifies the verb *close.*)

Adverbs have the following characteristics:

1. Adverbs are commonly distinguished from corresponding adjectives by the suffix *ly: warm, warmly; angry, angrily;* but some words ending in *ly* are adjectives (*manly, lonely, friendly*).

2. Certain adverbs are distinguished from corresponding nouns by the suffixes *wise* and *ways: lengthwise, sideways.*

3. Certain adverbs are distinguished from similarly spelled prepositions in not being connected to a following noun:

Adverb: He came *up.*
Preposition: He came *up* the street.

4. Like adjectives, but unlike nouns and verbs, adverbs may be preceded by words of the "very" group (intensifiers), such as *very, extremely, exceedingly, right:*

> The *very beautifully* dressed girl is the class queen.
> He went *right* by.

Adverbs modifying adjectives and other adverbs are usually placed just before the words they modify. Adverbs modifying verbs can be placed almost anywhere in the sentence, clearness and smoothness permitting.

Both adjectives and adverbs have changes in form to indicate three degrees of *comparison—positive, comparative, superlative: good, better, best; great, greater, greatest; slowly, more slowly, most slowly.* For discussion, illustration, and application, see Section 83e, f, g, h.

Errors in the use of adjectives and adverbs are discussed in Section 83.

For diagraming adjectives and adverbs in a sentence, see page 510.

JOINING WORDS: PREPOSITIONS AND CONJUNCTIONS

71j. Distinguish between the functions of prepositions and conjunctions.

A *preposition* (note its literal meaning: *pre*—"before," plus *position*) is a linking word used before a noun or pronoun to show its relationship to some other word in the sentence. The following list contains most of the prepositions used in English:

about	beside	in	since
above	besides	inside	through
across	between	into	throughout
after	beyond	like	till
against	but	near	to
along	by	notwithstanding	toward
alongside	concerning	of	under
amid	despite	off	underneath
among	down	on	until
around	during	onto	unto
at	ere	outside	up
before	except	over	upon
behind	excepting	per	with
below	for	regarding	within
beneath	from	save	without

Each preposition is of course followed by its object (see Section 75d)—noun, pronoun, noun phrase, or noun clause. In some word combinations the preposition may, paradoxically, follow its object:

> *In which house* do you live?
> *Which house* do you live *in?*
> The man *for whom* I am working . . . .
> The man *whom* I am working *for* . . . .

Compound prepositions, consisting of two or more words, serve the purpose of a single one-word preposition. The most common are the following:

as for	because of	by way of
as to	by means of	contrary to
aside from	by reason of	due to

497

exclusive of	in company with	pertaining to
for fear of	in favor of	regardless of
for the sake of	in regard to	with a view to
in accordance with	in spite of	with reference to
in addition to	in view of	with regard to
in behalf of	on account of	with respect to
in case of	owing to	with the exception of

Certain prepositions are used with other parts of speech, such as verbs, adjectives, adverbs, to form idiomatic combinations: *agree to, confused about, depend upon, independent of, jealous of.* Some hundreds of such idioms use prepositions; most of them are discussed in your dictionary. Further discussion with a list is also in Section **56**, pages 409–411.

A *conjunction* is a linking word used to connect words or groups of words in a sentence, or even to connect sentences. In some detail, conjunctions and their use are discussed in Section **84**.

These seven kinds of words—nouns, pronouns, verbs, adjectives, adverbs, prepositions, and conjunctions—are the principal parts of speech.

INTERJECTIONS

71k. Use interjections for effectiveness and appropriateness.

The eighth part of speech, the *interjection,* is an exclamatory or parenthetic word which has little connection with the remainder of the sentence; in fact, it frequently serves alone as a sentence: *Whoops! Ouch!* "*Oh,* must you go?" "And here, *alas,* our good fortune came to an abrupt end."

The following list contains most of the interjections found in English:

ah	bravo	here	mum
aha	encore	hey	O
ahoy	fie	hist	off
alas	good	ho	oh
amen	good-by (good-bye)	huh	ouch
ay	gosh	humph	pshaw
bah	halloo	hurrah	so
behold	heigh	hush	there
boo	hello	indeed	tush
botheration	hem	lo	tut

ugh	whist	whoopee	why
what	whoa	whoops	woe

Occasional interjections are effective, but overuse gives the effect of a strained or immature style. For their punctuation see Section **87a** and **88n2**.

EXERCISES

A. Copy the following sentences. Put one each on a page of paper, and put one word only on a line, in column form, beginning at the extreme left margin. After each word write the part of speech that it is: noun, pronoun, adjective, verb, adverb, preposition, conjunction, interjection.

1. Many students attend football games every week during the season, although we notice that some work busily in the library even while the games are in progress.
2. A Canadian humorist and professor of economics once said that for a great university only three things are needed: a library, a body of interested students, and a scholarly faculty; what do you think of that statement?
3. Ah, if only more of our students would put their studies above their activities, this college would become a great center of learning; will you be the student who will first set the example?
4. Words are a vital part of our everyday life, but we seldom stop and think whether or not the form and meaning were the same throughout the centuries that have passed.
5. I had always been brought up with the idea that going to college was just the thing to do; indeed, my parents always expected that I would some day go to college, they planned for it, and they planted their ideas firmly in my mind.

B. From the following sentences, copy in column form the italicized words; after each, write the part of speech it is.

1. It was a *very* warm day.
2. Susan was a most *intelligent* child.
3. He *caught* the book as it fell.
4. The *suit* will cost too much money.
5. He is sitting *by* a roaring fire.
6. They cannot go *because* it has rained.
7. This is the magazine of *which* you spoke.
8. He bought his books and *a* writing tablet.
9. *"Pshaw!"* she said; "I'm an hour late already."

499

10. It seems to me that he *talks* too *much*.
11. Carnations *and roses* make a *beautiful* bouquet.
12. *What!* six *hot* dogs in *one* afternoon!
13. The edge of the *razor* blade *resembled* a saw.
14. The tide *crept* imperceptibly *but relentlessly* on.
15. The rusty, *worn* old *chain* snapped in an instant.
16. The extent of the storm is *difficult* to *estimate*.
17. *Her* slant on life *is* a hard one to explain.
18. *Who* wrote the note is *his* problem, not *mine*.
19. *Come*, Thomas, can't you hurry up *quietly?*
20. *For* the life of *me*, I could *not* solve the problem.

PHRASES

72. Identify phrases correctly, both for clearness and effectiveness in writing and for avoiding unjustifiable sentence fragments.

A *phrase* is a group of related words which do not contain a subject and a predicate. It serves usually as a single part of speech.

Phrases classified according to use.

A phrase usually fulfills the functions of a single noun, adjective, verb, or adverb. Phrases containing adjectives modifying nouns or containing adverbs modifying verbs are labeled according to their stronger words, that is, noun phrases or verb phrases.

> Our city is proud of *its wide, well-paved, shady streets and boulevards.* (Noun phrase)
> Many a river *runs swiftly and silently to the sea.* (Verb phrase)

A phrase can be used in a sentence as a noun is used, as subject, object, etc. It is called a *noun phrase.*

> *Freshmen and sophomores* live in campus dormitories. (Noun phrase as subject)
> *Playing on a major football team* was his special ambition. (Noun phrase as subject)

A phrase may modify a noun or pronoun; it may function, that is, as a single adjective functions. Such a phrase is called an *adjective* (or adjectival) *phrase.*

> Our city is proud of *its wide, well-paved, shady* streets.
> The farmers *in the West* (cf. the *western* farmers) need rain.

A phrase may modify a verb, adjective, or adverb; it may function, that is, as a single adverb functions. Such a phrase is called an *adverb* (or adverbial) *phrase.*

> Many a river runs *swiftly and silently to the sea.*
> Our fullback fumbled *on the 2-yard line.*

If a modifying phrase is essential to explain or identify the word to which it is attached or refers, the phrase is called *restrictive.* If the phrase is not absolutely necessary, it is called *nonrestrictive.* Proper identification is necessary for clear punctuation. Restrictive and nonrestrictive phrases are discussed in Sections **88m-R** and **88m-N,** with examples of punctuation given.

A *verb phrase* consists of a group of words serving the function of a verb, such as an auxiliary verb with its main verb, or a verb with its modifiers. A *verb phrase* is not the same as a *verbal phrase:* participial, gerundial, infinitive, defined below.

> By June your first college year *will have been completed.*
> Every student *should write correctly, clearly, effectively, and appropriately.*

Phrases classified according to form.

Phrases may also be classified according to form; such phrases usually receive their name from their initial or more important word. Six common divisions are the following:

Prepositional (used as adjectives or adverbs, rarely as nouns):

> The house *on the corner* is the home of Mayor Williams. (Adjective)
> The road winds *through the mountains* and down *into a valley.* (Adverb)
> *Without saving* is to be without money when it is needed. (Noun)

Participial:

> *Having completed my assignments,* I went to bed.
> *Puffing like steam engines,* we reached the top of the tower.

Gerundial:

> *Winning first place in the speech contest* was his special ambition.
> The audience enjoyed *his playing of the Viennese waltzes.*

Prepositional-gerundial (a phrase introduced by a preposition which is followed by the gerund as noun):

> *After graduating from college,* I plan to go to medical school.
> We won *by having a superior line and a faster backfield.*

Infinitive:

> *To win games* is the aim of every team.
> He has worked hard *to achieve success.*

NOTE: Participial, gerundial, and infinitive phrases serve the same purpose that is served by single participles, gerunds, and infinitives. (See Section 71f.) Except for absolute phrases, these and prepositional phrases can also be classified according to use, since a phrase usually serves as a single part of speech.

Absolute:

> *Night coming,* we ceased our work.
> *My theme written,* I signed my name to it and turned it in.
> John went to bed, *his work being finished.*

The *absolute phrase,* a peculiar construction, consists usually of a noun followed and modified by a participle or participial phrase. It is a phrase because it cannot stand alone as a sentence; absolute, because it modifies no single word in the sentence of which it is a part, although it has a close thought relationship to the sentence or some word or phrase in it. (See also Section 88p.)

EXERCISES

A. From the following sentences compile a list of phrases and classify them under these headings: prepositional, participial, gerundial, prepositional-gerundial, infinitive, and absolute.

1. Through the night the plane roared on to its destination.
2. To get along well with people, you must learn to share their interests.
3. In the spring, according to the poet, a young man's fancy lightly turns to thoughts of love.
4. Having reached the age of 19, I have no desire ever to fall in love again.
5. A motion for adjournment having been made, the meeting disbanded.
6. Traveling by airplane is our swiftest mode of travel; traveling by oxcart is the slowest.

7. Your teacher has no objection to your turning in well-written themes.
8. John wrote to a friend in Chicago to inquire about obtaining employment for the summer.
9. Smith being pretty well battered, the coach sent in Jones to replace him at tackle.
10. Seen from a distance, the night train, creeping up the mountain grade, looked like an animated glowworm.
11. A motion was made to close the nominations, no other names being proposed.
12. After opening and reading your letter, I understood your not receiving my invitation in time to accept.
13. To get experience and not to make money was his goal in seeking a summer job.
14. Having been unanimously elected president, I expressed my gratitude for the honor bestowed upon me.
15. In catching 15 trout, we had a good day of fishing, the legal limit being 20.

B. After each phrase in the list you compiled according to A, indicate how the phrase was used: noun, adjective, adverb, or verb.

CLAUSES

73. A clause is a group of words having a subject and predicate and forming part of a sentence. Clauses are of two kinds: *independent* (or *main,* or *principal*) and *dependent* (or *subordinate*).

73a. Identify independent clauses carefully for effectiveness in writing and for correctness of punctuation.

An *independent clause* makes a complete grammatical statement and may stand alone; that is, it makes reasonable sense if the remainder of the sentence is omitted. It could stand as a sentence. Context, of course, is usually necessary for completely clear meaning.

> Although I should have studied last evening, *I watched several TV programs.* (Independent clause)
> I watched several TV programs. (Sentence)

More than one independent clause may be contained in a sentence.

> *My roommate studied,* but *I watched several TV programs.*

73b. Identify dependent clauses carefully, as a safeguard against writing unjustifiable sentence fragments and against incorrect punctuation.

A *dependent clause,* or *subordinate clause,* is not capable of standing alone but depends upon the remainder of the sentence for its meaning. Dependent clauses function as nouns, adjectives, or adverbs. Like an independent clause, a dependent clause contains a subject and predicate; it shows that it is dependent, usually, by the linking word which joins it to the independent clause.

Noun clauses.

In the following examples the dependent clause is used as a noun; each italicized clause functions exactly as would a single noun.

> *What you paid* was too much. (Noun clause used as subject. Compare: "The *price* was too much.")
>
> He promised *that he would give me the money.* (Noun clause used as object of verb *promised;* compare "promised a gift of money.")
>
> I am not aware of *what he has in mind.* (Noun clause used as the object of the preposition *of.*)
>
> Your remark *that you hate college* surprises me. (Noun clause used as an *appositive;* see **Appositive,** in glossary, Section **85.** Compare: "Your remark, hatred of college, . . .")
>
> His remarks usually were *whatever came to his mind first.* (Noun clause used as a *predicate complement;* see **Complement,** in glossary, Section **85.** Compare: ". . . were his first thoughts."

Adjective clauses.

In the following, the dependent clause is used as an adjective; each italicized clause functions as would a single adjective.

> The farmers *who live in the West* need rain. (Compare: "The *western* farmers need rain.")
>
> The price *which he paid* was too much. (Clause modifies *price.*)
>
> People *who rarely think* should say little. (Clause modifies *people.*)
>
> You are the very person *whom I wanted.* (Clause modifies *person.*)
>
> He is a boy *I never admired.* (Clause modifies *boy; whom* after *boy* is understood.)

Adverbial clauses.

Dependent clauses function as adverbs in the following; each italicized clause functions as would a single adverb.

I shall pay the bill *when you send it.* (Clause modifies the verb *shall pay;* compare: "I shall pay the bill *later.*"
You study more efficiently *than I do.* (Clause modifies the adverb *more efficiently.*)
As a residential town, West Liberty is more desirable *than East Liberty is.* (Clause modifies the adjective *more desirable.*)

If a dependent clause—usually adjective, sometimes adverb—is essential in order to explain or identify the word on which it depends or to which it refers, it is called restrictive. If the dependent clause is not necessary, if it is in the nature of a parenthetical remark which could be removed from the sentence, leaving the essential meaning intact, it is called nonrestrictive. Proper identification is necessary for clear punctuation. Restrictive and nonrestrictive clauses are discussed in Sections **88m-R** and **88m-N,** with examples of punctuation given.

Elliptical clauses.

A special kind of clause, the *elliptical clause,* is for practical purposes a dependent clause; its subject and frequently part of its predicate are omitted because they are understood from the main clause. In the following pairs, the first example contains full clauses, the second contains an elliptical clause. (See Section **40c.**)

Although I was ill, I insisted on attending class.
Although ill, I insisted on attending class.

When he was in New York, John went to the theater every night.
When in New York, John went to the theater every night.

While she was sewing, Mary listened to the radio.
While sewing, Mary listened to the radio.

Trouble arises when the omitted, understood parts are *not* those of the main clause. (See Section **40c.**)

When driving a car, the emergency brakes should be released.
When six years old, my mother married my stepfather.

EXERCISES

Copy the following sentences, leaving a blank line between each two lines. Underline each clause in the sentences. Above each clause indicate by these abbreviations its functions in the sentence: **N**—noun, **Adv.**—adverb, **Adj.**—adjective, **Ind.**—independent.

1. As it was getting late, we began looking for a place where we might land and camp for the night.

2. During the night we heard strange noises, which frightened us considerably, but they finally stopped, and we soon went back to sleep.
3. When school was out on Friday afternoons, a few of us stayed behind to take special instructions in learning how to typewrite.
4. Among other kinds of men we can single out these two: those who think and those who act.
5. I have often heard it said that people are funny, and I am sorry to have to admit that the statement is true.
6. I recommend a visit to Chicago, but when you go, remember that your impressions will be determined by where you get off the train.
7. Not all people in the library are scholars: across the table from me a boy is enjoying himself looking at the cartoons in a magazine; sitting farther away in a quiet corner are a boy and a girl having a library date.
8. The high light of my childhood summers was a visit to Grandfather's farm; letting a boy do everything under the sun, it seemed, was Grandfather's idea of showing me a good time.
9. I have now been on the campus for eight weeks, and I have long since overcome my fears of meeting new people.
10. The people of that section have been marketing a great quantity of vegetables in the city this summer.
11. The task which he has set himself is too heavy for his limited ability. He has been trying to recover his health, catch up with the class, and do the current assignments all at the same time.
12. Now that he has made a fortune, he is expected to start for Europe within the month.
13. He jumped up and down, he shouted and yelled; and yet, for some strange reason, no one paid him the slightest attention.
14. The men who have been working in the experiment station are trying to develop a plant that will grow in any kind of soil.
15. Whenever my high school friends assembled, we listened to the new records in anyone's collection.

SENTENCES

74.   "Grammatically defined, a sentence consists of a subject and predicate and expresses a complete thought. Yet various kinds of statements express a complete thought without a stated or implied subject or predicate."

This quotation from Section 31, attempting a usable definition of a sentence, is discussed, expanded, and qualified in Section 31, where are included statements giving complete meaning without a subject and predicate and where, in addition, justifiable and unjustifiable sentence fragments are considered and illustrated.

Most statements giving complete meaning contain a *subject* and a *predicate*. The subject is the name of the person (persons) or thing (things) about which the verb makes a statement. The predicate is that which is said of the subject; it contains a verb which agrees with the subject in number and person. Obviously, subject and predicate have to be defined in terms of each other: a statement without a subject has no predicate; a statement without a predicate has no subject. In clear and effective writing, it is worth remembering that participles, infinitives, and gerunds cannot serve as predicates.

A *simple subject* is only the noun or pronoun or series of nouns or pronouns serving as subject; a *complete subject* is the simple subject with all its modifiers. A *simple predicate* is only the verb, verb phrase, or series of verbs serving as predicate; a *complete predicate* is the simple predicate with all its modifiers.

To reinforce your knowledge of grammar, you may find diagraming of value. This is a mechanical device by which you are aided in identifying words as parts of speech, in identifying phrases and clauses, and in indicating the uses or functions in a sentence of these words, phrases, or clauses. These purposes of diagraming are accomplished through the use of lines: horizontal lines, perpendicular lines, slanting lines, curved lines, and dotted lines.

But diagraming, although it seems like a game, is only a *means* to an end, not an *end* in itself; it is simply a device to help you identify and see the relationships between various parts of a sentence.

The parts of the sentence are put on lines in the positions indicated in the following skeleton diagram; the three important parts, subject, predicate, object, are usually put on a horizontal line, and any modifiers are usually placed appropriately on lines underneath.

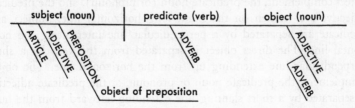

Filled in, such a diagramed sentence might read:

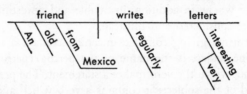

74a. Understand the grammatical classification of sentences in order to obtain variety in your expression of the relationship of ideas.

Sentences are classified—according to number of clauses they contain—as *simple, compound, complex,* or *compound-complex.*

A *simple sentence* contains only one subject and one predicate and expresses only one thought, although part of the thought can contain several related ideas. It could serve as an independent clause if other clauses were added to it. If the simple subject contains two or more nouns or pronouns joined by the proper conjunction, the descriptive term used is *compound subject.* If the simple predicate contains two or more verbs joined by the proper conjunction, the descriptive term used is *compound predicate.*

The simple sentence is excellent for the expression of one idea or two or more simple, uncomplicated ideas.

> Our campus has paved roads. (Simple subject, simple predicate)
> Oaks, maples, and elms line the campus roads. (Compound subject, simple predicate)
> The speaker arose and bowed. (Simple subject, compound predicate)
> My father and mother discuss and settle every important family matter. (Compound subject, compound predicate)
> Alumni, faculty, and students attended the game, cheered the team, and celebrated the victory. (Compound subject, compound predicate)

In a sentence diagram, the simple predicate, the direct object, the object complement, the predicate noun (or pronoun), and the predicate adjective are written on the main long horizontal line. Subject and predicate are separated by a perpendicular line intersecting the horizontal line. The direct object is separated from the verb by a short perpendicular line extending up from the horizontal line. The object complement, the predicate noun or pronoun, or the predicate adjective is separated by a short slanting line extending leftward from the horizontal line. The following four diagrams illustrate the preceding principles and are examples also of how simple sentences are diagramed.

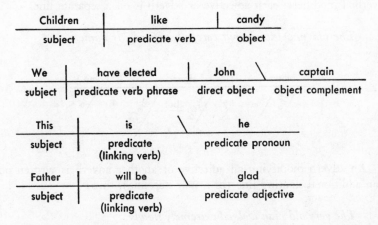

When conjunctions are used, dashes or dotted lines (usually perpendicular) are used to join, and the conjunction is written along or across such a line.

To diagram a simple sentence with a compound subject, compound predicate, and compound object:

Freshmen and sophomores read or write stories and essays.

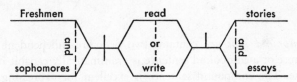

Englishmen, Canadians, and Americans speak, write, and understand the English language.

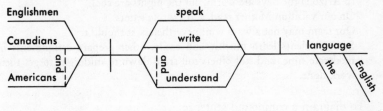

To diagram a sentence containing adjective and adverbial modifiers: Slanting lines below the horizontal line are used for adjective and adverbial modifiers; each adjective or adverb is on a separate line.

The old man slowly but carefully signed his name.

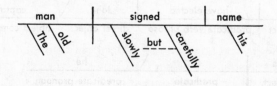

An adverb modifying an adjective or another adverb is written on an additional slanting line (or a stair-step line), thus:

The very old man walked extremely slowly.

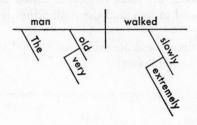

A *compound sentence* contains two or more independent clauses. Each clause of a compound sentence is grammatically capable of standing alone. The compound sentence is excellent for expressing two or more equally related parts of one main idea.

In Arizona the days are warm, but the nights are cool.
On our vacation Mother read, and I wrote letters.
Our team may not always win; nevertheless, it should try.
Some students learn quickly and easily, other prepare assignments in moderate time, and still others toil from dawn to midnight to get their work done.

To diagram a compound sentence:

I like movies, but John prefers radio dramas.

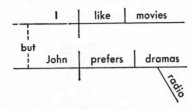

A *complex sentence* contains one independent clause and one or more dependent (subordinate) clauses. The complex sentence is excellent for expressing two ideas, one of which is not so important as the other.

> Leonard is a student who puts his studies above his activities.
> If the weather is fair, we shall go to the lake for the week end.
> Helen said that she had spent four hours writing her theme.

To diagram a complex sentence: Noun clauses usually occupy the position of subject or object; an adjective clause is linked with a vertical dotted line to the noun it modifies; an adverbial clause is linked with a vertical dotted line to the proper word it modifies in the independent clause. Any conjunction expressed is written across the dotted line.

Noun clause as subject:

What you say has convinced me.

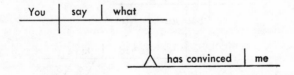

Noun clause as object:

John said that he had studied his lesson faithfully.

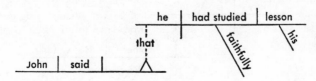

Adjective clauses:

Men who work diligently usually succeed.

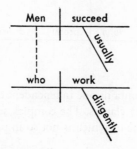

I met a friend whom I like.

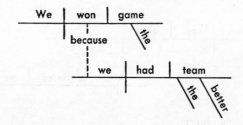

Adverbial clauses:

We won the game because we had the better team.

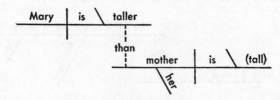

Mary is taller than her mother is.

John drives faster than he should drive.

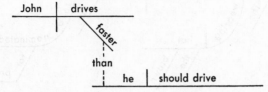

A *compound-complex sentence* contains two or more independent clauses and one or more dependent clauses. The compound-complex sentence is excellent for expressing two equally related parts of one larger idea and one or more ideas not so important as either of the two main ideas.

> Since the day was unpleasant, we spent Sunday indoors; John studied mathematics, and I wrote the first draft of my theme, which is due on Tuesday.

Simple, compound, complex, and compound-complex sentences may and usually do contain various kinds of phrases. Diagraming phrases can be done as follows:

Prepositional phrases are attached below the words they modify by a slanting line for the preposition and a horizontal line for the object of the preposition. Any adjectives modifying this object are, as already indicated, written on a slanting line.

A friend of my father gave me the book with the red cover.
(Note how *me*—the indirect object—is diagramed.)

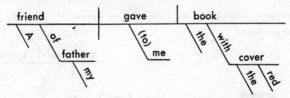

Participial and infinitive phrases (as adjectives or adverbs) are attached to the words they modify by means of a line that curves into a horizontal line. Any objects, adjectives, or adverbs in these phrases are placed as indicated above.

The man wearing the brown hat is the man to be nominated for president.

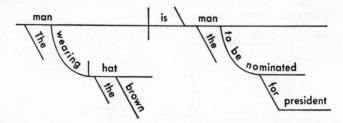

A gerund phrase or an infinitive phrase used as a noun is put on a horizontal line supported by a vertical line placed to indicate whether such phrase is the subject, object, predicate noun, etc. A noun clause or an infinitive "clause" is similarly supported. Within these phrases or clauses, objects, adjectives, adverbs, and the like, are placed as indicated above.

Gerund phrase as subject of a verb:

Occasionally reading a good book is a worthy achievement.

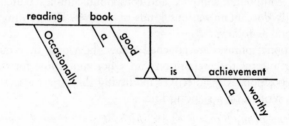

Infinitive phrase as predicate noun:

A precept worthy to be followed by everyone is freely to forgive your enemies.

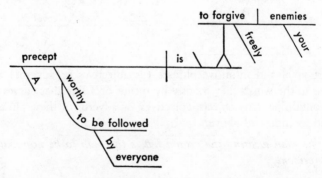

An infinitive "clause":

Henry asked me to lend him my dictionary.

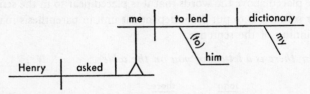

Sometimes a sentence may contain parts in inverted or transposed order; these parts must be put in the proper places in the diagram according to the directions already given.

Never again will John see so exciting a game.

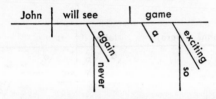

Certain other sentences cause diagraming trouble because we try to fit various constructions into a rigid pattern and order, like subject-verb-object, and often these constructions simply will not fit. Difficult to diagram are sentences containing what seem like independent units, i.e., material not directly modifying any word in the sentence. Such units are absolute phrases, nouns in direct address, and the expletive *there.*

Absolute phrases are placed on a vertically supported line but are enclosed in brackets:

The tire being repaired, we continued our journey.

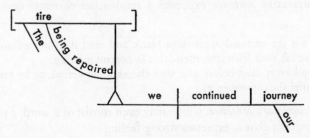

A noun in direct address or the expletive *there* may be placed on a line above the sentence diagram; its position is not important but it could be placed above the words that it is placed near to in the sentence. Another solution is to put the independent unit in parenthesis marks at the beginning of the sentence.

John, there is a letter for you on the table.

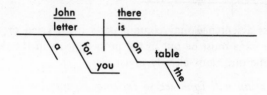

or

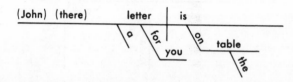

74b. Understand the classification of sentences for the expression of meaning and purpose in clear and effective writing.

Sentences are also classified according to *meaning* and *purpose,* that is, according to the kind of statement that each makes.

A *declarative sentence* makes an assertion or states a fact, a possibility, or a condition.

> This dormitory houses 120 students.
> It may rain before tomorrow.
> If it rains, we must change our plans for tomorrow.

An *imperative sentence* expresses a request, an entreaty, or a command.

> Fill out the enclosed application blank and send it in immediately.
> Please ask your friends to attend this important meeting.
> Attend every class before and after the vacation period, or be prepared to suffer the consequences.

An *exclamatory sentence,* which may even consist of a word, a phrase, or a dependent clause, expresses strong feeling.

Ouch! Stop!
Attention, please! Danger ahead!
Oh, if only you had telephoned!
Thank goodness, you are here at last!

Frequently the exclamatory sentence consists of an exclamatory word + complement + subject + predicate:

How lovely these roses are!
What a brilliant student you have become!
What a busy day we have had!

An *interrogative sentence* asks a question, makes a direct inquiry. It can be written in several different ways:

1. By placing the subject after the auxiliary verb: *Are* you going? *Have* you bought any oranges? *Did* you study last night?

2. By using an interrogative pronoun or adverb: *Who* is it? *Which* is my book? *Where* did you find it? *How* are you?

3. By adding an interrogative statement to a declarative sentence: You have many visitors here, *haven't you?* You did study, *didn't you?*

4. By a question mark after a declarative statement: *You're going home? You've been to the theater?*

74c. Understand the arrangement of ideas in sentences for effectiveness of expression.

Sentences are also classified according to the *arrangement* of their content. Depending upon this arrangement, sentences are classified as *periodic, loose,* and *balanced,* a variety of either the periodic or the loose sentence.

A *periodic* sentence is one in which the words are so arranged that the meaning is not completed until the end or near the end.

A *loose* sentence is one in which a full or moderate completeness of meaning is obtained long before the end of the sentence.

Conversation and informal writing contain many more loose sentences than periodic, because a loose sentence is, probably, a more natural means of expression. Yet a periodic sentence provides suspense and variety; it holds the interest and attention of reader or listener and thus contributes to effectiveness of expression. Although a natural form of expression also, the periodic sentence is less common—hence its effectiveness—but overuse makes for monotony.

Act quickly, or you will be too late to secure the bargain you want. (Loose)

He liked to play baseball and tennis but more than either he enjoyed dancing and ice skating. (Loose)

If you do not wish to go, please say so. (Periodic)

According to a former college president, to be at home in all lands and ages; to count Nature a familiar acquaintance and Art a familiar friend; to gain a standard for the appreciation of other men's work and the criticism of one's own; to make friends among men and women of one's own age who are to be the leaders in all walks of life; to lose one's self in generous enthusiasm and to cooperate with others for common ends; to learn manners from students who are gentlemen and gentlewomen, and to form character under professors who are dedicated—these are the returns of a college for the best four years of one's life. (Periodic)

A *balanced sentence* is so written that similar or opposing thoughts have similar grammatical phrasing. One part *balances* another: independent clause and independent clause, dependent clause and dependent clause, phrase and phrase (see "Parallelism," Section 44); most effective, however, is the use of independent clauses to make statements emphatic through comparisons and contrasts.

Spring is planting time; summer is growing time; autumn is harvest time.

In the morning I attend classes; in the afternoon I study; in the evening I work.

A wise man changes his mind, a fool never.

You can take a man out of the country; you can't take the "country" out of a man.

For further discussion of the sentence, see "The Sentence," Sections 31 to 49.

EXERCISES

A. On a blank sheet of paper, make a column of figures, 1 to 15. After each number, write for the corresponding number of the following sentences whether each sentence is a simple sentence, compound sentence, complex sentence, or compound-complex sentence.

1. Every street in the village is paved with wood blocks.
2. Whenever the postman rings twice, my sister knows that he has a letter for her from Jack.

3. The snow covered the roads to a depth of eight inches, but we had no difficulty in rolling right along.
4. If the gun jams easily, you should notify the corporal, and he will provide you with a new one.
5. Twelve hours is a long while to sleep, but our bodies need such a rest occasionally because we regularly overwork them.
6. Joan and Patricia, eager to make a real contribution to the bazaar, worked from early morning until after midnight.
7. Cheap cars soon begin to consume a great deal of oil, and I know of no inexpensive way to remedy the fault.
8. Literature is often difficult for engineers, it seems to me, because they have spent their youth working with gadgets instead of reading books.
9. Since red-shouldered hawks rarely utter a call, the bird you heard screaming must have been a red-tailed hawk.
10. I will go because you have invited me, but if the orchestra is poor and the girls are stupid, I won't stay late.
11. Why don't we get all the interested men, women, and children of the towns around Midvale to contribute toward the pool?
12. The folly of such wild spending ought to be patent enough, even to people of little education.
13. When I told about my plans, she agreed at once, and so did he.
14. A tornado is a cyclone which has small diameter but great intensity.
15. Hard work seems to have more than personal or social advantages.

B. On a blank sheet of paper, make a column of figures, 1 to 15. After each number, write for the corresponding number of the following sentences whether each sentence is a loose or periodic sentence.

1. Sometimes when we sit down to think things over, we somehow approach a detached attitude as we compose our thoughts.
2. At 5:30 in the evening Fred stepped off the bus about two blocks from his home; then he walked down the street to where his family awaited him.
3. Anyone interested will find that the University of Illinois is located in the twin cities of Urbana and Champaign.
4. As I walked down the east side of the street, I noticed numerous neon signs announcing that I was approaching the town's business district.
5. I put on my skis and started tracking up the side of the hill, in fear and trepidation of what was to come later.
6. Because I get very sleepy right after lunch, I usually take a nap just before my first afternoon class.
7. I recall vividly the little village in the southern part of Missouri, where I lived as a little girl.

8. When I started to write my outline for my research paper, I discovered that I had not investigated my subject very thoroughly.

9. Horse racing, once the so-called sport of kings, has long since become the sport of the common man.

10. Why, I often wonder, aren't parents compelled to lock up mean children just as owners are required to confine vicious dogs?

11. I never liked Uncle Anthony, because to me he represented the terrors of sarcasm and repression, epitomizing a generation as cold and brittle as ice.

12. Student government plays an important part in training young people to be responsible, well-informed citizens of tomorrow.

13. Even though it is customary for a bridge game to cease when the players leave the card table, bridge fanatics insist on a heated post-mortem of every hand played.

14. People of the West, that is, people who have grown up in the culture of Western civilization, have developed a biased view of history.

15. Our train was now coming into Washington, D.C., and I caught a glimpse of the famous Washington Monument.

C. Copy the following sentences with spaces between the lines. Then underline all simple subjects, all simple predicates, all compound subjects, and all compound predicates. Above each indicate what kind of subject (simple or compound) and what kind of predicate (simple or compound).

1. At our Homecoming exercises there have been honored in past years five women and seven men.

2. Nobody knows or cares about my troubles.

3. Our club is having a small party and is inviting a few friends; come early and stay late.

4. My father and my mother have been the best parents that any child could deserve.

5. Father has lent me money for my college education but says that he not only expects but believes that I can repay it and will repay it.

6. All during vacation we swam, played golf, hiked, played tennis, and, in general, just had a wonderful time.

7. A college preparatory course, a commercial course, and a vocational course are the three major courses that our high school offers its students.

8. When Father called and told me the bad news, I hurriedly packed my clothes, called a taxicab, rushed to the airport, and took the first plane home.

9. Unless you now speak forth or forever after hold your peace, the class will never vote for you as their president.

10. Football, basketball, and baseball are major sports on our campus; track, wrestling, fencing, swimming, and golf are minor sports.
11. I stood on the lawn, watched the stars, and wondered what kind of life might be lived there.
12. Suddenly, from every building on the campus, poured the freshmen, sophomores, juniors, seniors, and even the faculty; lunch hour had arrived!
13. There stands the Statue of Liberty, I proudly said to myself.
14. Chicago and New York are hundreds of miles apart but compete in all forms of friendly rivalry.
15. Every morning local delivery men and long-distance truck drivers come in, pick up their assignments, check their cargo, and set out for their destinations.

DIAGRAMING EXERCISES

A. Diagram the following sentences:

1. You may borrow my pen.
2. The Smiths saw many interesting sights on their trip.
3. I am painting my car green.
4. Father has appointed Mary his secretary.
5. You will be our next treasurer.
6. An athletic victory is usually a joyful occasion.
7. The day is becoming colder and more gloomy.
8. Edison has been famous for a long time.
9. Books, magazines, and newspapers are available in the library.
10. Busy people receive and send many letters.
11. Oak, maple, and locust trees grow profusely on our farm.
12. Some students are steady and persevering in their work.
13. Freshmen, sophomores, and juniors made the plans for the reception to the seniors.
14. Every one of us should have something to contribute to a discussion.
15. For most of the afternoon we talked, watched TV, and played bridge.

B. Diagram the following sentences:

1. Henry has worked faithfully to achieve his ambition.
2. Your winning the election so easily surprised everyone.
3. Tomorrow I shall begin taking regular exercise.
4. To recognize one's errors is to take the first step toward improvement.
5. The host invited us to come early and to stay late.
6. That I might have the pleasure of your company is my desire.
7. Father wrote that he would arrive on Friday.

8. We returned to college yesterday, our vacation having ended.
9. The college which I am attending is a small one.
10. I shall bring you the book when I go to the library tomorrow.
11. You must obey traffic rules, or some policeman may arrest you.
12. Father, who is kind and generous, does sometimes lose his temper.
13. My parents usually send me my allowance by Friday of each week.
14. If I were you and wished to improve my grades, I would not spend so much time watching TV.
15. The fancy of a young man turns in the spring to thoughts of love.

    C. Diagram the following sentences:

1. I am looking forward to your coming to the university in September.
2. John wrote to Mr. Brown, who had promised him a job for the summer.
3. Driving carefully on icy roads is necessary in order to prevent accidents.
4. On this wintry day the weather outside is frightful but the weather inside is delightful.
5. Our first item of business today is to call the roll.
6. I am telephoning what I have to say and I shall then confirm it by letter.
7. People who make no provision for the morrow are like the five foolish virgins who are mentioned in the Bible.
8. Charles claims to be a better golfer than I am, but I dare him to prove it.
9. When I received your telegram, I dropped everything and came at once.
10. You should remember that traffic regulations are devised and enforced for the safety of drivers, passengers, and pedestrians.
11. Though I work long and hard, I have difficulty in writing good English themes.
12. Trying to overcome the lead of his opponent was too difficult for the anchor man on our relay team.
13. Students, you need not bring your dictionaries to class unless we have a class theme.
14. Some students come to class so late that the instructor threatens to lock them out.
15. A day to be remembered will be the day when we are granted our diplomas and become alumni of this university.

CASE

75. *Case* is a grammatical term referring to one of the forms that a noun or pronoun takes to indicate its relation to other words. The three cases in English—subjective or nominative, possessive or genitive, objective or accusative—appear in the singular and plural.

In English, case and case endings are less important grammatically than in other languages you may be studying, such as German, Spanish, Italian, Latin, or Greek. For example, English nouns have no distinguishing endings to show the difference between nominative and objective case; in German and Latin, nouns are declined to show endings for nominative, possessive, dative (indirect object), and objective cases (see glossary, Section 85). In addition, Latin nouns have another case called the ablative case, with appropriate endings. In German and Latin, also, adjectives are fully declined, but English adjectives in general take no endings.

The following principles for use of nominative and objective cases rarely apply to nouns but are a guide for use of pronoun forms (see Sections 71d and 75a). Most difficulty comes from case forms of the personal pronouns and the relative or interrogative pronoun *who*. Grammatical problems arise because these pronouns, unlike nouns, have different forms for the nominative and objective cases.

75a.   Learn the different forms of personal, relative, and interrogative pronouns.

PERSONAL PRONOUNS

Singular

NOMINATIVE	POSSESSIVE	OBJECTIVE
1st person: I	my, mine	me
2nd person: you	your, yours	you
3rd person		
masculine: he	his	him
feminine: she	her, hers	her
neuter: it	its	it

Plural

1st person: we	our, ours	us
2nd person: you	your, yours	you
3rd person		
all genders: they	their, theirs	them

When there are two possessive forms of the personal pronoun, the first one given in the list above is followed by the noun it qualifies as a possessive adjective; the second is used alone, as a possessive pronoun.

My book is on the desk; *yours* is on the shelf.

The book on the desk is *mine*.

His appointment is in the morning; *hers* is in the afternoon.

RELATIVE AND INTERROGATIVE

Singular and Plural

NOMINATIVE	POSSESSIVE	OBJECTIVE
who	whose	whom

No change in form occurs in the use of *that* and *which*.

75b.   The subject of a sentence or a clause is in the nominative case.

If the subject is a noun, forget about it. Even the most illiterate American could not get its grammatical form wrong. If the subject is a pronoun, used as the first or even the second member of a compound subject, again only the most poorly prepared college freshman would be confused:

Incorrect: My father and *me* have gone on many a successful fishing trip.

        Himself has been the most desirable roommate that any freshman could ask for.

        As for my mother, Father and *her* have always encouraged me to do my best.

        Whom is speaking, please?

Correct: My father and *I* have gone on many a successful fishing trip.

        He has been the most desirable roommate that any freshman could ask for.

        As for my mother, Father and *she* have always encouraged me to do my best.

        Who is speaking, please?

75c.   A predicate complement is in the nominative case (see Complement, Section **85**).

Predicate complement means a noun (no problem), a pronoun (nominative case, essentially), or a predicate adjective (not an adverb) used after a linking or copulative (coupling) verb (Sections 78, 85). Not nouns, but only pronouns have different forms for nominative and objective. After a coupling or copulative verb the nominative, or subjective case, of pronouns is used, not the objective case.

524

This is *he* (not *him*) speaking.
That is *she* (not *her*) there at the desk.
It was *they* (not *them*) who made the decision.

The foregoing principle applies to the first person pronoun, plural, *we, us,* and to second and third person pronouns, singular and plural, *she, her, he, him, they, them.* Controversy exists over "This is *I*" or "It is *I*" versus "This is *me*" or "It is *me*." In one opinion poll among competent judges, 59 percent labeled the *me* use acceptable. Studies have shown that *both* "It is *I*" and "It is *me*" are avoided by careful speakers and writers in favor of "This is Jones" or "This is he" or a simple "Yes" to the question, "Is this Jones?"

75d. The object of a verb or preposition is in the objective case.

Again nouns, or *it* or *you,* cause no trouble. Only the pronouns—*who* vs. *whom, I* vs. *me, she* vs. *her, he* vs. *him, we* vs. *us, they* vs. *them*—must be carefully observed. Pay especial attention to the cases of pronouns which are used as the second member of a compound object.

The teacher blamed *her.*
This was good news for *us.*
A committee of *us* students is assisting in the planning.
We are inviting both *him* and *her* to go along with *us.*
No disagreement has ever arisen between my roommate and *me.*

75e. The indirect object of a verb is in the objective case.

The indirect object, like the direct object, is a source of trouble only with the pronouns mentioned in 75d. The indirect object is the noun or pronoun before which *to* or *for* is understood.

Give (to) *us* our daily bread.
Write (to) *me* a letter about your plans.
If you do (for) *him* a favor, he will never forget it.
Tell (to) *whom* my story? John? I should say not.

75f. The subject, object, or objective complement of an infinitive is in the objective case.

Infinitives are certain verb forms preceded by an expressed or implied *to.* As with the other principles in this section, pronouns, not nouns, cause trouble.

The fraternity made *him* do that. (Subject of *to do*)
The fraternity caused *him* to do that. (Subject of *to do*)

The class has named *me* to serve as treasurer. (Subject of *to serve*)

Whom did you take *her* to be? (I.e., did you take *her* to be *whom?*) (*Her* is the subject of *to be; whom* is an objective complement agreeing in case with *her*.)

Did you think *her* to be *me?* (*Her* is subject of *to be*, and *me* is an objective complement after *to be*.)

If the grammar in the five preceding examples seems unduly complicated, just pretend that the pronoun is the object of the verb preceding it and is modified by the infinitive. Your writing will turn out to be just as correct. If you write constructions like the foregoing and are puzzled about correcting them, revise and recast the sentence.

NOMINATIVE OR OBJECTIVE CASE

75g. An appositive should be in the same case as the noun or pronoun it explains or identifies.

This principle, again, demands care in use of proper case forms of pronouns.

We, *you* and *I,* are the only candidates with a chance to win. (Nominative)

The dean gave friendly advice to both of us, James and *me.* (Objective)

Last evening the club pledged two additional men, my roommate and *me.* (Objective)

75h. An elliptical clause of comparison, preceded by than or as, requires the case called for by the expanded construction.

An elliptical clause is one with a word or more missing; the omitted word or words are understood from other parts of the sentence (Section 85). If you supply the missing word or words, you should have little trouble about the correct case form.

I am as strong as *he* (is). (Nominative)

You are much taller than *I* (am). (Nominative)

Mother does not drive a car as well as *I* (do). (Nominative)

I do not like her as much as (I like) *him.* (Objective)

I do not like her as much as *he* (likes her). (Nominative)

This TV program amused you much more than (it amused) *me.* (Objective)

This TV program amused you much more than *I* (amused you). (Nominative)

75i. **Who** and <u>whoever</u> are used as subjects of verbs or predicate pronouns; <u>whom</u> and <u>whomever</u> are used as objects of verbs and prepositions.

Many grammatical errors arise from misunderstanding the pronoun forms *who* or *whom* and *whoever* or *whomever*. This discussion supplements and expands that given above, Section **75a-h.**

1. The following sentences illustrate proper use of *who* and *whoever,* nominative forms serving as subjects of the verbs in the dependent clauses:

> I demand membership for *whoever* wishes it (*Whoever* is the subject of the verb *wishes;* the whole dependent clause is the object of the preposition *for.*)
>
> The question of *who* can ask for membership should not arise. (*Who* is the subject of *can ask;* the whole dependent clause is the object of the preposition *of.*)
>
> This book tells *who* is *who* in America, and that one tells *who* was *who.* (Each *who* before *is* and *was* is the subject; each *who* after *is* and *was* is a predicate pronoun.)

In other words, subject of a verb takes precedence over object of a preposition or verb, when pronoun case forms are in question.

2. The following sentences illustrate proper use of *whom* and *whomever,* objective forms serving as objects in the dependent clauses:

> This is the same man *whom* I saw at Oak Bluffs last summer. (Direct object of *saw.*)
>
> Ask *whomever* you desire. (Direct object of *desire;* the dependent clause is the object of *ask.*)
>
> The letter began, "To *whom* it may concern." (Direct object of *concern;* the dependent clause is the object of the preposition *To.*)
>
> Grandfather tells the same yarns to *whomever* he meets. (Direct object of *meets;* the dependent clause is the object of the preposition *to.*)

3. The nominative and objective cases are frequently confused because of intervening words. The case of a pronoun depends upon its use in the sentence and must not be influenced by words which come between the pronoun and its antecedent.

> He asked me *who* I thought would be chosen. (Check by omitting *I thought.*)
>
> *Who* do you suppose drew up these plans? (Check by omitting *do you suppose.*)

I danced with the girl *whom* no one suspected we had chosen "Beauty Queen." (Check by omitting *no one suspected*.)

4. Whenever you are in doubt about *who* or *whom,* substitute *he* or *him* and see which makes sense:

Who/whom are you writing to? (to *who/whom* are you writing?)
He/him are you writing to? (To *he/him* are you writing?)
This is the kind of student *who/whom* we need.
. . . we need *who/whom.*
. . . we need *he/him.*

NOTE: Current-usage studies indicate that the distinction between *who* and *whom* is breaking down, partly because keeping them straight is difficult and partly because many people start a sentence or clause with *who,* not knowing how they are going to end. One dictionary says of *whom:* "the objective case of *who;* in colloquial usage, now often replaced by *who*" (*Webster's New World Dictionary*), i.e., in informal English *who* may replace *whom* when it stands before a verb or preposition of which it is the object. Precise speakers and writers probably will still observe the conventional distinctions of *who* vs. *whom: who* only as subject, *whom* only as object.

POSSESSIVE (GENITIVE) CASE

75j. Use the correct form of a particular noun in the possessive (genitive) case.

Although it is sometimes called the *genitive* case, the usual word in English is *possessive.* In other languages, such as German and Latin, the genitive case has various uses, including the expression of possession. In English the possessive case serves three purposes: (1) to indicate measurement of time or space (see Section **75m**); (2) to indicate ownership, the usual use of the case; and (3) to indicate association with or to identify, as in the following:

My father's profession differs from my grandfather's occupation.
Mark Twain's novels and Edgar Allan Poe's short stories are still enjoyed by millions of Americans.
Colonel Rufus M. Brown is in charge of our Reserve Officers' Training Corps.
New York City's airports are among the busiest in the world.

Misuse of nouns in the possessive case is usually due to carelessness. Many students write the plurals of nouns when such nouns should be in the possessive case, either singular or plural. Although it is a grammatical term, possessive case of nouns in English is formed by a punctuation mark, the apostrophe, according to the principles stated in Section 94a, b, c, d, e.

75k. Avoid awkwardness and incorrectness in the use of the possessive case; use an _of_ phrase instead.

For avoiding awkwardness in showing possession of inanimate objects, for avoiding other awkwardness and incorrectness, and for variety, possessive case is expressed by an *of* phrase. Occasionally and idiomatically, an inanimate object may be in the possessive case (see Section 75m), but the use is usually awkward.

Awkward possession of inanimate objects:
> The *trees'* leaves were turning green.
> The *house's* roof was on fire.
> We pledges waxed and polished the *dining room's* floor.

Improved:
> The leaves *of the trees* were turning green.
> The roof *of the house* was on fire.
> We pledges waxed and polished the floor *of the dining room*.

Both awkward and incorrect is the use of a phrase containing "one of the," then a plural possessive, and then a singular noun. Rephrasing is needed.

Awkward and incorrect:
> The waiter accidentally spilled coffee on *one of the girls' dress.*
> We held our after-graduation party at *one of the boys' home.*

Correct:
> The waiter accidentally spilled coffee on the dress of *one of the girls.* (Or: on *one girl's dress.*)
> We held our after-graduation party at the home of *one of the boys.* (Or: at *one boy's home.*)

Variety (either alternative is correct):
> The home *of my parents* (or: my *parents'* home) is on Laurel Avenue.
> The report *of the committee* (or: the *committee's* report) is due next week.
> The extracurricular activities *of any student* (or: any *student's* extracurricular activities) should not interfere with his studies.

75l.   A noun or pronoun linked immediately with a gerund should preferably be in the possessive case.

The possessive case with a gerund is usually clear, whereas the objective case with the gerund may not be.

Awkward: He resents *you* being more popular than he is.

Most of the members paid their dues without *me* asking them.

The teacher praised John for *him* taking careful notes of the lecture.

We objected to the *girl* being at the football banquet.

Improved: He resents *your* being more popular than he is.

Most of the members paid their dues without *my* asking them.

The teacher praised John for *his* taking careful notes of the lecture.

We objected to the *girl's* being at the football banquet.

When use of the possessive case with a gerund causes awkwardness as, for example, when other words come between the two, recast the sentence.

Awkward: No rules exist against *anyone's* in this class saying what he thinks.

We saw many *students'* carefully taking notes on the lecture.

Improved: No rules exist against any class *member's* saying what he thinks.

Do not confuse the possessive-with-gerund and noun-or-pronoun-with-participle constructions.

Clear: We saw many *students* carefully taking notes on the lecture.

The class members heard their *teacher* asking for greater care in their written work.

The class members responded to their *teacher's* asking for greater care in their written work.

75m.   Use the possessive case to express extent of time or space.

The principle stated in Section **75k** should not be followed implicitly if it produces awkwardness or violates good idiomatic usage. Although inanimate objects are rarely put in the possessive case, good English idiom prefers the possessive case of certain nouns of measure, time, and the like. It is not a question of ownership or possession; it is simply an effective expression of measure, extent of time, etc. Instead of an awkward "of" phrase, the following expressions are preferable and desirable:

a day's work	a dollar's worth
a moment's notice	a stone's throw
10 minutes' walk	at his wit's end
3 years' experience	the law's delay
a summer's work	tomorrow's weather report
2 semesters' study	4 inches' space

For some of these ideas, of course, hyphenated expressions are perfectly acceptable and sometimes preferable alternatives: *a 10-minute walk, a 5-mile drive, a 2-semester course, a 95-yard run* (vs. *a 95 yards' run*).

EXERCISES

A. On a separate page, write a list of numbers 1 to 20. Opposite each number write the correct form of the italicized words in the following sentences:

1. Every student in college will have teachers *who whom* he likes and teachers *who whom* he does not like.
2. My home economics teacher was the person *who whom* I thought I would like to model my life after.
3. Our family's first baby was a girl, *who whom* my mother named Susan.
4. I had four older brothers and sisters *who whom* I had to obey.
5. We marched around the campus with shouts of *who whom* we wanted for our class president.
6. I did not know *who whom* to be more frightened of, the policeman or my father.
7. In a fraternity you live with people *who whom* you want to be your best friends.
8. Our town has a doctor *who whom* we believe is a very clever surgeon.
9. The man *who whom* we were to work with was very pleasant.
10. Nothing on the envelope indicates *who whom* the letter is from.
11. My father always votes for the man *who whom* he thinks would do the best job regardless of party.
12. It is a pleasure to live with a friend *who whom* you can trust.
13. The first thing students do at a party is look around to see *who whom* they know.

14. The hero, *who whom* I thought was essentially shy, finally overcame his shyness.
15. But *who whom* can an only child share his toys with?
16. The actual giving of gifts is less of a problem than *who whom* to give them to.
17. Avoiding accidents often depends on *who whom* drives the car.
18. Next month's issue will answer these football questions: *Who whom* will our team beat? *Who whom* might they lose to? *Who'll whom'll* be the top players?
19. I can't remember now *who whom* I was employed by.
20. My brother was named after a lawyer *who whom,* I suspected, was my mother's childhood sweetheart.

B. Copy the following sentences, correcting all errors in the use of case. Specify each kind of error.

1. I used to put on an act, hoping to make Mother feel sorry for such a small unhappy girl as me.
2. After church our different relatives and us have a reunion.
3. Most people (me included) think of a superstitious person as one who does not use common sense.
4. Our family consists of my parents and their three children: my older brother, younger sister, and I.
5. From his whistle it is easy to tell it is him even before he enters the room.
6. Little brother followed my sister and I in becoming a very stubborn child.
7. Our government officials are chosen by we the people, and the power of government comes from us.
8. One of the fellows introduced my parents and I to other members of the fraternity.
9. I always remember Charles as being taller than the rest of his playmates and me.
10. We—Tom, Jerry, and me—had planned this camping trip for weeks.
11. Voting resulted in my friend being elected vice-president and I being chosen as president.
12. The town across the border is an hour slower than us.
13. This was a portrait of he who was later called the "radiant youth."
14. The guide told us, my father and I, to be ready at 5 o'clock the next morning.
15. Most of we teen-agers are constantly complaining about certain actions of our parents.

16. That experience brought his sister and he closer together.
17. Father talked the situation over with my brother and I and offered us the job.
18. Like you and I, she is a former member of the 4-H.
19. In the last of the six rooms that are occupied live my roommate and me.
20. In the fall of my senior year in high school his parents and him had my brother and I sold on going to college.

C. Copy the following sentences, correcting all errors in the use of possessive case. Explain each kind of error.

1. So far I have completed one semesters work satisfactorily.
2. Slowly we climbed the stage's stairs to receive our diplomas.
3. I spent the week at the home of one of my friends mother.
4. I shall never forget our three months residence in Miami Beach.
5. I really appreciate you sending me to school here.
6. It is the main offices duty to set the example for the different dormitories celebration.
7. Golf is a good way to let off steam after a hard days work.
8. I can remember me saying to my parents that I was now sixteen and should have a car.
9. We decided to take advantage of the cottage's cooking facilities and then go to bed.
10. Whenever we talked together, the conversation would end by us talking about drums.
11. Some say that walking under a ladder will bring seven years bad luck.
12. Everyone is fascinated by the trees' beauty in the autumn.
13. One day I persuaded Father to ride in one of my friends car.
14. What were the reasons for me not studying more in high school?
15. I overhauled my car in two weeks time.
16. October is our most beautiful month, and a great many things account for it being called thus.
17. Some people expect the possession of a rabbits foot or a four-leaf clover to bring them good luck.
18. The dictionarys principal use is still that of supplying definitions of words.
19. On Sundays we have dinner either at one of our relatives house or at our house.
20. We must learn the "how" and "why" of a machines operation before we can use it.

AGREEMENT OF SUBJECT AND PREDICATE

76.   Grammatical agreement means *unison* or *oneness* or *concord* or *harmony* of parts of a sentence. Thus when a subject agrees with its predicate, both subject and the verb in the predicate are alike in having the same *person* (first, second, or third) and *number* (singular or plural).

76a.   **A predicate normally agrees with its subject in person and number.**

Few problems in agreement arise because English verbs (except *to be*—see p. 554) have the same form for singular and plural and for *all* persons except the third person singular present tense. Most nouns and verbs form their plurals in directly opposite ways. Except for special groups, nouns form their *plurals* by adding s or *es: desk, desks; glass, glasses; lady, ladies.* (See Section **71c**.) Most verbs add an *s* in the third person singular. Do not be misled by an *s* sound in the verb. Examine carefully the following forms, 1st, 2nd, and 3rd person singular, present tense:

I do	go	ask	possess	exist	suppose
You do	go	ask	possess	exist	suppose
He does	goes	asks	possesses	exists	supposes
The man does	goes	asks	possesses	exists	supposes

In the plural, with *we, you, they,* the *men,* etc., only one plural form is used: *do, go, ask, possess, exist, suppose,* etc.

Errors in agreement which do occur are serious; they are usually subtle and so the principle—that subjects and predicates agree in number—seems difficult to apply. Usually errors appear when a writer or speaker is confused about the number of the subject because of other words intervening before the verb, or when he uses a verb to agree not with the grammatical form of a subject but with its meaning—as is sometimes logical and acceptable. In short, you need to know what the subject is, whether it is singular or plural, and what its true meaning is.

Section **76a** states the general rule; to understand variations and to avoid serious errors, study the following sections.

76b. **A verb should not agree with a noun which intervenes between it and the subject, when such noun is an appositive or the object in a phrase.**

Wrong: *I,* the delegate, *is* the one to determine the procedure.
The *architecture* of our college buildings *are* beautiful.
The *reason* for the sudden change in plans *were* not apparent.
He, together with John and David, *are* going.
Mary, as well as some members of her family, *were* determined to stay.

Right: *I,* the delegate, *am* the one to determine the procedure.
The *architecture* of our college buildings *is* beautiful.
The *reason* for the sudden change in plans *was* not apparent.
He, together with John and David, *is* going.
Mary, as well as some members of her family, *was* determined to stay.

76c. **Singular pronouns require singular verbs. The following pronouns are singular: <u>another</u>, <u>anybody</u>, <u>anyone</u>, <u>anything</u>, <u>each</u>, <u>either</u>, <u>everybody</u>, <u>everyone</u>, <u>everything</u>, <u>many a one</u>, <u>neither</u>, <u>nobody</u>, <u>no one</u>, <u>one</u>, <u>somebody</u>, <u>someone</u>.**

Each *has* his own money.
Someone *is* speaking now.
One of you *has* made a mistake.
No one *skates* better than Thomas.

76d. **Certain nouns or pronouns are considered singular or plural according to the singular or plural number of the key word in a modifying phrase.**

Examples are *some, all, half, none* (*no one* or *not any*), *what, which.*

Some of my *money has* been lost.
Some of our *students have* been awarded scholarships.
No food is left; *all* of *it has* been eaten.
No students are left on the campus; *all* of *them have* gone home for vacation.
Half of this *building is* to be completed by autumn.
Half of the *buildings* on our campus *are* of red-brick construction.
Which (one) of the rooms *is* reserved for the meeting?
Which (ones) of the rooms *are* reserved for students?

None (literally *no one,* but frequently meaning *not any*) may be followed by either a singular or a plural verb. Studies of the use of *none* have revealed that it is as frequently followed by a plural as by a singular verb, especially when the phrase which modifies *none* contains a plural noun.

> *None* (no one) of the students in our dormitory is a candidate for a class office.
>
> *None* (not any) of our students have recently disobeyed any college regulations.

A tricky subject-predicate combination is one beginning with *what*, a pronoun used in both the singular and plural. When it is used in the sense of *that which*, it has a singular predicate. When it is used in the sense of *those (persons) who* or *those (things) which*, it has a plural predicate.

> *What is* to come is not known.
>
> *What are* known are the things which happened yesterday.

76e. For nouns plural in form but singular in meaning use a singular verb.

The following are nearly always used with singular verbs: *molasses, news,* and *stamina;* a few others may be used with singular verbs: *amends, headquarters, means, summons,* and *whereabouts.* (For the use of *data,* see "Glossary of Faulty Diction," p. 463.) When in doubt about any particular word, especially those words ending in *ics* (*athletics, economics, mathematics, physics,* etc.), turn for guidance to your dictionary, which also has a brief discussion under the suffix *-ics.*

> Good news *was* in yesterday's newspaper.
>
> Politics *has* always been one of Father's major interests.

Subjects plural in form, which describe a quantity or number, require a singular verb when the subject is regarded as a unit.

> Ten miles *is* too far to walk.
>
> Two from five *leaves* three.
>
> Five dollars *was* asked for the lamp.
>
> Three-fourths of a bushel *does* not seem enough.

76f. Use a plural verb, ordinarily, with two or more nouns or pronouns joined by <u>and</u>.

> The house and the automobile *were* both painted green.
>
> Behind the wall *stand* a house and the garage.
>
> Both the secretary and the treasurer *have* agreed to be present.

When the two nouns or pronouns form a single thought or have a closely related meaning or mean one thing or one person, a singular verb is used.

The secretary and treasurer of our club *is* Harrison Thompson.
My oldest pal and best friend *was* my roommate this year.
The sum and substance of the speaker's remarks *has* caused much comment.
My house and home *is* at 1707 Maryland Drive.

NOTE: Idiomatically, two or more singular nouns joined by *and,* but with the first noun preceded by *every* or *each,* take a singular verb:

Every man, woman, and child here is an expert swimmer.
Each boy and girl here has received polio shots.

76g. Two or more singular subjects joined by or or nor or two singular subjects joined by either . . . or, neither . . . nor require a singular verb.

Father or Mother *is* to represent our family at the meeting.
Neither John nor Henry *makes* very high grades.
Either economics or history *is* the course I shall elect next semester.

76h. When the parts of the subject differ in number or person and are joined by or, nor, either . . . or, neither . . . nor, the verb agrees with the nearer subject member.

A European history course or any English courses *are* not among the courses that I like.
Neither the students nor the teacher *wants* to meet at 7 o'clock.
Either some of my classmates or I *am* willing to write the petition.
Either some of my classmates or Bill *is* willing to write the petition.
Either Bill or some of his classmates *are* willing to write the petition.

76i. Relative pronouns referring to plural antecedents require plural verbs; relative pronouns referring to singular antecedents require singular verbs.

Each house has its own elected *officers, who conduct* the business of the house.
Each house has its own *president, who conducts* the business of the house.
Our city has three excellent *beaches, which attract* many of our residents each summer.

Our city has an excellent *beach, which attracts* many of our residents each summer.

My dictionary concludes with some *pages that contain* a list of American universities.

My dictionary has *one page that contains* a guide to pronunciation.

1. A troublesome application of this principle concerns *one of those who* or *one of those which*.

My English teacher was one of those high school *teachers who were* always getting off the subject.

This is one of the most important *events that have* ever occurred to me.

I happen to be one of those *people who like* to travel.

I hope to get a ride from *one* of my friends *who is* driving to Philadelphia.

In sentences like these, check carefully to see which is the *true* antecedent of the relative pronoun. Sometimes putting the *of* phrase first will help.

Of the important sporting *events that take* place each year, the Indiana High School Basketball Tournament is one.

Of those *people who like* to travel, I happen to be one.

2. If *the only* or some similar qualifying words precede *one*, the relative pronoun and the verb are singular:

He is *the only one* of those present *who plays* well.

My English teacher was *the only one* of my high school teachers *who was* always getting off the subject.

3. Sometimes you can determine the antecedent by the proper use of *who* or *which*:

This is a *list* of students *which has* been prepared.

This is a list of *students who have* been invited.

76j.   Forms of <u>to be</u> agree with the subject, not with the predicate noun or pronoun.

In some constructions, between two nouns or pronouns comes some form of the verb *to be: am, is, are, was, were, have been, has been.* The noun or pronoun coming first is considered the subject.

The best part of the meal *is* the coffee and cookies.

Coffee and cookies *are* the best part of the meal.

76k. **After expressions like** <u>there is</u>, <u>there are</u>, <u>there was</u>, <u>there were</u>, <u>there has been</u>, <u>there have been</u>, **and other verbs, the verb is singular or plural according to the number of the subject, which in these constructions follows the predicate.**

There *seem* (not *seems*) to be one book and three magazines missing.
Fortunately, there *exist* (not *exists*) people who can help us.
There *have been* (not *has been*) many exciting games this fall.
At camp there *were* (not *was*) baseball, softball, tennis, and swimming.

The same principle applies when *there* is replaced by other words and the subject still follows the predicate:

In front of our Administration Building *stands* (not *stand*) a towering oak.
In front of our Union Building *stand* (not *stands*) an elm, two maples, and an oak.

NOTE: Sentences or clauses beginning with *there is, there are,* etc., can be correct, but such beginnings are often wordy, ineffective, and avoidable (Section **67c**).

76l. **A collective noun takes a singular verb when the group is regarded as a unit, a plural verb when the individuals of the group are regarded separately.**

Common collective nouns are *army, assembly, clergy, committee, company, couple, crew, crowd, family, flock, group, herd, jury, mob, multitude, orchestra, pair, personnel, squad, team, union.* Most of these nouns also have plural forms: *army, armies; assembly, assemblies; company, companies; crowd, crowds; team, teams;* etc.

Without the *s*, they are considered singular and take a singular verb and singular pronouns when the collection of individuals is thought of as a unit, as a whole; they are considered plural and take a plural verb and plural pronouns when the members of the group are thought of as individuals, acting separately. (For collective nouns as antecedents of pronouns, see Section **77c**.)

Our crew [a unit] *is* going to compete this afternoon.
Our crew [members] *have* been on shore leave and *are* coming aboard in a few hours.
The team *has* elected Robbins captain.
The team *have* been unable to agree on a man for captain.

The family next door *is* named Browne.
The family *were* seated in armchairs on the lawn.

EXERCISES

A. Make a list of numbers from 1 to 15. Opposite each, write the correct form of the verb from the italicized forms in the following sentences:

1. October is my favorite because of the many things there *are is* to do during this month.
2. Homecoming week end we freshmen had to sleep on the floor, for there *wasn't weren't* enough beds.
3. This dam along with the four or five other dams along the river *form forms* part of the network of hydroelectric plants.
4. Neither one of my parents *know knows* much about mathematics.
5. Whenever either of us *has have* a problem, we talk it over until we reach a solution.
6. Liking outdoor work is one of the reasons that *make makes* me want to go back to the farm.
7. The only other equipment you will need *are is* eating utensils, a flashlight, and a pocket knife.
8. The amount that it *cost costs* a person to fly will depend upon the class of travel he chooses.
9. Whenever any one of us *decide decides* to do anything, that person always lets the others know.
10. Water in the form of floods *has have* changed the landscape considerably.
11. The supplementary material in the dictionary *include includes* useful miscellaneous information.
12. Each of us *like likes* to play Santa Claus and give out the gifts.
13. My keeping New Year's resolutions *has have* always failed in past years.
14. I expect to solve the few problems which *confronts confront* me.
15. Some students think a college instructor *don't doesn't* care whether his students learn anything or not.

B. Directions given in A.

1. Clustered around the mill *are is* the restored homes of the early settlers.
2. Each of the houses in this restored village *has have* antique furniture.
3. I hope that neither of these things *happen happens*.
4. I am one of the millions of people who *has have* been bitten by the golf bug.
5. There *are is* in my family my mother, my father, my sister, and I.

6. The second criticism of these letters *concern concerns* the misspellings.
7. There *was were* ham, fried potatoes, eggs, and toast for breakfast.
8. Building model airplanes *require requires* a great deal of time and patience.
9. Great advances in communication, illumination, and power machinery *are is* still to come.
10. Upper Michigan has forests that *cover covers* thousands of acres.
11. The sounds of blaring horns and roaring motors *was were* everywhere.
12. The location of the complimentary close and of the signature *seem seems* unusual in some business letters.
13. Ellen, along with two or three of her friends, *plan plans* to tour the Southwest this summer.
14. Neither the other students nor the instructor *was were* surprised when I came in late.
15. Charles Dickens' greatest achievement *is are* the novels that he wrote.

C. Rewrite the following sentences, correcting the lack of agreement between subject and predicate.

1. Inside this building are many rooms, each of which are decorated in the tradition of some foreign country.
2. Package after package of paper napkins were stuffed into the tiny holes of the chicken wire.
3. This magazine offers no special services, nor do either of its competitors.
4. I enjoyed your advice to foreign students because I am one of your students who is scattered all over the world.
5. My first year of basic courses were completed in a junior college in my city.
6. In the card catalog every book, every author, and every subject are arranged systematically.
7. I have heard how beautiful California is and how many things there is to see.
8. The last main important topic are the rules for spelling.
9. The combination of a good offense and defense make a good football. team.
10. Included in the Air Force program is pilot training, navigation, technical skills, and nontechnical skills.
11. On the basketball court his twisting, turning, dribbling, and faking is enough to confuse just about anyone.
12. My maiden aunts are concerning themselves with things which does not have anything to do with them.

13. I too believe that a thousand words is worth more than a picture.
14. The coffee and rice pudding is brought out at the end of the meal.
15. The fishing party gets into the car and drive 30 miles to the lake.

   D. Directions given in C.

1. Neither Larry nor Dick have any outstanding or even ordinary peculiarities.
2. Just outside the gym is an archery range, a rifle range, and a short golf course.
3. The Clothing Department of our high school is interested in the purchase of sewing machines and have several questions to ask.
4. Poor spelling and bad grammar gives the impression that you are careless or stupid.
5. One of the pleasant features of our city are its fine recreational facilities.
6. The most common faults in this letter collection is the omission of the inside address and the salutation.
7. During the past decade the quality of television programs have increased tremendously.
8. Residence in the dormitories are obtained merely by application and signing of a contract.
9. In this accident, luckily neither of us were hurt.
10. Understanding the importance of English is one of the major things which contributes to your grades in college.
11. Descriptive and narrative exposition have been used in this theme.
12. Preparation for Homecoming festivities begin with the designing of signs.
13. If either of these hours are convenient for a conference with you, I would greatly appreciate one.
14. At the lower left of each letter is the writer's initials and the initials of the typist.
15. At the end of the scene exit the King, the Prince, and the councillors.

AGREEMENT OF PRONOUN AND ANTECEDENT

77.   A pronoun agrees with its antecedent in gender, number, and person, but its use with other words determines its correct case. Since a pronoun (*pro-* means "for") is a word used instead of a noun or a group of words serving as a noun, such noun or noun group—called the *antecedent* of the pronoun—must be unmistakably clear if your reader is not to be misled or confused.

The *woman* put on *her* hat. (Singular antecedent, feminine)
The *women* put on *their* hats. (Plural antecedent, feminine)
The *boy* misplaced *his* tickets. (Singular antecedent, masculine)
The *boys* misplaced *their* tickets. (Plural antecedent, masculine)

77a. Singular pronouns refer to singular antecedents. (See also Section **76c.**)

Has anyone here forgotten *his* dictionary?
The student was lucky to find the dictionary that *he* had lost.
In the new dormitory, each girl will have a room to *herself*.
Every person in favor will please raise *his* right hand.
Everybody is expected to do *his* share.

Since or when the sense of *everybody, anyone,* etc., is *many* or *all,* the plural personal pronoun referring to these indefinite pronouns is frequently found in both formal and informal English: "Everybody is expected to do *their* share of the work." Such use is preferable to the somewhat artificial and even awkward "Everybody is expected to do *his* or *her* share of the work." Notice, however, that a singular, not a plural verb form is used.

77b. A pronoun agrees with the nearer of two antecedents.
Occasionally, two antecedents, different in gender or in number, are in a sentence. With two antecedents and only one pronoun, the pronoun referring to the antecedent nearer to it is used.

He loves anything and everybody *who* is connected with his work.
He loves anybody and anything *which* is connected with his work.
Either the plant or the flowers will lose *their* freshness.

77c. A collective noun used as an antecedent takes either a singular or plural pronoun depending upon whether the collective noun is considered as a unified group or a group of individuals acting separately. (See Section **76l.**)

The crowd of men took off *their* hats. (The *crowd* acted as individuals.)
The crowd shouted *its* approval. (The *crowd* acted as a unit.)

Be consistent in the use of collective nouns with singular or plural predicates and with singular or plural pronouns.

Inconsistent: The class *was* unanimous in *their* choice of a president.
Consistent:　The class *was* unanimous in *its* choice of a president.

Inconsistent: The team *were* unable to agree on whom *it* considered *their* most valuable player.

Consistent: The team *were* unable to agree on whom *they* considered *their* most valuable player.

The team *was* almost immediately ready with *its* choice of *its* most valuable player—Harry Brown, the center.

77d. Do not confuse the relative pronouns <u>who</u>, <u>which</u>, and <u>that</u>.

Who usually refers only to persons; *which* usually refers only to things; and *that* refers to persons or things.

Wrong: The horse *who* stands there is a thoroughbred.

The person *which* you mentioned is away from the city.

(For the use of *that, which,* and *who,* in restrictive and nonrestrictive adjective clauses, see Section **88m.**)

77e. In the use of "I" in a compound subject, politeness suggests that the "I" come last.

The same politeness applies to *we* in a compound subject and to *me* and *us* in a compound object.

Dubious: *I* and my roommate are both studying engineering.

Last spring the fraternity pledged *me* and six other boys.

We and our neighbors have a community picnic each fall.

Preferable: My roommate and *I* are both studying engineering.

Last spring the fraternity pledged six other boys and *me.*

Our neighbors and *we* have a community picnic each fall.

77f. Do not use <u>myself</u>, <u>himself</u>, etc., unless an intensive or reflexive idea is present. (See Section **71d.**)

Incorrect: John and myself can carry it.

Correct: John and I can carry it.

Incorrect: This is a matter that concerns only you and myself.

This is a matter that concerns only you and himself.

Correct: This is a matter that concerns only you and me.

This is a matter that concerns only you and him.

In correcting the error just discussed, do not make a "frying pan" error (a worse error than the original one) by using the wrong case of the personal pronoun.

Wrong: John and me can carry it.

This is a matter that concerns only you and I.

This is a matter that concerns only you and he.

77g. Do not use illiterate forms for reflexive or intensive pronouns.

Such illiterate forms are *meself, mineself, youself, hisself, itsself, ourself* (see dictionary), *theyself, theyselves, theirself, theirselves, themself.*

The correct forms are the following: *myself, yourself, himself, itself, ourselves, yourselves, themselves.* (See Section 71d5, 6.)

77h. Avoid using personal pronouns directly after nouns and referring to them.

Repetition of pronoun after noun is useless for both clearness and effectiveness. (See Section 67a.) Avoid sentences like these:

My friends *they* expected me to go with them everywhere.

Father *he* thinks that sometimes I spend too much money.

Our high school English teacher *she* did more for us than she will ever realize.

77i. Avoid reference of pronouns to nouns in the possessive case.

The use of pronouns referring to nouns in the possessive case is grammatically correct but usually ineffective, since nouns as subjects or objects stand out more clearly. One method of improvement is reversing the case: pronoun in possessive, noun in nominative or objective.

Dubious: In my father's car he has installed two radios.

Mary borrowed her brother's car; he knows that she is a careful driver.

Improved: In his car my father has installed two radios.

Mary borrowed the car of her brother; he knows that she is a careful driver.

77j. Avoid implied reference for a pronoun.

The relation of a pronoun to its antecedent must be clear and unmistakable, except for indefinite pronouns (Section 71d7). The reference word should be placed close to its antecedent in order that no intervening words may cause confusion. A *relative* pronoun must be in the same sentence as its antecedent, but *personal* or *demonstrative* pronouns may be placed some distance away, frequently in other sentences, if there is no intervening noun or pronoun to cause confusion.

Implied reference occurs when the antecedent of a pronoun is not actually expressed but must be inferred from the context. One of the most common forms of implied reference is the use of the pronouns *it, this, that, which* to refer to an entire preceding statement rather than to some noun or pronoun in that statement.

You, as writer, must decide whether such words refer to an implied antecedent or whether their antecedent is contained, paradoxically, in a statement which follows. Frequent occurrence of implied reference is found in the work of many reputable writers, and when confusion is not possible, the use may be effective.

Faults in the implied reference of *it, which, this, that, these, those,* etc., may be corrected by (1) summing up the idea of the preceding statement in a noun which acts as the antecedent; (2) rephrasing the sentence so as to eliminate the pronoun or to give it a clear and appropriate antecedent.

Doubtful: I worked for the FBI last summer and fall and enjoyed *it* very much.

Improved: I was employed by the FBI last summer and fall and enjoyed the work very much.

Doubtful: Tuesday noon I became ill and *it* became steadily worse during the day.

Improved: Tuesday noon I became ill and felt steadily worse during the day.

Doubtful: Sometimes you have many facts and figures to memorize, and *this* can be very difficult.

Improved: Sometimes you have many facts and figures to memorize, a task that can be very difficult.

Doubtful: On the first floor we saw where the fiction books are kept. *This* concluded our library tour.

Improved: When we saw where the fiction books are kept on the first floor, we concluded our library tour.

Doubtful: For a vacation we had everything from camping stoves to sleeping bags. *That* influenced our decision.

Improved: For a vacation we had everything from camping stoves to sleeping bags. That equipment influenced our decision.

Doubtful: I am a trifle lazy, *which* is made obvious by my constant procrastinating.

Improved: I am a trifle lazy, a fact which is made obvious by my constant procrastinating.

Doubtful: I mislaid your address, *which* was the reason why I did not write sooner.
Improved: I mislaid your address, a fact which kept me from writing sooner.
I mislaid your address and therefore could not write to you until I found it.

Acceptable: I could also tell you of my experiences in Alaska, but *that* is another story. (Antecedent follows pronoun.)

Confusion also may arise when *this, that, these, those,* and *such* are used as demonstrative adjectives.

Doubtful: The dean's attitude gave me *that* sinking feeling.
Improved: The dean's attitude gave me a sinking feeling.
The dean's attitude depressed me.
The dean's attitude gave me that sinking feeling which accompanies frustration.

Doubtful: Every summer at Sunset Bay we meet *those* wonderful people.
Improved: Every summer at Sunset Bay we meet wonderful people.
Every summer at Sunset Bay we meet those wonderful people who make the town what it is.

Even the definite article *the* is sometimes misused as a kind of demonstrative adjective. This use is vague and ineffective; either avoid it or amplify it to clearness.

Vague: These island people were evidently in *the* early stage of cultural development.
Improved: These island people were evidently in *an* early stage of cultural development.
or
These island people were evidently in *that* early stage of cultural development which precedes any use of complex machines and mechanisms.

77k. Avoid the indefinite use of you.

In some informal and colloquial writing, an expression such as "*You* can see the importance of money" is permissible, even though *you* may refer to no particular person or group. In general, however, when using *you,* be sure that you mean the person or persons whom you are addressing. For example, the following is inappropriate in a paper designed for reading by an adult: "When you become a Boy Scout, *you* learn many useful things." (See Section **4b**.) If you wish to refer to a number of people in general and to no one in particular, use indefinite pronouns like *one* or *anyone,* or a general noun like *person* or *student.*

Dubious: In high school you should be compelled to do more theme writing.

Preferable: In high school the student should have to do more theme writing.

When a youngster becomes a Boy Scout, he learns many useful things.

For the use of *you* as an appropriate or inappropriate theme beginning, see Section **8g2**.

77l. Avoid the indefinite use of <u>it</u>.

It as a third person singular pronoun, neuter, should usually have an appropriate antecedent. Also, when *it* is used impersonally and acceptably (*it* seems, *it* is possible, *it* is raining, etc.), do not use another *it* in the same sentence to refer to a definite antecedent.

Dubious: In this picture *it* showed some of the dark side of city life.
Better: This picture showed some of the dark side of city life.

Dubious: In this magazine article *it* states that not all wars are victories for the victors.
Better: This magazine article states that not all wars are victories for the victors.

Dubious: Bar Harbor is a beautiful summer resort; we liked *it* very much and *it* is possible that we shall go there again.
Better: We liked Bar Harbor very much as a summer resort, and *it* is possible that we shall go there again.

Dubious: Our roof needs patching, and when *it* rains *it* leaks badly.
Better: Our roof needs patching, and *it* leaks badly in rainy weather.

77m. Avoid the indefinite use of <u>they</u>.

They, their, theirs, them, as plural forms of the third person personal pronoun, should have definite antecedents: plural nouns or other pronouns in the plural. Otherwise, do not use these pronouns.

Dubious: *They* have good roads in Texas.
Better: Texas has good roads.

Dubious: *They* said that Mexico is becoming very popular among tourists.

Better: Many people are saying that Mexico is becoming popular among tourists.

Dubious: We do our shopping in Chicago, for we like *their* large department stores.

Better: We do our shopping in Chicago, for we like the city's large department stores.

Dubious: In my high school *they* had excellent courses in English and mathematics.

Better: My high school had excellent courses in English and mathematics.

77n.   Avoid double reference for a pronoun.

Double reference occurs when two antecedents are possible for a single pronoun. The pronoun reference is therefore ambiguous; instead, the antecedent should be clear and definite.

Ambiguous reference can be corrected by (1) repeating the antecedent, (2) using a synonym for the antecedent, (3) changing the wording of the sentence so that the antecedent of each pronoun is unmistakable.

Dubious: When a salesman hands over an article to a customer, *he* is not always certain of its worth.

Better: A salesman is not always certain of the worth of an article when he hands it over to a customer.

Dubious: The professor told George that *he* should vote in the next election. (Who should vote: *George*? The *professor*?)

Better: The professor said, "I shall vote in the next election." (The *professor* will vote.)

The professor told George of his intention to vote in the next election. (The *professor* will vote.)

The professor advised George to vote in the next election. (*George* should vote.)

The professor told George that he, as a mature student, should vote in the next election. (*George* should vote.)

EXERCISES

A. Correct all errors of disagreement between pronoun and antecedent.

1. We knew where every stream was and where they went.
2. My high school days—ah, if I only had it to live over again!

3. Some high schools do very little to prepare its students for college.
4. When you are in the air, everything looks as though they were little toys.
5. Some people use big words in order to make an impression, but not many know what he is talking about.
6. I am returning the defective glassware by parcel post; will you please replace them and send them to me?
7. I do not know whether this has been the feelings of anyone before.
8. It is good to see the crocus peeping their heads above the snow.
9. Ask a child what Thanksgiving means to them, and they will say it means a big turkey dinner.
10. It is believed that if one carries a rabbit's foot, it will bring them luck.
11. Where is the skilled craftsman of yesterday? Very few of them are left.
12. If students fail to take advantage of the services of the library, he is losing a valuable helper.
13. I am sure that October, November, and December will always be as interesting to almost everyone as it is to me.
14. There are two ways you can judge a person when you first meet them.
15. The buildings are large, and this gives one the feeling that our university is powerful.
16. Concerning your knitting yarns, will you please tell me whether it is mothproof and whether it is dye-fast?
17. May is the month when the different classes have their proms. This is probably the biggest social event of the year.
18. I have heard of teachers who showed no interest in the future of his students.
19. We hear many rumors about different instructors. Some are that he gives terrible exams, or that his lectures are boring, or that he is unfair in grading.
20. Most students know about manners in the classroom and do not have to embarrass himself or the professor by not paying attention.

B. With numbers corresponding to the sentences, make a list of the pronoun forms which are correct in each sentence.

1. One of the reasons for not joining certain clubs is the people *which who whom* make up its membership.
2. I went backstage to visit the director *that which who whom* I had served under in the second play.
3. Two other fellows and *myself me I* were discussing our religions just yesterday.
4. Our college certainly has many alumni of *which who whom* to be proud.

5. In our state, we like to know that we have scores of sand dunes *which who whom* challenge our stamina.

6. A person can drive at high speed on an icy road, and *they he* can end up in a ditch.

7. Most of the college professors have received a doctor's degree in *his their* particular field.

8. Twenty girls, of *which who whom* I was one, boarded the bus for Girl Scout camp.

9. I have two brothers and two sisters *that who which* are all younger than *myself me I*.

10. You should select a major study and a minor or two; *this these* will give you a good deal of knowledge in a given area.

11. Another popular superstition is the curse of black cats *which who* walk across your path.

12. The girl *which who whom that* I marry will have to be attractive, intelligent, and capable.

13. On the island were stationed about 250 men, half of *which who whom* were U.S. Marines and half of *which who whom* were construction workers.

14. Many cars have safety belts now, and if *this does these do* not break, *you have one has* a good chance of surviving a crash.

15. *Yourself you* and *I me myself* should be able to make this project succeed.

C. Correct all errors in pronoun use in the following sentences:

1. Here in college they assume that you know everything that you covered in high school.

2. I have nearly completed one semester of college and I've about had it.

3. The water was crystal clear, which enabled us to see the sandy bottom of the pond.

4. We stopped in at a service station, where he checked the water and oil.

5. In the driving test, most have to make two or more attempts before they can get it properly parked.

6. My brother and myself have done most of the farm work this year.

7. My future includes a girl friend I knew in high school, which I hope to marry some day.

8. As for college, the average student who really works at it can make it through most of the time.

9. I attended the student church last Sunday, where they had a very inspiring service.

10. Proper spacing and margins give a business letter that distinguished look.

11. The characters are all well portrayed. This makes the book much more interesting.
12. The lights dim, the curtain rises, and there you are before an eager audience.
13. My mother and I went to the residence hall, where they showed us to my room.
14. This was an honor which I nor my teacher nor my band director expected.
15. The children were very shy, but that can only be expected.
16. Peanuts are good for me because they put iron in your stomach.
17. Joe, myself, and our other friends usually go swimming together.
18. The end of the semester also means the end of all those dull subjects.
19. A good friend told me that one should never brag about his home town. Let them visit it and find out for themselves.
20. Many times a student holds a grudge against an instructor because he feels he doesn't grade him as he thinks he should be graded.

LINKING AND AUXILIARY VERBS

78.   To write correctly, clearly, effectively, and appropriately, as well as to read satisfactorily, you need an adequate understanding of linking and auxiliary verbs. Such verbs, basic in many foreign languages, are also basic in English.

LINKING VERBS

Most verbs assert action but a few express a static condition or state of being (no action). Most, not all, of these "inactive" verbs are *linking* (or *joining* or *copulative*) verbs. They serve the purpose of coming between, or *coupling,* two substantives or a substantive and an adjective. The substantive following the linking verb is a *predicate noun* or *predicate pronoun* (never a direct object). Nouns cause no trouble; pronouns may present problems (see Section **75c**). An adjective following the linking verb is a *predicate adjective,* for it modifies the subject, not the predicate (see Section **83c**).

The most common linking verb is *to be,* in its various forms of number, person, tense, and mood (for table of these forms, see pp. 554–555; for the meaning of tense, see Section **80**; for the meaning of mood, see Section **82**). Other common linking verbs are *appear, become, feel, grow, look, prove, remain, seem, smell, sound, stand, taste, turn.* Except for forms of *to be,* these other linking verbs are followed by adjectives—rarely, if ever, by pronouns or nouns as predicate substantives. When these verbs are followed by nouns or pronouns as direct objects, they are not linking verbs but imply or express action. They are linking verbs if you can substitute some form of *to be* for them, especially *is, are, was, were.* Of course, some verbs not expressing action, such as *endure, exist, lie, sit, wait,* are not considered linking verbs. In the following examples, the linking verbs are in italics; the words linked are in small capitals.

> My NAME *is* JOHN.
> THIS *is* my ROOMMATE.
> MR. BROWNE *was* my English INSTRUCTOR last semester.
> My ROOMMATE *is* DARK-COMPLEXIONED.
> MR. BROWNE *will be* BUSY tomorrow.
> The WEATHER *seems* (*is*) COLD today; tomorrow IT may *turn* (*grow, become, be*) COLDER.
> The EXCITEMENT *became* (*seemed, grew, was*) GREATER as the game progressed.
> These CLOUDS *appear* (*look, seem, are*) SALMON-COLORED.

78a. Do not confuse a linking verb with a verb expressing action.

Distinguish carefully between the meanings of the same verb word when it asserts action of the subject in one meaning and does not assert action in another; in the latter sense only is it a linking verb, followed by an adjective, not by an adverb (See Section **83c**). Observe differences in the following:

> The river *looks* muddy this morning. (Linking)
> John *looked* steadily at the scene before him. (Action)
> Oranges *taste* sweet. (Linking)
> Mary carefully *tasted* the salad. (Action)
> We do not *feel* bad about our defeat. (Linking)
> In the dark John stumbled against the furniture and *felt* his way carefully across the room. (Action)

78b. Use correct grammatical agreement in a linking verb, the correct pronoun case after it, and, as predicate complement, an adjective, not an adverb.

For correct agreement, see Section **76**; for correct case, see Section **75**; for adjective-adverb use, see Section **83**. Remember that when the linking verb is specifically described, an adverb is used; when the subject is described, an adjective is used.

TABLE II. LINKING AND AUXILIARY VERBS

Principal Parts	TO BE	TO HAVE	TO DO
	be was been	have had had	do did done

INDICATIVE MOOD

Present Tense

	TO BE Singular	TO BE Plural	TO HAVE Singular	TO HAVE Plural	TO DO Singular	TO DO Plural
1st person	I am	we ⎫	I have	we ⎫	I do	we ⎫
2nd person	you are	you ⎬ are	you have	you ⎬ have	you do	you ⎬ do
3rd person	he is (she, it)	they ⎭	he has (she, it)	they ⎭	he does (she, it)	they ⎭

Past Tense

	TO BE Singular	TO BE Plural	TO HAVE Singular	TO HAVE Plural	TO DO Singular	TO DO Plural
1st person	I was	we ⎫	I ⎫	we ⎫	I ⎫	we ⎫
2nd person	you were	you ⎬ were	you ⎬ had	you ⎬ had	you ⎬ did	you ⎬ did
3rd person	he was	they ⎭	he ⎭	they ⎭	he ⎭	they ⎭

Future Tense

	TO BE Singular	TO BE Plural	TO HAVE Plural
1st person	I shall be	we shall be	we shall have
2nd person	you will be	you will be	you will have
3rd person	he will be	they will be	they will have

Present Perfect Tense

	TO BE Singular	TO BE Plural
1st person	I have been	we ⎫
2nd person	you have been	you ⎬ have been
3rd person	he has been	they ⎭

Past Perfect Tense

	TO BE Singular	TO BE Plural
1st person	I ⎫	we ⎫
2nd person	you ⎬ had been	you ⎬ had been
3rd person	he ⎭	they ⎭

NOTE: The present perfect, past perfect, and future perfect tenses of *have* and *do* are rarely, if ever, used as *auxiliary* verb forms, nor are the verbal forms of *do* (doing, done) so used. As *main* verbs, they form these tenses as does any other main verb. See pp. 570–581.

Future Perfect Tense

	Singular	Plural
1st person	I shall have been	we shall have been
2nd person	you will have been	you will have been
3rd person	he will have been	they will have been

SUBJUNCTIVE MOOD

Present Tense

Singular

(if) I
(if) you } be
(if) he (she, it)

Plural

(if) we
(if) you } be
(if) they

Singular

(if) I
(if) you } have
(if) he (it, she)

Plural

(if) we
(if) you } have
(if) they

Singular

(if) I
(if) you } do
(if) he (it, she)

Plural

(if) we
(if) you } do
(if) they

Past Tense

Singular

(if) I
(if) you } were
(if) he

Plural

(if) we
(if) you } were
(if) they

NOTE: The other tense forms, in the subjunctive mood, of *to be, to have, to do* are identical to the corresponding tense forms of the indicative mood.

Verbals (Non-finite Verb Forms)

Present infinitive:	to be	to have
Perfect infinitive:	to have been	to have had
Present participle:	being	having
Past participle:	been	had
Perfect participle:	having been	having had
Present gerund:	being	having
Perfect gerund:	having been	having had

NOTE: Gerunds have the same form as participles, except that there is no past gerund.

AUXILIARY VERBS

78c. Use the correct form of the auxiliary verb with a main verb.

An auxiliary verb "helps out" a main verb; that is, it helps to form some of the tenses and the tone (see Section **80**), the mood (see Section **82**), and the voice (see Section **81**) of the main verb. It may have little meaning of its own, but it changes the meaning of the main verb, which contains the central or "key" meaning of the verb phrase. In the following sentences, the italicized form is an auxiliary verb, the black-type form is the main verb.

> John *has* **gone** home.
> The furniture *will be* **shipped** by express.
> As we *were* **coming** home, we *were* **stopped** by a policeman.
> I *did* **mail** your letters.

The most common auxiliary verbs are forms of *to be, to have,* and *to do*. A table showing the various form of these as auxiliary verbs is given on pages 554–555. Other common auxiliary verbs are *shall, should, will, would, may, might, can, could, must,* and *ought*. Less frequently used are *let, need, used,* and *dare*. (See Section **78h**.)

78d. Never use <u>of</u> as a substitute for the auxiliary <u>have</u>.

The error of *of* used for *have* is frequently made after *shall, will, should, would, may, might, could,* and *must*. Sound, not grammar, causes the error: unless you are careful, you pronounce *have* (as infinitive) and *of* alike; then you might confuse them in your writing—an example of how careful speech helps in correct writing.

Wrong: You should *of* informed me sooner.
    I would *of* lent you the money if you had asked me.
    It might *of* been much worse.
    I could *of* gone yesterday.
    Mother must *of* paid this bill, for she has a receipt.

78e. Use the correct form of the main verb with the auxiliary verb.

Given the principal parts of the main verb (see Section **79**) and knowing the auxiliaries, you can form any desired tense, tone, mood, and voice, if such exist in good English usage. Present infinitive (with or without the sign *to*), past participle, and present participle ending in

556

ing are the parts of the main verb used with auxiliaries. (See Sections 71f and **85,** and tables on pp. 572–573, 584–585.)

78f.   Distinguish between a verb form used as an auxiliary and a verb form used as a main verb.

At least three specific verbs, dependent upon purpose, may be either auxiliary verbs or main verbs. *To be* may be a linking and therefore main verb, or it may help to express the progressive tone or the passive voice; *to have,* the auxiliary in the perfect tenses, and *to do,* expressing emphasis in the present and past tenses, are also used as main verbs. Notice the differences in the following:

> His name *was* John. (Main verb)
> He *was* named John. (Auxiliary verb)
> He *was* telephoning when I came. (Auxiliary verb)
> I *have* no money. (Main verb)
> I *have* lost my money. (Auxiliary verb)
> She *does* her work well. (Main verb)
> She *does* spend her money foolishly. (Auxiliary verb)

For the various meanings of *have* and *do* as main verbs, see your dictionary.

78g.   Do not use the same verb form to serve as both auxiliary verb and main verb.

Incorrect: His name *was* John and given him by his grandfather.
            She *does* her work well but spend money foolishly.
Correct: His name *was* John, and it *was* given him by his grandfather.
            She *does* her work well, but she *does* spend foolishly the money that she earns.

78h.   Use the correct auxiliary verb.

The meanings of the commonly used auxiliary verbs are in your dictionary. These verbs and their uses are as follows:

1. *to be*—
    used in all tenses in forming the progressive tone and the passive voice. (See Section **80b** and **81a.**)
2. *to have*—
    used in the present perfect, past perfect, and future perfect tenses; also in the perfect infinitive and the perfect participle. (See Section **80b.**)

3. *to do*—

     used to express emphasis (emphatic tone) in the present and past tenses. (See Section **80b.**)

     used to avoid repetition of a verb or full verb expression: "John slept as soundly as I *did*." "I shall go when you *do*."

4. *shall*—

     used as the precise auxiliary for the first person, future and future perfect tenses (but see pp. 575–576).

     used in the second and third persons to express command or determination: "You *shall* not fool me again."

5. *will*—

     used as the precise auxiliary for the second and third persons, future and future perfect tenses (but see pp. 575–576).

     used in all three persons to express willingness or consent: "I *will* write you tomorrow."

     used in the first person to indicate determination or resolution: "We *will* rush your order immediately."

6. *should*—

     used as a kind of "past" tense of *shall*, in the first person, but weaker in emphasis: "I *should* prefer not to come." "I *should* not judge him harshly."

     used frequently in a conditional meaning: "If I *should* decide, I shall let you know." "If John *should* call, tell him to leave a message."

     used in all three persons to express duty or propriety or necessity: "You *should* attend class regularly." "He *should* be ashamed of himself."

     used in all three persons to express expectation: "By dusk we *should* be halfway to St. Louis." "Mary *should* arrive home by noon if she left early this morning."

7. *would*—

     used as a kind of "past" tense of *will*, in the second and third persons, but less strong in meaning: "You *would* not recognize him."

NOTE: If the verb in the independent clause is in the past tense, use *would* to express futurity in the dependent clause; if the verb in the independent clause is in the present tense, use *will* in the dependent clause: "Henry *said* that he *would* go." "Henry *says* that he *will* go."

used frequently in a conditional meaning, or after a conditional clause: "If you *would* consent, everyone would be happy." "If the weather were good, he *would* walk in the park."

used to express determination: "He *would* do it, no matter how much we protested."

used in all three persons to express repeated or habitual action: "Last summer I *would* read three books every week."

used infrequently to express wish or desire: "*Would* that I had gone with you!"

8. *may*—

used to express permission: "*May* I borrow your book?" "You *may* have it until tomorrow." "If I *may* say so, the idea is absurd."

used to express probability or a wish: "It *may* rain tomorrow." "*May* your college years be happy ones!"

9. *might*—

used as a kind of "past" tense of *may* to express the same ideas of possibility or probability in a weaker manner: "You *might* find the address in the telephone directory."

10. *can*—

used to express ability or power or the idea of "being able to": "I *can* come at 6 o'clock." "He *can* do anything that you *can*."

11. *could*—

used as a kind of "past" tense of *can* to express the same ideas in a weaker manner: "John *could* not do all the assigned work."

12. *must*—

used to express obligation or compulsion: "Every man *must* do his part." "You *must* have your report in by next week."

used to express reasonable certainty: "John left for Louisville this morning, and he *must* be there by now." "It *must* be about ten o'clock."

13. *ought*—

used to express duty or obligation, one of the few auxiliary verbs followed by the sign of the infinitive (*to*) with the main verb: "You *ought* to write letters to your friends more frequently." "Everyone *ought* to pay his bills promptly."

NOTE: *Have* and *had* are never used before *ought* or *must*.

Wrong: I *had ought* to start studying.

Right: I *ought to have started* studying an hour ago.

14. *let*—

used to express the ideas of "allowing" or "permitting," "suggesting," "ordering": "*Let* me think a minute." "*Let* me call you tomorrow." "*Let's* go to the movies." "*Let* the man have his money."

15. *need*—

used to express necessity or obligation: "I *need* not tell you the reasons." "You *need* bring only your pen and theme paper."

NOTE: As auxiliary verb, 3rd person singular form is also *need:* "He *need* not doubt my word."

16. *used*—

in the past tense only, *used* expresses custom or habitual action: "On my vacation I *used* to lie in the sun for hours." "It *used* to rain every day in the mountains."

17. *dare*—

used, usually with *say,* to express probability: "I *dare* say it will be a good game." "I *dare* say you're right."

EXERCISES

A. In the following sentences, indicate which verbs are linking verbs and which express action:

1. Everyone was glad that the sea remained calm during our voyage.
2. The sentry, standing silently at attention, appeared statuesque.
3. On a bright Sunday morning, church bells sound peaceful and beautiful.
4. Farmers have never seen crops grow so rapidly.
5. If the water turns rough, we shall turn around rapidly and head for shore.
6. The runner seemed stronger at the finish than at the beginning.
7. The dog smelled the bone indifferently.
8. When you have a cold, you certainly feel bad.
9. You have misspelled five words; you are becoming careless.
10. As a good chef Henry tasted the unsavory mess wryly.
11. You surely look good to me.
12. When you lose an argument, you feel certain that you are miserable.
13. Put the dog outside; he smells.
14. The fighter looked sure of himself after the first round.
15. On a cold day a cup of hot coffee smells good and tastes better.

B. From the following sentences, list all the linking and auxiliary verbs. If the verb is an auxiliary verb, indicate the purpose that it serves or the meaning that it expresses.

1. Let everyone express an opinion; it will do us all good.
2. If the dean does not hear about this, no one need worry about excuses, I dare say.
3. I ought to go now; I should have gone an hour ago, don't you think?
4. Harry used to think he was a good golfer; now he is not so sure.
5. I did write carefully and my writing was legible, but I must have forgotten to proofread.
6. Must you go? You have not been here long.
7. We should have won the relay race; in fact, we might have won it if our anchor man had not stumbled on the last lap.
8. You may borrow my car, but can you drive it?
9. The roses are fresh and fragrant today, but by next week they will be wilted.
10. I will never permit a friend of mine to be without money.
11. Some people should buy a book of etiquette; they could certainly profit by reading it.
12. When I was a boy, Mother would serve us fried chicken at least once a week.
13. Have you tried hot lemonade? It might help you.
14. I shall be bowling this evening, but I can help you with your chemistry tomorrow morning.
15. One ought to obey traffic regulations; otherwise, he may find himself involved with an officer of the law.

PRINCIPAL PARTS OF VERBS

79. Knowing principal parts of verbs and using proper auxiliary verbs (see Section **78c, d, e, f, g, h**) when necessary, you can express both a great variety of meaning and precise shades of meaning. This variety is made possible through the proper use of tense (Section **80**) and of active and passive voice (Section **81**). Errors in tense and voice are often due to insufficient knowledge of the principal parts of verbs.

In every language, verbs have principal parts, sometimes three, as in German, sometimes five, as in French, Spanish, and Italian. The English verb has three principal parts: *present tense* (present infinitive), *past tense,* and *past participle.* Example: *see, saw, seen.* An excellent way to recall the principal parts of a verb is to substitute those of any verb for the following:

I *see* today.	I *work* today.
I *saw* yesterday.	I *worked* yesterday.
I *have seen* every day this week.	I *have worked* every day this week.

Almost a principal part and a necessary verb form is the present participle, formed by adding *ing* to the present infinitive form. This "fourth" part, if in any way irregular, is given in your dictionary. Examples: *seeing, working, doing, beginning, choosing, raising.* The present participial form has constant use both as part of the predicate and as adjective (see Section 71f).

79a. Add the proper endings, d, ed, or t, to form the past tense and past participle of regular verbs.

The past tense and past participle of *most* English verbs are formed by adding the endings *d, ed,* or *t* to the present infinitive: *move, moved, moved; walk, walked, walked; mean, meant, meant.* Any comparatively recent verb added to our language also forms its principal parts with these endings: *telegraph, telegraphed, telegraphed; telephone, telephoned, telephoned; radio, radioed, radioed.*

Verbs forming their principal parts by adding endings *d, ed,* or *t* are called *regular* verbs (or *weak* verbs). Notice that past tense and past participle forms are alike. When in doubt, look up the verb in your dictionary. If no additional forms follow the main entry, the past tense and past participle are formed with the endings *d, ed,* or *t.* Otherwise, the past tense and past participle, and even the present participle, are given immediately after the verb.

79b. Do not carelessly omit the ending of a regular verb, d, ed, or t, in the past tense or past participle.

Since regular verbs form past tense and past participle by adding the endings *d, ed,* or *t,* omitting these endings from these forms is a serious error in grammar. Common trouble-causers are *attack, ask, prejudice, suppose, use.*

Wrong: We are *suppose* to get our work in on time.
Last week I *ask* for permission to miss one class.
These children *use* to swim every day; now they are completely *use* to the water.
We should not be *prejudice* against those who don't agree with us.

Right: We are *supposed* to get our work in on time.

Last week I *asked* for permission to miss one class.

These children *used* to swim every day; now they are completely *used* to the water.

We should not be *prejudiced* against those who don't agree with us.

79c. Use your dictionary to find the principal parts of irregular verbs.

Irregular verbs, many of which are sometimes called *strong* verbs, are verbs which form their past tense and past participle by a vowel change within the verb as well as by the occasional addition of an ending: *see, saw, seen; do, did, done; give, gave, given; throw, threw, thrown; sleep, slept, slept.* A few have the same form for all three parts: *cut, cut, cut; burst, burst, burst; hurt, hurt, hurt; put, put, put.* All told, there are about 375 irregular verbs in English—survivals from the Anglo-Saxon language used in England one thousand years ago.

Principal parts of any irregular verb are given in your dictionary, your safest guide. Immediately after the entry word are the past tense, past participle, and present participle; any alternate forms are given also.

79d. Check carefully to see that you are using correctly the principal parts of commonly used regular and irregular verbs.

The following verbs, some regular, most of them irregular, are especially troublesome. Study them carefully; put them into the three expressions mentioned above on page 562; memorize them. If other regular or irregular verbs cause you trouble, copy their principal parts from your dictionary and memorize them also.

1.	arise	arose	arisen
2.	ask	asked	asked
3.	attack	attacked	attacked
4.	bear	bore	borne (born—given birth to)
5.	beat	beat	beaten
6.	become	became	become
7.	begin	began	begun
8.	bend	bent	bent
9.	bid	bid	bid (as in an auction)
10.	bid	bade, bid	bidden, bid (as in a command)
11.	bind	bound	bound
12.	bite	bit	bitten

13. bleed	bled	bled
14. blend	blended, blent	blended, blent
15. blow	blew	blown
16. break	broke	broken
17. bring	brought	brought
18. build	built	built
19. burn	burned, burnt	burned, burnt
20. burst	burst	burst
21. buy	bought	bought
22. cast	cast	cast
23. catch	caught	caught
24. choose	chose	chosen
25. climb	climbed	climbed
26. come	came	come
27. creep	crept	crept
28. cut	cut	cut
29. deal	dealt	dealt
30. dig	dug	dug
31. dive	dived, dove	dived
32. do	did	done
33. drag	dragged	dragged
34. draw	drew	drawn
35. dream	dreamed, dreamt	dreamed, dreamt
36. dress	dressed, drest	dressed, drest
37. drink	drank	drunk, drunken (see your dictionary)
38. drive	drove	driven
39. drown	drowned	drowned
40. drug	drugged	drugged
41. dwell	dwelt, dwelled	dwelt, dwelled
42. eat	ate	eaten
43. fall	fell	fallen
44. feed	fed	fed
45. feel	felt	felt
46. fight	fought	fought
47. find	found	found
48. flee	fled	fled
49. flow	flowed	flowed
50. fly	flew	flown
51. fly (baseball)	flied	flied
52. forecast	forecast, forecasted	forecast, forecasted
53. forget	forgot	forgotten, forgot

54. forsake	forsook	forsaken
55. freeze	froze	frozen
56. get	got	got, gotten
57. give	gave	given
58. go	went	gone
59. grind	ground	ground
60. grow	grew	grown
61. hang (object)	hung	hung
62. hang (person)	hanged	hanged
63. happen	happened	happened
64. hear	heard	heard
65. help	helped	helped
66. hide	hid	hidden
67. hit	hit	hit
68. hold	held	held
69. hurt	hurt	hurt
70. keep	kept	kept
71. kneel	knelt, kneeled	knelt, kneeled
72. know	knew	known
73. lay	laid	laid
74. lead	led	led
75. learn	learned, learnt	learned, learnt
76. leave	left	left
77. lend	lent	lent
78. let	let	let
79. lie (falsehood)	lied	lied
80. lie (recline)	lay	lain
81. light	lighted, lit	lighted, lit
82. loose	loosed	loosed
83. lose	lost	lost
84. make	made	made
85. mean	meant	meant
86. meet	met	met
87. pass	passed	passed, past (see dictionary)
88. pay	paid	paid
89. plead	pleaded, plead, pled	pleaded, plead, pled
90. prejudice	prejudiced	prejudiced
91. prove	proved	proved, proven
92. put	put	put
93. raise	raised	raised
94. read	read	read
95. ride	rode	ridden

96. ring	rang	rung
97. rise	rose	risen
98. run	ran	run
99. say	said	said
100. see	saw	seen
101. seek	sought	sought
102. sell	sold	sold
103. send	sent	sent
104. set	set	set
105. shake	shook	shaken
106. shine	shone	shone
107. shoot	shot	shot
108. show	showed	shown, showed
109. shrink	shrank, shrunk	shrunk
110. sing	sang	sung
111. sink	sank, sunk	sunk (see your dictionary)
112. sit	sat	sat
113. sleep	slept	slept
114. smell	smelled, smelt	smelled, smelt
115. speak	spoke	spoken
116. speed	sped, speeded	sped, speeded
117. spell	spelled, spelt	spelled, spelt
118. spend	spent	spent
119. spoil	spoiled, spoilt	spoiled, spoilt
120. spring	sprang, sprung	sprung
121. stand	stood	stood
122. steal	stole	stolen
123. stick	stuck	stuck
124. sting	stung	stung
125. stride	strode	stridden
126. strike	struck	struck, stricken
127. string	strung	strung
128. strive	strove, strived	striven, strived
129. suppose	supposed	supposed
130. swear	swore	sworn
131. sweep	swept	swept
132. swim	swam	swum
133. swing	swung	swung
134. take	took	taken
135. teach	taught	taught
136. tear	tore	torn

137. tell	told	told
138. think	thought	thought
139. thrive	throve, thrived	thrived, thriven
140. throw	threw	thrown
141. tread	trod	trodden, trod
142. use	used	used
143. wake	waked, woke	waked, woken
144. wear	wore	worn
145. weep	wept	wept
146. win	won	won
147. wind	wound	wound
148. work	worked, wrought	worked, wrought
149. wring	wrung	wrung
150. write	wrote	written

79e. Do not confuse an irregular with a regular verb.

For centuries, most strong and weak verbs in English have kept the principal parts that they now have. Only in a few isolated instances has a strong or irregular verb changed to weak or regular (*help, holp, holpen* to *help, helped, helped*) or a weak verb added an alternative strong-verb ending (*prove, proved, proved* or *proven*).

Confusion or carelessness may cause you to add regular-verb endings to irregular verbs or to treat an occasional regular verb like an irregular verb.

Wrong: I was *borned* on a small farm in Ohio.

All my early years were *pasted* there, and these *pasted* years were the happiest I have lived.

Once I was *losted* in downtown Atlanta.

In our drawing class we *drawed* plans for several new buildings.

The trouble with these shirts is that they have *shrinked* too much.

These are errors in verb forms; they can also be considered illiteracies—errors in diction or word choice (see Section 57).

Right: I was *born* on a small farm in Ohio.

All my early years were *passed* there, and these *past* years were the happiest I have lived.

Once I was *lost* in downtown Atlanta.

In our drawing class we *drew* plans for several new buildings.

The trouble with these shirts is that they have *shrunk* too much.

567

79f. **Do not misuse the past tense for the past participle, or the past participle for the past tense.**

The confusion of the past tense with the past participle is a serious grammatical error. Avoid it by memorizing the principal parts of all verbs used or, when in doubt, by consulting a dictionary.

Past tense wrongly used for past participle:

> We have *did* the best we could.
> We can skate tomorrow; the lake has *froze* over.
> Our second semester has already *began*.

Past participle wrongly used for past tense:

> I *seen* my duty and I *done* it.
> That night our Glee Club *sung* like angels.
> I *drunk* two cups of strong coffee to keep awake.

You may be helped by remembering that in predicates and other verb phrases, past tense forms are not preceded by auxiliary verbs and that past participle verb forms are preceded by auxiliary verbs.

Right:　The Army is *to attack;* the city is *to be attacked.*
　　　　Mother and Father *use* good English; I *am used* to hearing good English.
　　　　Three Boy Scouts *swam* across the river today; three others *had swum* across it last week.

EXERCISES

A. From each of the following sentences, make a list of the correct forms of the verb.

1. Some of the older buildings on the campus are being *tore torn* down.
2. Our team was *beaten beat* badly last Saturday.
3. The bread was *cast casted* to the fish.
4. Before the teacher had *spoken spoke* a word, he drank a glass of water.
5. The man was sentenced to be *hung hanged* on October 15.
6. Clark pulled off his clothes and *jump jumped* into the icy water.
7. The teacher saw immediately that I had *brung brought* the book.
8. I have *swum swam* across the lake nine times this summer.
9. She was so exhausted that she *laid lay* down to rest.
10. After a little while it *began begun* to rain.
11. The bell for assembly has already *rang rung* twice.

12. He *sprung sprang* into the saddle and galloped away.
13. Our captain has *drawn drew* the pole position.
14. He struck a blow that would have *felled fallen* a heavyweight boxer.
15. *Set sit* the book on the table and *set sit* down.

B. Give the correct forms of the verbs that appear in parentheses in the following sentences.

1. During the evening we were many times (bite) by mosquitoes.
2. He wasn't sure when he should have (sow) the wheat.
3. My teacher (lead) me into reading many good books.
4. For such simple questions every student should have (know) the answers.
5. It is not easy to remember how much money one has (give) to people who have (come) to the door.
6. No one wants to be (see) in his company.
7. Don't leave your books (lie) around; they may be (steal).
8. The twins were (bear) last Sunday morning.
9. The horse should easily have (spring) over the barrier.
10. Children like to have pictures (hang) on the walls of their rooms.
11. His shirts had (shrink) to the point of being almost unwearable.
12. Some students never have (bear) their share of responsibilities.
13. Crowds used to come to watch a man get (hang).
14. John has (dive) from the highest platform many times.
15. You should not have (lend) him so much money.

C. Correct all errors in the use of regular verbs in the following sentences:

1. In high school we were not use to such long assignments.
2. The plan seemed simple, and I was determine to adhere to it.
3. We couldn't have ask for any worse weather than we got.
4. When I finish basic work, I plan to enroll in some advance courses.
5. The most recent thing that has happen to me is an invitation to a dance.
6. I hope that I have consider everything in making out my list.
7. After that ceremony, a red-hair girl is crowned queen for the year.
8. I do not always use the right words where I am suppose to use them.
9. I am finding it difficult to become accustom to some of the regulations.
10. How a roommate can help you or harm you can be exemplify by numerous situations.
11. One morning we were awaken by the barking of our dog.
12. Two years ago our summer term was shorten to eight weeks.
13. In order to learn a foreign language, the student is subject to a somewhat different learning process.

14. It has been prove that handicapped people work as well as those not handicapped.
15. After a while we can become use to almost anything.

D. Correct all errors in the use of irregular verbs in the following sentences:

1. The game had began before we arrived.
2. I cannot say that 13 has always be luck for me.
3. His mouth seems to be froze in a half-hearted sneer.
4. Thanksgiving is now past, and never before have I ate so much.
5. During the year we gave two student-casted plays.
6. Not getting rid of excess energy could have lead to a nervous breakdown.
7. Overnight we became a basketball power, and all because we had beat the favorites.
8. Our teacher would read us stories that some of the students had wrote.
9. We were in New York for four days, and we seen most of the town around Times Square.
10. We all had drank some hot coffee before we started.
11. My mother had went to great lengths to prepare a good Thanksgiving dinner.
12. On the first play of the second half, our star halfback got his ankle broke.
13. Individuals and nations have either rose or fell on their sincere belief in superstitions.
14. All things considered, I must chose the lesser of the two evils.
15. In some of the parks in our city, people are not forbid to walk on the grass.

TENSE AND TONE

80.   Tense indicates time of the action or time of the static condition expressed by a verb. Three divisions of time, *past, present,* and *future,* are shown by six tenses in English: *present tense, past tense, future tense, present perfect tense, past perfect tense, future perfect tense.*

Within some tenses, verbs also have certain "tones" which express precisely what the writer wishes to say: *simple tone, progressive* or *continuing tone,* and *emphatic tone.*

English, unlike a highly inflected language such as German or Latin, has few distinctive tense *forms,* verbs with change of endings to indicate time. Instead, English tenses are revealed mainly through auxiliary verbs, and only occasionally by a verb ending.

Students frequently have difficulty in using tenses, but such difficulty is caused by ignorance of the functions of the six tenses, by the writer's not thinking out carefully the *time* expressed in his ideas, and by his not spending the small amount of effort necessary to learn how in English the various tenses and tones are formed.

Study carefully the following comments on the meaning of time in each tense and on the formation of tenses and tones. Study also Table III, pages 572–573.

80a. Use the correct tense to express precise time.

The first three tenses are *present tense, past tense,* and *future tense—* sometimes called primary tenses:

1. *Present tense* indicates that the action or condition is going on or exists *now.*

> A careful driver *watches* the road constantly.
> Our team *is playing* in Philadelphia today.
> Mary *does make* a nice appearance.

2. *Past tense* indicates that an action or condition took place or existed at some definite time in the past—before *now.*

> As we *drove,* we *watched* the road constantly.
> Our team *was playing* in Cleveland yesterday.
> Mary *did appreciate* the compliment.

3. *Future tense* indicates that action will take place, or that a certain condition will exist, in the future—after the present, after *now.*

> We *shall arrive* in Pittsburgh tomorrow.
> Our team *will be playing* in Pittsburgh on Tuesday.
> The weather *will be* warmer by mid-July.

The other three tenses—*present perfect, past perfect,* and *future perfect*—are called *secondary* or *compound* or *perfect* tenses. The key word is *perfect* or *perfected,* in the sense of *completed.* In these tenses

571

TABLE III. To see, INDICATIVE MOOD, ACTIVE VOICE

Principal Parts: see saw seen

	Singular			Plural	
	Simple	Progressive	Simple		Progressive

Present Tense

1st person	I see	am seeing
2nd person	you see	are seeing
3rd person	he sees (she, it)	is seeing

1st person	we |	are seeing
2nd person	you } see	
3rd person	they |	

Past Tense

1st person	I |	was seeing
2nd person	you } saw	were seeing
3rd person	he |	was seeing

1st person	we |	were seeing
2nd person	you } saw	
3rd person	they |	

Future Tense

1st person	I shall see	shall be seeing
2nd person	you will see	will be seeing
3rd person	he will see	will be seeing

1st person	we shall see	shall be seeing
2nd person	you will see	will be seeing
3rd person	they will see	will be seeing

Present Perfect Tense

1st person	I have seen	have been seeing
2nd person	you have seen	have been seeing
3rd person	he has seen	has been seeing

1st person	we |	have been seeing
2nd person	you } have seen	
3rd person	they |	have been seeing

Past Perfect Tense

1st person	I	} had seen	had been seeing
2nd person	you		
3rd person	he		
	we	} had seen	had been seeing
	you		
	they		

Future Perfect Tense

1st person	I shall have seen	shall have been seeing
2nd person	you will have seen	will have been seeing
3rd person	he will have seen	will have been seeing
	we shall have seen	we shall have been seeing
	you will have seen	you will have been seeing
	they will have seen	they will have been seeing

Verbals (Non-finite Verb Forms)

	Simple	Progressive
Present infinitive:	to see	to be seeing
Perfect infinitive:	to have seen	to have been seeing
Present participle:	seeing	(none)
Past participle:	seen	(none)
Perfect participle:	having seen	having been seeing
Present gerund:	seeing	(none)
Perfect gerund:	having seen	having been seeing

NOTE: Gerunds have the same form as participles, except that use of a past gerund is rare: "The battlefield was filled with the *injured* and *the slain*," i.e., really a form of ellipsis for "the injured and the slain soldiers."

The action or condition has begun.
The action or condition begins.
The action or condition has continued.
The action or condition continues.
The action or condition will continue.
and, in addition,
The action or condition has just been completed.
The action or condition is being completed.
The action or condition will be completed by a certain stated or implied period.

4. *Present perfect tense* indicates that an action or condition was begun in the past and has just been completed or is still going on. The present perfect tense presupposes some relationship with the present.

> You *have been* very ill. (Illness has just ended.)
> The ice on the lake *has melted*. (The melting has just been completed.)
> The class *has been writing* steadily for an hour. (The writing began an hour ago and is still going on.)

5. *Past perfect tense* indicates that an action or condition was begun at some point in the past and was completed at some point in the past, or has just been completed. It presupposes some action or condition expressed in the past tense, to which it is related.

> The roads were impassable because the snow *had fallen* so fast. (The falling of the snow *began* in the *past* and *ended* in the *past*.)
> Henry worked in a drug store; he *had been* there a year when he resigned. (His work there *began* in the *past* and *ended* in the *past*.)

6. *Future perfect tense* indicates that an action or condition began in the past or begins in the present and will be completed at some future time, stated or implied.

> I *shall have spent* all my money by June. (Spending *began* in the *past*, *will be finished* by June.)
> The snow *will have melted* before you arrive. (Melting of snow *has begun*, *is continuing*, and *will soon be completed*.)
> One year from now my father *will have been working* for his present employer exactly 20 years. (Work *began 19 years ago*, *is continuing*, and *will be completed* one year from now.)

HOW TO FORM TENSES AND TONES

80b.   **Use the correct tense form and tone form to express precise meaning.**

In the *active* voice, tense and tone are formed according to the directions given below (for a discussion of *voice* and of the *passive* voice, see Section 81).

Within certain tenses, verbs also have certain tones which express precisely what the writer wishes to say. These are the *simple* tone, the *progressive* or *continuing* tone, and the *emphatic* tone. For example, consider the differences in the following:

> I *study* my assignments every day. (Simple tone)
> Right now I *am studying* my history assignment. (Progressive tone)
> I *do study* each of my assignments two or three times. (Emphatic tone)

The *simple* tone is a concise statement, a kind of snapshot picture. The *progressive* tone indicates, in general, a kind of moving picture, a continuing action or state of being within a tense limit. The *emphatic* tone serves both to emphasize a statement and—by use of inverted order—commonly to ask a question.

Simple Tone

Present tense.

The present tense is the first principal part of the verb. All forms in the singular and plural are alike, *except* the third person singular, which varies from all the other forms by adding *s* or *es:*

I *go*	I *do*	I *come*	I *speak*
he *goes*	he *does*	she *comes*	she *speaks*

Past tense.

The past tense of the verb is the second principal part, given in your dictionary (see *regular* and *irregular* verbs in "Grammatical Terms Defined," Section 85). Except for *was* and *were,* all singular and plural forms are alike: *had, did, came, spoke, went.*

Future tense.

The future tense, as *future* tense, is formed by the auxiliary verb *shall* in the first person and the auxiliary verb *will* in the second and third persons preceding the present infinitive.

I *shall* come.	We *shall* come.
You *will* come.	You *will* come.
He *will* come.	They *will* come.

Careful writers and speakers still observe these distinctions between *shall* and *will* as auxiliaries in the future tense; but the distinction is breaking down in current use, partly because it does not seem important, partly because *will* suggests the idea of willingness, as in *I will speak* (i.e., *am willing to speak*) *before your group*. However, *shall* in the second and third persons is used only to express determination on the part of the speaker: "You *shall* not borrow my clothes, and your friends *shall* not play that trick on me again." So, too, *will* in the first person can express determination or emphasis: "I *will* speak."

Even careful and precise speakers and writers, however, have other perfectly acceptable and idiomatic ways of expressing future time. These include using the present tense accompanied by an adverb or adverbial phrase of time or using expressions like "going to" or "plan to." Expressions like the following express future time:

The new students arrive tomorrow.
I am taking my entrance examinations next week.
This Saturday the team leaves for University Park to play Penn State.
I am going to pay my tuition fees tomorrow.
We plan to attend the convention in Detroit in March.

Present perfect tense.

The present perfect tense is formed by using the auxiliary verb *have* (*has*) with the past participle. It expresses action or state of being which began in the past and has just been completed or is still continuing in the present.

I *have* just *completed* writing my theme.
We *have had* a wonderful time here.
John *has been* studying for over two hours.

Past perfect tense.

The past perfect tense is formed by using the auxiliary verb *had* with the past participle. It expresses action or state of being which began in the past and was completed at some point or time in the past.

By last June I *had finished* my first two years of college.

Our family *had* never *seen* a living President until we saw President Kennedy.

Before I came to college, I *had read* many of Shakespeare's plays.

Future perfect tense.

The future perfect tense is formed by using the future of the auxiliary verb *have* (*shall have, will have*) with the past participle. It expresses action or state of being which began in the past or begins in the present and which will not be completed until some specified or implied time in the future.

I am completing my freshman year, and three years from now I *shall have graduated* from this university.

By July 4, 1975, this country *will have celebrated* the 200th anniversary of its independence.

Verbals.

For *verbals,* or non-finite verb forms, the formation is as follows:

Present infinitive, usually without the sign *to,* is given as the first principal part of the verb: *to be, to do, to have, to see.*

Perfect infinitive of any verb is formed by using the present infinitive of the auxiliary verb, *to have,* followed by the past participle: *to have been, to have done, to have had, to have seen, to have come.*

Present participle is formed by adding *ing* to the present-infinitive form, equivalent in most verbs to the present-tense form: *being, doing, having, seeing, coming.* If the infinitive ends in silent *e,* the silent *e* spelling rule applies (Section 52e5).

Past participle is the third principal part of any verb. When in doubt about its formation, see your dictionary.

Perfect participle is formed by using the present participle of the auxiliary verb, *having,* followed by the past participle: *having been, having done, having had, having seen, having come.*

Progressive Tone

The progressive tone forms in each tense are built by using the proper tense forms of the auxiliary verb *to be* (pp. 554–555) followed by the present participle of the main verb: *am coming, were coming, will be coming, have been coming, had been coming, will have been coming.* (See Table III, on pp. 572–573.)

Emphatic Tone

The emphatic tone, used only in the present and past tenses, indicative mood, active voice, is formed by the auxiliary verb forms of *do* with the present infinitive of the main verb. The emphatic tone has two common uses: (1) to emphasize and (2) to ask a question: I *do* study. I *did* study. *Do* you plan to come? *Did* you know the answers?

Present		**Past**	
SINGULAR	PLURAL	SINGULAR	PLURAL
I do see	we do see	I did see	we did see
you do see	you do see	you did see	you did see
he does see	they do see	he did see	they did see

With the foregoing information mastered, you should have little difficulty in using the correct tense and tone form for any given time of action or state of being.

CONSISTENCY OF TENSE USE

When a verb is used alone in a sentence, the tense should express the precise time. When two or more verbs are used in a sentence (1) two or more members of a compound predicate expressing the same time should have the same tense; (2) verbs in the clauses of a compound sentence should be clear and consistent in their tenses; (3) the tense of the verb in a dependent clause is determined by the tense of the verb in the main clause.

80c.   **Use the present tense to express a timeless or universal truth or, in a dependent clause, a general truth.**

Iron, copper, and tin *are* metals.
The power of logical thinking *distinguishes* man from the animals.
In the Middle Ages some people did not believe that the earth *is* round.
In high school I learned that the speed of light *is* 186,000 miles a second.

80d.   **Avoid shifting needlessly from one tense to another.**

In consecutive sentences developing ideas and thoughts, do not needlessly shift tenses, as from present to past, or past to present. (See also Section 45a.)

Last summer we spent a few weeks at Bar Harbor, Maine. We fish nearly every day, but sometimes we drive around and enjoy the beautiful scenery. On rainy days we wrote letters or read.

Do not allow the tense of a verb to be attracted into the past when it should be present tense: "On our way home, we visited Gloucester, Massachusetts. The houses there were old and picturesque." Does the writer mean that the houses are no longer there?

80e.   Do not misuse the past tense for the present perfect tense or the present perfect tense for the past tense.

Bad: You received the check your father is to send?
             The snow fell heavily since yesterday. (It is still snowing.)
             Mr. Brown has died a year ago.
Improved: You have received the check your father was to send?
             The snow has fallen heavily since yesterday.
             Mr. Brown died a year ago.

80f.   Use the appropriate tense of participles.

Using participial forms depends upon the ideas you are expressing. Ordinarily, however, a present participle indicates action at the time expressed by the main verb (present or present perfect tense); a past or perfect participle indicates action previous to that of the time expressed by the main verb (past or past perfect tense). Notice participles and main verbs in the following:

Traveling constantly from coast to coast, my parents *see* much of this country. (Participle in present tense, main verb in present tense)
Traveling from coast to coast, my parents *have seen* much of this country. (Participle in present tense, main verb in present perfect tense)
Having traveled from coast to coast, my parents *saw* much of this country. (Participle in present perfect tense, main verb in past tense)
Making a good academic record, Henry *expects* to get excellent letters of recommendation. (Participle in present tense, main verb in present tense)
Having made a good academic record, Henry *obtained* many excellent letters of recommendation. (Participle in present perfect tense, main verb in past tense)

80g.   Use the appropriate tense of infinitives.

Your use of one of the infinitive tenses—present infinitive or perfect infinitive—likewise depends upon the ideas you are expressing.

579

Ordinarily the *present infinitive* expresses action occurring or state of being existing at the same time as the main verb or supposed to occur or exist at a time future to the main verb:

> Mr. Browne, I am happy *to meet* you.
> I have been asked *to invite* you to our meeting.

The perfect infinitive ordinarily indicates action which has occurred or state of being which has existed prior to the time of the main verb:

> Mr. Browne, I am happy *to have met* you.
> Every member is pleased *to have listened* to you as our speaker.

80h. Be consistent in the use of tense in dependent and independent clauses.

Consistency demands the correct "sequence of tenses," i.e., order of events in time and proper expression of that order. Note these principles:

1. When the tense in the independent clause is the *present,* the *future,* the *present perfect,* or the *future perfect,* any tense may be used in the dependent clause which will adequately express the thought.

> I always *tell* people that I *live* in Detroit.
> Henry *tells* me that he *will visit* Niagara Falls.
> Henry *will* also *tell* you that he *will visit* Niagara Falls.
> John *tells* me that he *has seen* Niagara Falls.
> I *have told* you that I *have* not *seen* Niagara Falls.
> By June I *shall have finished* all the courses that *are required* for graduation.

2. When the tense in the independent clause is *past* or *past perfect,* a past tense or past perfect tense should be used in the dependent clause (except to express a timeless or universal truth or general truth, Section 80c).

> John *told* me that he *saw* Niagara Falls yesterday.
> John *told* Henry that he *had seen* Niagara Falls a year ago.
> Our instructor *told* us yesterday that our themes *would be* (not *will be*) due tomorrow.
> I *had told* John last week that we *had worked* too hard the week before.

3. In conditions and contrary-to-fact statements (see Section **82c**), the *past* tense or *past perfect* tense is used in the dependent clause, and *should, would, could,* or *might* is used in the independent clause:

If you *were* I, you *would* do exactly the same thing.
If it *had* not *rained* yesterday, we *might* have seen two ball games.
We *could* have won the game if we *had played* better in the last quarter.

Note that ordinarily *should, would, could,* or *might* do not appear in both the *if* clause and the independent clause:

Dubious: If you *should* go to Chicago, you *would* see Lakeshore Drive.
If John *would* reconsider, I *would* offer him the position.
Better: If you *should* go to Chicago, you *will* see Lakeshore Drive.
If John reconsiders, I *would* offer him the position.

But note also: If *should* replaces *if* in the dependent clause:

Should you go to Chicago, you *would* (or *will*) see Lakeshore Drive.
Should John reconsider, I *would* (or *will*) offer him the position.

EXERCISES

A. Make a list of all the verbs and verb phrases in the following sentences; after each write the tense and the tone.

1. When I have finished writing my theme, I shall begin to prepare my history assignment.
2. Father and Mother will observe their silver wedding anniversary next month; they do not want a celebration.
3. Mary has been sending out letters of application, but by last evening she had not received any replies.
4. Our leaders said that they saw that a recession was inevitably coming.
5. You do believe, don't you, that to see a football game is better than to read about it in the Sunday newspaper?
6. Whenever John leaves me, he always says, "I'll be seeing you."
7. Having flown on numerous trips, I am wondering whether I shall have the patience ever to travel by automobile again.
8. Henry had never heard of our product before I mentioned it to him; now he is using it continuously.
9. I saw a new TV program last evening; I had never seen it before and I most certainly shall not see it again.
10. My family is going to travel abroad this summer, and when my summer school is over, I am flying over to join them.
11. If you live until January 1, 2000, you will have seen the birth of a new century.

12. Did you wonder what had happened to us when we did not meet you as we had planned?

13. Professor Jones does not know why Mary failed; she did study, she said, and he believes her.

14. When you reach the top of the hill, you will see an abandoned building on the left.

15. The outfielder ran back to the fence and caught the ball, but he did succeed only after a hard run.

B. Correct all errors in tense in the following sentences:

1. If I had started farming, I would have had to gone into debt.

2. At 6:30 P.M. I decide it was time to go to the airport.

3. All my life I wanted to become a nurse or a doctor.

4. Being from Indiana, I have never seen a palm tree before.

5. Thanksgiving was the first vacation I have had since I enter college.

6. When we reach this part of our trip, we turned due north.

7. Later in the evening we meet another couple and went to a drive-in to eat.

8. Many of the hearts of the alumni have skipped a beat when they hear the band play the Alma Mater.

9. I would have liked to have spent a day just wandering about the airport.

10. This theme is written for a person who was completed a high school education.

11. The next day we entered Oklahoma and eat dinner in a very unusual town.

12. I am glad the Indiana and Ohio Turnpikes are built because we make much better time.

13. My mother was a young bride, being married at the age of 18 years.

14. It was difficult to convince myself that I reached the end of 12 years of education.

15. When I let my dog in in the morning, he stays by me until I ate breakfast, and then he ate his own.

16. Just imagine! I am able to start college when it seems as if I should still be in high school. The time went so fast.

17. If all my plans work out, I will feel as if I had accomplished my goal in life.

18. People who smoked quite regularly find that they will save a lot of money by breaking the smoking habit.

19. We forgot cups and saucers, and therefore we drank our coffee out of plates and soup bowls.

20. At dawn on Monday we left for camp. We arrive about noon, eat our

lunch, get into our bathing suits, swim, and fish. Every day is about the same. The next Monday we came home.

VOICE (ACTIVE AND PASSIVE)

81. In the study of grammar, when you hear or use *voice*, think of verbs and of A and P (active and passive). *Voice* is the grammatical term indicating whether the subject of the sentence or clause is acting or being acted upon. In the *active voice* of verbs expressing action, the subject (person or thing) is literally the actor, the doer; in the *passive voice*, the subject does nothing, is literally passive or inactive, and has something done to it.

John *wrote* a short story. (Active voice)
A short story *was written* by John. (Passive voice)

Every day I *ride* my horse, Bulger. (Active voice)
My horse, Bulger, *is ridden* every day. (Passive voice)

Father *has changed* his place of residence three times in five years. (Active voice)
His place of residence *has been changed* by Father three times in five years. (Passive voice)

81a. **Use correct forms of the auxiliary and main verbs in forming the passive voice.**

Like verbs in the active voice, verbs in the passive also have tense (time) and tone. To form passive voice, use auxiliary verb *to be* in its various forms and the past participle of the main verb. Study the forms of this auxiliary verb (Table II, pp. 554–555), and then study Table IV (pp. 584–585), noting how auxiliary forms are applied.

Note also that in tone the passive voice has all the forms in the simple tone; it has none in the emphatic tone; and it uses, commonly, in the progressive tone the present, past, and future tenses only. The compound tenses (present perfect, past perfect, future perfect) in the progressive can be formed, but they are cumbersome, awkward, and uneuphonious. The ideas in the perfect progressive tenses (*have been being seen, had been being seen, shall have been being seen*) are more easily and effectively expressed by the simple tone of these tenses (*have been seen, had been seen, shall have been seen*).

TABLE IV. **To see, INDICATIVE MOOD, PASSIVE VOICE**

Principal Parts: see   saw   seen

Singular

Present Tense

		Simple	Progressive
1st person		I am seen	am being seen
2nd person		you are seen	are being seen
3rd person		he is seen (she, it)	is being seen

Past Tense

		Simple	Progressive
1st person		I was seen	was being seen
2nd person		you were seen	were being seen
3rd person		he was seen	was being seen

Future Tense

		Simple	Progressive
1st person		I shall be seen	shall be being seen
2nd person		you will be seen	will be being seen
3rd person		he will be seen	will be being seen

Present Perfect Tense

		Simple
1st person		I have been seen
2nd person		you have been seen
3rd person		he has been seen

Plural

Present Tense

	Simple	Progressive
we		
you	are seen	are being seen
they		

Past Tense

	Simple	Progressive
we		
you	were seen	were being seen
they		

Future Tense

	Simple	Progressive
we	shall be seen	shall be being seen
you	will be seen	will be being seen
they	will be seen	will be being seen

Present Perfect Tense

	Simple
we	
you	have been seen
they	

Past Perfect Tense

1st person	I	
2nd person	you	} had been seen
3rd person	he	

1st person	we	
2nd person	you	} had been seen
3rd person	they	

Future Perfect Tense

1st person	I shall have been seen
2nd person	you will have been seen
3rd person	he will have been seen

1st person	we shall have been seen
2nd person	you will have been seen
3rd person	they will have been seen

Verbals (Non-finite Verb Forms)

	Simple
Present infinitive:	to be seen
Perfect infinitive:	to have been seen
Present participle:	being seen
Past participle:	(none)
Perfect participle:	having been seen
Present gerund:	being seen
Perfect gerund:	having been seen

NOTE: Gerunds have the same form as participles.

81b. Do not use intransitive verb forms in a passive-voice construction.

With a transitive verb (see pp. 491–492) a direct object receives the action of the verb; with an intransitive verb no such object is needed. Only transitive verbs, therefore, can be used in the passive voice. In this process, the direct object of the transitive verb is shifted in front of the verb and becomes the subject, and the subject of the transitive active verb becomes the expressed agent (preceded by the preposition *by*) or the implied agent.

> John Brown writes novels. (Active voice, transitive verb)
> Novels are written by John Brown. (Passive voice)
> Our class has performed many experiments dealing with moisture condensation. (Active voice, transitive verb)
> Many experiments dealing with moisture condensation have been performed. (Passive voice; "by our class," the agent, is implied.)

A passive-voice construction is sometimes used when an indirect object is made the "passive" subject in a rephrased sentence.

> Father gave me some money. (Active voice)
> Some money was given me by Father. (Passive voice; direct object has become subject.)
> I was given some money by Father. (Passive voice; indirect object has become subject.)
>
> His company granted John a month's vacation. (Active voice)
> John was granted a month's vacation by his company. (Passive voice; indirect object has become subject.)
> A month's vacation was granted John by his company. (Passive voice; direct object has become subject.)

Verbs with intransitive meaning are not used in passive voice.

Incorrect: The river has been risen because of the recent rains.
Correct: The river has risen because of the recent rains.

Incorrect: The dog was sat on the chair.
Correct: The dog was made to sit on the chair.

Incorrect: Your letters have been lain on your desk.
Correct: Your letters have been laid on your desk.

NOTE: Idiomatic usage permits an *apparent* passive construction of a few intransitive verbs: Jesus is risen; Mary is gone; I am come to tell you the plans. Note, however, that the subject of the active and "apparent passive" remains unchanged.

81c. Do not shift needlessly from active voice to passive voice.

Clear, effective, appropriate use of voice is mainly a matter of being consistent. Do not, therefore, shift needlessly from active to passive voice, or from passive to active, since such a shift becomes annoying and troublesome to the reader. For discussion of consistency in the use of subject and voice in a sentence, see Section 45b.

81d. Use the passive voice in impersonal writing.

Writing is impersonal when it avoids use of personal pronouns; it is completely impersonal when it avoids even the use of the indefinite pronouns like *one, someone, everybody,* or nouns like a *person,* a *student.* In certain kinds of writing, as in recording of laboratory experiments, giving conclusions, making recommendations, and the like, completely impersonal expression may be desirable and is obtained by using the passive voice. The agent or doer is usually not expressed, only implied.

> The experiment was performed in order to . . . .
> The following facts were obtained . . . .
> The results were tabulated, and from them the following conclusions were reached . . . .
> On the basis of these conclusions, the following changes are recommended . . . .

81e. Avoid overfrequent use of the passive voice.

Since a subject being acted upon is rarely as effective as a subject acting, the use of the passive voice often detracts from effectiveness in a sentence. Active voice normally gives sentences greater force and strength. Use active voice, therefore, wherever or whenever you express or imply action, mental or physical, on the part of the subject.

Unemphatic: A lecture *is scheduled to be given* by Professor Brown on Wednesday.
This essay *was read* by me four times before it *was understood.*
Better: Professor Brown *will give* a lecture on Wednesday.
I *read* this essay four times before I *understood* it.

Occasionally, sentences do require a passive verb, especially when the agent is not expressed. Use the passive voice, therefore, whenever it is effectively appropriate, that is, when your purpose is to represent the subject of the sentence as acted upon and when you wish to emphasize the subject in the beginning position (Section **47a**).

Effective: A lecture on "Better Living at Less Cost" *will be given* on Wednesday by Professor Brown.

Our place of meeting *has been changed* from Room 414 to Room 24.

EXERCISES

A. Copy from the following sentences, in column form, all the verbs or verb phrases in the passive voice. After each, write also the tense or tone that it illustrates.

1. The cause of the accident was not determined until a thorough investigation had been completed.
2. The purse was lost on Main Street; if it is found, please telephone 92–2668.
3. This draft of the theme has been thoroughly revised; now the final draft must be written.
4. The contest will be closed Saturday night; all entries must be sent in by midnight, and winners will be announced on Monday.
5. When candidates are considered for class offices, it is an honor to be asked to be included among the nominees.
6. The work will be done, even if 100 men are needed for the job.
7. I am being considered as a candidate for class president.
8. Heavy-duty trucks are used in long-distance hauling; light trucks are utilized for local deliveries.
9. The subject of the address was not announced until the guests of honor had been ushered to their seats.
10. Five recommendations were proposed on the basis of the facts that had been established.
11. A famous movie star in person will be being seen all next week at the Acme Theater.
12. My having been elected vice-president last year was a stepping stone to my being chosen president this year.
13. To be forced from your home by floods is as tragic as to be driven from your home by fire.

14. Although the fact was not known to you, you were being heard on the radio by thousands of unseen listeners.
15. Old jokes have been told so often that script writers are hard pressed for material.

B. Change all passive-verb forms in the following sentences to active voice:

1. A few hours later a sad good-by was said to my parents, and I was alone in the world of the university.
2. Then a long trip was made by us to a room on the third floor, and a lecture on the library was given for approximately 25 minutes.
3. In between my courses in mathematics, courses in physics and chemistry have been taken.
4. In basketball, my awkward act of tossing was overcome and more skillful shooting the ball was accomplished.
5. The Christmas vacation is always looked forward to with eager anticipation by students.
6. All of the decorations were brought up from the basement, and the tree was begun to be decorated by our family.
7. My horse's wonderful disposition will always be remembered by me.
8. Any letters which will be written by me in the near future will probably be letters of inquiry and application.
9. You may not think you have ever been a litterbug, but you have if anything has been discarded out the automobile window.
10. The student was asked by the instructor to read the theme which had been written.
11. The roof was blown off by the storm, and the furniture was badly damaged by the rain.
12. When the question was asked by Mary, it was considered too difficult to be answered by the lecturer.
13. The vegetables are being cooked by the women and the dessert is being bought by the men.
14. Being seen in public for the first time in weeks, John was asked by us how his illness had been overcome.
15. When your theme has been finished, your paper is to be folded and handed in.

MOOD (MODE)

82. *Mood*, literally, is a state or temper of mind; *mode*, literally, is a prevailing fashion or manner. In grammar, the *mood* or *mode* of a verb indicates the state of mind or the manner in which a statement is made: a fact, a request or command, a condition or probability. English has commonly three moods: *indicative, imperative,* and *subjunctive.* Other "states of mind" or "prevailing manners"—such as willingness, duty, propriety, necessity, expectation, permission, ability, obligation, compulsion, custom—are expressed by auxiliary verbs (see Section **78h**).

82a. Use the indicative mood to express a fact or what seems to be a fact, or to ask a question of fact.

Verb forms in the indicative mood are the most frequently used verb forms in English. Outlines of the indicative mood of the auxiliary verbs *to be, to have, to do* and of the main verb *to see,* active and passive voice, are given in Tables II (pp. 554–555), III (pp. 572–573), and IV (pp. 584–585). Examples:

> When *are* the term papers due? (Question of fact)
> They *are* due on the second Friday in January. (Statement of fact)
> Oak trees *are* taller than maple trees. (Statement of fact)

82b. Use the imperative mood to express a command, a polite request, a strong request, an order.

The imperative mood of the verb has only one form, the same form as the present infinitive without the sign *to.* It is both singular and plural. Examples: *come, go, speak, do, be.*

> Forward, *march!* Company, *halt!* (Commands)
> *Line up* in a column of twos. (Command)
> *Come* to the meeting and *bring* a friend with you. (Polite request)
> This class will begin promptly at 8 A.M. *Be* here. (Strong request)
> Please *deliver* these flowers this afternoon. (Order)

82c. Use the subjunctive mood to express (a) a condition contrary to fact, (b) a supposition, (c) a highly improbable condition, (d) doubt or uncertainty, (e) necessity, (f) parliamentary motions, (g) a desire.

Distinctive subjunctive verb forms in current English have disappeared or are disappearing in favor of more commonly used indicative verb forms.

Former use: If it *be* possible, I shall come.
  A student, if he *write* well, will receive a high grade.

Current use: If it *is* possible, I shall come.

  A student, if he *writes* well, will receive a high grade.

The verb *to be* (both as linking and as auxiliary verb) has only two distinct subjunctive forms now in occasional use: the form *be* for all persons in singular and plural, present tense, and the form *were* for all persons in singular and plural, past tense. See Table II, "Subjunctive Mood," on page 555. The same table gives any currently used subjunctive forms of the verbs *have* and *do*.

For all other verb forms except *be,* and including *have* and *do,* the only subjunctive form different from the indicative in any tense is the third person singular present, which, by dropping the *s* ending, becomes exactly like the other forms:

(if) I do	(if) I have	(if) I see	(if) I come
(if) you do	(if) you have	(if) you see	(if) you come
(if) he do	(if) he have	(if) he see	(if) he come

Only rarely, however, can you find such main-verb subjunctive forms, third person singular present tense, in current writing. Instead, both subjunctive and other non-indicative mood and non-imperative mood ideas are expressed by the use of auxiliary verbs: *should, would, can, could, may, might, must, ought, let, dare, need, used* (see Section **78h**).

Rare: If she *come,* it will be a pleasure.

  If he *write* me, I shall reply.

Common: If she *can come,* it will be a pleasure.

  If he *should write* me, I shall reply.

Our language still retains a number of subjunctive forms in sayings handed down from times when this mood was more widely used: *Heaven forbid, Thy Kingdom come, if need be, he need not speak, suffice it to say, come what may,* etc. Also, careful speakers and writers employ the subjunctive mood to express the precise manner in which they make their statements, when the indicative mood would not serve effectively.

As indicated in the general principle introducing this section, current English uses subjunctive verb forms, especially of *to be* (*be* and *were*), to express

a. A condition contrary to fact, something that is not true, that could not be true.

If I *were* the king, I would have you decorated.
If she *were* I, would she succeed in doing better?
If it *were* not so cold, we could go swimming.

b. A supposition.

Suppose he *were* to ask you that question!
Let's assume that she *were* to be chosen campus queen.

c. A highly improbable condition even though not completely contrary to fact.

He worked as if he *were* never going to have another chance.
If I *be* [*am*] too talkative at the meeting, please inform me at once.
If the program *be* [*is*] deadly dull, let's not complain.

The bracketed words *am* and *is,* indicative forms, are usually used in current English.

d. Doubt or uncertainty.

He talks as if he *were* the only intelligent person in the group.
As though he *were* any smarter himself!

e. Necessity.

It is necessary that she *pass* this course in order to be initiated.
It is essential that Henry *appear* in person for the honor.
The dean of women insisted that Jane *come* to her office.
It is expected that every man *pay* his own way.

f. Parliamentary motion.

I move that the chairman *be authorized* to proceed.
The motion is that the remark of the last speaker *be expunged* from the record.
Resolved, that Henry *be made* an honorary member of this organization.
It is moved and seconded that he *pay* his dues in advance.

g. A wish, a desire, volition, recommendation.

She wishes that she *were* going to go along.
Our officers desire that you *be* rewarded.
"Thy Kingdom *come,* Thy Will *be done.*"
It is recommended that the class president *speak* at the reception and *give* the address of welcome.

82d. In parallel constructions, do not shift the mood of verbs.

Be consistent in the use of the subjunctive mood, or the indicative, or the imperative, as in compound predicates and in two or more parallel dependent clauses.

Inconsistent: If I *were* in your position and *was* not prevented, I should certainly go.

If it *does* not rain and if I *be* not called out of town, I shall attend the game.

If John *were* to resign and if Henry *was* elected to take his place, we should have more vigorous leadership.

Consistent: If I *were* in your position and *were* not prevented, I should certainly go.

If it *does* not rain and if I *am* not called out of town, I shall attend the game.

If John *were* to resign and if Henry *were* elected to take his place, we should have more vigorous leadership.

EXERCISES

A. Choose between the subjunctive and indicative forms in the following sentences and give reasons for your choice:

1. I move that the chairman (be, is) appointed our delegate to the state convention.
2. Write your friend that he (needs, need) not worry about the money he owes me.
3. If anyone here (have, has) a desire to speak, now (is, be) the time.
4. Resolved, that Jeremiah Wilson (be, is) given public recognition for his contribution to the Society for Kindness to Coeds.
5. You speak as though it (was, were) an easy matter to preside at such meetings.
6. I wish that I (were, was) you!
7. If this (were, was) December, I could pay you what I owe.
8. If she (were, was) pretty, he might love her more.
9. I wonder if the doctor (be, is) willing to operate.
10. If only he (were, was) in Detroit, and I (were, was) at Ann Arbor!
11. If I (were, was) going, I should begin to make preparations.
12. I wondered whether this (were, was) an intentional error.
13. Although every precaution (be, is) taken, the expedition will be hazardous.

14. If this (be, is) what you mean, you are in error.
15. If you (were, was) to meet him, what would you say?

B. From the following sentences make a list containing the italicized forms that you prefer. If you choose the subjunctive form, state which of the subdivisions under Section **82c** you are following.

1. Assume, now, that she *was were* to be our official delegate.
2. If she *be is* chosen our delegate and *was were* sent to Chicago, would we be well represented?
3. To put this campaign over, it *be is* necessary that the class president *be is* here Tuesday to make final plans.
4. My only hope is that John *receive receives* full recognition for his work.
5. Heaven *grant grants* that he *be is* not seriously injured.
6. It made no difference to me if he *were was* coming or not.
7. If I *was were* 30 instead of 20, I'd know what to do.
8. I strongly advocate that a vote of censure *be is* ordered.
9. It is imperative that there *is be* not the slightest delay.
10. We shall all suffer if the country *be is* invaded.
11. Even though extreme measures for our safety *are be* taken, the consequences are dubious.
12. My, how he wished he *was were* a few inches taller.
13. If the President were given a free hand and *were was* sent to negotiate, we would see some action.
14. It hardly seems possible that the doctor *is would be* willing to give that anesthetic to a baby.
15. You can be sure the corporal wished he *was were* miles away.

GENERAL EXERCISE: USE OF VERBS

Rewrite the following sentences, correcting all errors in the use of verbs (principal parts, tense, tone, mood, or voice):

1. The best solution to the problem would be not to sleep in class.
2. The total distance that we hike last Saturday was approximately eight miles.
3. If a student would attend every class meeting, his chances of passing that course would be greatly improved.
4. If I would have had more composition in high school, I would have been better prepared for college English.
5. In the fall of 1948, although it would have been four months until I would have been five years old, the teacher said that I could start to school if I wanted to do so.

6. Until last November I maintain average grades very easily.

7. The hardest thing this past semester is learning to study.

8. I feel that even if I wouldn't have received money for working, I was fully paid by the experience that I gained.

9. In high school my brother seem to be interest in mathematics and science.

10. I have always like arithmetic, algebra, geometry, and such.

11. I often wonder whether my grandfather truly believe the tales he told.

12. I would have been better prepared for college if I would have worked harder in high school.

13. A big deer jumps right across the road in front of us.

14. If I would have studied harder, I would have made some decent grades this semester.

15. If one would look up the name *Karl* in the dictionary, he would find it to be a German name for *Charles*.

16. Many a person may not have been dead today if they would have use safety devices in their cars.

17. Some people can tell of some incidents that would never have happen if they would have sought advice.

18. Another weak spot in American culture would be our fast way of living.

19. The trees were coated with ice, and when the sun shines, it looked as if everything was made out of diamond.

20. The difference between a person who follows the crowd and the one who stood up against the crowd when it is wrong is the difference between a follower and a leader. Have courage! Dare to be different!

ADJECTIVES AND ADVERBS

83. Ordinarily, determining when an adjective or adverb should be used is not difficult. An *adjective* modifies only a noun or pronoun; an *adverb* modifies only a verb, an adjective, or another adverb, or, infrequently, the general idea of a sentence. This rule is simple enough, and yet misuse of adjectives and adverbs is common. Part of the confusion is caused by the fact that after linking or coupling verbs the adjective is used, since it modifies the subject noun or pronoun, and after certain other verbs the adjective *or* adverb is used, depending upon the meaning of the verb.

More confusion comes because the form of a word does not always reveal whether it is an adjective or adverb. Most words ending in *ly* are adverbs, but some are not, such as *holy, sickly;* also *-ly* is an adjective suffix meaning "like": *saintly, manly, fatherly*. Many adverbs do not end in *ly*. Again, some adjectives and adverbs have identical forms (*quick, little, fast*), but these naturally cause no trouble. A few adverbs, also, have two forms which differ in meaning, like *sharp, sharply,* or *late, lately*.

In general, if the word or phrase about which you are in doubt modifies sensibly a noun or pronoun, the chances are that it is an adjective. If it modifies or even loosely applies to the verb, it is an adverb. (For additional discussion, see Section **71h, i**.)

83a.   Do not use an adjective to modify a verb.

Wrong: Our chemistry teacher talks too *rapid*.
              Some people take themselves too *serious*.
              On every occasion my sister dresses *neat*.
Correct: Our chemistry teacher talks too *rapidly*.
              Some people take themselves too *seriously*.
              On every occasion my sister dresses *neatly*.

83b.   Do not use an adjective to modify another adjective or an adverb.

Wrong: Joe is a *real* good boxer.
              This is a *strong* made box.
Dubious: Small auto racers are *plenty* fast.
Correct: Joe is a *really* good boxer.
              This is a *strongly* made box.
              Small auto racers are *very* fast.

83c.   After such verbs as <u>be</u> (<u>am, is, are, was, were</u>, etc.), <u>appear</u>, <u>become</u>, <u>feel</u>, <u>look</u>, <u>seem</u>, <u>smell</u>, <u>sound</u>, <u>taste</u>, <u>grow</u>, the modifier should be an adjective if it refers to the subject, an adverb if it describes or defines the verb. (See Section **78**.)

Correct: The cake tastes *good*. (Adjective)
              The girl looked *beautiful*. (Adjective)
              He looks *careful*. (Adjective: he appears to be a person who is careful.)
              After my illness, I feel *strong* again. (Adjective)
              She looked at him *angrily*. (Adverb)
              He looks *carefully*. (Adverb: describes the way in which he *looks*.)

The first four italicized modifiers are adjectives because they refer to the *subjects* of the sentences. The last two are adverbs because they modify *verbs*. (See Sections 78a, 78b.)

83d. Be accurate in the use of words that may be either adjectives or adverbs, and of adjectives that end in <u>ly</u>.

Cheap, deep, far, fast, well, wrong, and many other words are both adjectives and adverbs. Further, *cheap, deep, wrong,* and many others have *ly* forms, also. Words such as *friendly, goodly, lovely, manly, sickly, timely* are adjectives, normally. Consult your dictionary when in doubt; it tells which words are adjectives only, which are adverbs only, which may be either, and what their label is—colloquial, informal, formal.

Correct: The miler ran very *fast.* (Adverb)
He ran the mile in *fast* time. (Adjective)
Grandfather was a *kindly* (adjective) person; he spoke *kindly* (adverb) to everyone he met.

83e. Use the correct forms of adjectives and adverbs to indicate the three degrees of comparison.

Grammatically, comparison is the change in form of an *adjective* or *adverb* to indicate greater or smaller degrees of quantity, quality, or manner. The change is indicated by three methods: (1) by use of different words, a somewhat uncommon method; (2) by adding endings *er, est* to one-syllable words and some of two syllables; (3) by using adverbial modifiers, *more, most* (upward comparison) and *less, least* (downward comparison), with words of two or more syllables when awkwardness results from adding the *er, est* endings. The three degrees of comparison are *positive, comparative, superlative*. Examples:

Positive	Comparative	Superlative
good (well)	better	best
little	less	least
bad	worse	worst
many	more	most
small	smaller	smallest
wisely	more wisely	most wisely
beautiful	less beautiful	least beautiful

Positive degree, the first or simple form of an adjective or adverb, shows no comparison; *comparative degree* shows relationship between two persons, objects, or ideas; *superlative degree* shows relationships among three or more.

> Smith is a *tall* (*competent*) man. (Adjective, positive degree)
> Smith is a *taller* (*more competent*) man than I am. (Adjective, comparative degree)
> Smith is the *tallest* (*most competent*) man in our society. (Adjective, superlative degree)
>
> The Wabash River flows *fast* (*violently*) during the rainy season. (Adverb, positive degree)
> The Wabash River flows *faster* (*more violently*) in spring than in fall. (Adverb, comparative degree)
> The Wabash River flows *fastest* (*most violently*) in April, *least violently* in the winter months. (Adverbs, superlative degree)

83f. **Use the comparative degree for comparison between two things, the superlative degree for more than two.**

According to the discussion in Section **83e**, *positive degree* shows no comparison; *comparative degree* is used when two are compared; *superlative degree* is used when three or more are compared.

In incorrect and sometimes in informal usage we hear such statements as "In the Army-Navy series, Navy's team has been the best," or in a boxing match "May the best man win." In such statements, only two, not three or more, are being compared. Accurate speakers and writers would use *better* in such sentences.

> Let us vote for the *better* of the two candidates. (Only two are concerned.)
> Let us vote for the *best* of these five candidates. (More than two are concerned.)

In informal or colloquial English the superlative qualifying adverb *most* is sometimes used when no particular comparison is intended: "You are *most* generous." In such meaning, *most* is an intensive or a substitute for *very:* "You are very generous."

(For unjustifiable omissions in comparisons, see Section **35f**; for mixed and illogical comparisons, see Section **35d, e**.)

83g. **Avoid the trap of the double comparative or double superlative.**

When comparative and superlative forms of adjectives and adverbs are formed by adding *er* and *est* endings, the adverbs *more* and *most* should never be used, even though such a model as Shakespeare slipped with "This was the *most unkindest* cut of all" (*Julius Caesar,* III:ii). Such expressions are not permissible even in informal usage.

Wrong: This test was much *more longer* than the one last month.

Our high school senior queen was the *most prettiest* of any we had chosen during my four years of high school.

83h. Do not compare adjectives and adverbs that are in meaning logically incapable of comparison.

When their meaning is absolute, adjectives and adverbs are logically incapable of comparison; what they say is said once and for all. Such words are *perpendicular, horizontal, parallel, unique, excellent, perfect, accurate, absolute, round, square, final, fatal, impossible.*

More nearly accurate writing (not *more* accurate) uses qualifying adverbs: *nearly impossible,* not *completely impossible* or *more impossible; almost fatal,* not *completely fatal; almost square* or *more nearly square,* not *squarer; the most nearly round,* not *the roundest.*

EXERCISES

A. Rewrite the following sentences correcting all errors in the misuse of adjectives and adverbs.

1. My knees were shaking so bad I thought they would shake off.
2. For camping, dried foods take longer to prepare, but they pack easier.
3. Many of us take it for granted that English just comes natural.
4. It became apparent that I was not going to do good on the test.
5. In the evenings we have a real pleasant fire in the fireplace.
6. Such folding will cause the letter to be opened for reading easier.
7. I never learned near so much as I should have.
8. At Christmas everything is decorated so beautiful, it makes everyone joyful.
9. This road is one of the most heavy traveled roads in the state.
10. Two people can figure out the answer quicker than one can.
11. Exceptionally good designed pictures often attract the reader's attention.
12. Thanksgiving began as usually with all the relatives coming to our house.
13. Since I am the youngest one of two children, I really know what this means.
14. Formal education is good, but self-education is best.
15. Greenville is one of the more cleaner towns in our area.

B. Directions given in A.

1. I hope I can get back in the swing of things pretty quick.
2. The week end started off quiet, but more and more excitement soon developed.
3. At the last moment, my aunt, uncle, and three cousins arrived unexpected, but were welcome.
4. No one wants to be waited on by a sloppy dressed salesman.
5. Everyone should spend enough money to live comfortable and enjoy life.
6. At camp there are times when things go real smooth and then there are times when they don't.
7. On icy roads some people turn corners too sharp and they apply the brakes too sudden.
8. My roommate seems never to take anything serious.
9. Such activities help to draw the entire group of students closer together.
10. College students must learn to write clear and simple.
11. A student criticized openly in class will feel resentfully toward his teacher.
12. My sights are now fixed on two targets, and the second of these is the most important.
13. His large kindly eyes help to make his smile more friendlier and warmer.
14. Some of my most happiest years were spent in high school.
15. Christmas with all its traditions is one of the gayest and colorfulest holidays of the whole year.

C. From each of the following sentences, list the italicized form which is correct:

1. Under a poor teacher the student is not able to learn very *rapid rapidly*.
2. If you treat some people *rude rudely*, they will treat you *rude rudely* too.
3. Maybe Mother's life was not as *easy easily* as I thought.
4. Many auto drivers wonder why they should drive *careful carefully*.
5. At the fairs in the past we have done very *good well* with our cattle and sheep.
6. Everyone takes a written test and a driving test; the actual driving test is the *worse worst* of the two.
7. Doris Day fit into her role *perfect perfectly*, for she can dance, sing, and act.
8. I'm glad to say I'm doing *excellent excellently* in all my subjects.
9. Mother's health has improved *some somewhat* since you last saw her.

10. My high school years went by almost *uneventful uneventfully*.
11. *Different differently* positions on the football team are played *different differently*.
12. It is *remarkable remarkably* to see operations in this college function so *smooth smoothly*.
13. In rainy weather your brakes are not as *efficient efficiently* as on dry roads.
14. It takes more than money to make a person *real really* happy.
15. An owl sees much *clearer more clearly* at night than a hawk does.

CONJUNCTIONS

84. A *conjunction* is a word, sometimes several words with the force or meaning of one word, used to join words, phrases, clauses, and, occasionally, sentences. As a *joining* or *linking* or *connecting* or *relating* word, it has no other function than to couple two or more elements.

You must know the various kinds of conjunctions in order to write clearly, effectively, and appropriately. Conjunctions are divided into two main groups: (1) *coordinating* and (2) *subordinating*.

A *coordinating conjunction* joins words, phrases, clauses, or sentences of equal rank, that is, elements not dependent upon one another grammatically, although they may be in meaning. Three kinds of conjunctions are classified as coordinate:

a. *Pure* or *simple conjunctions—and, but, or, nor, neither, yet*, and some teachers add *for* and *so*. In their most common uses, these join two or more words or phrases or clauses or even sentences of equal rank.

b. *Correlative conjunctions*—words used in pairs and serving to emphasize the relationship between two ideas. Most frequently used of these pairs are *both . . . and, either . . . or, neither . . . nor*, and *not only . . . but also*. Sometimes other pairs are listed, but careful study reveals that they do not coordinate, but subordinate. For example, *whether . . . or* really means that two *whether* statements are joined by *or*, even though the second *whether* is understood: "Your English instructor does not care *whether* you attend *or* (*whether* you) don't attend the football games."

c. *Conjunctive adverbs*—ordinarily, adverbs used parenthetically in a sentence but frequently used to relate two independent clauses or two sentences: words or phrases like *however, thus, besides, still, then, in fact, for example* (see also Section **89b**).

A *subordinating conjunction* serves only one purpose: to relate a noun clause or an adverbial clause to its independent clause (the adjective clause is related to its noun or pronoun by a relative pronoun). Examples: *if, since, because, as, while, so that, although, unless, before.*

Conjunctions, particularly when they join clauses, must be chosen with care, for they should always show clear and appropriate relationships of ideas. Often, a careless writer will use *and* where the relationship of clauses needs to be more clearly expressed, probably by use of subordination. (Section **84a.**)

Table V, pages 605–607, classifies all the commonly used conjunctions according to whether they are *pure* or *simple, correlative, conjunctive adverb,* or *subordinating;* this table also shows their meaning and how this meaning can be expressed through either coordinating or subordinating relationships.

The following suggestions deal both with the right or appropriate conjunction as a matter of diction and with the right or appropriate conjunction to indicate proper relationship of ideas.

84a. Distinguish among the meanings of simple coordinating conjunctions. (See Table V, pp. 605–607.)

When independent clauses, or dependent clauses, or phrases are genuinely coordinated, respectively, with other independent clauses, or dependent clauses, or phrases, use the exact coordinating conjunction that relates them. Do not use *and* if *but* is the exact word, *or* for *but,* and the like.

Inaccurate: I wanted to buy the coat, *and* I had no money.
　　　　　　We had a flat tire, *but* we should have been here an hour ago.
　　　　　　I had hoped you would go, *or* you did.
　　　　　　The book may have been good in your opinion, *and* it was not good in mine.
Right:　　　I wanted to buy the coat, *but* I had no money.
　　　　　　We had a flat tire, *or* we should have been here an hour ago.
　　　　　　I had hoped you would go, *and* you did.
　　　　　　The book may have been good in your opinion, *but* it was not good in mine.

84b. Use correlative conjunctions to correlate only two ideas.

Since by definition correlative conjunctions are used in pairs, their

602

clear and logical use is to relate two ideas, not more than two. Each member of the pair is followed by the same grammatical construction. (Section **44b**.)

Dubious: *Both* my father, my mother, *and* my oldest sister are graduates of this university.

Neither rain, snow, hail, ice, *nor* tornado could have kept me from our high school Junior Prom.

At this early date it looks as if *either* Michigan, Ohio State, Illinois, Wisconsin, or Iowa will win the Big Ten Conference Championship.

NOTE: *Neither . . . nor* go together, not *neither . . . or*.

Wrong: Williamsport is *neither* the biggest *or* the most beautiful city in the state.

NOTE: As indicated in the "Glossary of Faulty Diction," Item 46, page 464, the use of *either . . . or, neither . . . nor* to coordinate more than two words, phrases, or clauses is sanctioned by some dictionaries but not by others. Logic and clearness suggest that they relate two only.

84c. Avoid using conjunctive adverbs to join words or phrases or dependent clauses. (See Section **89b**.)

The adverbs which can also serve as conjunctions relate only two independent clauses or two sentences.

Dubious: Mother's favorite colors are blue and yellow, *also* pink.

John, *also* Henry, will be at the meeting.

I worked on my theme for two hours, *then* revised it and went to bed.

At last reports the Channel swimmer had swum for 12 hours; *still* was going strong.

In such sentences a pure coordinating conjunction should be used before the adverb, which becomes weakly parenthetical, or a second independent clause can sometimes be used.

Right: Mother's favorite colors are blue, yellow, and also pink.

John, and also Henry, will be at the meeting.

I worked on my theme for two hours; then I revised it and went to bed.

At last reports the Channel swimmer had swum for 12 hours and was still going strong.

84d. Use the proper subordinating conjunction to express subordinate relationships. (See Section **37**.)

Faulty diction: *Being as how* I was small, I did not make the football team.

I do not know *as how* I trust such a person.

Father wrote me *how that* he had gone fishing.

I read *where* Joe had broken another track record.

He was so fond of mathematics *until* he didn't want to talk of anything else.

Expenses became so unbearable *until* I sold my car.

Right: *Because* I was small, I did not make the football team.

I do not know *how* I could trust such a person.

Father wrote me *that* he had gone fishing.

I read *that* Joe had broken another track record.

He was so fond of mathematics *that* he didn't want to talk of anything else.

Expenses became so unbearable *that* I sold my car.

84e. Be sparing in the use of <u>like</u> as a subordinating conjunction.

In recent years *like* (for *as* or *as if*) has been increasingly used as a subordinating conjunction and has reached the status of having dictionaries give it a "colloquial" label as a subordinating conjunction. Perhaps the chief objection to *like* in this meaning is not its use but its overuse (as with *so*, see Section **36c**).

1. Blood was running from my nose *like* a red river had been undammed.
2. My face felt *like* it had been baking in a kiln for a week.
3. College teachers don't keep after you to do an assignment *like* the teachers do in high school.
4. As a freshman I'm trying to study hard *like* the good students in the class are doing.
5. Some people try to live *like* they were millionaires.
6. I felt *like* I had been tied to the bottom of the lake.
7. My overcoat felt *like* it weighed a ton.
8. With everything going *like* I had hoped, the summer was a profitable one.
9. I was not named after my father *like* many sons are.
10. Do you go to classes at West Point *like* we do here?

Overuse of *like* makes readers wish that writers would use an occasional *as, as if, though, as though,* for the sake of effective variety. However, do not become so word-conscious of *like* that you avoid it as a necessary preposition. In the following sentences, *like* should replace *as:*

> I hope that there are more instructors *as* my third example, and not any examples *as* the first two I have described.
>
> Let us now discuss a spectator's sport *as* football and a participant's sport *as* bowling.

TABLE V. **CONJUNCTIONS**

This table contains all the more commonly used conjunctions: pure or simple coordinating conjunctions, correlative conjunctions, conjunctive adverbs, and subordinating conjunctions. The various kinds of relationships, through meaning, are suggested in parallel columns. Depending upon your purpose, you may coordinate ideas in one of several ways or you may subordinate one idea to another. Some of the conjunctions have overlapping, double, or additional meanings. When in doubt about their use, consult your dictionary.

PURPOSE EXPRESSED	COORDINATING CONJUNCTIONS			SUBORDINATING CONJUNCTIONS
	Pure or Simple	**Correlative**	**Conjunctive Adverbs**	
Along the same line or in the same direction of thought	and	both . . . and not only . . . but also	also besides furthermore in addition indeed likewise moreover similarly	whereby whereupon
Contrast	but yet	not only . . . but also	however instead nevertheless notwith- standing still yet	although whereas
Affirmative alterna-tion	or	either . . . or	anyhow moreover still	else whereas whether

TABLE V. CONJUNCTIONS (Continued)

PURPOSE EXPRESSED	COORDINATING CONJUNCTIONS			SUBORDINATING CONJUNCTIONS
	Pure or Simple	Correlative	Conjunctive Adverbs	
Negative alternation	nor neither	neither . . . nor	however instead otherwise nevertheless	except that only whereas
Reason, result, purpose, cause	for (?) so		accordingly as a result consequently hence thereby therefore thus so	as because for inasmuch as in order that since so that that whereas why
Example			for example in fact indeed namely	
Comparison			in fact indeed moreover	than as . . . as so . . . as
Time			henceforth meanwhile then	after as long as as soon as before once since till until when whenever while

TABLE V. **CONJUNCTIONS** (Continued)

PURPOSE EXPRESSED	COORDINATING CONJUNCTIONS			SUBORDINATING CONJUNCTIONS
	Pure or Simple	**Correlative**	**Conjunctive Adverbs**	
Place				whence
				where
				wherever
				whither
Condition				although
				as if
				as though
				if
				lest
				once
				provided
				providing
				though
				unless
Concession				although
				in so far as
				notwithstand- ing the fact that
				though
				unless
				while

EXERCISES

A. Rewrite the sentences given in Section **84e,** giving them greater variety and effectiveness.

B. Correct all the errors in the use of conjunctions in the following sentences:

1. It was hard for me to develop good study habits, and I think I have solved my problem.
2. We return home to watch the football games on television, also to eat Christmas dinner.

3. Using the tunnel, we pass under the Hudson River, therefore coming out on Manhattan Island.
4. It is a custom in our house, on Sunday, to visit my cousin, then my grandmother.
5. In college it doesn't matter to my teachers whether I study, where in high school the teachers were always after me to get my work done.
6. This old vacant house really looked like it was haunted.
7. I haven't found anything else as good, and when I do I'll let you know about it.
8. We drove around the campus for a while, then returned to the motel for the night.
9. Easter morning dawned bright and clear, therefore meaning many people would attend sunrise services.
10. I was so sleepy when I finished studying until I just tumbled into bed.
11. We had hardly left town than we had a puncture.
12. Being that I am a sociable person, I speak to many people to whom I have not been regularly introduced.
13. I don't know as they have any right to enforce this regulation.
14. I read where another swimming record was broken at a recent meet.
15. I went to my room early that evening, but I had much work to do.

GRAMMATICAL TERMS DEFINED

85.   Many writers have partially or entirely forgotten definitions of most grammatical terms. Some can well be forgotten. A knowledge of others is necessary if you wish to phrase your ideas correctly, clearly, effectively, and appropriately.

The following list defines briefly and illustrates some of the elements of grammar which you have most need for and have possibly forgotten. Refer to this glossary whenever you are in doubt about the definition of a grammatical term as you study the sections on grammar (71–84), punctuation (86–100), and the sentence (31–50). Cross references guide you to other pages where important matters are discussed in some detail.

1. **Absolute phrase** or **Absolute expression,** sometimes called **Nominative absolute.** An absolute phrase or expression usually consists of a noun or pronoun followed by a participle modifying it. The participle is usually expressed; it may be understood. The expression is "absolute" because it modifies no special word in the sentence; yet it does not stand alone as a sentence. Section **31d** and page 502.

My work finished, I left on my vacation with a clear conscience.
The meeting adjourned, *no one having anything more to say.*
The game (being) over, we started a victory parade.

2. **Abstract noun.** The name of a thing not evident to one of the senses, like a quality: *beauty, honor, duty, sadness.*

3. **Accusative.** A *case* name meaning the same as the *objective* (which see). The word is rare in English but common in a study of some foreign languages like German and Latin.

4. **Active voice.** The form of an action-expressing verb which tells that the subject does or performs the action. See **Voice,** below.

5. **Adjective.** A part of speech modifying a noun or pronoun by limiting or describing: *red* shoes, *happy* children, *six* eggs. See Section 83 for discussion of right and wrong use of adjectives.

6. **Adjective clause.** A dependent clause used to modify a noun or pronoun. See Sections 73b and 88m.

The book *which you borrowed* from the library is overdue.
Go to see Mr. Wells, *who will advise you about future courses of study.*

7. **Adverb.** A part of speech modifying a verb (he runs *swiftly*), an adjective (an *extremely* good dinner), or another adverb (she spoke *very* rapidly). Some adverbs, especially when used for transition, modify the whole statement ("Some students, *however,* are planning to spend the vacation in Florida.") See Section 83 for discussion of right and wrong use of adverbs.

8. **Adverbial clause.** A dependent clause used to modify a verb, an adjective, or an adverb. See Section 73b.

John works part-time *because he needs the money.* (Modifies verb *works.*)
This is better *than I usually do.* (Modifies adjective *better.*)
Do you work more rapidly *than your brother does?* (Modifies adverb *more rapidly.*)

9. **Agreement.** Correspondence or sameness in number, gender, and person—between subject and predicate, and between pronoun and antecedent. Subjects and predicates *agree* in number (both are singular or both are plural):

John is my brother. (Subject and predicate are singular.)
John and Harry are my brothers. (Subject and predicate are plural.)

Pronouns agree with their antecedents in having the same gender, person, and number:

A *man* hopes to attain *his* goal in life.
Many *men* attain *their* goal in life.
Sue is one of those *girls who* are always pleasant and gracious.

For fuller discussion, see Section **76** for subject-predicate agreement, and Section **77** for pronoun-antecedent agreement.

10. **Antecedent** (meaning, literally, *placed before*). The substantive (noun or pronoun) to which a pronoun refers, or for which it is substituted. See Section **77**.

The *girl* has lost *her* gloves. (*Girl* is the antecedent of *her*.)
A *man* hopes to attain *his* goal in life. (*Man* is the antecedent of *his*.)
Many *men* attain *their* goal in life. (*Men* is the antecedent of *their*.)

Although by definition the antecedent is placed before the pronoun, it is sometimes illogically, yet clearly, placed after:

When *he* finally arrived, *Father* explained why he was late.

11. **Appositive.** A substantive, usually a noun, added to or following another substantive to identify or explain it. The appositive signifies the same thing, and the second substantive is said to be in *apposition*.

One important product, *rubber,* this country had to import.
(*Rubber* is in apposition with *product*.)
More hardy than wheat are these grains—*rye, oats,* and *barley*.
(*Rye, oats,* and *barley* are in apposition with *grains*.)

An appositive agrees with its substantive in number and case; it is set off by commas if its relationship is loose (nonrestrictive) and is used without punctuation if the relationship is close (restrictive). See Section **88q.**

12. **Articles.** The *indefinite* articles *a* and *an* and the *definite* article *the* are adjectives since they always accompany nouns. Nothing is described, however, and not much is limited; but, for example, *the book* is somewhat more definite than *a book*.

13. **Auxiliary.** A verb used to "help" another verb in the formation of tenses, voice, mood, and certain precise ideas. *Be (am, is, are, was were, been), have (has, had), do (does), can, could, may, might, shall,*

should, will, would, must, ought, let, dare, need, used are examples. See Section **78.**

> Mother *has* gone to Cleveland for a visit.
> *Will* you please turn out the light?
> We *should have been* studying an hour ago.

14. **Balanced sentence.** A sentence so written that certain thoughts or ideas have similar phrasing for purposes of comparison, contrast, or emphasis. See Section **74c** and Section **44.**

> Diligently to seek advice is wise; blindly to follow it is foolish.
> We fought our enemy in the streets; they fought us from the housetops.

15. **Case.** A term referring to the forms that nouns or pronouns have (nominative, possessive, objective) to indicate their relation to other words in the sentence. See Section **75.**

16. **Clause.** A group of words containing a subject and predicate and forming part of a sentence. A one-word *imperative* (which see), with the understood subject *you,* can serve as an independent clause. See Section **73.**

> Knowledge is wisdom, and wisdom is power. (Two independent clauses)
> Come early and stay late. (Two independent clauses)
> When I arrive, I shall telephone you. (One dependent clause, one independent)
> Those who strive usually succeed. (One dependent clause, one independent)

17. **Collective noun.** The name of a group composed of individuals but considered as a unit: *team, class, audience, jury.*

18. **Common noun.** A noun naming a member or members of a common or general group: *street, coat, automobile.*

19. **Comparative degree.** The form of an adjective or adverb comparing two objects, two persons, etc. See **Comparison,** below.

20. **Comparison.** The change in form of an *adjective* or *adverb* to indicate greater or smaller degrees of quantity, quality, or manner. Comparison is discussed and explained in some detail in Section **83e,** which see.

21. **Complement.** A word or expression used to *complete* the idea indicated or implied by a verb. A *predicate complement* (sometimes called *subjective complement*) may be a noun, a pronoun, or an adjective

611

which follows a linking verb and describes or identifies the subject of the linking verb.

> This book is *a novel*.
> The leaves of this tree are *red*.

An *object* (*objective*) *complement* may be a noun or adjective which follows the direct object of a verb and completes the necessary meaning:

> We are painting our house *gray*.
> Our neighbors named their baby *Maryann*.
> His teammates elected Schmidt *captain*.

Note that the verb is transitive (see Item 145) in a sentence or clause containing an object complement.

22. **Complex sentence.** A sentence containing one independent clause and one or more dependent clauses. See Section **74a**.

> When I arrived, the first person I saw was my father, who had come to the station to meet me.

23. **Compound object.** See **Object,** below.
24. **Compound predicate.** See **Predicate,** below.
25. **Compound sentence.** A sentence containing two or more independent clauses. See Section **74a**.

> We planned to spend the day at the beach, but rain spoiled our plans.
> Give willingly; give promptly; give abundantly.

26. **Compound subject.** See **Subject,** below.
27. **Compound-complex sentence.** A sentence containing two or more independent clauses and one or more dependent clauses. See Section **74a**.

> Since I am not skillful with my hands, I like to read, but my brother, who is mechanically inclined, rarely opens a book.

28. **Concord.** In grammar, *concord* is a term meaning the same as **Agreement** (which see).
29. **Concrete noun.** A noun naming an object evident to one of the senses of sight, hearing, touch, taste, smell: *shoe, song, velvet, coffee, perfume*.
30. **Conjugation.** The inflectional changes in the form or uses of a

verb to show tense, mood, voice, number, and person. See these terms in this glossary and see also Sections **79, 80, 81, 82.**

31. **Conjunction.** A part of speech which serves as a linking or joining word to connect words or groups of words like phrases, dependent clauses, independent clauses, or sentences: *and, or, if, when, nevertheless, moreover,* etc. See Section **84.**

32. **Conjunctive adverb.** A certain kind of adverb which can also be used as a conjunction coordinating two independent clauses: *also, furthermore, nevertheless, besides, however, therefore, thus, so, consequently, hence, likewise, still, then, moreover,* etc. See pages 605–607 and also Section **89b.**

33. **Construction.** A somewhat vague word, meaning the *arrangement* and *connection* or *relation* of two or more words in the phrase, clause, or sentence. Poor or bad or faulty or awkward construction therefore means poor arrangement, bad arrangement, faulty arrangement, awkward arrangement of words; or poor connection, bad connection, faulty connection, or awkward connection between words.

34. **Coordinating conjunction.** A *conjunction* (which see) relating words or phrases or clauses of equal grammatical value or importance (*coordinate* literally means *of equal* rank). See Section **84.**

35. **Copula.** See **Linking verb,** below.

36. **Correlative conjunctions.** Coordinating conjunctions used in pairs. The most common are: *neither . . . nor, either . . . or, both . . . and, not only . . . but also.* Each member of the pair is followed by the same grammatical word or phrasing. See also Sections **44b** and **84.**

> *Both* Father *and* Mother are natives of Kansas. (Nouns co-related)
> My books are *either* at home *or* at school. (Prepositional phrases co-related)
> The lilies of the field *neither* toil *nor* spin. (Verbs co-related)

37. **Declarative sentence.** A sentence which states a fact, a possibility, a condition.

> Abraham Lincoln was born February 12, 1809.
> If more money is needed, another campaign for funds will be held later.

38. **Declension.** The inflectional changes in the form or use of a noun or pronoun to indicate case, number, and person. "To decline" means to give these grammatical changes.
Examples:

	SINGULAR			PLURAL		
Nominative	man	I	who	men	we	who
Possessive	man's	my, mine	whose	men's	our, ours	whose
Objective	man	me	whom	men	us	whom

39. Decline. See **Declension.**

40. Demonstrative pronoun. A pronoun identifying, pointing to, pointing out, calling attention to: *this, that, these, those, such.* See Section **71d.**

41. Dependent clause (or subordinate clause). A *clause* (which see) that does not provide complete meaning in itself, that "depends" on an independent clause. There are three kinds of dependent clauses: *noun clause, adjective clause,* and *adverbial clause* (which see).

42. Direct address. The noun or pronoun showing to whom speech is addressed (also called the *vocative*):

> *Mother,* where are you?
> When we finish rolling the court, *Fred,* we'll still have time for two sets of tennis.
> Tell me, *sir,* where the Administration Building is.

43. Direct quotation. Giving the exact words as written or spoken by someone.

> Father wrote, "I'll be there on Friday."
> "Please use your dictionary more often," the instructor said.

44. Elliptical clause. From *ellipsis,* the omission of a word or words from a clause or sentence; not needed because understood from other words or from context. An elliptical clause is occasionally an independent clause; usually it is a dependent clause with its subject and part of its predicate omitted, since these are clearly understood from the main clause. See Section **73b.** In the following examples, the words shown in brackets are often omitted in speaking and writing.

> Some of the patriots carried guns, others [carried] swords, still others [carried] clubs and sticks.
> While [we were] drifting downstream, we grounded on a sand bar.
> He was 18 years of age, his brother [was] 12 [years of age].
> Although [he is] in New York frequently, Father rarely goes to the theater.

45. Emphatic verb form. Present or past tenses using the auxiliary verb forms *do, does, did* for emphasis. See Section **80b.**

Though I *did* work and still *do* work, I make no progress.

46. Exclamatory sentence. A sentence or justifiable sentence fragment expressing surprise or strong feeling: *What a time! We're there!* See Section **74b.**

47. Expletive. Frequently when a writer is at a loss about beginning a sentence or independent clause, he resorts to an *expletive*—a word or words not needed for the sense but used merely to fill out a sentence. The most common expletive is *there;* the most common expletive phrases are *there is, there are, there was, there were.* Usually, *there is* no weaker or more ineffective way to begin a sentence; occasionally, however, expletives are desirable or even necessary, but as a general principle they should be avoided whenever *there is* a better, more effective way of beginning a statement. (See Section **67c.**) Compare for effectiveness the following:

There stands a castle on the hill.
On the hill stands a castle.

There are three students sharing this room.
Three students share this room.

48. Finite verb. A verb form or verb phrase that serves as a predicate; it has number and person. Opposed to the finite verb is the non-finite verb form, which cannot serve as a predicate; non-finite forms are participles, gerunds, and infinitives. See Section **71e, f.**

49. Future perfect tense. The time of the action of a verb beginning in the present and ending at some time in the future. See Section **80a, b.**

In 1975 Father will have finished 40 years of medical practice.

50. Future tense. The time of a verb expressing "after now" or "after the present." See Section **80a, b.**

In 1975 Father will be 75 years old.

51. Gender. The classification of nouns or pronouns according to sex. The four genders are masculine, feminine, neuter, and common (either masculine or feminine): *boy, girl, it, individual.* In modern English nearly all traces of grammatical gender, as these are indicated by endings, have disappeared: *poetess* is an obsolete word, *actress* is still in good use. Gender, when indicated, is clear from the noun or pronoun, and no one pays any attention to endings as such: *actor, actress, he, she, it.*

52. **Genitive.** A *case* name meaning the same as *possessive* (which see). The word is rare in English but common in a study of foreign languages such as German and Latin.

53. **Gerund.** A verbal noun ending in *ing,* that is, a noun formed from and based on a verb. A gerund has the same form as the present or perfect participle: "Your *speaking* is appreciated"; "Your *having spoken* to us is greatly appreciated." See also Section **71f.**

54. **Gerundial phrase.** A phrase introduced by a gerund. If begun by a preposition, the phrase is a prepositional-gerundial phrase. See Section **72.**

> *Memorizing poetry* is a pleasant pastime. (Gerundial phrase)
> *Upon achieving my first goal,* I aimed *at achieving my second.*
> (Prepositional-gerundial phrases)

55. **Grammar.** The science dealing with words and their relationships to one another. *Rhetoric* deals with the art of expressive speech and writing and with the principles of clear, effective writing. *Grammar,* a descriptive statement of the way language works, includes a discussion of the forms of words, their use in phrases, clauses, and sentences, their tenses, cases, or other changes in form according to their relationships with one another. See pages 480–481.

56. **Imperative.** The mood, or mode, of a verb expressing a command or a request. See **Mood,** below, and Section **82.**

57. **Imperative sentence.** A sentence expressing a command or a request. See Section **74b.**

> Please reply by return mail.
> Send the enclosed card immediately.
> Give generously if you can.

58. **Impersonal construction.** A method of phrasing in which neither personal pronoun nor a person as noun is stated as the actor. The passive voice is used, or words like *it* or *there.*

> I have three reasons for my choice. (Personal)
> Three reasons were given for this choice. (Impersonal)
> We must consider three proposals. (Personal)
> It is necessary to consider three proposals. (Impersonal)

> or, better, less wordy,

There are three proposals to be considered.

or, best, least wordy,

Three proposals must be considered.

59. **Indefinite pronoun.** A pronoun implying an antecedent but referring to no specific person, place, or thing: *one, someone, everyone, everybody, somebody, each, none, no one, nobody, everything, nothing,* etc. See Section **71d.**

60. **Independent clause.** A clause (which see) that is complete grammatically by having a subject and predicate, that makes complete sense in the light of its context, that could if necessary stand as a complete sentence. See Section **73a.**

Harry plans to be a chemist, but Roger will become a doctor. (Each clause here makes a complete statement.)
If he is admitted, Roger will enter medical school this September. (The first clause is dependent; the second one is independent.)

61. **Indicative.** The mood, or mode, of the verb expressing a fact or what seems to be a fact. See **Mood,** below, and Section **82.**

We sell books here.
I think that today is Tuesday.

62. **Indirect object.** A noun or pronoun preceding the direct object of a verb and before which the word *to* or *for* is understood. When such an object follows the direct object, the preposition *to* or *for* is used.

Yesterday I sent *him* a telegram.
(Yesterday I sent a telegram *to him*.)
Will you lend *her* your book until Monday?
(Will you lend your book *to her* until Monday?)
Do *me* a favor, please.
(Do a favor *for me*, please.)

63. **Indirect question.** Restatement by one person of a direct question asked by another (see **Interrogative sentence,** below).

Direct:　　When will you arrive?
Indirect:　Jane asked when I would arrive.

64. **Indirect quotation.** Restatement by one person in his own words of the exact words written or spoken by someone else. See also **Quotation,** below:

Direct: Father wrote, "I'll be there on Friday."
Indirect: Father wrote that he will be here on Friday.

65. **Infinitive.** A verb form which is the first of the three principal parts of a verb; the infinitive has the function of a verb (as part of the predicate), but it is also commonly used as a verbal or in a verbal phrase, like a noun, adjective, or adverb. In these last three uses—as verbal—it is usually preceded by the sign of the infinitive, the word *to*. See Section **71f.**

> I must *study* tonight. (Infinitive as part of predicate)
> Will you please *reply* by return mail? (Infinitive as part of predicate)
> *To succeed* in life is my ambition. (Infinitive as noun)
> The candidate *to elect* is the present president. (Infinitive as adjective)
> John is going *to tell* us of his trip to Mexico. (Infinitive as adverb)

66. **Infinitive phrase** and **Infinitive "clause."** An infinitive phrase is one introduced by an infinitive: *to study mathematics*. For other examples, see **Infinitive,** above. An infinitive "clause," sometimes so called, is a construction which is part of the predicate and in which a noun or pronoun in the objective case is followed by an infinitive or an infinitive phrase; the noun or pronoun is called its "subject" (Section **75f**):

> Mary invited *me to attend the concert*.
> The Dean advised *us to take courses in foreign languages*.

67. **Inflection.** A change in the form of a word to show a change in use or meaning. *Comparison* (see Section **83e**) is the inflection of adjectives and adverbs; *declension* (see Item 38, above) is the inflection of nouns and pronouns; and *conjugation* (see Item 30, above) is the inflection of verbs.

68. **Intensive pronoun.** A pronoun having the same form as the *reflexive pronoun* (which see) and usually used immediately after its antecedent for emphasis. See Section **71d.**

> My sister *herself* baked this cake.
> I *myself* will see that you are invited.
> Students *themselves* are responsible for their attendance at classes.

69. **Interjection.** A part of speech—an exclamatory word—expressing strong feeling or surprise, which has little connection with the remainder of the sentence. See Section **71k.**

Oh, so that's how it was.
Hurrah! We've finally won a game.

70. **Interrogative adverb.** An adverb used in asking a question: *where, when, how, why, and,* less commonly, *whence, whither.*

> *Where* is University Hall? *When* was it built? *How* large is it? *Why* is it called University Hall?

71. **Interrogative pronoun.** A pronoun used in asking a question: *who, which, what,* and, less commonly, *whoever, whatever.* (Note: *which* and *what* sometimes combine two duties: pronoun and adjective.) See Section **71d.**

> *Who* is arriving tonight? On *which* train? *Which* is the hotel where he will stay? *What* is he coming for? *Whoever* had the bright idea of inviting him?

72. **Interrogative sentence.** A sentence asking a question and followed by a question mark. See Section **74b.** In addition to the examples under **Interrogative adverb** and **Interrogative pronoun,** just above, note:

> Have you received your semester grades yet?
> You're planning to go tonight, aren't you?
> You're not going to accept this invitation?
> Do you accept responsibility easily?

73. **Intransitive verb.** A verb that does not require a direct object to complete its meaning; the meaning ends with itself and the verb therefore may have adverbial modifiers but not an object. See Section **71g.**

> The night plane *has arrived.* It *flew* in just before midnight.
> The speaker *paused* for a few minutes before he *replied.*

74. **Irregular verbs.** Sometimes called *strong* verbs, irregular verbs do not follow a regular system or pattern in forming their principal parts. Instead, the principal parts are usually formed by a change in the vowel: *see, saw, seen; drive, drove, driven; choose, chose, chosen; lose, lost, lost.* Your dictionary is your guide. See Section **79c** also.

75. **Linking verb.** (Also called a *joining verb,* a *copula,* a *copulative verb,* or *coupling verb*). A verb which does not express action but only a state of being or a static condition. It serves to link the subject with another noun (predicate noun) or pronoun (predicate pronoun) or with an adjective (predicate adjective). These words following the

linking verb are called predicate complements (which see) or subjective complements. Common linking verbs are the forms of *to be, look, seem, smell, sound, appear, feel, become, grow, prove, turn, remain, stand*, etc. See Section **78**.

> This man *is* my uncle.
> This *is* he speaking.
> I *feel* happy this morning.
> This price *seems* high.

76. **Loose sentence.** A sentence with its parts arranged so that its meaning is clear before the end of the sentence. See Section **74c**.

> I shall be in Chicago early next month, and I shall hope to see you then.

77. **Mode.** A term meaning the same as **Mood** (which see).
78. **Modify.** To describe or limit. Adjectives are used with nouns or pronouns, and adverbs are used with verbs, adjectives, or other adverbs to describe, limit, or make meaning more definite in some other closely related way. Descriptive: *blue* skies, *tall* buildings. Limiting: *seven* books, the *only* woman.
79. **Mood.** A characteristic of verbs, revealing how action or expression is thought of: as a fact (*indicative mood*), as a possibility or something desired (*subjunctive mood*), or as a command or request (*imperative mood*). See Section **82**. Other kinds of expression are possible through use of certain auxiliary verbs. See Section **78**.
80. **Nominative.** The *case* form of nouns or pronouns used as grammatical subject or predicate complement. See Section **75**.
81. **Nominative absolute.** See **Absolute phrase,** above.
82. **Non-finite verb.** A verb form which cannot serve as predicate, since it shows—neither person nor grammatical number. Non-finite verb forms—the verbals—are *gerunds, participles, infinitives* (which see; see also Section **71f**).
83. **Nonrestrictive.** A modifier that does not limit but describes or adds information. The term is ordinarily used with phrases and dependent clauses. See Section **88m**.

> Professor Brown, *having given out the test questions*, told us to begin.
> This hat, *which I borrowed from my roommate*, does not fit me.

84. **Noun.** A part of speech naming a person, place, thing, quality, idea, or action: *John, meadow, paper, beauty, realism, walking*. See Section **71a, b, c**.

85. Noun clause. A dependent clause serving the purpose of a single noun. See Section **73b.**

> *What I achieve* will depend upon me. (Noun clause as subject of sentence)
> My mother wrote *that she would come here for Mother's Day.* (Noun clause as object of verb)

86. Number. The change in the form of a noun, pronoun, or verb to show whether one or more than one is indicated. The formation of the plural of *nouns* is discussed in Section **71c;** the few *pronouns* that have plural forms are listed in Section **75a.**

Plurals of *verbs* are relatively simple. Main verbs have the same form for singular and plural except in the third person singular, present tense, which ends in *s* (*sees, moves, thinks,* etc.) or occasionally *es* (*goes*).

Of the verb *to be:* in the present tense, *am* (1st person) and *is* (3rd person) are singular, *are* is 2nd person singular and 1st, 2nd, 3rd person plural; in the past tense, *was* is 1st and 3rd person singular, *were* is 2nd person singular and 1st, 2nd, 3rd person plural.

Of the verb *to have, has* is the third person singular, present tense form. Of the verb *to do, does* is the third person singular, present tense form.

Use your dictionary when you are in doubt concerning the singular or plural form of a noun, pronoun, or verb.

87. Object. The noun, pronoun, or noun clause following a preposition or following a transitive verb.

> Your book is on the *table.* (Object of preposition)
> I have written many *themes.* (Object of verb)
> I am sending *what you have ordered.* (Object of verb)

A *simple object* is the noun or pronoun or noun clause alone. A *complete object* is a simple object together with its modifiers. A *compound object* consists of two or more nouns or pronouns or noun clauses.

88. Object complement. A word—usually a noun or adjective—used after a direct object of certain verbs to complete the meaning. See **Complement,** also.

> We have elected Mary *secretary.*
> Let me try to make this picture *clear.*

89. **Objective.** The *case* form of nouns or pronouns used as objects of prepositions or as direct or indirect objects of verbs. See above, **Object** and **Indirect object.**

90. **Participial phrase.** A phrase introduced by a participle or an adverbial modifier + participle. See Section **72.**

> *Writing steadily,* I soon finished my theme.
>
> *Having finished my theme,* I signed my name and turned in my paper.
>
> Carefully *watching the numbers,* we had no trouble following Route 303.

91. **Participle.** A verb form having the function either of a verb used as part of the predicate or of an adjective. See Section **71f.** The three forms are *present participle, past participle, perfect participle* (all of which see).

> I am *writing* my theme now. (Present participle, part of predicate)
>
> I have *finished* my theme. (Past participle, part of predicate)
>
> A *driving* rain delayed our progress. (Present participle, used as adjective)
>
> *Heard* melodies are sweet. (Past participle, used as adjective)
>
> *Having finished* my theme, I turned it in. (Perfect participle, used as adjective)

92. **Parts of speech.** The classifications to one of which every word must belong: *noun, pronoun, adjective, verb, adverb, preposition, conjunction, interjection.* See each of these terms in this glossary; see also Section **71.**

93. **Passive voice.** The form of an action-expressing verb which tells that the subject does not act but is acted upon. Literally and actually, the subject is *passive.* See **Voice,** below.

94. **Past participle.** The third principal part of a verb (see Section **79**) used as part of the predicate or as an adjective. Unless it is formed simply by adding *d* or *ed* or *t,* the correct form is given in your dictionary. See **Participle,** above.

95. **Past perfect tense.** The time of the action of a verb beginning at a point in the past and ending at a later point in the past. See Section **80a.**

> By last September I *had traveled* 3,500 miles.

96. **Past tense.** The second principal part of a verb (see Sections **79, 80**), and the time of a verb which expresses a before-now action.

Unless the past tense is formed simply by adding *d* or *ed* or *t*, you will find the correct form given in your dictionary.

97. **Perfect infinitive.** Formed by the auxiliary *to have* followed by the past participle: *to have seen, to have worked*.

98. **Perfect participle.** Formed by the auxiliary verb *having* followed by the past participle: *having seen, having worked*. See **Participle**, above.

99. **Periodic sentence.** A sentence with its parts arranged so that its meaning is not complete or clear until the end is reached or nearly reached. See Section **74c**.

When I received the telegram, I knew that I had won.

100. **Person.** The change in the form of a pronoun or verb—sometimes, merely a change in use as with verbs—to indicate whether the "person" used is the person speaking (*first person*) the person spoken to (*second person*), or the person or thing spoken about (*third person*): *I* read, *you* read, *he* reads, *she* reads, *we* read, *you* read, *they* read, *it* plays.

101. **Personal pronoun** (see **Person**, above). A pronoun referring to the speaker or person writing (first person, *I, we*), the person spoken or written to (second person, *you*), or the person spoken of or written of (third person, *he, she, it, they, them*). See Sections **71d, 75a**.

102. **Phrase.** A group of related words not containing a subject and a predicate, and serving as a single part of speech. See Section **72**.

103. **Plural.** A classification of nouns, pronouns, subjects, and predicates, to indicate two or more units or members. See Section **71c**. Note that a subject with two or more singulars joined by *and* becomes plural. See Section **76f**.

104. **Positive degree.** The simple form of an adjective or adverb in which no comparison is expressed: *red, tall, rapid, beautiful, swiftly*. See Section **83e**.

105. **Possessive.** The *case* form of nouns or pronouns indicating, usually, ownership or some idiomatic use, like extent of space or time: *the man's hat, my job, the people's choice, children's activities, a week's vacation, two years' experience*. See Section **75j, k, l, m**.

106. **Predicate.** The verb or verb phrase in a sentence which makes a statement—an assertion, an action, a condition, a state of being—about the subject. A *simple predicate* is a verb or a verb phrase alone, without an object or modifiers; a *complete predicate* consists of the verb with its object and all its modifiers; a *compound predicate* consists of two or more verbs or verb phrases. See Section **74a**.

Mr. Tyler drove the ball nearly two hundred yards. (*Drove* is the simple predicate; *drove the ball nearly two hundred yards* is the complete predicate.)

I *wrote* the letter last night *and mailed* it this morning. (Compound predicate)

107. Predicate adjective. An adjective used in the predicate after a linking or joining or coupling verb; this adjective modifies or qualifies the subject. See **Complement,** above.

> This task is *difficult.*
> Today seems *colder* than yesterday.
> The team appears *ready* for the game.

108. Predicate complement, also called **Subjective complement.** A *predicate noun* or *pronoun,* or a *predicate adjective.* See these terms in this glossary.

109. Predicate noun or pronoun. A noun or pronoun used in the predicate after a linking or joining or coupling verb and identifying the subject. See **Complement,** above.

> She was *the best teacher* I ever had.
> This is *he* speaking.

110. Preposition (literally, *placed before: pre-position*). A part of speech showing the relationship of a noun or pronoun (the object of the preposition) to some other word: *at* home, *to* school, *from* a book, *through* the tunnel, *across* the street. See Section **71j.**

111. Prepositional phrase. A phrase introduced by a preposition. For examples, see **Preposition.** Sometimes the preposition *follows* its object: *Which car* did you ride *in?* See Section **72.**

112. Present participle. A verb form (verbal) ending in *ing* and used as part of the predicate or as an adjective. See **Participle,** above.

> I am *working* every afternoon. (Part of predicate)
> This restaurant does a *thriving* business. (Adjective use)

113. Present perfect tense. The time of the action or state of being of a verb, beginning in the past and just ending or still going on in the present. See Section **80a, b.**

> I *have studied* until I am tired.
> I *have been studying* since early this morning.

114. Present tense. The "now" time of the verb, including the *simple present,* the *progressive present,* the *emphatic present* (which see): I *study,* I *am studying,* I *do study.* See Sections **79** and **80.**

115. **Principal parts.** The three parts of a verb (*present infinitive, past tense,* and *past participle*) from which all other forms and uses of verbs (tense, mood, tone, voice) can be expressed, sometimes without but most frequently with the necessary auxiliary verbs. In learning the principal parts of unfamiliar verbs, consult your dictionary. See **Regular verbs** and **Irregular verbs;** see also Section **79.**

116. **Progressive verb form.** A statement of continuing action or state of being within a tense, formed by the proper forms of the auxiliary *to be* followed by present participle. See Section **80b** and comparative table on pages 572–573.

> We *are writing* our themes today.
> John *was playing* golf when I arrived.
> *Are* you *coming* early? We *shall be leaving* before six o'clock.

117. **Pronoun** (literally, *pro,* "for," plus *noun,* "name"). A part of speech which is used instead of a noun, primarily to prevent overuse and repetition of the noun: *I, you, he, she, they, it, who, whom, which,* etc. See Section **71d.**

118. **Proper noun.** A noun naming a particular or individual member of a group: *Harry, Mrs. Jane Wilson, Mexico, Methodist.* Note that proper nouns are capitalized.

119. **Pure conjunction.** A short or simple commonly used coordinating conjunction, to connect words, phrases, clauses, or even sentences: *and, but, or, nor, neither, yet,* etc. See Sections **84** and **88d.**

120. **Quotation.** Words written or said by someone. If these are given exactly as written or spoken, the quotation is *direct;* if they are restated and given in the words of another person, the quotation is *indirect.* Note the differences in punctuation. See Section **95a, b, c, d, j, k.**

> Direct: Henry said, "I have finished my work."
> Indirect: Henry said that he had finished his work.

121. **Reciprocal pronoun.** A pronoun indicating interchange of action. The only two reciprocal pronouns in English are *each other* and *one another.* See Section **71d.**

> Father and Mother consult *each other* before they make an important decision.
> In our family we have the greatest confidence in *one another.*

122. **Reference.** A word used with pronouns and their antecedents to indicate the relationship between them. The pronoun *refers* to the antecedent, the antecedent is indicated or *referred* to by the pronoun.

123. **Reflexive pronoun.** A combination of *self* or *selves* with one of the forms of personal pronouns, usually placed after a verb or preposition and referring or reflecting back to the subject: *myself, yourself, himself, herself, itself, ourselves, yourselves, themselves, oneself.* See Section **71d.**

> We asked *ourselves* these questions.
> He sometimes whispers nonsense to *himself.*

124. **Regular verbs.** Also called weak verbs, these are the most common verbs in English because they usually form their past tense and past participle by adding *d, ed,* or *t* to the present infinitive form: *move, moved, moved; walk, walked, walked; mean, meant, meant.* See Section **79a.**

125. **Relative pronoun.** A pronoun *relating* or connecting an adjective clause to its antecedent, a noun or pronoun: *who, whom, which, that.* The relative pronoun has a double function: to connect the clauses and to serve as a substantive in the dependent clause. See Section **71d.**

> The man *whom* we met lives in the house *that* we just passed.
> A teacher *who* likes reading will recommend books *which* his students will enjoy.

126. **Restrictive.** A modifier that limits or identifies the word modified. The term is ordinarily used with phrases and dependent clauses. See Section **88m.**

> A man *who works hard* should succeed. (Restrictive adjective clause)
> The books *on the top shelf* belong to the college library. (Restrictive adjective phrase)
> He works well *when you watch him.* (Restrictive adverbial clause)

127. **Sentence.** A word or group of words which convey completeness of meaning from writer to reader or from speaker to listener. For fuller discussion, see pages 262–264 and Sections **31** and **74.**

128. **Sentence fragment.** A word or group of words, usually a phrase or a dependent clause, not expressing completeness of meaning. Exclamatory sentences, answers to questions, and broken conversation are allowable and frequently used sentence fragments. For discussion of justifiable and unjustifiable sentence fragments, see Section **31a** and **b.**

129. **Sequence of tenses.** When independent and dependent clauses occur in a sentence, the tense or time relationship in these clauses

should be clearly stated. Hence, sequence of tenses: the clear order of time in verb forms. For fuller discussion, see Section **80h.**

130. **Sign of the infinitive.** The word *to* accompanying the infinitive form of the verb: *to* go, *to* see, *to* arrive. "I plan *to* go." "I hope *to* arrive next week." In certain expressions, especially with certain auxiliary verbs, the *to* is not used: "He can *go*." "I do *see*."

131. **Simple sentence.** A sentence containing one subject (simple or compound) and one predicate (simple or compound). See Section **74a.**

> Weather conditions were perfect for flying.
> Books and magazines are read by some and are studied by others.

132. **Simple verb form.** Usually a statement of a "snapshot" or instantaneous action of a verb. Compare with **Emphatic verb form** and **Progressive verb form,** and see Section **80b** and comparative table on pages 572–573.

> You *win,* but I *won* yesterday and I *shall win* tomorrow.
> We *have read* seven books this semester.

133. **Singular.** The number classification of nouns, pronouns, subjects, and predicates to indicate *one: boy, student, woman, I, he, she, it, is, has, was, goes, studies.* See **Number,** above.

134. **Strong verbs.** See **Irregular verbs,** above.

135. **Subject.** The person or thing (noun, pronoun, noun phrase, noun clause) about which a statement or assertion is made in a sentence or clause. A *simple subject* is the noun or pronoun alone. A *complete subject* is a simple subject together with its modifiers. A *compound subject* consists of two or more nouns, pronouns, noun phrases, noun clauses. See Section **74a.**

> The green *house is* for sale. (Simple subject)
> *The green house on the hill* is for sale. (Complete subject)
> *The green house and two acres of land* are for sale. (Compound subject)
> *What you say and what you do* are no concern of mine. (Compound subject)

136. **Subjective complement.** See **Predicate complement,** above.

137. **Subjunctive.** The mood, or mode, of a verb expressing possibility, desire, or a condition contrary to fact. See Section **82.**

> I wish I *were* in New York right now.
> If I *had gone,* I should have regretted it.

138. Subordinate clause. Another name for **Dependent clause** (which see.)

139. Subordinating conjunction. A conjunction joining a dependent clause (noun or adverbial) to its independent clause: *when, if, since, because, that,* etc. For a list of subordinating conjunctions, see pages 605–607.

> Dues were increased *because* there was no money in the treasury.
> He thinks *that* he will come.
> *If* I had gone, I should have regretted it.

140. Substantive. An inclusive term for noun, pronoun, verbal noun (gerund, infinitive), or a phrase or a clause used like a noun. The practical value of the word *substantive* is that it saves repeating all the words which are included in this definition. The following italicized words are examples of substantives:

> My *dog* is three years old.
> *They* will arrive tomorrow; in fact *everyone* is arriving tomorrow.
> Your *coming* is looked forward to.
> *To improve* myself is my *aim.*
> *From Chicago to San Francisco* is a long *distance.*
> *What you say* is no *concern* of *mine.*
> Do *you* know *that he was here yesterday?*

141. Superlative degree. The form of an adjective or adverb comparing three or more objects, persons, etc. See Section **83e.**

> Of the three brothers, Alan is the *tallest.*
> In our family, Mother is the one who drives *most carefully.*

142. Syntax. For all practical purposes, not a very useful word. Compare these three dictionary definitions of *syntax:*

> "The patterns of formation of sentences and phrases from words in a particular language; the study and description thereof."— *American College Dictionary.*

> "Sentence structure; the due arrangement of word forms to show their mutual relations in the sentence; that part of grammar which treats of the expression of predicative, qualifying, and other word relations, according to established usage in the language under study."—*Webster's New Collegiate Dictionary.*

> "In grammar, the arrangement of words as elements in a sentence to show their relationship; sentence structure; the branch of grammar dealing with this."—*Webster's New World Dictionary.*

Let's use, then, the words *grammar* and *grammatical.*

143. Tense. The time of the action or the state of being expressed by the verb: *present, past, future, present perfect, past perfect, future perfect.* See these terms in this glossary. The first three of these six are sometimes named the *simple* or *primary* tenses; the last three are sometimes named the *compound* or *secondary* or *perfect* tenses. See Section **80.**

144. Tone. A word used in this handbook to distinguish a characteristic of tenses of verbs, indicating within any one tense or time limit *emphasis* or *progress* or just *simple* time. See **Emphatic verb form, Progressive verb form, Simple verb form,** above. See also Section **80b.**

145. Transitive verb. A verb accompanied or followed by a direct object which completes its meaning. See Section **71g.**

> The batter *hit* the ball.
> We have carefully *studied* the assignment.

146. Verb. A part of speech expressing action or a state of being (static condition). See Section **71e, f, g.**

> The river *flows* slowly.
> My name *is* John.
> Yesterday *seemed* warm.

147. Verb phrase. A verb together with an auxiliary or auxiliaries, or with its object or its modifiers: *is going, was finished, shall take, shall have taken, will have been taken, studied the assignments, flows slowly, whispers nonsense to himself.* Distinguish between a *verb phrase* and a *verbal* (participle, infinitive, gerund). See Sections **71f** and **72.**

148. Verbals. The verb forms—*participles, gerunds, infinitives* (which see). One or more of these serve at times as adjectives, adverbs, nouns, parts of the predicate—but *never* as the predicate alone. See Section **71f.**

149. Voice. The change in the form or use of a verb—a transitive verb only—to indicate whether the subject is the performer of the action (*active* voice) or is acted upon (*passive* voice). In the formation of the passive voice, some form of the auxiliary verb *to be* is used with the past participle. See Section **81.**

> Leonard Brown *wrote* the theme that I *have* just *read.* (Active voice)
> The theme *was written* by Leonard Brown. (Passive voice)

150. Weak verbs. See **Regular verbs,** above.

PUNCTUATION AND MECHANICS

Punctuation is a system or method by which, through the use of certain marks, the meaning of written or printed communication is made clear.

Mechanics, a somewhat vague word, here simply means the conventional or proper use of capitals and small letters, italics (underlining), abbreviations, and numbers in either figures or words.

Proper punctuation is an indispensable aid to correct, clear, effective, appropriate writing because it helps to express thoughts and to make clear the relationships of thoughts to a reader. Punctuation developed originally because without it written language could not indicate certain qualities of speech, in which a pause or a rising inflection, for example, conveys meaning. These and other qualities of speech are reproduced in writing by certain marks of punctuation. Similarly, relationship between parts in a sentence is revealed by word order, but since modern English is not a highly inflected language, word order is flexible. In written English, therefore, various marks of punctuation suggest and indicate grouping, relationship, position, and kind of expression needed to convey meaning clearly.

With only a few words—even one word—punctuation marks change meaning. Note the differences conveyed in the following:

See!	What a pity.	I'm not shouting.
See?	What a pity!	I'm not shouting!
	What? a pity?	I'm not shouting?

What do you think? I am giving you four tickets to the dance.
What! Do you think I am giving you four tickets to the dance?

630

Punctuation and Mechanics

> Henry Browne firmly believes my roommate is the best athlete on our campus.
>
> Henry Browne, firmly believes my roommate, is the best athlete on our campus.

Punctuation is thus an organic part of writing; it is neither mechanical nor arbitrary. Usage does vary with individual writers, but fundamental principles remain the same. These fundamental principles, or descriptive "rules," are drawn from thousands of examples of punctuation as applied in writing and printing by authors, printers, editors, and others whose knowledge and practice are respected. When enough examples of one use of a certain punctuation mark occur, we state this use as a general principle or rule, beginning it thus: "Use the . . ." or "*Always* use the. . . ." When most of the examples agree: "The mark is *usually* used . . ."; when not enough examples are found to make a generalization: "The mark is *occasionally used*. . . ." Correct punctuation permits individuality only to the extent that communication of ideas from writer to reader is aided, not impeded.

The most important marks of punctuation are:

.	Period	—	Dash
?	Question mark	-	Hyphen
!	Exclamation point	'	Apostrophe
,	Comma	" "	Double quotation marks
;	Semicolon	' '	Single quotation marks
:	Colon	( )	Parentheses

Less commonly used marks of punctuation are:

[ ]	Brackets	***	Asterisks
. . .	Ellipsis periods	∧	Caret

A few marks used mainly for pronunciation or spelling are listed in Section **92g, h.**

The Four Purposes of Punctuation

Ordinarily you will apply a principle or specific "rule" of punctuation to a specific instance or sentence element. You may be helped in such application by remembering that punctuation usually serves one of four general purposes:

1. To *end* or *terminate* a statement—use period, question mark, or exclamation point.

> Little progress was reported.
> Are you going home?
> What an occasion!

2. To *introduce*—use comma, colon, or dash.

> Only one quality is needed, perseverance.
> My purpose is simple: to succeed in life.
> My goal in life is simple—success.

3. To *separate* parts of a sentence or word—use comma, semicolon, dash, hyphen, or apostrophe.

> If you have any influence at all, try to have me excused.
> Some people prefer dinner at noon; others prefer it in the evening.
> Commas, periods, semicolons, and colons—these are common marks of punctuation.
> Mr. Brown was elected secretary-treasurer.
> It isn't 9 o'clock yet.

4. To *enclose* parts of a sentence or a whole section—use commas, dashes, quotation marks, single quotation marks, parentheses, brackets. *Enclosure marks are used in pairs, except when the capital letter at the beginning of a sentence takes the place of the first or when a terminating mark at the end takes the place of the second.*

> An elderly lady, Miss Eleanor Moorson, was my favorite high school teacher.
> Miss Eleanor Moorson, an elderly lady, was my favorite high school teacher.
> My favorite high school teacher was Miss Eleanor Moorson, an elderly lady.

> You are not—and everyone knows this—a very careful driver.
> You are not a careful driver—and everyone knows this.

> "The word 'lousy' is not in reputable use as a term in literary criticism," said the lecturer.

> You are referred to the United States Constitution (see especially Article VIII).

Different marks indicating these four principal purposes of punctuation are, obviously, not necessarily interchangeable. The comma and the dash, for example, can serve three of the purposes, but you must choose the appropriate mark which will best serve clearness and effectiveness.

Also, a progression in the strength of the punctuation marks indicates strength of ideas. For example: Very weak parenthetic material—no commas; weak—commas; strong—dashes; strongest—(possibly) parenthesis marks. Very weak separation—no comma; normal separation—comma; stronger separation—semicolon; strongest (between sentences) —period, question mark, or exclamation point.

A more specific approach to punctuation is a study of each punctuation mark and its uses. Many of the principles make use of grammatical terms; if in doubt about their meaning, study their definitions in Section 85. If you know what kinds of words, phrases, clauses, or sentences you have but are in doubt about the punctuation marks to use, consult "Glossary of Applied Punctuation," Section 100.

THE PERIOD
86. The period (.) is usually a mark of termination, although it has a special use after abbreviations and, in series, a special use to indicate separation.

86a.   Use a period at the end of a declarative sentence.

When autumn comes, birds begin flying south.
Some people read two or three newspapers a day.
Grandfather spends his winter vacations in Florida; Father spends his in Maine.

86b.   Use a period after a mildly imperative sentence (a command or a polite request).

Drive carefully and avoid accidents.
Come over this evening and watch TV.
Write all your business letters on business stationery.

86c.   Use a period after an indirect question (see Section **87c**).

Mr. Brown asked when I could report for work.
Tell me what he said.

86d. Use a period after a standard abbreviation.

> Mr. and Mrs. James Brown.
> Henry Smith, M.D. (b. 1900; d. 1950)
> Sept. 15; lbs.; n.b.; ff.; q.v.; a.m.; p.m.; i.e.
> (See Section **98c** for exceptions.)

If a declarative sentence ends with an abbreviation, one period only is used. If the sentence is interrogative or exclamatory, a question mark or exclamation point follows the abbreviation period. Inside the sentence, the abbreviation period is followed by any punctuation which would have been normally used.

86e. Use periods properly in an outline.

A period is conventionally used after each symbol in the outline— Roman and Arabic numbers and capital and small or lower-case letters. See illustrations in Section **6a**.

A period usually is not used at the ends of lines in the topic outline, but it is used at the ends of lines in sentence and paragraph outlines. See illustrations in Section **6a-c**.

86f. Use a period before a decimal, to separate dollars and cents, and to precede cents written alone.

> 4.25 percent $5.75 $0.52

86g. Use three spaced periods to indicate an intentional omission from a sentence or quotation.

Such periods, called ellipsis periods, are especially helpful when only part of a sentence or line of poetry is quoted. Thus:

> ". . . a man's reach should exceed his grasp,
> Or what's a heaven for?
> —Browning, "Andrea del Sarto"

> "In the spring a young man's fancy . . ."
> —Tennyson, "Locksley Hall"

When ellipsis periods follow a complete sentence, the end-of-sentence period is also used.

> The game was filled with dramatic moments. . . . No one will ever forget the long, spine-tingling, game-winning shot in the last second, just as the gun fired.

1. A question mark or exclamation point may follow ellipsis periods.

2. Do not use ellipsis periods as a substitute for the dash. See Section 91f.

3. Do not use ellipsis periods purely as a stylistic device. Students occasionally use them to indicate that much more could be said. Generally, they have nothing in mind.

4. Asterisks (***), three in number, serve the same purpose as ellipsis periods but are not frequently used to indicate omissions within a sentence. They are more likely to indicate omissions of paragraphs or long passages.

86h.   **Use no period at the end of a title or after a centered or side subhead in the body of a manuscript.**

86i.   **Use no period after a quotation mark that is preceded by a period.**

Wrong: He said, "Stop at the next corner.".
Right: He said, "Stop at the next corner."

86j.   **Do not punctuate sentence fragments as complete units of thought unless they obviously qualify as complete expressions.**

Correct: "Was that coat on sale?"
           "Yes."
           "A bargain?"
           "Naturally."
           "Did you buy it?"
           "Of course."
           "For how much?"
           "Thirty-five dollars."

Incorrect: I spend part of every afternoon at the library. *Reading a magazine or anything else that looks interesting.*
           We sat in the first balcony. *Although there were still a few seats available downstairs.*

For full discussion of the sentence fragment ("period fault") see Section 31.

EXCLAMATION POINT AND QUESTION MARK

87.   The exclamation point (!) and the question mark (?), like the period, are usually marks of termination.

87a.   Use the exclamation point to terminate a forceful interjection, or to express surprise, emphasis, strong emotion, or command (i.e., a vigorously imperative sentence).

> Ouch! That hurt!
> Oh, what a remark to make!
> Help! Help!
> What wonderful news!
> Come at once!
> Here's to Smithson, the Man of the Year!

An exclamation point also may be used after a phrase or sentence to express irony. Often the exclamation used for this purpose is put in parentheses.

> You're a fine friend!
> She said that she might possibly condescend (!) to write.

Do not overuse the exclamation point. The emotion must be strong, the surprise genuine, the command emphatic to call for this punctuation. Too frequent use of the exclamation point weakens its effectiveness. Notice that a comma, not an exclamation point, is used after the mild interjection, *oh,* in the second illustration above.

87b.   Use a question mark at the end of every direct question.

For various ways of asking questions in English, i.e., of stating ideas in interrogative sentences, see Section 74b.

> Do you really know?
> You really do know?
> Why are you so eager to go?
> Where is the Administration Building?
> Which student left his dictionary in the classroom?
> You're going home next week, aren't you?
> Who said, "What is Man?" (Note use of single question mark.)

636

87c.   Do not use a question mark after an indirect question.

An indirect question is a question repeated in different words by the same speaker or by another person. The usual mark is a period (Section **86c**).

Wrong: I asked whether I had heard the announcement correctly?
Right: I asked whether I had heard the announcement correctly.

Wrong: John wondered when we would be ready to go?
Right: John wondered when we would be ready to go.

87d.   Use question marks to indicate a series of queries in the same sentence.

> Will you be there? or your brother? or your parents?
> Who will be there from your house? You? Your brother? Your parents?
> Also: Will you be there—or your brother—or your parents?
> Will you be there, or your brother, or your parents?

Notice also the different possibilities of capitalization.

87e.   Use a question mark, enclosed in parentheses, to express doubt or uncertainty.

> This is a genuine (?) leather bag.
> The University of Socomber was founded in 1350 (?).
> Shakespeare was born on April 23 (?), 1564.

Do not overuse the question mark to express doubt or uncertainty. If it is impossible to find the exact information needed, use the question mark, but do not use it as an excuse for not trying to find exact information.

87f.   Do not use a question mark in parentheses to indicate an ironical or humorous meaning .

Undesirable: The ambitious candidate boasted in a modest (?) way and
never raised his voice above a gentle (?) roar.

EXERCISES (Sections **86, 87**)

A. Copy a paragraph of 100–300 words from an article in your book of readings or from a magazine, omitting all terminal punctuation marks and changing all sentence beginnings to small letters. Exchange your paper for a similar one prepared by a classmate. Each of you should recapitalize and reinsert all terminal marks in the other's paper.

B. Underline all the periods, question marks, and exclamation points on a page in your book of readings or in a current magazine. Account for the use of each mark by careful reference to one of the principles cited in Sections **86, 87.**

C. Use the period, exclamation point, and question mark correctly in the following sentences, or if any of these marks are misused, make the necessary corrections.

1. Having dates in the library is all right, but one wonders how much studying gets done?
2. How can we be a government of the people if the majority of the people do not vote.
3. Oh, how beautiful Mother Nature looked that morning.
4. I use my nickname, Chas, in writing to my parents and friends.
5. Don't you agree that action should be taken at once.
6. Now I am beginning to wonder whether college life is the life for me?
7. What fun it is to be on the deck of a boat and soak up the sun.
8. Nature is a wonderful artist, but what is there left for Nature to paint.
9. The president of our college has an honorary LL D from his alma mater.
10. I wonder whether you would give me your opinion about proper punctuation of indirect questions?
11. During our senior year Miss. Douglas was married, but we never did get used to calling her Mrs Brown.
12. I never gave you my physical characteristics, did I.
13. We started studying at 7:15 PM and finished at 2:30 AM.
14. Give thanks. Isn't that the real purpose of Thanksgiving.
15. Some of the main things that worry him now are these: will he really like engineering will he flunk out during the next four years and will his girl wait four years for him.

THE COMMA

88. The comma (,) serves the purpose of introducing, separating, or, with another comma, enclosing. Because it has varied and distinct uses and is the most frequently seen mark of punctuation, it is the most troublesome of all the punctuation marks. Always used within the sentence, it differs from terminal marks (the period, question mark, and exclamation point) in degree. It shows a brief pause, less separation than full stops.

Note also that the comma, the semicolon, and the period form a series having a relatively increasing strength. The *comma* is the weakest mark of the three, for it separates short groups within the sentence and indicates comparatively close connection. The *semicolon* is used between longer and more important groups within the sentence, or between those which have a comparatively less close relation in thought. The *period* is the strongest mark of the three: it points out the most important division of thought, the sentence; it also indicates separation of thought into independent units.

NOTE: Mastery of the comma depends upon the individual. Some teachers in reading themes prefer to give students a specific reference discussing and illustrating comma use, the plan followed in this handbook. Other teachers find satisfactory the assigning and use of six broad principles dealing with comma use. These are as follows (with some parenthetic references to more detailed sections):

88/1. **Use a comma to separate long independent clauses of compound sentences** (Section **88d**).

88/2. **Use a comma to set off long introductory subordinate elements, usually adverbial or participial** (Section **88f, g**).

88/3. **Use commas to set off parenthetical word groups, including nonrestrictive elements, whether words, phrases, or clauses** (Section **88m, n, o, p, q, r, s, t**).

88/4. **Use commas to divide elements in series** (Section **88h, i, j**).

88/5. **Use commas in the conventional uses of setting off or enclosing dates, initials, numbers, letter salutations, etc.** (Section **88b, c, q, r, s, t**).

88/6. **Use commas for clearness, that is, to prevent misreading.** (Section **88k**).

COMMAS TO INTRODUCE

88a. **Use a comma to introduce a word, a phrase, or, occasionally, a clause.**

My aim in this course is easily stated, a high grade.
Only one other possibility remains, to travel by air.

I had an important decision to make, whether I should drop out of school or borrow the money and continue.

I have need of only two things, money and more money.

This principle of the introducing comma applies also to asking a mental question or expressing a thought or musing aloud:

I wondered, should I tell Father the whole story?

I thought, you're in real trouble now.

I told myself, you can do this as well as anyone.

Our next problem is, where do we go from here?

For a comparison of the introducing comma, as a less emphatic mark, with the colon and dash, see page 632, and also Sections **90a** and **91a**.

88b. Use a comma to introduce, or separate, a short quotation.

Henry said, "I'll never do that again."

1. If the "he said" or its equivalent follows the quotation, it is separated from it by a comma, provided a question mark or exclamation point is not demanded.

"I'll never do that again," said Henry.

2. If the "he said" or its equivalent is inserted between the parts of a quotation, it is enclosed by commas—provided one part is dependent (otherwise, see Section **95b**):

"I'll never do that again," said Henry, "unless I lose my temper."

3. When the quotation being introduced is long or formal, the colon replaces the comma. (See Section **90d**.)

4. Make a careful distinction between quotations which are really quotations of speaking or writing and quoted material which is the subject or object of a verb or material stressed by quotation marks such as titles, slang, and special word use. As examples of such special uses, observe the following:

The usual remark is "May the better man win."

"Make haste slowly" is the motto that came to my mind.

When Patrick Henry thundered "Give me liberty or give me death," he contributed a great catch phrase to the world.

If the "he said" comes between parts of a quotation, it is enclosed by commas.

"Itty-bitty" is not the exact phrase to use for "very small."

88c.   Use a comma after the salutation to introduce a friendly or social letter. (See Section **90e.**)

Dear John,   Dear Mary,   Dear Father,   Dear Mr. Browne,

COMMAS TO SEPARATE

88d.   Use a comma to separate independent clauses joined by one of the pure or simple coordinating conjunctions: and, but, nor, or, neither, yet.

To this list, *for* (see Section **88e** for discussion of *for*) and *so* are sometimes added. *So* is a short word and as conjunction its meaning is *therefore* or *thus;* it assuredly coordinates, but the chief objection to it is its constant overuse (see Section **36c**).

> I have not seen John recently, nor has anyone else seen him.
> Commas are important marks of punctuation, and you will do well to master their use.
> I tried to show him the error of his argument, but he would not be convinced.
> "Consider the lilies of the field, how they grow; they toil not, neither do they spin."—Matthew vi:28.
> The dean had no specific objections, yet he would not approve our proposal.

The principle stated in Section **88d** is one of the most frequently used and illustrated in English writing. This frequency accounts for considerable flexibility in application, as follows:

1. If the independent clauses are short, the comma may be omitted before the pure conjunction. This statement, however, immediately brings up the question "How short is short?" If the independent clauses consist of only subject and predicate, or of three or four words each, then they are obviously short and the comma may be omitted, except perhaps before *neither* and *yet*. Examples:

> The rains came and the rivers rose.
> I made a motion but no one heard me.
> In the final judging, Mary did not win nor did Jane.

Sometimes lack of punctuation between short clauses may cause momentary misreading, and a comma is necessary for clearness.

Misleading: We ate *bacon and the Brownes* ate eggs.
Clear: We ate bacon, and the Brownes ate eggs.

2. Fairly long clauses are sometimes written without a comma between them if their connection is particularly close. The comma, for example, is frequently omitted before the pure conjunction when the subjects of both clauses are the same (same noun or noun and pronoun).

> I read for an hour or two and then I studied.
> Henry read the assignment over hurriedly and then he began a more careful rereading of it.

When the subject of the second clause is omitted, the sentence has merely a compound predicate and does not contain a comma before the conjunction, unless the members are unusually long. Use of a compound sentence or a simple sentence with a compound predicate depends upon a writer's view of which is more effective for a particular purpose.

> Henry came into the house and called excitedly to his mother.
> The last person spoke clearly and made a favorable impression upon the audience.

3. Use commas between short clauses to which you wish to give special emphasis.

> You must pay promptly, or you will be penalized.
> I did not expect to win, but I did.

4. Long independent clauses—but be sure they are *long*—which contain complicated internal punctuation (a sprinkling of three, four, or five commas) should be separated by a semicolon before the pure conjunction (see Section **89c**).

88e. Use a comma before the conjunction <u>for</u>.

The word *for* is used either as a conjunction or as a preposition. A comma before it is a fairly sure sign that the word is a conjunction, no comma that it is a preposition. Of course, a prepositional phrase beginning with *for* and used parenthetically is enclosed by commas.

Conjunction: I went home early last evening, *for* my parents did not wish to be alone.

We cannot pay a bill as large as this, *for* we do not have the money in our treasury.

Preposition: I went home early last evening *for the purpose* of getting a good night's sleep.

My high school, *for that matter,* has always had excellent teachers in English and mathematics.

One convincing argument, *for example,* concerns our pocket-book.

Because of its smallness, *for* is frequently listed with the other pure coordinating conjunctions (Section **88d**), even though its meaning is *because, as, since.* If you apply Section **88e**, the grammatical classification of *for* is of little importance.

88f. Use a comma to separate an introductory adverbial clause from the independent clause.

When you have finished the examination, sign your name and turn in your paper.
Before John started on his trip, he made a careful plan of his itinerary.
If I arrive first, I'll wait for you in the library.

This principle applies only to adverbial clauses. An introductory noun clause is not set off by a comma; an adjective clause follows, not precedes, the noun or pronoun that it modifies.

What you say is true.
That your theme was turned in late is unfortunate.

Many introductory adverbial clauses are simply transposed elements. Inserted in their natural order, they may or may not have commas, depending upon meaning. Inserted elsewhere, they are enclosed by commas.

After you arrive on the campus, various meetings will be held to help orient you.
Various meetings, after you arrive on the campus, will be held to help orient you.
Various meetings will be held to help orient you after you arrive on the campus.

When the adverbial clause follows the independent clause:
1. Omit the comma if the adverbial clause is necessary to complete (i.e., if it restricts) the meaning of the sentence.

The accident occurred as I turned into Tenth Street.
John works because he has no other way to live.

2. Use a comma if the clauses are fairly long, or if a slight pause is desired; omit it if the clauses are short.

> I'm quite willing to be a delegate to the convention, although there are others more capable than I.
> I'll go, if I have to go.
> I'll go if I have to go.

88g. Use a comma to set off an introductory modifying phrase containing a verb form.

Not universally applied, this principle is so commonly illustrated that it is still recommended for the student-writer. The introductory phrase may be participial or prepositional, adjective or adverb. If an adjective phrase, it is very likely nonrestrictive (see Section **88m**).

> Half-concealed in the bushes, the dog watched us go by.
> In order to play a vigorous game, you should be in good physical condition.
> By studying slowly and carefully, John mastered the subject.
> Because of his hidden fear of water, he refused to go swimming.

1. Neither an introductory gerund phrase nor an introductory infinitive phrase used as subject is a modifying phrase; therefore, neither one is set off by a comma unless for other reasons. Frequently even a short modifying infinitive phrase is not set off.

> Playing on a championship basketball team is a thrilling experience. (Gerund phrase as subject)
> Playing on a championship basketball team, according to my roommate, is a thrilling experience. (Gerund phrase as subject, followed by parenthetic element)
> To be a successful fisherman is not easy. (Infinitive phrase as subject)
> To be a successful fisherman I use only the best equipment. (Introductory modifying infinitive phrase)

2. An introductory modifying phrase without a verb form, unless it is fairly long, is usually not set off by a comma.

> Without fail I'll be there.
> Because of lack of money some students have to drop out of school.
> After careful consideration of the matter for a week or 10 days, we decided that the trip was too long to justify the expense.

NOTE: Many phrases containing verb forms do not come at the beginning of sentences, and usually they may be considered as some kind

644

of parenthetic element, such as absolute phrases (Section **88p**) or non-restrictive phrases (Section **88m**).

88h. Use commas to separate words, phrases, or clauses in a series.

1. One kind of series is represented by A, B, and C—three or more words, phrases, or clauses, with an appropriate pure conjunction joining the last two members.

> I have brought my textbook, my notebook, and some theme paper with me.
> You will find Henry around somewhere: in the living room, in the basement, or out in the garden.
> He whispered, he muttered, but finally he shouted.

Some writers omit the comma before the conjunction and use A, B and C. Since greater clearness is frequently obtained by the use of the comma before the conjunction, present practice favors the comma, a practice advocated by the United States Government Printing Office *Style Manual,* the University of Chicago's *A Manual of Style,* and the Modern Language Association *Style Sheet.*

2. Another kind of series is represented by A, B, C—three or more words, phrases, or clauses, with no conjunctions. Commas are used after each member except *after* the last, unless the clauses are all independent (see Sections **89a, 32a**).

> This store sells newspapers, magazines, books.
> Joe believes in good sportsmanship on the football field, on the basket-ball court, in the swimming pool, on the golf course.

3. Do not use commas separating members of a series, unless emphasis is desired, when a conjunction is used to join each pair.

> I have read nothing by Swift or Milton or Wordsworth.
> Billy says he is going to have ice cream and cake and pie and choco-late pudding for his dessert.
> At times I have no energy, or enthusiasm, or skill. (Emphasis)

88i. Use a comma to separate two or more adjectives when they modify, equally and coordinately, the same noun.

> I bought an old, dilapidated chair and a new, ugly, badly faded rug.
> Our Administration Building is surmounted by a tall, stately, ivy-covered tower.

When the adjectives are not coordinate, commas are omitted.

> A heavy steel cable spans the rugged green ravine.
> The old oaken bucket was covered with green wet moss.
> To me Colonel Smith is the supreme example of a fine old Southern gentleman.

Notice that a comma is never used to separate the last adjective from the noun.

Sometimes there may be doubt, as in "an old, dilapidated chair" above; then you must use your judgment in deciding, for, admittedly, it is sometimes difficult to determine whether the adjectives are coordinate or not. Several tests, although not infallible, may help. One way of testing is to insert the coordinate conjunction *and* between the adjectives; if the *and* fits naturally, use a comma when it is omitted, otherwise not. Another test: if the position of the adjectives can be reversed, the adjectives are coordinate. Another test: does the first adjective modify the idea of the second adjective and the noun? If so, the adjectives are not coordinate. Also, if one of the adjectives describes shape or material or color, the adjectives are probably not coordinate.

88j.   Use a comma to separate contrasted coordinate elements.

1. Such contrasted elements may be words or phrases:

> Psmith begins his name with a *P,* not an *S.*
> Your misspelling is due to carelessness, not to ignorance.
> The pitcher threw slowly, but effectively.
> This garden spray is effective, yet safe.
> Books should be kept on the table, not on the floor.

2. Two dependent clauses may contrast. A special kind of contrasting dependent clauses is in good use: neither clause makes sense alone, but taken together the two form a complete sentence.

> The higher we go into the air, the more rarefied the atmosphere becomes.
> The more tired the team became, the better it played.
> The less haste some people make, the more progress they achieve.

3. Two independent clauses contrast when the first is a declarative statement and the second is interrogative, a common way of asking a question:

You did telephone, didn't you?
We should have longer vacations at Thanksgiving, shouldn't we?
You believe I was justified, don't you?

88k. Use a comma to separate words or other sentence elements that might be misread.

Misleading: The day after a salesman called with the same product.
Outside the house needs a coat of paint; inside the walls need replastering.
Instead of a hundred thousands came.
In 1960 842 freshmen appeared on our campus.
Last week I was in bed with a cold and my mother took care of me.

Improved: The day after, a salesman called with the same product.
Outside, the house needs a coat of paint; inside, the walls need replastering.
Instead of a hundred, thousands came.
In 1960, 842 freshmen appeared on our campus.
Last week I was in bed with a cold, and my mother took care of me.

Constructions in which commas are needed to prevent misreading are usually questionable or faulty. If it is possible, rephrase such sentences to eliminate awkwardness and to increase clearness.

Instead of the hundred people expected, thousands came.
Last week, when I was in bed with a cold, my mother took care of me.

88l. Use the comma to separate thousands, millions, etc. (i.e., numbers of four or more digits except numbers indicating years, telephone numbers, and house numbers).

In the fall of 1961 our freshman class numbered exactly 1,961 students.
In this contest 5,612 entries have been received.
If you telephone Prospect 1452, you will learn that the population of our city is now 312,456.
The government deficit may reach $5,565,000,000 this year.
The Blacks have sold their home at 2455 Jefferson Street and have moved to 8634 Avondale Avenue.

COMMAS TO ENCLOSE

88m-N. Use commas to enclose <u>nonrestrictive</u> clauses and phrases within the sentence.

88m-R. Do not use commas to enclose <u>restrictive</u> clauses and phrases.

1. Clauses and phrases are *nonrestrictive* when they do not limit or restrict the word or words modified. Clauses and phrases are *restrictive* when they limit the word or words modified. Usually such clauses and phrases serve as adjectives and limit (one meaning of an adjective) or describe (another meaning of an adjective) the noun or pronoun they modify. Observe what the same clause does in each of the following sentences:

> Indianapolis, *which is the capital of Indiana,* has a population of 427,200.
> The city *which is the capital of Indiana* has a population of 427,200.

In the first sentence above, the omission of the adjective clause, *which is the capital of Indiana,* does not materially change the meaning of the sentence; its purpose is to give added information. In the second sentence, the same worded adjective clause, *which is the capital of Indiana,* is necessary for the complete expression of the idea; that is, it identifies, it tells which city (the capital of Indiana). The clause in the first sentence is *nonrestrictive,* and it is thus enclosed, or set off from the remainder of the sentence, by commas; the clause in the second sentence is *restrictive* and is not enclosed by commas. Adjective clauses usually begin with the expressed or understood relative pronouns, *who, which, that.* A *that* adjective clause is usually restrictive; a *who* or *which* adjective clause may be either restrictive or nonrestrictive, depending on meaning; and when the relative pronoun is omitted, the adjective clause is restrictive.

Note the labels attached to the following:

> Chapter 10, *which tells of the rescue,* is well written. (Nonrestrictive or nonlimiting clause)
> The chapter *which tells of the rescue* is well written. (Restrictive or limiting clause)

The car *that you saw* was a sports model. (Restrictive or limiting clause)

The books *that I own* are all by American authors. (Restrictive or limiting clause)

The man *my brother met in Chicago* has traveled widely (Restrictive or limiting clause)

Arthur Johnson, *whom my brother met in Chicago,* has traveled widely. (Nonrestrictive or nonlimiting clause)

The foregoing examples show that the adjective clause immediately follows the noun it modifies.

2. When an adjective phrase, not a series of adjectives, precedes its modifier, it is usually nonrestrictive; when it immediately follows, it may be restrictive or nonrestrictive; when it follows a few words farther on, with no sacrifice of clearness, it is usually nonrestrictive. Examples:

Living very simply and economically, Father and Mother have saved enough money to put me through college. (Nonrestrictive)

Having won the regional championship, our basketball team moved into the semifinals. (Nonrestrictive)

The book *lying there on the living-room table* has had hard use. (Restrictive)

Encyclopaedia Britannica, Volume II, *lying there on the living-room table,* has had hard use. (Nonrestrictive)

I thought only of college entrance, *fully realizing that the next four years would be important for me.* (Nonrestrictive)

Occasionally a student walks into a building, *leaving his companion outside to open the door for herself.* (Nonrestrictive)

3. The preceding examples show that the modifier (clause or phrase) may be either restrictive or nonrestrictive, depending upon the intended purpose. Restrictive phrases and clauses are therefore necessary to identify the word or words they modify. They answer such questions about the word or words as *who? which one?* Each of the restrictive modifiers above serves to identify the word it modifies.

The context sometimes determines whether a clause or phrase is restrictive or nonrestrictive. If the word or words are already identified by a phrase or clause, an additional modifier is likely to be nonrestrictive.

The man *who sharpens our lawn mower every summer* is a genius. (Restrictive)

We were fortunate in finding a little shop full of all kinds of mechanical gadgets and kept by a thin, undersized little old man. We have no doubt that the man, *who sharpens our lawn mower every summer,* is a genius.

The man *sitting across the aisle from us* was going to Los Angeles. (Restrictive)

The man in the blue serge suit and wearing a brown straw hat, *sitting across the aisle from us,* was going to Los Angeles. (Nonrestrictive)

4. Usually proper names, being already limited and identified, are modified by nonrestrictive phrases or clauses. But occasionally they, too, need identification.

The John Jones *who is our postman* is not the John Jones *who lives on University Avenue.* (Restrictive)

The Springfield *which is in Illinois* is a long way from the Springfield *which is in Massachusetts.*

NOTE: Occasionally proper names in apposition are restrictive and, unlike other appositional phrases, are not set off by commas. See Section **88q1.**

5. Avoid the error of double restrictions:

This is *my* new suit *that I bought last week.*

Both italicized elements are restrictive; the latter is the important limiting statement:

This is the new suit *that I bought last week.*
This is *my* new suit, which I bought last week.

88n. Use commas to enclose parenthetical words, phrases, or clauses.

A fairly adequate test of a parenthetical expression is this: it may be omitted without materially affecting the meaning of the sentence or, frequently, though not always, its position in the sentence may be shifted without any change in meaning.

However, we do not disagree too much.
We do not, *however,* disagree too much.
We do not disagree too much, *however.*
We must, *on the other hand,* discuss every aspect of the problem.
I believe, *if anyone should ask my opinion,* that action should be postponed.

Parenthetic elements vary in intensity, and you show by punctuation their relative strength.

1. Many words and phrases are so weak that they require no punctuation.

> I *also* believe in progress.
> *In fact* I am inclined to agree.

2. Other words, like *oh, well, yes, no, too, etc., i.e.,* when used parenthetically, are enclosed by commas.

> *Oh,* what a game!
> *Oh, yes,* I agree completely.
> *Well,* that was the remark that closed the discussion.
> Then, *too,* other problems need consideration.
> Am I going? *No,* I believe not.
> Dictionaries, paper, pencils, pens, erasers, *etc.,* are used in the writing laboratory.

The letter combinations *i.e.* (Latin, *id est,* "that is") and *e.g.* (Latin, *exempli gratia,* "for example") are parenthetical elements always followed by a comma and preceded by a comma or a semicolon (see Section **89a**).

> Please report to Room 217, *i.e.,* the Writing Laboratory.
> Your work has been satisfactory; *i.e.,* it has been accurate and it has been turned in promptly.
> Certain universities, *e.g.,* University of Illinois, Southern Illinois University, and Northern Illinois University, are primarily state-supported.

3. Some phrases and dependent clauses have enough parenthetic strength to require commas.

> Consider, *for example,* the benefits of extracurricular activities.
> Those activities, *as I said,* may require considerable time.

4. Independent clauses—as well as some phrases and dependent clauses used emphatically—are so strong, parenthetically, that enclosure marks should be dashes or parentheses. (See Sections **91e** and **92a**.)

> There is no reason—*no good reason, that is*—for spending so much money now.
> The lovely little town of Kickapoo Falls—*I was born there, you know*—hasn't changed much since I was a boy.

My father has been a physician (*he received his training at the University of Louisville*) in Kickapoo Falls for 30 years.

88o. Use commas to enclose inserted sentence elements.

Inserted sentence elements—emphatic, suspending, or transposed expressions—are somewhat similar to parenthetical words, phrases, and clauses. *Emphatic* expressions are set off because the writer indicates that he considers them emphatic. *Suspending* expressions interrupt or retard the movement of the sentence, holding important information until near the end of the sentence. *Transposed* expressions, like *I believe, I think, it seems to me, I suppose, you see,* and, frequently, adjectives following their nouns, are out of their normal order and require punctuation not used in normal word order. Such inserted expressions are frequently more essential to the thought of the sentence than purely parenthetical material, but they are nonrestrictive in function.

Emphatic insertion:	He did not make that statement, *as you will see if you read more carefully,* and I am certain that he did not mean it to be misunderstood.
Suspending:	This is a good novel, *not only because it contains plenty of action,* but because it fully develops three characters.
	Another secret for successful study, *and not many students know this,* is the preparation and use of a study schedule.
Transposed:	Action, *I believe,* should be postponed.
	On that night, *it seems,* there is to be a full moon.
	A maple tree, *tall and well shaped,* stood in front of the house.
Not transposed:	*I believe* action should be postponed.
	It seems on that night there is to be a full moon.
	A *tall and well-shaped* maple tree stood in front of the house.

88p. Use commas to enclose absolute phrases.

An absolute phrase, a group of words having no grammatical relation to any word in the sentence, consists of a noun and a participial modifier, the latter being sometimes omitted but understood.

NOTE: The last seven words in the preceding sentence form an absolute phrase, which can come at the beginning, in the middle, or at the end of a sentence. See also Section 72 and page 608.

The game (being) over, the crowd soon scattered.
The task having been finished, we started on our return trip.
I went to the first desk, *my application (held) in hand,* and asked for Mr. Brown.
We needed a fourth member for our bridge club, *Mary Ellen having moved to another town.*

An absolute phrase should not be punctuated as a sentence.

Wrong: We needed a fourth member for our bridge club. Mary Ellen having moved to another town.

88q.   Use commas to enclose words in apposition.

A word in apposition is a noun or pronoun (word or phrase) identifying in different words a preceding noun or pronoun. (See Section **85.**) Usually the appositional word or phrase is explanatory and therefore nonrestrictive (Section **88m-N**).

My father, *a physician,* has just retired from active practice.
This is Mr. Browne, *our newly elected president.*
My task, *to compose a short story,* seemed hopeless.

1. Sometimes the appositional word or phrase limits or restricts (Section **88m-R**). Omit the commas when the appositive is restrictive, or part of a proper name, or closely related to the preceding word.

The river Ohio is beloved of song writers.
We have recently seen an excellent performance of the play *Julius Caesar.*
Richard the Lion-Hearted was a famous English king.
My brother James is a senior in high school.

2. Omit the commas, usually, when the appositive is a noun clause.

The fact that I was ill caused my absence.

3. Frequently words in apposition are introduced by *namely, for example, for instance, i.e., e.g.,* etc. These words and phrases are enclosed by commas, as parenthetical expressions. If these and the apposition are fairly strong—that is, long and emphatic—dashes should enclose them. (See Section **91e1**.)

Two of the candidates, *namely,* John Smith and William Browne, are my friends.
Any difficult subject, *for example,* chemistry, needs careful study.

The various seasonal sports—*for example,* football in the fall, basketball in the winter, and baseball in the summer—attract millions of spectators.

4. When *such as* introduces an appositive word or phrase, it is preceded by a comma and has no punctuation following—*never* a comma or colon.

Wrong: Some of our cities, *such as,* New York, Chicago, and San Francisco, are thriving centers of commerce.

Some of our cities, *such as:* New York, Chicago, and San Francisco, are thriving centers of commerce.

Right: Some of our cities, *such as* New York, Chicago, and San Francisco, are thriving centers of commerce.

88r. Use commas to enclose nouns or pronouns or a noun phrase in direct address (vocatives).

Mr. Brown, will you speak next?

I am proud, *Father,* of what you have accomplished.

We are assembled, *ladies and gentlemen,* to discuss an important problem.

Will you please, *sir,* speak more distinctly?

Your class will not meet today, *George.*

88s. Use commas to enclose places and dates explaining preceding places and dates within a sentence.

Henry left on June 20, *1960,* to go to Cincinnati, *Ohio,* for an interview. (But note: Henry left on June 20th to go to . . .)

In October, *1960,* he was transferred to Albany, *N.Y.*

or

In October *1960* he was transferred to Albany, *N.Y.*

He told us to send his mail to him at 147 Prospect Avenue, *Albany 21, N.Y.,* his new address.

1. The second comma must be used when the state follows town or city and when the year follows both month and day. When only month and year are used, the use of commas around the year is optional: use two or do not use any.

2. Note the choice of punctuation in the date line of a letter:

February 23, 1961

14 June 1961

3. No comma is used before the postal-delivery zone number: Chicago 16; Philadelphia 27.

88t.   Use commas to enclose initials or titles following a person's name.

Abbett, H. M., Abner, T. W., and Adams, R. B., head the list of names.
James Norman, M.D., and Frank Hale, D.D., are the featured speakers on the program.

The abbreviations of Senior and Junior after a name are also enclosed:

The son of William McAdams, Sr., is listed as William McAdams, Jr., on our records.

UNNECESSARY COMMAS

88u.   Use no unnecessary commas; i.e., use commas only where needed and justifiable.

Comma usage varies with different writers, but the fact that a reputable writer deviates occasionally from conventional practices does not establish a new principle. When practice varies so widely that no principle of punctuation can be stated, remember that every comma used must be needed for sense construction, clearness, or effectiveness.

Modern punctuation usage omits many commas that were formerly used; therefore, be able to account for each comma in your writing. In general, avoid using the comma needlessly to separate closely related sentence elements. Some of the more common misuses or overuses of the comma are discussed in the following series of "do not use" statements.

1. Do not use a comma to separate a subject from its predicate or a verb from its object or complement. Noun phrases and clauses also act as subjects, objects, or complements of verbs and should not be separated by commas without logical reason.

Wrong: What you say, is true. (Noun clause as subject)
To do satisfactory work, is my aim. (Infinitive phrase as subject)
We asked, to hear the motion reread. (Infinitive phrase as object)
The reason is, that I have been ill. (Noun clause as predicate nominative)

655

I found, that college was not so hard after all. (Noun clause as object)

The coach believes, that the team will play a good game. (Noun clause as object)

2. Do not use a comma before the indirect part of a quotation. Frequently the indirect quotation is a noun clause used as the object of the verb.

Wrong: The letter informed me, that I should report for an interview.

John told me emphatically, to come as early as I could.

The speaker asserted, that he stood squarely for progress.

3. Do not use a comma indiscriminately to replace a word omitted. The word *that* in an indirect quotation, the word *that* in introducing other noun clauses as objects, and the relative pronouns *who, whom, which, that* are frequently omitted in informal writing; they should not be replaced by commas. (See Section 31f.)

Wrong: John replied, he would return next week. (Comma incorrectly substituted for *that* in an indirect quotation.)

Joe never realized, he could learn to write so easily. (Comma replaces, wrongly, *that* in introducing a noun clause as object of a verb.)

The man, I met was a friend of a friend of mine. (Comma incorrectly substituted for the relative pronoun *whom*.)

The last house, we lived in was just the right size for our family. (Comma incorrectly substituted for the relative pronoun *which*.)

4. Do not use a comma, ordinarily, to separate two words or two phrases joined by a pure coordinating conjunction or correlative conjunctions. (For contrasting elements, see Section 88j; for independent clauses, see Section 88d.)

Wrong: He has dignity, and integrity.

The leader has strength of body, and firmness of purpose.

5. Do not use a comma indiscriminately after a pure or simple conjunction. The use of other parenthetical or inserted elements may justify a comma after the conjunction.

Wrong: But, I shall never make that mistake again.

We are leaving early, and, I shall expect to receive your check before I go.

Right: But, as a lesson learned from experience, I shall never make that mistake again.

We are leaving early, and, to save trouble all around, I shall expect to receive your check before I go.

6. Do not use a comma to separate a *so . . . that* clause in a sentence.

Wrong: The game was so hard fought, that our players were completely exhausted.

I was so cold, that I thought I would never get warm again.

7. Do not use a comma before the first or after the last member of a series.

Wrong: Avoid a mixture of, red, yellow, green, blue, and brown paints.

We went swimming in a cool, clear, smooth-flowing, river.

8. Do not use a comma to set off quoted words which are not direct quotations but which use quotation marks to call attention to the words. For examples, see Section **88b.**

9. Do not overuse commas; sometimes they come at reasonable places in the sentence, but not one may be necessary. (See Section **88n.**)

Unneeded commas: After the game, my brother and I went home, by the long route, because we wanted, at all costs, to avoid the highway traffic.

Omitted commas: After the game my brother and I went home by the long route because we wanted at all costs to avoid the highway traffic.

88v. Avoid the comma splice: Do not use a comma to separate independent clauses not joined by one of the pure or simple conjunctions, and, but, or, nor, neither, yet (for, so).

The comma splice, a serious error also named "comma blunder" and "comma fault," is the joining or *splicing* of two separate complete statements by a comma. This punctuation is confusing to the reader, who expects a sharper break between such clauses. For discussion of this error and methods of correcting it, see Section **32.**

EXERCISES

A. Choose a page from your book of readings or from a current magazine. Underline or encircle every comma. Give a reason for each comma, or each pair of commas, according to the principles stated in Section **88**. Do not be surprised if a few of the commas are unconventionally used, unnecessary, or incorrectly placed.

B. Buy one of the larger popular magazines. Read at least three full pages. Underline all the A, B, and C series, the A, B, C series, and the coordinate adjectives (Section **88h** and **i**). What are your conclusions about the use of commas?

C. Read at least two full pages in the same magazine (Exercise B). Underline or encircle all restrictive and nonrestrictive adjective clauses and phrases (see Section **88m**). What are your conclusions about the use of commas?

D. In the following—mainly, introductory phrases and clauses and coordinate independent clauses (see Section **88d, e, f, g**)—commas are omitted. Where should they be properly used? For what reasons?

1. Should you take the wrong road you may never find the right road again.
2. You may choose easy courses and get high grades or you may choose difficult courses and really learn something.
3. When one gets there he has the feeling of having conquered the mountains for he can see for miles around.
4. Through a careful examination of himself as driver, his ability, and the requirements for safe driving everyone can live in a safer world.
5. Now that I am enrolled in college I would like to make a few suggestions about studying.
6. We have not made our decision yet nor can I tell you how soon we shall make it.
7. If everybody would ask himself what he has to be thankful for I know many of us would be surprised.
8. Once the plane takes off the stewardess is always there to help you.
9. After working there three months I was promoted to putting stock on the shelves.
10. Either some students are not fitted for college or society is paying huge sums for offering education to many loafers now in college.
11. As reckless drivers we are always one jump ahead of the safety experts for we can think of other ways to kill ourselves.
12. Florida is visited all the year round but the busy season starts in December and lasts through March.
13. The oftener we hear certain stories the more we want to hear them again.
14. After wandering through the woods all afternoon I found enough mushrooms for our supper.

15. To demonstrate what I mean by a mean trick I'll relate an experience that happened to me.
16. The atmosphere of Holland, Michigan, is of the old world and all the charm of old Holland can be found there.
17. The more education a person has the more capable he is of facing the problems of life.
18. Because the football stadium is not centrally located it is an inconvenience to most of the fans.
19. Before Grandfather became a marine engineer the family lived in Springfield.
20. Whenever a holiday comes the whole town moves to the beach.

E. Coordinate adjectives, the A, B, C series, and the A, B, and C series need commas (see Sections **88h** and **i**). In the following sentences, some commas are misused, and some are omitted. Where should commas be properly used? For what reasons?

1. I, like every other average, red-blooded, American boy, have a hobby.
2. We left my brother my sisters and my aunt, and started out to look for my father.
3. Aviation is dependent on electronics for its present operation, and future growth.
4. A person susceptible to colds should avoid exposure to cold wet or snowy weather.
5. It was a beautiful, sunny, June day.
6. Little brothers come in assorted sizes shapes and colors.
7. A tall good-looking boy sits next to me in class.
8. Let's use as examples winter spring and summer.
9. The difference between my dictionary, and an ordinary dictionary is that my dictionary has an encyclopedic section.
10. The outstanding landmark of the town is the huge old brick water tower.

F. Where are commas needed, for clearness, in the following sentences (see Section **88k**)? Why?

1. To learn the student must use books other than his regular textbook.
2. As far back as I can remember our family has been moving from place to place.
3. Just as we finished the policeman came and tried to catch us.
4. Yes, believe it or not many couples go to the library.
5. I went home early for supper, and after I had eaten my mother brought me back to school.

6. As we have observed the customs of other lands are very different from our own.
7. As I said above our farm is located about five miles south of where the last glacier stopped.
8. From my childhood on foreign and native superstitions and traditions have held a great deal of interest for me.
9. The electrical engineer must constantly be searching for new things are happening in his field every day.
10. When she was asked why Mary gave three or four good reasons.
11. Our city supports a Class D baseball team; other than this local sport fans must support the high school teams.
12. Besides our working my family took time out for summer vacations.
13. I was in bed with a cold and my dog kept me company.
14. After reading this one should begin to realize the value of a dictionary.
15. Whenever you have time to kill the boys on this floor will help you kill it.

G. The following sentences contain restrictive or nonrestrictive clauses or phrases (see Section **88m**). Indicate by your nonuse or use of commas which are restrictive and which are nonrestrictive.

1. Another course in which I am doing satisfactory work is Mathematics 112.
2. Parents having only one child should make every effort to keep him from becoming too selfish.
3. My sister Jane who will be 16 in December is a junior in high school.
4. Friday was a day which was filled with many activities.
5. Another contest and one that I liked best of all was the pony-riding contest.
6. Lake Jackson which extends into parts of Georgia and Florida is one of the prettiest lakes in the area.
7. The Library has a typing room for those people wanting to use typewriters.
8. The student who is writing this theme is having his troubles with English.
9. The next day we arrived at Lookout Mountain where we visited Point Park and Rock City Gardens.
10. Donaldson Cave is named after Mr. Harry Donaldson who previously owned part of the park and the land in the area.
11. Wolf Cave located at one end of the park is an outstanding natural attraction.

12. I expect to talk with our dean of boys who is coming here to interview his high school's graduates.
13. Our town has a population of 18,000 people most of whom commute to New York City which is just 20 miles away.
14. Mr. Lynn having no children left his property for a recreation center.
15. Mother being a shrewd woman knows how to get Father to do things for her.

H. In the following sentences, various parenthetic or inserted sentence elements (see Section **88n, o, p, q, r, s, t**) need commas. Where should the commas go, and why, specifically?

1. Most people seem to be in a hurry no matter where they are going.
2. This being our first day we didn't know where the different classrooms were.
3. The best-known and most popular building however is the Union Building.
4. Located on the Potomac River a few miles from Washington D.C. is the home of our first President George Washington.
5. William unlike many important people is modest and most courteous.
6. Whiting known as the "Oil City" is located in northern Indiana.
7. Let us take for instance Friday the 13th.
8. Mother likes to be with people though.
9. I Harry N. Wilson reside at 821 North Ferry Street Cincinnati Ohio.
10. I want you to meet Sharon my younger sister.
11. This I believe is the most important advantage of military life.
12. To get into too many activities at the start is not a good idea I have learned.
13. I attended grade school in Glen Park a small suburb of Pittsburgh.
14. All other equipment such as radio turn signals and fog lights should be checked.
15. Any one of these plans could keep me happy though and that is what I am looking for in a job.
16. After my two weeks are over at the Navy base I will fly to Clearwater Florida where I will meet my parents.
17. My name by the way is Wally Schmidt.
18. Grandfather a silver-haired old gentleman wears gold-rimmed glasses.
19. America has Hollywood movie capital of the world and Louisville home of the famous Kentucky Derby.
20. First of all I will be home for my first vacation from college, second my relatives will be at our house Thanksgiving day, and third our Thanksgiving dinner will be the best Mother has ever prepared.

I. Commas in the following sentences are misused (see Section **88u**). How?

1. Any boy, who is interested in a 4-H project, will learn many things of value to himself and his community.
2. I think, that the demand for pharmacists will increase.
3. Thanksgiving should be a time, when one gives thanks for his blessings.
4. I was so proud, that I ran and told all my playmates.
5. While working there I met a girl named, Amelia Bright.
6. The biggest responsibility, I ever had, was to drive a truck to California.
7. I know from experience, that smoking is harmful.
8. TV has done to reading, what the great Chicago fire did to Chicago. It has ruined it.
9. The most famous New Year's game is the one called, "The Rose Bowl."
10. Being able to enjoy college, is another thing that I have learned.
11. I received a pamphlet entitled, "Safe Driving Rules and Laws."
12. The main reason I think I am a careful driver, is the fact that I had a good driver-training course.
13. One of the most important activities of the camp every year, is the canoe trip.
14. Those themes, reaching the finals in the competition, are published in our college newspaper.
15. He explained further, that experts were hired by insurance companies to investigate accidents.
16. The most important thing I have learned, is not to cut classes.
17. That decision of course, was an important decision.
18. An inventor is a man, who finds new and easier ways of doing things.
19. Such simple questions must be answered along with more detailed, and complicated ones.
20. The evening of October 31, is the time children have looked forward to for weeks.

THE SEMICOLON

89. The semicolon (;) is a mark of separation only, a stronger mark than the comma, signifying a greater break or a longer pause between sentence elements. It is not, however, so strong as terminal marks of punctuation; its use indicates that two or more statements are not closely enough related to justify commas but are too closely related to justify being put in separate sentences. In all its uses, it separates coordinate elements.

89a. **Use the semicolon to separate independent clauses not joined by a pure or simple conjunction, such as <u>and</u>, <u>but</u>, <u>or</u>, <u>nor</u>, <u>neither</u>, <u>yet</u>.** (See Section **88d.**)

Except for conjunctive adverbs (Section **89b**), this principle is that the semicolon is used between two independent clauses with *no* conjunction between them.

> I am certain you will like this dress; it will suit you perfectly.
> Please close the window; the room is too cold.
> You have only ten more minutes; please stop writing and revise what you have written.

89b. **Use the semicolon to separate coordinate independent clauses joined by a conjunctive adverb or a phrase which serves as a conjunctive adverb: <u>also</u>, <u>anyhow</u>, <u>as a result</u>, <u>besides</u>, <u>consequently</u>, <u>for example</u>, <u>furthermore</u>, <u>hence</u>, <u>henceforth</u>, <u>however</u>, <u>in addition</u>, <u>in fact</u>, <u>indeed</u>, <u>instead</u>, <u>likewise</u>, <u>meanwhile</u>, <u>moreover</u>, <u>namely</u>, <u>nevertheless</u>, <u>notwithstanding</u>, <u>otherwise</u>, <u>similarly</u>, <u>so</u>, <u>still</u>, <u>then</u>, <u>therefore</u>, <u>thus</u>, <u>yet</u>.**

> I tried for two hours to solve the problem; *then* I gave up and worked on my English assignment.
> This road has many sharp curves; *however,* a careful driver will have no difficulty.
> Mr. Greene is a busy man; *in fact,* he seems busier than he really is.

To apply correctly and effectively the foregoing principle, keep in mind the following explanatory statements:

1. The semicolon is used immediately before the conjunctive adverb when the conjunctive adverb comes *between* the two independent clauses. If the conjunctive adverb is shifted to a position within the second clause, the semicolon separates the two clauses (see Section **89a**), and the adverb, depending upon its parenthetic strength, is or is not enclosed by commas (Section **88n**).

> I tried for two hours to solve the problem; I *then* gave up and worked on my English assignment.
> This road has many sharp curves; a careful driver, *however,* will have no difficulty.
> Mr. Greene is a busy man; he seems busier, *in fact,* than he really is.

2. When the conjunctive adverb comes between the clauses, should there be a comma after it? In the absence of an unvarying principle, use as a guide the weakness or strength of the word or phrase, parenthetically, in relation to the second clause. If it is weak, omit the comma; if it is strong, use a comma; if it is mildly strong (like *therefore,* for example), use or omit, depending upon your desire to indicate a pause. Another guide: a comma follows a long conjunctive adverb or phrase (*nevertheless, in fact, for example,* etc.), rarely follows a shorter one (*thus, hence, then,* etc.).

> I have trained myself to read rapidly and carefully; *thus* I save myself many hours a week.
> I did not favor spending the money; *nevertheless,* I did not vote against the proposal.
> This climate is subject to sudden weather changes; *therefore* (or *therefore,*) you should bring a variety of clothing.

3. Distinguish between conjunctive adverb and simple conjunction. A conjunctive adverb is both conjunction and adverb; as such it has an adverbial function which no simple conjunction possesses. Furthermore, it is used only between independent clauses, or sentences, whereas a simple conjunction may join words, phrases, dependent clauses, independent clauses, or even sentences.

4. Distinguish between a conjunctive adverb placed between independent clauses and a subordinating conjunction (*although, because, since, whereas, inasmuch as*) introducing a dependent clause coming between the two independent clauses. The subordinating conjunction is preceded by a semicolon in such uses only when no pure coordinating conjunction joins the independent clauses (see Section **89a, d**).

> I shall attend the lecture this evening, *although I can ill afford the time.* (Dependent clause follows independent clause.)
> I shall attend the lecture this evening; *although I can ill afford the time,* I believe that I shall learn something of profit. (Two independent clauses separated, second being introduced by a dependent clause.)
> I am having trouble with English and chemistry, *because my high school training in these subjects was inadequate.* (Dependent clause follows independent clause.)
> I am having trouble with English and chemistry; *because my high school training was inadequate,* I have been assigned to non-credit

sections in these subjects. (Two independent clauses separated, second being introduced by a dependent clause.)

To eliminate any possibility of confusion or misunderstanding, two sentences might be preferable.

89c. **Use the semicolon to separate independent clauses joined by a pure conjunction if the clauses are long or contain much internal punctuation.** (See Section **88d**4.)

In applying this principle, do not overuse the semicolon. The longer a sentence becomes, and the more involved its punctuation, the less likely it is to be clear. One, two, or even three commas in a sentence are scarcely enough to justify a semicolon before a pure conjunction, especially if the commas, or most of them, occur in the second clause.

> Grandfather has been a steady, industrious worker all his life, and now his income from stocks, bonds, and other investments enables him to live comfortably.
>
> Success in college, so some maintain, requires intelligence, industry, and honesty; but others, fewer in number, assert that only personality is important.
>
> Many books, particularly very cheap ones, are slapped together so hastily that they have little durability and cannot withstand the wear and tear a student must subject them to; but, with proper care such as the true lover of books would bestow, even these books can be made to serve during a student's college years, or even longer.

Whenever clearness might not otherwise be attained, use semicolons also to separate long phrases or long dependent clauses or a series of words.

> The nominations for class president include the following: Adams, J. B., of New Richmond, member of Skull and Bones; Davis, H. M., of Belleville, formerly secretary of the Camera Club; and Wilson, M. L., of Newtown, captain of the football team.

89d. **Do not use the semicolon to set off a phrase or a dependent clause.**

Ordinarily the semicolon serves the same purpose as the period: to indicate the end of one complete thought and the beginning of another; it is this break in thought that your reader expects when he sees a semicolon. *One fairly safe guide is this: no period, no semicolon.* Setting off dependent clauses or phrases with semicolons leads to the same confusion, in your reader's mind, that is caused by the *unjustifiable sentence fragment* (see Sections 31 and 89b4); therefore, do not use the semicolon between unequal grammatical elements, i.e., between one complete grammatical element and one incomplete (but see Section 89c). Such an error is named "semicolon fault."

Frequent misuses of semicolons concern dependent clauses and participial or absolute phrases:

> Inasmuch as Joe has a fiery temper; we have to be careful what we say to him. (Dependent clause)
> The next meeting of the club has been postponed two weeks; because most of the members are on an inspection trip to Detroit. (Dependent clause)
> I received an A on the test; although I was hoping for no more than a B. (Dependent clause)
> If I were you; I should ask for a recount of the ballots. (Dependent clause)
> Being careful to observe all traffic regulations; I am considered a good driver. (Participial phrase)
> The excitement of our mock political campaign having died down; we once again turned our attention to our studies and the approaching final examinations. (Absolute phrase)

To correct semicolon errors like these, use no punctuation or use the comma for the semicolon.

89e. Do not use a semicolon for a colon as a mark of introduction.

Wrong: My purpose is simple; to succeed in life.
> Yesterday the bookstores sold me the following; textbooks, theme paper, drawing instruments, and laboratory equipment.
> (In business letters) Dear Sir; Dear Mr. Woods; Gentlemen;

To correct semicolon errors like the foregoing, substitute colons for the semicolons.

89f. Do not use the semicolon for the dash as a summarizing mark. (See also Section 91d.)

Wrong: Class plays, debates, a newspaper, and the yearbook; these were the major non-athletic activities in our high school.
> Mathematics, chemistry, English; these give me more trouble than any other subjects.

Right: Class plays, debates, a newspaper, and the yearbook—these were the major non-athletic activities in our high school.

Mathematics, chemistry, English—these give me more trouble than any other subjects.

EXERCISES

A. The following sentences contain conjunctive adverbs or conjunctive-adverb phrases. Where should semicolons and commas go?

1. It takes my brother a long time to get over a fit of temper, and I am glad otherwise I would not be able to recuperate and be ready for the next argument.
2. Some people are not afraid of anything, at least they don't act as if they are.
3. While at home, I spent most of my time out of doors therefore I put in a great deal of time hunting and fishing.
4. Fred Waring and His Pennsylvanians were doing a show on the campus however no tickets were left when I went to buy mine.
5. Our star miler has a very sore leg consequently he will not run on Saturday.
6. Bob spent the larger part of his naval career at Great Lakes he was sent overseas however on special duty twice during that time.
7. Education is considered very desirable every student therefore should try to get at least a little while he is in college.
8. You should give that chair at least two coats of flat paint then in addition you should put on one coat of varnish.
9. He said the quotation was from Shakespeare nevertheless I was certain that it was from the Bible.
10. I disliked everything that went with English I never did learn much therefore about writing and reading.
11. I remember when I was in the sixth grade I then had dreams of going to college and studying medicine.
12. Our family expanded by a sister, three years younger than I, and a brother, five years younger as a result, our house became too small for us.
13. Mysterious noises rang in my ears in fact some of those noises I had never heard before.
14. My ambition then was to become a major-league baseball player henceforth I practiced baseball by day and dreamed baseball by night.
15. Jim and I shared many hobbies together for example we shared hobbies from stamp collecting to cross-country running.

B. Semicolons are misused in the following sentences. How?

1. My family is made up of four people; my father, my mother, my brother, and me.
2. It was our only full day there; although we had spent several previous afternoons visiting museums.
3. The more I learned about engineering; the more I became interested in this field.
4. If a student cannot rely on himself and make decisions; what good will all the facts in the world do him?
5. To drive in heavy traffic is folly; especially if there is a snowstorm brewing.
6. Being tired, I decided to see a show; so that I could sit down and rest.
7. Joe McGee was his name; a happy-go-lucky sort of fellow.
8. It would be difficult to see everything in this museum in two days; much less the two hours I spent there.
9. Al and I would get up early every Saturday morning; pack a lunch; grab our hiking gear; and trot off into the pine forest behind our house.
10. I'm sure that we have no witches today; at least, none that ride a broom.
11. Kenny is 22; about 3 years older than his brother.
12. Summer or winter; spring or fall; Florida offers a mild climate.
13. Life on a farm is not all fun and enjoyment; especially in the spring.
14. After the plans were drawn; they were given to the chairman for further checking.
15. As I had started, as a freshman, from the bottom in high school; accordingly I started from the bottom in my job.

C. How are semicolons misused in the following sentences?

1. We spent most of the day in the motorboat; but stopped to eat and refill the gas tank occasionally.
2. If the student still dozes off, there is only one conclusion I can come to; his is a hopeless case.
3. My friend's college is surprisingly big; much bigger than my own college.
4. Our going to a movie turned out to be a mistake; because the two pictures that we saw were ridiculous.
5. After the dance was over we went to Sue's house; where her mother gave us snacks.
6. Milltown is a quiet little town of approximately 3,000 people; most of whom have lived in this residential town all their lives.
7. I entered college thoroughly interested in outdoor life; and, therefore, chose forestry as my course of study.

8. I've enjoyed hearing a number of records; such as those of Beethoven and Brahms.
9. He was fond of the country and of books; and from these tastes had arisen his principal enjoyments.
10. My study habits had improved steadily; resulting in my becoming an above-average student.
11. Learn how to study in high school; for not knowing how is the greatest fault of students in college.
12. A veterinarian's private practice is of two kinds; large- and small-animal treatment.
13. Somehow I managed to keep from hitting the other car; as the driver hadn't turned an inch toward his side.
14. How beautifully Nature blends her colors in the autumn; reds, greens, yellows, and browns.
15. We were instructed in the use of the library; how to find books and magazines, and how to use the card catalog.

THE COLON

90. The colon (:) is usually a mark of introduction, sometimes a mark of separation. Unlike the semicolon, which is used to separate coordinate sentence elements, the colon is primarily a mark for introducing lists, series, and quotations.

90a. Use the colon to introduce a word, phrase, or, occasionally, dependent clause when emphasis is desired.

For a comparison of the colon, as a more emphatic mark, with the comma in such uses, see pp. 632–633 and Section **88a.**

My aim in this course is easily stated: a high grade.
Only one other possibility remains: to travel by air.
This is our next problem: where do we go from here?
I am positive there is one appeal which you cannot overlook: money.
These two things he loved: an honest man and a beautiful woman.

90b. Use the colon after an introductory statement which clearly shows that something is to follow: an enumeration, tabulation, list, etc.

You will need the following equipment for the trip: a change of clothes, a few toilet articles, and a supply of money.
Three reasons have been given for his success: integrity, industry, and a good personality.

Everything will be arranged: the paper provided, the pencils sharpened, the chairs placed.

A break must come between the introduction and what follows, and the best indication of this break is the use of words such as *the following* or *as follows*.

90c. **Use a colon to introduce a clause that summarizes or gives an example of or carries on the thought of a preceding clause.**

Only skillful and infrequent use of the colon for this purpose is effective. Its overuse is ineffective and misleading, because the reader expects the conventional mark between such clauses to be the semicolon, not an introducing but a separating mark.

The purpose of reading is not alone recreation: it is also information.

Many a man succeeds through sheer attention to industry: Benjamin Franklin was such a man.

I went to the fair for two reasons: first, I wanted to visit the various 4-H exhibits, and, second, I wanted to see about a job for the summer.

90d. **Use the colon to separate the introductory words from a quotation which follows, if the quotation is formal, long, or paragraphed separately.** (See also Sections **88b** and **95a**.)

General Robert E. Lee once said: "*Duty* is the sublimest word in the English language; no man should do more, nor should any man be expected to do less."

The mayor arose, wiped his spectacles, cleared his throat, and said: "It seems inevitable that we should have differences of opinion about this important community problem."

The most important suggestion was made by William Furniss, who spoke as follows: ". . . " (one or more paragraphs of the speech)

90e. **Use the colon after the salutation of a business letter.**

Dear Sir:
Dear Mr. Brown:
Gentlemen:
My dear Mr. Burns:

The usual practice is to place a colon after the salutation of a formal or business letter and a comma after the salutation of an informal, friendly letter. (Section 88c.)

90f. **Use the colon to separate the title of a book from the subtitle, hour and minute figures in writing time, the scene from the act of a play, the chapter from a verse in the Bible.**

Lew Wallace is the author of *Ben Hur: A Tale of the Christ.*
By my watch it is exactly 10:25 A.M.
The passage quoted occurs in Shakespeare's *Macbeth,* III:ii.
John iii:16 is my best-loved Bible verse.

In the last two examples and similar uses, the Modern Language Association *Style Sheet* suggests the following for documentation (Section **20f**): period instead of colon, with no spacing; no comma after the title; no italics for the books of the Bible; and small Roman numerals for play scenes and Bible chapters: *Macbeth* III.ii; I Chron. xxv.8; Luke xiv.5.

90g. **Do not use the colon to separate prepositions from their objects or verbs from objects or complements.**
Also, note especially that the expression *such as* is not followed by a colon (see Section **88q**4).

Wrong: I am fond of: books, newspapers, and magazines.
　　　　I like to read: novels, detective stories, and biographies.
　　　　The three Ohio cities Marvin visited were: Toledo, Cleveland, and Dayton.
　　　　In our community we enjoy a number of popular sports, such as: basketball, tennis, and bowling.
Right:　I am fond of the following: books, newspapers, and magazines.
　　　　I am fond of books, newspapers, and magazines.
　　　　I like to read the following: novels, detective stories, and biographies.
　　　　I like to read novels, detective stories, and biographies.
　　　　The three Ohio cities Marvin visited were as follows: Toledo, Cleveland, and Dayton.
　　　　The three Ohio cities Marvin visited were Toledo, Cleveland, and Dayton.
　　　　In our community we enjoy a number of popular sports, such as the following: basketball, tennis, and bowling.
　　　　or
　　　　In our community we enjoy a number of popular sports, such as basketball, tennis, and bowling.

671

90h. Do not use the colon for the dash as a summarizing mark.
(See Section **91d.**)

The colon looks ahead; the summarizing dash tells the reader what
has preceded.

Wrong: Class plays, debates, a newspaper, and the yearbook: these were
the major non-athletic activities in our high school.
Mathematics, chemistry, English: these gave me more trouble
than any other subjects.

To correct sentences like these, replace the colon by the dash.

EXERCISES

Some of the following sentences need colons and some already have
them correctly or incorrectly used. Check each sentence carefully and make
each one correct in its use of the colon.

1. I put the key in the hole and turned it, but the car would not start a
dead battery.
2. I became interested in Purdue because: I have many relatives in Indiana.
3. After breakfast we climbed aboard the bus again: this time for a trip
to Mount Vernon.
4. To prepare for the future I divided my time into three main courses
studies, athletics, and other activities.
5. I finally reached my goal I was awarded the Senior Red Cross Life-
Saving badge.
6. I always say to my younger brother "You don't know how lucky you
are."
7. English is a rather broad field which includes: grammar, punctuation,
spelling, writing, reading, and literature.
8. Many states now have an important law every automobile owner and
driver must carry automobile insurance.
9. The second superstition is this one if you break a mirror, you are supposed to have as many years of bad luck as there are broken pieces.
10. These subjects include the following mathematics, chemistry, English,
speech, graphics, and physics.
11. A few of my hobbies are: photography, printing, drawing, and building
tools and machinery.
12. The saying: "To thine own self be true," contains an important message for everyone.
13. In high school I participated in many extracurricular activities such as:
varsity wrestling, newspaper reporting, and band.

14. There are four major steps in the growing of corn preparing the seed-bed, planting the seeds, cultivating the corn after it comes up, and harvesting the corn at maturity.

15. In our dormitory each student gets: a bookcase, a modern lamp, large clothes press, and, of course, a bed.

16. There are four types of jet engines the rocket, the ramjet, the turbojet, and the turboprop.

17. The work consisted of: drawing plans, cutting out parts, pasting them together, and finally painting them.

18. The crops we raise are: corn, soybeans, wheat, oats, barley, and clover seed.

19. There is one major difference between my roommate and me we are of different religious beliefs.

20. I definitely agree with the statement in the newspaper "When Santa Claus comes to town, the shoppers do too."

THE DASH

91. The dash (—) serves the purpose of introduction, termination, separation, or, with another dash, enclosure.

The dash is a mark of punctuation most characteristically used to denote a sudden break or shift in thought. Although a stronger mark, it is approximately equivalent to a comma: both may be used in pairs or alone and between expressions of either coordinate or unequal rank. Logically, some other mark can usually be substituted for the dash, but its occasional use provides emphasis or surprise.

For those who type: the dash may be the only common mark of punctuation not on the standard keyboard of the typewriter. If so, to type a dash, use two hyphens together; no space precedes or follows the two hyphens. Example:

```
The dash--one of the important but less fre-
quently used marks of punctuation--adds variety
and emphasis to writing.
```

Only on the typewriter is the dash equal to two hyphens; the printed hyphen is somewhat smaller than half a dash. The double dash or long dash also finds occasional use in writing.

91a-d

91a. Use the dash to introduce a word, a phrase, or, occasionally, a clause when emphasis is desired.

For some of these purposes the comma or the colon is used. Compare the following illustrations with those in Sections **88a** and **90a**.

My aim in this course is easily stated—a high grade.
There is only one other possibility—to travel by air.
Our next problem is—where do we go from here?
There is only one thing he needs for his complete success and happiness—love.

91b. Use the dash, or double dash, to indicate an interruption, an unfinished statement, or an unfinished word (usually in dialogue).

George began, "May I ask—"
"You may not," snapped the judge.
"I hardly know how to express—" and then the speaker blushed, and sat down.
When John Smith comes in—oh, here you are now, John.
"I can't spell the word 'erysip—' "

The double dash is usually used at the end of the statement, the ordinary dash within the line. Omit the period when such statement terminates with a dash.

91c. Use the dash to indicate a break, shift, or turn in thought.

Here is a fuller explanation—but perhaps your class will not be interested.
Do we—can we—dare we propose such action to the trustees?
He is the most despicable—but I should not say any more.

91d. Use a dash to separate a final clause summarizing a series of ideas that precede it.

The usual summarizing words are *these, those, such.*

Mathematics, chemistry, English—these give me more trouble than any other subjects.
The meek, the kind, the gentle, the pure in heart—such are of the Kingdom of Heaven.
Food to eat, a place to sleep, a pleasant occupation, a congenial companion—what more can anyone ask from life?

No other marks of punctuation, such as the comma, semicolon, or colon, are used with the dash in this summarizing use; the semicolon or colon cannot be used in place of the summarizing dash (see Sections 89f, 90h).

91e. Use dashes to enclose sharply distinguished parenthetical matter in order to secure emphasis, suspense, or clearness.

We are in favor—completely in favor, we repeat—of the proposal.
I was surprised—in fact, pleasantly astonished—to hear of your splendid record.
My advice—if you will pardon my impertinence—is that you apologize to your friend.
My father is not afraid—he is a surgeon, you know—of performing the most delicate operation.

The following are special applications of the foregoing principle:

1. Long appositional phrases are likely to be enclosed by dashes.

Three candidates for public office—Wilson of New York, Matthews of Illinois, and Adams of Colorado—are in favor of larger old-age pensions.

For commas with shorter appositional phrases, see Section **88q**.

2. When the parenthetical material set off by dashes requires an exclamation point or question mark, such punctuation precedes the second dash:

If I should fail this course—heaven forbid!—I shall have to attend summer school.

91f. Use the dash to indicate the omission of words or letters (other than contractions), or to connect combinations of letters and figures.

General B— was an excellent soldier.
The First World War, 1914—1918, was fought to end all wars.
John Kline is a pilot on the Chicago—New York run.
Monday—Friday classes will have one meeting more next week than Tuesday—Thursday classes.
Please study pages 3—14 for tomorrow's assignment.

If you type your work, you could justifiably use hyphens in all the examples above, except the first.

91g.   Use the dash sparingly.

Overuse of the dash is inadvisable. It is legitimately used in the instances cited in this section, but other marks of punctuation have their functions, too, and are usually more commonly used. Frequent use of the dash detracts from its effectiveness.

91h.   Never use the dash as a substitute for the period.

Except for the use of the dash to mark unfinished statements or interrupted dialogue (Section 91b), the dash is never used for the period at the end of a sentence.

EXERCISES

A. Encircle all the dashes on two pages of a textbook, your book of readings, or a magazine. Account for the use of each.

B. Where should dashes be placed in the following sentences? Why?

1. My roommate kept me up quite late last night or should I say this morning?
2. "I remember when" what a wealth of memories these words bring.
3. I was defeated the only time all season in the regional track meet.
4. Joan and it's about time I told you her name was enjoying the flight very much.
5. Confusion, everywhere confusion this was the beginning of a week I shall never forget.
6. Father's years in college were 1934 1938; Mother's were 1938 1942.
7. My brother and sister I have a twin brother and sister who live at home usually put the trimmings on the Christmas tree.
8. Dirt, noise, and chaos such are the ideas one receives when thinking of a big city.
9. My roommate has made a rowboat actually it is a small barge that is so big he can't row it.
10. The numerous herds of deer, antelope, buffalo, and other wild animals what has happened to them?
11. My cousin learned to fly in the Navy, and so I asked begged is a better word him to let me have a ride.
12. My roommate is a carefree fellow classes, grades, knowledge these have no meaning to him.

13. Because our residence hall is so large, each wing there are four wings has its own dining room.
14. In this grease job you are now about half done oh, by the way, did you know that you have grease on your sleeve?
15. Father loves to fish in fact, he spends a lot of time at it and almost always has very good luck.
16. Three years old, 28 inches tall, full of pep and mischief that's my baby sister.
17. Instructors those people who stand before a class each day and try to drill knowledge into our heads aren't really so bad.
18. To be a courteous driver, you do not need to memorize every traffic situation this would be impossible but try to think of yourself as the driver of the other car.
19. Just how far I shall go with the idea of building a new hi-fi set well I'll have to wait and see.
20. After a day of hard driving we finally crossed the Wisconsin Minnesota border into Minnesota.

PARENTHESES, BRACKETS, AND LESS FREQUENTLY USED MARKS

92. Parentheses ( ), sometimes called "curves," and brackets [ ] are marks of enclosure. The former find occasional use. The latter are infrequently used; in fact, they are not included on the regular keyboard of standard typewriters.

92a. Use parentheses to enclose parenthetical material which is remotely connected with the context.

This punctuation (I am convinced it is important) should be carefully studied.

If you find any holly berries (surely they must be numerous now), please bring me some.

To justify parenthesis marks, be sure that your material is strongly parenthetic, i.e., usually long phrases, perhaps dependent clauses, or independent clauses—not words or most phrases or most dependent clauses. In such constructions the parenthetic material merely amplifies the thought. Thus many writers prefer dashes to parentheses (see Section 91e). These marks may frequently be used interchangeably, although parentheses are more commonly used when the strong parenthetic material is more remotely related to the main statement.

92b.   Use parentheses to enclose amplifying references, directions, and numbering figures.

Study carefully the assignment on credits. (See Chapter V.)
Gulliver among the Lilliputians (see Book I) had some exciting experiences.
Shakespeare was born on April 23 (?), 1564.
I am studying medicine for three reasons: (1) I like the subject; (2) my father and grandfather are doctors; and (3) our town needs additional doctors.

NOTE: The second) of the pair ( ) also could serve with the numbers in the last example above.

92c.   Do not use parentheses to cancel parts of your writing. Erase or draw lines through the words you wish to delete.

92d.   Use brackets to enclose your comment inserted or interpolated in a quoted passage.

For all practical purposes, this is the only use of brackets.

"On the first float rode the Queen of the Tournament [Miss Emily Miller], her attendants, and two boys dressed as pages."
"In April of that year [1942] Johnson took out his first patent."
"Milton portrays Satan as a fallen angle [*sic*] of tremendous size."

NOTE: Do not confuse brackets and parentheses. Brackets are used to set off inserted matter in someone else's writing, i.e., your addition to *quoted* material, such as corrections, comments, or explanations; parentheses are used to enclose your own parenthetic material, according to Section 92a.

92e.   Use other marks appropriately with parentheses and brackets.

Since parenthetic and bracketed materials go with what has preceded, any other needed punctuation mark follows the closing parenthesis mark or bracket. See second example under Section 92a and first example under Section 92d.

LESS FREQUENTLY USED MARKS

Ellipsis periods and brackets are among the less frequently used marks of punctuation. Asterisks (Section 86g4) and the marks discussed just below are not strictly punctuation marks, but symbols serving a purpose in writing. Except for the caret, this purpose concerns a mechanical method of indicating pronunciation.

92f.   Use a <u>caret</u> (∧) to insert an omitted expression or letter.

Place the caret below the line at the place of omission and write the inserted expression or letter directly above or in the margin.

92g.   Use a <u>dieresis</u> (¨) to show that the second of two vowels is pronounced in the following syllable.

With such words as *zoology, cooperation,* and *coordination,* present tendency is not to use this sign. It is useful, however, in words like *preëxistent, reënforce,* and *naïve,* in order to prevent momentary confusion or mispronunciation. A hyphen may also be used to indicate this separation of vowels in words like *pre-existent* and *re-enforce.* Consult your dictionary for guidance.

92h.   Use an <u>accent or other mark</u>, usually with words of foreign origin, where the spelling requires it.

Acute accent(´): *passé*
Grave (`): *à la mode*
Circumflex (^): *hôtel de ville*
Cedilla (ç): *façade*
Tilde (~): *cañon*
Umlaut (¨): *schön*

Again, let your dictionary be your guide.

EXERCISES

Copy the following sentences, inserting parentheses or brackets where they belong.

1. The four brothers are not unintelligent, in fact, they all own their own businesses, but they still go to their father for the final word in a big decision.
2. Some girls stopped at my house and asked us four of my girl friends were there too whether we would like to go somewhere with them.
3. It was in March I think it was in March that I was notified of my admission to Springfield University.
4. Not long ago Happy Hollow that was the name of the place before

it became a park was bought by the city as a place of recreation for our citizens.

5. The magazine article began: "People these days are to *sic* busy to care about anyone but themselves."

6. This article by James Jones you remember him? has been widely quoted.

7. The letter reads: "John the boy I met at the dance has been asking about you every day since you left."

8. *Plain Sense* was published early in the 19th century 1826 by a New York printer.

9. Totalitarianism see Chapter 10 was eagerly discussed.

10. This book the one I referred to earlier is an excellent example of 16th-century thought.

THE HYPHEN

93. The hyphen (-) is a mark of separation used only between parts of a word. Paradoxically, its most frequent use is unification, bringing together two or more separate words into a compound word which serves the purpose of a single part of speech. The hyphen, therefore, is more a mark of spelling than of punctuation, to indicate that two or more words or two or more parts of one word belong together.

No longer is the hyphen used—as it once was in older dictionaries—to indicate division of words into syllables. That purpose is now served by the dot: re·sist, ad·vo·cate, ir·re·sis·ti·ble (see Section 51c3). Hyphens used between syllables are an integral part of the word.

93a. Use your dictionary to determine whether certain word combinations are written as two words, as one word written solid, or as a compound word with a hyphen between parts.

→1. Do not write as one word two or more words that should be completely separated.

→2. Do not write as two separate words any two words which should be written solid.

→3. Do not write as two or more words any word combinations which should be hyphenated. (See expanded discussion, Section **93b**, below.)

The use of a hyphen in joining compound words (two or more words used as a unit) varies greatly. No rules cover all combinations, which are so numerous that many such are not in your dictionary. Fortunately, many are, and when in doubt, consult it as your guide in hyphenating and compounding. If the compound word you seek is not there, apply the principles given below.

The general principle of word joining derives from usage. When two or more words first become associated with a single meaning, they are written separately; as they grow to be more of a unit in common thought and writing, they are hyphenated; finally they are written together as one word. This evolution is seen in the following, the third word in each series now being the accepted form: *base ball, base-ball, baseball; basket ball, basket-ball, basketball; rail road, rail-road, railroad.*

Many common expressions are still in the first stage; *mother tongue, boy friend, Girl Scout, girl friend, high school.* The one-word combination *highschool,* for example, although used by a prominent educational magazine, has not yet been accepted by dictionaries.

93b. Use a hyphen to separate the parts of many compound words.

Many compounds are always written solid, many are written with a hyphen, and many are written either with a hyphen or as two words, depending upon meaning (examples are given below). Note the difference in these:

> After three years of service, Joe was a hardened, *battle-scarred* veteran.
> The *battle scarred* the bodies and souls of all who took part.

> The *above-mentioned* principles are frequently illustrated in writing.
> The poem *above, mentioned* several times by the speaker, has been one of my favorites.

> In the quarrel between Ellen and Sue, Jean served as a *go-between.*
> In a field goal, the ball must *go between* the goal posts and over the crossbar.

> Some politicians follow a *middle-of-the-road* course.
> A careful driver will never drive down the *middle of the road.*

Hyphens are generally used:

1. Between two or more words modifying a substantive and used as a single adjective, especially when placed before the substantive. These combinations may consist of

a. an adjective or noun united with a present or past participle: *sad-looking, able-bodied, absent-minded, soft-spoken, battle-scarred, bell-shaped, wind-blown.*

b. two adjectives, or an adjective and a noun, or a noun and an adjective: *light-blue, Latin-American, ocean-green, midnight-black.*
   NOTE: Use no hyphen with adjective-plus-noun as object: "We live in a *one-story* house." "Our house has only *one story.*"

c. a prefix or combining form attached to a capitalized word: *un-American, trans-Andean.*

   NOTE: Prefixes and suffixes attached to common words usually become part of the word, written solid; dictionaries often have long lists of these—see, for example, combining syllables like *non, over, un, under* in your dictionary.

d. an adverb and a present or past participle (unless the adverb ends in *ly*): *fast-moving, above-mentioned, ever-rising, swiftly moving.*

2. Between words of a compound noun:

a. three or more words: *mother-in-law, jack-of-all-trades.*

b. compounds having an adverb or a preposition as the second element: *go-between, looker-on, leveling-off.*

c. compounds having *fellow, father, mother, brother, sister, daughter,* or a similar word as the first element: *fellow-citizen, brother-classmates, sister-nations.*

3. Between compound words when, usually, *self, ex, half,* or *quarter* is the first element: *self-control, self-respect, ex-president, half-asleep, half-truth, quarter-share* (but *selfsame, halfback,* and *quarterback.*) See Section 93a.

4. Between a single capital letter joined to a noun or participle: *A-flat, H-bomb, S-curve, T-shaped, U-turn.*

5. Between elements of an improvised compound: *make-believe, know-it-all, never-say-die, never-to-be-forgotten.*

6. Between the parts of compound numerals if written out (from twenty-one to ninety-nine): *forty-three, sixty-seven, eighty-two.*

7. Between the numerator and denominator of a fraction if written out: *two-thirds, four-fifths, one-thousandth* (but omitted when the hyphen already appears in either numerator or denominator: *twenty-four thirty-fifths; three ten-thousandths*).

8. Between a numbered figure and its unit of measurement: *a 5-yard gain, 40-hour week, 10-day trip, 16-foot board.*

9. To avoid, usually, doubling a vowel or tripling a consonant: *anti-inflation, pre-existent, semi-independent, shell-like.*

10. To prevent mispronunciation: *co-op, re-cover* vs. *recover, re-creation* vs. *recreation, re-treat* vs. *retreat.*

11. As a "suspensive hyphen" in pairs or more, when the first or second part of a compound word is used only once:

> In literature, an elephantine style is *heavy-handed* or *-footed* writing.
> Your next theme is to be a *400-* to *600-word* theme.
> For our Homecoming display we brought some *8-, 10-,* and *16-foot* boards.

93c. **Use a hyphen to indicate the division of a word broken at the end of a line.**

> The rambling old house, it is true, would have looked considerably better if it had been freshly painted.

Occasionally, at the end of a longhand or typewritten line, a long word must be divided. Avoid such division if you possibly can, and do not divide the word if it is the last one on the page. When division is necessary, follow these directions:

1. Place the hyphen at the end of the first line, *never at the beginning of the second.*

2. Never divide a monosyllable. Five- to seven-letter one-syllable words like *breath, death, ground, thought,* and *through* cannot be divided. Write the entire monosyllable on the first line; if this is not possible, carry the whole word over to the next line.

3. Divide words of more than one syllable between syllables, but avoid dividing one-letter syllables from the remainder of the word, as well as any unpronounced *ed* in one- or several-syllable pronunciations. Undesirable: *a·bout; i·talics; man·y; ask·ed; dress·ed; attack·ed.* Also do not divide words with only four letters. Undesirable: *al·so, in·to, on·ly, op·en.*

4. When in doubt about correct syllabication, consult your dictionary in order to divide words properly. Several simple suggestions, however, apply to many words:

Prefixes and suffixes can be divided from the main words (but see 3, just above).

Compound words are divided between their main parts.

Two consonants are usually divided.

NOTE: If you have material you plan to have printed, do not end a line with a hyphen which separates parts of a compound word; the printer, in setting type, would probably make the compound a single word.

93d. Do not use a hyphen in place of a dash or a dash in place of a hyphen.

In longhand, make the hyphen and the dash distinct. In typing, a dash usually consists of two hyphens, and, in typing also, the hyphen may substitute for the dash in several uses (see Section 91f).

EXERCISES

A. Encircle all the hyphens on one page of your book of readings, another textbook, or a magazine. Give the reason for each.

B. With the aid of your dictionary, determine which of the following words are compounds and should be written with hyphens: *johnnycake, chickenhearted, helterskelter, schoolboy, downstairs, drawbridge, textbook, pitchdark, fatherinlaw, bulls'eye, laborsaving, airtight, selfstarter, runin, hangeron, thirtynine, offstage, blowout, quietspoken, campfire.*

C. Copy the following words in a list, and make a list of the same words without the hyphens. What is the difference in meaning when the same word is hyphenated or written solid? *re-treat, re-creation, re-view, re-claim, re-dress, re-lay, re-search, re-turn, re-treat, re-cover, re-act, re-collect, re-pose, re-tire, re-count, re-sign, re-prove, re-sound, re-solve, re-sort.*

D. Indicate where hyphens should be inserted in words in the following sentences:

1. We chartered a bus for an all day tour of the city.
2. With the never ending help of my father and my mother, I became an Eagle Scout.
3. They decided to make a three day trip to the Great Smoky Mountains.
4. He is a transmission specialist for a new and used car dealer.
5. Saturday afternoon we opened our gifts at my mother in law's and father in law's home.
6. After Christmas is over, our Christmas thank you notes are written.
7. That summer I made a 400 mile trip every week for my father.
8. Among the contests are a girl catch boy race, a turtle race, and a putting match.

9. We live on a 120 acre farm near Greencastle.
10. When I came home late, I received a short but to the point lecture from my father.
11. The road to the Grand Canyon leads through hot sun baked waste lands.
12. A six man team can play a two man line, a three man line, or a four man line.
13. In little theater we put our talents to work on behind the scene projects.
14. Our conversation soon developed into an all out, full scale major argument.
15. Twenty miles per hour signs are posted in the business district.
16. I thought it was a stupid looking hat to put on my three year old brother.
17. John turned out to be an average or run of the mill type of person.
18. In one league our team plays only out of town teams.
19. The conventional propeller is the oldest type of heavier than air aircraft propulsion.
20. Why not take advantage of the many uses of this heavy, thin paged, fact filled source of knowledge, the dictionary?

THE APOSTROPHE

94.   The apostrophe (') as a mark of separation is used to indicate the possessive case of nouns and of indefinite pronouns (*another, everybody, no one,* etc.). It is also used to mark omissions in contracted words and numerals and to indicate the plurals of letters and numbers. Since the apostrophe is used only as part of a word, its use is as much a matter of spelling as of punctuation.

94a.   **Use an apostrophe and <u>s</u> to form the possessive of a noun (singular or plural) not ending in <u>s</u>.**

The *doctor's* car is waiting at the door.
Our fire department is ready for service at a *second's* notice.
This store sells *men's, women's,* and *children's* shoes.
Mr. Smith's *office* is on the second floor.

94b.   **Use an apostrophe alone to form the possessive of a plural noun ending in <u>s</u>.**

The principle applies to both common and proper names: *boys', dogs', doctors', days', weeks', the Smiths'.*

685

Some *students'* attitude toward activities is not quite the same as their *professors'* attitude.

During my two *weeks'* vacation I worked in a store selling *boys'* clothing.

The *Smiths'* vacation was one that we all envied.

94c. Use the apostrophe alone, or the apostrophe with s, to form the possessive of singular nouns ending in s.

The principle applies usually to proper names. Most common nouns ending their singular in *s* are the names of nonhuman objects and form their possessive with an *of* phrase (see Section 75k).

> On *the cover of my atlas* (not *the atlas' cover*) was a drawing of the world.

One-syllable proper names ending in an *s* sound add an apostrophe and *s:*

> *Keats's* sonnets are among my favorites, but I've never cared much for Karl *Marx's* books.
> Robert *Burns's* cottage is a shrine in Scotland.

In words of more than one syllable ending in *s*, add the apostrophe only:

> Every student of Greek knows *Aristophanes'* comedies and *Demosthenes'* orations.

Some common nouns not ending in *s* but having an *s*-sound ending also add only the apostrophe:

> "For *goodness'* sake" was one of my grandmother's favorite expressions.
> Let's sing "Auld Lang Syne" for old *acquaintance'* sake.

But

> *Horace's* name is a somewhat unusual one.

94d. In compound nouns add the apostrophe and s to the element nearest the object possessed.

> John borrowed his *brother-in-law's* car.
> Charge these goods to *John Brown, Jr.'s,* account.
> I left the restaurant wearing *somebody else's* hat.

94e. Add the apostrophe and $\underline{s}$ to the last member of a group to indicate joint possession.

I always use *Mason and Brown's* sporting equipment.
Let's get a soda at *Johnson and Stover's* drug store.

NOTE: Indicate individual possession by using the possessive case of each element of the series.

I am interested in the *Army's* and *Navy's* recruiting campaigns.
Mary is a baby-sitter for *Mrs. Brown's* and *Mrs. Wilson's* children.

94f. Use an apostrophe to indicate that letters or figures have been omitted.

Father was a member of the class of *'40;* I'm a member of the class of *'65.*
I myself never met a body *comin'* through the rye.

Contractions, usually pronouns or nouns combined with certain verbs, or the word *not* with certain verbs, provide common examples of this principle: *he's, it's, isn't, aren't, wasn't, weren't, hasn't, don't, doesn't, won't,* etc.

John's in New York now; Joe is coming next week.
When *you're* careful, you *shouldn't* have any trouble in catching your serious errors in writing.
Come now; you *don't* have to say, *"What's o'clock?" That's* a stilted way of saying *"What's* the time?"

94g. Use an apostrophe and $\underline{s}$ to indicate the plurals of figures, alphabetical letters, and words considered as words.

I have trouble making legible *8's.*
Uncrossed *t's* look like *l's;* undotted *i's* are read as *e's.*
Don't overuse *and's, but's,* and *for's* in your writing.
My uncle spent the first half of the *1940's* in uniform.

NOTE: An apostrophe is used in forming the plural of some abbreviation initials:

Three *G.I.'s* in my uncle's battalion were *Ph.D.'s* from an eastern university.

Where no ambiguity is likely, many writers and printers omit the apostrophe in the foregoing uses:

My uncle spent the first half of the *1940s* in uniform.

Three *G.I.s* in my uncle's battalion were *Ph.D.s* from an eastern university.

Many air lines now have many Boeing *707s* in service.

94h. Do not use the apostrophe in forming the plural of nouns.

Wrong: The *Smith's* are playing bridge with us tonight.

Right: The *Smiths* are playing bridge with us tonight.

Wrong: There have been more *boys'* than *girls'* among our freshman *student's* the past few *year's*.

Right: There have been more *boys* than *girls* among our freshman *students* the past few *years*.

94i. Do not use the apostrophe to form the possessive case of the personal and relative pronouns.

Wrong:	our's	Right:	ours
	ours'		ours
	your's		yours
	yours'		yours
	his'		his
	her's		hers
	hers'		hers
	it's		its
	their's		theirs
	theirs'		theirs
	who's		whose

NOTE: *Never* use the apostrophe with the possessive *its*—one of the most common errors in student writing. *Its* is the possessive form of *it; it's* is the contraction for *it is*.

When a dog wags *its* tail, that's a sign *it's* happy.

94j. Use the apostrophe and s to form the possessive case of indefinite pronouns.

The possessive case of indefinite pronouns is illustrated as follows:

anybody's	another's
everybody's	either's
no one's	neither's
one's	neither one's
someone's	other's (plural, others')

You must have your father or mother sign this application; *either one's* (or *either's*) signature is satisfactory.
Everybody's business is usually *nobody's* business.

EXERCISES

A. Encircle all the apostrophes on a page of selected prose and give the reason for each.

B. Where are apostrophes needed in the following sentences? Why?

1. Each Sunday we drove to my grandparents home to spend the day with them.
2. Its girls like her that try men to the very limit.
3. So, lets see whats new about the new models.
4. Fanny (thats the dogs name) is now almost 10 years old.
5. We each take turns opening a present till were finished.
6. Halloween reminds me of the fun I used to have with my special witchs costume.
7. Johns playing the guitar for hours is enough to get on anyones nerves.
8. Lets discuss the responsibility of drivers in more detail.
9. The starting wage is not as high as an engineers starting wage, but advancement comes just as fast.
10. New Years resolutions are still made by many people.
11. In this world there are many ifs and maybes.
12. Dont forget that youre going to college to get an education!
13. An engineer and a mechanic are no good at doing each others jobs.
14. I hope sometime to be a buyer in a womens department store.
15. A rigid drivers test and physical examination is the only way to remove unqualified drivers from the highways.

C. Apostrophes are misused in the following sentences. Make necessary corrections and explain each.

1. Both my parent's joy will be expressed when my brother and I arrive home for Christmas.
2. That night we had a meeting at one of my friends' cottage.
3. My future is uncertain, as is everyones'.
4. Since you are'nt 21 years old, you can'not vote in the coming election.
5. The oldest child is a little girl 20 months old who's name is Sharon Lea.
6. Our city has three excellent restaurant's in it's general vicinity.
7. Our's is one of the newer consolidated high schools.
8. Christmas afternoon at home is one of our busier afternoon's of the year.
9. In the country there are'nt many people around to bother a boy at play.

10. Wednesday is my mother's-in-law day to go shopping.
11. After four years' of technical study, an engineer is ready for a job.
12. At this resort town the beaches are very near to most peoples' homes.
13. Many of the student's parents will be here for Homecoming.
14. Both boy's and girl's themes are published in our freshman magazine.
15. Our city has lost it's friendliness and rolls up its' sidewalks at 10 o'clock each night.

QUOTATION MARKS

95. Quotation marks, double (". . .") and single ('. . .'), are marks of enclosure for words, phrases, clauses, sentences, and paragraphs. By definition, *quotation* is repeating what someone has said or written, but the marks themselves have several specialized uses.

In some books, magazines, and newspapers either no quotation marks at all or single quotation marks are printed where, according to American convention, double ones would be used. Neither of these practices is any criterion because, in this country at least, they are usually experiments in typography or a kind of affectation.

The following principles explain conventional uses.

95a. Use quotation marks to enclose every complete direct quotation.

A direct quotation is the exact words of the person quoted, the original speaker or writer.

> John asked, "What time shall I come?"
> "Dinner will be served at seven," replied Mary.

> Abraham Lincoln closed his Gettysburg Address as follows: ". . . and that government of the people, by the people, for the people, shall not perish from the earth."

95b. Use quotation marks to enclose each part of an interrupted direct quotation.

> "Father," I said, "may I have the car this evening?"
> "And why," said Father, "do you need the car this evening?"

The *he said* or *said he* part, or its equivalent, inserted within a quotation is preceded by a comma, unless a question mark or exclamation point is required. It is followed by a comma, unless a stronger mark, period or semicolon, is demanded by the grammatical elements. The test: What mark would be used if the *he said* were omitted? Use that mark after the inserted part indicating the speaker.

Joe Smith is a friend of mine, but I haven't seen him for five years.
"Joe Smith is a friend of mine," I said, "but I haven't seen him for five years."

There is no vacancy at present; however, we will keep your name on file.
"There is no vacancy at present," the employment director said; "however, we will keep your name on file."

I bought my hat at Johnson's Stores. It was on sale.
"I bought my hat at Johnson's Stores," Henry told us. "It was on sale."

95c. In dialogue, use a separate paragraph for every change of speaker. (See also Section **29a.**)

"And where's Mr. Campbell?" Charlie asked.
"Gone to Switzerland. Mr. Campbell's a pretty sick man, Mr. Wales."
"I'm sorry to hear that. And George Hardt?" Charlie inquired.
"Back in America, gone to work."
—F. Scott Fitzgerald, "Babylon Revisited."

95d. If a direct quotation extends for several paragraphs, use quotation marks at the beginning of each paragraph but at the end of <u>only</u> the last paragraph.

95e. In formal writing or in good informal writing use quotation marks to enclose words which suggest a widely different level of usage.

If a word is appropriate, no quotation marks should be used as a form of apology. If it is not appropriate, the expression can usually be altered. In some instances, however, you may wish to shift to an expression having a specific, limited usage or usage label in order to communicate meaning realistically or emphatically. Such expressions may be illiteracies, slang, difficult technical words, or common words with a technical meaning (see Sections 57, 58, 59, 62).

The Mayor of our town, in my opinion, is a "stuffed shirt."
The policeman "lit into" me as if I had committed a major crime; when he finished, I "lit out" in a hurry.

Do not rely upon this use of quotation marks as an excuse for inexact choice of words. Find the word that means exactly what you wish to say (see Section 61). Also do not sprinkle your writing with quotation marks around words or expressions; enclose only those that would puzzle or mislead your reader. Words labeled *colloquial* in your dictionary are in good informal use and are not enclosed in quotation marks.

When words or expressions are enclosed in quotation marks in accordance with Section 95e, commas are *not* used around them unless required for other reasons. Note the examples above and see also Section 88b.

95f. Use quotation marks to enclose chapter headings, titles of articles, titles of short stories, titles of short poems, and the like, when used in a body of prose.

When both chapter heading and book are mentioned, or title of article and magazine, book and magazine names should be indicated by italics (see Section 96a).

> For such information consult the chapter, "Private Preparatory Schools," in the *American Educational Directory*.
>
> Some humorous theatrical experiences are discussed in Jean Kerr's article, "What Happens Out of Town," in a recent issue of *Harper's Magazine*.

If there is no chance of confusion, quotation marks may be used instead of italics to indicate the names of ships, trains, airplanes, and the like, but the use of italics is preferred (see Section 96a).

> "The City of Los Angeles" leaves the Union Station at 9 o'clock.
>
> We have booked passage to England on the liner "United States."

95g. Use single quotation marks to enclose a quotation within a quotation.

> "Tell me," Father asked Mother after the wedding, "whether the bride said, 'I promise to obey.'"
>
> Our instructor said, "When you say, 'I'll turn in my theme tomorrow,' I expect it to be turned in tomorrow, not next week."

On the very rare occasions when it is necessary to punctuate a quotation within a quotation within a quotation, the order is double marks, single marks, double marks:

The speaker said: "I shall quote from a letter of a Civil War veteran: 'When I was on sentry duty in Washington, a tall gaunt man stopped one day and said, "Good morning, soldier. How goes it?" It was Abraham Lincoln who thus greeted me.'"

95h. Use quotation marks always in pairs.

Since quotation marks are marks of enclosure, they are used in pairs. They come at both beginning and end of the quotation.

Wrong: "I like football better than baseball, he said, and I like tennis better than either."

Right: "I like football better than baseball," he said, "and I like tennis better than either."

NOTE: Quotation marks come at the beginning of each new paragraph of a speech or extended quotation, but the concluding quotation marks, closing the quotation, do not come until the end of the last quoted paragraph (Section **95d**).

95i. Place quotation marks correctly with reference to other marks.

1. The comma and the period come *inside* the quotation marks. This principle applies even when only the last word before the comma or the period is enclosed (but not alphabetical letters or figures).

"I need your help now," she said. "I need it more than ever."
Some praised the performance as "excellent," and others thought it was only "fair."

But

I live in Hall "X", but spend most of my time at the "Y".

2. A question mark, exclamation point, or dash comes *outside* the quotation marks unless it is part of the quotation.

Did she say, "I have enough money"?
She asked, "Have I enough money?"
"Have I enough money?" she asked.
What is meant by "dog eat dog"?
Our play was obviously a "bust"!
"The play was a 'bust'!" our coach exclaimed.

The question mark comes inside the quotation marks when both the nonquoted and the quoted elements are questions:

Wrong: Did Father ask, "Have you enough money?"?
Right: Did Father ask, "Have you enough money?"

3. Semicolon and colon come *outside* the quotation marks.

Read E. B. White's "Walden"; it is, I think, his best essay.
Look up the following in "A Glossary of Famous People": Theodore
Roosevelt, Woodrow Wilson, Charles E. Hughes.

95j. Do not put quotation marks around an indirect quotation.

In an indirect quotation, a writer or speaker puts into his own words
the words of someone else or, at a later time, his own words.

Wrong:	The employment manager said that "I should report for work on Monday."
Right (indirect):	The employment manager said that I should report for work on Monday.
Right (direct):	The employment manager said, "Report for work on Monday."
Right (indirect):	I replied that I should be happy to attend the dinner.
Right (direct):	I replied, "I shall be happy to attend the dinner."

Note that the following are or can serve as indirect quotations:

He answered yes.
To a question of that kind I shall have to say no.
Direct: He answered, "Yes."
To a question of that kind I shall have to say, "No."

**95k. Do not confuse in one sentence a direct and an indirect
quotation.**

The confusion arises from a blending of direct and indirect questions
(see Section **35c,** also).

Confused:	I asked him what grade did he receive in the course.
Indirect:	I asked him what grade he had received in the course.
Direct:	I asked him, "What grade did you receive in the course?"

Confused:	Mary asked her adviser hadn't she already obtained credit for History 12.
Indirect:	Mary asked her adviser whether she had not already obtained credit for History 12.
Direct:	Mary asked her adviser, "Haven't I already obtained credit for History 12?"

95l. Do not enclose in quotation marks the title at the beginning of a theme.

The only exception to this principle is the use of a quotation as the theme title.

Usual title: The Dangers of Too Little Learning
Quotation as title: "A Little Learning Is a Dangerous Thing"

EXERCISES

A. Study several pages of a short story or novel using dialogue. Examine the use of quotation marks and their position with other marks of punctuation. Discuss any uses which are not in accord with principles given in Section 95.

B. In the following sentences, make quotation marks, capitals, and commas conform to commonly accepted principles:

1. One day I learned one of the primary rules of sailing, Always keep your mind on what you are doing.
2. Not all courses in the School of Home Economics deal with "cooking and sewing".
3. Such a student knows when to say no to a friend when he is asked to go out, but he also learns when he can say yes.
4. It would be so easy to sleep through those early 8-o'clock classes is a favorite thought of most students.
5. As a pledge I must be 'Johnny on the spot,' but next year I hope to be 'dishing it out.'
6. You have asked me, "Why read"?
7. The saying, "All work and no play makes Jack a dull boy.", is true.
8. After a month of shooting practice, Grandfather said that, "I was ready for my first coon hunt."
9. Can this really be happening to me? I said to myself.
10. Who am I, and Why was I born? and How are other people thinking and living? are sample questions that literature should suggest.
11. Why, I never have caught poison ivy and I never will I said to John Woods.
12. Three outstanding themes were The Courtship of John, by Mary Consel; Christmas in the Loop, by Harry Whitesell; and Sea Trip, by Joseph Thompson.
13. The home of 600 happy people and a few soreheads—this is the sign that the traveler sees as he enters my town.
14. I have read Keats's The Eve of St. Agnes and I think I have never read a more beautiful poem.

15. After you leave college and obtain a job the adviser told Henry you will find that coming in late and not appearing once or twice a week will have serious consequences.

ITALICS (UNDERLINING)

96. Words italicized in print, i.e., slanting letters, are underlined once, when you typewrite or write in longhand. Quotation marks may also be used to set off such words, but since these marks have various other uses (see Section 95), underlining is preferable.

96a. Use italics (underlining) to indicate titles of magazines, newspapers, pamphlets, books, long poems, plays, motion pictures, and the names of ships, trains, and airplanes.

I came from California to New York on the streamlined trains the *City of Denver* and the *City of Philadelphia,* and sailed for England on the *United States.* From the ship's library I borrowed a copy of *Newsweek, The New York Times,* and Thomas Hardy's novel *The Return of the Native.* As I was reading, I heard an airplane overhead and was reminded of Charles Lindbergh's trans-Atlantic flight in the *Spirit of St. Louis.* Every night, on shipboard, a revival of some famous movie was shown, like *The Birth of a Nation, Duel in the Sun,* and *It Happened One Night.*

1. When you use the title of an article or story and the magazine in which it appears, in order to distinguish them use quotation marks to enclose the former and italicize the latter; apply the same principle to the chapter title of a book and the book. But do not italicize the title of your theme used in the position of the title. Note that titles of articles and short stories are not italicized in their position as titles.

Be sure to read Wilbur Carter's article, "Non-Military Uses of Atomic Energy," in *Harper's Magazine.*
Your parents will enjoy reading Chapter 17, "How to Stretch Dollars," in Allen Brown's book, *The Quest for Security.*

2. Include the definite or indefinite article if it forms part of the title: *The Merchant of Venice* (not *Merchant of Venice*); *A Fable for Critics* (not *Fable for Critics*).

3. Do not add an article to a title if none appears in the original

work: Shakespeare's *Two Gentlemen of Verona* (not *The Two Gen-tlemen of Verona*).

4. Italicize the name of the city and the definite article if it is in-cluded in the title of a newspaper: *The New York Times; Chicago Tribune*. (Some teachers and style manuals suggest not italicizing the name of the city or the definite article in the title of a newspaper.)

5. According to convention, the names of the books of the Bible are not italicized or enclosed in quotation marks: Matthew 14:12 (Mat-thew xiv:12).

96b. Use italics (underlining) to indicate foreign words or phrases.

Foreign words which have not been naturalized in English should be either italicized or enclosed in quotation marks. Your dictionary will tell you whether foreign words and phrases are naturalized, i.e., are in good English use or still considered distinctly foreign.

There is a *je ne sais quoi* quality about this painting.
The foreign student in America must work out a *modus vivendi*.
A vicious cartoon of that kind has no *raison d'être*.

96c. Use italics (underlining) to refer to a word, letter, or number spoken of as such.

Your undotted *i's* look exactly like *e's*.
You have written *6* every time that you meant to write *9*.
I stupidly wrote *Rode 39* when I had meant to write *Road 39*.
The four most frequently misused pairs of words in English are the following: *to* and *too*, *it's* and *its*, *their* and *there*, and *your* and *you're*.

96d. Use italics (underlining) to emphasize a word, a phrase, or a statement.

Always sign your name to a letter.
Never, *under any conditions*, keep poisonous substances in your medi-cine cabinet.

Used sparingly, italics for emphasis are effective. Overused, they be-come monotonous and ineffective.

EXERCISES

Recopy the following sentences, underlining the words that should be italicized. What are your reasons?

1. The name October comes from the word octo, which means eight, even though it is the tenth month.
2. My first move was to subscribe to The Model Railroader, a magazine for those interested in model railroading.
3. Dirty, smoky, filthy, mean, and dishonest are some of the adjectives used to describe my city.
4. My sister has now worked for a year as associate editor of The Indianapolis Daily News.
5. In New York City we saw the two large liners, United States and Queen Elizabeth, docked beside each other in the harbor.
6. Monitor comes from the Latin word monere, which means to warn; the word monitor has been used (capitalized thus, Monitor) as the name of a ship.
7. Our music director adds spice by the way he pronounces words, such as do-reem' for dream and ka-rye' for cry.
8. A good example of a historical novel is Charles Dickens' A Tale of Two Cities, a story of the French Revolution.
9. The American College Dictionary, Webster's New Collegiate Dictionary, and the New World Dictionary are sold in our local bookstores.
10. Some people say au revoir and some say auf Wiedersehen; I'll stick with the plain, old-fashioned American good-by.
11. On our campus the title of the magazine of freshman themes is Trial Flight; at the University of Illinois the title of the magazine is The Green Caldron.
12. Sentences and paragraphs should be linked by such transitional words as and, also, moreover, afterwards, and so on.
13. When we were in New York, we went to see the long-running play, My Fair Lady.
14. Some textbooks say you should not abbreviate company, street, and avenue in business letters.
15. Careful proofreading will prevent such errors as writing here for hear, know for no, and women for woman.

CAPITALS

97. The applications of capitalization are so numerous that rules or principles cannot be given to apply to every possible example. Stylebooks of various publishing firms usually contain from 20 to 40 pages dealing with capitals and lists of examples, but for the student-writer a few underlying principles may be helpful.

97a.   **Capitalize each important word in titles of themes, articles, pamphlets, books, plays, motion pictures, poems, magazines, newspapers, musical compositions, songs, etc.**

Capitalize, in accordance with this principle, the first and each important word in titles, but within titles do not capitalize articles, infinitive sign, prepositions, or conjunctions, unless they consist of five or more letters, a curious convention which is quite generally observed.

Autumn Days on the Farm   Brown's *Other Worlds than Ours*
A Journey Through Louisiana   Steinbeck's *The Grapes of Wrath*
The Stars Pass By   *A Midsummer Night's Dream*
History as a Literary Art   Gray's *Elegy Written in a Country*
How to Study Under Difficulties   *Churchyard*
     The Saturday Evening Post

If you were to write an essay on "The Value of the Liberal Arts" for *The Journal of Engineering Education,* you might well include a critical discussion of Sheridan's play, *The School for Scandal,* Rossini's opera, *The Barber of Seville,* and the Steinbeck motion picture, *The Grapes of Wrath.*

NOTE 1: Both common nouns in a hyphenated compound are capitalized when capitals are needed, as in titles: Tennyson's poem, "The Lotos-Eaters."

NOTE 2: The Library of Congress now advocates capitalizing only the first word and any proper nouns or adjectives in the title. Until such practice is more widely adopted, you are advised to use the principle stated above.

97b.   **Capitalize the first word of every sentence and the first word of every quoted sentence.**

The rule of capitalizing the first word of every sentence is illustrated on every printed page.
Can you attend the meeting tonight?
Our teacher said, "Don't miss seeing that movie."

When only part of a direct quotation is included within a sentence, it is usually not begun with a capital letter.

The press secretary, after a talk with Dr. Snyder, said that the President was "fine," and added that the doctor "just didn't want to take any chances with the flu."

97c.   Capitalize the first word of every line of poetry.

> We look before and after,
>   And pine for what is not:
> Our sincerest laughter
> With some pain is fraught;
> Our sweetest songs are those that tell of saddest thought.
>
> —SHELLEY, "To a Skylark"

The foregoing illustrates traditional poetry. Some modern poetry is written without capital letters. If and when you quote poetry, use the capitalization employed in the poem.

97d.   Capitalize proper nouns.
These include:

1. Names of people and titles used in place of specific persons: William Shakespeare, Theodore Roosevelt, the President, the Senator, the Treasurer, the General, Mr. Chairman, Father, Mother.

2. Names of countries, states, regions, localities, other geographic areas, and the like: United States, England, Pennsylvania, the Far East, the Midwest, the Solid South, the Rocky Mountains, the Sahara Desert, the Mississippi River, Lake Michigan, the Badlands, the North Pole.

3. Names of streets: Michigan Boulevard, Fifth Avenue, Ross Street, Ravinia Road (see 97e).

4. Names of the Deity and personal pronouns referring to Him: God, Heavenly Father, Son of God, Jesus Christ, Savior (Saviour), His, Him, Thy, Thine.

5. Names for the Bible and other sacred writings: Bible, the Scriptures, Book of Genesis, Revelations, Koran.

6. Names of religions and religious groups: Protestantism, Roman Catholicism, Presbyterian, Jesuit, Unitarian.

7. Names of the days and the months (but *not* the seasons—see 97h3): Monday, Tuesday, etc.; January, February, etc.

8. Names of schools, colleges, universities: Hill School, Morton Grade School, Horace Mann High School, Kentucky Military Institute, Wabash College, Cornell University.

9. Names of historic events, eras, and holidays: Revolutionary War, Christian Era, Middle Ages, Renaissance, the Fourth of July, Labor Day, Thanksgiving.

10. Names of races, organizations, and members of each: Indian, Negro, Malay, League of Women Voters, American Academy of Science, National League, New York Giants, Big Ten Conference, an Elk, a Shriner, a Socialist.

11. Vivid personifications: Fate, Star of Fortune, Destiny, the power of Nature, the paths of Glory, the chronicles of Time.

12. Trade names: Bon Ami, Jello, Magnavox, Palmolive, Ry-Krisp, Wheaties.

13. All names similar or comparable to those in the foregoing 12 groups.

NOTE: If the second member of a hyphenated compound is a proper noun or proper adjective, it is capitalized: Latin-American, Pre-Raphaelite, un-American, trans-Pacific.

97e. Capitalize a common noun or adjective when it is a part of or helps to make a proper name.

Missouri River, Rocky Mountains, Wall Street, Fifth Avenue, Blackstone Theatre, Washington High School, Swarthmore College, New York University, Roosevelt Dam, Yosemite National Park, Lake Erie, U.S. Highway 40, Route 33, Room 117, Chapter 26.

Common nouns and adjectives used alone are not capitalized: avenue, bay, building, college, county, dam, high school, island, lake, library, mountain, ocean, park, river, sea, strait, street, theater, university, and the like.

He is not a professor.
This is Professor Smith.

My father is a dean in a college.
My father is Dean Williams of Seneca University.

These students attend the local high school.
John is a graduate of Rocktown High School.

The street in front of our house needs paving.
Three houses on Forest Street are vacant.

The Brenta River is a well-known river in northern Italy, just outside Venice.
I have explored many of the rivers in our country.

The Great Smoky Mountains are well worth a visit.
The mountains in eastern Tennessee are known as the Great Smokies.

NOTE: Interjections, except *O*, are common words, and within a sentence are not capitalized.

Sail on, O Ship of State.
On that day, alas, our high school days came to an end.

97f. Capitalize words derived from proper nouns.

Shakespearian (Shakespearean), American, Episcopalian, Biblical, Scriptural, Italian, Pennsylvanian, British.

Note two important specific applications and a list of exceptions.

1. The word *English* is always capitalized in reference to language and literature as well as its geographical application.

2. The first personal pronoun "I" is always capitalized. None of the other pronouns are capitalized unless they begin a sentence or a direct quotation.

3. Some proper nouns and derivatives of proper nouns (the number is approaching 200) have been used in specific meanings so frequently that they are now considered common and are not capitalized. When in doubt, consult your dictionary. A fair sampling of such a list includes:

braille	morocco leather
britannia metal	pasteurized
castile soap	quisling
delftware	quixotic
frankfurter	roman type
graham bread	simon-pure
herculean	turkish towel
klieg light	utopian
lyonnaise potatoes	watt
madras cloth	wiener

97g. Avoid careless writing of capitals.

Do not carelessly write small letters so large that they resemble capitals. You disconcert and confuse your reader by this carelessness.

97h. Avoid unnecessary use of capitals.

1. Do not capitalize names of points of the compass unless they refer to a specific section.

Correct: My home is in the East.
Texas is the largest state in the Southwest.
John lives west of the Allegheny Mountains.
I should like to live in the southern part of California.
Walk two blocks west; then turn north.

2. Do not capitalize earth, sun, moon except when they are used in association with other astronomical bodies that are capitalized:

Mercury and Venus are farther from the Sun than are the Earth, Mars, and Jupiter.

The sun is bright today, and the moon will be full tonight.

3. Do not capitalize the names of the seasons: spring, summer, autumn, fall, winter. Of course, if any season is personified, use a capital.
4. Do not capitalize nouns of kinship unless they are used as a substitute for a proper name. When preceded by an article or a possessive, they are common nouns.

Correct: My father is a dean.
At Seneca College, Father (i.e., Mr. Smith) is Dean of Men.
My sister thinks I am quiet, but Grandma and Mother say that I talk too much.
Every autumn my cousin Harry and I go hunting.
Every autumn Cousin Harry and I go hunting.

5. Do not capitalize a noun or adjective if the reference is to any one of a class of persons or things rather than a specific person or thing. For example, do not capitalize names of professions or occupations.

Wrong: My roommate is studying Engineering and expects to become a Teacher; I hope to become either a Doctor or a Dentist.

In capitalizing names of classes or college class members as members, follow the principle of consistency. One suggestion is that you do not capitalize the noun or adjective indicating college class members but that you do capitalize the name of a specific class.

Four of us are sharing a double room; Joe is a freshman, I am a sophomore, Bill is a junior, and Mike is a senior. On the floor below us every resident is a member of the Senior class and on the floor above us every one is a member of the Freshman class.

6. Do not capitalize names of general college subjects unless they are proper names, but capitalize titles of specific courses:

> Next year I shall have courses in history, Spanish, and journalism, and although I do not like science courses, I shall be required to take Mathematics 2 and Biology 12.

7. Do not capitalize unimportant words in titles (Section **97a**), or the first word of part of a direct quotation (Section **97b**), or common nouns and adjectives not part of or helping to make a proper name (Section **97e**).

8. Do not be misled by current practices of some magazines and book publishers: using small letters for every word in titles.

Undesirable: "lincoln land in illinois"

> *a book of readings for english and american literature*

EXERCISES

A. Encircle all the capitals on a page of prose selected from a textbook or magazine. Give the reason for each capital.

B. Rewrite the following sentences, making the misuse or nonuse of capitals conform to the principles stated in Section **97.**

1. My father shouted, "put on your brake."
2. Every boy was dressed in a beautiful indian costume.
3. I took U.S. highway 52 to junction 24, turned left on state route 24, and drove to Chatsworth.
4. Many fine laboratories are located in the electrical engineering building.
5. Last thursday I went to the library to begin work on my term paper.
6. On our trips we have traveled through most of the west and the southwest.
7. In High School my philosophy was, "don't do today what you can put off until tomorrow."
8. In one corner of the Library you will find the latest College Catalogs from many of the Colleges and Universities in the United States.
9. My Father and Mother have always been very helpful to me all my life.
10. One thing every tourist should see is the old restored water mill, with its early american antiques.
11. Here in college, I am studying to become a Pharmacist.
12. As a Glee Club member, you will have the opportunity to attend such functions as Weddings, Banquets, Special Parties, and Formal Dances.

13. My Uncle owns a farm North of Springvale.
14. My schedule allows free time tuesday and wednesday afternoons between one and five, and saturday morning between eight and nine.
15. Spring and Fall weather in our state is delightful.
16. I hope to graduate from the college of Civil Engineering here at Atwood university.
17. Last week end my roommate and I went to visit an Aunt's home.
18. I have chosen to work in the Teaching field rather than in the field of Art and Design.
19. During his term of service, my father was sent to teach in several Eastern and Southern colleges.
20. My high school preparatory course included algebra, english literature, biology, and english composition.

ABBREVIATIONS

98a. Use only acceptable abbreviations in formal writing or in informal writing.

In all writing intended for information and convenience of a reader, avoid abbreviations that would be puzzling or unusual to him; write out words and expressions in full, unless condensation seems necessary or the spelled-out words are unconventional like *Mister* for *Mr.* or *Missus* (*Mistress*) for *Mrs.*

In the following examples, exaggerated for illustration, puzzling and unusual abbreviations occur:

Incorrect: A new sec. is to be elected to replace the sec.-treas. who has resigned.

Many a chem. prof. grades too severely; many a lit. prof. grades too easily.

Meet me in the Penn. Station Wed. P.M.

Chicago, Ill., lies n.e. of the Miss. R.

1. Themes and other college written work are or should be formal writing or good idiomatic informal writing. Usually, use abbreviations only in footnotes and bibliographies of term and research papers. Specifically and as a general rule, avoid in continuous prose the abbreviations for:

a. Names of states, rivers, mountains, etc.: Ala., Pa., Ill. R., Appalach. Mtns.

b. Parts of geographic names: Ft. Wayne (for Fort Wayne), N. Dakota (for North Dakota), Pt. Arthur (for Port Arthur). (*Saint,* however, is abbreviated before a place name: St. Louis, St. Bonaventure.)

c. Christian names: Jos. (for Joseph), Benj. (for Benjamin), Thos. (for Thomas).

d. Names of months and days: Jan., Feb., Sun., Mon.

e. Most titles: Prof., Gen., Lieut., Pres.

f. Names of schools and college subjects: chem., math., ed., P.E.

g. Words denoting length, time, weight, or capacity: in., ft., yd., sec., min., hr., mo., yr., oz., lb., qt., gal., pk., bu., bbl.

NOTE: Words of measurement and numerous other words are abbreviated in tables, footnotes, and bibliographies.

h. Miscellaneous words like st. for street, ave. for avenue, blvd. for boulevard, dr. for drive, pl. for place, r. for river, mt. for mountain; a.m. and p.m. (as substitutes for *morning* and *afternoon:* "this a.m. and p.m."); & for *and.*

2. Certain abbreviations are permissible and should be used instead of the full word. These are usually conventional titles used before names of people and the letters after names indicating identification or educational degrees.

Mr. William Brown; Mrs. John Smith; Messrs. William Brown and John Smith; Dr. Albert Jones; Hon. James E. Mason; Rev. Gordon Graham (but note: *The Honorable* James E. Mason, *The Reverend* Gordon Graham, but *never* Rev. Smith).

William Brown, A.B., A.M.; John Smith, Ph.D., LL.D.; Rev. Gordon Graham, D.D.
William Brown, Sr., and William Brown, Jr., were elected delegates.
Harry Jones, M.D., and his brother, Henry Jones, D.D.S., share an office.

Other necessary abbreviations include the following: a.m. and p.m. or A.M. and P.M., with numbers (7 a.m., 8:25 a.m., 2:10 p.m.); F. (for Fahrenheit); C. (for Centigrade), B.C. (before Christ); A.D. (Anno Domini, i.e., in the year of the Lord).

NOTE: B.C. follows the year, A.D. precedes it: 73 B.C., A.D. 1960.

98b. Do not use contractions in formal writing.

A contraction is a form of abbreviation: a word written with an apostrophe to indicate the omission of a letter. Usually considered as colloquial expressions, proper in speech and in informal writing, such contractions as *aren't, isn't, can't, couldn't, don't, doesn't, hasn't, haven't, shan't, shouldn't, wasn't, weren't, won't, wouldn't, mustn't* are out of place in formal writing. See Sections 55, 69.

In reporting dialogue or conversation, however, use contractions correctly to convey the exact words of the speaker. Do not avoid contractions and other colloquialisms to the extent of making reports of conversation seem artificial and forced.

98c. Use a period after abbreviations, with few exceptions.

The few exceptions are

1. Contractions such as *don't, won't, isn't, haven't,* etc.
2. The ordinal numbers when written *1st, 2nd, 35th,* etc.
3. Shortened forms like *ad, phone, exam, lab* (see Section **70**).
4. Nicknames such as Bill, Joe, Al, etc.
5. A few specialized abbreviations, including broadcasting companies and stations: percent or per cent (avoid %), TV, ABC, NBC, CBS, WEND, WBBM, WILL, KDAD, etc.
6. Letters for certain associations, unions, and government divisions and agencies: AMVETS, CARE, FBI, FTC, ICC, NAM, PGA, SPARS, TVA, UNESCO, etc.

For similar abbreviations, the use or omission of periods is optional; for others, periods are required. When in doubt, follow the punctuation given in your dictionary.

EXERCISES

Correct all errors in the use of abbreviations in the following sentences:

1. That night I learned that I was the proud brother of a new 6 lb. 9 oz. sister.
2. My uncle came over on Wed. and stayed until Sun. night.
3. Much progress has been made in commercial & short-wave radio.
4. At that time I was a student in Jr. High School and my brother was a student in Sr. High School.
5. In the story the Capt. was afraid that he would be disinherited by his uncle, the Lieut.-Col.

6. The road was a glare of ice, and traffic was slowed down to 35 mph.
7. I went to Springfield, Ill., to interview the manager of an electric motor company, and then I returned to my home in Terre Haute, Ind.
8. My sister was graduated from Ohio State Univ. in Aug., 1959.
9. This fish will sometimes weigh between 60 and 80 lbs.
10. I was born on 15 Dec. 1945 in Harrisonburg, Va., lived in Franklin, W. Va., until 1948, and then moved in Sept. 1951, to W. Phila., Penna.
11. Last summer I sold my 1957 Chev. convertible and bought a 1959 Olds.
12. I hope to continue in R.O.T.C. during my four years and be commissioned a 2nd Lt. when I graduate.
13. The other car was about 200 yds. in front of us.
14. Our high school chem department was not as good as it might have been, and it didn't have much of a lab.
15. The library stacks contain the bound magazines which are 10 yrs. or older; the storage room is about 50 ft. by 75 ft.

NUMBERS

99a. Be consistent in your use of words or figures for numbers (numerals).

Writing words for numbers or using figures for words, in sustained prose writing, is a matter of convention and custom. For most themes and other college writing, two principles serve; with an occasional variation, the two agree:

1. When a number can be expressed in one word or two words, write it out; otherwise, use figures: two, twenty-two, two hundred, 101, 749, 2,412, etc.

or

2. Use words for numbers between one and ninety-nine; use figures for words above ninety-nine: 100, 200, 314, etc.

Some variations from the foregoing occur, as in the following suggestions (99b, c, d), which are not for memorization but for reference only. These suggestions are adapted from the United States Government Printing Office *Style Manual* (1959), which follows this policy: "Most rules for the use of numerals are based on the general principle that the reader comprehends numerals more readily than numerical word expressions, particularly in technical, scientific, or statistical matter. However, for special reasons numbers are spelled out in indicated instances." This *Style Manual* also suggests that within a sentence a word be used for a single number from one to nine, inclusive, and that a figure be used for a single number of 10 or more. In its use of numbers, this handbook consistently follows the suggestions of the U.S. Government Printing Office *Style Manual*. (For the use of commas with four or more figures, see Section **88l**.)

99b.   Use words to represent numbers in special uses.

1. Indefinite expressions or round numbers.

> This theater will seat several thousand persons.
> Right now I am wishing for a million dollars.
> We have a hundred cows and six hundred chickens on our farm.
> The mid-fifties will probably be known as the atomic fifties.
> but
> The 1950's will probably be known as the atomic decade.

2. One number or related numbers at the beginning of a sentence.

> Three of our class officers are from the College of Engineering.
> Twenty to thirty students will be absent on an inspection trip to Detroit.

Use common sense in applying this principle:

Undesirable: Three thousand two hundred and thirty-nine students are enrolled as freshmen this year.
3,239 students are enrolled as freshmen this year.
Desirable: A total of 3,239 freshmen . . .
Enrolled as freshmen this year are 3,239 students.

3. Numbers preceding a compound modifier containing a figure.

> To line this wall we need twelve ½-inch pieces of plywood.
> Our tent is supported by two 8-foot poles.

4. Fractions standing alone or followed by *of a* or *of an*.

> Be sure that the plywood is one-half inch thick.
> I live about one-fourth of a mile from the campus.

5. Numbers used with serious and dignified subjects.

> Pennsylvania is proud to be listed among the Thirteen Original Colonies.
> This bill was given serious consideration in the Seventy-eighth Congress.

NOTE: A spelled-out number is not repeated in figures in parenthesis marks, except in legal documents.

Undesirable: I enclose my check for ten dollars ($10).
        Thirty (30) claims were made for damages.

99c.   Use figures to represent numbers in special uses.

1. Dates, including the day or the day and the year.

> Please return the blank by June 1.
> My parents were married on June 28, 1940.
> I worked on a farm from July 1 to September 1, 1960.

The proper date line for a letter is

> February 1, 1960
> or
> 1 February 1960 (no comma)
> not figures like 2/1/61, except on the second page of business letters.

2. House, room, telephone, and postal zone numbers.

> I live at 1607 Ravinia Road, Columbus 14, Ohio; my telephone number
> is Lawndale 82-2784.
> Send your request to 3 Park Street, Lincoln 5, Vermont.
> Tomorrow this class will meet in Room 6, University Hall.
> We are staying at the Greenbriar Hotel, Room 712.

3. Highway or comparable numbers.

> Take U.S. Highway 40 into Columbus and turn north on Route 33.
> Our best TV reception comes in over Channel 6.
> Trains for Chicago leave on Track 3.
> Flight 808, New York to Paris, leaves Idlewild Airport each night;
> use Gate 7 to the plane.

4. Measurements: age; degrees of temperature, longitude, latitude;
distance; size; weight; containers; etc.

> Father is 42 years old, Mother is 39, and my baby sister is 6.
> The temperature has varied from 2° to 8° below 0.
> The white lines on a football field are 5 yards apart.
> Standard stationery is 8½-by-11 inches in size.

¾-inch pipe	1-inch margin	5-foot pole
7 bushels	5 acres	2 gallons

> The parcel-post package weighed 6 pounds and 9 ounces.
> Everyone knows that 2 pints make a quart and 4 quarts make a gallon.

710

5. Time.

> 8 a.m. (not 8:00 a.m.)   12 m. (noon)   3:25 p.m.   half past 3
> 10 o'clock (*not* 10 o'clock a.m., or 10 a.m. in the morning)
> 8 years, 4 months, 27 days
> 6 days   3 minutes   2 months   9-hour day   5-day week
> I completed my assignment in 3 hours, 9 minutes, and 35 seconds.

(See also Item 15, Section 70.)

6. Percentage and other mathematical expressions.

> 10 percent   one-half of 1 percent   4¼ percent bonds
> Many students waste 15 to 20 percent of their time just fooling around.
> To obtain the answer, multiply by 3 and divide by 6.
> The proportion of women to men on our campus is 1 to 4.

7. Money.

> $4.55 $0.60   60 cents $6 per bushel (not $6.00)   35 cents apiece

8. Chapter, page, and footnote numbers.

> Chapter 12   See p. 144   pp. 312–15
> Footnote 3 on page 7 is a good example of a footnote.

Sometimes chapters and preliminary pages of a book are numbered with small-capital Roman numerals (see Section 99e below).

99d. Use figure-and-letter combinations appropriately.

Occasionally, a writer needs to use figures and alphabetical letters in combination, especially in expressing the ordinal numbers: 1st for first, 2nd or 2d for second; 3d or 3rd for third; fourth through twentieth, 4th, 9th, 12th, 18th, 20th; others as they apply, 21st, 33rd, or 33d, 99th, etc.

Such combinations are appropriately used as follows: in tables; sometimes in numbering ideas in a paragraph or a succession of paragraphs; sometimes in dates, but not when the year follows immediately; and usually in expressing a numbered street from 10th on.

> Your May 15th letter (or your letter of May 15th) has been received.
> Your letter of May 15, 1960, has been received.
> 121 North First Avenue
> Corner of Fifth Avenue and 10th Street
> 49 East 33d Street   South 199th Street
> After June 1st my address will no longer be 12 West Second Street; it will be 833 East 24th Street.

Notice, 1st, that no period follows the figure-and-letter combinations, and 2nd, that the principles about figures versus words (Sections 99b, c) apply usually to figure-and-letter combinations.

99e. Use Roman numerals correctly.

Our numbers were Roman letters used as numerals until the 10th century. Our present figures came from the Arabs and are called Arabic numerals. Although these Arabic numbers are generally preferable, Roman numerals still find occasional use in current writing, as in preparing outlines (Section 6), numbering the preliminary pages of a book, occasionally marking the date for a year, and frequently indicating acts and scenes of plays, volume numbers of books and magazines, and chapter numbers of books.

Large-capital Roman numerals are used after book (Book VI), volume (Volume or Vol. VII), part (Part II), unit or individual in a series (Charles XII, Elizabeth II), and sometimes the year. Small-letter Roman numerals, or sometimes small capitals, may be used for numbering preliminary pages, play scenes, tables and plates in printed or graphic materials, and sometimes Bible chapters.

> Prince Hal and Falstaff first appear in Act I, Scene ii, of Shakespeare's *Henry IV,* Part I.
>
> George I, George II, and George III reigned in the 18th century, George V and George VI in the 20th.
>
> The article "Grecian Architecture" is printed in Volume XII of the *Universal Encyclopedia.*
>
> This imposing building bears the date when it was constructed— MDCCCLXXIV.
>
> The preliminary pages in my textbook are numbered from v through xi.

Table VI, below, shows how Roman numerals are formed: "a repeated letter repeats its value; a letter placed after one of greater value adds to it; a letter placed before one of greater value subtracts from it; a dashline over a letter denotes multiplied by 1,000." (From United States Government Printing Office *Style Manual,* 1959 Edition, from which the following "Roman Numerals" table is also taken.)

TABLE VI. **ROMAN NUMERALS**

I	1	LXX	70
II	2	LXXV	75
III	3	LXXIX	79
IV	4	LXXX	80
V	5	LXXXV	85
VI	6	LXXXIX	89
VII	7	XC	90
VIII	8	XCV	95
IX	9	XCIX	99
X	10	C	100
XV	15	CL	150
XIX	19	CC	200
XX	20	CCC	300
XXV	25	CD	400
XXIX	29	D	500
XXX	30	DC	600
XXXV	35	DCC	700
XXXIX	39	DCCC	800
XL	40	CM	900
XLV	45	M	1,000
XLIX	49	MD	1,500
L	50	MM	2,000
LV	55	MMM	3,000
LIX	59	MMMM or M$\overline{\text{V}}$	4,000
LX	60	$\overline{\text{V}}$	5,000
LXV	65	$\overline{\text{M}}$	1,000,000
LXIX	69		

Dates

MDC	1600	MCMXX	1920
MDCC	1700	MCMXXX	1930
MDCCC	1800	MCMXL	1940
MCM or MDCCCC	1900	MCML	1950
MCMX	1910	MCMLX	1960

EXERCISES

Correct any errors in the use of numbers in the following sentences:

1. My classes end every day at three-forty-five p.m.
2. 1945 saw the beginning of a new scientific age—The Atomic Age.
3. The nearest town to our farm has a population of only one hundred and seventy-five.

4. In closing I would like to quote the Bible from John, chapter 3, verse sixteen.
5. The damage to my car was three hundred and fifty-seven dollars, according to the insurance estimate.
6. During high school I studied diligently, and at graduation I was ranked twenty-six in a class of three hundred and fifty-four.
7. We got our first surprise that morning by seeing 2 trucks overturned.
8. 4-H teaches its members many important things about cooperation.
9. I traded my nineteen fifty-seven Ford coupe for a nineteen fifty-nine Chevrolet convertible.
10. This past vacation I traveled about twenty-three hundred miles.
11. My home town lies south of Gary on State Highway number fifty-three.
12. 11:30 that night the doctor performed the operation.
13. An engineering card-index service can be purchased for fifteen hundred dollars.
14. 5′ 4″, brown eyes, brown hair, and one hundred and six pounds—that's me.
15. I was born in Goshen, West Virginia, on December seventeen, nineteen hundred and thirty-eight, and lived there until nineteen hundred and forty, when my family moved to South Carolina.

GENERAL EXERCISES

A. Choose any two pages from your book of readings or from a current magazine. Underline or encircle every mark of punctuation. Give a reason for each separate mark, or pair of marks, according to the principles stated in the preceding sections.

B. Punctuate the following sentences according to the commonly accepted principles of punctuation. Give a reason for each mark that you use.

1. When I was six years old we moved to Bradley Illinois where we lived for nine years.
2. We should leave for the Stadium early otherwise we'll miss the exciting moment of the kick-off.
3. To my parents were born three children Lois Jane John Jr and Richard Lee.
4. My sister Marie who attends college in New York City is also coming home for Christmas.
5. One thing has been accomplished I said to Mother I passed my written test with a perfect score.
6. The more practice that is done the better the student should be able to write.

General Exercises

7. The great Mississippi longest river in North America twists and turns its way to the Gulf of Mexico.
8. On the other side of Fairfield is Westport another residential town.
9. I have to be getting some sleep now for tomorrow is another hard and lonely day.
10. It is no fun playing football in below freezing weather.
11. On January 28 1944 my parents received quite a surprise the bouncing baby boy that they had been expecting turned out to be a girl.
12. Children are allowed to drive these toy automobiles around on a fenced in track.
13. My 16 year old sister Charlene never ceases to amaze me.
14. Tennis, softball, hikes, camping trips, and fishing these are some of the activities which come along with the season of spring.
15. Would my roommate be tall short fat thin all these things I wondered as I approached my room.
16. What a hot day our first day on the campus turned out to be.
17. In rushed my aunt's children four of the most bloodthirsty savage heartless cute little blondheaded girls on this earth.
18. For Christmas I received as a treasured gift a bowling outfit bowling ball bag and shoes.
19. All at once a strange sensation came over me a sensation many young fliers get when they make their first solo flight.
20. Mother being the gentle person she is no problem of ours is too minor for her to consider.

C. Correct the faulty punctuation in the following sentences. Tell why the punctuation is faulty, and give reasons for the punctuation marks that you use.

1. That night I was one of many, tired little boys.
2. The poem, that I consider the greatest ever written has the title 'If.'
3. My grades this semester will be above average; even though I got off to a poor start at the first of the semester.
4. It is the dream of many-a-small boy to play professional baseball.
5. I took my time and sank the putt for my second eagle of the day; and the best game of my life.
6. Our town has long been known as, "the pottery center of the world."
7. When the teacher saw the dog, she asked who had brought it to class?
8. Rich and poor, young and old; all can enjoy the scenic beauties of Nature.
9. The first mistake I made occurred during my sophomore year in high school.

10. What college should I attend? Should it be large or small; all-male or coeducational?
11. We should have no trouble writing if we remember the many rules of English, that have been taught to us.
12. My father, I love, respect, and obey, because: first, he is my father, and second, he is the best man I know.
13. Whether this is my problem or my parent's problem remains to be seen.
14. I might compare my young brother to the, long-dreamed-of, perpetual motion machine.
15. Among these books are: books of biography, books of travel; and books of short stories.
16. My remaining subjects, English and mathematics are taught in the Arts Building.
17. Grandfather is still a dear and wise old man; the one man in the world I shall never forget.
18. We took a trip through Colorado, Utah, and Nevada; then down the California coast to Los Angeles.
19. We fished for a long time and caught many fish, the main ones were pike.
20. By the time I had finished moving into my room and visited the recreation room and its surroundings—it was time to attend my first orientation program.

D. Punctuated or written in one way, the following sentences have one meaning; punctuated in another way, they have a different meaning. Explain at least two possible meanings in each sentence.

1. Attention please Smith the director has a few words to say.
2. Mother said Father is always hopelessly late.
3. At the last filling station we stopped asking where County Road 5 is.
4. The alibi he told us was foolproof.
5. Mary said June is a good pianist.
6. Some of the students I know have already gone home.
7. My intention to be perfectly honest was not carried out.
8. Merle my little brother is nine years old.
9. The driver in the first car said the policeman did not yield the right of way.
10. You should have asked Henry when the directions became involved.
11. Henry has six year old rabbits for sale.
12. Why didn't you know there was a meeting of our committee last evening?

13. I have always been a small town boy.
14. Every day occurrences of this kind get noticed in the newspapers.
15. On the way home I stopped believing that I had another errand to do.

GLOSSARY OF APPLIED PUNCTUATION

100. In applying to your writing the general and specific punctuation principles reviewed in the preceding pages, answer the following questions when you have a problem about punctuation:

1. Exactly what is here that requires punctuation? That is, what kinds of sentences? What kinds of elements within sentences? What kinds of relations between elements?

2. What purpose do I want my punctuation to serve? Termination? Introduction? Separation? Enclosure? Correctness? Clearness? Effectiveness?

3. What punctuation mark or marks will best accomplish that purpose?

When you have answered the first question—"Exactly what is here that requires punctuation?"—use the following to answer the second and third questions. Figures in parentheses refer to sections providing detailed discussion and illustration.

1. **Abbreviations.** Use a period after a standard abbreviation. **(86d)**
2. **Absolute phrase** (nominative absolute). Use commas. **(88p)**
3. **Act—scene.** Separate by a colon. **(90f)**
4. **Adjectives.** Two or more adjectives modifying, coordinately, the same noun, separate by commas. See also **Series,** below. **(88i)**
5. **Adjective clauses** and **Adjective phrases.** See **Clauses, dependent,** below, and see **Phrases,** below.
6. **Adverbial clauses.** See **Clauses, dependent,** below.
7. **Although.** Never preceded by a semicolon, unless other conditions warrant. See **Conjunctions, subordinating,** below.
8. **Apposition.** Use commas. For long or emphatic appositional phrases, use dashes. **(88q, 91e)**
9. **Because.** Never preceded by a semicolon, unless other conditions warrant. See **Conjunctions, subordinating,** below.
10. **Break or shift in thought..** Use a dash. **(91c)**
11. **Cancellation.** Do not use parenthesis marks to cancel. Erase or draw a line through the material. **(92c)**

12. **Chapter headings.** In a body of prose, enclose in quotation marks. As the heading of a chapter, use no punctuation. **(95f)**

13. **Clauses.**

Independent clauses. (1) Joined by pure coordinating conjunction, use a comma. If the clauses are long with complicated internal punctuation, use a semicolon. **(88d, 89c)** (2) Not joined by any conjunction, use a semicolon. **(89a)** (3) Joined by a conjunctive adverb, use a semicolon. **(89b)** (4) Used parenthetically, enclose in dashes or parentheses. **(91e, 92a)** (5) Between contrasting independent clauses, use a comma. **(88j)**

Dependent clause. (1) Adverbial clause preceding independent clause, use a comma. **(88f)** (2) Adverbial clause following independent clause: if restrictive, use no punctuation; otherwise, use commas if adverbial clause is nonrestrictive or fairly long. **(88f)** (3) Adjective clause: if nonrestrictive, use commas; if restrictive, omit punctuation. **(88m)** (4) Noun clauses: used as subject or object or complement, no punctuation. **(88u)** (5) Dependent contrasting clauses, use a comma. **(88j)**

14. **Complex sentence.** See **Clauses, dependent,** above.

15. **Compound predicate.** With two members only, usually no commas; with three or more, commas. See **Series,** below.

16. **Compound sentence.** See **Clauses, independent,** above.

17. **Compound words.** Separate the parts by a hyphen or hyphens. **(93a, b)**

18. **Conjunctions, coordinating.** (1) Pure conjunctions joining independent clauses, use a comma before, but not after. **(88d)** (2) Pure conjunctions joining two words or two phrases, no punctuation; joining three or more, commas. **(88h)** (3) Conjunctive adverb (see **Conjunctive adverb,** below). (4) Correlative conjunctions: apply same principle as for pure conjunctions. **(88d, h)**

19. **Conjunctions, subordinating.** Never place a comma or a semicolon after, unless for other reasons; place a comma before if the clause is adverbial, is nonrestrictive, and follows the independent clause. **(88f, 88u, 89b)**

20. **Conjunctive adverb.** Use a semicolon before when placed between two independent clauses. Use a comma or no mark after, depending upon parenthetic strength. **(89b)**

21. **Contractions.** Use an apostrophe. **(94f)**

22. **Contrasted coordinate elements.** Use a comma. **(88j)**

23. **Coordinate adjectives.** See **Adjectives,** above.

24. **Correlative conjunctions.** See **Conjunctions, coordinating,** above.

25. **Dates and places.** Enclose in commas when they explain preceding dates and places. **(88s)**
26. **Decimal.** Use a period preceding. **(86f)**
27. **Declarative sentence.** See **Sentence,** below.
28. **Dependent clause.** See **Clauses,** above.
29. **Dialogue.** Use quotation marks and commas. **(88b, 95a, b, c)**
30. **Diction.** Provincialisms, slang expressions, misnomers, and unusual technical terms, use quotation marks. **(95e)**
31. **Direct address (Vocative).** Use commas. **(88r)**
32. **Dollars and cents.** Use a period between. **(86f)**
33. **Doubt or uncertainty.** Use a question mark in parentheses. **(87e)**
34. **Emphasis.** Italicize. **(96d)** Also see **Surprise,** below.
35. **Exclamatory sentence.** See **Sentence,** below.
36. **Figures.** Four or more figures, use a comma in front of each three numbers. **(88l)**
37. **For.** As a conjunction, use a comma preceding. As a preposition, use no punctuation. **(88e)**
38. **For example, for instance, namely,** etc. Used parenthetically, enclose in commas, unless they are followed by an independent clause; then use a colon or semicolon before, a comma after. **(88n, 88q)**
39. **Fractions.** Use a hyphen between the numerator and the denominator. **(93b)**
40. **Hour—minute.** Separate by a colon. **(90f)**
41. **Imperative sentence.** See **Sentence,** below.
42. **Independent clauses.** See **Clauses,** above.
43. **Indirect question.** Use a period, not a question mark. **(86c, 87c)**
44. **Indirect quotation.** Use neither commas nor quotation marks. **(88u, 95j)**
45. **Inserted material.** (1) Inserted sentence elements, use comma or commas. **(88o)** (2) Omitted material inserted later, indicate by a caret $(_\wedge)$. **(92f)**
46. **Interjections.** Mild, use a comma; strong or fairly strong, use an exclamation point! **(87a, 88n)**
47. **Interpolated material.** Use brackets. **(92d)**
48. **Interrogative sentence.** See **Sentence,** below.
49. **Interruption in dialogue.** Use a dash. **(91b)**
50. **Introduction.** Before a word, phrase, or clause being introduced, use a comma, colon, or dash. **(88a, 90a, b, 91a)**
51. **Irony.** Occasionally, indicate by an exclamation point within parentheses. **(87a)**
52. **Misreading.** Between words and elements that may be misread, use a comma, or recast. **(88k)**

53. **Namely.** See **For example,** above.
54. **Names of ships, trains, airplanes.** Use quotation marks or italics. **(95f, 96a)**
55. **Nominative absolute.** See **Absolute phrase,** above.
56. **Nonrestrictive clause.** See **Clauses, dependent,** above.
    Nonrestrictive phrase. See **Phrases,** below.
57. **Noun clause.** See **Clauses, dependent,** above.
58. **Numbers.** See **Figures,** above.
59. **Numerals.** Use a hyphen between the parts if they are written out (from twenty-one to ninety-nine). **(93b)**
60. **Object.** Use no comma between a verb and its object or a preposition and its object (except for additional reasons). **(88u)**
61. **Oh.** As a mild interjection, use a comma following; as a strong interjection, use an exclamation point. Before a vocative, O (spelled thus) is followed by no punctuation. **(87a, 88n)**
62. **Omission of letters.** In a contraction, use an apostrophe. **(94f)** Other omitted letters from a word, use a dash. **(91f)**
63. **Omission of words.** Use ellipsis periods or asterisks. **(86g)**
64. **Outline symbols.** Use a period after each. **(86e)**
65. **Parenthetic words, phrases, clauses.** Weak, no punctuation; fairly to moderately strong, use commas; strong, use dashes or parentheses. **(88n, 91e, 92a)**
66. **Phrases.** (1) An introductory modifying phrase containing a verb form, use a comma; not containing a verb form, use no punctuation, unless fairly long and then use a comma. **(88g)** (2) Nonrestrictive phrases, use commas; restrictive phrases, use no punctuation. **(88m)**
67. **Places.** See **Dates and places,** above.
68. **Plurals.** Formed by adding *s, es,* or change in form. *Never* use an apostrophe, except to form the plurals of words as words, of letters, and of figures. **(94g, h)**
69. **Possessive case.** Use the apostrophe in forming the possessive case of nouns and indefinite pronouns. Do *not* use the apostrophe in forming the possessive case of other classes of pronouns. **(94a–e, i, j)**
70. **Predicate.** See **Compound predicate,** above.
71. **Preposition and object.** Use no comma or colon between. **(88u)**
72. **Provincialisms.** See **Diction,** above.
73. **Pure conjunctions.** See **Conjunctions, coordinating,** above.
74. **Queries, series of.** Use question marks. **(87d)**
75. **Question.** After a direct question, use a question mark; after an indirect question, use a period. **(87b, 86c)**
76. **Quotation.** (1) Enclose a direct quotation in quotation marks; use no quotation marks with an indirect quotation. **(95a, b, c, j)** (2) A

short direct quotation is set off by a comma; an indirect quotation is not set off by a comma. **(88b)** (3) A long formal quotation is introduced by a colon. **(90d)**

77. **Quotation extending over one paragraph.** Use quotation marks at the beginning of each paragraph, but at the end of only the last paragraph. **(95d)**

78. **Quotation marks with other marks of punctuation.** See Section **95i.**

79. **Quotation within a quotation.** Use single quotation marks. **(95g)**

80. **References and directions.** When these amplify, enclose in parentheses. **(92b)**

81. **Restrictive clause.** See **Clauses, dependent,** above.
    Restrictive phrase. See **Phrases,** above.

82. **Salutation.** In a business letter, use a colon after; in a friendly letter, use a comma. **(88c, 90e)**

83. **Sentence.** (1) After a declarative sentence, use a period. **(86a)** (2) After a mildly imperative sentence, use a period; if it is vigorous, an exclamation point. **(86b, 87a)** (3) After an interrogative sentence, use a question mark. **(87b)** (4) After an exclamatory sentence, use an exclamation point. **(87a)**

84. **Series.** Three or more words or phrases or clauses, separate by commas, including one before but not after the conjunction. **(88h)** When the conjunction joins each two members of the series, except independent clauses, use no punctuation. **(88h)** See **Clauses,** above.

85. **Slang.** See **Diction,** above.

86. **Subheads.** Use no period following. **(86h)**

87. **Subject—predicate.** Use no comma to separate, unless parenthetic elements requiring commas intervene. **(88u, 88n)**

88. **Subordinating conjunctions.** See **Conjunctions, subordinating,** above.

89. **Such as.** Use a comma or no punctuation preceding; use no punctuation following. **(88q, 90g)**

90. **Summarizing final clause.** Use a dash preceding. **(91d)**

91. **Surprise, emphasis, strong emotion.** Use an exclamation point. **(87a)**

92. **Suspended elements.** Use commas, usually. **(88o)**

93. **Technical words.** See **Diction,** above.

94. **Title—subtitle.** Separate by a colon. **(90f)**

95. **Titles.** (1) Titles of books, long poems, pamphlets, magazines, newspapers, motion pictures, use italics, or, less preferably, quotation marks. **(95f, 96a)** (2) Titles of magazine articles, short stories,

and short poems, use quotation marks. **(95f)** (3) Titles at the beginning of a theme or paper or chapter, use neither quotation marks around nor a period following. **(95l, 86h)** (4) Titles (personal) and initials following a name, use comma preceding. **(88t)**

96. **Transposed elements.** Use commas, usually. **(88o)**
97. **Unfinished statement or word.** Use a dash. **(91b)**
98. **Verb—object and verb—complement.** Use no comma or colon to separate. **(88u, 90g)**
99. **Vocative.** See **Direct address,** above.
100. **Word division.** Use a hyphen at the end of the line, between syllables, when the word is continued on the next line. Never use a hyphen at the beginning of a line. **(93c)**

APPENDIX:
WRITING LETTERS

The letter is a widely used form of written communication. During your college years you probably will write many more letters than formal themes, and after graduation you will find it necessary to write even more letters than in college. So widely used a form of writing deserves attention; from the standpoint of utility only, training in no other form is so important, for the ability to write a good letter indicates much more than is commonly realized. Important businessmen and firms waste little time, for example, on applications written in slipshod style; friends frequently drift away when they receive hastily written notes instead of sincere, attractive, detailed letters. Often our business and social contacts are affected by ignorance of proper letter forms and conventions.

Your letters are an unfailing reflection and representation of you. What you say and how, the paper and ink you use, even the way in which you address the envelope and affix the stamp reflect your personality just as do your diction, smiles, and gestures.

This universally used, important, and highly personal form of communication called a letter is, in a sense, a theme governed by the same rules and principles as other kinds. It should be *correct, clear, effective,* and *appropriate.* A good letter is rarely dashed off; instead it is the result of careful planning, writing, and rewriting.

The two main kinds of letters are business letters and informal, friendly letters. Other kinds are formal invitations and replies, but the conventional patterns of formal social correspondence may be found in any standard book of etiquette. Business letters and informal letters, however, are more variable. Each group deserves attention, and each

723

illustrates admirably the process of communication: you, *the writer,* sending some specific question or information, *the subject,* to some specifically named person or company, *the reader.*

BUSINESS LETTERS

The business letter is largely utilitarian: its object is to convey information by clear exposition. As a writer of business letters, you are primarily concerned with *presentation* and *content,* or, respectively, the way in which you arrange and express your material and the subject matter that you include. Later in college you may take one or more courses in general business correspondence. Since, however, fewer than one-fifth of our colleges and universities offer even one such basic course, and since only a small number of students take advantage of it when offered, the following material introduces you to some general principls for use now or later in business correspondence.

1. PRESENTATION

A good business letter creates a pleasing impression the moment it is taken from its envelope. Quality of paper, neatness of typing or writing, and arrangement of letter parts are almost as important to total effect as content is. Correctness and attractiveness in *form* reflect a courteous attitude toward the reader.

Stationery

Business letters should be written on good-quality white unruled paper, preferably of the standard 8½-x-11-inch size, although the half-size sheet (8½-x-5½) is acceptable, using either the longer or the shorter measurement for the horizontal lines. Colored and unusual-sized sheets and fraternity, club, and hotel stationery are in doubtful taste for business correspondence.

Typing

Letters should be typewritten if possible, but legible longhand, in black or blue-black ink, is permissible. For typing, a black ribbon fresh enough to insure legibility should be used; the letter must be neat in every detail, with no strike-overs or visible erasures. (For typing conventions, see Section 1c.)

Appendix: Writing Letters

Form

Good business letters are arranged in a form which has now become so standardized that it is easy to follow. It consists of six parts:

1. The Heading
2. The Inside Address
3. The Greeting or Salutation

4. The Body
5. The Complimentary Close
6. The Signature

Each part has certain set forms which must not be ignored or altered if your letter is to be conventional, attractive, and easy to read. Study the letters on pages 731–740, not only for observing the position of the parts but also for illustration of the correct use and balanced arrangement of these conventionalized forms.

The Heading. The heading contains the sender's full address—street, city, postal zone, state—and the date of writing. It is usually placed in the upper right-hand part of the sheet (but see p. 731), an inch or more below the top edge (see "Margins," p. 730), and it ends flush with the right margin. It is single spaced. Avoid abbreviations and using *st, nd, rd,* or *d* after the day of the month. On stationery with a letterhead, you add only the date, placed flush with the right-hand margin or centered directly beneath the letterhead. For position of lines and punctuation, see "Full Block and Modified Block Forms" and "Open and Closed Systems," pages 730–732, and the letters on pages 736–740.

The Inside Address. The name and address of the person or company written to should appear from two to four spaces below the heading and flush with the left-hand margin of the letter. It is usually single spaced and harmonizes with the heading in being punctuated according to the closed or open system.

Some title should always precede the name of the person addressed: *Mr., Mrs., Miss.* A business title rarely precedes the name, but a person of professional standing may be addressed as *Dr., The Reverend, President, Dean, Professor, General,* etc. The title *Honorable,* preceded by *The,* is widely used for a person holding an important government position.

If only the last name of the person written to is known, the letter is directed to the firm, with *Attention: Mr. —* or *Attention of Mr. —* added. The attention line usually appears two spaces below the inside address and two above the greeting; it has no bearing on the greeting

725

itself, which is always determined from the first line of the inside address. (See pp. 727–728.)

The following list indicates proper forms for addressing and greeting various persons:

	Inside Address	*Greeting*
One man	Mr. James T. Wilcox 49 Nottingham Road Silver Spring, Utah	Dear Mr. Wilcox:
One woman	Mrs. Robert Fitch 2 Park Place Troy 65, Ohio	Dear Mrs. Fitch:
Partnership	Messrs. Herd and Tims 1350 Sumter Boulevard Tallahassee, Florida	Gentlemen:
Company	Cobblestone Paving Co. 569 West Shore Drive Chicago 25, Illinois	Gentlemen:
Firm of women	The Dora Dress Shop 14 Wilton Boulevard Portland, Maine	Ladies:
One man in a firm	Mr. Victor C. Woll Art Printing Company 332 Aiken Building Nashville 10, Florida	Dear Mr. Woll:
An officer in a firm	Mr. Lee Fox, Treasurer The Mayo Corporation West Falls, Montana or Mr. Walter Stephens Treasurer, Lea & Sons, Inc. 1659 Glenham Street Oak Park 4, Illinois	Dear Mr. Fox: Dear Mr. Stephens:
A college official (with professional title)	President Roy G. Wild Charlotte College Jackson, Arizona	Dear President Wild:
An officer in an organization, when individual name is unknown	The Registrar Polk University Brighton, New York	Dear Sir:
A clergyman	The Reverend Samuel Clark (or, if he has a doctor's degree, The Reverend Dr. Samuel Clark) Park Street Methodist Church 223 Park Street Buffalo 19, New York	Dear Sir: or Dear Mr. Clark: or Dear Dr. Clark:

Appendix: Writing Letters

	Inside Address	*Greeting*
A priest	The Reverend Father Smith or The Reverend Leo L. Smith 919 Euclid Avenue Pershingville, New York	Dear Father Smith: or Dear Reverend Father: or Dear Father:
Member of a sisterhood	Sister Mary Agnes Riverview Academy Riverview, Pennsylvania	Dear Sister: or Dear Sister Agnes:
Rabbi	Rabbi Joseph Simon or The Reverend Joseph Simon Temple of Israel North Ninth Avenue Cincinnati 12, Ohio	Dear Sir: or Dear Rabbi Simon:

PUBLIC OFFICIALS

	Inside Address	*Greeting*
The President	The President The White House Washington 25, D.C.	Mr. President: or My dear Mr. President:
Cabinet member	The Secretary of — Washington 25, D.C. or The Honorable John Foy Secretary of — Washington 25, D.C.	Dear Sir: or My dear Mr. Secretary:
Senator	The Honorable John Rae The United States Senate Washington 25, D.C.	Dear Sir: or Dear Senator: or Dear Senator Rae:
Representative	The Honorable R. B. Burns The House of Representatives Washington 25, D.C.	Dear Sir: or Dear Mr. Burns:
Governor	The Honorable Paul Key Governor of Colorado Denver, Colorado	Dear Sir: or Dear Governor Key:
Mayor	His Honor, the Mayor City Hall Bangor, Maine	My dear Mr. Mayor: or Dear Mayor Woods:

The Greeting or Salutation. The greeting or salutation is placed two spaces below the inside address and flush with the left-hand margin. It is usually punctuated with a colon only, never a comma, semicolon, dash, or colon and dash. The following forms of salutation, arranged in decreasing formality, are correct. The one chosen should be in harmony with the first line of the inside address and the general tone of your letter. However, for most business correspondence, the *last form* listed in each group is preferable (see also greetings shown above with the list of inside addresses). Notice that "dear" is capitalized only when it is the first word.

To a Man	To a Woman
Dear Sir:	Dear Madam:
My dear Mr. Pollock:	My dear Mrs. Lord:
Dear Dr. Bard:	Dear Mrs. Lord:
To a Firm of Men	*To a Group or Firm of Women*
Gentlemen:	Ladies:

NOTE: The more personal form using the name of the person addressed is preferred to the more formal *Dear Sir* or *Dear Madam*. However, *Dear Sir* and *Dear Madam* are commonly used for addressing officials. *Dear Sirs,* as greeting for a firm of men, is no longer used.

The Body. The body of the letter contains the message and begins two spaces below the greeting. Most business letters are single spaced, although a short message may be double spaced for attractive arrangement on a large page. Single-spaced letters require two spaces between each paragraph. Paragraphs may be in block form (if the heading and inside address correspond in form) or indented. They may be indented, for clearness and effectiveness, even when the block system is used in other parts. If double spacing is used in the body of the letter, paragraphs are more clearly separated by indentation. On the typewriter, indentation may be five or ten spaces, or one space beyond the length of the greeting line.

Messages too long for one page are continued on a second page, never on the back of a sheet. However, the second page must contain at least two lines, preferably more, in addition to the complimentary close and signature. A paragraph may be continued from one page to another, but at least two lines of the paragraph should appear on the page on which it begins or ends. Each additional page should carry a top line containing some sort of identification, such as the addressee's initials or name, the page number, and the date: H. M. Brown, 9/12/60. Page 2.

The Complimentary Close. The close is usually placed at the middle or slightly to the right of the middle of the page, two or three spaces below the last line of the body of the letter. Only the first word is capitalized. The punctuation mark is usually a comma. Correct forms, arranged in order of decreasing formality and used to harmonize with the formality or semi-informality of the greeting, are as follows:

Yours truly,	Sincerely yours,
Very truly yours,	Yours sincerely,
Yours very truly,	Cordially yours,
Yours very sincerely,	Yours cordially,
Very sincerely yours,	Cordially,

Respectfully yours (never *Respectively yours*) is commonly used in letters to public officials, to clergy and others in religious orders, and to those ranking above the writer in academic circles, like a college dean or president. *Cordially yours* is frequently used among business friends or by older people writing to younger.

The close is independent of the last paragraph of the letter and is not linked to it by a participial phrase such as *Thanking you in advance, I remain,* or *Hoping for an early reply, I am.* Clever or original forms such as *Enthusiastically yours, Apologetically yours, Yours for lower taxes, Yours for a cheery Homecoming* are to be avoided.

The Signature. The signature is placed directly below the complimentary close. If the signature (name) is typewritten, four spaces are needed for the insertion of the handwritten signature. Unless a letter is mimeographed or is plainly a circular letter, it should always have, in ink, a legible handwritten signature.

An unmarried woman places the title *Miss* in parentheses before her name; if *Miss* is included in the typewritten signature, it is not needed in the written signature:

(Miss) Elizabeth West

A married woman should sign her own full name, followed by her married name:

Anne Marie Shelton
(Mrs. Paul R. Shelton)

A man places no title before his written or typed name, such as academic degrees and courtesy or professional titles, *Mr., Dr., Rev.,* etc.; but the writer's business title is often given after, *General Man-*

ager, Superintendent, Vice-President, etc. Letter convention opposes putting the writer's address under the signature; its proper place is in the heading.

Margins

Balanced layout of the letter on the page is determined by the length of the message. The entire letter, including heading, inside address, complimentary close, and signature, should have the appearance of a rectangle, with top and bottom margins slightly wider than those at the sides. Side margins should be at least an inch wide, and particular care must be taken to maintain as even a right margin as possible. If division is necessary, long words should be divided according to their proper syllables. Short business letters should be approximately centered, with wide margins.

Full block and modified block forms

Arrangement of the lines of the heading and of the inside address may follow the *full block* or the *modified block* system. In both, the second and third lines of the heading and of the inside address, respectively, begin directly underneath the beginning of the first line. In the full block form, all the parts of the letter, including the heading, complimentary close, and signature, begin at the left-hand margin. In the modified block form, the heading, complimentary close, and signature are in their conventional place, on the right side of the letter.

Formerly popular but rarely seen in a present-day business letter is the indented system, in which each line of the heading and of the inside address was indented a few spaces to the right of the preceding line.

Open and closed systems

Punctuation of the heading and inside and outside addresses may follow the *open* or the *closed system*. In the open system, no commas or final periods, except after abbreviations, are used after the separate lines, and some letterwriters prefer, also, to omit the colon after the salutation and the comma after the complimentary close (see the two examples on pp. 736, 737 and p. 740). In the closed system, commas are used after each line of the heading and inside address, except the last, at the end of which a period is used. Because of time-saving and convenience, most letter writers now use open punctuation.

Appendix: Writing Letters

FULL BLOCK FORM

1934 Travis Street
Louisville 8, Kentucky
February 3, 19--

Miss Lucy Irwin
Secretary, Society of Commerce
375 East Boone Street
Arlington, Kentucky

Dear Miss Irwin:

This letter is an illustration of the "full block"
or the "modified military" form, since all parts
of the letter, including heading, complimentary
close, and signature, begin flush with the left-
hand margin. Where two or more lines appear in a
part, each line begins directly under the line just
above. Note the spacing between the various parts
of the letter.

The paragraphs also illustrate block form; that is,
each paragraph begins flush with the left-hand
margin. Division between paragraphs is indicated
by double spaces. Within the paragraphs and within
each part of the letter, single spacing is used.

No punctuation marks are used after the lines in
the heading, inside address, and signature. This
system, called open punctuation, may or may not
apply, however, to the greeting and the complimentary close; the writer's preference must decide.

This letter form--full block and open punctuation--
is widely used by businessmen, secretaries, and
stenographers, for it saves considerable time and
trouble by its elimination of indentions and some
of the end-punctuation marks.

Sincerely yours,

Wilson F. Johnson

Wilson F. Johnson
Correspondence Consultant
Louisville Mercantile Corporation

MODIFIED BLOCK FORM

516 Tudor Place,
Detroit 22, Michigan,
November 2, 19--.

Rinebeck & Company,
1224 East Denver Avenue,
Chicago 12, Illinois.

Gentlemen:

 This letter is an example of "modified block"
or "semi-block" form; that is, heading, complimentary close, and signature are on the right side
of the letter, the other parts on the left. But
within the parts the block form is used.

 The paragraphs are indented here, but they
could be block form. In fact, blocked paragraphs
are optional; indented paragraphs can be used, if
the writer so desires, with even the full-block
form.

 Closed punctuation--now rarely seen in business letters--is illustrated here: commas at the
end of each line in the heading and the inside
address except the last, which has a period.

 These two letters--this one and the one pre-
ceding--also illustrate variety in the use of
greeting and complimentary close. The tone of the
complimentary close likewise is in harmony with the
tone of the greeting, in each of the letters.

Very truly yours,

Rodney R. Rhodes

Rodney R. Rhodes

Appendix: Writing Letters

The envelope

The envelope carries the sender's return address in the upper left-hand corner and the addressee's name slightly below center and to the right. The full address should be used in harmony with the inside address on the letter, although double spacing of a three-line address on an envelope is helpful to the Post Office Department, which prefers indented lines as well as the placing of the state on a separate line.

Conventional folding of the letter depends upon the size of the envelope. When the large No. 10 ($9\frac{1}{2}$-x-$4\frac{1}{8}$) envelope is used, fold the lower third of the sheet over the message, fold the upper part down to within a half inch of the creased edge, and put the upper folded edge in the envelope first.

For the smaller No. $6\frac{3}{4}$ ($6\frac{1}{2}$-x-$3\frac{5}{8}$) envelope, fold the lower part of the letter page over the message to within approximately one-half inch of the top of the page. Next, fold from the right slightly more than one third, then from the left, leaving the left flap edge slightly short of the right folded edge. Insert the left folded edge in the envelope first.

The reason for these folds is obvious—courtesy to the reader. If he opens your letter in the conventional way, the letter comes out of the envelope literally half-unfolding itself, top edge and written face up, ready to be read. The conventional way of opening for a right-handed person is as follows: the envelope is held in the left hand, with the address side face down, and the envelope flap at the top; the envelope is slit along the top long edge, and the letter is withdrawn by the right hand.

2. CONTENT

In addition to adhering to general principles of effective writing, business letters should be clear, concise, complete, and courteous, four important C-words in letter writing. Since the object of a business letter is to convey information by precise exposition, and since you hope to secure the reader's attention, you should carefully plan every letter and its phrasing.

Opening sentence

Open the letter with a statement of its subject or its purpose, a courteous request, a direct question, a simple direct important statement, or several of these in combination. Avoid rubber-stamp and abbreviated expressions like those listed under "Language" (below). Include briefly in the opening sentences or paragraph any pertinent background information which will clarify your message. Make the purpose of your letter evident, and arrange your thoughts in logical, easy-to-follow units. Separate ideas require separate paragraphs and should be developed according to the principles discussed in Sections 23, 24.

Paragraphing

Business-letter paragraphs are shorter than those in most other kinds of prose. They usually vary in length from two to six lines. Longer paragraphs are rare; not infrequently one-line paragraphs are used. Such paragraphing enables the reader to get the message of each paragraph, and of the letter, easily, quickly, clearly, and effectively.

Closing sentence

Your letter should close strongly and effectively. As indicated above under "The Complimentary Close," avoid weak participial or prepositional phrases. Make your last group of words a complete sentence: an invitation, a direct question, a courteous request, a restatement of the subject of the letter, or a significant and important statement.

Language

Remember your reader: avoid using too formal English, but at the other extreme avoid using trite, outworn, "business" expressions, sometimes referred to as "letter killers." The following is a representative list of such expressions:

according to my records	in receipt of
am pleased to advise	meets your approval
as per	past favors
as soon as possible	permit us
at an early date	recent date
at this writing	regret to advise
at your earliest convenience	take the liberty of
attached hereto	thank you in advance
beg to acknowledge (state, advise, etc.)	under separate cover
	valued wishes
contents noted	we trust
enclosed herewith	wish to advise (state, inform)
enclosed please find	would advise (state, inform)
has come to hand	you may rest assured

Appendix: Writing Letters

Use instead an informal and soundly idiomatic style. Colloquialisms are permissible, but avoid a telegraphic style. Effective business letters use the same courteous and friendly language that is used in a business conversation over the telephone.

Types of business letters

The numerous kinds of business letters are classified according to their content or message. The most common are

1. Order letters and acknowledgments of orders.
2. Inquiries and replies; also, other letters of information.
3. Sales letters.
4. Letters asking or granting adjustments.
5. Credit letters (designed to encourage buying now and paying later).
6. Collection letters (designed to encourage paying, *now*).
7. Letters of application.
8. Letters of introduction or recommendation.

The four types you are likely to use, now and later, are represented below. For more detailed discussion of all the various types of letters in the transaction of business, you are referred to recent books which you will find listed in the card catalog of your library under "Business Letters" or "Letter-Writing—Business."

Order letters

Make your order letter—if you do not have a printed order blank available—brief, clear, and exact. Single-item order letters may concern tickets for the theater or a sports event, hotel reservations, a magazine subscription, a book, and the like. In multiple-item order letters, give a full description of the goods which you wish to buy, including quantity, size, color, price, and any other available identifying data such as catalog number and trade name. List separately, to facilitate reading, two or more items ordered in the same letter. Always specify methods of shipment and payment, and remember to mention any special information such as delivery of the order by a certain date.

In the lower left-hand corner, several spaces under the last line of the body, write "Encl." (i.e., enclosure) if something is to be sent with the letter (check, sample, etc.). Whenever this is done, it serves to remind you, or whoever folds the letter, to be sure that the enclosure mentioned in the body of the letter is made; it is also a further indication, to the reader, of the enclosure.

ORDER LETTERS (1)

1809 North Locust Avenue
Davenport 6, Iowa
October 31, 19--

Box Office
Globe Theater
114 West Adams Street
Chicago 2, Illinois

Gentlemen:

For the matinee performance, Saturday, November 25, 1961, please send me 6 tickets for "The Lonely Way," at $6.60 each, $39.60 total.

If tickets at this price are not available, please substitute those in the next-lower price range.

A money order for $39.60 and a stamped, addressed envelope are enclosed.

Very truly yours,

Jane Smith

(Miss) Jane Smith

Encl.

(2)

612 East Maple Road
Kokomo, Indiana
February 10, 19--

Cincinnati Film Supply Co.
412 West Main Street
Cincinnati 6, Ohio

Gentlemen

736

From your February catalog, please send me by parcel post the following 2"-x-2" color slides:

Cat. No.	No. of sets	Name	Unit Price	Total
CK 159	1	California Highways	$2.20	$2.20
CK 312	1	California Beaches	3.30	3.30
PK 168	1	Yosemite National Park	2.75	2.75
PK 169	1	Yellowstone National Park	2.75	2.75
TK 98	3	1961 Tournament of Roses	3.30	9.90
				20.90
		Estimated parcel post charge		.35
		Total.....................		21.25

My check for $21.25 is enclosed.

Very truly yours

Edward J. Ryan, Jr.

Edward J. Ryan, Jr.

Encl.

Inquiries

Most inquiry letters are written to obtain information about the products or services of a business firm. Some may be written to an individual for information concerning a subject on which he is an authority. Always make your request understandable; avoid vague and general questions, and supply any information the reader needs in order to answer your questions definitely.

Routine requests for catalogs, price lists, or other prepared data may be limited to a one-sentence letter clearly identifying the desired material. If your letter is phrased as a question (*Will you please send me . . . ?*), punctuate it as a question.

Nonroutine inquiries require more detailed letters. For example, a letter asking about an organization's policies must explain the use to which the information will be put. A request stemming from a personal problem must give a clear explanation of the problem and an indication of the type of help needed.

The general plan for the inquiry letter, usually from two to four paragraphs long, is as follows: (1) reason for the inquiry, (2) the inquiry, (3) expression of appreciation (*never* a "thank you in advance"). Sometimes material may be included to show the reader how he will benefit by replying. When the inquiry includes several questions, these are more effective when numbered and paragraphed separately.

If the person or firm addressed will eventually profit, no postage should be enclosed. Otherwise, apply this principle: When you ask for that which is of benefit only or primarily to you, enclose a stamped envelope addressed to yourself.

LETTER OF INQUIRY

919 Fowler Avenue
Athens 12, Missouri
September 25, 19—

Secretary-Treasurer
American Institute of Electrical Engineers
33 West 38th Street
New York 18, New York

Dear Sir:

As a student in the College of Electrical Engineering at Athens University, I am interested in eventually obtaining full membership in the American Institute of Electrical Engineers.

I shall appreciate your answers to the following questions:

(1) Can an undergraduate student of electrical engineering obtain a junior membership in the A.I.E.E.? If so,
(2) What is the cost of such membership?
(3) Is such junior membership transferable to full membership when the student graduates from college?

(4) Does the junior membership fee include a year's subscription to the official magazine, *Electrical Engineering*?

Very truly yours,
[written signature]
Wilson Hargrove

Letter asking adjustment

The letter asking adjustment—sometimes called a claim, or complaint, letter—is written not to accuse, blame, or threaten but to point out an error, such as shipment of wrong goods, damaged goods, failure to ship goods, an overcharge in a bill, and the like. Clarity is es-

Letters Asking Adjustment (1)

1809 North Locust Avenue
Davenport 6, Iowa
November 7, 19--

Box Office
Globe Theater
114 West Adams Street
Chicago 2, Illinois

Gentlemen:

I received today the six tickets, ordered on October 31, for the matinee performance of "The Lonely Way," for Saturday, November 25. Presumably you had no $6.60 tickets for this performance, for these are marked at $4.40 each.

You inadvertently did not send me the price difference, $2.20 on each ticket. A rebate of $13.20 is therefore due me.

Very truly yours,

Jane Smith

(Miss) Jane Smith

sential, brevity is desirable, and courtesy is diplomatic. Present the facts fairly; identify the unsatisfactory article or service, explain how it is unsatisfactory, and suggest or give the reader an opportunity to suggest adjustment. The letter that the reader writes to you is the adjustment letter.

If you have to write an angry letter, by all means write it, but lay it aside for a day; then destroy it, and write the kind of letter you would like to receive if your position were that of the reader.

Usually your adjustment-asking letter will consist of two to four paragraphs containing (1) a specific explanation of what is wrong, (2) the course of action you desire the reader to take, (3) sometimes, the inconvenience resulting to the writer, and (4) sometimes, the reader's gain by his making prompt adjustment. Circumstances determine the order in which these paragraphs come.

(2)

612 East Maple Road
Kokomo, Indiana
February 16, 19--

Cincinnati Film Supply Co.
412 West Main Street
Cincinnati 6, Ohio

Gentlemen

My February 10, 1961, order, which arrived today, contained three sets of the 1960 Tournament of Roses instead of the three sets of the 1961 Tournament of Roses.

I am therefore returning by parcel post these three sets, to be replaced by the 1961 sets ordered.

Very truly yours

Edward J. Ryan, Jr.

Edward J. Ryan, Jr.

Appendix: Writing Letters

Letters of application

An effective letter of application stresses, throughout, the applicant's desire and ability to be of benefit to the prospective employer. Always emphasize what you, the applicant with your qualifications, can do for the employer, not what the latter can do for you. The letter must be courteous, straightforward, and sincere in tone, offering services without pleading or demanding.

Open your letter by applying for a specific position and indicating how you learned of the opening: from a teacher, another friend, an agency, a "Help Wanted" advertisement. If your application is unsolicited, give your special reason for applying. Present your qualifications—education, experience, interest, and aptitude—and emphasize those particularly useful to the employer. Devote a brief paragraph to personal information: age, health, and any other pertinent details. Include two or three references, listing them separately, either in the body of the letter or immediately after the close, with full names, titles, and addresses. Close your letter by requesting an interview at the employer's convenience. If you are in the same city, indicate where you may be reached by telephone. An example of a letter of application is given below.

NOTE: Always secure permission from the persons whom you wish to suggest as references and remember that it is courteous to write letters thanking them for their help.

Letters Accompanying Data Sheets. Many applicants prepare a separate data sheet which should be labeled *Information Record Concerning* . . . , listing education, experience, personal information, and references. Such a record can be a full page, or even more, of information pertinent to the position desired; it will also have room, preferably in the upper right-hand corner, for a good photograph. Subheadings should be used for ready reading. The letter accompanying such a sheet should not repeat information. It is usually in three to six paragraphs. The first applies for the position; the middle ones stress the information on the data sheet which especially qualifies the applicant for the position; the last requests an interview.

Letters Replying to Newspaper or Magazine Advertisements. In responding to "Help Wanted" advertisements in newspapers or in certain professional magazines, you as applicant must first analyze the

912 Stanford Street
Concord, Illinois
November 15, 19—

Mr. James R. Kirby
Director, Izaak Walton Boys' Camp
Mennedota, Michigan

Dear Mr. Kirby:

Mr. Frank McLane, Y.M.C.A. Director of Boys' Work here, informs me that you will be employing boys' counselors at your camp this coming summer. Please consider me an applicant for one of the positions. I offer the following qualifications:

EDUCATION:

By June I shall have completed my Junior year here at the University of Central Illinois. Courses which bear on the summer's work include:

Speech 212—Informal Speaking
Speech 214—Debating
Speech 321—Group Discussion

Psychology 120—Introduction to Psychology
Psychology 334—Psychology of Adolescence

Education 262—Summer Work Experience
Education 304—Principles of Teaching

During the second semester I shall be studying Psychology 345—Psychology of Leadership; Education 360—Methods of Teaching Vocational Subjects; and Physical Education 325—Principles and Types of Recreational Leadership. In June, 1962, I hope to obtain a Bachelor of Science degree in the field of recreational management.

EXPERIENCE:

During my last two years of high school and first two years of college, I was an assistant Boy Scout leader. This college year I am assisting, for three afternoons a week, the Boys' Director of the local Y.M.C.A.; my assignment is supervising swimming and basketball activities. The past two summers I worked as life guard at the outdoor swimming pool in my home town, Audubon, Michigan.

SPECIAL ASSETS:

I played basketball and baseball all through high school; have been active in Boy Scout work since I was 8 years old; have been an excellent swimmer since boyhood; hold the Red Cross First-Aid and Life-Saving certificates; and am a member of the college service fraternity, Alpha Gamma Mu, which concerns itself with helping young people.

All these activities have given me experience in getting along with young people, whom I genuinely like. When I graduate from college, I plan to make working with boys my career.

PERSONAL
INFORMATION:

Age: 20. Height: 6 feet, 2 inches. Weight: 180 pounds. Health: excellent. College scholarship standing: upper fourth of class. Religion: Methodist. Home address: 116 Main Street, Audubon, Michigan.

REFERENCES:

For information concerning my education, experience, and character, I refer you, with their permission, to the following:

Professor Harold J. Creek, Department of Education, University of Central Illinois, Concord, Illinois.

Mr. Frank McLane, Director, Boys' Work Y.M.C.A., Concord, Illinois.

Mr. Thomas R. Masters, Superintendent, Columbia Memorial Park, Audubon, Michigan.

Dr. Thomas J. Bloom, Pastor, First Methodist Church, Audubon, Michigan.

May I have an interview? I shall be home for the Thanksgiving vacation November 22 to 25, and for the Christmas vacation December 20 to January 3. During those vacation days, I can come to Mennedota at your convenience.

Very sincerely yours,

(written signature)

(typed signature)   Richard M. Taylor

743

information given to determine the required qualifications. *Blind advertisements* give neither name nor address of the advertiser and often provide scant information about the opening. The applicant must judge as best he can the qualifications needed and offer in his letter whatever details seem pertinent.

Here is an example of a blind advertisement:

Stenographer: Good beginner considered. 5-day week. Opportunity for advancement. M4089 Tribune.

The applicant has no way of knowing the name of the firm, the kind of business, or exactly what "advancement" is suggested. It is likely that the work does not require knowledge of technical terminology since a beginner will be considered. In replying, the applicant can only express interest in a position which offers further opportunity and give details about her stenographic skill. She should of course include past experience in stenography, usually without referring to employers by name.

Open classified advertisements ordinarily include the name of the firm and more detailed information about the position. The following advertisement clearly outlines the employer's needs:

Wanted: Young man to check reports of public accountants, prove figures, check references, etc. Prefer accounting education and background, ability to assist in preparing reports. Excellent opportunity young man studying for CPA. Reply in detail. Brown, Merrill and Scott, CPA, 35 National Bank Building.

The applicant analyzes the advertisement by listing in detail the qualifications desired; his letter, if he expects it to gain him an interview, must show precisely how he meets these qualifications. For the position just quoted, an applicant must indicate (1) strong interest in an accounting career; (2) experience, if any, in checking reports, etc.; (3) education; (4) ability to compile data and write reports.

Unusual Letters of Application. The purpose of the letter of application is to gain for its writer an interview; rarely is a position obtained solely through the letter. Therefore, to make your letters of application effective and to assure yourself of an interview, make your letters unusual; make them secure the favorable attention of the prospective employer.

Do not be vain, assertive, overconfident, but try to convey routine information in an unusual way. For example, you can use subheads: centered, or in the left margin, or on the left third of the page with the material developing the subheads filling the right two-thirds. One attention-getting letter of application had the applicant's picture centered at the top, with position desired at the left and date available at the right; a three-paragraph letter occupied the center of the page, enclosed by ruled lines; surrounding the letter were statements of the applicant's attainments and qualifications: educational background, campus activities, business experience, personal data, and references. Your own ingenuity may suggest other letters of application which are unusual without being freakish.

INFORMAL, FRIENDLY LETTERS

An old saying, "The best way to have a friend is to be one," applies particularly to the writing and receiving of friendly letters. Nearly everyone is prone to say, "I love to get letters but, oh, how I hate to write them!" It is unfortunately true that good informal letters require careful planning and writing; they can no more be dashed off than can effective business letters.

Writing friendly letters is not exactly an art, but you can approximate artistry in your personal correspondence provided you take time and pains to plan and write your letters thoughtfully. They should, however, never seem or sound labored, strained, or artificial, nor should they be hastily scrawled, disconnected notes on a half-dozen random subjects. You can improve your friendly letter writing by practicing the following suggestions:

1. *Give details.* Full, clear description of one person or one place is likely to prove far more interesting than a series of choppy notes on numerous people or places. The detailed account of one interesting conversation which you have had is far more revealing and entertaining than a kaleidoscopic series of random comments quoted from a dozen people whom you have met. The vivid narration of a single experience proves more readable than scrappy accounts of several incidents. Try to write letters made up of unified details, not random notes which really are only topic sentences needing expansion. Think of each letter as a *theme* with a central purpose. Keep your central purpose in mind, reject all irrelevant details, and focus attention upon one

745

primary incident or one piece of conversation, upon description of one person or place, or exposition of one idea. Of course, a letter may contain more than one topic, but the topics should be clearly related and each should be fully developed. In writing informal letters follow the principles of preliminary analysis (Section 4), outlining (Section 6), and paragraph development (Section 24b).

2. *Adapt your letters and make them appropriate.* Friends and relatives differ in their tastes and interests. An incident one would enjoy reading about might not be particularly interesting to another. Friendship implies many obligations, one of which is to detect and respect individual differences. Rarely is it possible to give friends similar Christmas presents, and it is equally obvious that the recipients of letters have a right to expect individual treatment. In other words, adapt each letter and its content to your specific reader.

3. *Don't devote your letter entirely to yourself.* Although everyone wants to talk and write about himself, your reader is not greatly interested in *only* the writer's personal affairs and activities. In addition to accounts of other persons, places, and events, show sincere interest in your reader's affairs and activities. Don't use too many *I's, my's, me's, we's.* Keep in mind the moral of the note written by a young lady to a long-absent friend: "I don't like you any more; your *I's* are too close together."

4. *Take time.* No one can write a long, interesting letter in five or ten minutes. The best friendly letters are usually written by people who plan their letters before writing. They do not sit down to write a letter saying, "Well, I owe Bill a letter and I can't put it off any longer. What can I tell him?" They sit down to write about people, places, and events in which they know their reader will be interested and about which they have made mental notes for the very purpose of using them in a letter to him. Nor do good letter writers try to write six or eight letters at a sitting. They write only one or two, and thus give each letter all the freshness, spontaneity, and chattiness which they can. No one writes good letters when he considers the task tiresome and laborious, but most people can write letters with charm by not stinting the care lavished upon them. Friendships, often kept alive necessarily through the medium of correspondence, are too precious to throw away for the lack of a little time. Many a friend is occasionally irritated at receiving a long-expected letter which begins "I am sorry that this

746

letter will be brief, for I am in a great rush" or ends with a "Hastily yours," with·little interesting content between such a beginning and ending.

5. *Don't write illegibly or sloppily.* The friendly letter is different in form and purpose from business and formal correspondence. It is more intimate, much more informal. But hastily scrawled notes on odd pieces of paper do not show much interest in or respect for the persons written to. Informality is not only permissible but desirable in friendly letters, but liberty must not become license. The illegibility and general carelessness which fairly scream, "I haven't time to write you a good letter—take this or leave it," are neither effective nor appropriate. It is now conventional and proper to type many friendly letters. Only intimately personal letters, such as those of condolence, should always be written in longhand.

Use letter paper of good quality. White or cream or pale-gray paper is preferable to that of other colors. Stationery in good taste is on sale at a good book or stationery store. Avoid the use of heavily perfumed paper. Do not use violet or red or green ink. Your letters, even in their paper, ink, and handwriting, reflect your possession or lack of good taste and refinement.

Types of friendly letters

In addition to long letters giving information to friends and relatives, everyone must write brief sincere notes to fit certain specific circumstances: an inquiry, an invitation, the reply to an invitation, appreciation for a favor, thanks for a gift, thanks for hospitality (sometimes called a bread-and-butter letter), congratulations, *bon voyage* (farewell), and sympathy.

These notes are so varied that no single suggestion can be offered to cover them all. But for each of them, follow the directions given above; for each, make mental or written notes of the details you plan to include and the order in which you will treat them.

Remember also that the *form* of friendly letters is not nearly so important as their *content*. Notice, however, that a comma, not a colon, usually follows the greeting. It is suggested, too, that your address and the actual date (not just the day of the week) be given in the usual place for the heading or in the lower left-hand corner of the last page of the letter. No inside address is necessary, but the outside address on the envelope of the friendly letter must be as accurate and full as that on a business-letter envelope.

The letters that follow may be helpful to you in suggesting solutions to some letter-writing problems, but you should not follow any models slavishly. Let your letters represent you and your personality and not someone else's.

AN INVITATION

> Phi Beta Mu House
> 457 College Avenue
> Meridian, Indiana
> October 10, 19—

Dear Bob,

Are you planning to follow your team to our campus for our Homecoming festivities on October 21? If you are, will you be my week-end guest here at the house?

If you drive or get a ride, transportation is no problem. Buses also run every two hours. Come Friday afternoon or evening if you can, or sometime Saturday morning. I've a date lined up for you at our big dance Saturday night.

We have so many notes to compare, concerning our freshman year in college. And barring a tie, the Homecoming game will prove that one of us can be a good loser.

I hope you can come.

> Sincerely,
> Bill

A BREAD-AND-BUTTER LETTER

> Room 115, Residence Center
> University of Central Illinois
> Concord, Illinois
> October 23, 19—

Dear Bill,

Thanks very much for everything. The week end was perfect—the good gabfest Friday night, the chance to visit classes with you Saturday morning (you're lucky, or unlucky; we don't have Saturday classes here), the game, and the date for the dance with that gorgeous roommate of your campus sweetheart.

Your house cook is superb—or was she just "putting out everything" for the week end?

And the game! Who ever dreamed it would end in a 33–33 tie? So, no hard feelings!

Now it's back to the books. I'll see you at home Thanksgiving—and I hope to have you here at some major event during the spring semester.

Thanks again, and best luck on your mid-term exams.

> Sincerely,
> Bob

A "THANK-YOU" NOTE

Dear Uncle Jim,

I know that I wasn't the prettiest girl at the dance (although Jack, who took me, said I was); and I didn't get the biggest rush either, but then again I wasn't exactly a wallflower. And yet I'm positive about one thing— I was the happiest girl there. No one else was wearing such beautiful costume jewelry, and I could just see the looks of admiration on the other girls' faces.

I have always known that you knew the way to a girl's heart, but what I didn't know was that you thought enough of me to take the time and trouble to select and send me such an exquisite gift. I'm very grateful and the next time that I see you I'll tell you in person just how happy you have made me.

> Your devoted niece,
> Louise

923 Athens St.
New Orleans 6, La.
January 20, 19—

A NOTE OF CONGRATULATION

> 1567 Park Lane
> Forest Dell, Wisconsin
> October 30, 19—

Dear Alice,

No doubt you have received dozens of letters congratulating you on being chosen Homecoming queen. Let me add my note to the others. I am genuinely happy for you and congratulate not only you but the judges for their good judgment in choosing you. The pictures in this morning's *Tribune* were superb. It will be a long time, I'm sure, before Central has again such a lovely and regal queen.

Sincerely,
Martha

A NOTE OF SYMPATHY

Dear Barbara,

As I sat in the church today, a whole host of memories came crowding about me. I remember so well when I met your mother; she received me, as your friend, with her arms literally open. And for all the months that I have been privileged to know her, she has always been graciously hospitable to me. I recall dozens of good times which she made possible for us; I remember especially how she helped me with that fancy dress costume when I was almost in tears because I couldn't get it to hang just exactly right.

Nothing that I can say will lessen either the shock of her passing or your grief. But I want you to know that as I paid her my last respects this afternoon, my own heart was heavy with a sense of personal loss. Her kindliness, thoughtfulness, and complete integrity will serve as a constant challenge to you and to me.

With sincere sympathy,
Alice

Hamilton Hall
Lake College
October 9, 19—

EXERCISES

1. Collect and bring to class at least ten examples of business letters. (Perhaps you can supply these from your own correspondence; or a relative or business acquaintance may lend you some letters from his files.) Study the letterheads used; note especially both the usual and the unusual features about the six parts of the letters (heading, inside address, greeting, body, complimentary close, signature). Notice the stock of paper used, the spacing and length of the paragraphs, the tone of the letters.

Exercises

2. Classify the letters in your collection (Exercise 1) according to the types of business letters listed on pages 735–743. For one example of each type that you find, make a paragraph outline of the content. Compare this outline with the plan of organization given for the order letter, inquiry letter, claims letter, and application letter (see pp. 735–743).
3. Write a letter answering an advertisement in a magazine, in which you request a catalog.
4. From a magazine advertisement, write a letter ordering the item or items advertised.
5. Look through the advertisements of a magazine until you find some article or articles in which you are interested. Write for further specific information about the product.
6. You notice the announcement of an essay contest for college students being sponsored by a national publisher. Write a letter asking for details.
7. Write a letter to your dean asking permission to leave college before the close of the college year in order that you may accept a good summer position starting on June 1.
8. Assume that you are preparing a paper or a speech on the history of your home town. Write a letter to the state historical society asking for information on the early shops and industries in the town.
9. Write a letter asking an entertainer or a guest speaker to appear on a program sponsored by your class or some organization of which you are a member. Then assume that the entertainment has been given; write the speaker a "thank-you" letter.
10. Write a formal letter to the editor of your local newspaper, calling attention to some matter which you believe will interest your fellow-townsmen or fellow-students.
11. Write a letter to a railroad or bus company asking for a refund on an unused ticket.
12. Assume that some of your luggage has been lost on your way to or from college. Write a claims letter to the railroad or the express company.
13. Write a letter applying for a summer job on a cruise boat or for some kind of summer employment other than that mentioned in No. 14 and No. 15.
14. Answer the following "Want Ad": WANTED: Counselors and leaders for boys' and girls' camps, June through August. Youngsters are from 8 to 12. Give full details concerning qualifications. Acme Summer Camp Chain, Lake Onestoga Village, New York.
15. Answer the following "Want Ad": WANTED: Male college students to serve as lifeguards at public beaches, park pools, and summer camps.

Three months' summer employment. Excellent salary and working conditions for those properly qualified. Lifeguard Agency, Inc., 412 North Wyoming Avenue, Indianapolis, Indiana.

16. Answer the following "Want Ad": WANTED: Student to be night cashier in local restaurant. Hours 8 to 12. Time for study during work. Give references and previous experience. Dept. S-7, *Citizen,* Columbus, Ohio.

17. Write a letter of application in answer to an advertisement in the "Help Wanted" section of a newspaper or magazine. Choose an advertisement giving a reasonable amount of information.

18. With a specific position in mind, prepare a record sheet giving pertinent information about yourself. Write a letter of application to accompany the record.

19. Write a completely self-contained letter of application (i.e., without use of a record sheet). Use one or two unique or unusual devices to make your letter distinctive.

20. Write a letter to a high school teacher or former college instructor asking permission to use his name as reference in your application for a position.

21. Write an informal invitation to a friend asking him to join you and your family on a week's automobile tour.

22. Write a "bread-and-butter" letter to a friend who has entertained you for a week end in his (her) home. Write a letter also to your friend's mother.

23. Write a letter to a friend who is in the hospital for a long stay following a serious operation.

24. Assume that you are spending some time in a foreign country or in a section of the country considerably removed from your home. Write a "travel" letter to a friend at home.

25. Write a "thank-you" note to a friend's parents who have given you a "going-away-to-college" present.

26. Write a letter of advice to a friend who is a high school senior and who plans coming in the fall to the college which you are attending.

27. Write a letter to a friend attending another college, inviting him (or her) to one of the important social functions of your college.

28. Write a letter to a relative, asking him (her) to be your guest at some college activity in which you know that he (she) is greatly interested.

29. Send a letter of information to your high school principal, or your favorite high school teacher, giving your impressions of some phase of college life.

30. Write a letter to a former high school friend reminding him of, or suggesting, a reunion of your class or some other organization during the next vacation period.

INDEX

Index

Index

Index

Index

Index

761

Index

It, indefinite use, 546, 548
"It-does-not-follow" error, 92–93
Italics, 696–697; emphasis, 697; footnotes, 183–188; foreign words or phrases, 697; magazine, book, and other titles, 184–191, 696; misuse, 696–697; or quotation marks, 696; reference to word, letter, or number, 697
Its, it's, its', 468, 688

Jackson, Allen, quoted, 242–243
James, William, quoted, 68
Jameson, Robert U., quoted, 257
Jerky sentences, 336–337
Job, 468
Johnson, Burges, 49–50, 53–54
Johnson, Samuel, quoted, 331–332, 360 n.
Joining: conjunctions, 481, 498; prepositions, 481, 497–498; verb, *see* Linking verbs; words, 482, 497–498; words and hyphens, 680–684
Jones, Howard Mumford, quoted, 71
Jr., 655

Keats, John, quoted, 145
Kind of (a), sort of (a), 468
Known to unknown order, 132

Lab, 458, 707
Langewiesche, Wolfgang, quoted, 214–215
Language, business letters, 734; figurative, 429–431; literal, 429; misuse of, in thinking, 95
    See also Diction; Words
Lardner, Ring, quoted, 252–253
Lay, lie, 469, 491–492
Leave, let, 468
Legibility, manuscript, 27; friendly letters, 747
Length, paragraph, 211, 246–249; sentences, 346, 350
Less, 465
Let, leave, 468; as auxiliary verb, 560
Letter, date line, 710; punctuation, 639, 641, 670; salutation, 726–728
Letter writing, 127
    See also Business letters; Friendly letters
Letters, forming of, 27; omission of, 675; plural of, 687–688; use of italics, 697
Levels of usage, 357–359, 368–369, 454–456; punctuation, 691–692
Lewis, C. S., quoted, 70

Liable, likely, 460
Library, 149–169; aids to use, 150–152; card, 164–165; card catalog, 164–169; guide to use, 150–169; main book collection, 164–169; periodical material, 162–164; reference books, 150–162; special bibliographies, 153–162
Library of Congress Classification, 168–169
Lie, lay, 469, 491–492
Like, 469, 604–605
Likely, 460
Limiting adjectives, 494
Lincoln, Abraham, quoted, 331
"Lincoln the Soldier," research paper, 192–201
Linking verbs, 495, 552–555, 619–620; adjectives, 552–553, 596–597; agreement, 553; table of forms, 554–555
List, colon, 669–670
Listening, as communication, 9–12; directions for, 9–12; lectures, 9–10; movies, radio, and television, 11–12; speeches, 10–11
Literal language, 429
Loc. cit., 187–188
Localisms, 404–405
Logic, order of, 241
    See also Thinking
Longfellow, Henry Wadsworth, quoted, 147
Loose sentence, 349–350, 517–518, 620
Lots of, a lot of, 469
Ludwig, Emil, quoted, 101

McGhee, Paul A., quoted, 342
Mad, 469
Magazines, titles, 696, 699; use of quotation marks, 692
Main clause, 503
    See also Independent clause
Main verb, 556–557; omitted, 286–287
    See also Verbs
Manuscript form, 25–28; beginning, 26; cancellations, 26; endorsement, 27; final draft, 28; indentations, 26; insertions, 26; legibility, 27; margins, 26; page order, 26; paper, 26; proofreading, 28, 117–123; recopying, 28; title, 26; typewriting, 27–28, 122
Margins, business letters, 730; themes, 26
Mathematical expressions, 711
Maverick, Maury, 441
May, can, 462

Index

Index

Index

Rhyme, 450
Right along, right away, right then, 472
Rise, raise, 471, 491–492
Roane, T. H., quoted, 128–129
Roberts, Paul, quoted, 455–456
Robinson, Francis P., quoted, 256
Robinson, James Harvey, quoted, 67, 142, 222
Rogow, Lee, quoted, 252
Roman numerals, form, 711–713; in outline form, 55
Roueche, Berton, quoted, 69–70
Royal Bank of Canada Monthly Letter, quoted, 434
Rules for spelling, 385–391
Running-on sentences, 295
Russell, Bertrand, quoted, 76

St. John, Seymour, quoted, 69
Salutation and punctuation, 639, 641, 670, 726–728, 747
    See also Business letters
Saw, seen, 472
Scene and play, 671
"Scratch" outline, 48–49
Seasons, 703
Second person, 102, 485–486, 523–524, 623
Secondary tenses, 571, 629
Seen, saw, 472
Seesaw sentences, 296
Semicolon, 632, 662–666, 694; conjunctive adverb, 663–664; coordinate independent clauses, 663–665; "fault," 666; misused, 19, 665–666; phrases and dependent clauses, 665–666; quotation marks, 694; series, 665; vs. colon, 666; vs. comma, 642; vs. dash, 666–667
Sentence, 262–355, 506–518, 626; appropriateness, 264, 348–350; arrangement, 340–343, 517–518; beginning, 340–341, 345–346; beginning with numeral, 709; blends, 288–289; capitalization, 699; choppy, 336–338; clearness, 263–264, 283–321; 349–350; climax, 342; conciseness, 322–324, 443–448; consistency, 333–335; construction errors, 20, 286–292; correctness, 263–282; defined, 262–263, 506–507, 626; emphasis, 340–343; ending, 340–341; faulty coordination, 295–298; faulty subordination, 300–302; forms, 346–347; glossary of sentence

errors, 351–355; grammatical classification, 349, 516–517; illogical dependent clauses, 303–304; importance of, 262–264; incompleteness of meaning, 270, 286–291; kinds, 508–513; length, 346; meaning, 516–517; misplaced modifiers, 305–307; misused as complement, 304; mixed and illogical constructions, 282–292; omissions, 271, 286–291; outline, 50–52; parallelism, 326–330; period, 633; position and arrangement, 340–343; problems in writing, 263–264; purpose, 516–517; rambling, 284; running-on, 295; "seesaw," 296; split constructions, 314–317; stringy, 295; telegraphic style, 271; thesis, 39, 49–51, 58–59; topic, 39, 212–216; types of, 349–350; unity, 283–285; unrelated ideas, 284–285; varied length and forms, 344–350
    See also Balanced sentences; Comma splice; Complex sentence; Compound-complex sentence; Compound sentence; Dangling modifiers; Declarative sentence; Diagraming; Effectiveness; Elliptical sentence; Exclamatory sentence; Fragments; Fused sentences; Imperative sentence; Interrogative sentence; Loose sentence; Periodic sentence; Simple sentence
Separation, unnecessary, 314–317; improper punctuation, 655–657, 671
Sequence of tenses, 580–581, 626–627
Series of words, phrases, clauses, 639, 645, 665; misuse of punctuation, 656–657; questions, 637
Set, sit, 473, 491–492
Shakespeare, William, quoted, 96, 146
Shall, will as auxiliary verbs, 472–473, 558, 575–577
Shift, in mood, 333–335, 593; number, 335; person, 335; point of view, 101–104; subject, 334; tense, 333–334, 578–579; thought, 674; voice, 334, 587
Ships, names of, 692, 696
Shores, Louis, quoted, 75
Shorter Oxford Dictionary, 361
Should, would as auxiliary verbs, 473, 558–559, 580–581
Signature, business letters, 729–730
Similar-sounding words, overuse, 452–453
Simile, 429–430, 437

Index

Index

Theme Record (with Number of Serious Errors)

(Figures and letters in parentheses refer to *Handbook* sections)

Number of Theme	1	2	3	4	5	6	7	8	9	10	11	12	13	14	15	16
Grade on theme																
Adjective and adverb (83)																
Capitals, abbreviations, italics (97, 98, 96)																
Comma splice (32)																
Comma misuse (88)																
Coordination, subordination, parallelism (36, 37, 38, 44)																
Dangling modifiers (40)																
Diction (53-70)																
Fused sentences (33)																
Paragraphing (21-30)																
Possessive case (75j-m, 94a-e)																
Pronouns, nominative and objective case (75)																
Pronouns, antecedents—agreement, reference (77)																
Punctuation marks other than commas and semicolons (86, 87, 90-95)																
Semicolon misuse (89)																
Sentence fragment and incompleteness of meaning (31)																
Spelling (52)																
Subject, predicate—agreement in number (76)																
Variety in sentences (46, 47, 48)																
Verb forms—mood, tense, etc. (78-82)																

(Make a copy of this chart for additional theme records.)

Symbols Used in Indicating Errors in Writing

(Figures and letters in parentheses refer to *Handbook* sections)

ab   use of abbreviations (98)

agr   agreement of subject and predicate in number (76)

amb   ambiguous word or meaning (61)

ant   antecedent not clear (77)

awk   awkward phrasing (64, 68, 69)

C to R   not clear to reader

ca   wrong case (75)

cap   use a capital (97)

cl   lacking in clearness (12, 61)

comb   combine two or more simple sentences in a complex or compound-complex sentence (46)

comp   faulty comparison (83e-h)

con   consistency (13, 45)

cont   content vague and general (24)

coord   faulty coordination (36)

cs   comma splice (32)

cst   awkward or faulty construction (35, 36, 37, 38, 41)

d   faulty diction (70)

da   inappropriate diction (69)

dcol   colloquialism (55)

dcon   concise diction needed (67)

dem   emphatic diction (64)

deu   euphony (68)

dfw   "fine writing" (66)

dict   see your dictionary (51)

did   idiom (56)

dil   illiteracy (57)

dim   impropriety (58)

dl   localism (54)

dm   dangling modifier (40)

dmf   mixed figure (63)

dp   precise diction (61)

dr   useless repetition (67)

dsl   slang (59)

dtc   technical word (62)

dtr   triteness (65)

dw   word wrongly divided (93)

e   poor emphasis (64)

ef   effectiveness of word or sentence construction (44, 47, 61, 64)

ff   following rules or pages

fig   use of numbers (99)

fn   footnote form and punctuation (20f)

fp   "frying pan" error (32a, 36c, 77f)

fs   fused sentences (33)

fw   use figures for words (99)

gl   see Glossary (Sentence, 50; Diction, 70; Grammar, 85; Punctuation, 100)

gr   grammatical error (75, 76, 77, 79, 83)

id   wrong idiom, unidiomatic (56)

il   illegible handwriting (1b)

imp   important

ir   irrelevant

it   italics (96)

l   illogical in thought (12c)

lc   lower-case letter, no capital (97)

m   wrong mood (82)

mf   questionable manuscript form (1)

mm   misplaced modifier (39)

mod   use of *a, an* (70, 1); adjective vs. adverb (83)

n   wrong number (71c, 76)

nc   no capital (97)

n¶   make no new paragraph (22)

np   no punctuation